EPISTEMOLOGY

Epistemology: Contemporary Readings is a comprehensive anthology that draws together classic and contemporary readings from leading philosophers writing on the major themes in epistemology. The book begins with an extended introduction by Robert Audi, one of the leading experts in the field of epistemology, in which he sets the stage for the themes of the reader. Chapters appear under the headings:

- Perception
- Memory
- Reason and the a priori
- Testimony
- Inference in general
- Inductive inference
- The architecture of knowledge
- The analysis of knowledge
- Skepticism

Each section is prefaced by an introductory essay by the editor which guides students gently into each topic. Study questions follow every article and a bibliography is provided at the end of each chapter.

Articles by the following leading philosophers are included:

Alston
J.L. Austin
Ayer
Berkeley
BonJour
Carnap
Carroll
Chisholm
Coady
DeRose
Descartes
Dretske
Edwards
Foster
Fumerton
Gettier
Goldman
Haack
Hume
Kant
Klein
Lehrer
Locke
Malcolm
G.E. Moore
Nozick
Plato
Pollock
Putman
Quine
Reid
Russell
Stove

Ideal for any philosophy student, this book will prove essential reading for epistemology courses. The anthology is designed to complement Robert Audi's textbook *Epistemology: A Contemporary Introduction to the Theory of Knowledge* (Routledge, 1998).

Michael Huemer is Assistant Professor of Philosophy at the University of Colorado, Boulder. He is the author of *Skepticism and the Veil of Perception* (2001).

Robert Audi is Charles J. Mach Distinguished Professor of Philosophy at the University of Nebraska, Lincoln. He is regarded as one of the top experts in epistemology and has published widely in the field. His previous publications include *Epistemology: A Contemporary Introduction* (1998), *Practical Reasoning* (1996), *Moral Knowledge and Moral Character* (1997). He is also the editor of the *Cambridge Dictionary of Philosophy* (1999).

For my students

First published 2002
by Routledge
2 Park Square, Milton Park, Abingdon, Oxon OX14 4RN

Simultaneously published in the USA and Canada
by Routledge
270 Madison Avenue, New York, NY 10016

Reprinted 2006 (three times), 2007 (twice), 2008

Routledge is an imprint of the Taylor & Francis Group, an informa business

Typeset in Sabon by RefineCatch Limited, Bungay, Suffolk
Printed and bound in Great Britain by
MPG Books Ltd, Bodmin

British Library Cataloguing in Publication Data
A catalogue record for this book is available from the British Library

Library of Congress Cataloging in Publication Data
A catalog record for this book has been requested

ISBN 10: 0–415–25920–7 (hbk)
ISBN 10: 0–415–25921–5 (pbk)

ISBN 13: 978–0–415–25920–0 (hbk)
ISBN 13: 978–0–415–25921–7 (pbk)

CONTENTS

Preface vii
Acknowledgements ix

Introduction: A Narrative Survey of Classical and Contemporary Positions in Epistemology 1

PART I: SOURCES OF JUSTIFICATION AND KNOWLEDGE

1 PERCEPTION 27
John Locke, *Essay Concerning Human Understanding* 32
George Berkeley, *Of The Principles of Human Knowledge* 37
David Hume, "Of the Academical or Sceptical Philosophy" 46
Thomas Reid, *Essays on the Intellectual Powers of Man* 51
Bertrand Russell, *The Problems of Philosophy* 64
J.L. Austin, *Sense and Sensibilia* 74
2 MEMORY 85
Bertrand Russell, "Memory" 88
Norman Malcolm, "A Definition of Factual Memory" 91
John Pollock and Joseph Cruz, "Reasoning and Memory" 104
Michael Huemer, "The Problem of Memory Knowledge" 113
3 REASON AND THE A PRIORI 125
Plato, *Meno* 131
Immanuel Kant, *Critique of Pure Reason* 142
Bertrand Russell, *The Problems of Philosophy* 152
A.J. Ayer, "The Elimination of Metaphysics" 166
W.V. Quine, "Two Dogmas of Empiricism" 176
Rudolf Carnap, *Philosophical Foundations of Physics* 194
Laurence BonJour, "Appendix: Non-Euclidean Geometry and Relativity" 208
4 TESTIMONY 217
John Locke, *Essay Concerning Human Understanding* 219
David Hume, "Of Miracles" 221
Thomas Reid, *Inquiry into the Human Mind* 234
C.A.J. Coady, "Testimony and Observation" 239

PART II: THE STRUCTURE AND GROWTH OF JUSTIFICATION AND KNOWLEDGE

5 INFERENCE IN GENERAL 253
Lewis Carroll, "What the Tortoise said to Achilles" 256
Richard Fumerton, "Inferential Justification and Empiricism" 259
David Hume, "Of Scepticism with Regard to Reason" 270
Hilary Kornblith, "Distrusting Reason" 275
6 INDUCTIVE INFERENCE 293
David Hume, *An Enquiry Concerning Human Understanding* 298
Paul Edwards, "Russell's Doubts about Induction" 311
Nelson Goodman, "The New Riddle of Induction" 320
John Foster, "Induction, Explanation and Natural Necessity" 333
Colin Howson and Peter Urbach, *Scientific Reasoning: The Bayesian Approach* 344
David Stove, "Another Attempt to Prove that Induction is Justified: The Law of Large Numbers" 352
7 THE ARCHITECTURE OF KNOWLEDGE 369
Sextus Empiricus, "The Five Modes" 372
I.T. Oakley, "An Argument for Scepticism Concerning Justified Beliefs" 375
Laurence BonJour, *The Structure of Empirical Knowledge* 387
William Alston, "Has Foundationalism Been Refuted?" 402
Susan Haack, "A Foundherentist Theory of Empirical Justification" 417

PART III: THE NATURE AND SCOPE OF JUSTIFICATION AND KNOWLEDGE

8 THE ANALYSIS OF "KNOWLEDGE" 435
A.J. Ayer, "Knowing as Having the Right to be Sure" 440
Edmund Gettier, "Is Justified True Belief Knowledge?" 444
Michael Clark, "Knowledge and Grounds: A Comment on Mr. Gettier's Paper" 447
Alvin Goldman, "A Causal Theory of Knowing" 450
Keith Lehrer and Thomas Paxson, "Knowledge: Undefeated Justified True Belief" 464
Robert Nozick, "Knowledge" 475
Keith DeRose, "Contextualism and Knowledge Attributions" 491
9 SKEPTICISM 507
René Descartes, *Meditations on First Philosophy* 513
Hilary Putnam, "Brains in a Vat" 524
Fred Dretske, "The Pragmatic Dimension of Knowledge" 539
Peter Klein, "Skepticism and Closure: Why the Evil Genius Argument Fails" 552
Michael Huemer, "Direct Realism and the Brain-in-a-Vat Argument" 575
Roderick Chisholm, "The Problem of the Criterion" 590
G.E. Moore, "Proof of an External World" 602
G.E. Moore, "Hume's Theory Examined" 606

Index 613

PREFACE

This anthology is designed primarily for use in undergraduate courses in epistemology, although it may also provide a useful reference for graduate students studying the subject. The topics have been chosen to enable it to serve as a useful companion to Robert Audi's comprehensive and widely-used *Epistemology: A Contemporary Introduction to the Theory of Knowledge*. Professor Audi's introduction indicates many of the points of contact between this book and his. Alternatively, this collection may be used as a standalone text.

I will use this preface to say a few words about the usefulness of this collection. The choice of readings is the most important factor. My guideline in choosing the readings for this volume has been to select, for each chapter, readings that in my view are paradigms of several important, competing approaches to the topic of that chapter. Thus, for instance, the chapter on perception includes paradigmatic examples of representationalism, direct realism, and idealism. Within that constraint, I have sought to choose well-known or influential philosophers. I have included a mixture of both classic and contemporary readings, ranging from Plato to Quine. This reflects the fact that many of the debates in epistemology are perennial. And it reflects my beliefs, both that the terms of these debates were set by the great philosophers of the past, and that recent analytic philosophers have made important advancements in these debates. Beyond that, I will let the table of contents speak for itself.

In addition, for each selection, I have included a few simple "study questions." These are short-answer, objective questions about the contents of the readings, which can be used by the student to remind himself or herself of what the reading was about, or by the instructor to test students' familiarity with the readings. Although it cannot in general be assumed that a student who is able to answer these questions has an adequate grasp of the readings, it *can* be assumed that a student who is unable to answer the questions does not.

I was prompted to edit this anthology in part by a dissatisfaction with the existing alternatives. Most existing anthologies, I discovered, included *only* examples of recent work, while at least one included *only* classic writings. Many of them were narrowly focused on only a few topics of recent interest, neglecting some of the classic, perennial issues of epistemology—such as the problem of induction, or the debate between rationalism and empiricism. Some books even omitted the topic of perception. I have sought in this book, as Audi has in his, to remedy such omissions, without, I hope, introducing any equally serious omissions of my own. It is my opinion that a student who follows all the readings in this book will have a solid education in epistemology. For a single, introductory course, however, most instructors will want to select perhaps four or five chapters to focus on.

Lastly, I would like to thank a number of people without whom this anthology would not have existed, or would not have been nearly as good as it is: Robert Audi, for his advice and assistance at various stages; Peter Klein and the other (anonymous) reviewers for Routledge; my students, whose feedback on my classes has helped me to learn what works and what doesn't; and the staff at Routledge, including Tony Bruce and Siobhan Pattinson, for all their work in bringing this project to fruition.

Michael Huemer
University of Colorado

ACKNOWLEDGMENTS

The editors and publishers would like to thank the following copyright holders for permission to reprint material:

Locke, John, from *Essay Concerning Human Understanding*, edited by Peter H. Nidditch. © Oxford University Press, 1975. Reprinted by permission of the publisher.

Berkeley, George, from *Principles of Human Knowledge*. Reprinted by kind permission of Open Court Publishing, a division of Carus Publishing Company.

Hume, David, from *Enquiries Concerning Human Understanding and Concerning the Principles of Morals*, ed. by L.A. Selby-Bigge (2nd edition, 1902). Reprinted by permission of Oxford University.

Reid, Thomas, from *Inquiry and Essays*, ed. Ronald Beanblossom and Keith Lehrer. Reprinted by permission of Hackett Publishing Company, Inc. © 1983 by Hackett Publishing Co. All rights reserved.

Russell, Bertrand, from *The Problems of Philosophy* (1912), pp. 7–26 & 82–110. Reprinted by permission of Oxford University Press.

Austin, J.L., from *Sense and Sensibilia*, edited by G.J. Warnock. © Oxford University Press 1962. Reprinted by permission of Oxford University Press.

Russell, Bertrand, "Memory" from *Analysis of Mind*. Reprinted by permission of Routledge and the Bertrand Russell Peace Foundation.

Malcolm, Norman, from *Knowledge and Certainty*. © 1963 Cornell University Press. Used by permission of Cornell University Press.

Huemer, Michael, "The Problem of Memory Knowledge", reprinted from *Pacific Philosophical Quarterly* 80 (1999): 346–57 by permission of Blackwell Publishers. © 1999 Blackwell.

Pollock, John and Joseph Cruz, "Reasoning and Memory" from *Contemporary Theories of Knowledge*, 2nd edition (Rowman and Littlefield, 1999). Reprinted by permission of the publisher.

Kant, Immanuel, from *Critique of Pure Reason*, trans. Norman Kemp Smith (1965). Copyright © Macmillan & Co. Reprinted by permission of Palgrave.

Plato, from *Plato's Meno in Focus*, trans. and ed. Jane M. Day (London: Routledge, 1994). Reprinted by permission of the publisher.

Ayer, A.J., "The Elimination of Metaphysics." Reprinted with permission of Dover Publications from *Language, Truth, and Logic*.

Quine, W.V. "Two Dogmas of Empiricism," *Philosophical Review* 60 (1951). © 1951 Cornell University. Reprinted by permission of the publisher.

Carnap, Rudolph, "Philosophical Foundations of Physics." Reprinted from *Philosophical Foundations of Physics* (Basic Books, 1966).

BonJour, Laurence, reprinted from *In Defense of Pure Reason*, with the permission of Cambridge University Press. © Laurence BonJour 1998.

Coady, C.A.J., "Testimony and Observation" from *American Philosophical Quarterly* 10 (1973): 149–55. Reprinted by permission of the journal.

Carroll, Lewis, "What the Tortoise said to Achilles." Reprinted from *Mind* 4 (1895): 278–80 with permission of Oxford University Press.

Fumerton, Richard, "Inferential Justification and Empiricism." Reprinted from the *Journal of Philosophy* 73 (1976): 557–69 by permission of the author and the journal.

Kornblith, Hilary, "Distrusting Reason." Reprinted from *Midwest Studies in Philosophy* 23 (1999): 181–96 by permission of Blackwell Publishers. © 1999 Blackwell.

Edwards, Paul, "Russell's Doubts about Induction." Reprinted from *Mind* 58 (1949) with permission of Oxford University Press.

Goodman, Nelson, "The New Riddle of Induction." Reprinted by permission of the publisher from *Fact, Fiction and Forecast* by Nelson Goodman, pp. 59–83, Cambridge, Mass.: Harvard University Press, © 1979, 1983 Nelson Goodman.

Foster, John, "Induction, Explanation, and Natural Necessity." Reprinted from *Proceedings of the Aristotelian Society* 83 (1982/83): 87–102 by courtesy of the editor of the Aristotelian Society. © 1983.

Howson, Colin and Peter Urbach, from *Scientific Reasoning*. Reprinted by permission of Open Court Publishing Company, a division of Carus Publishing Company, Peru, Ill. © 1989 Open Court Publishing Company.

Stove, David, from *The Rationality of Induction*. © D.C. Stove 1986. Reprinted by permission of Oxford University Press.

Sextus Empiricus, reprinted from *Scepticism, Man and God: Selections from the Major Writings of Sextus Empiricus*, ed. Philip Hallie, trans. Sanford Etheridge (Wesleyan University Press, 1964), by permission of the publisher.

Oakley, I.T., "An argument for Skepticism Concerning Justified Beliefs." Reprinted from *American Philosophical Quarterly* 13 (1976): 221–8 by permission of the journal.

BonJour, Laurence, from *The Structure of Empirical Knowledge*. Reprinted by permission of the publisher (Cambridge, Mass.: Harvard University Press) © 1985 President and Fellows of Harvard College.

Alston, William, "Has Foundationalism been Refuted?" Reprinted from *Philosophical Studies* 29 (1976): 287–305 with kind permission from Kluwer Academic Publishers.

Haack, Susan, "A Foundherentist Theory of Empirical Justification." © 1997 Susan Haack. This paper first appeared in *The Theory of Knowledge*, ed. Louis Pojman, 2nd edition (Belman, Calif.: Wadsworth, 1998), pp. 283–93, and was reprinted in *Epistemology: An Anthology*, eds Ernest Sosa and Jaegwon Kim (Oxford: Blackwell, 1999), pp. 226–36. It also appeared in Spanish in *Agora* 18, 1 (1999): 35–53 (Santiago de Compostela, Spain), and will appear in French in *Carrefour* (Ottawa, Canada). Reprinted by permission of the author.

ACKNOWLEDGMENTS

Ayer, A.J., "Knowing as Having the Right to be Sure." © A.J. Ayer, 1956. Reprinted from *The Problem of Knowledge* by A.J. Ayer, with permission of Penguin Books.

Gettier, Edmund, "Is Justified, True Belief Knowledge?" Reprinted from *Analysis* 23 (1963): 121–3 by permission of the author.

Clark, Michael, "Knowledge and Grounds: A Comment on Mr Gettier's Paper." Reprinted from *Analysis* 24 (1963): 46–8 by permission of the author.

Goldman, Alvin, "A Causal Theory of Knowing." Reprinted from the *Journal of Philosophy* 64 (1967): 357–72 by permission of the author and the journal.

Lehrer, Keith and Thomas Paxson, "Knowledge: Undefeated Justified True Belief." Reprinted from the *Journal of Philosophy* 66 (1969): 225–37 by permission of the author and the journal.

Nozick, Robert, "Knowledge." Reprinted by permission of the publisher from *Philosophical Explanations* by Robert Nozick, pp. 172–8, 198–211 (Cambridge, Mass.: Harvard University Press). © 1981 Robert Nozick.

Descartes, René, *Meditations on First Philosophy*. Trans. John Cottingham. © Cambridge University Press 1996. Reprinted with the permission of Cambridge University Press.

Putnam, Hilary, "Brains in a Vat." © Cambridge University Press 1981. Reprinted with the permission of Cambridge University Press.

Dretske, Fred, "The Pragmatic Dimension of Knowledge." Reprinted from *Philosophical Studies* 40 (1981): 363–78 with kind permission of Kluwer Academic Publishers.

Klein, Peter, "Skepticism and Closure." Reprinted from *Philosophical Topics* 23 (1995) by permission of the journal and the author.

Chisholm, Roderick, "The Problem of the Criterion." Reprinted from *The Problem of the Criterion* (Aquinas Lecture, 1973) by Roderick Chisholm, with permission from Marquette University Press.

While reasonable effort has been put into obtaining permissions prior to publication, there are some cases where it has been impossible to trace the copyright holder or to secure a reply. The author and the publishers apologize for any errors and omissions and, if notified, the publisher will endeavor to rectify these at the earliest possible opportunity.

INTRODUCTION:

A Narrative Survey of Classical and Contemporary Positions in Epistemology

Robert Audi

This book presents a quite comprehensive set of readings that are excellent for courses in epistemology at several levels and can be used even without an accompanying textbook. They are organized by topic in a way that invites sequential study; the readings in each major area are presented in an order that both indicates historical development and facilities comprehension; and the volume as a whole has a good balance: it contains classical contributions by great philosophers, influential recent essays, and contemporary papers that illustrate cutting-edge work in the field.

The book is also specially designed to be a good companion to my *Epistemology: A Contemporary Introduction to the Theory of Knowledge*, and at appropriate points I will indicate connections between a particular reading and my book. A glance at the contents of the two books will make it obvious that their overall content and organization are parallel. There are, however, far more connections than I can bring out here: nearly every main point in the readings is addressed in one or another part of *Epistemology*—which has a detailed index meant to facilitate research and comparisons.

Both Huemer and I have presented epistemology not only as the theory of knowledge but also as the theory of justification. We have also presented it in the light of its history, but have given primary emphasis to bringing out its distinctive questions, positions, and methods. The aim is to help readers achieve an understanding of the field that is both broad and—given serious study of the materials—significantly deep. A mastery of these readings, particularly in combination with *Epistemology*, should provide a good sense of the field and a capacity for critical reading of the contemporary literature.

There are at least two further aims shared by this book and my *Epistemology*. First, both books aim at making connections between epistemology and other branches of philosophy, above all general metaphysics and philosophy of mind and language. Second, both are sensitive to the importance of approaching epistemology with an eye on the psychological aspects of the subject. This is in part because knowledge is constituted by belief (of a certain kind), which is a central psychological concept, and because knowledge and justification are both closely connected with perception, inference, memory, and other elements in human life that are crucial in psychology as well as in philosophy. But it is also because epistemology should be studied in a way that enables us both to get a psychologically realistic picture of human knowers and to accommodate the findings of psychological and neurobiological research.

The rest of this introduction will discuss the readings with a view to helping instructors and other readers decide what to select and in what order. This should be useful whether or not an accompanying textbook is used; but the connection between the readings and my *Epistemology* will be obvious from the part titles and section titles in this volume (which closely parallel mine), and I will indicate some further connections.

Suggested course outlines

The comprehensive study

One natural approach for a course in epistemology, particularly an undergraduate course, is simply to select readings from each part of this book and, depending on the number to be covered, add parts of a supporting book, such as *Epistemology*. But regardless of the level of the course, instructors and readers may have special interests. Let me indicate how some of these might yield a selection.

The basic texts approach

For those interested in the historically most influential "basics," it might be possible to select readings most heavily from Parts I and III, with, say, Hume and Edwards on induction in Part II. In Part III, for this kind of emphasis just two or three items on the nature of knowledge might serve. Descartes's version of skepticism is of course historically crucial, and the responses by Chisholm, Putnam, and Moore would provide variety and can give students a sense of some major approaches to dealing with skeptical problems.

The contemporary problems approach

If, on the other hand, the aim of a course is above all to help students get "up to speed" in dealing with contemporary problems, then much less time can be devoted to Part I, and the emphasis throughout can be on recent literature. In Part I an instructor might select just a few readings on perception and memory and concentrate on the a priori, with Quine an obvious choice for emphasis. Here my own chapter on reason (in *Epistemology*) gives a broad but also quite fine-grained picture of options other than the Quinean view. Part II is designed to be useful with or without the readings on inference in general. The works on inductive inference are independently intelligible, as are those on the architecture of knowledge, which treat the structure of a body of justified beliefs or knowledge. For Part II, then, one might use only the classical short treatment of the problem of induction by Hume, introduce the "grue problem" with the selection from Goodman's *Fact, Fiction, and Forecast*, and choose at least one of the contemporary responses to skepticism about induction. The chapter on inference in *Epistemology* is meant to go with either kind of selection, but is particularly suited to those interested in the philosophy-of-mind aspects of inference and how its epistemological role is connected with meeting skepticism. As to Part III, for students who—whether as advanced undergraduates or graduates—are good candidates to get "up to speed," the "Gettier Problem" can be quickly introduced and a selection made from the works by Goldman, Lehrer and Paxon, Nozick, and DeRose. The same students would be capable of dealing with skepticism mainly in connection with the contemporary readings.

Special topics approaches

Beyond the common kinds of aims for a course in epistemology so far discussed, one might have a special interest that determines the main readings. Suppose it is perception, or skepticism, or the a priori, or the nature of knowledge. On each of these, there are not only the readings so labeled but related ones—and of course there are chapters on these topics in *Epistemology*, which also deals with perception in comparison with memory and with consciousness (inner perception, in a sense). Let me briefly suggest some the possible combinations.

Perception

The readings on perception are a substantial set, and the perception chapter in *Epistemology* ranges over many of the recurring issues. Moreover, the selections on perception are nicely supplemented by, for instance, Coady on testimony, Alston on foundationalism, Dretske on knowledge, and Putnam and Huemer on brains in a vat.

Skepticism

The selections on skepticism are supplemented by Russell on memory, Hume on induction and Edward's critique of Russell's Humean treatment of induction, Sextus on the five modes, Oakley on justification, and DeRose on contextualism. The final chapter of *Epistemology* deals with most of these approaches and constructs a defense of a common-sense epistemology.

The a priori

In the case of the a priori, again there are many readings to choose from and the chapter on reason in *Epistemology* provides basic definitions and a perspective of its own. Chisholm's paper on the problem of the criterion and Kornblith's on distrusting reason are among the useful supplemental readings one might choose.

The analysis of knowledge

As to the nature of knowledge, in addition to the selections specifically on that, there are connected readings on all of the other topics. These can present data crucial for a good analysis as well as a perspective to be accommodated, as with, say, Quine, or BonJour.

The psychology of cognition

This can be a theme in any epistemology course or the main focus in specially designed ones. Particularly relevant among the readings would be Goldman's "Causal Theory of Knowing" taken together with the readings on perception by Locke and Hume, those by Pollock and Huemer on memory, the paper by Kornblith on "Distrusting Reason," and Putnam's paper on "Brains in a Vat" (which also makes connections between epistemology and philosophy of language). In *Epistemology*, Chapter 1 has much on the psychological and causal elements in perception (dovetailing with some of Goldman's theory); Chapter 5 explores the psychology of testimony; and Chapters 6 and 7, on the nature of inference and the structure of knowledge and belief, present a psychologically detailed account of the epistemology of those topics.

It should help in orienting readers if I address the contents of the parts of the book in some detail. In doing this, I will try to say enough to help instructors with selection and to aid readers—including students—in acquiring a sense of the issues and of connections among them.

The readings: content and further connections

What follows will be an indication of both some of the drift of the readings and how they are interconnected. I will also pose some of the larger questions they raise and identify some points of contact with the corresponding parts of *Epistemology*. In various places study questions will be suggested, although there is no explicit listing of them.

Perception

Locke
The short selection from John Locke's *Essay* presents the idea, so influential in empiricism, that the mind is a *tabula rasa* (blank tablet) at our birth, and that its initial and basic content is inscribed by the hand of experience. We also hear of "ideas" produced in the mind by experience—specifically, through the senses—and these ideas "bear witness" to truth. Here we have one classical picture of how perceptual knowledge arises. It is a version of *representationalism*.

Berkeley
In the selection from George Berkeley's *Principles*, we find experience producing ideas in us, but this time without causation by external objects. Rather, Berkeley defends the phenomenalist view that physical objects themselves are constituted by stable groupings of ideas. Perception is still, however, seen as a source of knowledge of the physical world.

Hume
In the short selection from Hume's *Treatise*, we again see "ideas," but with an apparent acknowledgment of the mind-independent existence of external objects that cause them: "[t]he existences, which we consider, when we say *this house*

and *that tree*, are nothing but perceptions or representations in the mind, and fleeting copies or representations of other existences, which remain uniform and independent" (p. 48).

Reid

The views of the three great British empiricists, Locke, Berkeley, and Hume, are criticized by the Scottish philosopher Thomas Reid, whose *Essays* represent what many today continue to regard as the enduring common sense of humanity. Reid astutely attacks Berkeley's phenomenalism and resolutely defends a common-sense view of perception as caused by objects and capable of giving us genuine knowledge of them. Perception involves "*First*, Some conception or notion of the object perceived; *Secondly*, A strong and irresistible conviction and belief of its presence; and *Thirdly*, That this conviction and belief are immediate, and not the effect of reasoning" (p. 51). A noteworthy element here is the apparent assumption that perception is *conceptual* (involving a conception of what is perceived) and even *doxastic* (belief-entailing regarding the object perceived). These are both views that are critically assessed at some length in the chapter on perception in *Epistemology*.

Russell

In Bertrand Russell, we find a more scientifically oriented version of the kind of representationalist theory articulated by Locke. But for Russell as for Locke, "sense-data," as opposed to physical objects, are taken to be what we are immediately acquainted with in perception and what represent the external world to the mind. We also find in Russell an affirmation of the "irresistibility" of which Reid spoke; and there are other common-sensical elements in Russell that are fruitfully compared with some found in the selection from Reid.

Austin

The sense-datum theory is criticized at length by J.L. Austin in the selections from *Sense and Sensibilia*, as well as (more comprehensively) in Chapter 1 of *Epistemology*. Austin is famous for his astute sense of the distinctions reflected in ordinary English. He brings this sense to bear on the idea that in illusions and hallucinations our experience can be "intrinsically indistinguishable" from what it normally is. It is an interesting question to what extent a sense-datum theorist can meet the objections Austin raises and whether an adverbial theory of perception (such as the one outlined in *Epistemology*) can provide an adequate account of perception. In any case, the readings on perception are an excellent source of theories and problems concerning what perception is, what its immediate objects are, whether it involves some kind of inference, and indeed whether it must produce beliefs at all.

Memory

Memory is perhaps best understood in comparison with perception. Perception is standardly taken to be the chief or only source of our knowledge of things in the present—at least if we include consciousness of what is in our own minds as a kind of (inner) perception. (In Chapter 3 of *Epistemology* consciousness is examined in the light of the idea that it may be conceived as "inner" perception.) Memory might similarly be taken to be the chief or only source of our knowledge of things in the past and to yield only knowledge of the past. This conception would, however, be a mistake on two counts: first, we remember such timeless things as propositions of mathematics; second, we seem to have inferential knowledge of the past from its footprints in the present—smouldering embers, dried-up stream beds, fossils of living creatures.

Russell

In Russell's treatment of memory in *The Analysis of Mind*, he says that its "images are recognized as 'copies' of past sensible experience" (p. 88). This discussion is the source of his famous statement that it is logically possible that "the world sprang into being five minutes ago, exactly as it then was" (p. 88). A copy, after all, can be a forgery. More positively, he introduces the notions of feelings of pastness and of familiarity and suggests how these feelings figure in generating trust in memory. A question he leaves us with here is what role these phenomenological aspects of memory play in justifying memory beliefs. That role is discussed in Chapter 2 of *Epistemology*. A central question to think about here is how *recalling*, which clearly involves the capacity of memory, is related to *remembering*.

Malcolm

By contrast, Norman Malcolm is concerned much less with the phenomenology of memory and far more with what constitutes knowledge from memory. His view is that we remember that *p* (some proposition) if and only if we know it because we *knew* it (p. 91). Malcolm does not here contrast the way memory figures in relation to knowledge—by preserving it, in his view—and the way it figures in relation to justification (a contrast that is developed in some detail in Chapter 2 of *Epistemology*), but he does consider the question of how one can know one has dreamt, given that (for him) one cannot know one is dreaming when one is. Here Russell's view would perhaps allow what Malcolm's does not: that the sense of pastness is enough for justification, whatever we say about the status of memorial knowledge.

Pollock

The contemporary essay by John Pollock covers territory left uncharted by Russell and Malcolm. Pollock is concerned to show how reasoning can justify belief when not all of the premises of the reasoning are actually held in active memory as a basis for the conclusion. He takes only one's "dynamic argument"—the kind one has through reasoning that is in consciousness at the time one draws the conclusion—to be "directly relevant to the assessment of the [conclusion] belief as justified or unjustified" (p. 112).

Huemer

Michael Huemer, in contrast to Pollock, considers justified belief in general, whether it rests on reasoning or not, and gives a direct role to both memorial and other aspects of its basis. He contends that justification for believing a proposition on the basis of memory requires *both* justification for adopting the belief and justification for retaining it (p. 117). These views differ from mine in *Epistemology*. I take memory to be preservative with respect to knowledge (and here share part of Malcolm's view), but generative with respect to justification (perhaps differing with Huemer on this). On that last point I stress something only implicit in the other treatments. I leave open, however, just how memory can preserve justification. A central question here is whether, if one has a belief justified on the basis of memory, one at least *can* remember the justificatory elements, even if only with effort or cues.

Reason and the a priori

In what might be called the epistemological tradition, perception (including such "inner perception" as consciousness) and memory are considered *experiential* sources of knowledge and justification, whereas reason is viewed as a distinct kind of source. It might be called intuitive, ratiocinative, or simply rational. The contrast is misleading insofar as it suggests that the thinking that is crucial for a priori justification is not part of one's experience or that people do not normally need experience to supply raw materials for knowledge of any kind; but if the basis of a priori justification is something like understanding concepts or propositions or their relations, the contrast has a point. This is apparently not the basis of justification in the other, "experiential" cases. In any event, the readings in this section all concern the kind of justification yielded by the use of reason in application to what would generally be agreed to be something abstract.

Plato

The opening reading from Plato is a splendid expression of a *nativist* conception of mathematical knowledge (and by implication, all a priori knowledge and presumably other knowledge as well). Socrates, Plato's spokesperson here, claims simply to bring to articulation what the slave boy already knows. Socrates takes the boy's answers to his questions to reveal not inference or discovery, but previously unarticulated knowledge. If, however, we distinguish—as I do throughout *Epistemology*, and especially in Chapter 1—between dispositions to *form* beliefs and, on the other hand, beliefs one already *holds* in dispositional form (roughly, in memory rather than in mind), then it is not at all clear that nativism gains significant support in the dialogue. For it is easy to *produce* belief by asking questions, as where, in asking you whether you are less than ten and five-hundredths feet tall, I cause you to believe this when previously you believed only that your height was some smaller measure and immediately saw that it was less than this. You were of course disposed to believe this, but did not already believe it. This is not to suggest that it is *easy* to tell what we already believe and what we quickly come to believe (and perhaps to know) upon considering some matter; but the question is important. It is crucial both for the psychology of cognition and for understanding what we know and how we acquire knowledge.

Kant

The selections from Immanuel Kant's monumental *Critique of Pure Reason* serve to introduce both the notion of a priori knowledge as "knowledge absolutely independent of all experience" (p. 143) and the distinction between analytic and synthetic propositions. He also lays out a famous case for the existence of some propositions that are synthetic yet a priori. Among these Kant counts some quite substantive mathematical (and other) propositions. Here he sets the stage for Quine's critique of the analytic–synthetic distinction and Laurence BonJour's discussion of the synthetic a priori in relation to geometry.

Russell

In the selection from Russell, Kant's view is critically examined, and although Russell accepts the basic distinction between the a priori and the empirical, he quite plausibly questions Kant's idea that the constitution of our nature underlies certain a priori truths (pp. 154–5). Russell goes on to characterize universals (here exhibiting connections with Plato, Berkeley, and Hume). His account of a priori knowledge construes it as dealing wholly with relations of universals (p. 161). In the same chapter he introduces the notion of *intuitive knowledge*, which is always direct (non-inferential) and is the basis for derivative knowledge (here conceived as knowledge deductively based on intuitive knowledge). He articulates both a notion of self-evidence and a foundationalist conception of knowledge. The selection is outstanding for its combination of brevity, readability, and scope. It nicely connects the epistemology of the a priori with the metaphysical question of the status of universals.

Ayer

A.J. Ayer's "The Elimination of Metaphysics" is also concerned with the a priori: but whereas Russell embraced a metaphysical view of universals to account for the a priori, Ayer argued that metaphysical sentences lack cognitive meaning. He defended the position (earlier expressed by David Hume) that "tautologies and empirical hypotheses form the entire class of significant propositions" (p. 171), where by "tautologies" Ayer meant to include all and only truths of logic and analytic propositions (these are described in detail in Chapter 4 of *Epistemology*). Like Carnap and other logical positivists, Ayer sought to account for the a priori through a philosophy of language. He conceived tautologies as true in virtue of the meanings of the crucial (linguistic) terms in which they are expressed; as to the empirical (factual), "a sentence is factually significant if, and only if he [its user] knows how to verify the proposition which it purports to express" (p. 167), that is, knows what "observations" would confirm or disconfirm it. By contrast, "no statement which refers to a 'reality' transcending the limits of all possible experience [by which he meant a metaphysical statement] can possibly have any literal significance" (p. 167). In this linguistic, empirically oriented strategy for determining what kinds of discourse are intellectually admissible, he foreshadows much contemporary philosophy.

Quine

The position Ayer arrived at left the heart of empiricism intact: like Hume, he countenanced the analytic–synthetic distinction, put logic and (presumably) pure mathematics on the analytic side, and took all knowledge of other kinds to be empirical: grounded in experience. If philosophical inquiry could fit into this framework, he could account for it; if not, as with traditional metaphysics, he had no place for it as a cognitive (roughly, truth-seeking) enterprise. It was against both the analytic–synthetic distinction and the associated conception of the cognitive enterprise that W.V. Quine so influentially argued in "Two Dogmas of Empiricism." In "Two Dogmas," Quine examines a number of criteria for analyticity and finds them wanting. For instance, he attacks the appeal to definitions as a way to secure the analytic–synthetic distinction. A correct definition would have to capture *synonymy* (sameness of linguistic meaning), and Quine finds that notion obscure. This is not because we do not understand the concept of sameness; it is because the notion of meaning is obscure. The verification theory of meaning (whose core I quoted in Ayer's formulation) does not help (pp. 187–8). Verificationism is committed to the second dogma Quine attacks: *reductionism*, which "survives in the supposition that each statement, taken in isolation from its fellows, can admit of confirmation or infirmation [disconfirmation] at all" (p. 188). Rather, using a now well-known metaphor, Quine contends that "statements about the external world face the tribunal of sense experience not individually but only as a corporate body" (p. 188). This view supports rejection of the other dogma; there can be no analytic statements: "no statement is immune to revision" (p. 190). Non-Euclidean geometry furnishes examples of propositions, such as Euclid's parallel postulate, that apparently illustrate the universal fallibility that Quine here affirms.

Carnap

If Quine is right, it is no surprise that there should be non-Euclidean geometries, and these are described briefly in the readings from Carnap on the nature and scientific rationale for development of such geometries. Here a crucial focus is the status of Euclid's famous parallel postulate, according to which, for any line and any point not on that line, there is exactly one line parallel to the first and passing through the point.

BonJour

Laurence BonJour critically explores the significance of such geometries for the rationalist view that, contrary to empiricism, there are synthetic a priori propositions, and hence, in principle, there can be substantive knowledge accessible to reason without dependence on sensory experience. He concludes that we cannot rule out the possibility that there is "an *a priori* insight or apparent insight that . . . a non-physical and also not merely formal geometry provides a correct account of the necessary features of space" (p. 213).

Readers of the section on the a priori may notice that there is little analysis of the *way* in which a priori knowledge is supposed to be "independent" of experience. This notion merits careful exploration, and in various parts of *Epistemology* I do one thing needed here by distinguishing between negative and positive dependence on experience (and independence of it). This distinction also bears on the sense in which a single proposition may or may not individually admit of "confirmation or infirmation."

Readers may also notice that, particularly in the contemporary readings, there are references not only to propositions as the focus of concern but also to sentences and statements. What difference might this make, and how is it related to the question of the bearing on the analytic–synthetic distinction of the possibility of definitions? If what is a priori is the proposition that if *A* is taller than *B*, then *B* is shorter than *A*, and if that proposition can be expressed in indefinitely many languages, why is the possibility of a definition of terms—which are peculiar to a single language—crucial for the issue?

Testimony

The classical sources of knowledge and justification, as we might call them—perception (including consciousness conceived as "inner perception"), memory, and reason—might all be called *intrapersonal.* They yield knowledge for a single person without essential dependence on another person. Testimony is different. It is *interpersonal.* We get it from one or more other people (apart from the metaphorical case of the testimony of the senses). What, then, is its status as a basis of knowledge or justification?

Locke

In the short selection from Locke's *Essay*, we find little credit given to testimony as a source of knowledge. He goes so far as to say, "So much as we our selves consider and comprehend of Truth and Reason, so much we possess of real and true Knowledge" (p. 219).

Hume

In the selection on the subject from David Hume's *Treatise of Human Nature*, he is only a little more concessive than Locke: "It is experience only, which gives authority to human testimony" (p. 230). Hume's positive view is apparently that our experience of natural patterns outweighs even the testimony of a great many people claiming to have witnessed miracles (which, for Hume, must be violations of natural law—p. 223). Even if a miracle were to occur, then, he thinks that we could not be justified in believing it did.

Reid

Here, as on other matters, Reid opposes the Humean view. In the selection on testimony drawn from his *Inquiry*, Reid articulates two important, interconnected principles. That "Truth is always uppermost, and is the natural issue of the mind" he called "the principle of veracity." That we have "a disposition to confide in the veracity of others" he called "the principle of credulity" (pp. 236–7). I do not find him treating testimony as exactly the same kind of source of knowledge as perception; but it is clear that he takes it to be a *major* source, and he sees our accepting it where there is no special reason not to as reasonable.

Coady

C.A.J. Coady is even more at odds with Hume's position than is Reid. Coady attacks what he calls "the reductionist thesis," which he quotes from the same passages in Hume's *Enquiry* just referred to: "The reason why we place any credit in witnesses and historians, is not derived from any *connexion*, which we perceive *a priori*, between testimony and reality, but because we are accustomed to find conformity between them" (p. 223). Coady argues that we are in no position to live up to finding such conformity; our experience is far too limited. His positive conclusion is an anticipation of the idea that a condition for meaningful language is a certain degree of accuracy regarding the world. Coady says, "I do not understand the idea that testimony could exist in a community and yet it be possible to discover empirically that it had no 'connection with reality.'" Indeed, it "constitutes a fundamental category of evidence" (p. 247). It is an interesting question how much support this last, epistemological claim receives from the previous, impossibility claim.

In the chapter on testimony in *Epistemology*, I have raised the question of whether testimony is a basic source of knowledge or justification. This is not the same as the question of whether testimony is a "basic category of evidence." The type of evidence is one thing, its source another. Even if we cannot receive testimony without relying on perception, the evidence we get may not be perceptual—or indeed of any other specific kind. Suppose, however, that the person giving testimony did not have perceptual (or memorial or a priori) grounds for the proposition attested to (nor did anyone in a testimonial chain ending with that person, if the person is the last in such a chain of attesters to the proposition in question). Could we then come to *know*, through the testimony, what is attested to? And if we could not, how does this bear on the sense in which testimonial evidence is a basic category? Moreover, since we can become justified through testimony even if the attester is lying and asserts a falsehood, might our grounds for testimony-based justification be different from our grounds for testimony-based knowledge? These and other questions raised by the readings on testimony are addressed in detail in *Epistemology*, and the topic is currently a lively source of discussion in the field.

Inference

Even if testimony is not a basic source of knowledge or justification, it is like those sources in one important way: it can yield non-inferential beliefs. Ordinarily, I just believe what you attest to without drawing any inferences; I presuppose your veracity, as Reid would say, rather than infer from a premise that you are veracious that I should accept what you say. Much of what we know, however, we do know by inference. What is inference, and under what conditions do we come to know something through it?

Carroll

The charming piece from Lewis Carroll brings out that we cannot take the (or a) principle governing an inference to be a premise in it. If we do, we simply have another inference with an additional premise; then the principle governing *that* inference must be added as a premise, and so on to infinity. A related issue is whether, in order to know one's conclusion on the basis of one's premises, one must *believe* the (or a) principle governing the inference. In this case, one would not get a regress *provided* the principle need not itself be known inferentially.

Fumerton

An intermediate view here is that one need only be *capable* of knowing or justifiedly believing a governing principle in order to know or have justified belief of the conclusion of the inference. Richard Fumerton's "Inferential Justification and Empiricism" defends something closer to the second of these. One reason it is difficult to tell whether he does is that he is not distinguishing between dispositions to believe and dispositional beliefs (p. 264). In any event, he is concerned to defend an empiricist version of the foundationalist view that we can have knowledge inferentially based on non-inferential knowledge.

Hume

Nothing I have said so far distinguishes between deductive and inductive inference. The kinds of questions we have considered and the main points made by Carroll and by Fumerton can be applied to both kinds. But Hume, in his section on "Skepticism with Regard to Reason," is especially concerned with inductive inference and defends the specific thesis that all our inferences ("reasonings") "*concerning causes and effects are deriv'd from nothing but custom*" (p. 272). He refers to customary transitions of thought, as opposed to formal reasoning that is deductively valid or invalid. He leaves much open regarding the psychology of inference, but seems not to be positing even a dispositional belief of any principle governing inductive inferences.

Kornblith

It is largely with psychological aspects of inference and reason-giving that Hilary Kornblith is concerned in "Distrusting Reason." He notes that "The difference between truth-responsive reason-giving and rationalization does not lie in features intrinsic to the arguments given" (p. 278). His point here is not about the conditions necessary for the premises of an inference to justify its conclusion in the abstract; that is, his concern is not with deductive validity or inductive strength (notions discussed in some detail in Chapter 6 of *Epistemology*). It is with what is needed for a *belief* of the conclusion of an inference to be justified or to constitute knowledge. For instance, I can give a good argument for a proposition from premises that are only rationalizations: either I do not believe them at all, or at least my belief of my conclusion is not *based* on my believing them. In that case, assuming I have no other basis for that belief, it is ill-founded and apparently does not constitute knowledge. The belief has, one might argue, potential but not actual support from my reasons. There remains some controversy in epistemology about whether this is so and, especially, why.

Inductive inference

With valid deductive inferences, there are questions about *how* justification and knowledge are transmitted from our premises to our conclusion and about *how much* is transmitted, but there is little doubt that they are transmitted. With even the best of inductive inferences, there are questions about whether any justification or knowledge is transmitted from the premises to the conclusion, and many skeptics have doubted that they are.

Hume

In the much-discussed and enormously influential passages from Hume's *Enquiry* included in this section, he formulates this Problem of Induction. He says:

> These two propositions are far from being the same, *I have found that such an object has always been attended with such an effect*, and *I foresee, that other objects, which are, in appearance, similar, will be attended with similar effects.* I shall allow, if you please, that the one proposition may be justly inferred from the other . . . it always is inferred. But if you insist that the inference is made by a chain of reasoning, I desire you to produce that reasoning. The connection between these propositions is not intuitive. (p. 303)

One might think that there is an unstated premise in such reasonings: roughly that nature is uniform. But to claim that nature is uniform would beg the question, for one would be entitled to hold such a premise only on the basis of the kinds of inference whose capacity to transmit justification and knowledge is in question (see, for example, p. 305). Given these points, one might also wonder why Hume entitles his next chapter "Skeptical Solution of These Doubts." There has been much discussion of whether in the end Hume really is a skeptic about induction. It may be that he intends a kind of pragmatic solution. He says, for instance, "Nature will always retain her rights, and prevail in the end over any abstract reasoning whatever" (pp. 306–7). But does it solve an intellectual problem to say that we are built so that our intellectual conduct will in the end ignore it?

Edwards

Paul Edwards is among the majority of contemporary philosophers in thinking it does not solve the problem. In "Russell's Doubts About Induction" he attacks the view, held by Hume and, in a different form, by Russell, that the connection between what we properly consider good inductive grounds and the conclusion we take them to support is, as Hume said, "not intuitive." Edwards's special focus is the notion of a reason. He grants that the premises of a valid deductive argument can provide a (deductive) reason for their conclusion. But he contends that this is not the only kind of reason. To deny that the premise of a good inductive argument can also provide a reason is made to seem plausible only by in effect redefining inductive reasons in accord with deductive standards. Thus, it is plausible to say that our repeated experience of things thrown from a window falling to the ground provides no "reason" to believe the next one will fall only if one means by "reason" *deductively entailing ground.* It is uncontroversial that there is not *this* kind of reason here; but why is the inference to the conclusion that the object will fall any less "intuitive" than in the deductive case? Edwards sees no good reason, then, in Russell (or Hume) for denying that if you have a good inductive argument for a conclusion and you know or justifiedly believe your premises, your knowledge or justification can be transmitted from your premises to the conclusion you infer from them.

Goodman

One might think that if the problem of induction could be solved, whether along the lines Edwards proposes or in some other way, inductive inferences might be taken to be unproblematic to the extent that deductive inferences are. But that is not so. Nelson Goodman has posed what he calls "The New Riddle of Induction." To see it, suppose that by standard inductive inference we are justified in believing that all emeralds are green. Notice that our evidence is a matter of emeralds being observed before midnight tonight and found to be green. But suppose that we had noted that they were also "grue": that is, observed before midnight tonight and found to be green, or otherwise blue. Don't we now have just as good inductive ground for saying that all emeralds are grue? But if we do, why shouldn't we have as much justification for expecting a so far unobserved emerald to be found to be blue after midnight as to be found to be green? After all, we have apparently confirmed that all emeralds are grue, and since the emerald in question is not observed before midnight the only way it can satisfy that confirmed hypothesis *after* midnight is by being blue. There have been many attempts to deal with this problem. Goodman's own (given later in *Fact, Fiction, and Forecast* and not reprinted here) appeals to the "entrenchment" of certain terms, such as "green," as against the artificiality of predicates like "grue." This is reminiscent of Hume's comfortable appeal to the sovereignty of nature in our habits of inductive inference.

Foster

It may be, however, that John Foster's "Induction, Explanation and Natural Necessity" can be plausibly viewed as addressing both the Humean problem (as it is mainly intended to do) and the new riddle. Foster above all makes use of the idea that explanatory inferences have a special status, and he takes the hypothesis of underlying natural law to explain best the kinds of regularities whose observation provides a basis for inductive inference. One might say, on this kind of basis, that whereas the proposition that all emeralds are green might explain our past observations of their color, this is not explained by the hypothesis that all emeralds are grue. But what constitutes an explanation? And when are we *justified* in thinking we have one? These are among the enduring questions overlapping epistemology and the philosophy of science.

Howson and Urbach and Stove

The selections from Howson and Urbach and from Stove lead to yet another attempt to deal with the problem of induction, this time on the basis of considerations concerning probability. Howson and Urbach set out some basic elements in probability theory. These are important in understanding reasoning and justification in general (and they help in understanding the chapter on inference in *Epistemology*). They also set the stage for Stove's proposed solution to the problem of induction. In general terms, his contention is that "most large samples are, because most large samples arithmetically must be, representative ones" (p. 358). Suppose we have experience (as we do) with huge numbers of "heavy" objects falling to the ground when released in mid-air: many pieces of tableware, many pencils, many stones, etc. Can anyone doubt that most of the samples are representative of a genuine natural pattern?

I am afraid that where the question is "Can anyone doubt . . .?" the answer usually is "At least some philosopher can." Goodman would perhaps ask: just what pattern is represented by the confirmatory findings? Others might ask: what if there is an infinite number of specimens? Hume might point out, after all, that it is not intuitive that there cannot be an infinite number of objects of the broad "kind" we have observed falling. Still, it does seem *incredible* that there not be a *representativeness* in such cases, to use a term that straddles the psychological notion of what we cannot—by nature, as Hume might put it—believe and the normative notion of what we may justifiedly reject. The problem of induction remains a challenge to philosophy.

The architecture of knowledge

Whatever we say about the capacity of inference to transmit justification and knowledge from premises to conclusions, our normal common-sense assumption is that we do have not only non-inferential knowledge and non-inferential justified belief, but inferential knowledge and inferentially justified belief. Suppose this is so. There will then be interesting questions about the *structure* of the body of knowledge or of justified belief on the part of any given person. The natural picture, prominent in the history of philosophy and evident in many of the readings in this book, is that a body of knowledge consists of a foundation of non-inferential knowledge and a superstructure of knowledge that is in some sense inferentially based on the foundations. The same seems a natural picture for justified beliefs—which, when true, may constitute knowledge. This picture has been challenged.

Sextus Empiricus

In the selection from Sextus Empiricus we find what seems to be a presupposition that the foundationalist picture just sketched is structurally correct together with a rejection of the assumption that the foundations are solid. He is a skeptic, and he maintains, in effect, that foundations can always be undermined by certain forces. Dialectical challenges—the kind that occur in argumentative discourse—are what he chiefly has in mind (p. 373). The relation between the admissibility of certain foundational elements and the person's capacity to defend them is discussed in *Epistemology*, both in Chapter 8, on the architecture of knowledge, and in the final chapter, on skepticism.

Oakley

There is another way in which the common-sense version of the foundationalist view can be skeptically challenged. The paper by I.T. Oakley claims that even our most confident perceptual beliefs—which a plausible foundationalism is likely to construe as commonly constituting perceptual *knowledge*—are dependent on background assumptions in a way that defeats the common-sense view. He holds that "to be justified in a perception-based belief . . . it is necessary that he [the person in question] be justified in believing, *inter alia*, that he has the relevant skills, and also that there are no special circumstances currently interfering with his exercise of them" (p. 377). But how would one be justified in those beliefs without depending on still others (perhaps including some perceptual ones)? The same strategy can be used against other claims to possess justified belief, and Oakley concludes with a quite general skepticism.

BonJour

The selections from BonJour indicate how a coherentist might criticize the foundationalist picture and at the same time make a case against skepticism. In "The

Elements of Coherentism" he lays out a conception of how knowledge can be accounted for without appeal to foundations in experience, but rather in terms of how the beliefs constituting knowledge cohere (or in a special way "hang together"). In his treatment of coherence and observation (drawn from his next chapter in the book from which the selections come), he grants that if a coherent body of beliefs is to contain knowledge of the external world, it must incorporate some beliefs that in some way are tied to observation. His point is not that justification of beliefs about the world requires more than coherence; it is that a coherent system of justified beliefs about the world should not *also* be taken to constitute knowledge, and hence to be true, unless some are tied to observation. After all, he is not maintaining a coherence theory of truth, only of justification and of knowledge *given* the assumption of observations of the world that knowledge is supposed to represent. Truth, as opposed to justification, is not supposed to be analyzed in terms of coherence; hence it should be no surprise that knowledge, which entails truth, requires something more than coherence. This does not force him to treat observational beliefs as non-inferentially justified, as a foundationalist would tend to do; but it does require giving such beliefs a role that is not earned entirely through coherence among beliefs, and it implies according them a measure of epistemic privilege.

In his next chapter, "Answers to Objections," BonJour replies to a number of charges against coherentism that have appeared in the literature. One in particular deserves mention, and it would likely be pressed from the perspective of Oakley's understanding of justification and knowledge. It is that in granting that we may assume that we are approximately right about what beliefs we have, BonJour is in effect presenting "a version of weak foundationalism in which the foundational beliefs are the person's metabeliefs about the composition of his own system of beliefs" (p. 400). BonJour grants that "there is *something* to this objection," but argues that metabeliefs are not treated as they would be on a foundationalist view (p. 400). Oakley would reply that our justification for the assumption that we are generally right about what our beliefs are depends on many other assumptions. To this BonJour would rejoin that coherence among the relevant assumptions is sufficient for the justification of each.

Alston

It is in William P. Alston's "Has Foundationalism been Refuted?" that we find points that support the traditional foundationalist picture against both the kind of coherentist objections posed by BonJour and the skeptical attack of Oakley. A central point of Alston's is that "Minimal Foundationalism [the kind supported by the classical regress argument, which he states and discusses on pp. 412–13] does not require one to be able to *show* that one's foundations have the required status, but only that they *do*" (p. 406). Thus, if sensory experience justifies an observational belief, that belief can serve as a foundation even if one cannot find some *other* justified belief to supply a premise for the observational one. And unless one simply assumed that *having* justification entails being able to show that one has it, why would one demand the higher-order capacity to show this, a capacity that both BonJour and Oakley apparently think one needs?

An analogy may help here. We can have virtues we cannot show we have. Indeed, with the virtue of humility it might be quite easy to see why. Why can't justification be similar on this count? A related point is this. If, with foundationalists, one thinks that justification cannot be grounded in an infinite or circular chain of "justifications," one would, on quite systematic grounds, reject the showing requirement. For if to be justified in believing *p*, one must be able to show that *p*, and if we can show that *p* only if we bring to bear a justified belief of some premise supporting *p*, then we cannot show anything without having an infinite number of justified beliefs or circling back to, say, *p* itself as justifying some premise for it. The burden of proof is surely on the skeptic or other proponents of the showing requirement here.

I should add that there is another point (developed in Chapter 7 of *Epistemology*) that can be used to undermine both the showing requirement and Oakley's dependency argument. It is that there is a distinction between positive and negative epistemic and justificatory dependency, and only the former is needed for justification. Consider an analogy. We should not say that your source of income is the institution of money and banking, even though your income negatively depends on that, in the sense that you would not have income apart from it. The source is (say) your salary, and your income positively depends on that. Similarly, your justification does not positively depend on justification for denying skeptical possibilities. Granting that you might not be justified in believing there is paper before you if you knew that you had recently been hallucinating paper when there was none before you, why should we say that your justification for this normally depends on your knowing, or even on your justification for believing, that you have not been hallucinating? You might need such a premise to rebut an attack on your justification. But do we *have* only what we can protect from attack? It seems not, and the skeptic in any case apparently cannot show otherwise.

Haack

In the last selection on the architecture of knowledge, Susan Haack proposes a "foundherentist" view meant to capture the advantages of both foundationalism and coherentism without the deficiencies of either. Her central analogy is that of justification for beliefs formed in doing a crossword puzzle: both foundational assumptions, such as that a line in the puzzle must fit a clue, and coherence considerations involving the mutual fit among different lines, figure essentially. Her paradigmatic coherentist is BonJour; her paradigmatic foundationalists seem to be less recent writers. A fruitful comparison is with the moderate foundationalism I have set out in Chapter 7 of *Epistemology*. An interesting question to pose for her foundherentist view is whether the data supporting it can be accommodated by a moderate foundationalism in which (as would be normal) the principle that what best explains propositions we are justified in believing is itself prima facie justified. This is a principle on which, if one is perceptually justified in believing there is smoke pouring from a window, one thereby acquires justification for believing that there is a fire inside. The latter proposition certainly coheres with the former. But is that what justifies it, or is its coherence with the former a *consequence* of its being inferrable from that by a principle that some foundationalists would take to be a priori, or at least non-inferentially, justified?

The analysis of knowledge

It is fortunate for epistemological inquiry that much can be illuminatingly said about knowledge without our having a wholly satisfactory analysis of the concept and even if we have reason to doubt that such an analysis can be found. This point is illustrated by the readings in the previous sections. But as difficult as the task is, we should surely not give up the quest, and promising attempts have been and continue to be made in the field.

Ayer

The selection from Ayer sets the stage for the problem of analyzing knowledge (strictly speaking, the concept of knowledge). Ayer conceives knowledge as surety regarding a true proposition that one is, and has the right to be, sure of (p. 442). Since being sure of a proposition entails believing it, and since having the right to be sure seems to be equivalent to having justification for believing it, this characterization and others like it have come to be conceived as the view that knowledge is analyzable as justified true belief.

Gettier

Edmund Gettier's famous little paper shows that this analysis is too broad. An example different from his (drawn from Chapter 8 of *Epistemology*) illustrates the point more briefly. You enter an apartment and see a very lifelike picture of your hostess right before you. It looks to you as if she is in front of you facing in your direction, and she *is—behind* the wall on which the picture hangs. So (having no reason to suspect that there is such a picture), you are justified in your true belief. But you do not even see her and do not know she is facing you. There are many ways to respond to the problem.

Clark

Michael Clark, in the next selection, requires that one's belief be "fully grounded." But granting that my belief about my hostess is not grounded in the right *way*, why is it not *fully* grounded? My sensory experience can be just what it would be if my hostess were standing directly before me.

Goldman

In Alvin I. Goldman's "A Causal Theory of Knowing," we get an answer: there is no causal chain running from her to my senses, but only from the picture to them. Among the theoretical questions raised by this approach, however, is how it accounts for a priori knowledge. If Russell and others are right in thinking that such knowledge rests on a grasp of relations between universals, which are abstract, must we then say that universals can figure as *causes—or* figure in causal connections in a way appropriate to ground a priori knowledge of the propositions in which those universals are central?

Lehrer and Paxson

Keith Lehrer and Thomas Paxson make use not of causal concepts, but of the notion of *defeasibility*, in understanding knowledge. This rescues the spirit of the justified true belief account; we must simply require that the justification not be defeated. There are, however, difficulties in understanding the notion of defeasibility, which is quite complicated (see, for example, p. 468). One question that arises here, as with other accounts of knowledge, is whether a notion presupposed in the account is sufficiently clear to advance our understanding of the concept under analysis. Whatever we say about this in connection with defeasibility, the notion provides a distinctive way to seek an understanding of knowledge.

Nozick

In the selection from Robert Nozick, a quite different strategy is pursued, one that helps in dealing with skepticism as well as in understanding knowledge. The analysis is, on the face of it, simple. The intuitive idea is that knowledge "tracks" the truth of the proposition known. This suggests a causal conception, as in the case of tracking an animal, but is not expressed in causal language. Rather, the idea is that knowledge is a true belief such that if the proposition in question were not true, you would not believe it and, if it were true, you would (pp. 477–8). A major question here is how to figure out what one would believe and what one would not. This is a difficult question. Whatever we say about it, we should grant that at least we have intuitions about such matters and these can be useful in understanding knowledge whatever analysis we give of the notion.

DeRose

So far, I have (generally in line with the readings mentioned) spoken as if, in attributing knowledge to people, we were presupposing a constant standard of grounding of the belief in question. But Keith DeRose denies this. He considers two cases in which he is asked by his wife whether the bank is open. In one, the matter is routine; in the other, it is of great importance. He knows it is open in the first, but in the second he does not know without getting further evidence. The context of her question is crucial; hence the name "contextualism" for the view. Specifically, "Attributor factors set a certain standard the putative subject of knowledge must live up to in order to make the knowledge attribution true" (p. 497). This is why he can know in one case—in which the context does not demand a high standard for truly attributing knowledge to someone—and not in the other. The implications of this position for skepticism, as well as for understanding knowledge in ordinary cases (on almost any analysis of knowledge we might plausibly give), are significant. We can maintain that the skeptic provides a context in which the attributor standards are artificially high. If we do not meet them, then, it does not follow that we do not have knowledge in the ordinary sense of the term, but at most that we do not meet the jacked-up standards invoked by the skeptic and hence do not have knowledge in the sense that the skeptic is (at least implicitly) giving to the term. We may, then, still have knowledge more or less when we reflectively think we do.

Skepticism

On the basis of the epistemological readings and reflections now behind us, we can fruitfully consider the difficult problem of skepticism. It has already surfaced, but let us begin with a word about its Cartesian form as a background commonly presupposed in the field of epistemology.

Descartes

In René Descartes's first two Meditations (reprinted below after a synopsis of his entire set of Meditations), he formulates a powerful skeptical challenge (First Meditation) and then overcomes it to his satisfaction (Second Meditation). One of the noteworthy elements in these meditations is the notion of certainty that emerges. In some contexts it sounds as if he may be speaking of *psychological certainty*, roughly a virtually maximal degree of conviction regarding a proposition. But most of the time it seems clear that his concern is to achieve *epistemic certainty*, which is roughly a matter of being both true and utterly beyond any reasonable doubt. Psychological certainty is quite possible regarding a false proposition; epistemic certainty is not. I can *be* certain of a falsehood; but a falsehood cannot be *a certainty*. Descartes has a high standard for certainty, and later skeptics have tended to adopt a similarly high one, although it is possible to be skeptical about whether there is even justification of a kind possible without achieving epistemic certainty. Chapter 8 of *Epistemology* distinguishes these kinds of certainty in some detail and connects both with the notion of knowledge.

The standard of certainty that emerges in Descartes's Second Meditation is that of *clarity and distinctness*. Much can (and has been) said about what this is, but it is important to see that it is a status possible for beliefs about the external world, such as that the same piece of wax endures through the transformative changes it undergoes upon being melted. Moreover, that case is significant because for Descartes "the nature of this piece of wax . . . is perceived by the mind alone" (p. 522). This is one among many places in which his rationalism emerges: for him (putting the point in rough terms), reason rather than experience is the most important element in grounding knowledge. Indeed, later in the work he uses reason (together with data available to pure thought) to prove that God exists and that, since God is not a deceiver, we are not created in a way that allows our truly clear and distinct ideas, as opposed to our uncritically formed ones, to be false. God has built us so that, through (say) carelessness we can misuse our native intellectual equipment, but not with a design defect that would allow our truly competent efforts to fail. Here Descartes's theology plays a central role in his epistemology.

Putnam

If Descartes's theology is rejected, his First Meditation still stands as a powerful statement of the idea that one could be a lone ego hallucinating a non-existent external world. A contemporary version of the idea is that one could be a "brain in a vat," i.e., a brain that (with or without scientists to control the inputs) sustains one's thoughts and provides all the sense experience one now has. Hilary Putnam, however, is quite anti-Cartesian in this matter. He makes a case that, owing to how language and conceptualization work, "although the people in that possible world [in which they are brains in a vat over their whole existence] can think and 'say' any words we can think and say, they cannot (I claim) *refer* to what we can refer to. In particular they cannot think or say that they are brains in a vat (*even by thinking 'we are brains in a vat'*)" (p. 529). If this is right, then regardless of what we say, we cannot raise the Cartesian skeptical worry. This sort of strategy is sometimes called a *dissolution* of a problem, as opposed to a solution.

The other selections in the section of the book on skepticism do not attempt a dissolution (at least not of this kind), but concentrate on meeting the skeptic in a more direct way. They grant (at least for the sake of argument) that we *can* formulate the problem in the way Descartes did (or in terms of the possibility of being just a brain in a vat) and defend the common-sense view that we do have a good deal of knowledge of external things.

Dretske

Fred Dretske's paper foreshadows the contextualist view put forward by DeRose. When we see a zebra in a zoo (to use Dretske's example), do we, under the usual conditions, know that it is one even though we could not distinguish it, at the distance from which we see it, from a mule painted to look like one? It would be one thing if zoos were known to pull off such pranks, but this is not so. In the context, the possibility that we see only a painted mule is not a "relevant alternative." On the kind of view Dretske is presenting—now called *relevant alternatives theory*—one can know that *p* even if one cannot discriminate it from irrelevant alternatives. We do need to be able to distinguish it from *relevant* ones, as where zoos *are* known for such substitutions.

Another question that comes to the fore in Dretske's paper is the problem of "closure" for knowledge. In one form the question is whether there is a sort of closed though potentially expanding circle around knowledge, in the sense that for anything that one knows, one also knows every deductive consequence of it (every proposition entailed by it). Thus, suppose I know that I cannot tell the zebra I see (at the distance in question) from a mule painted to look like a zebra. Still, since its being a zebra entails that it is not a mule and I know that it is a zebra, don't I still know that it is not a mule? Dretske, Nozick, and others say we do not and do not need to know this. Others hold that we need to and we do. Skeptics maintain that we "need" to and we do not. In Chapter 6 of *Epistemology* I argue that we do not need to, and my final chapter, on skepticism, develops this position.

Klein

Peter Klein, by contrast, argues that skeptics cannot show that we would not know in such a case that the animal is not a mule (his focus is on justification, but he apparently intends his main points to apply to knowledge as well). Among the things he does are two of special interest here. First, he defends a closure principle for justification, roughly that if one is justified in believing that *p*, and *p* entails *q*, one is also justified in believing *q* (and here he critically discusses in detail an example I introduced against such a principle in Chapter 6 of *Epistemology*). Second, he argues that the skeptic cannot *motivate* the skeptical attack without granting to common sense enough to rebut skepticism in the ways he outlines. A distinctive element of this approach is the way it combines a rejection of skepticism with an acceptance of a major principle the skeptic uses and an account of how skepticism may be plausible.

Huemer
The paper on this issue by Michael Huemer deals with both Dretske's and Klein's papers. Arguing that neither succeeds against the skeptic, he contends that a direct realist account can supplement what they have done in a way that does succeed. Huemer's strategy is to take perceptual beliefs as a direct realist does: they are foundational and in general not in need of explanation. They are "not inferred from evidence" (p. 588)—a view defended in detail in Chapter 1 and elsewhere in *Epistemology*. Given this, we may properly appeal to their content in explanations in a way we may not appeal to the content of skeptical scenarios, and "the direct realist can easily refute the brain-in-a-vat hypothesis on the basis of his beliefs about the external world" (p. 587). These beliefs give us a reason to reject the kinds of artificial explanations of our experience which the skeptic would have to give.

Chisholm
The entire debate between main-line epistemologists and skeptics is placed in a broader context by R.M. Chisholm in his widely discussed paper "The Problem of the Criterion". The problem—called the "diallelus" by the ancients—is quite general, affecting any attempt at philosophical analysis. As applied to the notion of knowledge, it is this: if we have no criterion for knowledge, how do we recognize an instance of knowledge?—but if we cannot recognize an instance, then how can we ever have a criterion for knowledge? Chisholm notes three important responses:

> there is scepticism (you cannot answer either question without presupposing an answer to the other, and therefore the questions cannot be answered at all); there is "methodism" (you begin with an answer to B [the first question]); and there is "particularism" (you begin with an answer to A [the second question]). I suggest the third possibility is more reasonable. (p. 596)

What follows in the paper is an articulation of some of the basic epistemological categories we must understand in order to be critical particularists. Chisholm does not claim to prove that particularism is correct. He does, however, conclude with an affirmation it licenses: "in favor of our approach there is the fact that we *do* know many things, after all" (p. 601).

Moore
It seems fitting to close the section on skepticism with the selections from G.E. Moore's classic affirmation of common sense against skepticism, "Proof of an External World". How might we know that there is an external world? Cutting the Gordian knot, Moore simply held up his hands and said "Here is one hand" and "Here is another" (p. 602) Isn't it obvious that this "proves" there is an external world? Responses have varied: there is, for instance, annoyance, incredulity, and amusement. For this book, the interesting thing is to compare what Moore says with what the other defenders of common sense have maintained. One question is what constitutes a *proof* (a topic discussed in Chapter 9 of *Epistemology* in the section that explores the sense, if any, in which scientific

hypotheses are "proved"). Chisholm, for instance, does not claim the possibility of a proof when he says that we do know many things.

It might seem that Moore is loose in speaking of proof, but he is more discriminating than one might at first sight think. He grants, for instance, that he does not have a proof that he is not dreaming. Rather, he has "conclusive reasons for asserting that I am not now dreaming" (p. 605). We might wonder just how much of a concession this is to Cartesian skepticism—if any. But it is not only Cartesian skepticism that Moore rejects. In "Hume's Theory Examined" Moore also rejects a similar skeptical position he finds in Hume, and he does so in a way that suggests he endorses a kind of closure principle, perhaps one like the kind defended by Klein. "I *do* know that this pencil exists; but I could not know this, if Hume's principles were true; *therefore*, Hume's principles, one or both of them, are false" (p. 606). The underlying strategy Moore uses is, like Chisholm's, a foundationalist version of what might be called *epistemological commonsensism*. Moore says:

> It is certain, then, that if any proposition whatever is ever known by us mediately [roughly, inferentially], or because some other proposition is known from which it follows, some one proposition at least, must also be known by us *immediately* . . . hence it follows that the conditions necessary to make an argument good and conclusive may just as well be satisfied, when the premiss is only known *immediately*, as when there are other arguments in its favour . . . . Therefore my argument: "I know this pencil to exist; therefore, Hume's principles are false"; may be just as good an argument as any other, even though its premiss . . . is only known immediately. (p. 609)

Moore is, then, appealing to "the argument from a particular case" (pp. 609–10). Here he is fruitfully compared with Chisholm.

Another comparison worth pursuing is to my chapter on skepticism in *Epistemology*. There and elsewhere I distinguish between simple perceptual propositions, such as that there is a pencil in my hand, and epistemic propositions built from these, such as that I *know* that there is a pencil in my hand. In various parts of my book I defend the view that we have non-inferential justification for propositions of the first kind. But it is more difficult to defend the position, held by Moore and probably Chisholm, that we have non-inferential knowledge of epistemic propositions. It may be, however, that we do; and even if we do not, there are many things that can be said against the skeptic.

One simple point to keep in mind here is this. We should distinguish between *rebutting* a skeptical case, which is showing that it is unsound, and *refuting* it, which is showing that its main conclusion is false, for instance that there is, contrary to skepticism, knowledge of the external world. Much of the argumentation against skepticism laid out in this section of the volume is devoted to its attempted refutation. But although refutation suffices for rebuttal, rebuttal does not require refutation. We can show a skeptical argument unsound, for example, without showing its conclusion to be false. The prospects for refutation of skepticism in its most plausible forms may be good; but whatever they are, the prospects for rebuttal are better. Chapter 10 of *Epistemology* discusses both the distinction between refutation and rebuttal and its implications for the assessment of the controversy between common-sense epistemology and skepticism.

It would be misleading to conclude this introduction without emphasizing that although skeptical concerns are pervasive in epistemology, they are not the central rationale for studying the subject. They surely provide a sufficient reason for doing so, but the nature of knowledge and justification is of enormous interest even apart from skepticism. This is particularly so if they are seen in context, as arising in perception, consciousness, memory, reflection, and through testimony; as extended by inference and structured in accordance with both our psychological and our epistemological nature; and as extending (I think) into ethics as well as science and, for people of appropriate experience and understanding, into the aesthetic and theological realms. The study of all this does not make it obvious just what constitutes knowledge or how to vindicate the common-sense view that we have a great deal of it. But this volume contains a great deal of what is needed to search out plausible solutions to those intriguing problems.

PART I

SOURCES OF JUSTIFICATION AND KNOWLEDGE

1

PERCEPTION

According to common sense, *perception*, the exercise of the five senses, is the chief means by which we know about the world around us. For this reason, a basic understanding of the nature of perception is important to epistemology. A theory of perception should answer such questions as: *What is it to perceive something?*, *What sorts of things does perception make us aware of?*, and *How does perception enable us to gain knowledge of the world around us?* The reading selections in this chapter discuss four traditional philosophical positions, each of which addresses one or more of those questions:

1. *Representationalism*, also known as "indirect realism," maintains that in perception, we are directly aware of certain internal, mental states or entities—referred to by various philosophers as "ideas" (Locke), "impressions" (Hume), "mental images," or "sense data" (Russell)—and we are *indirectly* aware of external things (that is, our awareness of them depends on our awareness of the images). The mental images are usually said to be caused by external, physical objects/events and to "represent" the latter. Representationalists usually also say that we can have knowledge or justified beliefs about the external world by inferring facts about external objects from the character of the mental images. Usually, it is thought that the hypothesis of external objects (objects existing independent of the mind) having certain characteristics provides the best explanation for why we have the sort of sense data that we do. Representationalism, more than any other position, probably deserves to be called the traditional theory of perception among philosophers.
2. By contrast, *direct realists* maintain that in perception, we are directly aware of external objects, that is, that our awareness of external objects does not depend upon the awareness of mental images or any other non-external things. Direct realists also generally claim that we have immediate (non-inferential) knowledge of the existence of, and some of the properties of, the external objects that we perceive. This view has sometimes been called "naive realism" (chiefly by its opponents), partly because it seems to be the view of common sense and also, probably, partly because its opponents have considered it too simplistic.
3. *Idealism* holds that there is no external world; all there are are minds and "ideas" in the mind. Perception, on this view, is simply the process of experiencing a certain particularly vivid sort of idea. (Note that "idea" is here used in an extended sense—it covers all mental phenomena.) There is thus no problem about how we know about external objects. Very few philosophers hold this

position today, although it enjoyed surprising popularity during the nineteenth century.

4. Finally, *skepticism* holds that we cannot know whether there is an external world or not; nor can we know, if there is, what it is like. Note that this position is not idealism, because the skeptic, unlike the idealist, does not *deny* the existence of external objects; he merely says that we do not *know* they exist.

Each of the selections in this chapter discusses one or more of the above theories.

John Locke in the seventeenth century gave what is perhaps the classic exposition of representationalism, to which later thinkers would respond. Locke uses the term "idea" to refer to any mental object that we are immediately aware of. In his view, all our "ideas" come either from "sensation" (meaning the five senses) or from "reflection" (meaning one's introspective observation of the operations of one's own mind). In normal sense perception, an external object causes us to experience an idea that represents that object. It was Locke's view that the external object resembles the idea we have of it in respect of spatial properties—e.g., if you see a round tomato, then you will have a round (tomato-shaped) image in your mind.

Locke also thought (although this is not discussed in the selection printed here) that there were other properties—including colors, tastes, smells, and sounds—that either were not really in the external object or existed only as *dispositions* the object had to cause certain kinds of sensations in us. For instance, your sensation of redness (*unlike* your idea of roundness) does *not* resemble any property in the physical tomato; the tomato just has a power to produce that sensation in you. The latter properties (colors, tastes, etc.) he called "secondary qualities." The properties of objects that resemble our ideas (chiefly spatial properties and mathematical properties, such as quantity) he called "primary qualities." We won't here go into the reasons that Locke believed in this distinction, although it comes up again in the Berkeley selection.

How do we know that there actually are external objects? Locke admits that one cannot be as certain of the existence of external things as one can of one's own existence (that is, of the existence of one's own mind), but he thinks it is rational to assume that our senses are trustworthy. Among other things, he states that our sensory ideas must be caused by external objects, since we do not have control over our sense perceptions, whereas we would have control over them if we caused them. He also points out that the information we acquire from different senses tends to fit together, which would be unlikely if our senses were generally unreliable. For instance, when one sees an object, one can usually also reach out and touch that object, and the shape it looks to have will generally be the same as the shape one feels. The things one perceives also have steady characteristics and obey regular laws; for instance, one can write down some words on a page, and the words will stay there, and be perceived by other people, just as you originally wrote them, even if you have forgotten what you wrote. This tends to show that the perceptions you experience are caused by things that exist independent of your mind, i.e., external objects.

Reacting in large part to Locke, Bishop George Berkeley became the first idealist in Western philosophical history, declaring that only minds and ideas in the mind existed. Odd as this sounds, it was a natural development after Locke: if the only things we are immediately aware of are ideas, why think that anything other than ideas exists? If we had the same ideas but there were no external objects, Berkeley argued, everything would seem exactly the same as it does now. As for what causes our ideas, Berkeley proposed that God plants certain ideas in our minds on an ongoing basis and makes sure to coordinate different people's ideas (so that you and I can both see a table at the same time, for instance). The ideas caused by God are the really vivid ones that we have no control over—otherwise known as "sense perceptions." (There are also some less vivid ideas that we have control over—the ideas created in imagination—which are not caused by God.) Berkeley insisted that he was not denying the reality of tables, rocks, and so on; rather, he was just saying that those things are collections of ideas (tables are real because ideas are perfectly real *as* ideas in the mind). However, most other philosophers have thought that he *was* denying the reality of those objects, in spite of his claim to the contrary.

What arguments did Berkeley have? Three main ones. One was the argument given in the last paragraph, that we have no reason for believing in external objects. Second, Berkeley argued that we could not have any coherent conception of what external objects were like. Locke had said that they resembled our ideas, but Berkeley argued that nothing could resemble an idea, except another idea. Locke had deployed arguments to show that our ideas of "secondary qualities" did not resemble qualities in the external objects. Berkeley showed that the same kind of arguments could be used to argue that primary qualities were not in external objects either, leaving external objects with no (comprehensible) qualities at all, and it did not seem reasonable to believe in things with no qualities. Third, Berkeley argued that the concept of an external object—a thing existing completely independent of the mind—was self-contradictory. Roughly, he argued that one could not conceive of anything existing outside the mind, because if one tried to conceive of such a thing, the thing would then, by the very fact that one was conceiving of it, be in one's own mind (section 23). Since he also thought that anything that was inconceivable was impossible, he concluded that external objects could not exist.

Most of his contemporaries in the eighteenth century seem to have regarded Berkeley's position as absurd, although they could not refute his arguments on an intellectual level. Dr. Samuel Johnson was informed of Berkeley's theory and asked how he would refute it. Johnson, famously, proceeded to kick a rock, saying, "I refute it thus." Berkeley, of course, would have said that the pain Johnson felt in his foot was just another idea in his mind.

David Hume (writing in the eighteenth century, shortly after Berkeley) criticizes direct realism, using a famous argument called "the argument from illusion." The argument begins by observing that the character of our sensory experiences often varies even when there is no change in the physical object we are putatively perceiving. For example, as one moves farther away from a table, the table looks smaller, but there is no objective change in the physical table. This allegedly shows that one is not genuinely perceiving the real table. Rather, one is perceiving an *image* of the table in one's mind. Ordinary people, Hume thinks, commonly confuse this image with the real object. The image represents the physical table but is not identical with it, since the image can get smaller while the real table stays the same size. Hume thus favors indirect realism over direct realism.

Hume also puts forward a skeptical argument. Since we are only directly aware of sensory images, in order to have any knowledge of the external world, we must be able to verify that sensory images of a particular kind are caused by physical objects of a particular kind. For instance, in order to have knowledge of a physical table, we must be able to verify that table-images are caused by real, physical tables. According to Hume, the only way we can ever know that one kind of thing, *A*, causes another kind of thing, *B*, is by experience: specifically, we must observe instances of *A* being followed by instances of *B*, on a number of occasions.[1] But we have already established that one can never really observe physical objects but only their images; therefore, we cannot know anything about the causal relations physical objects stand in.

Thus, Hume holds an unusual combination of indirect realism and skepticism: he believes that our sensory images are representations of real things existing outside the mind, but he also believes that that belief cannot be rationally defended. These seemingly conflicting beliefs are to some extent reconciled when we note that in Hume's view, it is a mistake to demand rational justifications for all our beliefs; many (perhaps all) of our beliefs are the product of ineradicable instincts, rather than reason, and Hume does not see this as a problem.

Thomas Reid developed his direct realist theory of perception mainly in response to Hume and Berkeley. He conceded that Berkeley's arguments would be irrefutable *if* one accepted the premise (which Locke and Hume had both adopted) that we can only directly perceive ideas. Reid, in fact, had been a follower of Berkeley at one time in his life, until he (Reid) noticed that if Berkeley's theory were true, there would be no reason to believe that other people were conscious, since the "other people" he perceived were just ideas in his own mind. He considered this consequence to be unacceptable, so he turned to questioning Berkeley's starting premise. Reid concluded, against Berkeley, Hume, and Locke, that we do not perceive ideas; rather, we perceive physical objects, directly. He also concluded that we are justified in believing in external objects without the need for any argument for their existence. He compares the principle that the things we perceive exist, to the axioms of a mathematical system—both, he thinks, should be accepted as self-evident.

The only argument Reid could find against direct realism was Hume's argument from illusion (see above). Reid proposed to explain Hume's phenomenon by drawing a distinction between the "apparent magnitude" and the "real magnitude" of the table. What he probably meant by the "apparent magnitude" of the table was its *angular* size, relative to the eye. To explain: imagine drawing a line connecting one extremity of the table to your eye. Draw another line connecting the other extremity of the table to the same eye. The angle that the two lines make where they meet is the angular size of the table, relative to the point where the eye is located. The "real magnitude" of the table is just its length, as measured in feet, inches, etc. Reid explains that the table "appears smaller" as you move away from it, not because you are perceiving an image, but because you perceive the angular magnitude of the table by the sense of sight (the real magnitude is perceived by the sense of touch), and the angular magnitude of the table decreases with distance, as dictated by the laws of geometry. In fact, the phenomenon is exactly what you should expect if you are seeing a real table; therefore, if anything, Hume's experiment gives evidence that we *are* perceiving the real table.

Bertrand Russell (one of the most important twentieth-century philosophers) defended a form of indirect realism. His view came to be called "the sense data theory," since he used the term "sense data" to refer to the mental images that, in his view, we are directly aware of in perception. Russell deploys versions of the argument from illusion, noting that the apparent shape and color of a table depend not just upon the properties of the table, but also upon the location of the observer and the lighting conditions. He thinks that this refutes direct realism, and he goes on to ask whether and how we can have knowledge of external, physical objects. While he concedes that we can never be certain that external objects exist, he argues that it is highly probable that they do. The reason is that the hypothesis of a world of external objects, which exist even when we are not looking at them, provides the simplest explanation for our sense data (our sense data behave just the way they would behave if they were caused by physical objects), and we have no positive reason to doubt the existence of external objects.

Lastly, the selections from John Austin (based on a series of lectures that he gave) criticize the argument from illusion and the sense data theory. Austin responds specifically to A.J. Ayer, whose views were very similar to those of Russell. Austin practised a style of philosophy popular in the twentieth century known as "ordinary language philosophy," which held that the job of philosophers was to analyze the way people use language. He argues that the argument from illusion draws plausibility from various misuses of language. Austin also points out an important *non sequitur* in the argument as Ayer presents it: Ayer discusses the famous optical illusion in which a straight stick, when halfway immersed in water, appears bent. Ayer claims that in this case what one sees cannot be the real stick. As Austin notes, from the fact that the stick looks bent, it does not follow that one is seeing something that is bent, nor does it follow that one is not seeing the actual stick. Rather, one is seeing a *straight* stick that *appears bent*. Austin sees no difficulty in this. Other versions of the argument from illusion seem to involve the same fallacy. Austin does not put forward any positive arguments for an alternative theory of perception (although presumably he would endorse direct realism), preferring instead to focus on criticizing the motivations offered for sense data.

Note

1. He discusses this point at greater length in section IV of his *Enquiry Concerning Human Understanding*, reprinted in Chapter 6 of this volume.

John Locke, *Essay Concerning Human Understanding*

(Book I, Chapter i)

§ 8. Thus much I thought necessary to say concerning the Occasion of this Enquiry into humane Understanding. But, before I proceed on to what I have thought on this Subject, I must here in the Entrance beg pardon of my Reader, for the frequent use of the Word *Idea*, which he will find in the following Treatise. It being that Term, which, I think, serves best to stand for whatsoever is the Object of the Understanding when a Man thinks, I have used it to express whatever is meant by *Phantasm, Notion, Species*, or whatever it is, which the Mind can be employ'd about in thinking; and I could not avoid frequently using it.

I presume it will be easily granted me, that there are such *Ideas* in Men's Minds; every one is conscious of them in himself, and Men's Words and Actions will satisfy him, that they are in others.

Our first Enquiry then shall be, how they come into the Mind.

(Book II, Chapter i)

§ 2. Let us then suppose the Mind to be, as we say, white Paper, void of all Characters, without any *Ideas*; How comes it to be furnished? Whence comes it by that vast store, which the busy and boundless Fancy of Man has painted on it, with an almost endless variety? Whence has it all the materials of Reason and Knowledge? To this I answer, in one word, From *Experience*: In that, all our Knowledge is founded; and from that it ultimately derives it self. Our Observation employ'd either about *external, sensible Objects; or about the internal Operations of our Minds, perceived and reflected on by our selves, is that, which supplies our Understandings with all the materials of thinking*. These two are the Fountains of Knowledge, from whence all the *Ideas* we have, or can naturally have, do spring.

§ 3. First, *Our Senses*, conversant about particular sensible Objects, do *convey into the Mind*, several distinct *Perceptions* of things, according to those various ways, wherein those Objects do affect them: And thus we come by those *Ideas*, we have of *Yellow, White, Heat, Cold, Soft, Hard, Bitter, Sweet*, and all those

J. Locke, *Essay Concerning Human Understanding*, ed. P.H. Nidditch (Oxford: Oxford University Press, 1975).

which we call sensible qualities, which when I say the senses convey into the mind, I mean, they from external Objects convey into the mind what produces there those *Perceptions*. This great Source, of most of the *Ideas* we have, depending wholly upon our Senses, and derived by them to the Understanding, I call *SENSATION*.

(Book II, Chapter xxxii)

§ 3. But 'tis not in that metaphysical Sense of Truth, which we enquire here, when we examine, whether our *Ideas* are capable of being *true* or *false*; but in the more ordinary Acceptation of those Words: And so I say, that the *Ideas* in our Minds, being only so many Perceptions, or Appearances there, none of them are *false*. The *Idea* of a Centaur, having no more Falshood in it, when it appears in our Minds; than the Name Centaur has Falshood in it, when it is pronounced by our Mouths, or written on Paper. For Truth or Falshood, lying always in some Affirmation, or Negation, Mental or Verbal, our *Ideas* are *not capable* any of them *of being false*, till the Mind passes some Judgment on them; that is, affirms or denies something of them.

§ 4. When-ever the Mind refers any of its *Ideas* to any thing extraneous to them, they are then *capable to be called true or false*. Because the Mind in such a reference, makes a tacit Supposition of their Conformity to that Thing: which Supposition, as it happens to be *true* or *false*; so the *Ideas* themselves come to be denominated.

(Book IV, Chapter xi)

Of our Knowledge of the Existence of other Things

§ 1. THE Knowledge of our own Being, we have by intuition. The Existence of a GOD, Reason clearly makes known to us, as has been shewn.

The *Knowledge of the Existence* of any other thing we can have only by *Sensation*: For there being no necessary connexion of *real Existence*, with any *Idea* a Man hath in his Memory, nor of any other Existence but that of GOD, with the Existence of any particular Man; no particular Man can know the *Existence* of any other Being, but only when by actual operating upon him, it makes it self perceived by him. For the having the *Idea* of any thing in our Mind, no more proves the Existence of that Thing, than the picture of a Man evidences his being in the World, or the Visions of a Dream make thereby a true History.

§ 2. 'Tis therefore the actual receiving of *Ideas* from without, that gives us notice of the *Existence* of other Things, and makes us know, that something doth exist at that time without us, which causes that *Idea* in us, though perhaps we neither know nor consider how it does it: For it takes not from the certainty of our Senses, and the *Ideas* we receive by them, that we know not the manner wherein they are produced: *v.g.* whilst I write this, I have, by the Paper affecting my Eyes, that *Idea* produced in my Mind, which whatever Object causes, I call *White*; by which I know, that that Quality or Accident (*i.e.* whose appearance before my Eyes, always causes that *Idea*) doth really exist, and hath a Being without me. And of this, the greatest assurance I can possibly have, and to which my Faculties can attain, is the Testimony of my Eyes, which are the proper and sole Judges of this thing, whose Testimony I have reason to rely on, as so certain, that I can no more doubt, whilst I write this, that I see White and Black, and that something really exists, that causes that Sensation in me, than that I write or move my Hand; which is a Certainty as great, as humane Nature is capable of, concerning the Existence of any thing, but a Man's self alone, and of GOD.

§ 3. *The Notice we have by our Senses, of the existing of Things without* us, though it be not altogether so certain, as our intuitive Knowledge, or the Deductions of our Reason, employ'd about the clear abstract *Ideas* of our own Minds; yet it is an assurance that *deserves the name of Knowledge*. If we persuade our selves, that our Faculties act and inform us right, concerning the existence of those Objects that affect them, it cannot pass for an ill-grounded confidence: For I think no body can, in earnest, be so sceptical, as to be uncertain of the Existence of those Things which he sees and feels. At least, he that can doubt so far, (whatever he may have with his own Thoughts) will never have any Controversies with me; since he can never be sure I say any thing contrary to his Opinion. As to my self, I think GOD has given me assurance enough of the Existence of Things without me: since by their different application, I can produce in my self both Pleasure and Pain, which is one great Concernment of my present state. This is certain, the confidence that our Faculties do not herein deceive us, is the greatest assurance we are capable of, concerning the Existence of material Beings. For we cannot act any thing, but by our Faculties; nor talk of Knowledge it self, but by the help of those Faculties, which are fitted to apprehend even what Knowledge is. But besides the assurance we have from our Senses themselves, that they do not err in the Information they give us, of the Existence of Things without us, when they are affected by them, we are farther confirmed in this assurance, by other concurrent Reasons.

§ 4. *First*, 'Tis plain, those Perceptions are produced in us by exteriour Causes affecting our Senses: Because *those that want the Organs of any Sense, never can have the* Ideas *belonging to that Sense* produced in their Minds. This is too evident to be doubted: and therefore we cannot but be assured, that they come in by the Organs of that Sense, and no other way. The Organs themselves, 'tis plain, do not produce them: for then the Eyes of a Man in the dark, would produce Colours, and his Nose smell Roses in the Winter: but we see no body gets the relish of a Pine-apple, till he goes to the *Indies*, where it is, and tastes it.

§ 5. *Secondly*, Because *sometimes I find, that I cannot avoid the having those* Ideas *produced in my Mind*. For though when my Eyes are shut, or Windows fast, I can at Pleasure re-call to my Mind the *Ideas* of *Light*, or the *Sun*, which former Sensations had lodg'd in my Memory; so I can at pleasure lay by that *Idea*, and take into my view that of the *smell* of a Rose, or *taste* of Sugar. But if I turn my Eyes at noon towards the Sun, I cannot avoid the *Ideas*, which the Light, or Sun, then produces in me. So that there is a manifest difference, between the *Ideas* laid up in my Memory; (over which, if they were there only, I should have constantly the same power to dispose of them, and lay them by at pleasure) and those which force themselves upon me, and I cannot avoid having. And therefore it must needs be some exteriour cause, and the brisk acting of some Objects without me, whose efficacy I cannot resist, that produces those *Ideas* in my Mind, whether I will, or no. Besides, there is no body who doth not perceive the difference in himself, between contemplating the Sun, as he hath the *Idea* of it in his Memory, and actually looking upon it: Of which two, his perception is so distinct, that few of his *Ideas* are more distinguishable one from another. And therefore he hath certain knowledge, that they are not both Memory, or the Actions of his Mind, and Fancies only within him; but that actual seeing hath a Cause without.

§ 6. *Thirdly*, Add to this, that *many of those* Ideas *are produced in us with pain, which afterwards we remember without the least offence*. Thus the pain of Heat or Cold, when the *Idea* of it is revived in our Minds, gives us no disturbance; which, when felt, was very troublesome, and is again, when actually repeated: which is occasioned by the disorder the external Object causes in our Bodies, when applied to it: And we remember the pain of *Hunger*, *Thirst*, or the *Head-ach*, without any pain at all; which would either never disturb us, or else constantly do it, as often as we thought of it, were there nothing more but *Ideas* floating in our Minds, and appearances entertaining our Fancies, without the real Existence of Things affecting us from abroad. The same may be said of Pleasure, accompanying several actual Sensations: And though mathematical demonstrations depend not upon sense, yet the examining them by Diagrams, gives great credit to the Evidence of our Sight, and seems to give it a Certainty approaching to that of the Demonstration it self. For it would be very strange, that a Man should allow it for an undeniable Truth, that two Angles of a Figure, which he measures by Lines and Angles of a Diagram, should be bigger one than the other; and yet doubt of the Existence of those Lines and Angles, which by looking on, he makes use of to measure that by.

§ 7. *Fourthly*, Our *Senses*, in many cases bear *witness* to the Truth of each other's report, concerning the Existence of sensible Things without us. He that sees a *Fire*, may, if he doubt whether it be any thing more than a bare Fancy, feel it too; and be convinced, by putting his Hand in it. Which certainly could never be put into such exquisite pain, by a bare *Idea* or Phantom, unless that the pain be a fancy too: Which yet he cannot, when the Burn is well, by raising the *Idea* of it, bring upon himself again.

Thus I see, whilst I write this, I can change the Appearance of the Paper; and by designing the Letters, tell before-hand what new *Idea* it shall exhibit the very next moment, barely by drawing my Pen over it: which will neither appear (let me fancy as much as I will) if my Hand stands still; or though I move my Pen, if my Eyes be shut: Nor when those Characters are once made on the Paper, can I chuse afterwards but see them as they are; that is, have the *Ideas* of such Letters as I have made. Whence it is manifest, that they are not barely the Sport and Play of my own Imagination, when I find, that the Characters, that were made at the pleasure of my own Thoughts, do not obey them; nor yet cease to be, whenever I shall fancy it, but continue to affect my Senses constantly and regularly, according to the Figures I made them. To which if we will add, that the sight of those shall, from another Man, draw such Sounds, as I before-hand design they shall stand for, there will be little reason left to doubt, that those Words, I write, do really exist without me, when they cause a long series of regular Sounds to affect my Ears, which could not be the effect of my Imagination, nor could my Memory retain them in that order.

QUESTIONS

1 For Locke, what is an "idea"?
2 According to Locke, can we know of the existence of external objects? Can we be certain of it?
3 Locke says that there are some ideas he cannot avoid having. What is this supposed to show?
4 Locke gives an example of writing some words on a page. How can he tell that the written words exist outside of his mind?

George Berkeley, *Of the Principles of Human Knowledge*

It is evident to any one who takes a survey of the *objects* of human knowledge, that they are either ideas actually imprinted on the senses; or else such as are perceived by attending to the passions and operations of the mind; or lastly, ideas formed by help of memory and imagination—either compounding, dividing, or barely representing those originally perceived in the aforesaid ways. By sight I have the ideas of light and colours, with their several degrees and variations. By touch I perceive hard and soft, heat and cold, motion and resistance, and of all these more and less either as to quantity or degree. Smelling furnishes me with odours; the palate with tastes; and hearing conveys sounds to the mind in all their variety of tone and composition. And as several of these are observed to accompany each other, they come to be marked by one name, and so to be reputed as one thing. Thus, for example, a certain colour, taste, smell, figure and consistence having been observed to go together, are accounted one distinct thing, signified by the name *apple*; other collections of ideas constitute a stone, a tree, a book, and the like sensible things—which as they are pleasing or disagreeable excite the passions of love, hatred, joy, grief, and so forth.

2. But, besides all that endless variety of ideas or objects of knowledge, there is likewise something which knows or perceives them, and exercises divers operations, as willing, imagining, remembering, about them. This perceiving, active being is what I call *mind, spirit, soul*, or *myself*. By which words I do not denote any one of my ideas, but a thing entirely distinct from them, wherein, they exist, or, which is the same thing, whereby they are perceived—for the existence of an idea consists in being perceived.

3. That neither our thoughts, nor passions, nor ideas formed by the imagination, exist without the mind, is what everybody will allow. And it seems no less evident that the various sensations or ideas imprinted on the sense, however blended or combined together (that is, whatever objects they compose), cannot exist otherwise than in a mind perceiving them.—I think an intuitive knowledge may be obtained of this by any one that shall attend to what is meant by the term *exists*, when applied to sensible things. The table I write on I say exists, that is, I see and feel it; and if I were out of my study I should say it existed—meaning thereby that if I was in my study I might perceive it, or that some other spirit actually does perceive it. There was an odour, that is, it was smelt; there was a

George Berkeley, *The Principles of Human Knowledge* (Chicago: Open Court, 1904).

sound, that is, it was heard; a colour or figure, and it was perceived by sight or touch. This is all that I can understand by these and the like expressions. For as to what is said of the absolute existence of unthinking things without any relation to their being perceived, that seems perfectly unintelligible. Their *esse* is *percipi*, nor is it possible they should have any existence out of the minds or thinking things which perceive them.

4. It is indeed an opinion strangely prevailing amongst men, that houses, mountains, rivers, and in a word all sensible objects, have an existence, natural or real, distinct from their being perceived by the understanding. But, with how great an assurance and acquiescence soever this principle may be entertained in the world, yet whoever shall find in his heart to call it in question may, if I mistake not, perceive it to involve a manifest contradiction. For, what are the fore-mentioned objects but the things we perceive by sense? and what do we perceive besides our own ideas or sensations? and is it not plainly repugnant that any one of these, or any combination of them, should exist unperceived?

5. If we thoroughly examine this tenet it will, perhaps, be found at bottom to depend on the doctrine of *abstract ideas*. For can there be a nicer strain of abstraction than to distinguish the existence of sensible objects from their being perceived, so as to conceive them existing unperceived? Light and colours, heat and cold, extension and figures—in a word the things we see and feel—what are they but so many sensations, notions, ideas, or impressions on the sense? and is it possible to separate, even in thought, any of these from perception? For my part, I might as easily divide a thing from itself. I may, indeed, divide in my thoughts, or conceive apart from each other, those things which, perhaps I never perceived by sense so divided. Thus, I imagine the trunk of a human body without the limbs, or conceive the smell of a rose without thinking on the rose itself. So far, I will not deny, I can abstract—if that may properly be called *abstraction* which extends only to the conceiving separately such objects as it is possible may really exist or be actually perceived asunder. But my conceiving or imagining power does not extend beyond the possibility of real existence or perception. Hence, as it is impossible for me to see or feel anything without an actual sensation of that thing, so is it impossible for me to conceive in my thoughts any sensible thing or object distinct from the sensation or perception of it.

6. Some truths there are so near and obvious to the mind that a man need only open his eyes to see them. Such I take this important one to be, viz., that all the choir of heaven and furniture of the earth, in a word all those bodies which compose the mighty frame of the world, have not any subsistence without a mind, that their *being* is to be perceived or known; that consequently so long as they are not actually perceived by me, or do not exist in my mind or that of any other created spirit, they must either have no existence at all, or else subsist in the mind of some Eternal Spirit—it being perfectly unintelligible, and involving all the absurdity of abstraction, to attribute to any single part of them an existence independent of a spirit. To be convinced of which, the reader need only reflect, and try to separate in his own thoughts the *being* of a sensible thing from its *being perceived*.

7. From what has been said it follows there is not any other Substance than *Spirit*, or that which perceives. But, for the fuller proof of this point, let it be

considered the sensible qualities are colour, figure, motion, smell, taste, etc., *i.e.* the ideas perceived by sense. Now, for an idea to exist in an unperceiving thing is a manifest contradiction, for to have an idea is all one as to perceive; that therefore wherein colour, figure, and the like qualities exist must perceive them; hence it is clear there can be no unthinking substance or *substratum* of those ideas.

8. But, say you, though the ideas themselves do not exist without the mind, yet there may be things like them, whereof they are copies or resemblances, which things exist without the mind in an unthinking substance. I answer, an idea can be like nothing but an idea; a colour or figure can be like nothing but another colour or figure. If we look but never so little into our thoughts, we shall find it impossible for us to conceive a likeness except only between our ideas. Again, I ask whether those supposed originals or external things, of which our ideas are the pictures or representations, be themselves perceivable or no? If they are, then they are ideas and we have gained our point; but if you say they are not, I appeal to any one whether it be sense to assert a colour is like something which is invisible; hard or soft, like something which is intangible; and so of the rest.

9. Some there are who make a distinction betwixt *primary* and *secondary* qualities. By the former they mean extension, figure, motion, rest, solidity or impenetrability, and number; by the latter they denote all other sensible qualities, as colours, sounds, tastes, and so forth. The ideas we have of these they acknowledge not to be the resemblances of anything existing without the mind, or unperceived, but they will have our ideas of the primary qualities to be patterns or images of things which exist without the mind, in an unthinking substance which they call Matter. By Matter, therefore, we are to understand an inert, senseless substance, in which extension, figure, and motion do actually subsist. But it is evident from what we have already shown, that extension, figure, and motion are only ideas existing in the mind, and that an idea can be like nothing but another idea, and that consequently neither they nor their archetypes can exist in an unperceiving substance. Hence, it is plain that the very notion of what is called *Matter* or *corporeal substance*, involves a contradiction in it.

10. They who assert that figure, motion, and the rest of the primary or original qualities do exist without the mind in unthinking substance, do at the same time acknowledge that colours, sounds, heat, cold, and such-like secondary qualities, do not—which they tell us are sensations existing in the mind alone, that depend on and are occasioned by the different size, texture, and motion of the minute particles of matter. This they take for an undoubted truth, which they can demonstrate beyond all exception. Now, if it be certain that those original qualities are inseparably united with the other sensible qualities, and not, even in thought, capable of being abstracted from them, it plainly follows that they exist only in the mind. But I desire any one to reflect and try whether he can, by any abstraction of thought, conceive the extension and motion of a body without all other sensible qualities. For my own part, I see evidently that it is not in my power to frame an idea of a body extended and moving, but I must withal give it some colour or other sensible quality which is acknowledged to exist only in the mind. In short, extension, figure, and motion, abstracted from all other qualities, are inconceivable. Where therefore the other sensible qualities are, there must these be also, to wit, in the mind and nowhere else.

11. Again, *great* and *small, swift* and *slow*, are allowed to exist nowhere without the mind, being entirely relative, and changing as the frame or position of the organs of sense varies. The extension therefore which exists without the mind is neither great nor small, the motion neither swift nor slow, that is, they are nothing at all. But, say you, they are extension in general, and motion in general: thus we see how much the tenet of extended movable substances existing without the mind depends on the strange doctrine of *abstract ideas*. And here I cannot but remark how nearly the vague and indeterminate description of Matter or corporeal substance, which the modern philosophers are run into by their own principles, resembles that antiquated and so much ridiculed notion of *materia prima*, to be met with in Aristotle and his followers. Without extension solidity cannot be conceived; since therefore it has been shewn that extension exists not in an unthinking substance, the same must also be true of solidity.

12. That number is entirely the creature of the mind, even though the other qualities be allowed to exist without, will be evident to whoever considers that the same thing bears a different denomination of number as the mind views it with different respects. Thus, the same extension is one, or three, or thirty-six, according as the mind considers it with reference to a yard, a foot, or an inch. Number is so visibly relative, and dependent on men's understanding, that it is strange to think how any one should give it an absolute existence without the mind. We say one book, one page, one line, etc.; all these are equally units, though some contain several of the others. And in each instance, it is plain, the unit relates to some particular combination of ideas arbitrarily put together by the mind.

13. Unity I know some will have to be a simple or uncompounded idea, accompanying all other ideas into the mind. That I have any such idea answering the word *unity* I do not find; and if I had, methinks I could not miss finding it: on the contrary, it should be the most familiar to my understanding, since it is said to accompany all other ideas, and to be perceived by all the ways of sensation and reflexion. To say no more, it is an *abstract idea*.

14. I shall farther add, that, after the same manner as modern philosophers prove certain sensible qualities to have no existence in Matter, or without the mind, the same thing may be likewise proved of all other sensible qualities whatsoever. Thus, for instance, it is said that heat and cold are affections only of the mind, and not at all patterns of real beings, existing in the corporeal substances which excite them, for that the same body which appears cold to one hand seems warm to another. Now, why may we not as well argue that figure and extension are not patterns or resemblances of qualities existing in Matter, because to the same eye at different stations, or eyes of a different texture at the same station, they appear various, and cannot therefore be the images of anything settled and determinate without the mind? Again, it is proved that sweetness is not really in the sapid thing, because the thing remaining unaltered the sweetness is changed into bitter, as in case of a fever or otherwise vitiated palate. Is it not as reasonable to say that motion is not without the mind, since if the succession of ideas in the mind become swifter, the motion, it is acknowledged, shall appear slower without any alteration in any external object?

15. In short, let any one consider those arguments which are thought manifestly to prove that colours and taste exist only in the mind, and he shall find they

may with equal force be brought to prove the same thing of extension, figure, and motion. Though it must be confessed this method of arguing does not so much prove that there is no extension or colour in an outward object, as that we do not know by sense which is the true extension or colour of the object. But the arguments foregoing plainly show it to be impossible that any colour or extension at all, or other sensible quality whatsoever, should exist in an unthinking subject without the mind, or in truth, that there should be any such thing as an outward object.

16. But let us examine a little the received opinon.—It is said extension is a mode or accident of Matter, and that Matter is the *substratum* that supports it. Now I desire that you would explain to me what is meant by Matter's *supporting* extension. Say you, I have no idea of Matter and therefore cannot explain it. I answer, though you have no positive, yet, if-you have any meaning at all, you must at least have a relative idea of Matter; though you know not what it is, yet you must be supposed to know what relation it bears to accidents, and what is meant by its supporting them. It is evident "support" cannot here be taken in its usual or literal sense—as when we say that pillars support a building; in what sense therefore must it be taken?

17. If we inquire into what the most accurate philosophers declare themselves to mean by *material substance*, we shall find them acknowledge they have no other meaning annexed to those sounds but the idea of Being in general, together with the relative notion of its supporting accidents. The general idea of Being appeareth to me the most abstract and incomprehensible of all other; and as for its supporting accidents, this, as we have just now observed, cannot be understood in the common sense of those words; it must therefore be taken in some other sense, but what that is they do not explain. So that when I consider the two parts or branches which make the signification of the words *material substance*, I am convinced there is no distinct meaning annexed to them. But why should we trouble ourselves any farther, in discussing this material *substratum* or support of figure and motion, and other sensible qualities? Does it not suppose they have an existence without the mind? And is not this a direct repugnancy, and altogether inconceivable?

18. But, though it were possible that solid, figured, movable substances may exist without the mind, corresponding to the ideas we have of bodies, yet how is it possible for us to know this? Either we must know it by sense or by reason. As for our senses, by them we have the knowledge only of our sensations, ideas, or those things that are immediately perceived by sense, call them what you will: but they do not inform us that things exist without the mind, or unperceived, like to those which are perceived. This the materialists themselves acknowledge. It remains therefore that if we have any knowledge at all of external things, it must be by reason, inferring their existence from what is immediately perceived by sense. But what reason can induce us to believe the existence of bodies without the mind, from what we perceive, since the very patrons of Matter themselves do not pretend there is any necessary connexion betwixt them and our ideas? I say it is granted on all hands (and what happens in dreams, phrensies, and the like, puts it beyond dispute) that it is possible we might be affected with all the ideas we have now, though there were no bodies existing without resembling them. Hence, it is evident the supposition of external bodies is not necessary for the producing

our ideas; since it is granted they are produced sometimes, and might possibly be produced always in the same order, we see them in at present, without their concurrence.

19. But, though we might possibly have all our sensations without them, yet perhaps it may be thought easier to conceive and explain the manner of their production, by supposing external bodies in their likeness rather than otherwise; and so it might be at least probable there are such things as bodies that excite their ideas in our minds. But neither can this be said; for, though we give the materialists their external bodies, they by their own confession are never the nearer knowing how our ideas are produced; since they own themselves unable to comprehend in what manner body can act upon spirit, or how it is possible it should imprint any idea in the mind. Hence it is evident the production of ideas or sensations in our minds can be no reason why we should suppose Matter or corporeal substances, since that is acknowledged to remain equally inexplicable with or without this supposition. If therefore it were possible for bodies to exist without the mind, yet to hold they do so, must needs be a very precarious opinion; since it is to suppose, without any reason at all, that God has created innumerable beings that are entirely useless, and serve to no manner of purpose.

20. In short, if there were external bodies, it is impossible we should ever come to know it; and if there were not, we might have the very same reasons to think there were that we have now. Suppose—what no one can deny possible—an intelligence without the help of external bodies, to be affected with the same train of sensations or ideas that you are, imprinted in the same order and with like vividness in his mind. I ask whether that intelligence hath not all the reason to believe the existence of corporeal substances, represented by his ideas, and exciting them in his mind, that you can possibly have for believing the same thing? Of this there can be no question—which one consideration were enough to make any reasonable person suspect the strength of whatever arguments he may think himself to have, for the existence of bodies without the mind.

21. Were it necessary to add any farther proof against the existence of Matter after what has been said, I could instance several of those errors and difficulties (not to mention impieties) which have sprung from that tenet. It has occasioned numberless controversies and disputes in philosophy, and not a few of far greater moment in religion. But I shall not enter into the detail of them in this place, as well because I think arguments *a posteriori* are unnecessary for confirming what has been, if I mistake not, sufficiently demonstrated *a priori*, as because I shall hereafter find occasion to speak somewhat of them.

22. I am afraid I have given cause to think I am needlessly prolix in handling this subject. For, to what purpose is it to dilate on that which may be demonstrated with the utmost evidence in a line or two, to any one that is capable of the least reflexion? It is but looking into your own thoughts, and so trying whether you can conceive it possible for a sound, or figure, or motion, or colour to exist without the mind or unperceived. This easy trial may perhaps make you see that what you contend for is a downright contradiction. Insomuch that I am content to put the whole upon this issue.—If you can but conceive it possible for one extended movable substance, or, in general, for any one idea, or anything like an idea, to exist otherwise than in a mind perceiving it, I shall readily give up the cause. And, as for all that compages of external bodies you contend for, I

shall grant you its existence, though you cannot either give me any reason why you believe it exists, or assign any use to it when it is supposed to exist. I say, the bare possibility of your opinion's being true shall pass for an argument that it is so.

23. But, say you, surely there is nothing easier than for me to imagine trees, for instance, in a park, or books existing in a closet, and nobody by to perceive them. I answer, you may so, there is no difficulty in it; but what is all this, I beseech you, more than framing in your mind certain ideas which you call books and trees, and the same time omitting to frame the idea of any one that may perceive them? But do not you yourself perceive or think of them all the while? This therefore is nothing to the purpose; it only shews you have the power of imagining or forming ideas in your mind: but it does not shew that you can conceive it possible the objects of your thought may exist without the mind. To make out this, it is necessary that you conceive them existing unconceived or unthought of, which is a manifest repugnancy. When we do our utmost to conceive the existence of external bodies, we are all the while only contemplating our own ideas. But the mind taking no notice of itself, is deluded to think it can and does conceive bodies existing unthought of or without the mind, though at the same time they are apprehended by or exist in itself. A little attention will discover to any one the truth and evidence of what is here said, and make it unnecessary to insist on any other proofs against the existence of *material substance*.

24. It is very obvious, upon the least inquiry into our thoughts, to know whether it is possible for us to understand what is meant by the *absolute existence of sensible objects in themselves, or without the mind*. To me it is evident those words mark out either a direct contradiction, or else nothing at all. And to convince others of this, I know no readier or fairer way than to entreat they would calmly attend to their own thoughts; and if by this attention the emptiness or repugnancy of those expressions does appear, surely nothing more is requisite for the conviction. It is on this therefore that I insist, to wit, that . . . the absolute existence of unthinking things . . . are words without a meaning, or which include a contradiction. This is what I repeat and inculcate, and earnestly recommend to the attentive thoughts of the reader. . . .

33. The ideas imprinted on the Senses by the Author of nature are called *real things*; and those excited in the imagination being less regular, vivid, and constant, are more properly termed *ideas*, or *images of things*, which they copy and represent. But then our sensations, be they never so vivid and distinct, are nevertheless ideas, that is, they exist in the mind, or are perceived by it, as truly as the ideas of its own framing. The ideas of Sense are allowed to have more reality in them, that is, to be more strong, orderly, and coherent than the creatures of the mind; but this is no argument that they exist without the mind. They are also less dependent on the spirit, or thinking substance which perceives them, in that they are excited by the will of another and more powerful spirit; yet still they are *ideas*, and certainly no idea, whether faint or strong, can exist otherwise than in a mind perceiving it.

34. Before we proceed any farther it is necessary we spend some time in answering objections which may probably be made against the principles we have hitherto laid down. In doing of which, if I seem too prolix to those of quick apprehensions, I hope it may be pardoned, since all men do not equally

apprehend things of this nature, and I am willing to be understood by every one.

First, then, it will be objected that by the foregoing principles all that is real and substantial in nature is banished out of the world, and instead thereof a chimerical scheme of *ideas* takes place. All things that exist, exist only in the mind, that is, they are purely notional. What therefore becomes of the sun, moon and stars? What must we think of houses, rivers, mountains, trees, stones; nay, even of our own bodies? Are all these but so many chimeras and illusions on the fancy? To all which, and whatever else of the same sort may be objected, I answer, that by the principles premised we are not deprived of any one thing in nature. Whatever we see, feel, hear, or anywise conceive or understand remains as secure as ever, and is as real as ever. There is a *rerum natura*, and the distinction between realities and chimeras retains its full force. This is evident from sect. 29, 30, and 33, where we have shewn what is meant by *real things* in opposition to *chimeras* or ideas of our own framing; but then they both equally exist in the mind, and in that sense they are alike *ideas*.

35. I do not argue against the existence of any one thing that we can apprehend either by sense or reflexion. That the things I see with my eyes and touch with my hands do exist, really exist, I make not the least question. The only thing whose existence we deny is that which *philosophers* call Matter or corporeal substance. And in doing of this there is no damage done to the rest of mankind, who, I dare say, will never miss it. The Atheist indeed will want the colour of an empty name to support his impiety; and the Philosophers may possibly find they have lost a great handle for trifling and disputation.

36. If any man thinks this detracts from the existence or reality of things, he is very far from understanding what hath been premised in the plainest terms I could think of. Take here an abstract of what has been said:—There are spiritual substances, minds, or human souls, which will or excite ideas in themselves at pleasure; but these are faint, weak, and unsteady in respect of others they perceive by sense—which, being impressed upon them according to certain rules or laws of nature, speak themselves the effects of a mind more powerful and wise than human spirits. These latter are said to have more *reality* in them than the former:—by which is meant that they are more affecting, orderly, and distinct, and that they are not fictions of the mind perceiving them. And in this sense the sun that I see by day is the real sun, and that which I imagine by night is the idea of the former. In the sense here given of *reality* it is evident that every vegetable, star, mineral, and in general each part of the mundane system, is as much a *real being* by our principles as by any other. Whether others mean anything by the term *reality* different from what I do, I entreat them to look into their own thoughts and see.

37. It will be urged that thus much at least is true, to wit, that we take away all corporeal substances. To this my answer is, that if the word *substance* be taken in the vulgar sense—for a combination of sensible qualities, such as extension, solidity, weight, and the like—this we cannot be accused of taking away: but if it be taken in a philosophic sense—for the support of accidents or qualities without the mind—then indeed I acknowledge that we take it away, if one may be said to take away that which never had any existence, not even in the imagination.

38. But after all, say you, it sounds very harsh to say we eat and drink ideas, and are clothed with ideas. I acknowledge it does so—the word *idea* not being used in common discourse to signify the several combinations of sensible qualities which are called *things*; and it is certain that any expression which varies from the familiar use of language will seem harsh and ridiculous. But this doth not concern the truth of the proposition, which in other words is no more than to say, we are fed and clothed with those things which we perceive immediately by our senses. The hardness or softness, the colour, taste, warmth, figure, or suchlike qualities, which combined together constitute the several sorts of victuals and apparel, have been shewn to exist only in the mind that perceives them; and this is all that is meant by calling them *ideas*; which word if it was as ordinarily used as *thing*, would sound no harsher nor more ridiculous than it. I am not for disputing about the propriety, but the truth of the expression. If therefore you agree with me that we eat and drink and are clad with the immediate objects of sense, which cannot exist unperceived or without the mind, I shall readily grant it is more proper or conformable to custom that they should be called things rather than ideas.

39. If it be demanded why I make use of the word *idea*, and do not rather in compliance with custom call them *things*; I answer, I do it for two reasons:—first, because the term *thing* in contradistinction to *idea*, is generally supposed to denote somewhat existing without the mind; secondly, because *thing* hath a more comprehensive signification than *idea*, including spirit or thinking things as well as ideas. Since therefore the objects of sense exist only in the mind, and are withal thoughtless and inactive, I chose to mark them by the word *idea*, which implies those properties.

40. But, say what we can, some one perhaps may be apt to reply, he will still believe his senses, and never suffer any arguments, how plausible soever, to prevail over the certainty of them. Be it so; assert the evidence of sense as high as you please, we are willing to do the same. That what I see, hear, and feel doth exist, that is to say, is perceived by me, I no more doubt than I do of my own being. But I do not see how the testimony of sense can be alleged as a proof for the existence of anything which is not perceived by sense. We are not for having any man turn sceptic and disbelieve his senses; on the contrary, we give them all the stress and assurance imaginable; nor are there any principles more opposite to Scepticism than those we have laid down, as shall be hereafter clearly shewn.

QUESTIONS

1 According to Berkeley, what kinds of things are there?
2 Does Berkeley believe in abstract ideas?
3 According to Berkeley, what is the cause of our ideas?
4 Does Berkeley think that physical objects such as rocks, tables, etc. do not exist?

David Hume "Of the Academical or Sceptical Philosophy"

Part I

THERE is not a greater number of philosophical reasonings, displayed upon any subject, than those, which prove the existence of a Deity, and refute the fallacies of *Atheists*; and yet the most religious philosophers still dispute whether any man can be so blinded as to be a speculative atheist. How shall we reconcile these contradictions? The knights-errant, who wandered about to clear the world of dragons and giants, never entertained the least doubt with regard to the existence of these monsters.

The *Sceptic* is another enemy of religion, who naturally provokes the indignation of all divines and graver philosophers; though it is certain, that no man ever met with any such absurd creature, or conversed with a man, who had no opinion or principle concerning any subject, either of action or speculation. This begets a very natural question; What is meant by a sceptic? And how far it is possible to push these philosophical principles of doubt and uncertainty?

There is a species of scepticism, *antecedent* to all study and philosophy, which is much inculcated by Des Cartes and others, as a sovereign preservative against error and precipitate judgement. It recommends an universal doubt, not only of all our former opinions and principles, but also of our very faculties; of whose veracity, say they, we must assure ourselves, by a chain of reasoning, deduced from some original principle, which cannot possibly be fallacious or deceitful. But neither is there any such original principle, which has a prerogative above others, that are self-evident and convincing: or if there were, could we advance a step beyond it, but by the use of those very faculties, of which we are supposed to be already diffident. The Cartesian doubt, therefore, were it ever possible to be attained by any human creature (as it plainly is not) would be entirely incurable; and no reasoning could ever bring us to a state of assurance and conviction upon any subject.

It must, however, be confessed, that this species of scepticism, when more moderate, may be understood in a very reasonable sense, and is a necessary

David Hume, "Of the Academical or Sceptical Philosophy," *An Enquiry Concerning Human Understanding*, in *Enquiries Concerning Human Understanding and Concerning the Principles of Morals*, 2nd edn, ed. L.A. Selby-Bigge (Oxford: Clarendon Press, 1902).

preparative to the study of philosophy, by preserving a proper impartiality in our judgements, and weaning our mind from all those prejudices, which we may have imbibed from education or rash opinion. To begin with clear and self-evident principles, to advance by timorous and sure steps, to review frequently our conclusions, and examine accurately all their consequences; though by these means we shall make both a slow and a short progress in our systems; are the only methods, by which we can ever hope to reach truth, and attain a proper stability and certainty in our determinations.

There is another species of scepticism, *consequent* to science and enquiry, when men are supposed to have discovered, either the absolute fallaciousness of their mental faculties, or their unfitness to reach any fixed determination in all those curious subjects of speculation, about which they are commonly employed. Even our very senses are brought into dispute, by a certain species of philosophers; and the maxims of common life are subjected to the same doubt as the most profound principles or conclusions of metaphysics and theology. As these paradoxical tenets (if they may be called tenets) are to be met with in some philosophers, and the refutation of them in several, they naturally excite our curiosity, and make us enquire into the arguments, on which they may be founded.

I need not insist upon the more trite topics, employed by the sceptics in all ages, against the evidence of *sense*; such as those which are derived from the imperfection and fallaciousness of our organs, on numberless occasions; the crooked appearance of an oar in water; the various aspects of objects, according to their different distances; the double images which arise from the pressing one eye; with many other appearances of a like nature. These sceptical topics, indeed, are only sufficient to prove, that the senses alone are not implicitly to be depended on; but that we must correct their evidence by reason, and by considerations, derived from the nature of the medium, the distance of the object, and the disposition of the organ, in order to render them, within their sphere, the proper *criteria* of truth and falsehood. There are other more profound arguments against the senses, which admit not of so easy a solution.

It seems evident, that men are carried, by a natural instinct or prepossession, to repose faith in their senses; and that, without any reasoning, or even almost before the use of reason, we always suppose an external universe, which depends not on our perception, but would exist, though we and every sensible creature were absent or annihilated. Even the animal creation are governed by a like opinion, and preserve this belief of external objects, in all their thoughts, designs, and actions.

It seems also evident, that, when men follow this blind and powerful instinct of nature, they always suppose the very images, presented by the senses, to be the external objects, and never entertain any suspicion, that the one are nothing but representations of the other. This very table, which we see white, and which we feel hard, is believed to exist, independent of our perception, and to be something external to our mind, which perceives it. Our presence bestows not being on it: our absence does not annihilate it. It preserves its existence uniform and entire, independent of the situation of intelligent beings, who perceive or contemplate it.

But this universal and primary opinion of all men is soon destroyed by the slightest philosophy, which teaches us, that nothing can ever be present to the mind but an image or perception, and that the senses are only the inlets, through which these images are conveyed, without being able to produce any immediate intercourse between the mind and the object. The table, which we see, seems to diminish, as we remove farther from it: but the real table, which exists independent of us, suffers no alteration: it was, therefore, nothing but its image, which was present to the mind. These are the obvious dictates of reason; and no man, who reflects, ever doubted, that the existences, which we consider, when we say, *this house* and *that tree*, are nothing but perceptions in the mind, and fleeting copies or representations of other existences, which remain uniform and independent.

So far, then, are we necessitated by reasoning to contradict or depart from the primary instincts of nature, and to embrace a new system with regard to the evidence of our senses. But here philosophy finds herself extremely embarrassed, when she would justify this new system, and obviate the cavils and objections of the sceptics. She can no longer plead the infallible and irresistible instinct of nature: for that led us to a quite different system, which is acknowledged fallible and even erroneous. And to justify this pretended philosophical system, by a chain of clear and convincing argument, or even any appearance of argument, exceeds the power of all human capacity.

By what argument can it be proved, that the perceptions of the mind must be caused by external objects, entirely different from them, though resembling them (if that be possible) and could not arise either from the energy of the mind itself, or from the suggestion of some invisible and unknown spirit, or from some other cause still more unknown to us? It is acknowledged, that, in fact, many of these perceptions arise not from anything external, as in dreams, madness, and other diseases. And nothing can be more inexplicable than the manner, in which body should so operate upon mind as ever to convey an image of itself to a substance, supposed of so different, and even contrary a nature.

It is a question of fact, whether the perceptions of the senses be produced by external objects, resembling them: how shall this question be determined? By experience surely; as all other questions of a like nature. But here experience is, and must be entirely silent. The mind has never anything present to it but the perceptions, and cannot possibly reach any experience of their connexion with objects. The supposition of such a connexion is, therefore, without any foundation in reasoning.

To have recourse to the veracity of the supreme Being, in order to prove the veracity of our senses, is surely making a very unexpected circuit. If his veracity were at all concerned in this matter, our senses would be entirely infallible; because it is not possible that he can ever deceive. Not to mention, that, if the external world be once called in question, we shall be at a loss to find arguments, by which we may prove the existence of that Being or any of his attributes.

This is a topic, therefore, in which the profounder and more philosophical sceptics will always triumph, when they endeavour to introduce an universal doubt into all subjects of human knowledge and enquiry. Do you follow the instincts and propensities of nature, may they say, in assenting to the veracity of sense? But these lead you to believe that the very perception or sensible image is the external object. Do you disclaim this principle, in order to embrace a more rational opinion, that the perceptions are only representations of something external? You here depart from your natural propensities and more obvious sentiments; and yet are not able to satisfy your reason, which can never find any convincing argument from experience to prove, that the perceptions are connected with any external objects.

There is another sceptical topic of a like nature, derived from the most profound philosophy; which might merit our attention, were it requisite to dive so deep, in order to discover arguments and reasonings, which can so little serve to any serious purpose. It is universally allowed by modern enquirers, that all the sensible qualities of objects, such as hard, soft, hot, cold, white, black, &c. are merely secondary, and exist not in the objects themselves, but are perceptions of the mind, without any external archetype or model, which they represent. If this be allowed, with regard to secondary qualities, it must also follow, with regard to the supposed primary qualities of extension and solidity; nor can the latter be any more entitled to that denomination than the former. The idea of extension is entirely acquired from the senses of sight and feeling; and if all the qualities, perceived by the senses, be in the mind, not in the object, the same conclusion must reach the idea of extension, which is wholly dependent on the sensible ideas or the ideas of secondary qualities. Nothing can save us from this conclusion, but the asserting, that the ideas of those primary qualities are attained by *Abstraction*, an opinion, which, if we examine it accurately, we shall find to be unintelligible, and even absurd. An extension, that is neither tangible nor visible, cannot possibly be conceived: and a tangible or visible extension, which is neither hard nor soft, black nor white, is equally beyond the reach of human conception. Let any man try to conceive a triangle in general, which is neither *Isosceles* nor *Scalenum*, nor has any particular length or proportion of sides; and he will soon perceive the absurdity of all the scholastic notions with regard to abstraction and general ideas.[1]

Thus the first philosophical objection to the evidence of sense or to the opinion of external existence consists in this, that such an opinion, if rested on natural instinct, is contrary to reason, and if referred to reason, is contrary to natural instinct, and at the same time carries no rational evidence with it, to convince an impartial enquirer. The second objection goes farther, and represents this opinion as contrary to reason: at least, if it be a principle of reason, that all sensible qualities are in the mind, not in the object. Bereave matter of all its intelligible qualities, both primary and secondary, you in a manner annihilate it, and leave only a certain unknown, inexplicable *something*, as the cause of our perceptions; a notion so imperfect, that no sceptic will think it worth while to contend against it.

Note

1 This argument is drawn from Dr. Berkeley; and indeed most of the writings of that very ingenious author form the best lessons of scepticism, which are to be found either among the ancient or modern philosophers, Bayle not excepted. He professes, however, in his title-page (and undoubtedly with great truth) to have composed his book against the sceptics as well as against the atheists and freethinkers. But that all his arguments, though otherwise intended, are, in reality, merely sceptical, appears from this, *that they admit of no answer and produce no*

conviction. Their only effect is to cause that momentary amazement and irresolution and confusion, which is the result of scepticism.

QUESTIONS

1. In Hume's example, what happens to the table we see as we move away from it?
2. What happens to the real table?
3. According to Hume, what is "present to the mind" when we look at the table?
4. According to Hume, how, if at all, could it be proved that the perceptions of the mind must be caused by external objects?

Thomas Reid, *Essays on the Intellectual Powers of Man*

Essay Two Of the powers we have by means of our external senses

Chapter 5 Of perception

In speaking of the impressions made on our organs in perception, we build upon facts borrowed from anatomy and physiology, for which we have the testimony of our senses. But, being now to speak of perception itself, which is solely an act of the mind, we must appeal to another authority. The operations of our minds are known, not by sense, but by consciousness, the authority of which is as certain and as irresistible as that of sense.

In order, however, to our having a distinct notion of any of the operations of our own minds, it is not enough that we be conscious of them; for all men have this consciousness. It is farther necessary that we attend to them while they are exerted, and reflect upon them with care, while they are recent and fresh in our memory. It is necessary that, by employing ourselves frequently in this way, we get the habit of this attention and reflection; and, therefore, for the proof of facts which I shall have occasion to mention upon this subject, I can only appeal to the reader's own thoughts, whether such facts are not agreeable to what he is conscious of in his own mind.

If, therefore, we attend to that act of our mind which we call the perception of an external object of sense, we shall find in it these three things:—*First*, Some conception or notion of the object perceived; *Secondly*, A strong and irresistible conviction and belief of its present existence; and, *Thirdly*, That this conviction and belief are immediate, and not the effect of reasoning.

First, It is impossible to perceive an object without having some notion or conception of that which we perceive. We may, indeed, conceive an object which we do not perceive; but, when we perceive the object, we must have some conception of it at the same time; and we have commonly a more clear and steady notion of the object while we perceive it, than we have from memory or imagination when it is not perceived. Yet, even in perception, the notion which our senses give of the object may be more or less clear, more or less distinct, in all possible degrees.

Thus we see more distinctly an object at a small than at a great distance. An

Thomas Reid, *Essays on the Intellectual Powers of Man*, in *Inquiry and Essays*, ed. R. Beanblossom and K. Lehrer (Indianapolis, Ind.: Hackett, 1983).

object at a great distance is seen more distinctly in a clear than in a foggy day. An object seen indistinctly with the naked eye, on account of its smallness, may be seen distinctly with a microscope. The objects in this room will be seen by a person in the room less and less distinctly as the light of the day fails; they pass through all the various degrees of distinctness according to the degrees of the light, and, at last, in total darkness they are not seen at all. What has been said of the objects of sight is so easily applied to the objects of the other senses, that the application may be left to the reader.

In a matter so obvious to every person capable of reflection, it is necessary only farther to observe, that the notion which we get of an object, merely by our external sense, ought not to be confounded with that more scientific notion which a man, come to the years of understanding, may have of the same object, by attending to its various attributes, or to its various parts, and their relation to each other, and to the whole. Thus, the notion which a child has of a jack for roasting meat, will be acknowledged to be very different from that of a man who understands its construction, and perceives the relation of the parts to one another, and to the whole. The child sees the jack and every part of it as well as the man. The child, therefore, has all the notion of it which sight gives; whatever there is more in the notion which the man forms of it, must be derived from other powers of the mind, which may afterwards be explained. This observation is made here only that we may not confound the operations of different powers of the mind, which by being always conjoined after we grow up to understanding, are apt to pass for one and the same.

Secondly, In perception we not only have a notion more or less distinct of the object perceived, but also an irresistible conviction and belief of its existence. This is always the case when we are certain that we perceive it. There may be a perception so faint and indistinct as to leave us in doubt whether we perceive the object or not. Thus, when a star begins to twinkle as the light of the sun withdraws, one may, for a short time, think he sees it without being certain, until the perception acquire some strength and steadiness. When a ship just begins to appear in the utmost verge of the horizon, we may at first be dubious whether we perceive it or not; but when the perception is in any degree clear and steady, there remains no doubt of its reality; and when the reality of the perception is ascertained, the existence of the object perceived can no longer be doubted.

By the laws of all nations, in the most solemn judicial trials, wherein men's fortunes and lives are at stake, the sentence passes according to the testimony of eye or ear witnesses of good credit. An upright judge will give a fair hearing to every objection that can be made to the integrity of a witness, and allow it to be possible that he may be corrupted; but no judge will ever suppose that witnesses may be imposed upon by trusting to their eyes and ears. And if a sceptical counsel should plead against the testimony of the witnesses, that they had no other evidence for what they declared but the testimony of their eyes and ears, and that we ought not to put so much faith in our senses as to deprive men of life or fortune upon their testimony, surely no upright judge would admit a plea of this kind. I believe no counsel, however sceptical, ever dared to offer such an argument; and, if it was offered, it would be rejected with disdain.

Can any stronger proof be given that it is the universal judgment of mankind that the evidence of sense is a kind of evidence which we may securely rest upon in the most momentous concerns of mankind; that it is a kind of evidence against which we ought not to admit any reasoning; and, therefore, that to reason either for or against it is an insult to common sense?

The whole conduct of mankind in the daily occurrences of life, as well as the solemn procedure of judicatories in the trial of causes civil and criminal, demonstrates this. I know only of two exceptions that may be offered against this being the universal belief of mankind.

The first exception is that of some lunatics who have been persuaded of things that seem to contradict the clear testimony of their senses. It is said there have been lunatics and hypochondriacal persons, who seriously believed themselves to be made of glass; and, in consequence of this, lived in continual terror of having their brittle frame shivered into pieces.

All I have to say to this is, that our minds, in our present state, are, as well as our bodies, liable to strange disorders; and, as we do not judge of the natural constitution of the body from the disorders or diseases to which it is subject from accidents, so neither ought we to judge of the natural powers of the mind from its disorders, but from its sound state. It is natural to man, and common to the species, to have two hands and two feet; yet I have seen a man, and a very ingenious one, who was born without either hands or feet. It is natural to man to have faculties superior to those of brutes; yet we see some individuals whose faculties are not equal to those of many brutes; and the wisest man may, by various accidents, be reduced to this state. General rules that regard those whose intellects are sound are not overthrown by instances of men whose intellects are hurt by any constitutional or accidental disorder.

The other exception that may be made to the principle we have laid down is that of some philosophers who have maintained that the testimony of sense is fallacious, and therefore ought never to be trusted. Perhaps it might be a sufficient answer to this to say, that there is nothing so absurd which some philosophers have not maintained. It is one thing to profess a doctrine of this kind, another seriously to believe it, and to be governed by it in the conduct of life. It is evident that a man who did not believe his senses could not keep out of harm's way an hour of his life; yet, in all the history of philosophy, we never read of any sceptic that ever stepped into fire or water because he did not believe his senses, or that shewed in the conduct of life less trust in his senses than other men have. This gives us just ground to apprehend that philosophy was never able to conquer that natural belief which men have in their senses; and that all their subtile reasonings against this belief were never able to persuade themselves.

It appears, therefore, that the clear and distinct testimony of our senses carries irresistible conviction along with it to every man in his right judgment.

I observed, *Thirdly*, That this conviction is not only irresistible, but it is immediate, that is, it is not by a train of reasoning and argumentation that we come to be convinced of the existence of what we perceive; we ask no argument for the existence of the object, but that we perceive it; perception commands our belief upon its own authority, and disdains to rest its authority upon any reasoning whatsoever.

The conviction of a truth may be irresistible, and yet not immediate. Thus, my conviction that the three angles of every plain triangle are equal to two right angles, is irresistible, but it is not immediate; I am convinced of it by demonstrative reasoning. There are other truths in mathematics of which we have not only an irresistible but an immediate conviction. Such are the axioms. Our belief of the axioms in mathematics is not grounded upon argument—arguments are grounded upon them; but their evidence is discerned immediately by the human understanding.

It is, no doubt, one thing to have an immediate conviction of a self-evident axiom; it is another thing to have an immediate conviction of the existence of what we see; but the conviction is equally immediate and equally irresistible in both cases. No man thinks of seeking a reason to believe what he sees; and, before we are capable of reasoning, we put no less confidence in our senses than after. The rudest savage is as fully convinced of what he sees, and hears, and feels, as the most expert logician. The constitution of our understanding determines us to hold the truth of a mathematical axiom as a first principle, from which other truths may be deduced, but it is deduced from none; and the constitution of our power of perception determines us to hold the existence of what we distinctly perceive as a first principle, from which other truths may be deduced; but it is deduced from none. What has been said of the irresistible and immediate belief of the existence of objects distinctly perceived, I mean only to affirm with regard to persons so far advanced in understanding as to distinguish objects of mere imagination from things which have a real existence. Every man knows that he may have a notion of Don Quixote, or of Garagantua, without any belief that such persons ever existed; and that of Julius Caesar and Oliver Cromwell, he has not only a notion, but a belief that they did really exist. But whether children, from the time that they begin to use their senses, make a distinction between things which are only conceived or imagined, and things which really exist, may be doubted. Until we are able to make this distinction, we cannot properly be said to believe or to disbelieve the existence of anything. The belief of the existence of anything seems to suppose a notion of existence—a notion too abstract, perhaps, to enter into the mind of an infant. I speak of the power of perception in those that are adult and of a sound mind, who believe that there are some things which do really exist; and that there are many things conceived by themselves, and by others, which have no existence. That such persons do invariably ascribe existence to everything which they distinctly perceive, without seeking reasons or arguments for doing so, is perfectly evident from the whole tenor of human life.

The account I have given of our perception of external objects, is intended as a faithful delineation of what every man, come to years of understanding, and capable of giving attention to what passes in his own mind, may feel in himself. In what manner the notion of external objects, and the immediate belief of their existence, is produced by means of our senses, I am not able to shew, and I do not pretend to shew. . . .

Chapter 10 Of the sentiments of Bishop Berkeley

George Berkeley, afterwards Bishop of Cloyne, published his "New Theory of Vision," in 1709; his "Treatise concerning the Principles of Human Knowledge," in 1710; and his "Dialogues between Hylas and Philonous," in 1713; being then a Fellow of Trinity College, Dublin. He is acknowledged universally to have great merit, as an excellent writer, and a very acute and clear reasoner on the most abstract subjects, not to speak of his virtues as a man, which were very conspicuous; yet the doctrine chiefly held forth in the treatises above mentioned, especially in the two last, has generally been thought so very absurd, that few can be brought to think that he either believed it himself, or that he seriously meant to persuade others of its truth.

He maintains, and thinks he has demonstrated, by a variety of arguments, grounded on principles of philosophy universally received, that there is no such thing as matter in the universe; that sun and moon, earth and sea, our own bodies, and those of our friends, are nothing but ideas in the minds of those who think of them, and that they have no existence when they are not the objects of thought; that all that is in the universe may be reduced to two categories—to wit, *minds*, and *ideas in the mind*.

But, however absurd this doctrine might appear to the unlearned, who consider the existence of the objects of sense as the most evident of all truths, and what no man in his senses can doubt, the philosophers who had been accustomed to consider ideas as the immediate objects of all thought, had no title to view this doctrine of Berkeley in so unfavourable a light.

They were taught by Des Cartes, and by all that came after him, that the existence of the objects of sense is not self-evident, but requires to be proved by arguments; and, although Des Cartes, and many others, had laboured to find arguments for this purpose, there did not appear to be that force and clearness in them which might have been expected in a matter of such importance. Mr Norris had declared that, after all the arguments that had been offered, the existence of an external world is only probable, but by no means certain. Malebranche thought it rested upon the authority of revelation, and that the arguments drawn from reason were not perfectly conclusive. Others thought that the argument from revelation was a mere sophism, because revelation comes to us by our senses, and must rest upon their authority.

Thus we see that the new philosophy had been making gradual approaches towards Berkeley's opinion; and, whatever others might do, the philosophers had no title to look upon it as absurd, or unworthy of a fair examination. . . .

In the "Theory of Vision," he goes no farther than to assert that the objects of sight are nothing but ideas in the mind, granting, or at least not denying, that there is a tangible world, which is really external, and which exists whether we perceive it or not. Whether the reason of this was, that his system had not, at that time, wholly opened to his own mind, or whether he thought it prudent to let it enter into the minds of his readers by degrees, I cannot say. I think he insinuates the last as the reason, in the "Principles of Human Knowledge."

The "Theory of Vision," however, taken by itself, and without relation to the main branch of his system, contains very important discoveries, and marks of great genius. He distinguishes more accurately than any that went before him, between the immediate objects of sight, and those of the other senses which are early associated with them. He shews that distance, of itself and immediately, is not seen; but that we learn to judge of it by certain sensations and perceptions which are connected with it. This is a very important observation; and, I believe, was first made by this author. It gives much new light to the operations of our senses, and serves to account for many phaenomena in optics, of which the greatest adepts in that science had always either given a false account, or acknowledged that they could give none at all.

We may observe, by the way, that the ingenious author seems not to have attended to a distinction by which his general assertion ought to have been limited. It is true that the distance of an object from the eye is not immediately seen; but there is a certain kind of distance of one object from another which we see immediately. The author acknowledges that there is a visible extension, and visible figures, which are proper objects of sight; there must therefore be a visible distance. Astronomers call it angular distance; and, although they measure it by the angle, which is made by two lines drawn from the eye to the two distant objects, yet it is immediately perceived by sight, even by those who never thought of that angle.

He led the way in shewing how we learn to perceive the distance of an object from the eye, though this speculation was carried farther by others who came after him. He made the distinction between that extension and figure which we perceive by sight only, and that which we perceive by touch; calling the first, visible, the last, tangible extension and figure. He shewed, likewise, that tangible extension, and not visible, is the object of geometry, although mathematicians commonly use visible diagrams in their demonstrations.

The notion of extension and figure which we get from sight only, and that which we get from touch, have been so constantly conjoined from our infancy in all the judgments we form of the objects of sense, that it required great abilities to distinguish them accurately, and to assign to each sense what truly belongs to it; "so difficult a thing it is," as Berkeley justly observes, "to dissolve an union so early begun, and confirmed by so long a habit." This point he was laboured, through the whole of the essay on vision, with that uncommon penetration and judgment which he possessed, and with as great success as could be expected in a first attempt upon so abstruse a subject.

He concludes this essay, by shewing, in no less than seven sections, the notions which an intelligent being, endowed with sight, without the sense of touch, might from of the objects of sense. This speculation, to shallow thinkers, may appear to be egregious trifling. To Bishop Berkeley it appeared in another light, and will do so to those who are capable of entering into it, and who know the importance of it, in solving many of the phaenomena of vision. He seems, indeed, to have exerted more force of genius in this than in the main branch of his system.

In the new philosophy, the pillars by which the existence of a material world was supported, were so feeble that it did not require the force of a Samson to bring them down; and in this we have not so much reason to admire the strength of Berkeley's genius, as his boldness in publishing to the world an opinion which the unlearned would be apt to interpret as the sign of a crazy intellect. A man who was firmly persuaded of the doctrine universally received by philosophers concerning ideas, if he could but take courage to call in question the existence of a material world, would easily find unanswerable arguments in that doctrine. "Some truths there are," says Berkeley, "so near and obvious to the mind, that a man need only open his eyes to see them. Such," he adds, "I take this important one to be, that all the choir of heaven, and furniture of the earth—in a word, all those bodies which compose the mighty frame of the world—have not any subsistence without a mind." Princ. § 6.

The principle from which this important conclusion is obviously deduced, is laid down in the first sentence of his principles of knowledge, as evident; and, indeed, it has always been acknowledged by philosophers. "It is evident," says he, "to any one who takes a survey of the objects of human knowledge, that they are either ideas actually imprinted on the senses, or else such as are perceived, by attending to the passions and operations of the mind; or, lastly, ideas formed by help of memory and imagination, either compounding, dividing, or barely representing those originally perceived in the foresaid ways."

This is the foundation on which the whole system rests. If this be true, then indeed, the existence of a material world must be a dream that has imposed upon all mankind from the beginning of the world.

The foundation on which such a fabric rests ought to be very solid and well established; yet Berkeley says nothing more for it than that it is evident. If he means that it is self-evident, this indeed might be a good reason for not offering any direct argument in proof of it. But I apprehend this cannot justly be said. Self-evident propositions are those which appear evident to every man of sound understanding who apprehends the meaning of them distinctly, and attends to them without prejudice. Can this be said of this proposition, That all the objects of our knowledge are ideas in our own minds? I believe that, to any man uninstructed in philosophy, this proposition will appear very improbable, if not absurd. However scanty his knowledge may be, he considers the sun and moon, the earth and sea, as objects of it; and it will be difficult to persuade him that those objects of his knowledge are ideas in his own mind, and have no existence when he does not think of them. If I may presume to speak my own sentiments, I once believed this doctrine of ideas so firmly as to embrace the whole of Berkeley's system in consequence of it; till, finding other consequences to follow from it, which gave me more uneasiness than the want of a material world, it came into my mind, more than forty years ago, to put the question, What evidence have I for this doctrine, that all the objects of my knowledge are ideas in my own mind? From that time to the present I have been candidly and impartially, as I think, seeking for the evidence of this principle, but can find none, excepting the authority of philosophers.

We shall have occasion to examine its evidence afterwards. I would at present only observe, that all the arguments brought by Berkeley against the existence of a material world are grounded upon it; and that he has not attempted to give any evidence for it, but takes it for granted, as other philosophers had done before him.

But, supposing this principle to be true, Berkeley's system is impregnable. No demonstration can be more evident than his reasoning from it. Whatever is perceived is an idea, and an idea can only exist in a mind. It has no existence when it is not perceived; nor can there be anything like an idea, but an idea. . . .

Berkeley foresaw the opposition that would be made to his system, from two different quarters: *first*, from the philosophers; and, *secondly*, from the vulgar, who are led by the plain dictates of nature. The first he had the courage to oppose openly and avowedly; the second, he dreaded much more, and, therefore, takes a great deal of pains, and, I think, uses some art, to court into his party. This is particularly observable in his "Dialogues." He sets out with a declaration, Dial. 1, "That, of late, he had quitted several of the sublime notions he had got in the schools of the philosophers, for vulgar opinions," and assures Hylas, his fellow-dialogist, "That, since this revolt from metaphysical notions to the plain dictates of nature and common sense, he found his understanding strangely enlightened; so that he could now easily comprehend a great many things, which before were all mystery and riddle." Pref. to Dial. "If his principles are admitted for true, men will be reduced from paradoxes to common sense." At the same time, he acknowledges, "That they carry with them a great opposition to the prejudices of philosophers, which have so far prevailed against the common sense and natural notions of mankind."

When Hylas objects to him, Dial. 3, "You can never persuade me, Philonous, that the denying of matter or corporeal substance is not repugnant to the universal sense of mankind"—he answers, "I wish both our opinions were fairly stated, and submitted to the judgment of men who had plain common sense, without the prejudices of a learned education. Let me be represented as one who trusts his senses, who thinks he knows the things he sees and feels, and entertains no doubt of their existence.—If by material substance is meant only sensible body, that which is seen and felt, (and the unphilosophical part of the world, I dare say, mean no more,) then I am more certain of matter's existence than you or any other philosopher pretend to be. If there be anything which makes the generality of mankind averse from the notions I espouse, it is a misapprehension that I deny the reality of sensible things: but, as it is you who are guilty of that, and not I, it follows, that, in truth, their aversion is against your notions, and not mine. I am content to appeal to the common sense of the world for the truth of my notion. I am of a vulgar cast, simple enough to believe my senses, and to leave things as I find them. I cannot, for my life, help thinking that snow is white and fire hot."

These passages shew sufficiently the author's concern to reconcile his system to the plain dictates of nature and common sense, while he expresses no concern to reconcile it to the received doctrines of philosophers. He is fond to take part with the vulgar against the philosophers, and to vindicate common sense against their innovations. What pity is it that he did not carry this suspicion of the doctrine of philosophers so far as to doubt of that philosophical tenet on which his whole system is built—to wit, that the things immediately perceived by the senses are ideas which exist only in the mind!

After all, it seems no easy matter to make the vulgar opinion and that of Berkeley to meet. And, to accomplish this, he seems to me to draw each out of its line towards the other, not without some straining.

The vulgar opinion he reduces to this, that the very things which we perceive by our senses do really exist. This he grants; for these things, says he, are ideas in our minds, or complexions of ideas, to which we give one name, and consider as one thing; these are the immediate objects of sense, and these do really exist. As to the notion that those things have an absolute external existence, independent of being perceived by any mind, he thinks that this is no notion of the vulgar, but a refinement of philosophers; and that the notion of material substance, as a *substratum*, or support of that collection of sensible qualities to which we give the name of an apple or a melon, is likewise an invention of philosophers, and is not found with the vulgar till they are instructed by philosophers. The substance not being an object of sense, the vulgar never think of it; or, if they are taught the use of the word, they mean no more by it but that collection of sensible qualities which they, from finding them conjoined in nature, have been accustomed to call by one name, and to consider as one thing.

Thus he draws the vulgar opinion near to his own; and, that he may meet it half way, he acknowledges that material things have a real existence out of the mind of this or that person; but the question, says he, between the materialist and me, is, Whether they have an absolute existence distinct from their being perceived by God, and exterior to all minds? This, indeed, he says, some heathens and philosophers have affirmed; but whoever entertains notions of the Deity, suitable to the Holy Scripture, will be of another opinion.

But here an objection occurs, which it required all his ingenuity to answer. It is this: The ideas in my mind cannot be the same with the ideas of any other mind; therefore, if the objects I perceive be only ideas, it is impossible that the objects I perceive can exist anywhere, when I do not perceive them; and it is impossible that two or more minds can perceive the same object.

To this Berkeley answers, that this objection presses no less the opinion of the materialist philosopher than his. But the difficulty is to make his opinion coincide with the notions of the vulgar, who are firmly persuaded that the very identical objects which they perceive, continue to exist when they do not perceive them; and who are no less firmly persuaded that, when ten men look at the sun or the moon, they all see the same individual object.

To reconcile this repugnancy, he observes, Dial. 3—"That, if the term *same* be taken in the vulgar acceptation, it is certain (and not at all repugnant to the principles he maintains) that different persons may perceive the same thing; or the same thing or idea exist in different minds. Words are of arbitrary imposition; and, since men are used to apply the word *same*, where no distinction or variety is perceived, and he does not pretend to alter their perceptions, it follows that, as men have said before, *several saw the same thing*, so they may, upon like occasions, still continue to use the same phrase, without any deviation, either from propriety of language, or the truth of things; but, if the term *same* be used in the acceptation of philosophers, who pretend to an abstracted notion of identity, then, according to their sundry definitions of this term, (for it is not yet agreed wherein that philosophic identity consists,) it may or may not be possible for divers persons to perceive the same things; but whether philosophers shall think fit to call a thing the *same* or no is, I conceive, of small importance. Men may dispute about identity and diversity, without any real difference in their thoughts and opinions, abstracted from names."

Upon the whole, I apprehend that Berkeley has carried this attempt to reconcile his system to the vulgar opinion farther than reason supports him; and he was no doubt tempted to do so, from a just apprehension that, in a controversy of this kind, the common sense of mankind is the most formidable antagonist.

Berkeley has employed much pains and ingenuity to shew that his system, if received and believed, would not be attended with those bad consequences in the conduct of life, which superficial thinkers may be apt to impute to it. His system does not take away or make any alteration upon our pleasures or our pains: our sensations, whether agreeable or disagreeable, are the same upon his system as upon any other. These are real things, and the only things that interest us. They are produced in us according to certain laws of nature, by which our conduct will be directed in attaining the one, and avoiding the other; and it is of no moment to us, whether they are produced immediately by the operation of some powerful intelligent being upon our minds; or by the mediation of some inanimate being which we call *matter*.

The evidence of an all-governing mind, so far from being weakened, seems to appear even in a more striking light upon his hypothesis, than upon the common one. The powers which inanimate matter is supposed to possess, have always been the stronghold of atheists, to which they had recourse in defence of their system. This fortress of atheism must be most effectually overturned, if there is no such thing as matter in the universe. In all this the Bishop reasons justly and acutely. But there is one uncomfortable consequence of his system, which he seems not to have attended to, and from which it will be found difficult, if at all possible, to guard it.

The consequence I mean is this—that, although it leaves us sufficient evidence of a supreme intelligent mind, it seems to take away all the evidence we have of other intelligent beings like ourselves. What I call a father, a brother, or a friend, is only a parcel of ideas in my own mind; and, being ideas in my mind, they cannot possibly have that relation to another mind which they have to mine, any more than the pain felt by me can be the individual pain felt by another. I can find no principle in Berkeley's system, which affords me even probable ground to conclude that there are other intelligent beings, like myself, in the relations of father, brother, friend, or fellow-citizen. I am left alone, as the only creature of God in the universe, in that forlorn state of *egoism* into which it is said some of the disciples of Des Cartes were brought by his philosophy.

Of all the opinions that have ever been advanced by philosophers, this of Bishop Berkeley, that there is no material world, seems the strangest, and the most apt to bring philosophy into ridicule with plain men who are guided by the dictates of nature and common sense. . . .

Chapter 14 Reflections on the common theory of ideas

There remains only one other argument that I have been able to find urged against our perceiving external objects immediately. It is proposed by Mr Hume, who, in the essay already quoted, after acknowledging that it is an universal and primary opinion of all men, that we perceive external objects immediately, subjoins what follows:—

"But this universal and primary opinion of all men is soon destroyed by the slightest philosophy, which teaches us that nothing can ever be present to the mind but an image or perception; and that the senses are only the inlets through which these images are received, without being ever able to produce any immediate intercourse between the mind and the object. The table, which we see, seems to diminish as we remove farther from it: but the real table, which exists independent of us, suffers no alteration. It was, therefore, nothing but its image which was present to the mind. These are the obvious dictates of reason; and no man who reflects ever doubted that the existences which we consider, when we say *this house*, and *that tree*, are nothing but perceptions in the mind, and fleeting copies and representations of other existences, which remain uniform and independent. So far, then, we are necessitated, by reasoning, to depart from the primary instincts of nature, and to embrace a new system with regard to the evidence of our senses."

We have here a remarkable conflict between two contradictory opinions, wherein all mankind are engaged. On the one side stand all the vulgar, who are unpractised in philosophical researches, and guided by the uncorrupted primary instincts of nature. On the other side stand all the philosophers, ancient and modern; every man, without exception, who reflects. In this division, to my great humiliation, I find myself classed with the vulgar. . . .

To judge of the strength of this argument, it is necessary to attend to a distinction which is familiar to those who are conversant in the mathematical sciences—I mean the distinction between real and apparent magnitude. The real magnitude of a line is measured by some known measure of length—as inches, feet, or miles; the real magnitude of a surface or solid, by known measures of surface or of capacity. This magnitude is an object of touch only, and not of sight; nor could we even have had any conception of it, without the sense of touch; and Bishop Berkeley, on that account, calls it *tangible magnitude*.

Apparent magnitude is measured by the angle which an object subtends at the eye. Supposing two right lines drawn from the eye to the extremities of the object making an angle, of which the object is the subtense, the apparent magnitude is measured by this angle. This apparent magnitude is an object of sight, and not of touch. Bishop Berkeley calls it *visible magnitude*.

If it is asked what is the apparent magnitude of the sun's diameter, the answer is, that it is about thirty-one minutes of a degree. But, if it is asked what is the real magnitude of the sun's diameter, the answer must be, so many thousand miles, or so many diameters of the earth. From which it is evident that real magnitude, and apparent magnitude, are things of a different nature, though the name of magnitude is given to both. The first has three dimensions, the last only two; the first is measured by a line, the last by an angle.

From what has been said, it is evident that the real magnitude of a body must continue unchanged, while the body is unchanged. This we grant. But is it likewise evident, that the apparent magnitude must continue the same while the body is unchanged? So far otherwise, that every man who knows anything of mathematics can easily demonstrate, that the same individual object, remaining in the same place, and unchanged, must necessarily vary in its apparent magnitude, according as the point from which it is seen is more or less distant; and that its apparent length or breadth will be nearly in a reciprocal proportion to the distance of the spectator. This is as certain as the principles of geometry.

We must likewise attend to this—that, though the real magnitude of a body is not originally an object of sight, but of touch, yet we learn by experience to judge of the real magnitude in many cases by sight. We learn by experience to judge of the distance of a body from the eye within certain limits; and, from its distance and apparent magnitude taken together, we learn to judge of its real magnitude.

And this kind of judgment, by being repeated every hour and almost every minute of our lives, becomes, when we are grown up, so ready and so habitual, that it very much resembles the original perceptions of our senses, and may not improperly be called *acquired perception*.

Whether we call it judgment or acquired perception is a verbal difference. But it is evident that, by means of it, we often discover by one sense things which are properly and naturally the objects of another. Thus I can say, without impropriety, I hear a drum. I hear a great bell, or I hear a small bell; though it is certain that the figure or size of the sounding body is not originally an object of hearing. In like manner, we learn by experience how a body of such a real magnitude and at such a distance appears to the eye. But neither its real magnitude, nor its distance from the eye, are properly objects of sight, any more than the form of a drum or the size of a bell, are properly objects of hearing.

If these things be considered, it will appear that Mr Hume's argument hath no force to support his conclusion—nay, that it leads to a contrary conclusion. The argument is this: the table we see seems to diminish as we remove farther from it; that is, its apparent magnitude is diminished; but the real table suffers no alteration—to wit, in its real magnitude; therefore, it is not the real table we see. I admit both the premises in this syllogism, but I deny the conclusion. The syllogism has what the logicians call two middle terms; apparent magnitude is the middle term in the first premise; real magnitude in the second. Therefore, according to the rules of logic, the conclusion is not justly drawn from the premises; but, laying aside the rules of logic, let us examine it by the light of common sense.

Let us suppose, for a moment, that it is the real table we see: Must not this real table seem to diminish as we remove farther from it? It is demonstrable that it must. How then can this apparent diminution be an argument that it is not the real table? When that which must happen to the real table, as we remove farther from it, does actually happen to the table we see, it is absurd to conclude from this, that it is not the real table we see. It is evident, therefore, that this ingenious author has imposed upon himself by confounding real magnitude with apparent magnitude, and that his argument is a mere sophism.

I observed that Mr Hume's argument not only has no strength to support his conclusion, but that it leads to the contrary conclusion—to wit, that it is the real table we see; for this plain reason, that the table we see has precisely that apparent magnitude which it is demonstrable the real table must have when placed at that distance.

This argument is made much stronger by considering that the real table may be placed successively at a thousand different distances, and, in every distance, in a thousand different positions; and it can be determined demonstratively, by the rules of geometry and perspective, what must be its apparent magnitude and apparent figure, in each of those distances and positions. Let the table be placed successively in as many of those different distances and different positions as you will, or in them all; open your eyes and you shall see a table precisely of that apparent magnitude, and that apparent figure, which the real table must have in that distance and in that position. Is not this a strong argument that it is the real table you see? . . .

Thus, I have considered every argument I have found advanced to prove the existence of ideas, or images of external things, in the mind; and, if no better arguments can be found, I cannot help thinking that the whole history of philosophy has never furnished an instance of an opinion so unanimously entertained by philosophers upon so slight grounds.

A *third* reflection I would make upon this subject is, that philosophers, notwithstanding their unanimity as to the existence of ideas, hardly agree in any one thing else concerning them. If ideas be not a mere fiction, they must be, of all objects of human knowledge, the things we have best access to know, and to be acquainted with; yet there is nothing about which men differ so much.

A *fourth* reflection is, that ideas do not make any of the operations of the mind to be better understood, although it was probably with that view that they have been first invented, and afterwards so generally received.

We are at a loss to know how we perceive distant objects; how we remember things past; how we imagine things that have no existence. Ideas in the mind seem to account for all these operations: they are all by the means of ideas reduced to one operation—to a kind of feeling, or immediate perception of things present and in contact with the percipient; and feeling is an operation so familiar that we think it needs no explication, but may serve to explain other operations.

But this feeling, or immediate perception, is as difficult to be comprehended as the things which we pretend to explain by it. Two things may be in contact without any feeling or perception; there must therefore be in the percipient a power to feel or to perceive. How this power is produced, and how it operates, is quite beyond the reach of our knowledge. As little can we know whether this power must be limited to things present, and in contact with us. Nor can any man pretend to prove that the Being who gave us the power to perceive things present, may not give us the power to perceive things that are distant, to remember things past, and to conceive things that never existed. . . .

QUESTIONS

1. What three elements does Reid find in every perception?
2. According to Reid, what premise does Berkeley's whole system rest on?
3. What does Reid mean by the "visible magnitude" of an object?
4. According to Reid, what does Hume's experiment with the table really show?

Bertrand Russell, *The Problems of Philosophy*

Chapter I Appearance and reality

Is there any knowledge in the world which is so certain that no reasonable man could doubt it? This question, which at first sight might not seem difficult, is really one of the most difficult that can be asked. When we have realized the obstacles in the way of a straightforward and confident answer, we shall be well launched on the study of philosophy—for philosophy is merely the attempt to answer such ultimate questions, not carelessly and dogmatically, as we do in ordinary life and even in the sciences, but critically, after exploring all that makes such questions puzzling, and after realizing all the vagueness and confusion that underlie our ordinary ideas.

In daily life, we assume as certain many things which, on a closer scrutiny, are found to be so full of apparent contradictions that only a great amount of thought enables us to know what it is that we really may believe. In the search for certainty, it is natural to begin with our present experiences, and in some sense, no doubt, knowledge is to be derived from them. But any statement as to what it is that our immediate experiences make us know is very likely to be wrong. It seems to me that I am now sitting in a chair, at a table of a certain shape, on which I see sheets of paper with writing or print. By turning my head I see out of the window buildings and clouds and the sun. I believe that the sun is about ninety-three million miles from the earth; that it is a hot globe many times bigger than the earth; that, owing to the earth's rotation, it rises every morning, and will continue to do so for an indefinite time in the future. I believe that, if any other normal person comes into my room, he will see the same chairs and tables and books and papers as I see, and that the table which I see is the same as the table which I feel pressing against my arm. All this seems to be so evident as to be hardly worth stating, except in answer to a man who doubts whether I know anything. Yet all this may be reasonably doubted, and all of it requires much careful discussion before we can be sure that we have stated it in a form that is wholly true.

To make our difficulties plain, let us concentrate attention on the table. To the eye it is oblong, brown and shiny, to the touch it is smooth and cool and hard; when I tap it, it gives out a wooden sound. Any one else who sees and feels and

Bertrand Russell, *The Problems of Philosophy* (New York: Oxford University Press, 1997).

hears the table will agree with this description, so that it might seem as if no difficulty would arise; but as soon as we try to be more precise our troubles begin. Although I believe that the table is "really" of the same colour all over, the parts that reflect the light look much brighter than the other parts, and some parts look white because of reflected light. I know that, if I move, the parts that reflect the light will be different, so that the apparent distribution of colours on the table will change. It follows that if several people are looking at the table at the same moment, no two of them will see exactly the same distribution of colours, because no two can see it from exactly the same point of view, and any change in the point of view makes some change in the way the light is reflected.

For most practical purposes these differences are unimportant, but to the painter they are all-important: the painter has to unlearn the habit of thinking that things seem to have the colour which common sense says they "really" have, and to learn the habit of seeing things as they appear. Here we have already the beginning of one of the distinctions that cause most trouble in philosophy—the distinction between "appearance" and "reality", between what things seem to be and what they are. The painter wants to know what things seem to be, the practical man and the philosopher want to know what they are; but the philosopher's wish to know this is stronger than the practical man's, and is more troubled by knowledge as to the difficulties of answering the question.

To return to the table. It is evident from what we have found, that there is no colour which preeminently appears to be *the* colour of the table, or even of any one particular part of the table—it appears to be of different colours from different points of view, and there is no reason for regarding some of these as more really its colour than others. And we know that even from a given point of view the colour will seem different by artificial light, or to a colour-blind man, or to a man wearing blue spectacles, while in the dark there will be no colour at all, though to touch and hearing the table will be unchanged. This colour is not something which is inherent in the table, but something depending upon the table and the spectator and the way the light falls on the table. When, in ordinary life, we speak of *the* colour of the table, we only mean the sort of colour which it will seem to have to a normal spectator from an ordinary point of view under usual conditions of light. But the other colours which appear under other conditions have just as good a right to be considered real; and therefore, to avoid favouritism, we are compelled to deny that, in itself, the table has any one particular colour.

The same thing applies to the texture. With the naked eye one can see the grain, but otherwise the table looks smooth and even. If we looked at it through a microscope, we should see roughnesses and hills and valleys, and all sorts of differences that are imperceptible to the naked eye. Which of these is the "real" table? We are naturally tempted to say that what we see through the microscope is more real, but that in turn would be changed by a still more powerful microscope. If, then, we cannot trust what we see with the naked eye, why should we trust what we see through a microscope? Thus, again, the confidence in our senses with which we began deserts us.

The *shape* of the table is no better. We are all in the habit of judging as to the "real" shapes of things, and we do this so unreflectingly that we come to think we actually see the real shapes. But, in fact, as we all have to learn if we try to draw, a given thing looks different in shape from every different point of view. If our table is "really" rectangular, it will look, from almost all points of view, as if it had two acute angles and two obtuse angles. If opposite sides are parallel, they will look as if they converged to a point away from the spectator; if they are of equal length, they will look as if the nearer side were longer. All these things are not commonly noticed in looking at a table, because experience has taught us to construct the "real" shape from the apparent shape, and the "real" shape is what interests us as practical men. But the "real" shape is not what we see; it is something inferred from what we see. And what we see is constantly changing in shape as we move about the room; so that here again the senses seem not to give us the truth about the table itself, but only about the appearance of the table.

Similar difficulties arise when we consider the sense of touch. It is true that the table always gives us a sensation of hardness, and we feel that it resists pressure. But the sensation we obtain depends upon how hard we press the table and also upon what part of the body we press with; thus the various sensations due to various pressures or various parts of the body cannot be supposed to reveal *directly* any definite property of the table, but at most to be *signs* of some property which perhaps *causes* all the sensations, but is not actually apparent in any of them. And the same applies still more obviously to the sounds which can be elicited by rapping the table.

Thus it becomes evident that the real table, if there is one, is not the same as what we immediately experience by sight or touch or hearing. The real table, if there is one, is not *immediately* known to us at all, but must be an inference from what is immediately known. Hence, two very difficult questions at once arise; namely, (1) Is there a real table at all? (2) If so, what sort of object can it be?

It will help us in considering these questions to have a few simple terms of which the meaning is definite and clear. Let us give the name of "sense-data" to the things that are immediately known in sensation: such things as colours, sounds, smells, hardnesses, roughnesses, and so on. We shall give the name "sensation" to the experience of being immediately aware of these things. Thus, whenever we see a colour, we have a sensation *of* the colour, but the colour itself is a sense-datum, not a sensation. The colour is that *of* which we are immediately aware, and the awareness itself is the sensation. It is plain that if we are to know anything about the table, it must be by means of the sense-data—brown colour, oblong shape, smoothness, etc.—which we associate with the table; but, for the reasons which have been given, we cannot say that the table *is* the sense-data, or even that the sense-data are directly properties of the table. Thus a problem arises as to the relation of the sense-data to the real table, supposing there is such a thing.

The real table, if it exists, we will call a "physical object". Thus we have to consider the relation of sense-data to physical objects. The collection of all physical objects is called "matter". Thus our two questions may be re-stated as follows: (I) Is there any such thing as matter? (2) If so, what is its nature?

The philosopher who first brought prominently forward the reasons for regarding the immediate objects of our senses as not existing independently of us was Bishop Berkeley (1685–1753). His *Three Dialogues between Hylas and Philonous, in Opposition to Sceptics and Atheists*, undertake to prove that there is no such thing as matter at all, and that the world consists of nothing but minds and their ideas. Hylas has hitherto believed in matter, but he is no match for Philonous, who mercilessly drives him into contradictions and paradoxes, and makes his own denial of matter seem, in the end, as if it were almost common sense. The arguments employed are of very different value: some are important and sound, others are confused or quibbling. But Berkeley retains the merit of having shown that the existence of matter is capable of being denied without absurdity, and that if there are any things that exist independently of us they cannot be the immediate objects of our sensations.

There are two different questions involved when we ask whether matter exists, and it is important to keep them clear. We commonly mean by "matter" something which is opposed to "mind", something which we think of as occupying space and as radically incapable of any sort of thought or consciousness. It is chiefly in this sense that Berkeley denies matter; that is to say, he does not deny that the sense-data which we commonly take as signs of the existence of the table are really signs of the existence of *something* independent of us, but he does deny that this something is non-mental, that it is neither mind nor ideas entertained by some mind. He admits that there must be something which continues to exist when we go out of the room or shut our eyes, and that what we call seeing the table does really give us reason for believing in something which persists even when we are not seeing it. But he thinks that this something cannot be radically different in nature from what we see, and cannot be independent of seeing altogether, though it must be independent of *our* seeing. He is thus led to regard the "real" table as an idea in the mind of God. Such an idea has the required permanence and independence of ourselves, without being—as matter would otherwise be—something quite unknowable, in the sense that we can only infer it, and can never be directly and immediately aware of it.

Other philosophers since Berkeley have also held that, although the table does not depend for its existence upon being seen by me, it does depend upon being seen (or otherwise apprehended in sensation) by *some* mind—not necessarily the mind of God, but more often the whole collective mind of the universe. This they hold, as Berkeley does, chiefly because they think there can be nothing real—or at any rate nothing known to be real—except minds and their thoughts and feelings. We might state the argument by which they support their view in some such way as this: "Whatever can be thought of is an idea in the mind of the person thinking of it; therefore nothing can be thought of except ideas in minds; therefore anything else is inconceivable, and what is inconceivable cannot exist."

Such an argument, in my opinion, is fallacious; and of course those who advance it do not put it so shortly or so crudely. But whether valid or not, the argument has been very widely advanced in one form or another; and very many philosophers, perhaps a majority, have held that there is nothing real except minds and their ideas. Such philosophers are called "idealists". When they come to explaining matter, they either say, like Berkeley, that matter is really nothing but a collection of ideas, or they say, like Leibniz (1646–1716), that what appears as matter is really a collection of more or less rudimentary minds.

But these philosophers, though they deny matter as opposed to mind, nevertheless, in another sense, admit matter. It will be remembered that we asked two questions; namely, (1) Is there a real table at all? (2) If so, what sort of object can it be? Now both Berkeley and Leibniz admit that there is a real table, but Berkeley says it is certain ideas in the mind of God, and Leibniz says it is a colony of souls. Thus both of them answer our first question in the affirmative, and only diverge from the views of ordinary mortals in their answer to our second question. In fact, almost all philosophers seem to be agreed that there is a real table: they almost all agree that, however much our sense-data—colour, shape, smoothness, etc.—may depend upon us, yet their occurrence is a sign of something existing independently of us, something differing, perhaps, completely from our sense-data, and yet to be regarded as causing those sense-data whenever we are in a suitable relation to the real table.

Now obviously this point in which the philosophers are agreed—the view that there *is* a real table, whatever its nature may be—is vitally important, and it will be worth while to consider what reasons there are for accepting this view before we go on to the further question as to the nature of the real table. Our next chapter, therefore, will be concerned with the reasons for supposing that there is a real table at all.

Before we go farther it will be well to consider for a moment what it is that we have discovered so far. It has appeared that, if we take any common object of the sort that is supposed to be known by the senses, what the senses *immediately* tell us is not the truth about the object as it is apart from us, but only the truth about certain sense-data which, so far as we can see, depend upon the relations between us and the object. Thus what we directly see and feel is merely "appearance", which we believe to be a sign of some "reality" behind. But if the reality is not what appears, have we any means of knowing whether there is any reality at all? And if so, have we any means of finding out what it is like?

Such questions are bewildering, and it is difficult to know that even the strangest hypotheses may not be true. Thus our familiar table, which has roused but the slightest thoughts in us hitherto, has become a problem full of surprising possibilities. The one thing we know about it is that it is not what it seems. Beyond this modest result, so far, we have the most complete liberty of conjecture. Leibniz tells us it is a community of souls; Berkeley tells us it is an idea in the mind of God; sober science, scarcely less wonderful, tells us it is a vast collection of electric charges in violent motion.

Among these surprising possibilities, doubt suggests that perhaps there is no table at all. Philosophy, if it cannot *answer* so many questions as we could wish, has at least the power of *asking* questions which increase the interest of the world, and show the strangeness and wonder lying just below the surface even in the commonest things of daily life.

Chapter II The existence of matter

In this chapter we have to ask ourselves whether, in any sense at all, there is such a thing as matter. Is there a table which has a certain intrinsic nature, and continues to exist when I am not looking, or is the table merely a product of my imagination, a dream-table in a very prolonged dream? This question is of the greatest importance. For if we cannot be sure of the independent existence of objects, we cannot be sure of the independent existence of other people's bodies, and therefore still less of other people's minds, since we have no grounds for believing in their minds except such as are derived from observing their bodies.

Thus if we cannot be sure of the independent existence of objects, we shall be left alone in a desert—it may be that the whole outer world is nothing but a dream, and that we alone exist. This is an uncomfortable possibility; but although it cannot be strictly *proved* to be false, there is not the slightest reason to suppose that it is true. In this chapter we have to see why this is the case.

Before we embark upon doubtful matters, let us try to find some more or less fixed point from which to start. Although we are doubting the physical existence of the table, we are not doubting the existence of the sense-data which made us think there was a table; we are not doubting that, while we look, a certain colour and shape appear to us, and while we press, a certain sensation of hardness is experienced by us. All this, which is psychological, we are not calling in question. In fact, whatever else may be doubtful, some at least of our immediate experiences seem absolutely certain.

Descartes (1590–1650), the founder of modern philosophy, invented a method which may still be used with profit—the method of systematic doubt. He determined that he would believe nothing which he did not see quite clearly and distinctly to be true. Whatever he could bring himself to doubt, he would doubt, until he saw reason for not doubting it. By applying this method he gradually became convinced that the only existence of which he could be *quite* certain was his own. He imagined a deceitful demon, who presented unreal things to his senses in a perpetual phantasmagoria; it might be very improbable that such a demon existed, but still it was possible, and therefore doubt concerning things perceived by the senses was possible.

But doubt concerning his own existence was not possible, for if he did not exist, no demon could deceive him. If he doubted, he must exist; if he had any experiences whatever, he must exist. Thus his own existence was an absolute certainty to him. "I think, therefore I am," he said (*Cogito, ergo sum*); and on the basis of this certainty he set to work to build up again the world of knowledge which his doubt had laid in ruins. By inventing the method of doubt, and by showing that subjective things are the most certain, Descartes performed a great service to philosophy, and one which makes him still useful to all students of the subject.

But some care is needed in using Descartes' argument. "*I* think, therefore *I* am" says rather more than is strictly certain. It might seem as though we were quite sure of being the same person to-day as we were yesterday, and this is no doubt true in some sense. But the real Self is as hard to arrive at as the real table, and does not seem to have that absolute, convincing certainty that belongs to particular experiences. When I look at my table and see a certain brown colour, what is quite certain at once is not "*I* am seeing a brown colour", but rather, "a brown colour is being seen". This of course involves something (or somebody) which (or who) sees the brown colour; but it does not of itself involve that more or less permanent person whom we call "I". So far as immediate certainty goes, it might be that the something which sees the brown colour is quite momentary, and not the same as the something which has some different experience the next moment.

Thus it is our particular thoughts and feelings that have primitive certainty. And this applies to dreams and hallucinations as well as to normal perceptions: when we dream or see a ghost, we certainly do have the sensations we think we have, but for various reasons it is held that no physical object corresponds to these sensations. Thus the certainty of our knowledge of our own experiences does not have to be limited in any way to allow for exceptional cases. Here, therefore, we have, for what it is worth, a solid basis from which to begin our pursuit of knowledge.

The problem we have to consider is this: Granted that we are certain of our own sense-data, have we any reason for regarding them as signs of the existence of something else, which we can call the physical object? When we have enumerated all the sense-data which we should naturally regard as connected with the table, have we said all there is to say about the table, or is there still something else—something not a sense-datum, something which persists when we go out of the room? Common sense unhesitatingly answers that there is. What can be bought and sold and pushed about and have a cloth laid on it, and so on, cannot be a *mere* collection of sense-data. If the cloth completely hides the table, we shall derive no sense-data from the table, and therefore, if the table were merely sense-data, it would have ceased to exist, and the cloth would be suspended in empty air, resting, by a miracle, in the place where the table formerly was. This seems plainly absurd; but whoever wishes to become a philosopher must learn not to be frightened by absurdities.

One great reason why it is felt that we must secure a physical object in addition to the sense-data, is that we want the *same* object for different people. When ten people are sitting round a dinner-table, it seems preposterous to maintain that they are not seeing the same tablecloth, the same knives and forks and spoons and glasses. But the sense-data are private to each separate person; what is immediately present to the sight of one is not immediately present to the sight of another: they all see things from slightly different points of view, and therefore see them slightly differently. Thus, if there are to be public neutral objects, which can be in some sense known to many different people, there must be something over and above the private and particular sense-data which appear to various people. What reason, then, have we for believing that there are such public neutral objects?

The first answer that naturally occurs to one is that, although different people may see the table slightly differently, still they all see more or less similar things when they look at the table, and the variations in what they see follow the laws of perspective and reflection of light, so that it is easy to arrive at a permanent object underlying all the different people's sense-data. I bought my table from the former occupant of my room; I could not buy *his* sense-data, which died when he went away, but I could and did buy the confident expectation of more or less similar sense-data. Thus it is the fact that different people have similar sense-data, and that one person in a given place at different times has similar sense-data, which makes us suppose that over and above the sense-data there is a permanent public object which underlies or causes the sense-data of various people at various times.

Now in so far as the above considerations depend upon supposing that there are other people besides ourselves, they beg the very question at issue. Other people are represented to me by certain sense-data, such as the sight of them or the sound of their voices, and if I had no reason to believe that there were physical objects independent of my sense-data, I should have no reason to believe that other people exist except as part of my dream. Thus, when we are trying to show that there must be objects independent of our own sense-data, we cannot appeal to the testimony of other people, since this testimony itself consists of sense-data, and does not reveal other people's experiences unless our own sense-data are signs of things existing independently of us. We must therefore, if possible, find, in our own purely private experiences, characteristics which show, or tend to show, that there are in the world things other than ourselves and our private experiences.

In one sense it must be admitted that we can never *prove* the existence of things other than ourselves and our experiences. No logical absurdity results from the hypothesis that the world consists of myself and my thoughts and feelings and sensations, and that everything else is mere fancy. In dreams a very complicated world may seem to be present, and yet on waking we find it was a delusion; that is to say, we find that the sense-data in the dream do not appear to have corresponded with such physical objects as we should naturally infer from our sense-data. (It is true that, when the physical world is assumed, it is possible to find physical causes for the sense-data in dreams: a door banging, for instance, may cause us to dream of a naval engagement. But although, in this case, there is a physical *cause* for the sense-data, there is not a physical object *corresponding* to the sense-data in the way in which an actual naval battle would correspond.) There is no logical impossibility in the supposition that the whole of life is a dream, in which we ourselves create all the objects that come before us. But although this is not logically impossible, there is no reason whatever to suppose that it is true; and it is, in fact, a less simple hypothesis, viewed as a means of accounting for the facts of our own life, than the common-sense hypothesis that there really are objects independent of us, whose action on us causes our sensations.

The way in which simplicity comes in from supposing that there really are physical objects is easily seen. If the cat appears at one moment in one part of the room, and at another in another part, it is natural to suppose that it has moved from the one to the other, passing over a series of intermediate positions. But if it is merely a set of sense-data, it cannot have ever been in any place where I did not see it; thus we shall have to suppose that it did not exist at all while I was not looking, but suddenly sprang into being in a new place. If the cat exists whether I see it or not, we can understand from our own experience how it gets hungry between one meal and the next; but if it does not exist when I am not seeing it, it seems odd that appetite should grow during non-existence as fast as during existence. And if the cat consists only of sense-data, it cannot be *hungry*, since no hunger but my own can be a sense-datum to me. Thus the behaviour of the sense-data which represent the cat to me, though it seems quite natural when regarded as an expression of hunger, becomes utterly inexplicable when regarded as mere movement and changes of patches of colour, which are as incapable of hunger as a triangle is of playing football.

But the difficulty in the case of the cat is nothing compared to the difficulty in the case of human beings. When human beings speak—that is, when we hear certain noises which we associate with ideas, and simultaneously see certain motions of lips and expressions of face—it is very difficult to suppose that what we hear is not the expression of a thought, as we know it would be if we emitted the same sounds. Of course similar things happen in dreams, where we are mistaken as to the existence of other people. But dreams are more or less suggested by what we call waking life, and are capable of being more or less accounted for on scientific principles if we assume that there really is a physical world. Thus every principle of simplicity urges us to adopt the natural view, that there really are objects other than ourselves and our sense-data which have an existence not dependent upon our perceiving them.

Of course it is not by argument that we originally come by our belief in an independent external world. We find this belief ready in ourselves as soon as we being to reflect: it is what may be called an *instinctive* belief. We should never have been led to question this belief but for the fact that, at any rate in the case of sight, it seems as if the sense-datum itself were instinctively believed to be the independent object, whereas argument shows that the object cannot be identical with the sense-datum. This discovery, however—which is not at all paradoxical in the case of taste and smell and sound, and only slightly so in the case of touch—leaves undiminished our instinctive belief that there *are* objects *corresponding* to our sense-data. Since this belief does not lead to any difficulties, but on the contrary tends to simplify and systematize our account of our experiences, there seems no good reason for rejecting it. We may therefore admit—though with a slight doubt derived from dreams—that the external world does really exist, and is not wholly dependent for its existence upon our continuing to perceive it.

The argument which has led us to this conclusion is doubtless less strong than we could wish, but it is typical of many philosophical arguments, and it is therefore worth while to consider briefly its general character and validity. All knowledge, we find, must be built up upon our instinctive beliefs, and if these are rejected, nothing is left. But among our instinctive beliefs some are much stronger than others, while many have, by habit and association, become entangled with other beliefs, not really instinctive, but falsely supposed to be part of what is believed instinctively.

Philosophy should show us the hierarchy of our instinctive beliefs, beginning with those we hold most strongly, and presenting each as much isolated and as free from irrelevant additions as possible. It should take care to show that, in the form in which they are finally set forth, our instinctive beliefs do not clash, but form a harmonious system. There can never be any reason for rejecting one instinctive belief except that it clashes with others; thus, if they are found to harmonize, the whole system becomes worthy of acceptance.

It is of course *possible* that all or any of our beliefs may be mistaken, and therefore all ought to be held with at least some slight element of doubt. But we cannot have *reason* to reject a belief except on the ground of some other belief. Hence, by organizing our instinctive beliefs and their consequences, by considering which among them is most possible, if necessary, to modify or abandon, we can arrive, on the basis of accepting as our sole data what we instinctively believe, at an orderly systematic organization of our knowledge, in which, though the *possibility* of error remains, its likelihood is diminished by the interrelation of the parts and by the critical scrutiny which has preceded acquiescence.

This function, at least, philosophy can perform. Most philosophers, rightly or wrongly, believe that philosophy can do much more than this—that it can give us knowledge, not otherwise attainable, concerning the universe as a whole, and concerning the nature of ultimate reality. Whether this be the case or not, the more modest function we have spoken of can certainly be performed by philosophy, and certainly suffices, for those who have once begun to doubt the adequacy of common sense, to justify the arduous and difficult labours that philosophical problems involve.

QUESTIONS

1 What are "sense data"?
2 What is "idealism"?
3 According to Russell, what sorts of things can we be certain of?
4 Briefly, what sort of reason does Russell say we have for believing in the existence of matter?
5 According to Russell, when should we reject an instinctive belief?

J.L. Austin, *Sense and Sensibilia*

III

The primary purpose of the argument from illusion is to induce people to accept "sense-data" as the proper and correct answer to the question what they perceive on certain *abnormal, exceptional* occasions; but in fact it is usually followed up with another bit of argument intended to establish that they *always* perceive sense-data. Well, what is the argument?

In Ayer's statement it runs as follows.[1] It is "based on the fact that material things may present different appearances to different observers, or to the same observer in different conditions, and that the character of these appearances is to some extent causally determined by the state of the conditions and the observer". As illustrations of this alleged fact Ayer proceeds to cite perspective ("a coin which looks circular from one point of view may look elliptical from another"); refraction ("a stick which normally appears straight looks bent when it is seen in water"); changes in colour-vision produced by drugs ("such as mescal"); mirror-images; double vision; hallucination; apparent variations in tastes; variations in felt warmth ("according as the hand that is feeling it is itself hot or cold"); variations in felt bulk ("a coin seems larger when it is placed on the tongue than when it is held in the palm of the hand"); and the oft-cited fact that "people who have had limbs amputated may still continue to feel pain in them".

He then selects three of these instances for detailed treatment. First, refraction—the stick which normally "appears straight" but "looks bent" when seen in water. He makes the "assumptions" (*a*) that the stick does not *really change its shape* when it is placed in water, and (*b*) that it *cannot be* both crooked and straight.[2] He then concludes ("it follows") that "at least one of the *visual appearances* of the stick is *delusive*". Nevertheless, even when "what we see is not the *real quality* of a *material thing*, it is supposed that we are still seeing something"—and this something is to be called a "sense-datum". A sense-datum is to be "the object of which we are *directly* aware, in perception, if it is not *part* of any *material thing*". (The italics are mine throughout this and the next two paragraphs.)

Next, mirages. A man who sees a mirage, he says, is "not perceiving any material thing; for the oasis which he thinks he is perceiving *does not exist*". But "his *experience* is not an experience of nothing"; thus "it is said that he is experiencing sense-data, which are similar in character to what he would be

J.L. Austin, *Sense and Sensibilia* (Oxford: Clarendon Press, 1962).

experiencing if he were seeing a real oasis, but are delusive in the sense that *the material thing which they appear to present* is not *really there*".

Lastly, reflections. When I look at myself in a mirror "my body *appears to be* some distance behind the glass"; but it cannot actually be in two places at once; thus, my perceptions in this case "cannot all be *veridical*". But I do see *something*; and if "there really is no such material thing as my body in the place where it appears to be, what is it that I am seeing?" Answer—a sense-datum. Ayer adds that "the same conclusion may be reached by taking any other of my examples".

Now I want to call attention, first of all, to the name of this argument—the "argument from *illusion*", and to the fact that it is produced as establishing the conclusion that some at least of our "perceptions" are *delusive*. For in this there are two clear implications—(*a*) that all the cases cited in the argument are cases of *illusions*; and (*b*) that *illusion* and *delusion* are the same thing. But both of these implications, of course, are quite wrong; and it is by no means unimportant to point this out, for, as we shall see, the argument trades on confusion at just this point.

What, then, would be some genuine examples of illusion? (The fact is that hardly any of the cases cited by Ayer is, at any rate without stretching things, a case of illusion at all.) Well, first, there are some quite clear cases of *optical* illusion—for instance the case we mentioned earlier in which, of two lines of equal length, one is made to look longer than the other. Then again there are illusions produced by professional "illusionists", conjurors—for instance the Headless Woman on the stage, who is made to look headless, or the ventriloquist's dummy which is made to appear to be talking. Rather different—not (usually) produced on purpose—is the case where wheels rotating rapidly enough in one direction may look as if they were rotating quite slowly in the opposite direction. Delusions, on the other hand, are something altogether different from this. Typical cases would be delusions of persecution, delusions of grandeur. These are primarily a matter of grossly disordered beliefs (and so, probably, behaviour) and may well have nothing in particular to do with perception.[3] But I think we might also say that the patient who sees pink rats has (suffers from) delusions—particularly, no doubt, if, as would probably be the case, he is not clearly aware that his pink rats aren't real rats.[4]

The most important differences here are that the term "an illusion" (in a perceptual context) does not suggest that something totally unreal is *conjured up*—on the contrary, there just is the arrangement of lines and arrows on the page, the woman on the stage with her head in a black bag, the rotating wheels; whereas the term "delusion" *does* suggest something totally unreal, not really there at all. (The convictions of the man who has delusions of persecution can be *completely* without foundation.) For this reason delusions are a much more serious matter—something is really wrong, and what's more, wrong *with* the person who has them. But when I see an optical illusion, however well it comes off, there is nothing wrong with me personally, the illusion is not a little (or a large) peculiarity or idiosyncrasy of my own; it is quite public, anyone can see it, and in many cases standard procedures can be laid down for producing it. Furthermore, if we are not actually to be taken in, we need to be *on our guard*; but it is no use to tell the sufferer from delusions to be on his guard. He needs to be cured.

Why is it that we tend—if we do—to confuse illusions with delusions? Well, partly, no doubt the terms are often used loosely. But there is also the point that people may have, without making this explicit, different views or theories about the facts of some cases. Take the case of seeing a ghost, for example. It is not generally known, or agreed, what seeing ghosts *is*. Some people think of seeing ghosts as a case of something being conjured up, perhaps by the disordered nervous system of the victim; so in their view seeing ghosts is a case of delusion. But other people have the idea that what is called seeing ghosts is a case of being taken in by shadows, perhaps, or reflections, or a trick of the light—that is, they assimilate the case in their minds to illusion. In this way, seeing ghosts, for example, may come to be labelled sometimes as "delusion", sometimes as "illusion"; and it may not be noticed that it makes a difference which label we use. Rather, similarly, there seem to be different doctrines in the field as to what mirages are. Some seem to take a mirage to be a vision conjured up by the crazed brain of the thirsty and exhausted traveller (delusion), while in other accounts it is a case of atmospheric refraction, whereby something below the horizon is made to appear above it (illusion). (Ayer, you may remember, takes the delusion view, although he cites it along with the rest as a case of illusion. He says not that the oasis appears to be where it is not, but roundly that "it does not exist".)

The way in which the "argument from illusion" positively trades on not distinguishing illusions from delusions is, I think, this. So long as it is being suggested that the cases paraded for our attention are cases of *illusion*, there is the implication (from the ordinary use of the word) that there really is something there that we perceive. But then, when these cases begin to be quietly called delusive, there comes in the very different suggestion of something being conjured up, something unreal or at any rate "immaterial". These two implications taken together may then subtly insinuate that in the cases cited there really is something that we are perceiving, but that this is an immaterial something; and this insinuation, even if not conclusive by itself, is certainly well calculated to edge us a little closer towards just the position where the sense-datum theorist wants to have us.

So much, then—though certainly there could be a good deal more—about the differences between illusions and delusions and the reasons for not obscuring them. Now let us look briefly at some of the other cases Ayer lists. Reflections, for instance. No doubt you *can* produce illusions with mirrors, suitably disposed. But is just *any* case of seeing something in a mirror an illusion, as he implies? Quite obviously not. For seeing things in mirrors is a perfectly *normal* occurrence, completely familiar, and there is usually no question of anyone being taken in. No doubt, if you're an infant or an aborigine and have never come across a mirror before, you may be pretty baffled, and even visibly perturbed, when you do. But is that a reason why the rest of us should speak of illusion here? And just the same goes for the phenomena of perspective—again, one *can* play tricks with perspective, but in the ordinary case there is no question of illusion. That a round coin should "look elliptical" (in one sense) from some points of view is exactly what we expect and what we normally find; indeed, we should be badly put out if we ever found this not to be so. Refraction again—the stick that looks bent in water—is far too familiar a case to be properly called a case of illusion. We may perhaps be prepared to agree that the stick looks bent; but then we can see that it's partly submerged in water, so that is exactly how we should expect it to look.

It is important to realize here how familiarity, so to speak, takes the edge of illusion. Is the cinema a case of illusion? Well, just possibly the first man who ever saw moving pictures may have felt inclined to say that here was a case of illusion. But in fact it's pretty unlikely that even he, even momentarily, was actually taken in; and by now the whole thing is so ordinary a part of our lives that it never occurs to us even to raise the question. One might as well ask whether producing a photograph is producing an illusion—which would plainly be just silly.

Then we must not overlook, in all this talk about illusions and delusions, that there are plenty of more or less unusual cases, not yet mentioned, which certainly aren't either. Suppose that a proof-reader makes a mistake—he fails to notice that what ought to be "causal" is printed as "casual"; does he have a delusion? Or is there an illusion before him? Neither, of course; he simply *misreads*. Seeing after-images, too, though not a particularly frequent occurrence and not just an ordinary case of seeing, is neither seeing illusions nor having delusions. And what about dreams? Does the dreamer see illusions? Does he have delusions? Neither; dreams are *dreams*. . . .

Next, let us have a look at the account Ayer himself gives of some at least of the cases he cites. (In fairness we must remember here that Ayer has a number of quite substantial reservations of his own about the merits and efficacy of the argument from illusion, so that it is not easy to tell just how seriously he intends his exposition of it to be taken; but this is a point we shall come back to.)

First, then, the familiar case of the stick in water. Of this case Ayer says (*a*) that since the stick looks bent but is straight, "at least one of the visual appearances of the stick is *delusive*"; and (*b*) that "what we see [directly anyway] is not the real quality of [a few lines later, not part of] a material thing". Well now: does the stick "look bent" to begin with? I think we can agree that it does, we have no better way of describing it. But of course it does *not* look *exactly* like a bent stick, a bent stick out of water—at most, it may be said to look rather like a bent stick partly immersed *in* water. After all, we can't help seeing the water the stick is partly immersed in. So exactly what in this case is supposed to be *delusive*? What is wrong, what is even faintly surprising, in the idea of a stick's being straight but looking bent sometimes? Does anyone suppose that if something is straight, then it jolly well has to *look* straight at all times and in all circumstances? Obviously no one seriously supposes this. So what mess are we supposed to get into here, what is the difficulty? For of course it has to be suggested that there *is* a difficulty—a difficulty, furthermore, which calls for a pretty radical solution, the introduction of sense-data. But what is the problem we are invited to solve in this way?

Well, we are told, in this case you are seeing *something*; and what is this something "if it is not part of any material thing"? But this question is, really, completely mad. The straight part of the stick, the bit not under water, is presumably part of a material thing; don't we see that? And what about the bit *under* water?—we can see that too. We can see, come to that, the water itself. In fact what we see is *a stick partly immersed in water*; and it is particularly extraordinary that this should appear to be called in question—that a question should be raised about *what* we are seeing—since this, after all, is simply the description of the situation with which we started. It was, that is to say, agreed at the start that we were looking at a stick, a "material thing", part of which was under water. If, to take a rather different case, a church were cunningly camouflaged so that it looked like a barn, how could any serious question be raised about what we see when we look at it? We see, of course, *a church* that now *looks like a barn*. We do *not* see an immaterial barn, an immaterial church, or an immaterial anything else. And what in this case could seriously tempt us to say that we do?

Notice, incidentally, that in Ayer's description of the stick-in-water case, which is supposed to be prior to the drawing of any philosophical conclusions, there has already crept in the unheralded but important expression "visual appearances"—it is, of course, ultimately to be suggested that all we *ever* get when we see is a visual appearance (whatever that may be).

Consider next the case of my reflection in a mirror. My body, Ayer says, "appears to be some distance behind the glass"; but as it's in front, it can't really be behind the glass. So what am I seeing? A sense-datum. What about this? Well, once again, although there is no objection to saying that my body "appears to be some distance behind the glass", in saying this we must remember what sort of situation we are dealing with. It does not "appear to be" there in a way which might tempt me (though it might tempt a baby or a savage) to go round the back and look for it, and be astonished when this enterprise proved a failure. (To say that A is *in* B doesn't always mean that if you open B you will find A, just as to say that A is *on* B doesn't always mean that you could pick it off—consider "I saw my face in the mirror", "There's a pain in my toe", "I heard him on the radio", "I saw the image on the screen", &c. Seeing something in a mirror is not like seeing a bun in a shop-window.) But does it follow that, since my body is not actually located behind the mirror, I am not seeing a material thing? Plainly not. For one thing, I can see the mirror (nearly always anyway). I can see my own body "indirectly", *sc.* in the mirror. I can also see the reflection of my own body or, as some would say, a mirror-image. And a mirror-image (if we choose this answer) is not a "sense-datum"; it can be photographed, seen by any number of people, and so on. (Of course there is no question here of either illusion or delusion.) And if the question is pressed, what actually *is* some distance, five feet say, behind the mirror, the answer is, not a sense-datum, but some region of the adjoining room.

The mirage case—at least if we take the view, as Ayer does, that the oasis the traveller thinks he can see "does not exist"—is significantly more amenable to the treatment it is given. For here we are supposing the man to be genuinely deluded, he is *not* "seeing a material thing".[5] We don't actually have to say, however, even here that he is "experiencing sense-data"; for though, as Ayer says above, "it is convenient to give a name" to what he is experiencing, the fact is that it already has a name—a *mirage*. Again, we should be wise not to accept too readily the statement that what he is experiencing is "*similar in character* to what he would be experiencing if he were seeing a real oasis". For is it at all likely, really, to be very similar? And, looking ahead, if we were to concede this point we should find the concession being used against us at a later stage—namely, at the stage where we shall be invited to agree that we see sense-data always, in normal cases too.

V

I want now to take up again the philosophical argument as it is set out in the texts we are discussing. As I mentioned earlier, the argument from illusion is intended primarily to persuade us that, in certain exceptional, abnormal situations, what we perceive—directly anyway—is a sense-datum; but then there comes a second stage, in which we are to be brought to agree that what we (directly) perceive is *always* a sense-datum, even in the normal, unexceptional case. It is this second stage of the argument that we must now examine.

Ayer expounds the argument thus. There is, he says, "no intrinsic difference in kind between those of our perceptions that are veridical in their presentation of material things and those that are delusive. When I look at a straight stick, which is refracted in water and so appears crooked, my experience is qualitatively the same as if I were looking at a stick that really was crooked. . . ." If, however, "when our perceptions were delusive, we were always perceiving something of a different kind from what we perceived when they were veridical, we should expect our experience to be qualitatively different in the two cases. We should expect to be able to tell from the intrinsic character of a perception whether it was a perception of a sense-datum or of a material thing. But this is not possible. . . ." Price's exposition of this point,[6] to which Ayer refers us, is in fact not perfectly analogous; for Price has already somehow reached the conclusion that we are always aware of sense-data, and here is trying to establish only that we cannot distinguish *normal* sense-data, as "parts of the surfaces of material things", from *abnormal* ones, not "parts of the surfaces of material things". However, the argument used is much the same: "the abnormal crooked sense-datum of a straight stick standing in water is qualitatively indistinguishable from a normal sense-datum of a crooked stick"; but "is it not incredible that two entities so similar in all these qualities should really be so utterly different: that the one should be a real constituent of a material object, wholly independent of the observer's mind and organism, while the other is merely the fleeting product of his cerebral processes?"

It is argued further, both by Ayer and Price, that "even in the case of veridical perceptions we are not directly aware of material things" [or *apud* Price, that our sense-data are not parts of the surfaces of material things] for the reason that "veridical and delusive perceptions may form a continuous series. Thus, if I gradually approach an object from a distance I may begin by having a series of perceptions which are delusive in the sense that the object appears to be smaller than it really is. Let us assume that this series terminates in a veridical perception.[7] Then the difference in quality between this perception and its immediate predecessor will be of the same order as the difference between any two delusive perceptions that are next to one another in the series. . . ." But "these are differences of degree and not of kind. But this, it is argued, is not what we should expect if the veridical perception were a perception of an object of a different sort, a material thing as opposed to a sense-datum. Does not the fact that veridical and delusive perceptions shade into one another in the way that is indicated by these examples show that the objects that are perceived in either case are generically the same? And from this it would follow, if it was acknowledged that the delusive perceptions were perceptions of sense-data, that what we directly experienced was always a sense-datum and never a material thing." As Price puts it, "it seems most extraordinary that there should be a total difference of nature where there is only an infinitesimal difference of quality".[8]

Well, what are we to make of the arguments thus set before us?

1. It is pretty obvious, for a start, that the terms in which the argument is stated by Ayer are grossly tendentious. Price, you remember, is not producing the argument as a proof that we are always aware of sense-data; in his view that question has already been settled, and he conceives himself to be faced here only with the question whether any sense-data are "parts of the surfaces of material objects". But in Ayer's exposition the argument *is* put forward as a ground for the conclusion that what we are (directly) aware of in perception is always a sense-datum; and if so, it seems a rather serious defect that this conclusion is practically assumed from the very first sentence of the statement of the argument itself. In that sentence Ayer uses, not indeed for the first time, the term "perceptions" (which incidentally has never been defined or explained), and takes it for granted, here and throughout, that there is at any rate some kind of entities of which we are aware in absolutely all cases—namely, "perceptions", delusive or veridical. But of course, if one has already been induced to swallow the idea that every case, whether "delusive" or "veridical", supplies us with "perceptions", one is only too easily going to be made to feel that it would be straining at a gnat not to swallow sense-data in an equally comprehensive style. But in fact one has not even been told what "perceptions" *are*; and the assumption of their ubiquity has been slipped in without any explanation or argument whatever. But if those to whom the argument is ostensibly addressed were not thus made to concede the essential point from the beginning, would the statement of the argument be quite such plain sailing?

2. Of course we shall also want to enter a protest against the argument's bland assumption of a simple dichotomy between "veridical and delusive experiences". There is, as we have already seen, *no* justification at all *either* for lumping all so-called "delusive" experiences together, *or* for lumping together all so-called "veridical" experiences. But again, could the argument run quite so smoothly without this assumption? It would certainly—and this, incidentally, would be all to the good—take rather longer to state.

3. But now let us look at what the argument actually says. It begins, you will remember, with an alleged statement of fact—namely, that "there is no intrinsic difference in kind between those of our perceptions that are veridical in their presentation of material things and those that are delusive" (Ayer), that "there is no qualitative difference between normal sense-data as such and abnormal sense-data as such" (Price). Now, waiving so far as possible the numerous obscurities in and objections to this manner of speaking, let us ask whether what is being alleged here is actually true. Is it the case that "delusive and veridical experiences" are not "qualitatively different"? Well, at least it seems perfectly extraordinary to say so in this sweeping way. Consider a few examples. I may have the experience (dubbed "delusive" presumably) of dreaming that I am being presented to the Pope. Could it be seriously suggested that having this dream is "qualitatively indistinguishable" from *actually being* presented to the Pope? Quite obviously not. After all, we have the phrase "a dream-like quality"; some waking experiences are said to have this dream-like quality, and some artists and writers occasionally try to impart it, usually with scant success, to their works. But of course, if the

fact here alleged *were* a fact, the phrase would be perfectly meaningless, because applicable to everything. If dreams were not "qualitatively" different from waking experiences, then *every* waking experience would be like a dream; the dream-like quality would be, not difficult to capture, but impossible to avoid.[9] It is true, to repeat, that dreams are *narrated* in the same terms as waking experiences: these terms, after all, are the best terms we have; but it would be wildly wrong to conclude from this that what is narrated in the two cases is *exactly alike*. When we are hit on the head we sometimes say that we "see stars"; but for all that, seeing stars when you are hit on the head is *not* "qualitatively" indistinguishable from seeing stars when you look at the sky.

Again, it is simply not true to say that seeing a bright green after-image against a white wall is exactly like seeing a bright green patch actually on the wall; or that seeing a white wall through blue spectacles is exactly like seeing a blue wall; or that seeing pink rats in D.T.s is exactly like really seeing pink rats; or (once again) that seeing a stick refracted in water is exactly like seeing a bent stick. In all these cases we may *say* the same things ("It looks blue", "It looks bent", &c.), but this is no reason at all for denying the obvious fact that the "experiences" are *different*.

4. Next, one may well wish at least to ask for the credentials of a curious general principle on which both Ayer and Price seem to rely,[10] to the effect that, if two things are not "generically the same", the same "in nature", then they can't be alike, or even very nearly alike. If it were true, Ayer says, that from time to time we perceived things of two different kinds, then "we should expect" them to be qualitatively different. But why on earth should we?—particularly if, as he suggests would be the case, we never actually found such a thing to be true. It is not at all easy to discuss this point sensibly, because of the initial absurdity in the hypothesis that we perceive just *two* kinds of things. But if, for example, I had never seen a mirror, but were told (*a*) that in mirrors one sees reflections of things, and (*b*) that reflections of things are not "generically the same" as things, is there any reason why I should forthwith *expect* there to be some whacking big "qualitative" difference between seeing things and seeing their reflections? Plainly not; if I were prudent, I should simply wait and see what seeing reflections was like. If I am told that a lemon is generically different from a piece of soap, do I "expect" that no piece of soap could look just like a lemon? Why should I?

(It is worth noting that Price helps the argument along at this point by a bold stroke of rhetoric: how *could* two entities be "qualitatively indistinguishable", he asks, if one is a "real constituent of a material object", the other "*a fleeting product of his cerebral processes*"? But how in fact are we supposed to have been persuaded that sense-data are *ever* fleeting products of cerebral processes? Does this colourful description fit, for instance, the reflection of my face in a mirror?)

5. Another erroneous principle which the argument here seems to rely on is this: that it *must* be the case that "delusive and veridical experiences" are not (as such) "qualitatively" or "intrinsically" distinguishable—for if they were distinguishable, we should never be "deluded". But of course this is not so. From the fact that I am sometimes "deluded", mistaken, taken in through failing to distinguish A from B, it does not follow at all that A and B must be *indistinguishable*. Perhaps I should have noticed the difference if I had been more careful or attentive; perhaps I am just bad at distinguishing things of this sort (e.g. vintages); perhaps, again, I have never learned to discriminate between them, or haven't

had much practice at it. As Ayer observes, probably truly, "a child who had not learned that refraction was a means of distortion would naturally believe that the stick really was crooked as he saw it"; but how is the fact that an uninstructed child probably would not discriminate between *being refracted* and *being crooked* supposed to establish the allegation that there *is* no "qualitative" difference between the two cases? What sort of reception would I be likely to get from a professional tea-taster, if I were to say to him, "But there can't be any difference between the flavours of these two brands of tea, for I regularly fail to distinguish between them"? Again, when "the quickness of the hand deceives the eye", it is not that what the hand is really doing is *exactly like* what we are tricked into thinking it is doing, but simply that it is *impossible to tell* what it is really doing. In this case it may be true that we can't distinguish, and not merely that we don't; but even this doesn't mean that the two cases are exactly alike.

I do not, of course, wish to deny that there may be cases in which "delusive and veridical experiences" really are "qualitatively indistinguishable"; but I certainly do wish to deny (*a*) that such cases are anything like as *common* as both Ayer and Price seem to suppose, and (*b*) that there *have* to be such cases to accommodate the undoubted fact that we are sometimes "deceived by our senses". We are not, after all, quasi-infallible beings, who can be taken in only where the avoidance of mistake is completely impossible. But if we are prepared to admit that there may be, even that there are, *some* cases in which "delusive and veridical perceptions" really are indistinguishable, does this admission require us to drag in, or even to let in, sense-data? No. For even if we were to make the prior admission (which we have so far found no reason to make) that in the "abnormal" cases we perceive sense-data, we should not be obliged to extend this admission to the "normal" cases too. For why on earth should it *not* be the case that, in some few instances, perceiving one sort of thing is exactly like perceiving another?

6. There is a further quite general difficulty in assessing the force of this argument, which we (in common with the authors of our texts) have slurred over so far. The question which Ayer invites us to consider is whether two classes of "perceptions", the veridical and the delusive, are or are not "qualitatively different", "intrinsically different in kind"; but how are we supposed to set about even considering this question, when we are not told what "a perception" *is*? In particular, how many of the circumstances of a situation, as these would ordinarily be stated, are supposed to be included in "the perception"? For example, to take the stick in water again: it is a feature of this case that part of the stick is under water, and water, of course, is not invisible; is the water, then, part of "the perception"? It is difficult to conceive of any grounds for denying that it is; but *if* it is, surely this is a perfectly obvious respect in which "the perception" differs from, is distinguishable from, the "perception" we have when we look at a bent stick *not* in water. There is a sense, perhaps, in which the presence or absence of water is not the *main thing* in this case—we are supposed to be addressing ourselves primarily to questions about the stick. But in fact, as a great quantity of psychological investigation has shown, discrimination between one thing and another very frequently depends on such more or less extraneous concomitants of the main thing, even when such concomitants are not consciously taken note of. As I said, we are told nothing of what "a perception" is; but could any defensible account, if such an account were offered, completely exclude all these highly

significant attendant circumstances? And if they *were* excluded—in some more or less arbitrary way—how much interest or importance would be left in the contention that "delusive" and "veridical" perceptions are indistinguishable? Inevitably, if you rule out the respects in which A and B differ, you may expect to be left with respects in which they are alike.

I conclude, then, that this part of the philosophical argument involves (though not in every case equally essentially) (*a*) acceptance of a quite bogus dichotomy of all "perceptions" into two groups, the "delusive" and the "veridical"—to say nothing of the unexplained introduction of "perceptions" themselves; (*b*) an implicit but grotesque exaggeration of the *frequency* of "delusive perceptions"; (*c*) a further grotesque exaggeration of the *similarity* between "delusive" perceptions and "veridical" ones; (*d*) the erroneous suggestion that there *must* be such similarity, or even qualitative *identity*; (*e*) the acceptance of the pretty gratuitous idea that things "generically different" could not be qualitatively alike; and (*f*)—which is really a corollary of (*c*) and (*a*)—the gratuitous neglect of those more or less subsidiary features which often make possible the discrimination of situations which, in other *broad* respects, may be roughly alike. These seem to be rather serious deficiencies.

Notes

1 A.J. Ayer, *The Foundations of Empirical Knowledge* (London: Macmillan & Co., 1963).

2 It is not only strange, but also important, that Ayer calls these "assumptions". Later on he is going to take seriously the notion of denying at least one of them, which he could hardly do if he had recognized them here as the plain and incontestable facts that they are.

3 The latter point holds, of course, for *some* uses of "illusion" too; there are the illusions which some people (are said to) lose as they grow older and wiser.

4 Cp. the white rabbit in the play called *Harvey*.

5 Not even "indirectly", no such thing is "presented". Doesn't this seem to make the case, though more amenable, a good deal less useful to the philosopher? It's hard to see how normal cases could be said to be *very like* this.

6 *Perception* (London: Methuen & Co., 1950), p. 31.

7 But what, we may ask, does this assumption amount to? From what distance *does* an object, a cricket-ball say, "look the size that it really is"? Six feet? Twenty feet?

8 I omit from consideration a further argument cited by both Price and Ayer, which makes play with the "causal dependence" of our "perceptions" upon the conditions of observation and our own "physiological and psychological states".

9 This is part, no doubt *only* part, of the absurdity in Descartes' toying with the notion that the whole of our experience might be a dream.

10 Ayer in fact expresses qualms later: see p. 12.

QUESTIONS

1 According to Austin, what is the difference between "illusions" and "delusions"?
2 What are the two stages of the argument from illusion?
3 According to Austin, what conclusion can we draw from the fact that the phrase "a dream-like quality" is meaningful?
4 According to Austin, does either stage of the argument from illusion succeed?

FURTHER READING ON PERCEPTION

Adler, Mortimer, *Ten Philosophical Mistakes* (New York: Macmillan, 1985).
Armstrong, David, *Perception and the Physical World* (London: Routledge & Kegan Paul, 1961).
Ayer, A.J., *The Foundations of Empirical Knowledge* (London: Macmillan, 1964).
Berkeley, George, *Principles, Dialogues, and Correspondence* (Indianapolis, Ind.: Bobbs-Merrill, 1965).
Chisholm, Roderick, *Perceiving: A Philosophical Study* (Ithaca, N.Y.: Cornell University Press, 1957).
Crane, Tim (ed.) *The Contents of Experience* (Cambridge: Cambridge University Press, 1992).
Fales, Evan, *A Defense of the Given* (Lanham, Md.: Rowman & Littlefield, 1986).
Fumerton, Richard, *Metaphysical and Epistemological Problems of Perception* (Lincoln, Nebr.: University of Nebraska Press, 1985).
Grice, H.P., "The Causal Theory of Perception," *Proceedings of the Aristotelian Society*, supplementary volume 35 (1961): 121–68.
Huemer, Michael, *Skepticism and the Veil of Perception* (Lanham, Md.: Rowman & Littlefield, 2001).
Hume, David, *Enquiries Concerning Human Understanding and Concerning the Principles of Morals*, ed. L.A. Selby-Bigge (Oxford: Clarendon, 1975).
Jackson, Frank, *Perception: A Representative Theory* (Cambridge: Cambridge University Press, 1977).
Kelley, David, *The Evidence of the Senses* (Baton Rouge, La.: Louisiana State University Press, 1986).
McDowell, John, *Mind and World* (Cambridge, Mass.: Harvard University Press, 1994).
Peacocke, Christopher, *Sense and Content* (Oxford: Clarendon, 1983).
Pollock, John and Joseph Cruz, *Contemporary Theories of Knowledge*, 2nd edn (Lanham, Md.: Rowman & Littlefield, 1999).
Price, H.H., *Perception* (London: Methuen, 1950).
Reid, Thomas, *Inquiry and Essays*, ed. Ronald Beanblossom and Keith Lehrer (Indianapolis, Ind.: Hackett, 1983).
Wright, Edmond (ed.) *New Representationalisms* (Brookfield, Vt.: Ashgate, 1993).

2

MEMORY

The epistemology of memory is a neglected topic in philosophy, but memory plays an essential role in almost all of our knowledge—almost all of what you now know consists of things that you learned before now and that you presently remember—for instance, who Abraham Lincoln was, what is the product of 7 and 4, and what the beginning of this sentence was about. Epistemological questions about memory (as distinct from psychological questions) include the likes of "How do we know that the events we seem to remember actually happened?" and "What sort of justification do we have for believing *p* when we 'remember that *p*'?"

It is useful to distinguish "event memory," or "episodic memory" (remembering an event that one previously witnessed), from factual memory (remembering a fact that one previously learned). It is possible to have factual memory in the absence of any relevant event memory. For instance, I remember that the Battle of Hastings took place in 1066 (factual memory), but I am not old enough to remember the Battle of Hastings itself, nor do I even remember my experience of first learning about the battle. Both of these kinds of memory play an important role in our retention of knowledge, although factual memory seems to be more ubiquitous (it may be entailed by event memory, even though the reverse entailment does not hold).

In the selection from *The Analysis of Mind*, Bertrand Russell makes two important points about the nature of memory. The first is that our memory beliefs (and, presumably, our memory experiences as well) are present states, even though they are *about* past states. Thus, the occurrence of a given memory belief cannot logically entail anything about the past. He illustrates this by introducing his famous "five minute hypothesis": the hypothesis that the world came into existence just five minutes ago, with all of us complete with false memories of the past. Though not a *plausible* hypothesis, this is logically possible, since past events are distinct events from our present memories of them. Russell's second main observation is that event memory cannot be merely a matter of having images. He says that one's memory images are also accompanied by (a) a feeling of pastness, which enables us to judge roughly how long ago the remembered event occurred, and (b) a feeling of familiarity, which we use to judge how reliable a memory image is.

Norman Malcolm provides a definition of factual memory. His definition states that a person remembers that *p* if and only if the person knows that *p* because he previously knew that *p*. Malcolm goes on to explain this definition and defend it from objections. Along the way, he addresses three epistemological questions concerning memory beliefs. (a) When a person, S, remembers that *p*, what kind of knowledge does S have? Malcolm answers that S's knowledge is of the same kind as it was when *S* originally came to know that *p*. For example, if *S* first learned *p* through perception, and he remembers it now, then *S*'s present knowledge is perceptual knowledge. The reason for this is that *S* presently has the very same item of knowledge that he previously had; memory does not produce new items of knowledge, but only enables one to *retain* knowledge. (b) When *S* remembers that *p*, does *S* have grounds for believing that *p*? For similar reasons, Malcolm answers that *S* has the same grounds, if any, that he originally had when he first formed the belief that *p*. (c) When *S* remembers that *p*, how certain is it that *p*? Malcolm answers that it is exactly as certain that *p* as it was when *S* first formed the belief. This seems to follow from the answer to (b).

Malcolm's theory does seem to have two problems. First, it does not seem to be true that the level of certainty of a memory belief is the same as that of the original belief. Since our memories are fallible (sometimes your memory plays tricks on you, as we say), a memory belief that *p* is open to new possibilities of error not present when one first formed the belief that *p*; therefore, at least some of the time, a memory belief ought to be counted *less* certain than the original belief. Second, Malcolm denies that a memory experience (the experience of seeming to remember that *p*) is part of one's grounds for believing that *p*. But this seems to be mistaken. Imagine a case in which, unbeknownst to him, *S*'s memory is deceiving him, so that he seems to remember that *p* even though he actually never knew that *p*. As a result, *S* quite understandably accepts *p*. It does not seem correct to say that in this case *S* believes *p for no reason*, still less that he is entirely unjustified in believing *p*. But this is what Malcolm's theory would imply, since *S* never previously had reasons for believing *p* and memory experiences do not generate new reasons for beliefs.

Because of the latter objection, Pollock and Cruz propose a different conception of the justification of memory beliefs. They propose that memory beliefs are "epistemologically basic," meaning that having an experience of seeming to remember that *p* gives one a (new) justification for believing *p*, distinct from the grounds one previously had. This is similar to the way in which perceptual experiences justify one in believing propositions about the physical world.

Pollock and Cruz focus on the role that memory plays in reasoning. Often, a person's beliefs depend upon a complex chain of reasoning which he cannot hold all in mind at once. At any given time, he is only thinking of, say, the present step that he is on and the step immediately preceding it. What makes one now justified in accepting the present step, then, is one's memory of the previous step (rather than the entire series of previous steps). Pollock and Cruz distinguish the "genetic argument," the whole series of steps one goes through, from the "dynamic argument," the steps one is thinking of at the moment. Although one's belief that *p*, when one comes to the end of the chain of reasoning, is justified by the dynamic argument one is then entertaining, the genetic argument remains relevant, because if one acquires grounds for doubting that the genetic argument was correct (they call this having a "defeater" for the genetic argument), then one ought to withhold belief from the ultimate conclusion. A criticism of the genetic argument is a criticism of the belief that *p*.

Pollock and Cruz's view of the epistemology of memory is subject to two objections. First, it seems to imply that the level of justification for one's belief can increase (so the belief becomes more certain) merely by the passage of time. For if I keep in mind my original justification for believing *p*, while at the same time remembering that *p*, according to Pollock and Cruz, I would then have *two* reasons for believing *p*. This would seem to mean that I should now be more certain that *p* than I was before. Second, a person might adopt the belief that *p* irrationally at first but later (perhaps after forgetting how he initially adopted the belief) have an experience of seeming to remember that *p*. In Pollock and Cruz's view, it appears, the initially unjustified belief would now be justified.

The reading selection by the editor criticizes the theories of both Malcolm and Pollock and Cruz. It proposes an alternative, "dualistic" view according to which the justification for a memory belief has two components: (a) the justification one had for adopting the belief initially and (b) the justification, provided by one's memory experiences, that one has since had for retaining it. The *degree* of justification of a memory belief will be the product of the degree of justification for adopting it and the degree of justification for retaining it. It is argued that this theory avoids the objections cited above to Malcolm's theory and to Pollock and Cruz's theory.

Bertrand Russell, "Memory"

One reason for treating memory at this early stage is that it seems to be involved in the fact that images are recognized as "copies" of past sensible experience. In the preceding lecture. I alluded to Hume's principle "that all our simple ideas in their first appearance are derived from simple impressions, which are correspondent to them, and which they exactly represent." Whether or not this principle is liable to exceptions, everyone would agree that is has a broad measure of truth, though the word "exactly" might seem an overstatement, and it might seem more correct to say that ideas *approximately* represent impressions. Such modifications of Hume's principle, however, do not affect the problem which I wish to present for your consideration, namely: Why do we believe that images are, sometimes or always, approximately or exactly, copies of sensations? What sort of evidence is there? And what sort of evidence is logically possible? The difficulty of this question arises through the fact that the sensation which an image is supposed to copy is in the past when the image exists, and can therefore only be known by memory, while, on the other hand, memory of past sensations seems only possible by means of present images. How, then, are we to find any way of comparing the present image and the past sensation? The problem is just as acute if we say that images differ from their prototypes as if we say that they resemble them; it is the very possibility of comparison that is hard to understand.[1] We think we can know that they are alike or different, but we cannot bring them together in one experience and compare them. To deal with this problem, we must have a theory of memory. In this way the whole status of images as "copies" is bound up with the analysis of memory.

In investigating memory-beliefs, there are certain points which must be borne in mind. In the first place, everything constituting a memory-belief is happening *now*, not in that past time to which the belief is said to refer. It is not logically necessary to the existence of a memory-belief that the event remembered should have occurred, or even that the past should have existed at all. There is no logical impossibility in the hypothesis that the world sprang into being five minutes ago, exactly as it then was, with a population that "remembered" a wholly unreal past. There is no logically necessary connection between events at different times; therefore nothing that is happening now or will happen in the future can disprove the hypothesis that the world began five minutes ago. Hence the occurrences which are *called* knowledge of the past are logically independent of the past; they

Bertrand Russell, *The Analysis of Mind* (London: Allen & Unwin, 1921).

are wholly analysable into present contents, which might, theoretically, be just what they are even if no past had existed.

I am not suggesting that the non-existence of the past should be entertained as a serious hypothesis. Like all sceptical hypotheses, it is logically tenable, but uninteresting. All that I am doing is to use its logical tenability as a help in the analysis of what occurs when we remember.

In the second place, images without beliefs are insufficient to constitute memory; and habits are still more insufficient. The behaviourist, who attempts to make psychology a record of behaviour, has to trust his memory in making the record. "Habit" is a concept involving the occurrence of similar events at different times; if the behaviourist feels confident that there is such a phenomenon as habit, that can only be because he trusts his memory, when it assures him that there have been other times. And the same applies to images. If we are to know—as it is supposed we do—that images are "copies," accurate or inaccurate, of past events, something more than the mere occurrence of images must go to constitute this knowledge. For their mere occurrence, by itself, would not suggest any connection with anything that had happened before.

Can we constitute memory out of images together with suitable beliefs? We may take it that memory-images, when they occur in true memory, are (*a*) known to be copies, (*b*) sometimes known to be imperfect copies (cf. footnote on previous page). How is it possible to know that a memory-image is an imperfect copy, without having a more accurate copy by which to replace it? This would *seem* to suggest that we have a way of knowing the past which is independent of images, by means of which we can criticize image-memories. But I do not think such an inference is warranted.

What results, formally, from our knowledge of the past through images of which we recognize the inaccuracy, is that such images must have two characteristics by which we can arrange them in two series, of which one corresponds to the more or less remote period in the past to which they refer, and the other to our greater or less confidence in their accuracy. We will take the second of these points first.

Our confidence or lack of confidence in the accuracy of a memory-image must, in fundamental cases, be based upon a characteristic of the image itself, since we cannot evoke the past bodily and compare it with the present image. It might be suggested that vagueness is the required characteristic, but I do not think this is the case. We sometimes have images that are by no means peculiarly vague, which yet we do not trust—for example, under the influence of fatigue we may see a friend's face vividly and clearly, but horribly distorted. In such a case we distrust our image in spite of its being unusually clear. I think the characteristic by which we distinguish the images we trust is the feeling of *familiarity* that accompanies them. Some images, like some sensations, feel very familiar, while others feel strange. Familiarity is a feeling capable of degrees. In an image of a well-known face, for example, some parts may feel more familiar than others; when this happens, we have more belief in the accuracy of the familiar parts than in that of the unfamiliar parts. I think it is by this means that we become critical of images, not by some imageless memory with which we compare them. I shall return to the consideration of familiarity shortly.

I come now to the other characteristic which memory-images must have in order to account for our knowledge of the past. They must have some characteristic which makes us regard them as referring to more or less remote portions of the past. That is to say if we suppose that A is the event remembered, B the remembering, and the interval of time between A and B, there must be some characteristic of B which is capable of degrees, and which, in accurately dated memories, varies as *t* varies. It may increase as *t* increases, or diminish as *t* increases. The question which of these occurs is not of any importance for the theoretic serviceability of the characteristic in question.

In actual fact, there are doubtless various factors that concur in giving us the feeling of greater or less remoteness in some remembered event. There may be a specific feeling which could be called the feeling of "pastness," especially where immediate memory is concerned. But apart from this, there are other marks. One of these is context. A recent memory has, usually, more context than a more distant one. When a remembered event has a remembered context, this may occur in two ways, either (*a*) by successive images in the same order as their prototypes, or (*b*) by remembering a whole process simultaneously, in the same way in which a present process may be apprehended, through akoluthic sensations which, by fading, acquire the mark of just-pastness in an increasing degree as they fade, and are thus placed in a series while all sensibly present. It will be context in this second sense, more specially, that will give us a sense of the nearness or remoteness of a remembered event.

There is, of course, a difference between knowing the temporal relation of a remembered event to the present, and knowing the time-order of two remembered events. Very often our knowledge of the temporal relation of a remembered event to the present is inferred from its temporal relations to other remembered events. It would seem that only rather recent events can be placed at all accurately by means of feelings giving their temporal relation to the present, but it is clear that such feelings must play an essential part in the process of dating remembered events.

We may say, then, that images are regarded by us as more or less accurate copies of past occurrences because they come to us with two sorts of feelings: (1) Those that may be called feelings of familiarity; (2) those that may be collected together as feelings giving a sense of pastness. The first lead us to trust our memories, the second to assign places to them in the time-order.

Note

1 How, for example, can we obtain such knowledge as the following: "If we look at, say, a red nose and perceive it, and after a little while *ekphore* its memory-image, we note immediately how unlike, in its likeness, this memory-image is to the original perception" (A. Wohlgemuth, "On the Feelings and their Neural Correlate with an Examination of the Nature of Pain," *Journal of Psychology*, vol. viii, part iv, June, 1917).

QUESTIONS

1 Describe Russell's five-minute hypothesis.
2 According to Russell, what does the "feeling of pastness" enable us to judge?
3 According to Russell, what does the "feeling of familiarity" enable us to judge?

Norman Malcolm, "A Definition of Factual Memory"

Enough has been said in the previous two lectures to show that factual memory (remembering that *p*) holds an important position in the family of concepts of memory. Some forms of memory can be defined in terms of factual memory plus the purely logical notion of existential quantification. Other forms are related to factual memory as *species* to *genus*.[1] Still other forms, not related to factual memory in either of these two ways, *imply* it.[2] I have not been able to discover any form of memory which does not have at least this latter relation to factual memory. I will not undertake to provide an account of the exact position that factual memory occupies among the concepts of memory, but it has sufficient importance to make it worthwhile to attempt to *define* it.

In my second lecture I produced definitions of perceptual and personal memory. As we noted they are not definitions of *memory*, but only of the adverbs "personally" and "perceptually," as these modify the verb "remember." That they are not definitions of *memory* is shown by the fact that the verb "remember" occurs in the *definiens* of each of those definitions. The definition of factual memory which I shall propose will really be a definition of *memory*—not of memory in general, but of one use of the verb "remembers." In this definition that verb will not occur in the *definiens*.

The definition is very simple. It is the following: A person, B, remembers that *p* if and only if B knows that *p* because he knew that *p*. It will be convenient to say that this definition is composed of three elements: the present knowledge that *p*, the previous knowledge that *p*, and the relationship between the present and the previous knowledge expressed by saying that B knows that *p* *because* he previously knew that *p*. Each element is a logically necessary condition and the conjunction of them a logically sufficient condition of factual memory.

I wish to discuss each of these three elements in turn. But before I do so I want to anticipate one objection to the definition. Let us suppose that a man saw a bird of striking appearance in his bird feeder last week, but did not know what bird it was. While looking through a book about birds he comes upon a picture of a cardinal and now knows it was a cardinal he saw. He might naturally say "I remember that I saw a cardinal in the feeder last week." But it is false that *previously* he knew that he saw a cardinal. It might be concluded that the element

Norman Malcolm, *Knowledge and Certainty* (Englewood Cliffs, NJ: Prentice/Hall, 1963).

of *previous* knowledge is shown not to be a necessary condition of factual memory.

I deal with this kind of case by distinguishing between what I call "elliptical" and "nonelliptical" uses of the expression "remembers that *p*." I believe that the man in our example would agree to substitute for his sentence "I remember that I saw a cardinal" the *conjunctive* sentence "I remember that I saw this bird (or: a bird of this kind) *and* now I know it was a cardinal." The sentence he originally uttered was an ellipsis, in the grammarian's sense, the meaning of which is given by the conjunctive sentence. In this conjunction the first conjunct expresses factual memory, the second conjunct expresses the new information. Another way of putting the distinction is to say that the original sentence did not express "pure" factual memory. In the conjunctive sentence substituted for it, the first conjunct expresses pure factual memory, the second conjunct expresses something other than memory. The whole conjunction expresses "impure" memory.

There could be many different kinds of impure factual memory. For example, suppose that someone had often noticed, as a boy, that the house in which he lived faced the setting sun. Years later, when conversing with someone, he suddenly realizes, for the first time, that this implied that his house faced the west, and he says "I remember that our house faced the west." This sentence of his expresses impure factual memory, which is a compound of pure factual memory and present inference or realization. The definition I am presenting is intended solely to be a definition of *pure* factual memory, with no admixture of inference or present realization.

I turn now to a consideration of the three elements in the definition. The first two elements are present and previous knowledge, and so whatever is true of knowledge will apply equally to both. In the history of the philosophy of memory there has been a considerable amount of puzzlement and confusion about the relation of memory to knowledge. First, if memory involves knowledge what *kind* of knowledge is it? Second, if a person remembers that *p* just *how certain* is it that *p*? Third, when a person remembers that *p* does he have *grounds* for saying that *p*? These are some of the questions that puzzle us, and I hope that this discussion will help to answer them.

Obviously one necessary condition for the knowledge that *p* is that *p* that should be *true*. If *p* is false then B does not know, and did not know, that *p*; and also B does not remember that *p*.

A second necessary condition for someone's knowing that *p* may be expressed, roughly, as the condition that he should be *sure* that *p*. Being unsure whether *p* is true counts both against knowing that *p* and against remembering that *p*. If a man previously knew that *p* and now not only is not sure but does not even believe that *p*, we are sometimes ready to say "He really remembers it": but what we mean would also be expressed by saying "He *will* remember it" or "His forgetting it is only *temporary*." We should have to admit that at present he does not remember it.

Of course there are many differences of degree in the confidence with which one believes or is sure of something. A person can be *inclined* to believe something and at the same time be quite unsure about it. Sometimes we should say he knows the thing in question and sometimes that he does not, depending on what contrasts we were making. Suppose some pupils were being tested on their knowledge of Roman history. They are supposed to tell who killed Caesar. Suppose that one of them, A, is inclined to think it was Brutus, but has little confidence in this answer. Should we say A *knows* that Brutus killed Caesar? If we were comparing him with B, who believes that Cassius was the assassin, we should say that A knows the answer but B does not. If we were comparing A with C, who is *certain* that Brutus slew Caesar, we should say that C knows the answer but A does not "really *know*" it, or does not know it "very well." The same considerations apply to the question of whether A *remembers* that Brutus killed Caesar. Thus we can say, in summary, that if someone has *no* inclination to believe that *p*, this counts absolutely against either his knowing or remembering that *p*. If he has some inclination to believe that *p* but is unsure about it, whether we say he does or does not know, or remember, that *p* depends on the comparisons we are making. In short, if one is unsure about something this *can serve*, in some circumstances, to justify the claim that one does not know, and does not remember, the something.

The considerations about truth and certainty, so far adduced, apply equally to knowledge and memory. A third consideration is that of *grounds* for being sure that *p*.[3] It has often been supposed that, in addition to being right and being sure, a further thing necessary for knowledge is the possession of grounds, or adequate grounds, or conclusive grounds. I am not convinced that this third feature is a requirement for knowledge, although I admit that not just any true belief is knowledge. My discussion of this difficult point will necessarily be skimpy.

In the first place, I call attention to the knowledge that human beings normally have of their own voluntary actions, both of what they are doing and what they are going to do. Suppose a man was for a while undecided as to whether he would quit his job, but now *knows* he will quit it. Should we expect him to have *grounds* for being sure he will quit it? It is hard to see what this could mean.[4] Could one say that his grounds for being sure he will quit is his *decision* to quit? But in the case, which is common enough, where a person is trying to make up his mind whether or not he will quit his job, not through the consideration of evidence that he will or will not quit it, but of reasons for and against quitting it—in this case, what *is* his deciding to quit other than the transition from his being unsure about it to his being sure that he will quit? In this example, his deciding what he will do is the same thing as his becoming sure what he will do, and is not his grounds for being sure. Nothing can be put forward as his grounds for being sure he will quit: yet it is correct to say "He knows now that he will quit his job."

In the second place, sometimes people know in advance about things they do *in*voluntarily. A nervous amateur actor, about to make his first appearance on the stage, might say with conviction, "I know I shall forget my lines." Sure enough, he does forget them. This use of "know" is entirely natural. Did he have grounds? He could have been relying on some statistics—but that would not be the normal case. We are willing to say that he knew he would forget his lines, yet we do not expect him to have had evidence or grounds.[5]

In the third place, I can imagine a man who has unusual knowledge of the whereabouts of various persons, of what they are engaged in, what will happen to them, and so on. The man I am imagining (let us call him "the seer") is sure about these things and apparently is always right, but he does not have *grounds* for being sure. He has no special sources of information, he does not make use of tips or hints, and he does not guess. But he can tell someone the whereabouts of the son who left home five years ago and has not since been heard from. As his powers became known, people would come to him to inquire about their relatives and friends. I am supposing that in a large number of cases his answers have proven true and in no cases have they proven false. It is unquestionable that people would regard the seer as a source of *information*. "He informed me of the whereabouts of my son" would be a natural thing to say about him: and also "He knew the whereabouts of my son." The seer, as said, does not have grounds for being sure of the things he is sure of. He might even admit that he does not know *how* he knows the things in question. Sometimes when a question is put to him he has to wait a bit until the answer comes to him, like an inspiration; and sometimes he knows the answer immediately. But never is it a matter of grounds, evidence, or reasoning.

It is sometimes held that a person cannot properly be said to know something unless he is *in a position* to know it. But one might say that what is extraordinary about the seer is that he knows things which he is *not in a position to know*. A.J. Ayer says that "the necessary and sufficient conditions for knowing that something is the case are first that what one is said to know be true, secondly that one be sure of it, and thirdly that one should have the right to be sure."[6] I question the third condition. I believe Ayer would agree with me that the seer *knows* the things he reports, for Ayer says that if someone "were repeatedly successful in a given domain" although "without appearing to have any adequate basis for it," then "we should grant him the right to be sure, simply on the basis of his success."[7] But I think it is odd to say that the seer has a right to be sure of what he is sure of. The rest of us would have a right to be sure of something because the seer told us so, and because (to the best of our knowledge) he is invariably right. *We* have grounds for being sure. But the seer does not have our grounds, or any other grounds. As said, he is not, in the ordinary meaning of the phrase, *in a position to know* what he tells us. I cannot understand, therefore, the expression "has a right to be sure" when it is applied to the seer, unless it merely means "*knows* what he is sure of," in which case it cannot express an element in the *analysis* of knowledge.

I have argued, from several different kinds of cases, that having grounds for being certain of something is not a necessary condition of knowing it. I imagine there are still other kinds of cases. I suspect that a stronger candidate than grounds or evidence, for being a necessary condition of knowledge, is the negative requirement that to know something one should not be certain of it because of a *mistake*, e.g., because of mishearing what someone said or because of fallacious reasoning.

The connection of this discussion of grounds with the definition of factual memory is that if having grounds is not a necessary condition of knowing something there is then no reason to suppose it is a necessary condition of remembering something.

When people do have grounds for being sure of something the grounds can differ in strength. If an American living in England converts his dollar holdings into pounds because he is sure that the American government is going to devalue the dollar, his grounds for being sure could be of many sorts. Let us suppose there are three people, A, B, and C, each of whom converts from dollars to pounds because he is sure the dollar will be devalued. A's grounds for being sure of this are that several of his friends, who are "generally well-informed about developments in international finance," are convinced it will happen. B's grounds are that a friend of his was told in confidence by an American Treasury official that it was "bound to happen." C's grounds are that the Secretary of the Treasury himself, in his last news conference, said he "did not see how this step could be avoided." All three are right; the dollar is devalued.

A person commenting on the matter afterwards could correctly say that all three *knew* the devaluation would occur (in contrast, for example, with D, whom the devaluation took by surprise). The person commenting on the matter would allow that B's grounds for being sure of it were stronger than A's, and that C's grounds were stronger still. Indeed, he would think that C's grounds were "just about as strong (or conclusive) as one could have in a matter of that sort." As he might put it, A's grounds were pretty good, B's grounds were even better, and C's grounds were as good as one could have. Another way to express the difference would be to say that on A's grounds it was "reasonably certain" it would happen; on B's grounds it was still more certain; and on C's grounds it was as certain as could be. Finally, another way to express it would be to say that although A knew it would happen his knowledge of it *was less certain* than B's, and B's knowledge was more certain than A's although not as certain as C's, and C's knowledge of it was as certain as knowledge can be in such matters. The interesting point here, if I am right, is that in ordinary discourse we conceive of *knowledge* as being *more or less certain*. We *grade* knowledge in terms of certainty. This grading of knowledge is solely in terms of the strength of the grounds. Grading *knowledge* as more or less certain is *equivalent* to grading *grounds* as more or less conclusive. If this is right, the assumption we are often tempted to make in philosophy, that if someone really knows that *p* then he must have grounds which make it perfectly certain or perfectly conclusive that *p*, is shown to be false. Knowledge is not all wool and a yard wide.

Our definition of factual memory requires the elements of present and previous knowledge. Let us raise again the questions that we put before: First, what *kind* of knowledge is involved in memory? Second, when someone remembers that *p* does he have *grounds* for being sure that *p*? Third, when someone remembers that *p*, just *how certain* is it that *p*?

Let us consider the first question, keeping in mind that memory involves both previous and present knowledge. The element of *previous* knowledge involved in memory can be any kind of knowledge at all. It might be the knowledge that a person has of his own voluntary or involuntary actions; it might be knowledge based on a newspaper report, or on a mathematical demonstration, or on an inference from what someone said; it might be the kind of knowledge that the seer has. Of what kind is the *present* knowledge involved in memory? Of exactly the *same* kind that the previous knowledge was. I think that here it may be misleading to speak of *two* elements of knowledge in memory, previous and present knowledge. There are not two pieces of knowledge but one piece. Memory is the *retention* of knowledge. One knew something and still knows it. The present knowledge in memory is the *same* as the previous knowledge.

Let us go to the second question: When someone remembers that *p* does he have grounds for being sure that *p*? The answer is that he has the same grounds, if any, that he previously had.[8] If B remembers that his friend, Robinson, was ill last year, then B previously knew of the illness. His previous knowledge may have been based on perception (He saw Robinson when the latter was ill); or on testimony (Jones told him about Robinson's illness); or on inference (B inferred that Robinson was ill from his absence from work). B's *present* knowledge that Robinson was ill, if it is solely memory, has the *same* grounds. If the ground of his previous knowledge was testimony then the ground of his present knowledge is that same previous testimony. And so on. If what made him sure, previously, that Robinson was ill was that Jones told him so, his present ground for being sure is that Jones told him so previously. If a man's previous knowledge that *p* had *no* grounds, then in remembering that *p* his present knowledge has *no* grounds.

There is an interesting problem that arises here. If a man previously had grounds for being sure that *p*, and now remembers that *p*, but does not remember what his grounds were, does he *have* grounds for being sure that *p*? I will not go into this point, but I am inclined to say that he *has* the *same* grounds he previously had. In some cases if a man cannot give any grounds for believing something it follows that he has no grounds. But I think this does not hold for the special case of his *forgetting* what his grounds were. I should say it does not follow that he *has* no grounds for being certain that *p*, any *more* than it follows that he *had* no grounds. But by hypothesis he had grounds.

Our third question was: When someone remembers that *p*, how *certain* is it that *p*? The answer I give is that his present knowledge that *p* has the *same* degree of certainty that his previous knowledge that *p* had. Of course, if he has forgotten what his grounds were, *he* may be less certain than he was—but that is a different matter.

One thing which is obvious is that no matter how well a person remembers something, his present knowledge cannot be *superior* to his previous knowledge. His present knowledge that *p*, if it is solely memory, cannot be *more* certain than was his previous knowledge that *p*. This fact provides one clear sense for the claim that memory is not a *source* of knowledge.

When I remember that *p*, does my *remembering* it have grounds? If we are not merely asking again whether my certainty that *p* has grounds, then this seems a nonsensical question. If by "my remembering it" is meant the *relation* between my present and my previous knowledge that *p*, then my remembering it cannot be said to have or to lack grounds. This is reflected in the definition of factual memory—knowing that *p* because one previously knew that *p*. It would be unintelligible as well as ungrammatical to ask whether one had grounds for *that*.

Let us try to summarize briefly the place of knowledge in factual memory. If a person remembers that *p* then he knows that *p* and he knew it before. Knowing implies being sure, save for the qualification noted. There can be and are cases in which people know things without having *grounds* for being sure. If the previous knowledge was without grounds then the present knowledge is without grounds (if the present knowledge is solely memory). When a man had grounds for his previous knowledge that *p*, his previous knowledge was more or less certain, depending on the strength of his grounds; and his present knowledge (if it is solely memory) has this same degree of certainty regardless of whether he *remembers* his grounds.

I turn now to the third element in the definition of factual memory. What does it mean to say that someone knows that *p because* he previously knew that *p*? Could it mean that the past knowledge *caused* the present knowledge? W. von Leyden says that "it is part of the meaning of memory that, when it is correct, it is causally dependent upon a previous perception."[9] He is saying, for example, that someone's memory of having seen the *Queen Mary* in drydock is causally dependent on his having seen the *Queen Mary* in drydock. One might object to the idea that the supposed effect is *causally* dependent on the supposed cause, for the reason that the "effect" is *logically* dependent on the "cause." It is logically impossible that one should remember having seen *x* unless one saw it.

But we are concerned now with factual memory and whether it is a possibility that the present *knowledge* that *p* is causally dependent on the previous *knowledge* that *p*. Here it is not true that there is logical implication, in either direction, between supposed effect and supposed cause. Furthermore, one might think that we must be justified in speaking of a "causal dependence" here, simply because it is a natural use of language to say that someone knows that *p* "because" he knew it before, or to say that his present knowledge is "due to" his previous knowledge.

Granting this to be so, it does not tell us what this "causal dependence" *means*. There is an important sense of "cause" in which a singular causal statement of the form "*x* caused *y*" implies a general proposition of the form "In like circumstances, whenever *x* then *y*." But *this* meaning of "cause" cannot be involved in factual memory, since in saying that someone remembers that *p*, we are certainly not committing ourselves to the truth of the general proposition that "In like circumstances, whenever a person has previously known that *p* then he knows that *p*," even if we could give any clear meaning to it.

To come back to von Leyden, he holds that recollecting something implies that there is "a memory process or causal chain stretching continuously from the occurrence of *x* and the original experience of *x* up to the present recollection of *x*."[10] Another way he puts it is to say that there is a "continuous connexion" between a remembered fact and a present memory of it.[11] Sometimes he calls it an *unbroken* connection.[12] But this requirement, he holds, creates a problem about knowing whether *anyone* remembers *anything!* For, "the process of retention," says von Leyden, is "unobservable."[13] The "causal chain" implied by memory is "elusive."[14] It is difficult if not impossible, he says, to prove that an unbroken connection or persisting process intervened between a past experience and one's present recollection of it.[15] The conclusion drawn by him is that "no memory statement is, strictly speaking, verifiable."[16] I think he means by this remark that it is *never* verifiable that someone remembers something!

I should have thought a more reasonable conclusion would be that the concept of memory carries *no* implication of a continuous process of retention or of an unbroken causal connection. The imagery suggested by what von Leyden says is fairly definite. Remembering consists in a certain *process* which begins at the time a person witnesses or learns something. What the process is *in its own nature* is not known. But it is there, going on, and the person's occasional recollection of what he witnessed or learned is a *manifestation* of this underlying process.

This picture gives rise to two sorts of skeptical reflection. First, perhaps the underlying process is not *always* in operation during the intervals between the manifestations of it, and consequently we are sometimes mistaken in thinking that we remember certain things even though we give the right answers. Second, perhaps the required process is *never* there, and occurrences of so-called "recollection" are *never* manifestations of a process of remembering, and we are *always* deceived in thinking we remember something. It merely *looks as if* people remember!

Rather than to dwell on the absurdity of this conclusion, I want to try to explain the third element in the definition of factual memory. What does it mean to say that A knows that *p because* he previously knew that *p*? It does not mean that there is a "continuous" or "unbroken" connection between the previous and the present knowledge, even if this were an intelligible notion. I am afraid my explanation of the meaning of the "because" will be disappointing. I believe its meaning is essentially *negative*. This will be brought out by reflecting on one sort of consideration which would *disprove* the claim that A remembers that *p*. Suppose we know that A had known at a previous time that Robinson walked across Cayuga Lake when it was frozen. Suppose we also know that A knows it now. Could it turn out that A's present knowledge is not memory? Yes. If A were to tell us that he would not have had his present knowledge of the incident had not someone informed him of it *just now*, or had he not read about it in his diary a moment ago, or had he not inferred it from some remarks he overheard just now, then we should know that A's present knowledge that Robinson walked across the lake is not memory.

In this example, A had *forgotten* that *p*. But his having previously forgotten it is not a sufficient condition of his not remembering it. He might have forgotten it and then later remembered it, just as it often happens that one is for a time unable to remember a name and then finally does remember it. What keeps it from being true that A remembered the incident is not that he had previously forgotten it, but that he had just now *learned about it over again*. To say that A knows that *p because* he previously knew that *p* implies that A has *not* just now learned over again that *p*. This brings out, in part, the negative sense of the "because."

Another expression we can use here is "source," i.e., the *source* of A's present knowledge that *p* is his previous knowledge of it. This word carries a certain physical imagery. A river has a source and stretches continuously from its source to its mouth. The imagery of this word might play some part in producing von Leyden's inclination to postulate a "continuous connexion." But when the word "source" is used in the analysis of memory it must, like "because," be understood in a negative sense. To say "His previous knowledge is the source of his present knowledge" implies that he has not just now learned over again that *p*.

The meaning of "just now" is, however, pretty indefinite. If I was told something two hours ago would that be "just now"? Or would "just now" have to be ten minutes or ten seconds ago? I believe this is an artificial problem. I think that when we say "A remembers that *p*," we refer, more or less vaguely, to a more or less definite previous time when A knew that *p*. We are asserting that A remembers that *p from that time*. This will imply that A has not learned over again that *p* since that time. If this is correct we can get rid of the phrase "just now" in stating our analysis of factual memory. The statement "He remembers that *p*" will imply: "He knows that *p*, and at a previous time, *t*, he knew that *p*, and he has not learned over again that *p* since *t*." It would be up to the person who made the original statement to specify the time, *t*, to which he refers.

There is another objection to this analysis of factual memory. Let us imagine the following case: A man, B, learned that *p*. B then suffered an injury to a certain part of his brain, as a result of which he no longer knew that *p*. Later an operation was performed on his brain which had the effect that again he knew that *p*. At this later time it would be true that B knows that *p* and also that he knew that *p* at a previous time, *t*, and that he had not learned over again that *p* since *t*. (The operation on his brain, or the effect of it, cannot be called "*learning* over again" that *p*.) Our proposed definition of factual memory is satisfied: yet should we really wish to say that B remembers that *p*?

Whether we should say this or not may depend on what we suppose to be the efficacy of the brain surgery.[17] If we supposed that what was done to B's brain would cause him to know that *p*, *regardless of what his previous knowledge had been*[18] (i.e., he would know that *p* even if he had not ever previously known that *p*) then we should be disinclined to say that the operation had "restored his memory," and also disinclined to say, "Now he remembers that *p*." If, on the other hand, this operation could cause a person to know that *p only if* he had previously known that *p*, then we should be inclined to say those things.

It appears, therefore, that in this described case we should call B's present knowledge that *p memory*, only if we supposed that he would not now know that *p* had he not previously known that *p*. This fits in with the general feature of knowing something on the basis of memory, namely, that the present knowledge must be dependent on previous knowledge. As suggested before, when we claim that someone remembers a certain thing, we refer (more or less tacitly) to a previous time, t_1, when he knew the thing, and we are claiming that he remembers it *from* that time. Our claim implies that he has not learned the thing over again since t_1.[19] More generally, our claim implies that nothing whatever has occurred at some later time, t_2, such that his knowledge "dates" from t_2 instead of from t_1. This general requirement eliminates the possibility that, for example, a brain operation at t_2 should have been a sufficient condition of B's present knowledge.

The most concise and accurate formulation of this requirement which I have been able to think of is this: A person, B, remembers that *p* from *t*, only if it is the case that had B not known that *p* at *t*, he would not now know that *p*. The negative counter-factual conditional statement "If B had not known at *t* that *p*, he would not now know that *p*" does not express a *law*. It is similar in meaning to such a statement as the following: "If you had not given me a cigar I should not have one now." This would simply mean that, in fact, no other opportunity of my obtaining a cigar presented itself. Similarly, our negative counterfactual conditional about B's knowledge means that, as a matter of fact, if he had not obtained this knowledge at *t* he would not have it now. This is a kind of thing we often know to be true, just as we often know it to be true that this man would not have a cigar now if someone had not given him the one he has. Nothing is implied, in either case, about the existence of a causal chain or of a continuous process.

I have been trying to explain the meaning of the third element in our definition of factual memory, namely, the meaning of saying that someone now knows that *p because* he previously knew it. Our definition of factual memory can now be stated in full as follows: A person, B, remembers that *p* from a time, *t*, if and only if B knows that p, *and* B knew that p at t, and if B had not known at t that p he would not now know that p.

One point should be mentioned here. Something may *remind* one of some fact. You remember the latter *because* of something you saw or heard or thought. This meaning of "because" is different from the meaning it has in the definition of factual memory. Without going further into the matter, I will say that these two meanings of "because" are quite compatible. It can be true both that a man should now remember that p (which implies that he now knows that p *because* he previously knew it) and also that something made him remember that p (i.e., he remembered it *because* of something he perceived or thought). I think that this second "because" has a genuine *causal* meaning.

It must be admitted that one feels some mystification about my negative interpretation of the words "because" or "source" in our definition of factual memory. It seems mysterious that a man should know that p, having previously known it, unless there is something that comes *between* his previous and present knowledge and *ties them together*. It is probably this feeling that chiefly contributes to von Leyden's view of memory. We feel that there is a *gap* between the previous and the present knowledge, but at the same time we do not know how to fill in the gap. Should we say that what fills it is some persisting state of the brain or neural process? Whether or not it makes sense to postulate a specific brain-state or neural process persisting between the previous and the present knowledge that p, such a postulation is obviously not required by an analysis of the *concept* of remembering. Our everyday verifications of whether some person does or does not remember that p are not bound up with any questions about what is and has been going on in his brain. Our use of the language of memory carries no implications about inner physiology. Nor can we fill the gap with a continuous process of thinking about what is remembered. People could not think, continuously and simultaneously, of all the things they remember. If we resorted to *unconscious* thoughts in order to bridge the gap, we should then be in a difficulty about the *criterion* we should use for the existence of those unconscious thoughts. If we had no criterion our "solution" would, in a sense, be unintelligible. If we used the existence of the gap itself as our criterion for the existence of the unconscious thoughts that bridge the gap, then our solution would solve nothing.

This feeling of the mysteriousness of memory, unless we assume a persisting state or process between the previous and the present knowledge, provides one *metaphysical* aspect of the topic of memory. I believe this feeling explains why it is so commonly taken for granted, by philosophers, psychologists, and physiologists, that there is a "*process* of retention." It would be a valuable piece of philosophical work to explain why we have this feeling—what comparisons, what analogies, give rise to it. My own guess would be that our strong desire for a mechanism (either physical or mental) of memory arises from an abhorrence of the notion of action at a distance-in-time.

Leaving aside the question of why we have it, the idea of there being a gap between the previous and the present knowledge in memory is certainly a confusion. There is a gap only if there is something *missing*. But what is missing? We have no idea.

What *could* fill the gap? I have mentioned three candidates: a persisting physiological state or process; continuous thinking about what is remembered; continuous unconscious thinking about what is remembered. We see that for different reasons none of these candidates can be included in the truth conditions for statements of the form "A remembers that *p*." I believe we do not have the conception of anything else that might fill the gap. In a sense, therefore, we do not know what it means to speak of a *gap* here.

All of us (myself too) tend to have a piece of imagery, namely, of a *physical* gap. I can express that imagery with gestures. With a wave of the hand I can say, "Over *there* is the previous knowledge that *p*, and over *here* is the present knowledge that *p*: but what *connects* the two?" Yet if someone were to take seriously my pointing gestures and my expressions "Over there" and "Over here," I should be embarrassed. I have the imagery, together with the feeling that it illustrates something significant; but at the same time I cannot take it seriously. This is a frequent predicament in philosophy.

Two additional objections to our definition of factual memory must be considered. The first one is the following: Bodily sensations are among the objects of memory. A person can remember that he had an earache and that the pain was excruciating. But it is senseless, it may be said, to speak of someone's *knowing* that he is in pain.[20] Our definition cannot be satisfied, therefore, since it requires that a person who remembers that he had an earache should have previously known that he had one. The time at which he had this previous knowledge would have to be the very time at which he had the earache. For if it were at a later time, his knowledge at this later time would itself be memory and, by our definition, would require a previous knowledge. And so on. Our definition really requires that a person who remembers that he had a certain sensation (solely on the basis of having had it) must have shown that he was having it at the time he was having it. But since this latter is nonsense, it would follow that one could not remember a sensation. We can and do remember sensations, and so the definition is wrong.

My reply to this objection is to point out that *a* sense can be given to saying that a person knows that he has a sensation at the time he has it. He knows it in the sense that *he can tell you* that he has it. This is a significant thing to say, because a dog or a human baby *cannot* tell you that he has a painful ear, although it could be determined that he has one. In this sense, there are various sensations that lower animals and human infants have without knowing it, whereas human adults both have them and know it. As a human being learns language he acquires the capacity to know that he has those sensations. Therefore he can subsequently remember that he had them. Our definition of factual memory in terms of knowledge does not presuppose that knowledge is always the *same kind* of thing. Any legitimate sense of "know" yields a legitimate sense of "remember."[21]

The second and final objection to our definition, which I am going to consider, is the following: A person can remember that he had a dream and what it was. But a person cannot know that he is dreaming *while* he is dreaming. Remembering that one had a dream cannot be analyzed, therefore, into knowing that one had a dream because one previously knew it.

I believe this argument is sound. In my monograph on dreams I argue that the sentence "I am asleep" cannot be used to express a judgment about one's own condition, i.e., one cannot judge that oneself is asleep.[22] If this is correct then there cannot be such a thing as knowing that oneself is asleep, and from this it follows that one cannot know that one is dreaming. One can know that one *dreamt* but not that one is dreaming.

Is this knowledge that one dreamt *memory*, and if so, does our definition of factual memory fit it? There is no doubt that often the knowledge that one had a dream is memory, e.g., when one knows that one had a dream last week or last month. But if a person awakened suddenly from sleep and immediately declared that he had a dream, should we call this *remembering* that he had a dream? I am not sure: but if so then this use of "He remembers that *p*" does not fall under our analysis of factual memory. We cannot hold that here "He remembers that he dreamt" is equivalent to "He knows that he dreamt because he knew that he dreamt," since we should not know how to determine a previous time at which he knew that he dreamt. It would not be satisfactory to hold that "At some previous time he knew that he dreamt" means the same as "If he had been awakened at some previous time he would have said that he dreamt," since, in our example, the latter might be false.

The conclusion I draw is, not that our definition of factual memory is wrong, but that this special sense of remembering that one dreamt differs sharply from the central use of the factual memory locution.[23] Our definition gives a correct account of the central use, but perhaps not of absolutely every use of this locution.

Notes

1 For example, if a man "remembered to" water his horse it follows that he remembered that he should water his horse and also that he watered it. Remembering *to* do something appears to consist of remembering that one should do it plus doing it.

2 Both personal and perceptual memory imply factual memory.

3 It is worth noting that we do not speak of a person's grounds for *knowing* something, but of his grounds for believing it, being sure of it, asserting it, denying it, saying it, or doubting it. On the other hand, we ask *how* he knew it.

4 Of course we might expect him to have grounds or reasons *for* quitting his job—a different matter.

5 A friend of mine died after an illness of several weeks. Those who were with him reported to me that *he knew* he would die on the night he did die. Am I supposed to think that either they were wrong, or else that he had grounds for his conviction? "He felt his life ebbing away." What does this mean, except that he knew he was dying?

6 *The Problem of Knowledge* (London: Macmillan & Co., Ltd., 1956), p. 34.

7 *Ibid.*, p. 32.

8 This is true insofar as his present knowledge that *p* is solely *memory*. I am not dealing with the case in which it is partly memory and partly present evidence.

9 *Remembering* (London: Gerald Duckworth & Co., Ltd., 1961), p. 31.

10 *Ibid.*, p. 42.

11 *Ibid.*, p. 45.

12 E.g., *ibid.*, p. 40.

13 *Ibid.*, p. 55.

14 *Ibid.*, p. 46.
15 *Ibid.*, p. 53.
16 *Ibid.*, p. 43.
17 In my discussion of this point, I am indebted to John Rawls and David Sachs.
18 I do not assume that this is, or ever will be, a factual possibility. I am not entirely sure that it even makes sense. But it is not clear to me that it does not, and so my analysis of factual memory should take account of it.
19 It is worth remarking that if I have forgotten something temporarily, and then suddenly remember it, it cannot be said that I have *learned* the thing over again. This is because my present knowledge of it is "due" to my previous knowledge of it.
20 "It can't be said of me at all (except perhaps as a joke) that I *know* I am in pain" (Ludwig Wittgenstein, *Philosophical Investigations*, tr. G. E. M. Anscombe [New York: The Macmillan Company, 1953], sec. 246. See p. 110).
21 I do not believe there is any sense in which a dog or infant can be said to know that it has some sensation. I accept the consequence that a dog cannot be said to remember that he had a painful ear, and also the more interesting consequence that a human being cannot be said to remember that he had one, if he had it at a time before he knew enough language to be able to tell anyone that he had it. This point is connected with what Wittgenstein says about William James's Ballard (*Investigations*, sec. 342).
22 Norman Malcolm, *Dreaming*, second impression (New York: Humanities Press and London: Routledge & Kegan Paul, Ltd., 1962). See especially Chapters 3 and 9.
23 See *Dreaming*, pp. 56–59, for a discussion of the notion of remembering dreams.

QUESTIONS

1 What is Malcolm's definition of factual memory?
2 According to Malcolm, when S remembers that *p*, what grounds does S have for believing that *p*?
3 According to Malcolm, when S remembers that *p*, how certain is it that *p*?
4 According to Malcolm, is memory a source of knowledge? (If no, what is it?)

John Pollock and Joseph Cruz, "Reasoning and Memory"

On the foundationalist's proposal, epistemic ascent proceeds by reasoning, which leads to the formation of new beliefs on the basis of previously held beliefs. But now a surprising new issue arises. Just what are the beliefs from which we can form new beliefs on the basis of argument?

Occurrent thoughts

We have thus far implicitly adopted a kind of "mental blackboard" picture of reasoning according to which (1) we have an array of interconnected beliefs all available for simultaneous inspection and evaluation and (2) arguments are built out of these beliefs and are evaluated by such inspection. That is the picture normally adopted, but it is unrealistic. To see this, let us begin by distinguishing between thoughts and beliefs. At any given time, we are not thinking about most of the things we believe at that time. We all believe that 2+2 = 4, but this is not something that is likely to have "occurred to" the reader in the past five minutes. It is not something that she has actually *thought*. Thoughts, on the other hand, are what we are occurrently thinking. At any given time we are apt to have many beliefs but few thoughts. It is difficult to hold very many thoughts in mind at one time. In particular, we rarely hold an entire argument (even a simple one) in mind at one time. Psychological evidence indicates that people can hold about seven items in mind at one time. There is some evidence that the number may be even smaller for complex items like complicated propositions.[1]

The term "thought" is normally used to refer to either occurrent beliefs or to a more general class of mental events that includes our entertaining ideas without mentally endorsing them. In the latter sense thoughts may include hypotheses, fears, musings, daydreams, and so on. However, we will restrict our use of the term to occurrent beliefs. So thoughts are beliefs, but most beliefs are not thoughts. Given this distinction, which are involved in arguments and in the determination of justification—beliefs in general or just thoughts? Reasoning is an occurrent process, so it might seem that insofar as justification emerges from reasoning it can only be thoughts that enter into considerations of justification. The trouble with this is that we have too few occurrent thoughts at any one time

John L. Pollock and Joseph Cruz, *Contemporary Theories of Knowledge* (Lanham, Md.: Rowman & Littlefield, 1999).

to be able to construct arguments out of them. Although reasoning is an occurrent process, that does not mean that we occurrently hold an entire argument in mind. Rather, we progress through the argument one step at a time, occurrently holding each step in mind as we come to it but not holding the entire argument in mind. Memory plays an indispensable role in such reasoning, in at least two ways. On the one hand, we employ memory to supply us with premises for arguments. These premises will typically be the conclusions of earlier arguments, but we do not have to rehearse those arguments in order to make new use of their conclusions. We also keep track of the course of an argument by relying upon memory to ensure that the first part (which we are no longer holding in mind) went all right and to alert us when there is a step in the argument for which we subsequently acquire a defeater.

Memory as a source of knowledge

How do these observations about the role of memory in reasoning fit into the foundationalist picture of epistemic justification? The foundationalist must say different things about the different roles played by memory in reasoning. Let us begin with what might be called "premise memory." Most of the information at our disposal at any given time is stored in memory and recalled when we need it. What are we to say about the justifiedness of beliefs held on the basis of memory? Reasoning is an occurrent process. It can proceed only in terms of what we occurrently hold in mind. We do not have to hold the entire argument in mind in order for it to justify its conclusion, but we do have to hold each step in mind as we go through it. Thus memory can only contribute premises to an argument insofar as we occurrently remember those premises. Furthermore, we can have varying degrees of difficulty in recalling beliefs that are stored in memory. If we remember something (hold it in memory) but are unable to occurrently recall it just now, then it can play no role in justifying new beliefs. In other words, only occurrent memory can supply premises for arguments.

Granted that only occurrent memory can supply premises, what are we to say about the justification of those premises and the justification of conclusions inferred from those premises? A common view has been that when we hold a belief on the basis of remembering it, what determines whether the latter belief is justified is the argument we instantiated when we first acquired it.[2] On this picture we have an evolving network of arguments that grows longer and more complex over time. Old arguments are extended as we continue to reason from their conclusions, and new arguments are added as we acquire new basic beliefs and reason from them, but the old arguments do not drop out of the picture just because we are no longer thinking about them. They continue to represent the justificatory structure underlying our beliefs.

Critics of foundationalism commonly associate this picture with foundationalism,[3] but foundationalists need not adopt such a picture and they would be well advised not to. The difficulty with the picture is that it overlooks some important facts about memory. It has already been noted that we can have varying degrees of difficulty recalling things, and our memory is not infallible. Sometimes we "remember" incorrectly. When that happens, what are we to say about the justifiedness of beliefs inferred from the incorrect memories? We do not automatically regard a person as unjustified in holding a belief just because that belief is inferred from false memories. If he has no reason to suspect that his memory is faulty, we regard his behavior as epistemically beyond reproach. This is true even if he is misremembering. For example, consider a person who has all of his memories altered artificially without his knowing it. Is he then unjustified in everything he believes? Surely not. Recall that when we talk about justification we have in mind the reason-guiding sense of justification. If a person has no reason to be suspicious of his apparent memories, then he is doing the best he can if he simply accepts them. Consequently, he is justified. But if he is misremembering, the belief in question is not one that he previously held or for which he previously had reasons. This seems to indicate that it is the process of remembering itself that confers justification on the use of a memory in a present argument, and not whatever reasons one may or may not have had for that belief originally.

The only way the foundationalist can allow that the process of remembering can confer justification on a belief is by supposing that memory provides us with epistemologically basic beliefs. It is important to realize that *what* is remembered can be a proposition of any sort at all. Sometimes there is a temptation to suppose that we can only remember facts about the past, but memory is just the process of retrieving stored information, and that information can be of any sort. For example, I can remember that 4+7 = 11. This is a timeless truth. I can remember general truths, e.g., that birds fly. And I can even remember facts about the future, such as that there will not be another solar eclipse visible in North America until 2032. By definition, epistemologically basic beliefs comprise a privileged subclass of the set of all possible beliefs, so it cannot be true that the proposition remembered is always epistemologically basic. Rather, memory must operate on analogy with sense perception. Sense perception provides us with beliefs about material objects, but according to foundationalism it does so only indirectly by providing us with beliefs about appearances from which we can infer beliefs about material objects. Similarly, if we are to accommodate memory within foundationalism, memory must provide us with beliefs about what we "seem to remember" and then we infer the truth of what are ordinarily regarded as memory beliefs from these apparent memories. The viability of such an account turns in part on whether there is such a psychological state of "seeming to remember" that is analogous to being appeared to in some way or other. Some philosophers have denied that there is any such state,[4] but it is not too hard to see that they are wrong. It is possible to hold the same belief on the basis of memory, or perception, or for no reason at all, and when we hold the belief we can tell introspectively which is the case. In other words, we can discriminate between memory beliefs and other beliefs.[5] But to say this is just to say that memory has an introspectively distinguishable mental characteristic. The mental state so characterized is the state of "seeming to remember." This can be made clearer by considering an example. Imagine that you are trying to quote the first line of a poem. It is on the tip of your tongue, but you cannot quite get it. Finally, a friend tires of watching you squirm and tells you the line. This can have two possible effects. It may jog your memory so that the line comes flooding back and you now remember it clearly. Alternatively, it may fail to jog your memory. You believe your friend when he tells you how the lines goes, but you still do not remember it. In either case you come to have the same occurrent belief about the line, but there is a clear introspectible difference between the two cases. The difference is precisely that in the first case you come to be in the state of seeming to remember that the line goes that way, whereas in the second case you have no such recollection. Cases like this show that there is such a psychological state as that of seeming to remember.

Given that there is such a state as seeming to remember, the natural move for the foundationalist is to treat memory as a source of knowledge parallel to sense perception and posit the following "mnemonic" defeasible reason:

"*S* seems to remember *P*" is a defeasible reason for *S* to believe *P*.

This becomes the foundationalist's explanation for how memory can supply premises for arguments that confer justification on new beliefs. Furthermore, it seems to be the only possible way to integrate premise memory into a foundationalist theory.

Genetic arguments and dynamic arguments

What about the other aspects of memory as it is used in reasoning? We were led to the topic of memory by the observation that the mental blackboard picture of reasoning is wrong. We do not hold an entire argument in mind at one time. Rather, we step through it sequentially, holding no more than a few lines at a time in occurrent thought. Insofar as we have to know that the earlier parts of the argument were all right, we must rely upon memory. It is tempting to try to assimilate this use of memory to premise memory in the following way. Suppose we reason through the complicated argument in Figure 1 and on that basis come to believe P_n.

As we occurrently step through the *i*th line of the argument we may occurrently recall nothing earlier than the *i*-1st line. At that point, only memory can certify that the earlier parts of the argument were all right. This suggests that the basis upon which we actually come to believe P_i is not argument (1) at all, but rather a much shorter argument whose first premise is supplied by memory; see argument (2), Figure 2. Having inferred P_{i-1}, in order to proceed to P_i all we have to do is remember P_{i-1}. Premise memory certifies P_{i-1}, and then we infer P_i from P_{i-1}. This is what justifies us in coming to believe P_i.

But this is puzzling. It seems to indicate that argument (1) is not doing any work. It is not on the basis of that argument that we become justified in holding the individual beliefs comprising it. That argument represents the historical genesis of the beliefs, but in an important sense it does not represent the dynamics of their justification. The latter is represented by lots of little arguments of the form of argument (2). An apparent problem for this view is that we do not regard argument (1) as irrelevant to our justification. If we discover inadequacies in early stages of argument (1) (e.g., if we acquire a defeater for a defeasible reason used early in argument (1)), we take that to make us unjustified in holding the later beliefs in the argument. How can it do that if we do not hold those beliefs on the basis of argument (1)?

Argument (1) and argument (2) are both important in understanding the justification of P_i. We will distinguish between them by calling them the *genetic*

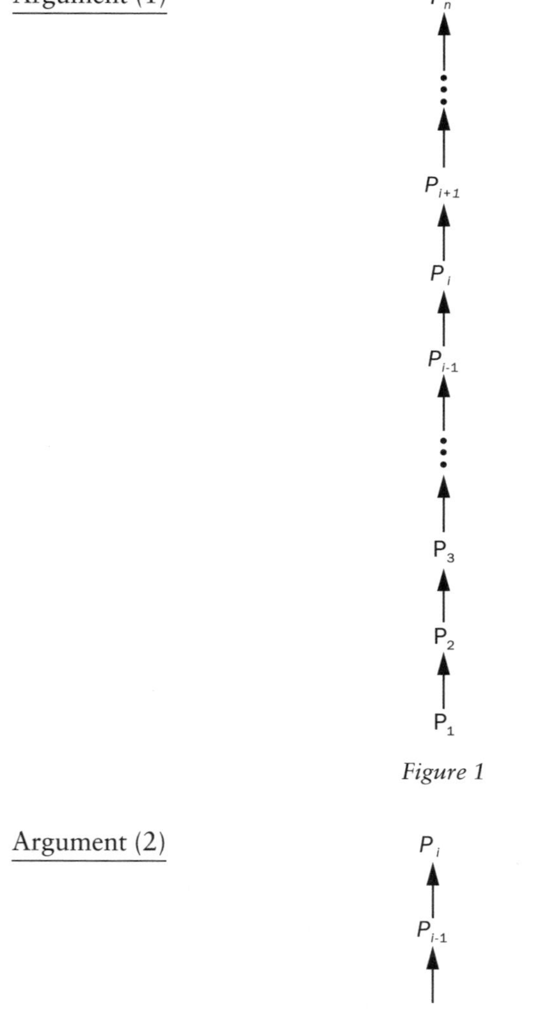

Figure 1

Figure 2

argument and the *dynamic argument*, respectively. Note that as we are using the term, dynamic arguments do not always begin with apparent memories. They might begin instead, for instance, with an appearance belief and infer a physical-object belief. The important thing about dynamic arguments is that they represent what we are currently thinking. To use a computer metaphor, the dynamic argument is short and fits into "working memory". We can regard the mental blackboard picture as true of dynamic arguments.

The genetic argument and the dynamic argument are both relevant to justification, but in different ways. The dynamic argument is "positively relevant" in that it tells us what makes us currently justified in believing P_i. The genetic argument is not positively relevant in the same way. If we are no longer able to recall the earlier steps of the genetic argument, it can play no positive role in the justification of our occurrent belief in P_i. On the other hand, the genetic argument is "negatively relevant" to the justification for our occurrently believing P_i because if (a) we know that the genetic argument underlies our having come to believe P_i and (b) we acquire a defeater for some step of the genetic argument, we regard that as defeating our justification for P_i.

How can we put these observations together into a coherent account of the relationship between reasoning and justification? Earlier it was suggested that justification can be identified with holding a belief on the basis of an undefeated argument. But justification *cannot* be identified with holding a belief on the basis of an undefeated genetic argument. The genetic argument for a belief may stretch back over a period of years as you slowly accumulate the diverse premises. If you can no longer recall the arguments for some of those premises (which is quite likely), then if you presently acquire a defeater for one of those early steps in the argument but do not realize that it is a defeater or do not in any way appreciate its relevance to P_i we would not regard the acquisition of that defeater as making it unreasonable for you to believe P_i. (Intuitively, this is because you currently believe P_i on the basis of the dynamic argument rather than the genetic argument.) Consequently, it is not a necessary condition for justified belief in P_i that your genetic argument for P_i be undefeated.

Can we instead identify justification with holding a belief on the basis of an undefeated dynamic argument? We can once we recognize that genetic arguments play a role in determining whether a dynamic argument based on memory is undefeated. Such a dynamic argument proceeds in terms of the following mnemonic defeasible reason:

> "I seem to remember *P*" is a defeasible reason for me to believe *P*.

It is obvious upon reflection that one kind of defeater for this defeasible reason is any reason for thinking that I do not actually remember *P*. A necessary condition for remembering *P* is that one originally knew *P*. If, for instance, my original belief in *P* was unjustified, but was retained in memory, then even though I now *seem* to remember *P*, it would be incorrect to describe me now as remembering *P*. Thus, any reason for thinking that I did not originally know *P* is also a reason for thinking that I do not remember *P* now. I did not originally know *P* if there is a true undefeated defeater for some step of the reasoning (i.e., the genetic argument) underlying my belief in *P*. Thus the following is a defeater for the mnemonic defeasible reason:

> *Q* is true, and *Q* is a defeater for some step of my genetic argument for *P*.[6]

We will call this "the genetic defeater." The concepts of a defeater and a genetic argument seem like technical philosophical concepts not shared by the person on the street. On this ground, it might be doubted that ordinary people actually have beliefs of the form of the genetic defeater. But our contention is that they do. They could not formulate them using this technical terminology, but they could formulate them less clearly by saying things like, "In coming to believe *P* in the first place I assumed *A* and concluded *B*, but because *Q* is true, I should not have done that." There does not seem to be anything psychologically unrealistic about supposing that people often have thoughts they could formulate in such a way as this, and these are the thoughts expressed more precisely by the above formulation of the genetic defeater.

Our proposal is that, on a foundationalist picture, justification should be identified with holding a belief on the basis of an undefeated dynamic argument. What we mean by this is that the arguments to which we appeal in determining whether a dynamic argument is undefeated must all be in working memory at the same time as the dynamic argument. This makes the requirement of being undefeated a rather minimal one, because we cannot get much into working memory at one time. From one point of view, formulating the requirement in this way seems obviously correct—if we do not occurrently remember an argument for a defeater, we *cannot* take it into account in deciding what to believe, and so we should be deemed epistemically beyond reproach if we ignore it. On the other hand, this makes the requirement that the dynamic argument be undefeated seem so weak as to be virtually useless. It seems we will almost never have any defeating arguments in working memory at the same time as the argument to be defeated, and so a dynamic argument will almost always be undefeated in this sense. We contend, however, that this objection is wrong. As a matter of psychological fact, when we acquire a new belief that constitutes a defeater for the genetic argument, we often remember that it does, and thus we add the dynamic argument in Figure 3 to working memory.

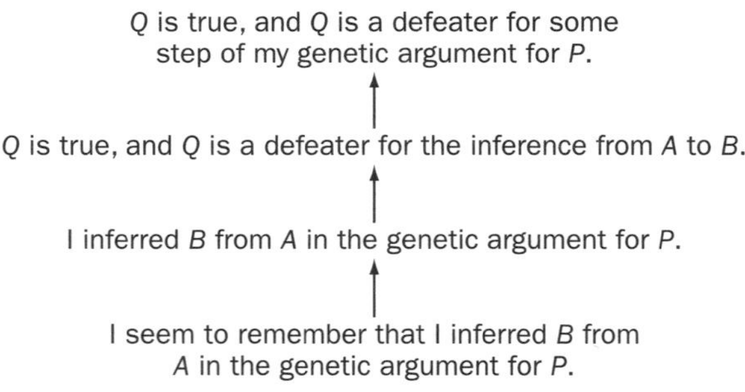

Figure 3

Thus working memory comes to contain both argument (2) and argument (3), and the latter is a defeating argument for the former. Hence argument (2) is not undefeated.

Primed search

According to this account, if we have a defeater for the inference from *A* to *B* but we do not remember inferring *B* from *A* in the genetic argument for *P*, then our present belief in *P* is justified. That seems to be correct. The reason this does not trivialize the requirement that the dynamic argument be undefeated is that we frequently have the requisite memories. Memory allows us to monitor the course of our arguments and alerts us when we subsequently encounter a defeater for an earlier stage of an argument. This is how memory supplies us with genetic defeaters. This aspect of memory is intriguing, partly because it does not fit into naive models of memory that would attempt to reduce all memory to premise memory. In this connection, it might be tempting to suppose that we acquire genetic defeaters by occurrently recalling the earlier parts of the genetic argument and inspecting them to see whether each newly drawn conclusion constitutes a defeater for any of the earlier steps. This would reduce the monitoring function of memory to premise memory. But obviously, we do not really do it that way. To suppose we must is to adopt a simplistic view of memory. This is best illustrated by considering memory searches. When we search our memory for something, we do not have to proceed sequentially through all the beliefs held in memory, calling each to consciousness, inspecting it to see if it is what we are looking for, and if it is not, then rejecting it and going on to the next item. For example, in trying to remember someone's name, despite the fact that this is something that we can voluntarily undertake to do, the process whereby we do it is not a conscious process. We set ourselves to do it, and then we wait a moment and see whether anything emerges into occurrent thought. If we are able to remember the name, the only thing that occurs at a conscious level is the recollection of the name. If we are unable to remember the name, we may feel frustrated and we may continue to "try" to remember it, but nothing happens at the conscious level. The point is that, to use computer jargon, human recollection involves built-in search procedures. If asked to name a famous composer, my memory can find one. It does it by searching my unconscious memory for someone remembered as a famous composer, and because it is searching unconscious memory, this search is not something I do consciously.

Human recollection also involves a somewhat more complicated operation that we might call "primed search." Consider a birdwatcher who has a mental list of rare birds he would like to observe. This need not be a fixed list. Each month he may add new birds to the list when he reads about them in his birdwatcher's magazine, and he strikes items off the list when he observes them. Furthermore, the way in which the list evolves need not consist of his recalling the entire list to mind and then altering it. He can alter such a mental list by adding or deleting items without ever thinking about the list as a whole. Given such a list, when our birdwatcher sees a bird on the list, he immediately recalls that it is one of the listed birds and he may get very excited. The point is that one can prime oneself to be on the lookout for things on such a nonoccurrent mental list. This is an unconscious mental function that humans are capable of performing, and it involves memory in accessing the list itself, but the memory processes involved cannot be reduced to any kind of simple memory of individual facts.

Primed search is what is involved in monitoring our reasoning and being on the lookout for newly inferred defeaters for previous steps of reasoning. We remember what those earlier steps were, although we do not do so occurrently, and we remain on the lookout for defeaters for those earlier steps, and when we encounter such a defeater we then occurrently remember the earlier step and note that we have a defeater. The only conscious output of this primed search consists of occurrently remembering that a certain step occurred in the argument, and we combine that with the observation that a particular newly acquired belief is a defeater for that step. This is how we acquire a genetic defeater for a dynamic argument.

To recapitulate, reflections on the role of memory in reasoning have led us to a radically different picture of the relationship between reasoning and epistemic justification. We have been led to distinguish between the genetic argument for a belief and the dynamic argument, concluding that it is only the latter that is directly relevant to the assessment of the belief as justified or unjustified. The genetic argument is indirectly relevant because genetic defeaters for the dynamic argument appeal to the genetic argument and are supplied by some of the more sophisticated operations of memory. Without these innovations, foundationalism would be much less plausible.

Notes

1 The classic article on the limits of memory is George Miller, "The Magical Number Seven, Plus or Minus Two: Some Limits on our Capacity for Processing Information" (*Psychological Review* 63, 1956: 81–97). Also see W. Kintsch and J.M. Keenan, "Reading Rate and Retention as a Function of the Number of the Propositions in the Base Structure of Sentences" (*Cognitive Psychology* 5, 1973: 257–74), and W. Kintsch, *The Representation of Meaning in Memory* (Hillsdale, N.J.: Lawrence Erlbaum Associates, 1974). For a thorough overview, see the chapters on memory in John Anderson, *Cognitive Psychology and Its Implications* (New York: W.H. Freeman, 1995).

2 See Norman Malcolm [this volume, pp. 95–6], and Robert Squires, "Memory Unchained" (*The Philosophical Review* 77, 1969: 178–97). Of course, we can also come to instantiate new arguments for old beliefs, in which case the source of justification may change, but the view is that that is not what is involved in memory.

3 See Gilbert Harman, "Positive versus Negative Undermining in Belief Revision" (*Nous* 18, 1984: 39–49)

4 Norman Malcolm [this volume, pp. 95–6], and Robert Squires, "Memory Unchained".

5 By "memory beliefs" we mean "putative memory beliefs." We do not mean that we can tell introspectively whether we are correctly remembering what we take ourselves to be remembering.

6 There are other kinds of defeaters as well. The kind of defeater operative in cases where we discover that we are misremembering is "I did not originally believe *P*."

QUESTIONS

1 According to Pollock and Cruz, in what way is the "mental blackboard" picture of reasoning mistaken?

2 According to Pollock and Cruz, when S remembers that *p*, what sort of justification does S have for believing that *p*?

3 What is a "dynamic argument"?

Michael Huemer, "The Problem of Memory Knowledge"

The sun is about 93 million miles away from the earth. How do I know that? Well, I learned it once. I don't know when or how I learned it, but I did, and I now remember it. I couldn't tell you how the distance to the sun was calculated either, but it's something that scientists have discovered. How do I know that scientists have discovered it? Well, I don't know how I learned that either, but I remember it, too.

Even granting the reliability of scientists and other experts, this does not sound like a very impressive justification. Yet arguably, *most* of our knowledge is like that. A few more examples: there is a 3-hour time difference between Los Angeles and New York; Abraham Lincoln was President of the United States during the Civil War; the word "tree" refers in English to a certain kind of plant; the square on the hypotenuse of a right triangle equals the sum of the squares on the other two sides; wood is a poor conductor of heat and electricity; China is in Asia. I don't know how I learned any of those facts, but however I learned them, I kept them in memory since then (doubtless I gained numerous confirmations of them since the first time I learned them, and I can't specifically remember any of those occasions either), and I have no serious doubt about any one of them.

What justifies me in believing that the sun is 93 million miles from the earth? The fact that I don't remember my original reason for adopting that belief suggests that whatever that reason was, it can not be considered a reason I *now* have for my belief.[1]

In general, when S remembers that P, what kind of justification does S have for believing P? Three possible answers to this question naturally come to mind:

1. The inferential theory

First, perhaps my justification is inferential. And perhaps it is something like this: I now seem to remember that the earth is 93 million miles away from the sun. In the past, I have generally found that expectations formed on the basis of my seeming memories have been borne out. For example, I seemed to remember my address, and when I went to that address, I found an apartment of just the sort I

Michael Huemer, "The Problem of Memory Knowledge," *Pacific Philosophical Quarterly* 80 (1999), 346–57.

was expecting. This strongly confirms that my seeming memories are highly reliable. Therefore (probably), it is true that the sun is 93 million miles away from the earth.

The most obvious problem here is one of circularity. How do I know that in the past, my seeming memories have been corroborated? Well, I seem to remember that that's generally been the case. But, on the present theory of memory knowledge,[2] I cannot trust that until I *first* prove the reliability of my memory. Therefore, I cannot use my past experiences in this way—nor, in fact, in any other way—in my argument for the reliability of memory.

Thus, if any inferential account is to work, the premises of my argument must rely solely on my present experiences and/or a priori insights. I can't use any previously-gained knowledge. It seems unlikely that I could derive the reliability of memory from premises of this kind; at any rate, I have no idea how such an inference would go. Additionally, an inferential theory would face two further constraints that increase its difficulties. First, the argument would have to be short and simple, such that one could hold it all in mind at once. Otherwise, completion of the argument would depend on one's *remembering* that the earlier stages of the argument had been correctly executed, and this would illicitly presuppose the reliability of memory.

Second, I would have to be in some sense using the argument *every time* I had a justified memory belief. It would not be enough for me to go through the argument once, and thenceforth merely remember that I had demonstrated the reliability of memory. For if merely remembering that my memory is reliable were enough for me to be justified in believing my memory is reliable, then merely remembering that the sun is 93 million miles away from the earth should be sufficient for me to be justified in believing that the sun in 93 million miles away from the earth—contrary to the present theory, but in accord with the theory to be considered in section 2.

Given that my belief that the sun is 93 million miles from the earth is continuously present (it remains as a dispositional belief even when I'm not thinking about it), I will apparently need to be employing the argument for the reliability of memory continuously, if I am to keep my justification. The defender of the inferential account may claim that I am using this argument (whatever it is) for the reliability of memory only unconsciously, but it remains implausible that I am using it all the time, even unconsciously. Indeed, there is no evidence that I have ever employed any such argument at all, so skepticism seems to be the price of the inferential account.

2. The foundational theory

Perhaps, then, my justification is non-inferential. Perhaps memory experiences create the same sort of foundational justification that (some epistemologists argue) sensory experiences do. Just having an experience of seeming to perceive that P makes one prima facie justified in believing that P, and similarly, having an experience of seeming to remember that P makes one prima facie justified in believing that P.[3]

This view has counter-intuitive results. Suppose I initially learn that P by means of an a priori proof of it (the proof is short, so I can hold it all in mind at once and do not need to use memory). So I have an adequate justification for believing P from the start, although the possibility of mistakes, even in short proofs, makes my justification less than completely conclusive. However, a few moments pass, and I now am able, in addition, to *recall* that P. If I entertain the proof while also remembering that P, I will now have *two* justifications for P, one inferential and one foundational. Thus, my warrant becomes more secure with the passage of time.[4]

Here's another case. Suppose that I initially adopt the unjustified belief that P (perhaps by wishful thinking or some such irrational process). The next day, however, my belief is adequately justified, because I now seem to remember that P. The passage of time has transformed my irrational belief into a rational one.

It might be argued that in this latter case, I have a defeater for P, since I can recall that I adopted P by wishful thinking.[5] Therefore, modify the case as follows: a number of years pass, and I no longer recall how I initially "learned" that P, but I still clearly "remember" that P.[6] For example, suppose that I initially accepted the existence of life after death by wishful thinking. I now no longer remember where I got that belief, but I just seem to remember that that's something I know. On the other hand, my brother Pete adopted the same belief in exactly the same way. However, his memory is better than mine, so he also remembers how he got the belief. As a result, my belief system is rational and his is not. That seems wrong.

To further confirm that this result is wrong, Thomas Senor (1993) asks us to consider an analogy to moral philosophy. Suppose there is a certain ruthless tyrant, call him "Saddam," who decides to viciously attack a neighboring country. Suppose that at the time he makes this choice, Saddam's character is such that it would be psychologically impossible for him to behave in any other way. Suppose, however, that Saddam, having begun as a normal boy, *acquired* this deplorable character as a result of a series of evil choices that he made of his own free will. In this case, we would surely not excuse Saddam's present actions on the ground that he could not do otherwise. Rather, Saddam's culpability in his past choices follows him to the present day, rendering him culpable for the present evil actions that flow from them. Similarly, argues Senor, a person's previous *epistemic* irresponsibility follows him, making him epistemically blameworthy for any present likely-to-be-false beliefs that result from his previous irrationality. A present-day belief cannot be rendered epistemically justified by the fact that, doing the best one can do *now* results in acceptance of the belief, if this situation results from previous epistemic irrationality—just as a present-day action can not be rendered morally blameless by the fact that, doing the best one can do *now* results in performance of the action, if this situation results from previous immorality.[7]

Both of the above cases—the case where memory would increase one's justification for a belief, and the case where memory would convert an unjustified belief into a justified one—point up the following general, intuitive constraint on a theory of memory justification: the justification for a belief cannot be increased by its passing into memory; it can only be lowered. The foundational theory fails to account for this.[8]

3. The preservation theory

Here is a third view. When I remember that P, my justification for believing P is whatever it was to begin with. Memory just preserves the justification (or lack of it) of my beliefs.[9] So my justification for thinking that the sun is about 93 million miles away is, perhaps, that Mrs. Kim in second grade told me that it was—even if I don't know that that is my justification. On this view, the fact that I don't remember what my original justification for P was does not prevent me from still having that justification for P. This seems more natural than the preceding two theories.

But now recall Russell's five-minute hypothesis.[10] Suppose God created someone five minutes ago in exactly the state that I was in five minutes ago, surrounded by exactly the same kinds of things. Call this person Mike2. Mike2 was created complete with false memories of his past life, identical to my memories of my past life. He thinks his name is "Mike" and is presently writing a paper about the problem of memory knowledge. His situation would be (to him) indistinguishable from my actual situation. Usually, this scenario is mentioned for the purpose of asking, How do I know I'm not actually in that situation? But here I mention it to make a positive point. What sort of things would it be *rational* for Mike2 to believe? Pretty clearly, just the same things that it is rational for me, now, to believe (modulo appropriate changes in indexical references). Most of Mike2's beliefs about his own past are *false*, but he has no way of knowing that, and no more reason for suspecting it than I have for suspecting that my beliefs about my past are false. So if I am justified in believing that I ate a bagel this morning, Mike2 is justified (though mistaken) in believing that *he* ate a bagel this morning. Furthermore, it seems that he has the same degree and kind of justification that I now have.

But of course, this contradicts the present theory of memory knowledge. According to the present view, memory merely preserves one's initial justification, if any, for a belief.[11] So I am adequately justified in believing that I ate a bagel this morning, on the basis of the sensory experiences I had then. Mike2 has no such justification, since he never had any sensory experience of eating a bagel. At minimum, he does not have the same sort of justification that I have, and it appears that he has no justification at all, since, on the preservation theory, memory experiences are not themselves a *source* of justification.[12] On this theory, then, Mike2 is highly irrational (unlike myself), even though he is intrinsically identical to me.[13]

Thus, there is an interesting problem of memory knowledge. The three most obvious theories of the justification of memory beliefs are all unacceptable. How can we find a theory that is not subject to any of the preceding objections? Our verdict on the case of Mike2 seems to demand that the justification of memory beliefs depend only on the current state of the believer, and not on his past; otherwise, Mike2 would be found to be drastically less rational than myself. But if the past history of a memory belief is thus irrelevant to its justification, won't this allow us to construct cases where memory transforms an irrational belief into a rational one (as in our objection to the foundational theory)? How, that is, can we reconcile the principle that the degree of justification of a remembered belief can never exceed the original degree of justification one had for its adoption, with the apparent lesson of the five-minute hypothesis, that the past history of a belief is irrelevant to its present justification? It seems that our intuitions are simply contradictory.

4. A solution: the dualistic theory

Not so. There is a theory that accommodates our intuitions about all of the cases, incorporating elements of both the foundational view and the preservation view. I call it the "dualistic theory" because it holds that the question, "What is my justification for believing that P?" requires a two-part answer: first, why I was justified in *adopting* the belief that P; and second, why I was justified in *retaining* it.[14] On this view, a belief is justified full stop if and only if one had an adequate justification for adopting it at some point, and thenceforward one was justified in retaining it. The normal functioning of memory, in the absence of specific reasons for revising a belief, constitutes an epistemically acceptable manner of retaining beliefs.

So far, this sounds exactly like the preservation theory. However, we will see in a moment how, having distinguished two parts of a belief's justification, the dualistic theory is in a position to make an appropriate concession to the foundationalist account that avoids the major objection to the preservation theory.

It is already clear that the present view avoids the foundationalist's main problem. The dualistic view does not allow an initially irrational belief to become rational merely by passing into memory, since a rational belief, in the full sense, requires *both* rational acquisition and rational retention.

How, then, can the dualistic theory avoid the objection from the five-minute hypothesis—how can it secure Mike2's epistemic rationality? Simply by this posit: coming to believe something by seeming to remember it (in the absence of defeaters that one is aware of) is an epistemically rational way of acquiring the belief. This posit captures the foundationalist intuition, that I am rational in believing something I seem to remember even if on this particular occasion, unbeknownst to me, my memory is deceiving me – even if, that is to say, I never really had that belief before. From the standpoint of epistemic responsibility, this is surely correct. The unfortunate Mike2 has not committed any epistemic wrongs; he has done the best that could be expected of him. Our theory credits him this: since Mike2 acquired his belief that he ate a bagel this morning by seeming to remember it, he is rational in accepting it.[15]

But this posit does not introduce the possibility of memory's converting an irrational belief into a rational one. For the principle only applies to a case in which having a seeming memory that P was actually one's way of acquiring the belief that P. Recall the case where I believe P by wishful thinking and later seem to remember that P. Having a seeming memory in this case is not my method of acquiring the belief; wishful thinking is. Apparent memory is only my way of *retaining* the belief. Since a justified belief must have both a rational acquisition method and a rational retention method, this belief is unjustified.

It must be admitted that this view can not maintain the supervenience of epistemic justification on the current, intrinsic state of the believer. That seemingly desirable characteristic is genuinely inconsistent with the conjunction of two other principles we have been assuming: first, that memory can not convert unjustified belief to justified belief; and second, that in typical circumstances our remembered beliefs are justified. For it is possible to have two people who are in the same state presently, each having forgotten his original reason for adopting P, one of whom did and the other of whom did not originally have a good reason for accepting P. The one person must be counted justified in his present belief (else we have memory skepticism), and the other must be counted unjustified (else we have an unjustified belief converted to a justified belief by the passage of time). It follows that the justificatory status of the belief that P does not supervene on the current, intrinsic state of the believer. Of course, it may still supervene on the total history of intrinsic states of the believer.

To illustrate, return to the case of myself and Mike2. Let's suppose that, among many beliefs I have for which I do not remember my original reasons for adopting them, there are some rational beliefs and a few irrational ones. I am justified in believing P, say, but unjustified in believing Q. Mike2, likewise, will be justified in believing P. But unlike me, on the present theory, Mike2 will *also* be justified in believing Q, since he, unlike me, acquired the belief through apparent memory. So there is one way in which the victim of the five-minute hypothesis would be epistemically better off than we actually are—he has no fewer, and possibly more, justified beliefs.

On reflection, we can see that this result is correct and that the principle of current time-slice supervenience is therefore mistaken. For Mike2, there is no relevant difference between his belief that Q and his belief that P. Both are adopted in the same way, so if we grant that his belief that P is justified, we have to allow his belief that Q to be justified similarly. Recall Senor's analogy with moral philosophy. Suppose that a person (call him "Saddam2") were created and placed at the head of a country, with a compulsion to invade a neighboring country. Saddam2 is born lacking free will, his decision to invade already predetermined. In that case, Saddam2 could not be morally blamed for his action. We have already said that Saddam, who acquired a similar psychological compulsion through earlier bad choices, *can* be blamed for the same action. So the moral culpability of a decision does not supervene on the internal state of the agent at the time of decision-making; it depends, too, on the agent's past choices. Likewise, we should not be surprised that the epistemic status of a belief depends in part on the believer's past thought processes.

5. The theory extended: degrees of justification

So far, I have stated the dualistic theory as a theory of when a memory belief is *justified* or *unjustified*. But we can generalize the theory to give an account of the *degree* of justification that a belief has, and this generalization provides a further demonstration of the superiority of the dualistic view. The natural extension of the simple dualistic view would be to say that there are two degrees of justification involved in any belief—a degree of justification associated with the adoption of the belief, and a degree of justification associated with its retention—and that the overall level of justification of a belief is the product of those two quantities. The first of these two quantities is simply a matter of the conclusiveness of the grounds one originally had (again, this holds true even if one has forgotten those grounds). We can think of it as a number between 0 and 1, with 1 representing infallible justification for believing the proposition in question, and 0 representing infallible justification for disbelieving it. The second quantity is a matter of the credibility of one's memory, and it too, can be thought of as a number between 0 and 1. If one has a relatively faint memory, such that one is quite unsure whether one really remembers that P or not, then this number will be close to ½ (not 0, for even the faintest of memories would not be evidence *against* P). If one has a very firm and clear memory, the number will be close to 1. If one has special reason for doubting the reliability of one's memory (e.g., one knows that one has misremembered similar things in the past), this can lower the second number further.

One of our objections to the foundationalist account was based on the principle that the justification of a belief can be lowered through its passing into memory but cannot be raised. The foundationalist could not accommodate this fact, because for him, the past justification of a belief is irrelevant to its present justification. But the generalized dualistic view easily accommodates the principle—when one multiplies the original degree of justification by a number less than or equal to 1 representing the credibility of the memory, one necessarily gets something less than or equal to the original degree of justification.

The dualistic view also surpasses the straight preservation theory in the treatment of degrees of justification. Under the straight preservation view, the justification I *now* have for P when I remember that P is the same as the justification I had for P originally. Given this, the only natural view to take as to the *degree* of justification I now have for P is that it is identical to the degree of justification I originally had, on the principle that the degree of one's justification for P is a function of what one's justification for P is. For example, suppose my original justification for P consisted in a conclusive, deductive proof of P, although I have since forgotten what my justification was. On the preservation view, I nevertheless retain my original justification for P. Therefore, my belief that P continues to be supported by a conclusive proof (the memory can hardly preserve the argument but turn it into an inconclusive one). Therefore, my degree of justification for P is the degree appropriate to having a conclusive proof, that is, conclusive justification.

But this result is wrong—one should not be as confident that P ten years after learning it as one was when it was fresh in one's mind. One should not have 100% confidence in one's memory. The passage of time introduces new possibilities of error; therefore, it lowers one's justification for believing a proposition. Here, as elsewhere, the dualistic view succeeds in accommodating our intuitions about justification, escaping the objections that tell against the two main alternatives.[16]

The preservation theorist might try arguing that as time passes, one's justification for P typically decreases, not because one's justification acquires a new, fallible component, but because one acquires new defeaters. For instance, the proposition that my memory is unreliable, or even the proposition that this particular memory experience is faint, would be defeaters for P when I seem to recall that P. In order to explain why one's justification *typically* (perhaps always) decreases with time, rather than only decreasing in certain special circumstances, the preservation theorist would have to maintain that even so weak a proposition as "my memory is not infallible" or "this memory is not *absolutely* clear" can be a defeater.

There seems to be something ad hoc about introducing a defeater that is always or nearly always present and that functions to lower one's justification for P by just the amount that one's justification would fall short of its original level *if* one's having a memory experience were part of one's justification for P. But be that as it may, there is a more serious problem. Suppose that I initially learned that P through sensory observation, and I am now, ten years later, genuinely remembering that P. According to the preservation theory, my justification for believing P, now, consists in the same sensory experience. If this is the case, then why would a proposition about the reliability of my *memory* be a defeater for my belief? Certainly, at the time I was initially observing that P, "my memory is unreliable" would not have defeated my justification for believing P. "My memory is unreliable" is not a rebutting defeater for P (it is merely neutral with respect to the truth of P), and nor is "my memory is unreliable" an undercutting defeater for a *perceptual* justification of P—only something like "my senses are unreliable" would undercut a perceptual justification. Therefore, if my present justification for P consists in my (earlier) sensory experience, my justification should be unaffected by the discovery that my memory is unreliable.

An analogy here is instructive: suppose that I believe Q on the basis of Jones' testimony. Now suppose you come along and succeed in convincing me that *Smith* is an unreliable witness. Would this defeat my justification for believing Q? Of course not. You would have to show that *Jones* was unreliable in order to undermine my justification for Q; either that, or my justification for believing Q would have to depend at least in part on Smith's testimony (perhaps in addition to Jones'). According to the preservation theory, when I observe that P and later recall that P, my belief at the later time is based solely on the observation, not on the memory experience. Therefore, a criticism of my senses would undermine the belief, but a criticism of my memory should not. On the other hand, the dualistic view naturally explains the significance of a criticism of my memory as affecting the second factor involved in the justification of a memory belief—the factor neglected by the preservationist.

One of the two main theories of memory knowledge locates the justification of a memory belief solely in the memory impression. The other locates it solely in the original acquisition of the belief. As a result, one theory implies that memory can raise a belief's justification, while the other implies that memory cannot lower a belief's justification. The solution is to locate a belief's justification *both* in the circumstances of its initial acquisition *and* in the nature of the present memory experience.[17]

Notes

1 So argues Ginet (1975), pp. 153–6.

2 I am assuming that knowledge is a kind of justified belief, where justification is understood in terms of epistemic responsibility (see Alston's (1985) discussion of "deontological" notions of justification for more on this kind of justification). If this is not what knowledge is, then what I am looking for should be described as "a theory of the justification of memory beliefs" rather than "a theory of memory knowledge."

3 Pollock (1986), pp. 50–2 appears to defend this view. However, he has since

indicated that he is addressing a different sense of "justification" than mine (personal communication).

4 Pollock (1995), pp. 101–2 points out that it need not be the case that the conjunction of two reasons for believing P provides better justification for P than either reason alone provides. As an example, he considers a case in which S_1 and S_2 are each generally reliable witnesses, but you know that S_1 tends to corroborate S_2's testimony only when the latter is a fabrication (otherwise, S_1 keeps his mouth shut). However, nothing like this is going on in my example (it isn't as if you tend to remember that P only when your argument for P was fallacious), so it's hard to see why getting a second justification for P shouldn't increase your degree of justification for P. See also the analogy below, in note 5.

5 Pollock's (1986), p. 54 remarks imply such a response, although it is not clear that the response works. Consider a similar case: suppose I initially adopt P by wishful thinking, but later I perceive that P. At this point, my belief becomes justified. The fact that I initially adopted P through wishful thinking is merely irrelevant to the truth of P—it does not count against P in the event that I discover a new justification for P. Since Pollock assimilates the epistemology of memory to that of perception, it is unclear why the same assessment would not apply when a memory experience is substituted for a perception—i.e., the memory experience provides a new justification for the initially irrational belief.

6 Annis (1980), pp. 325–6 raises this kind of counter-example to Pollock's view.

7 Senor (1993), pp. 468–9.

8 Malcolm (1963), pp. 230–1 almost says this, except he does not seem to allow the possibility of one's justification being lowered.

9 This view is defended by Malcolm (1963), pp. 229–30; Annis (1980); Naylor (1983); and Owens (2000).

10 See Russell (1971), p. 159.

11 See Malcolm (1963), p. 230: "When someone remembers that *p* does he have grounds for being sure that *p*? The answer is that he has the same grounds, if any, that he previously had."

12 Owens (2000), chapter 9 is particularly explicit about this point.

13 Pollock (1986), p. 50 poses a related objection to the preservation theory, based on ordinary cases in which your memory deceives you: He thinks that in such cases, provided you have no reason for suspecting that your memory is deceiving you, you are justified in believing what you seem to remember; yet the preservation theory implies that these beliefs are unjustified. Pollock concludes that memory must be accepted as a source of justification, and hence that the foundational theory is true.

14 Owens (2000) makes use of this distinction, but he does not take advantage of the opportunity it provides to avoid the five-minute-hypothesis objection.

15 The following objection could be pressed: Mike2 is created with a host of *dispositional* beliefs implanted in him. Having never consciously entertained the propositions that these beliefs are about, he has not had any (occurrent) experiences of seeming to remember them, so the present theory cannot account for Mike2's justification for his dispositional beliefs. An obvious response would be to say that Mike2's beliefs are justified by virtue of his *dispositional* seeming-memories (quasi-memories). But a more interesting response, and the one I favor, is that Mike2 does not (cannot) have the same dispositional beliefs that I

have. A detailed discussion of this point would take us too far afield, but briefly: in order to genuinely believe that P, it is not enough that one *would* occurrently believe P if one considered it—"dispositional belief" does not merely mean "disposition to believe." To believe P, a person must either (i) occurrently believe it, (ii) have once believed it, having never changed his mind about it, (iii) believe something else which *presupposes* it, or (iv) believe something else which obviously entails it. So there are three ways of dispositionally believing something, but each presupposes another belief or belief at an earlier time. For this reason, Mike2 cannot be created with dispositional beliefs already implanted in him; he can't have any dispositional beliefs prior to his first occurrent belief.

16 I don't count the inferential theory as one of the main alternatives, because I do not know of any philosopher who actually defends it.

17 My thanks are due to David Owens for stimulating my interest in and initial thoughts on this topic, and to both David Owens and John Pollock for discussion of various ideas in this paper. Unfortunately, I do not believe either of these philosophers would agree with more than half of what I have said here.

References

Alston, William P. (1985) "Concepts of Epistemic Justification," *The Monist* 68, pp. 57–89.

Annis, David B. (1980) "Memory and Justification," *Philosophy and Phenomenological Research* 40, pp. 324–33.

Ginet, Carl (1975) *Knowledge, Perception, and Memory* (Boston: D. Reidel).

Malcolm, Norman (1963) *Knowledge and Certainty* (Englewood Cliffs, N.J.: Prentice Hall).

Naylor, Andrew (1983) "Justification in Memory Knowledge," *Synthese* 55, pp. 269–86.

Owens, David (2000) *Reason without Freedom* (London: Routledge), chapter 9.

Pollock, John L. (1986) *Contemporary Theories of Knowledge* (Totowa, N.J.: Rowman & Littlefield).

Pollock, John L. (1995) *Cognitive Carpentry: A Blueprint for How to Build a Person* (Cambridge, Mass.: MIT Press).

Russell, Bertrand (1971) *The Analysis of Mind* (London: Allen & Unwin).

Senor, Thomas D. (1993) "Internalistic Foundationalism and the Justification of Memory Belief," *Synthese* 94, pp. 453–76.

QUESTIONS

1 According to Huemer, what are the two elements in the justification of a memory belief?

2 Huemer describes a case in which a person adopts a belief irrationally, and later seems to remember it. (a) According to Huemer, is the later belief justified? (b) What theory is this example supposed to refute?

3 Huemer alludes to Russell's five-minute hypothesis. (a) According to Huemer, in

this example, does the person have justified beliefs? (b) What theory is this example supposed to refute?

FURTHER READING ON MEMORY

Annis, David, "Memory and Justification," *Philosophy and Phenomenological Research* 40 (1980): 324–33.

Burge, Tyler, "Interlocution, Perception, and Memory," *Philosophical Studies* 86 (1997): 21–47.

Christensen, David and Hilary Kornblith, "Testimony, Memory and the Limits of the 'A Priori,'" *Philosophical Studies* 86 (1997): 1–20.

Ginet, Carl, *Knowledge, Perception, and Memory* (Boston: D. Reidel, 1975).

Meinong, Alexius, "Toward an Epistemological Assessment of Memory," trans. Linda L. McAlister and Margarete Schätte, pp. 253–70 in *Empirical Knowledge: Readings from Contemporary Sources*, ed. Roderick M. Chisholm and Robert J. Swartz (Englewood Cliffs, N.J.: Prentice Hall, 1973).

Naylor, Andrew, "Justification in Memory Knowledge," *Synthese* 55 (1983): 269–86.

Naylor, Andrew, "In Defense of a Nontraditional Theory of Memory," *Monist* 62 (1985): 136–50.

Owens, David, *Reason Without Freedom* (London: Routledge, 2000).

Senor, Thomas, "Internalistic Foundationalism and the Justification of Memory Belief," *Synthese* 94 (1993): 453–76.

3

REASON AND THE A PRIORI

There has been a longstanding debate in epistemology over the role of reason in cognition. The *empiricists* argue, roughly, that all knowledge is derived from observation (sensory experience and introspection), and that the role of reason is therefore only to operate on, or make inferences from, the information provided by experience. In contrast, the *rationalists* say that we have some substantive knowledge that is independent of experience, and that the faculty of reason can be a source of new knowledge.

The rationalist position goes back at least to Plato. Plato believed in a realm of abstract objects called "Forms," which existed independent of the mind. The Forms were supposed to explain what multiple concrete, particular things had in common and how we could have concepts of perfect things (such as a perfect circle) that did not exist in the physical world. The Forms included such things as the number 2, Justice (in the abstract), and the perfect circle.

Plato argues, through the character of Socrates, that people have some sort of innate understanding of mathematics. This is allegedly demonstrated by a dialogue between Socrates and a slave boy who, though previously uneducated in geometry, is able to answer correctly a series of questions that Socrates poses about a geometrical figure, culminating in the conclusion that a square built on the diagonal of another square will have twice the area of the latter square. Since Socrates was only questioning the slave boy and not *telling* him the answers, the slave boy must have already known the answers in some sense (perhaps unconsciously?). This leads into Plato's unusual theory that human beings had knowledge of the Forms in a previous existence, prior to birth, and just need to be reminded of what they previously knew.

Few philosophers would accept Plato's argument here. Empiricists would argue that the episode with the slave boy fails to demonstrate Plato's conclusion, because the slave boy was acquiring new experience as Socrates questioned him, by looking at the figures Socrates drew. Most modern rationalists, on the other hand, would say, not that the slave boy had *innate* knowledge of the facts of geometry, but that his faculty of reason was supplying him with knowledge of geometrical truths *as* Socrates questioned him; that is, he was acquiring the knowledge then, but he was acquiring it through the exercise of his reason (and not solely through observation).

Immanuel Kant, in the eighteenth century, advanced the debate between rationalists and empiricists by drawing two important distinctions: the distinction between *analytic* and *synthetic* judgments, and the distinction between *a priori* and *a posteriori* (or empirical) judgments. Kant defined these terms as follows:

- *Analytic judgment:* A judgment in which the concept of the subject contains the concept of the predicate. Example: "All bachelors are unmarried" (because the concept "bachelor" contains the concept "unmarried"). In more recent times, the definition has been modified as follows: an analytic *statement* is a statement that can be derived using just the laws of logic and the substitution of synonymous expressions. Example: The statement "All bachelors are unmarried" is analytic. Since "bachelors" is synonymous with "unmarried men," we can substitute the latter for the former, obtaining the sentence, "All unmarried men are unmarried," which is a logical truth. Analytic statements are also called "true by definition" and are commonly thought to contain no real information about the world.
- *Synthetic judgment:* A judgment that is not analytic. Example: "All bachelors are slobs." Similarly, a synthetic statement is any statement that is not analytic.
- *A priori judgment:* A judgment that is not based on experience. Here, "experience" includes sensory experience and introspection. "Based on" is intended in the sense of "justified by" (n.b. *not* "caused by"). In modern times, we usually speak of a priori justification or knowledge (rather than merely a priori judgments).
- *A posteriori/empirical judgment:* A judgment that is based on experience.

The modern definitions of empiricism and rationalism, post Kant, are as follows. *Rationalists* are people who believe that there is some synthetic, a priori knowledge. *Empiricists* deny this; hence, they believe either that there is no a priori knowledge at all—the extreme empiricist position—or that there is only analytic a priori knowledge—the moderate empiricist position.

It is important to distinguish a priori knowledge from innate knowledge. All innate knowledge (if there is any) is a priori, but not all a priori knowledge need be innate. The slave boy's knowledge of geometry might be a priori (if it is produced by the faculty of reason, rather than observation), even if it is not innate (existing at birth).

It is likewise important to distinguish a belief that is *caused* by experience (because, for instance, experience stimulated one to form the concepts contained in the belief, or to consider the proposition) from a belief that is *justified* by experience. There is a famous story about the chemist Kekulé, who discovered the ring structure of the benzene molecule. It is said that he came up with the idea as a result of a dream in which he saw a snake turn around and bite its tail. In this case, the dream *caused* him to think of the idea that benzene had a ring structure. But obviously, the dream is not a *justification* for the claim that benzene has a ring structure (if he had presented the dream as evidence at a scientific conference, he would have been laughed at). In light of this distinction, we can say that the rationalist position is that there is some knowledge which is not justified by experience; the position is *not* that experience plays no role in causing us to think of the propositions that are known.

Besides the above distinctions, there are two important points that the student should get from the reading selections from Kant. The first is Kant's defense of the existence of synthetic, a priori knowledge. He gives several putative examples of such knowledge. The second point is how Kant tries to explain how such knowledge is possible. Stated very briefly, he thinks that the mind imposes a sort of structure on the world, which determines certain aspects of how we perceive (and conceive of) things. Our synthetic, a priori knowledge derives from and reflects this imposed structure. For example, we have a priori knowledge of the laws of Euclidean geometry, not because reality is necessarily contained in Euclidean space as other rationalists have thought (Kant denies that space exists independent of the mind), but because the human mind is so constituted that we can only perceive things as in Euclidean space.

Bertrand Russell criticizes Kant's theory on two main grounds. First, he says, Kant's theory cannot explain why the truths of mathematics are *necessary* (e.g., 2 + 2 *must* equal 4), since Kant's theory implies that if the nature of the human mind were to change, the truths of mathematics would also change. This is a problem, since Kant had held that all a priori knowledge (including all mathematical knowledge) was indeed necessary. Second, it was a consequence of Kant's theory (as Kant himself insisted) that the truths of mathematics could only apply to "things as they appear to us," and not to "things in themselves." But Russell argues that arithmetic should apply to things in themselves, even if we never perceive things-in-themselves: two things-in-themselves plus two more things-in-themselves make four things-in-themselves.

Russell's own theory of a priori knowledge held that we have a priori knowledge because of our acquaintance with *universals*. Universals are properties or relationships that can be shared by multiple things. For instance, multiple things can share the property of redness, so redness is a universal. Similarly, multiple things can be on top of something else, so the relation *being on top of* is a universal. Russell held that we have an intellectual grasp of the natures of at least some of these universals, and that this grasp enables us to discern the relationships of universals to each other. All a priori knowledge, then, is knowledge of the relations of universals. For instance, I know a priori that 1 + 2 = 3: this is knowledge of a relationship holding among the numbers 1, 2, and 3.

A.J. Ayer is a representative of a school of thought popular early in the twentieth century known as "logical positivism." Logical positivism embodied two main theses. The first was empiricism, the view that there is no synthetic, a priori knowledge (but positivists admit the existence of analytic a priori knowledge). The second thesis was *verificationism*, or the *verification criterion of meaning*, which held that the cognitive meaning of a statement is determined by the conditions under which it is verified or refuted, and that therefore a statement that cannot be verified or refuted is cognitively meaningless. ("Cognitive meaning," the kind of meaning a statement has when it asserts something about reality, is distinguished from "emotive meaning," the kind of "meaning" a sentence has when it expresses the speaker's feelings or other attitudes.) The positivists used the word "metaphysics" to refer to all statements allegedly expressing synthetic a priori knowledge. Based on their empiricism and verificationism, they concluded that all metaphysical statements were cognitively meaningless—hence Ayer's campaign for "the elimination of metaphysics." They applied this doctrine not only to the traditional metaphysical systems in philosophy, of the sort that you find in Leibniz and Spinoza for instance, but also to the fields of ethics and religion, which the positivists considered equally unverifiable.

Quine, an extreme empiricist, criticizes two "dogmas" that have commonly been accepted by other empiricists, especially positivists. The first "dogma" is the idea that there is a distinction between analytic and synthetic statements. He considers several ways of trying to define the notion of an "analytic" statement and argues that none of them works, because each requires the use of some other undefined and obscure term (e.g., "meaning," "synonymous," and "definition"). The second "dogma" is what Quine calls "reductionism," the view that every statement can be translated into a statement or collection of statements about sensory experiences (idealists hold this view). He considers the positivist view that each statement can be associated with a class of possible experiences that would confirm it and another class that would disconfirm it, to be a weakened form of reductionism.

So Quine proposed a radical revision of epistemology, in which (a) there is no such thing as an analytic statement, and (b) an individual statement cannot be confirmed or disconfirmed. Instead, he thought, one can only confirm or disconfirm a *system* of statements. To get some idea of what this means, consider only one miniature example. Is it possible to confirm or disconfirm Newton's theory of gravity, considered by itself? It is usually thought that the answer is yes: you can try dropping a rock and observing its motion. If it did not fall, that would disconfirm the theory of gravity. But Quine would say that in fact, the theory of gravity by itself does not predict anything about the object's motion and so is not tested by that sort of observation. For the theory of gravity only says that all massive bodies exert a force on each other proportional to their masses and inversely proportional to the distance between them. In order to infer that the rock will fall, you would have to add all of the following statements, at least:

- The rock is massive.
- The Earth is massive.
- There is a finite distance between the Earth and the rock.
- There are no other forces acting on the rock.
- When a body has a force acting on it, it will tend to move in the direction of the force.

If the rock fails to fall, then, you will have tested that *system* of statements; you will know that the whole system of statements cannot be correct. But you will not have tested any one statement considered individually. Quine believes that this sort of lesson applies much more generally, and that our beliefs are all interconnected in such a way that only our belief system as a whole enables us to make predictions about what we will observe. Therefore, when our observations fail to go the way we expect, we have a choice of many beliefs that we could revise. There are some beliefs that we are just *less willing* to revise than others—the statements other philosophers have called "analytic" are the ones that they are least willing to revise. But since willingness to revise a statement comes in degrees, there really is no principled distinction between analytic and synthetic statements, for Quine. Quine's views have extremely far-reaching implications and have been much discussed among philosophers in several branches of philosophy.

The debate over a priori knowledge was strongly influenced by the development in the nineteenth and twentieth centuries of non-Euclidean geometries. Hitherto, it had been thought (particularly by Kant) that geometry was a paradigmatic example of our synthetic, a priori knowledge. However, when Einstein, in his general theory of relativity, adopted a non-Euclidean geometry to describe our space–time, many philosophers and scientists concluded that Kant had been wrong: they concluded that geometry was in fact an empirical science, and that Euclidean geometry was so far from being a priori knowledge that it was not even *true*.

The reading selections from Carnap explain the basic ideas of non-Euclidean geometry. Essentially, there are now three kinds of geometry:

1. *Euclidean geometry* includes the axiom (known as the axiom of parallels): given a line and a point not on the line, there exists *exactly one* line (in a single plane) that passes through the given point and is parallel to the given line.
2. *Riemannian geometry* substitutes the following axiom: given a line and a point not on the line, there exist *no* lines (in the plane) that pass through the given point and are parallel to the given line. (Also called elliptical geometry, since it is the geometry of the surface of an ellipsoid.)
3. *Lobachevskian geometry* instead assumes: given a line and a point not on the line, there exist *many* lines (in the plane) that pass through the given point and are parallel to the given line. (Also called hyperbolic geometry, since it is the geometry of the surface of a hyperboloid.)

Is it possible, by measurements, to determine what sort of space we are living in? One might try drawing a triangle and measuring the interior angles. In a Euclidean space, they must add up to 180°; in other spaces, they will not.

A complication for this proposal is brought out by Carnap's following chapter, "Poincaré versus Einstein" (using an example derived from Reichenbach). If we find that the angles of our triangle add up to more than 180°, there will still be at least two possible explanations of this observation. The first explanation would be that we are living in a non-Euclidean space (this is what Einstein would say).

The second explanation is that we are living in a Euclidean space in which an unusual sort of force operates. This force causes bodies to expand in certain predictable ways when they enter certain regions of space (for instance, it might be that bodies expand as they move closer to other, very massive bodies). This expansion is not directly measurable because any ruler or other measuring rod that you take into the region also expands by exactly the same ratio. However, it can be shown that one effect of this expansion would be that when a "triangle" is drawn in the region, its sides will be bowed outward, such that the interior angles will add up to more than 180°. (This is compatible with the fact that the space is Euclidean, because it would not be a true triangle, since its sides would be curved, rather than straight lines.)

It can be shown that the two theories would predict the same observations, so one cannot distinguish between them by means of observation. Carnap, being a positivist, concludes that the two theories therefore are really equivalent in meaning (remember the verification criterion of meaning). Most who consider Carnap's example find this claim to be implausible (for one thing, the two theories contain statements that are contradictory on their face). Note, however, that Carnap would not claim that any one statement of the one theory is synonymous with any particular statement in the other theory; it is only the whole system of statements that constitute the first theory which is equivalent to the system that constitutes the second theory (compare Quine's holism).

Laurence BonJour gives a different response to the example. BonJour defends a "moderate rationalism," which holds that we have some intuitions, or "rational insights," which should be accorded some evidential weight in deciding what to believe. On BonJour's view, these intuitions are fallible and can sometimes be overridden by countervailing evidence, just as our sensory experiences are fallible (consider cases of illusions and hallucinations) and can sometimes be overridden. This does not invalidate intuition as a possible source of knowledge, any more than the possibility of sensory illusions invalidates sense perception as a source of knowledge. Thus, even if the Euclidean axiom of parallels were mistaken, this fact would not threaten BonJour's form of rationalism. But BonJour goes on to suggest that we lack strong reasons for thinking the axiom of parallels is mistaken. The second of the two theories discussed above may be superior to the first, on the grounds that the second theory is more consistent with our intuitions (such as the intuitive sense that the axiom of parallels is true), while both are equally consistent with our observations.

Plato, *Meno*

Meno Can you tell me, Socrates—does virtue come from teaching? Or does it come not from teaching but from practice? Or does it come to people neither from practice nor from being learnt, but by nature or in some other way?
Socrates Well, Meno, in the past it was for horsemanship and wealth that the Thessalians were famous among the Greeks and admired, but now, I think, it is for wisdom too, especially your friend Aristippus' fellow-citizens in Larisa. You owe all this to Gorgias. When he went to that city, he won over the most eminent people as lovers for his wisdom—both those within the Aleuad family (including your own lover Aristippus) and those among the other Thessalians. In particular he trained you in the habit of answering any questions anyone asks with the grand confidence that suits people with knowledge, just as he himself too volunteers to be asked anything that anyone in the Greek world may wish, and never leaves anyone unanswered. But here in Athens, my dear Meno, the opposite has happened. A sort of drought of wisdom has developed, and it seems that wisdom has left these parts for yours. At any rate, if you want to ask one of the people here such a question there's no one who won't laugh and say: "Well, stranger, perhaps you think I'm some specially favoured person—I'd certainly need to be, to know whether virtue comes from teaching or in what way it does come—but in fact I'm so far from knowing whether it comes from teaching or not, that actually I don't even know at all what virtue itself is!"

And that's the situation I'm in too, Meno. I'm as impoverished as my fellow-citizens in this respect, and confess to my shame that I don't know about virtue at all. And if I don't know what something is, how could I know what that thing is like? Or do you think it possible, if someone doesn't know who Meno is at all, that this person should know whether he's beautiful or rich, or whether he's well-born, or whether he's the opposite of all these? Do you think that possible?
Meno No I don't. But is it really true about *you*, Socrates, that you don't even know what virtue is? Is this the report about you that we're to take home with us?
Soc. Not just that, my friend, but also that I don't think I've yet met anyone else who does, either.
Meno What? Didn't you meet Gorgias when he was here?
Soc. Yes I did.

Plato's Meno in Focus, trans. and ed. Jane M. Day (London: Routledge, 1994).

Meno You mean you didn't think he knew?

Soc. I don't remember things very well, Meno, so I can't now say what I thought about him then. But perhaps he does know, and perhaps you know what he used to say, so remind me what that was. Or if you like, *you* tell me yourself, for I expect you think the same as he does.

Meno Yes I do.

Soc. Well then, let's leave him out of it, since after all he isn't here—and Meno, by all the gods, what do you yourself say that virtue is? Tell me and don't keep it back. Make it a really lucky false statement I've uttered, if what comes to light is that you and Gorgias do know, all the time I've been saying I'd never yet met anyone who did.

Meno But it's not hard to tell you, Socrates. First, if it's virtue for a man you wish to know, that's easy: virtue for a man is the ability to conduct the city's affairs and, in so doing, to help his friends, hurt his foes, and take good care not to get hurt himself. Or if it's virtue for a woman you wish for, that's not hard to describe: she must run the home well, looking after everything in it and obeying her husband. And there is another virtue for a child, whether female or male, and another for an older man, free or slave, whichever you wish. And there are a great many other virtues, so that there's no perplexity about saying what virtue is. For there is virtue for every field of practice and time of life, in connection with every activity, and for every one of us; and vice too in the same way, I think, Socrates.

Soc. I seem to be having a lot of luck, Meno, if in searching for just one virtue I've found a positive swarm of virtues in your possession. But Meno, to follow up this metaphor of swarms: if I had asked about the nature of a bee and what that is, and you had said that bees were many and varied, how would you answer me if I then asked, "Do you say they are many and varied and different from one another *in respect of being bees*? Or is it not at all in *this* respect that they differ, but in some *other* respect, such as beauty or size or something else like that?" Tell me, how would you answer if you were asked that?

Meno I would say that in respect of being bees they are no different from one another.

Soc. Then if I said next, "Well, tell me then, Meno, what do you say this thing itself is, in respect of which they are not different but all the same?", I expect you would have an answer for me?

Meno Yes I would.

Soc. Then it's the same with the virtues too: even if they are many and various, they must still all have one and the same form which makes them *virtues*. Presumably it would be right to focus on this in one's answer and show the questioner what virtue actually *is*. Or don't you understand what I mean?

Meno I think I understand. But I don't yet grasp the question quite as clearly as I'd like to.

Soc. Well, is it only about virtue, Meno, that you think as you do—that there is one for a man, another for a woman, and so on—or do you think the same about health and size and strength too? Do you think there is one health for a man and another for a woman? Or is it the same form in every case, if it really *is* health, whether in a man or in anything else?

Meno With health, I think it is the same in both man and woman.

Soc. And isn't it so with size and strength too? If a woman is strong, won't it be the same form, the same strength, that makes her strong? What I mean by "the same" is that whether strength is in a man or in a woman makes no difference with respect to its being *strength*. Or do you think it does make a difference?

Meno No I don't.

Soc. Well, will whether *virtue* is in a child, in an old man, in a woman or in a man make any difference with respect to its being *virtue*?

Meno I think this is somehow no longer like those other cases, Socrates.

Soc. Well now, didn't you say that for a man, virtue was running a city well and for a woman, running a home well?

Meno Yes I did.

Soc. And is it possible to run a city or home or anything else well without running it temperately and justly?

Meno No indeed.

Soc. And to run it temperately and justly will mean running it with temperance and justice, won't it?

Meno It must.

Soc. So they both need the same things if they're going to be good—both the man and the woman—justice and temperance?

Meno Apparently they do.

Soc. And what about a child or old man? Surely they could never come to be good by being undisciplined and unjust?

Meno No indeed.

Soc. But rather, by being temperate and just?

Meno Yes.

Soc. So people are all good in the same way, since they all come to be good by attaining the same things?

Meno It seems so.

Soc. Now presumably they would not have been good in the same way if the virtue they'd had were not the same?

Meno No indeed.

Soc. Well then, since virtue is the same for everyone, try to remember and tell me what Gorgias, and you with him, say it is.

Meno What else but the ability to rule over people, if what you are searching for is some one thing covering them all.

Soc. That is indeed what I'm searching for. But does a child have the same virtue too, Meno, or a slave—the ability to rule over his master? Do you think he would still *be* a slave, if he were the ruler?

Meno I don't think so at all, Socrates.

Soc. It's certainly unlikely, my good chap. For consider this too. You say "ability to rule." Won't we add to this the words "justly, and not unjustly"?

Meno Yes, I think so. For justice is virtue, Socrates.

Soc. Virtue, Meno, or *a* virtue?

Meno What do you mean by that?

Soc. The same as I would with anything else. For instance, if you like, with roundness, I'd say that it's *a* shape, not simply that it's shape. The reason I'd say this is that there are also other shapes.

Meno You're quite right, since I too say that besides justice there are also other virtues.

Soc. What are these? Tell me. Just as I'd name some other shapes if you told me to, so you tell me some other virtues.
Meno Well then, courage is virtue in my opinion, and so are temperance and wisdom and grandeur, and all the many others.
Soc. The same thing has happened to us as before, Meno. Once again, though in a different way from last time, we've found many virtues while searching for one. But as for the one virtue which extends through all these, that we can't discover.
. . .
Meno And how are you going to search for this when you don't know at all what it is, Socrates? Which of all the things you don't know will you set up as target for your search? And even if you actually come across it, how will you know that it *is* that thing which you didn't know?
Soc. I know what you mean, Meno. Do you see what a disputatious argument you're bringing down on us—how it's impossible for a person to search either for what he knows or for what he doesn't? He couldn't search for what he knows, for he knows it and no one in that condition needs to search; on the other hand he couldn't search for what he doesn't know, for he won't even know what to search for.
Meno And don't you think that's a fine argument, Socrates?
Soc. No I don't.
Meno Can you tell me why?
Soc. Yes I can. I've heard men and women wise in matters divine—
Meno Saying what?
Soc. Something both true and beautiful in my opinion.
Meno What is it, and who are the people saying it?
Soc. The people saying it are those priests and priestesses who have made it their concern to be able to give an account of their practices; Pindar says it too and many other divinely inspired poets. And as for what they say, it's this—but consider if you think what they say is true. They say the soul of man is immortal; sometimes it comes to an end—which people call dying—while at other times it is reborn, but it never perishes. So because of this one should live out one's life in the holiest possible way, since for those from whom

> "Persephone receives
> Requital for long grief, their souls she yields
> In the ninth year once more to the sun above;
> From whom grow noble kings, and men
> Swift in strength and great in wisdom;
> And to the end of time men call them heroes holy."

Well, since the soul is immortal, and has been born many times and seen both what is here, and what is in Hades, and everything, there is nothing it has not learnt. So no wonder it's possible that it should recollect both virtue and other things, as after all it did know them previously. For seeing that the whole of nature is akin and the soul has learnt everything, there's nothing to prevent someone who recollects—which people call learning—just one thing, from discovering everything else, if he's courageous and doesn't give up searching;—for searching and learning are just recollection. So we shouldn't be persuaded by that disputatious argument. That argument would make us lazy, and weak-willed people love to hear it, but this one makes us industrious and eager to search. It's because I'm confident that this one is true that I'm ready to search with you for what virtue is.

Meno Yes Socrates—but what do you mean by saying we don't learn, but what we call learning is recollection? Can you teach me how that is so?

Soc. Only a minute ago I said you were a rascal, Meno, and now you ask me if I can teach you—I who say there's no teaching, only recollecting—obviously all to show me up as immediately contradicting myself.

Meno No by Zeus, Socrates, I didn't speak with any such thought, but out of habit. But if there's any way you can show me that it is as you say, do show me.

Soc. Well, it's not easy, but all the same I'm ready to do my best for your sake. Call me one of these many attendants you have, whichever one you wish, so that I can demonstrate on him for you.

Meno Yes, certainly. Come here!

Soc. First, is he Greek and does he speak Greek?

Meno Very much so; he was born in our home.

Soc. Observe carefully then which of the two things he shows himself to be doing, recollecting or learning from me.

Meno I shall, do.

Soc. Tell me now, boy, you know that a square figure is like this?

Boy Yes I do.

Soc. So a square figure is one which has all these four lines equal?

Boy Yes indeed.

Soc. And it is one which also has these lines through the middle equal, isn't it? [*See Figure 1. Throughout his conversation with the slave we must imagine Socrates drawing figures as he describes them.*]

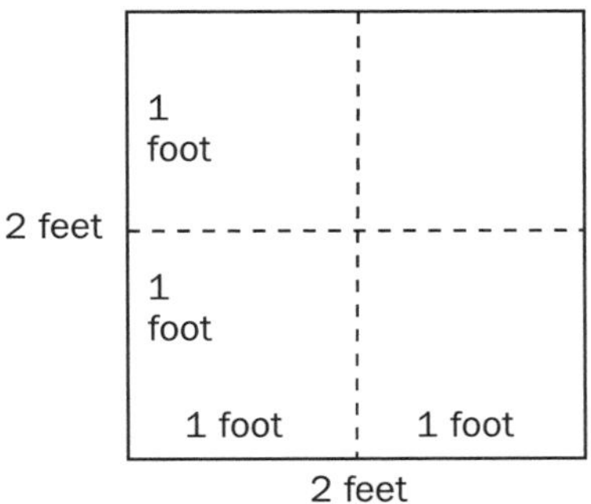

Figure 1

Boy Yes.

Soc. And there could be both bigger and smaller figures like this, couldn't there?

Boy Yes indeed.

Soc. Well, if this side were two feet long and this other side two feet, how many feet big would the whole be? Think of it like this: if it had been two feet this way and only one foot that way, wouldn't the figure have been two feet times one?

Boy Yes.
Soc. But since it's two feet that way also, doesn't it come to two times *two*?
Boy It does.
Soc. So it comes to two times two feet?
Boy Yes.
Soc. Well, how many are two times two? Work it out and tell me.
Boy Four, Socrates.
Soc. Well, there could be another figure twice the size of this one but like it, couldn't there, having all its lines equal just like this one?
Boy Yes.
Soc. How many feet big will it be, then?
Boy Eight.
Soc. Well now, try to tell me how long each line of that one will be. The line for this one is two feet long; what about the line for that one which is twice the size?
Boy Clearly it'll be twice the length, Socrates.
Soc. Do you see, Meno, how I'm not teaching him anything but instead asking him everything? And at present he supposes he knows what kind of line the eight-foot figure will come from—or don't you think he does?
Meno Yes I do.
Soc. And does he know?
Meno No indeed.
Soc. But he supposes it will come from a line twice the length?
Meno Yes.
Soc. Then watch him recollecting in order, as one has to do.

Now, you tell me. You say that a figure twice the size comes from a line twice the length? I mean a figure like this one, not long one way and short the other, but it's to be equal in each direction just like this one, only twice the size, eight feet big—but see whether you still think it will come from the line twice the length.
Boy I do.
Soc. Well, *this* line comes to twice the length of this one, doesn't it, if we add on another of the same length starting here?
Boy Yes indeed.
Soc. Then this is the line you say the eight-foot figure will come from, if there came to be four lines of the same length.
Boy Yes.
Soc. Let's draw four equal lines starting from it, then. Isn't this what you say would be the eight-foot figure?
Boy Yes indeed.
Soc. And inside it, aren't there these four figures, of which each one is equal to this four-foot figure? [*See Figure* 2]
Boy Yes.
Soc. How big is it then? Isn't it four times the size?
Boy Yes, of course.
Soc. So what's four times the size is twice the size?
Boy No, by Zeus.
Soc. But how many times the size *is* it?
Boy Four times.
Soc. So it's not a figure *twice* the size that comes from a line twice the length, my

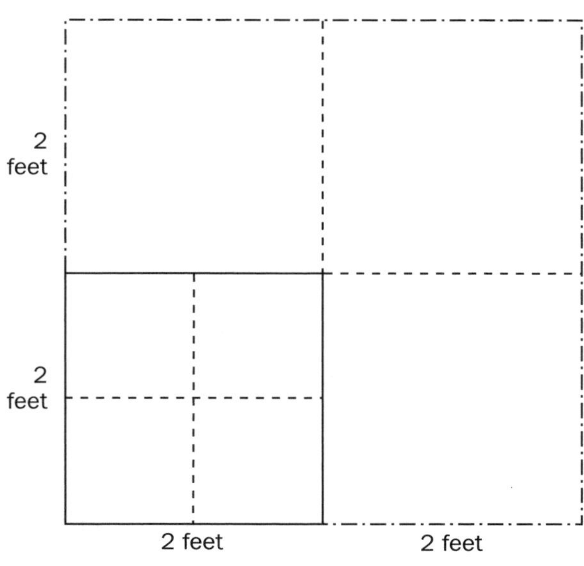

Figure 2

boy, but one *four times* the size.

Boy What you say is true.

Soc. For four times four is sixteen, isn't it?

Boy Yes.

Soc. But what line does an *eight*-foot figure come from? From this line comes a figure four times the size, doesn't it?

Boy I agree.

Soc. And this quarter-size figure comes from this half-length line, doesn't it?

Boy Yes.

Soc. Right. The eight-foot figure is twice the size of this one and half the size of that one, isn't it?

Boy Yes.

Soc. Won't it be from a line bigger than this one but smaller than that? Or not?

Boy I think that is so.

Soc. Fine; always answer what you think. And tell me, wasn't this line two feet long and the other one four feet?

Boy Yes.

Soc. So the line for the eight-foot figure needs to be bigger than this two-foot line, but smaller than the four-foot one.

Boy It does.

Soc. Then try to tell me how long a line you say it is.

Boy Three feet.

Soc. Well, if it's to be three feet long, we'll add on half as much again of this line and that will be three feet, won't it?—these two feet here, plus this one more. And over here in the same way there will be these two feet here plus this one more, and here comes the figure you say. [*See Figure 3*]

Boy Yes.

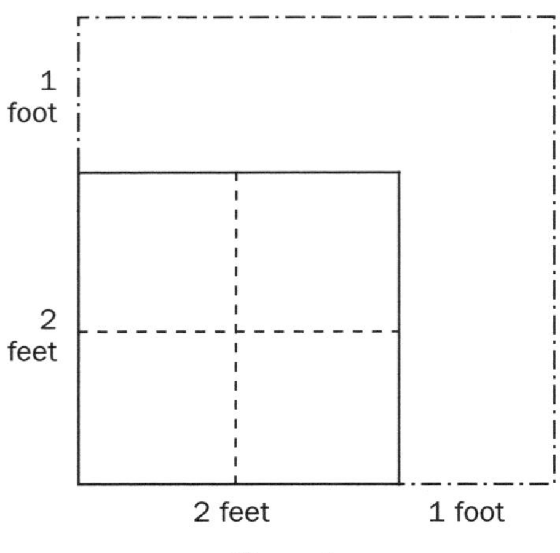

Figure 3

Soc. Then if it's three feet this way and three feet this way, doesn't the whole figure come to three times three feet?
Boy Apparently:
Soc. And how many feet are three times three?
Boy Nine.
Soc. And how many feet big did the figure which is twice the size have to be?
Boy Eight.
Soc. So a three-foot line is still not what an eight-foot figure comes from, either?
Boy No indeed.
Soc. But what line *is*? Try to tell us exactly, and if you don't wish to put a number to it, *show* us what it is instead.
Boy But by Zeus, Socrates, *I* certainly don't know.
Soc. Are you observing again, Meno, what stage he's reached now in recollecting? At first he didn't know what the baseline of the eight-foot figure was, just as he still doesn't know it now either, but at that time he supposed he *did* know, and answered boldly like someone with knowledge, and didn't think he was perplexed. But now he *has* begun to think he's perplexed, and besides not knowing, he doesn't suppose he knows either.
Meno What you say is true.
Soc. And isn't he in a better state now in relation to the thing he doesn't know?
Meno I think that is so too.
Soc. Well, in making him perplexed and torpifying him like a torpedo fish does, we've done him no harm, have we?
Meno No, I don't think so.
Soc. In fact it seems we've done him a service towards finding the real answer, for now he'd gladly search for what he doesn't know, whereas then he'd have supposed he could speak well with ease in front of many people and on many occasions, about how a figure twice the size has to have its baseline twice the length.
Meno It seems so.
Soc. Well, do you think he would have attempted to search out or learn what he

supposed he knew but in fact didn't, till he fell into perplexity on coming to think he didn't know, and began longing for knowledge?

Meno I don't think so, Socrates.

Soc. So he has benefited from being torpified?

Meno I think so.

Soc. Now look what he'll go on from this state of perplexity to discover as he searches with me, while I do nothing but ask questions, not teach him. Watch out in case you ever find me teaching and instructing him instead of drawing out his own opinions.

You tell me, this is our four-foot figure, isn't it? You understand?

Boy Yes I do.

Soc. And we could add on to it this other equal one here.

Boy Yes.

Soc. And this third one equal to each of the others?

Boy Yes.

Soc. Then we could fill in this one in the corner as well, couldn't we?

Boy Yes indeed.

Soc. And these would come out four equal figures, wouldn't they?

Boy Yes.

Soc. Now then, how many times the size of this one here does this whole thing here come to?

Boy Four times the size.

Soc. While what we had to get was one twice the size. Or don't you remember?

Boy I do indeed.

Soc. Then there's a line here from corner to corner, isn't there, cutting each of the figures in two?

Boy Yes.

Soc. And these four lines come out equal, don't they, and surround this figure here? [*See Figure 4*]

Boy Yes they do.

Soc. Now consider. How big is this figure?

Boy I don't understand.

Soc. Of these four figures here, hasn't half of each been cut off and enclosed by each line? Or is that not so?

Boy Yes.

Soc. Then how many bits of that size are there inside here?

Boy Four.

Soc. And how many inside here?

Boy Two.

Soc. And how much is four as compared to two?

Boy Twice as much.

Soc. Then how big does this figure come out?

Boy Eight feet big.

Soc. And what line does it come from?

Boy This one.

Soc. The one stretching from corner to corner of the four-foot figure?

Boy Yes.

Soc. What the experts call that is the diagonal. So if the diagonal is the name of

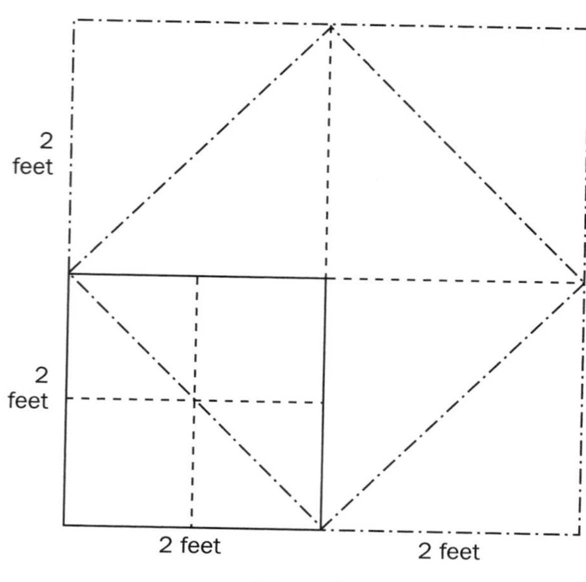

Figure 4

this line then you, Meno's boy, say that a figure of twice the size would come from the diagonal.

Boy Yes indeed, Socrates.

Soc. What do you think, Meno. Has he answered with any opinions but his own?

Meno No, only with his own.

Soc. And yet he certainly didn't *know*, as we said a little while ago.

Meno What you say is true.

Soc. But he certainly had these opinions in him—or didn't he?

Meno Yes.

Soc. So someone who doesn't know something, whatever it may be he doesn't know, has true opinions in him about the very thing he doesn't know?

Meno It appears so.

Soc. And at present it's as though in a dream that these opinions have just been aroused in him. But if someone questions him many times and in many ways about the same things as now, you may be sure he will end up knowing them as precisely as anyone does.

Meno It seems so.

Soc. And it won't be through being taught by anyone that he knows, will it, but through being questioned, recovering the knowledge from within him for himself?

Meno Yes.

Soc. And recovering knowledge which is within one for oneself is recollecting, isn't it?

Meno Yes indeed.

Soc. Well, the knowledge which this boy has now—he either acquired it sometime or else always had it, didn't he?

Meno Yes.

Soc. Then if he always had it, it follows that he was always in a state of knowledge. On the other hand, if he acquired it sometime, it could certainly not be in his present life that he has done so. Or has someone taught him geometry? For he will do just the same with anything in geometry or any other subject of knowledge. *Has* someone taught him everything, then? Presumably you should know, especially as he's been born and brought up in your home.

Meno No, I know that no one ever taught him.

Soc. And does he have these opinions or not?

Meno Apparently he must, Socrates.

Soc. And if that is without acquiring them in his present life, doesn't it clearly follow that he had them and had learnt them at some other time?

Meno Apparently.

Soc. And that means the time when he was not a human being, doesn't it?

Meno Yes.

Soc. Well, if both during the time that he is a human being, and during the time that he is not, there are going to be true opinions within him which become knowledge when aroused by questioning, isn't his soul going to be for *all* time in a state of having learnt? For it's clear that at every time he either is, or is not, a human being.

Meno Apparently.

Soc. Then if the truth about the things which are is in our souls always, the soul must be immortal, must it not? So shouldn't you boldly try to search for and recollect what you happen not to know—that is, not to remember—at present?

Meno I think that is well said, somehow or other, Socrates.

Soc. Yes, I think so too, Meno. I wouldn't be absolutely adamant about the rest of the argument, but that we shall be better people, more manly and less slothful, by supposing that one should enquire about things one doesn't know, than if we suppose that when we don't know things we can't find them out either and needn't search for them—*this* is something for which I absolutely *would* fight, both in word and deed, to the limit of my powers.

QUESTIONS

1 Socrates claims not to teach the slave boy anything. What is he doing instead?

2 When Socrates shows the slave boy his ignorance, why is this supposed to be good?

Immanuel Kant, *Critique of Pure Reason*

Introduction

I. The distinction between pure and empirical knowledge

There can be no doubt that all our knowledge begins with experience. For how should our faculty of knowledge be awakened into action did not objects affecting our senses partly of themselves produce representations, partly arouse the activity of our understanding to compare these representations, and, by combining or separating them, work up the raw material of the sensible impressions into that knowledge of objects which is entitled experience? In the order of time, therefore, we have no knowledge antecedent to experience, and with experience all our knowledge begins.

But though all our knowledge begins with experience, it does not follow that it all arises out of experience. For it may well be that even our empirical knowledge is made up of what we receive through impressions and of what our own faculty of knowledge (sensible impressions serving merely as the occasion) supplies from itself. If our faculty of knowledge makes any such addition, it may be that we are not in a position to distinguish it from the raw material, until with long practice of attention we have become skilled in separating it.

This, then, is a question which at least calls for closer examination, and does not allow of any off-hand answer:—whether there is any knowledge that is thus independent of experience and even of all impressions of the senses. Such knowledge is entitled *a priori*, and distinguished from the *empirical*, which has its sources *a posteriori*, that is, in experience.

The expression "*a priori*" does not, however, indicate with sufficient precision the full meaning of our question. For it has been customary to say, even of much knowledge that is derived from empirical sources, that we have it or are capable of having it *a priori*, meaning thereby that we do not derive it immediately from experience, but from a universal rule—a rule which is itself, however, borrowed by us from experience. Thus we would say of a man who undermined the foundations of his house, that he might have known *a priori* that it would fall, that is, that he need not have waited for the experience of its actual falling. But still he could not know this completely *a priori*. For he had first to learn through

Immanuel Kant, *Critique of Pure Reason*, trans. Norman Kemp Smith (New York: St Martin's Press, 1963).

experience that bodies are heavy, and therefore fall when their supports are withdrawn.

In what follows, therefore, we shall understand by *a priori* knowledge, not knowledge independent of this or that experience, but knowledge absolutely independent of all experience. Opposed to it is empirical knowledge, which is knowledge possible only *a posteriori*, that is, through experience. *A priori* modes of knowledge are entitled pure when there is no admixture of anything empirical. Thus, for instance, the proposition, "every alteration has its cause," while an *a priori* proposition, is not a pure proposition, because alteration is a concept which can be derived only from experience.

II. We are in possession of certain modes of a priori *knowledge, and even the common understanding is never without them*

What we here require is a criterion by which to distinguish with certainty between pure and empirical knowledge. Experience teaches us that a thing is so and so, but not that it cannot be otherwise. First, then, if we have a proposition which in being thought is thought as *necessary*, it is an *a priori* judgment; and if, besides, it is not derived from any proposition except one which also has the validity of a necessary judgment, it is an absolutely *a priori* judgment. Secondly, experience never confers on its judgments true or strict, but only assumed and comparative *universality*, through induction. We can properly only say, therefore, that, so far as we have hitherto observed, there is no exception to this or that rule. If, then, a judgment is thought with strict universality, that is, in such manner that no exception is allowed as possible, it is not derived from experience, but is valid absolutely *a priori*. Empirical universality is only an arbitrary extension of a validity holding in most cases to one which holds in all, for instance, in the proposition, "all bodies are heavy." When, on the other hand, strict universality is essential to a judgment, this indicates a special source of knowledge, namely, a faculty of *a priori* knowledge. Necessity and strict universality are thus sure criteria of *a priori* knowledge, and are inseparable from one another. But since in the employment of these criteria the contingency of judgments is sometimes more easily shown than their empirical limitation, or, as sometimes also happens, their unlimited universality can be more convincingly proved than their necessity, it is advisable to use the two criteria separately, each by itself being infallible.

Now it is easy to show that there actually are in human knowledge judgments which are necessary and in the strictest sense universal, and which are therefore pure *a priori* judgments. If an example from the sciences be desired, we have only to look to any of the propositions of mathematics; if we seek an example from the understanding in its quite ordinary employment, the proposition, "every alteration must have a cause," will serve our purpose. In the latter case, indeed, the very concept of a cause so manifestly contains the concept of a necessity of connection with an effect and of the strict universality of the rule, that the concept would be altogether lost if we attempted to derive it, as Hume has done, from a repeated association of that which happens with that which precedes, and from a custom of connecting representations, a custom originating in this repeated association, and constituting therefore a merely subjective necessity. Even without appealing to such examples, it is possible to show that pure *a priori* principles are indispensable for the possibility of experience, and so to prove their existence *a priori*. For whence could experience derive its certainty, if all the rules, according to which it proceeds, were always themselves empirical, and therefore contingent? Such rules could hardly be regarded as first principles. At present, however, we may be content to have established the fact that our faculty of knowledge does have a pure employment, and to have shown what are the criteria of such an employment.

Such *a priori* origin is manifest in certain concepts, no less than in judgments. If we remove from our empirical concept of a body, one by one, every feature in it which is [merely] empirical, the colour, the hardness or softness, the weight, even the impenetrability, there still remains the space which the body (now entirely vanished) occupied, and this cannot be removed. Again, if we remove from our empirical concept of any object, corporeal or incorporeal, all properties which experience has taught us, we yet cannot take away that property through which the object is thought as substance or as inhering in a substance (although this concept of substance is more determinate than that of an object in general). Owing, therefore, to the necessity with which this concept of substance forces itself upon us, we have no option save to admit that it has its seat in our faculty of *a priori* knowledge.

III. Philosophy stands in need of a science which shall determine the possibility, the principles, and the extent of all a priori *knowledge*

But what is still more extraordinary than all the preceding is this, that certain modes of knowledge leave the field of all possible experiences and have the appearance of extending the scope of our judgments beyond all limits of experience, and this by means of concepts to which no corresponding object can ever be given in experience.

It is precisely by means of the latter modes of knowledge, in a realm beyond the world of the senses, where experience can yield neither guidance nor correction, that our reason carries on those enquiries which owing to their importance we consider to be far more excellent, and in their purpose far more lofty, than all that the understanding can learn in the field of appearances. Indeed we prefer to run every risk of error rather than desist from such urgent enquiries, on the ground of their dubious character, or from disdain and indifference. These unavoidable problems set by pure reason itself are *God, freedom*, and *immortality*. The science which, with all its preparations, is in its final intention directed solely to their solution is metaphysics; and its procedure is at first dogmatic, that is, it confidently sets itself to this task without any previous examination of the capacity or incapacity of reason for so great an undertaking.

Now it does indeed seem natural that, as soon as we have left the ground of experience, we should, through careful enquiries, assure ourselves as to the foundations of any building that we propose to erect, not making use of any knowledge that we possess without first determining whence it has come, and not trusting to principles without knowing their origin. It is natural, that is to say, that the question should first be considered, how the understanding can arrive at all this knowledge *a priori*, and what extent, validity, and worth it may have. Nothing, indeed, could be more natural, if by the term "natural" we signify what fittingly and reasonably ought to happen. But if we mean by "natural" what ordinarily happens, then on the contrary nothing is more natural and more intelligible than the fact that this enquiry has been so long neglected. For one part of this knowledge, the mathematical, has long been of established reliability, and so gives rise to a favourable presumption as regards the other part, which may yet be of quite different nature. Besides, once we are outside the circle of experience, we can be sure of not being *contradicted* by experience. The charm of extending our knowledge is so great that nothing short of encountering a direct contradiction can suffice to arrest us in our course; and this can be avoided, if we are careful in our fabrications—which none the less will still remain fabrications. Mathematics gives us a shining example of how far, independently of experience, we can progress in *a priori* knowledge. It does, indeed, occupy itself with objects and with knowledge solely in so far as they allow of being exhibited in intuition. But this circumstance is easily overlooked, since this intuition can itself be given *a priori*, and is therefore hardly to be distinguished from a bare and pure concept. Misled by such a proof of the power of reason, the demand for the extension of knowledge recognises no limits. The light dove, cleaving the air in her free flight, and feeling its resistance, might imagine that its flight would be still easier in empty space. It was thus that Plato left the world of the senses, as setting too narrow limits to the understanding, and ventured out beyond it on the wings of the ideas, in the empty space of the pure understanding. He did not observe that with all his efforts he made no advance—meeting no resistance that might, as it were, serve as a support upon which he could take a stand, to which he could apply his powers, and so set his understanding in motion. It is, indeed, the common fate of human reason to complete its speculative structures as speedily as may be, and only afterwards to enquire whether the foundations are reliable. All sorts of excuses will then be appealed to, in order to reassure us of their solidity, or rather indeed to enable us to dispense altogether with so late and so dangerous an enquiry. But what keeps us, during the actual building, free from all apprehension and suspicion, and flatters us with a seeming thoroughness, is this other circumstance, namely, that a great, perhaps the greatest, part of the business of our reason consists in analysis of the concepts which we already have of objects. This analysis supplies us with a considerable body of knowledge, which, while nothing but explanation or elucidation of what has already been thought in our concepts, though in a confused manner, is yet prized as being, at least as regards its form, new insight. But so far as the matter or content is concerned, there has been no extension of our previously possessed concepts, but only an analysis of them. Since this procedure yields real knowledge *a priori*, which progresses in an assured and useful fashion, reason is so far misled as surreptitiously to introduce, without itself being aware of so doing, assertions of an entirely different order, in which it attaches to given concepts others completely foreign to them, and moreover attaches them *a priori*. And yet it is not known how reason can be in position to do this. Such a question is never so much as thought of. I shall therefore at once proceed to deal with the difference between these two kinds of knowledge.

IV. The distinction between analytic and synthetic judgments

In all judgments in which the relation of a subject to the predicate is thought (I take into consideration affirmative judgments only, the subsequent application to negative judgments being easily made), this relation is possible in two different ways. Either the predicate B belongs to the subject A, as something which is (covertly) contained in this concept A; or B lies outside the concept A, although it does indeed stand in connection with it. In the one case I entitle the judgment analytic, in the other synthetic. Analytic judgments (affirmative) are therefore those in which the connection of the predicate with the subject is thought through identity; those in which this connection is thought without identity should be entitled synthetic. The former, as adding nothing through the predicate to the concept of the subject, but merely breaking it up into those constituent concepts that have all along been thought in it, although confusedly, can also be entitled explicative. The latter, on the other hand, add to the concept of the subject a predicate which has not been in any wise thought in it, and which no analysis could possibly extract from it; and they may therefore be entitled ampliative. If I say, for instance, "All bodies are extended," this is an analytic judgment. For I do not require to go beyond the concept which I connect with "body" in order to find extension as bound up with it. To meet with this predicate, I have merely to analyse the concept, that is, to become conscious to myself of the manifold which I always think in that concept. The judgment is therefore analytic. But when I say, "All bodies are heavy," the predicate is something quite different from anything that I think in the mere concept of body in general; and the addition of such a predicate therefore yields a synthetic judgment.

Judgments of experience, as such, are one and all synthetic. For it would be absurd to found an analytic judgment on experience. Since, in framing the judgment, I must not go outside my concept, there is no need to appeal to the testimony of experience in its support. That a body is extended is a proposition that holds *a priori* and is not empirical. For, before appealing to experience, I have already in the concept of body all the conditions required for my judgment. I have only to extract from it, in accordance with the principle of contradiction, the required predicate, and in so doing can at the same time become conscious of the necessity of the judgment—and that is what experience could never have taught me. On the other hand, though I do not include in the concept of a body in general the predicate "weight," none the less this concept indicates an object of experience through one of its parts, and I can add to that part other parts of this same experience, as in this way belonging together with the concept. From the start I can apprehend the concept of body analytically through the characters of extension, impenetrability, figure, etc., all of which are thought in the concept. Now, however, looking back on the experience from which I have derived this concept of body, and finding weight to be invariably connected with the above characters, I attach it as a predicate to the concept; and in doing so I attach it synthetically, and am therefore extending my knowledge. The possibility of the synthesis of the predicate "weight" with the concept of "body" thus rests upon experience. While the one concept is not contained in the other, they yet belong to one another, though only contingently, as parts of a whole, namely, of an experience which is itself a synthetic combination of intuitions.

But in *a priori* synthetic judgments this help is entirely lacking. [I do not here have the advantage of looking around in the field of experience.] Upon what, then, am I to rely, when I seek to go beyond the concept A, and to know that another concept B is connected with it? Through what is the synthesis made possible? Let us take the proposition, "Everything which happens has its cause." In the concept of "something which happens," I do indeed think an existence which is preceded by a time, etc., and from this concept analytic judgments may be obtained. But the concept of a "cause" lies entirely outside the other concept, and signifies something different from "that which happens," and is not therefore in any way contained in this latter representation. How come I then to predicate of that which happens something quite different, and to apprehend that the concept of cause, though not contained in it, yet belongs, and indeed necessarily belongs, to it? What is here the unknown = X which gives support to the understanding when it believes that it can discover outside the concept A a predicate B foreign to this concept, which it yet at the same time considers to be connected with it? It cannot be experience, because the suggested principle has connected the second representation with the first, not only with greater universality, but also with the character of necessity, and therefore completely *a priori* and on the basis of mere concepts. Upon such synthetic, that is, ampliative principles, all our *a priori* speculative knowledge must ultimately rest; analytic judgments are very important, and indeed necessary, but only for obtaining that clearness in the concepts which is requisite for such a sure and wide synthesis as will lead to a genuinely new addition to all previous knowledge.

V. In all theoretical sciences of reason synthetic a priori *judgments are contained as principles*

1. *All mathematical judgments, without exception, are synthetic.* This fact, though incontestably certain and in its consequences very important, has hitherto escaped the notice of those who are engaged in the analysis of human reason, and is, indeed, directly opposed to all their conjectures. For as it was found that all mathematical inferences proceed in accordance with the principle of contradiction (which the nature of all apodeictic certainty requires), it was supposed that the fundamental propositions of the science can themselves be known to be true[2] through that principle. This is an erroneous view. For though a synthetic proposition can indeed be discerned in accordance with the principle of contradiction, this can only be if another synthetic proposition is presupposed, and if it can then be apprehended as following from this other proposition; it can never be so discerned in and by itself.

First of all, it has to be noted that mathematical propositions, strictly so called, are always judgments *a priori*, not empirical; because they carry with them necessity, which cannot be derived from experience. If this be demurred to, I am willing to limit my statement to *pure* mathematics, the very concept of which implies that it does not contain empirical, but only pure *a priori* knowledge.

We might, indeed, at first suppose that the proposition 7 + 5 = 12 is a merely analytic proposition, and follows by the principle of contradiction from the concept of a sum of 7 and 5. But if we look more closely we find that the concept of the sum of 7 and 5 contains nothing save the union of the two numbers into one, and in this no thought is being taken as to what that single number may be which combines both. The concept of 12 is by no means already thought in merely thinking this union of 7 and 5; and I may analyse my concept of such a possible sum as long as I please, still I shall never find the 12 in it. We have to go outside these concepts, and call in the aid of the intuition which corresponds to one of them, our five fingers, for instance, or, as Segner does in his *Arithmetic*, five points, adding to the concept of 7, unit by unit, the five given in intuition. For starting with the number 7, and for the concept of 5 calling in the aid of the fingers of my hand as intuition, I now add one by one to the number 7 the units which I previously took together to form the number 5, and with the aid of that figure [the hand] see the number 12 come into being. That 5 should be added to 7, I have indeed already thought in the concept of a sum = 7 + 5, but not that this sum is equivalent to the number 12. Arithmetical propositions are therefore always synthetic. This is still more evident if we take larger numbers. For it is then obvious that, however we might turn and twist our concepts, we could never, by the mere analysis of them, and without the aid of intuition, discover what [the number is that] is the sum.

Just as little is any fundamental proposition of pure geometry analytic. That the straight line between two points is the shortest, is a synthetic proposition. For my concept of *straight* contains nothing of quantity, but only of quality. The concept of the shortest is wholly an addition, and cannot be derived, through any process of analysis, from the concept of the straight line. Intuition, therefore, must here be called in; only by its aid is the synthesis possible. What here causes us commonly to believe that the predicate of such apodeictic judgments is already contained in our concept, and that the judgment is therefore analytic, is merely the ambiguous character of the terms used. We are required to join in thought a certain predicate to a given concept, and this necessity is inherent in the concepts themselves. But the question is not what we *ought* to join in thought to the given concept, but what we *actually* think in it, even if only obscurely; and it is then manifest that, while the predicate is indeed attached necessarily to the concept, it is so in virtue of an intuition which must be added to the concept, not as thought in the concept itself.

Some few fundamental propositions, presupposed by the geometrician, are, indeed, really analytic, and rest on the principle of contradiction. But, as identical propositions, they serve only as links in the chain of method and not as principles; for instance, $a = a$; the whole is equal to itself; or $(a + b) > a$, that is, the whole is greater than its part. And even these propositions, though they are valid according to pure concepts, are only admitted in mathematics because they can be exhibited in intuition.

2. *Natural science (physics) contains* a priori *synthetic judgments as principles*. I need cite only two such judgments: that in all changes of the material world the quantity of matter remains unchanged; and that in all communication of motion, action and reaction must always be equal. Both propositions, it is evident, are not only necessary, and therefore in their origin *a priori*, but also synthetic. For in the concept of matter I do not think its permanence, but only its presence in the space which it occupies. I go outside and beyond the concept of

matter, joining to it *a priori* in thought something which I have not thought *in* it. The proposition is not, therefore, analytic, but synthetic, and yet is thought *a priori*; and so likewise are the other propositions of the pure part of natural science.

3. *Metaphysics*, even if we look upon it as having hitherto failed in all its endeavours, is yet, owing to the nature of human reason, a quite indispensable science, and *ought to contain* a priori *synthetic knowledge*. For its business is not merely to analyse concepts which we make for ourselves *a priori* of things, and thereby to clarify them analytically, but to extend our *a priori* knowledge. And for this purpose we must employ principles which add to the given concept something that was not contained in it, and through *a priori* synthetic judgments venture out so far that experience is quite unable to follow us, as, for instance, in the proposition, that the world must have a first beginning, and such like. Thus metaphysics consists, at least *in intention*, entirely of *a priori* synthetic propositions. . . .

Space

. . .

§3 The transcendental exposition of the concept of space

I understand by a transcendental exposition the explanation of a concept, as a principle from which the possibility of other *a priori* synthetic knowledge can be understood. For this purpose it is required (1) that such knowledge does really flow from the given concept, (2) that this knowledge is possible only on the assumption of a given mode of explaining the concept.

Geometry is a science which determines the properties of space synthetically, and yet *a priori*. What, then, must be our representation of space, in order that such knowledge of it may be possible? It must in its origin be intuition; for from a mere concept no propositions can be obtained which go beyond the concept—as happens in geometry (Introduction, V). Further, this intuition must be *a priori*, that is, it must be found in us prior to any perception of an object, and must therefore be pure, not empirical, intuition. For geometrical propositions are one and all apodeictic, that is, are bound up with the consciousness of their necessity; for instance, that space has only three dimensions. Such propositions cannot be empirical or, in other words, judgments of experience, nor can they be derived from any such judgments (Introduction, II).

How, then, can there exist in the mind an outer intuition which precedes the objects themselves, and in which the concept of these objects can be determined *a priori*? Manifestly, not otherwise than in so far as the intuition has its seat in the subject only, as the formal character of the subject, in virtue of which, in being affected by objects, it obtains *immediate representation*, that is, *intuition*, of them; and only in so far, therefore, as it is merely the form of outer *sense* in general.

Our explanation is thus the only explanation that makes intelligible the *possibility* of geometry, as a body of *a priori* synthetic knowledge. Any mode of explanation which fails to do this, although it may otherwise seem to be somewhat similar, can by this criterion[1] be distinguished from it with the greatest certainty.

Conclusions from the above concepts

(*a*) Space does not represent any property of things in themselves, nor does it represent them in their relation to one another. That is to say, space does not represent any determination that attaches to the objects themselves, and which remains even when abstraction has been made of all the subjective conditions of intuition. For no determinations, whether absolute or relative, can be intuited prior to the existence of the things to which they belong, and none, therefore, can be intuited *a priori*.

(*b*) Space is nothing but the form of all appearances of outer sense. It is the subjective condition of sensibility, under which alone outer intuition is possible for us. Since, then, the receptivity of the subject, its capacity to be affected by objects, must necessarily precede all intuitions of these objects, it can readily be understood how the form of all appearances can be given prior to all actual perceptions, and so exist in the mind *a priori*, and how, as a pure intuition, in which all objects must be determined, it can contain, prior to all experience, principles which determine the relations of these objects.

It is, therefore, solely from the human standpoint that we can speak of space, of extended things, etc. If we depart from the subjective condition under which alone we can have outer intuition, namely, liability to be affected by objects, the representation of space stands for nothing whatsoever. This predicate can be ascribed to things only in so far as they appear to us, that is, only to objects of sensibility. The constant form of this receptivity, which we term sensibility, is a necessary condition of all the relations in which objects can be intuited as outside us; and if we abstract from these objects, it is a pure intuition, and bears the name of space. Since we cannot treat the special conditions of sensibility as conditions of the possibility of things, but only of their appearances, we can indeed say that space comprehends all things that appear to us as external, but not all things in themselves, by whatever subject they are intuited, or whether they be intuited or not. For we cannot judge in regard to the intuitions of other thinking beings, whether they are bound by the same conditions as those which limit our intuition and which for us are universally valid. If we add to the concept of the subject of a judgment the limitation under which the judgment is made, the judgment is then unconditionally valid. The proposition, that all things are side by side in space, is valid under the limitation that these things are viewed as objects of our sensible intuition. If, now, I add the condition to the concept, and say that all things, as outer appearances, are side by side in space, the rule is valid universally and without limitation. Our exposition therefore establishes the *reality*, that is, the objective validity, of space in respect of whatever can be presented to us outwardly as object, but also at the same time the *ideality* of space in respect of things when they are considered in themselves through reason, that is, without regard to the constitution of our sensibility. We assert, then, the *empirical reality* of space, as regards all possible outer experience; and yet at the same time we assert its *transcendental ideality*—in other words, that it is nothing at all, immediately we withdraw the above condition, namely, its limitation to possible experience, and so look upon it as something that underlies things in themselves.

With the sole exception of space there is no subjective representation, referring to something *outer*, which could be entitled [at once] objective [and] *a priori*. For there is no other subjective representation from which we can derive *a priori* synthetic propositions, as we can from intuition in space (§ 3). Strictly speaking, therefore, these other representations have no ideality, although they agree with the representation of space in this respect, that they belong merely to the subjective constitution of our manner of sensibility, for instance, of sight, hearing, touch, as in the case of the sensations of colours, sounds, and heat, which, since they are mere sensations and not intuitions, do not of themselves yield knowledge of any object, least of all any *a priori* knowledge.

The above remark is intended only to guard anyone from supposing that the ideality of space as here asserted can be illustrated by examples so altogether insufficient as colours, taste, etc. For these cannot rightly be regarded as properties of things, but only as changes in the subject, changes which may, indeed, be different for different men. In such examples as these, that which originally is itself only appearance, for instance, a rose, is being treated by the empirical understanding as a thing in itself, which, nevertheless, in respect of its colour, can appear differently to every observer. The transcendental concept of appearances in space, on the other hand, is a critical reminder that nothing intuited in space is a thing in itself, that space is not a form inhering in things in themselves as their intrinsic property, that objects in themselves are quite unknown to us, and that what we call outer objects are nothing but mere representations of our sensibility, the form of which is space. The true correlate of sensibility, the thing in itself, is not known, and cannot be known, through these representations; and in experience no question is ever asked in regard to it.

QUESTIONS

1. What is meant by an “analytic” truth?
2. What is “a priori” knowledge?
3. Give three examples of what Kant would consider to be synthetic, a priori knowledge.
4. According to Kant, what is space?
5. According to Kant, about what sorts of things can we know that they are all side by side in space?

Bertrand Russell, *The Problems of Philosophy*

Chapter VIII How *a priori* knowledge is possible

Immanuel Kant is generally regarded as the greatest of the modern philosophers. Though he lived through the Seven Years War and the French Revolution, he never interrupted his teaching of philosophy at Königsberg in East Prussia. His most distinctive contribution was the invention of what he called the "critical" philosophy, which, assuming as a datum that there is knowledge of various kinds, inquired how such knowledge comes to be possible, and deduced, from the answer to this inquiry, many metaphysical results as to the nature of the world. Whether these results were valid may well be doubted. But Kant undoubtedly deserves credit for two things: first, for having perceived that we have *a priori* knowledge which is not purely "analytic," i.e. such that the opposite would be self-contradictory; and secondly, for having made evident the philosophical importance of the theory of knowledge.

Before the time of Kant, it was generally held that whatever knowledge was *a priori* must be "analytic." What this word means will be best illustrated by examples. If I say, "A bald man is a man," "A plane figure is a figure," "A bad poet is a poet," I make a purely analytic judgement: the subject spoken about is given as having at least two properties, of which one is singled out to be asserted of it. Such propositions as the above are trivial, and would never be enunciated in real life except by an orator preparing the way for a piece of sophistry. They are called "analytic" because the predicate is obtained by merely analysing the subject. Before the time of Kant it was thought that all judgements of which we could be certain *a priori* were of this kind: that in all of them there was a predicate which was only part of the subject of which it was asserted. If this were so, we should be involved in a definite contradiction if we attempted to deny anything that could be known *a priori*. "A bald man is not bald" would assert and deny baldness of the same man, and would therefore contradict itself. Thus according to the philosophers before Kant, the law of contradiction, which asserts that nothing can at the same time have and not have a certain property, sufficed to establish the truth of all *a priori* knowledge.

Hume (1711–76), who preceded Kant, accepting the usual view as to what makes knowledge *a priori*, discovered that, in many cases which had previously

Bertrand Russell, *The Problems of Philosophy* (Oxford: Oxford University Press, 1959).

been supposed analytic, and notably in the case of cause and effect, the connexion was really synthetic. Before Hume, rationalists at least had supposed that the effect could be logically deduced from the cause, if only we had sufficient knowledge. Hume argued—correctly, as would now be generally admitted—that this could not be done. Hence he inferred the far more doubtful proposition that nothing could be known *a priori* about the connexion of cause and effect. Kant, who had been educated in the rationalist tradition, was much perturbed by Hume's scepticism, and endeavoured to find an answer to it. He perceived that not only the connexion of cause and effect, but all the propositions of arithmetic and geometry, are "synthetic," i.e. not analytic: in all these propositions, no analysis of the subject will reveal the predicate. His stock instance was the proposition 7 + 5 = 12. He pointed out, quite truly, that 7 and 5 have to be put together to give 12: the idea of 12 is not *contained* in them, nor even in the idea of adding them together. Thus he was led to the conclusion that all pure mathematics, though *a priori*, is synthetic; and this conclusion raised a new problem of which he endeavoured to find the solution.

The question which Kant put at the beginning of his philosophy, namely "How is pure mathematics possible?" is an interesting and difficult one, to which every philosophy which is not purely sceptical must find some answer. The answer of the pure empiricists, that our mathematical knowledge is derived by induction from particular instances, we have already seen to be inadequate, for two reasons: first, that the validity of the inductive principle itself cannot be proved by induction; secondly, that the general propositions of mathematics, such as "two and two always make four," can obviously be known with certainty by consideration of a single instance, and gain nothing by enumeration of other cases in which they have been found to be true. Thus our knowledge of the general propositions of mathematics (and the same applies to logic) must be accounted for otherwise than our (merely probable) knowledge of empirical generalizations such as "all men are mortal."

The problem arises through the fact that such knowledge is general, whereas all experience is particular. It seems strange that we should apparently be able to know some truths in advance about particular things of which we have as yet no experience; but it cannot easily be doubted that logic and arithmetic will apply to such things. We do not know who will be the inhabitants of London a hundred years hence; but we know that any two of them and any other two of them will make four of them. This apparent power of anticipating facts about things of which we have no experience is certainly surprising. Kant's solution of the problem, though not valid in my opinion, is interesting. It is, however, very difficult, and is differently understood by different philosophers. We can, therefore, only give the merest outline of it, and even that will be thought misleading by many exponents of Kant's system.

What Kant maintained was that in all our experience there are two elements to be distinguished, the one due to the object (i.e. to what we have called the "physical object"), the other due to our own nature. We saw, in discussing matter and sense-data, that the physical object is different from the associated sense-data, and that the sense-data are to be regarded as resulting from an interaction between the physical object and ourselves. So far, we are in agreement with Kant. But what is distinctive of Kant is the way in which he apportions the shares of ourselves and the physical object respectively. He considers that the crude material given in sensation—the colour, hardness, etc.—is due to the object, and that what we supply is the arrangement in space and time, and all the relations between sense-data which result from comparison or from considering one as the cause of the other or in any other way. His chief reason in favour of this view is that we seem to have *a priori* knowledge as to space and time and causality and comparison, but not as to the actual crude material of sensation. We can be sure, he says, that anything we shall ever experience must show the characteristics affirmed of it in our *a priori* knowledge, because these characteristics are due to our own nature, and therefore nothing can ever come into our experience without acquiring these characteristics.

The physical object, which he calls the "thing in itself,"[1] he regards as essentially unknowable; what can be known is the object as we have it in experience, which he calls the "phenomenon." The phenomenon, being a joint product of us and the thing in itself, is sure to have those characteristics which are due to us, and is therefore sure to conform to our *a priori* knowledge. Hence this knowledge, though true of all actual and possible experience, must not be supposed to apply outside experience. Thus in spite of the existence of *a priori* knowledge, we cannot know anything about the thing in itself or about what is not an actual or possible object of experience. In this way he tries to reconcile and harmonize the contentions of the rationalists with the arguments of the empiricists.

Apart from minor grounds on which Kant's philosophy may be criticized, there is one main objection which seems fatal to any attempt to deal with the problem of *a priori* knowledge by his method. The thing to be accounted for is our certainty that the facts must always conform to logic and arithmetic. To say that logic and arithmetic are contributed by us does not account for this. Our nature is as much a fact of the existing world as anything, and there can be no certainty that it will remain constant. It might happen, if Kant is right, that to-morrow our nature would so change as to make two and two become five. This possibility seems never to have occurred to him, yet it is one which utterly destroys the certainty and universality which he is anxious to vindicate for arithmetical propositions. It is true that this possibility, formally, is inconsistent with the Kantian view that time itself is a form imposed by the subject upon phenomena, so that our real Self is not in time and has no to-morrow. But he will still have to suppose that the time-order of phenomena is determined by characteristics of what is behind phenomena, and this suffices for the substance of our argument.

Reflection, moreover, seems to make it clear that, if there is any truth in our arithmetical beliefs, they must apply to things equally whether we think of them or not. Two physical objects and two other physical objects must make four physical objects, even if physical objects cannot be experienced. To assert this is certainly within the scope of what we mean when we state that two and two are four. Its truth is just as indubitable as the truth of the assertion that two phenomena and two other phenomena make four phenomena. Thus Kant's solution unduly limits the scope of *a priori* propositions, in addition to failing in the attempt at explaining their certainty.

Apart from the special doctrines advocated by Kant, it is very common among philosophers to regard what is *a priori* as in some sense mental, as concerned rather with the way we must think than with any fact of the outer world. We noted in the preceding chapter the three principles commonly called "laws of thought." The view which led to their being so named is a natural one, but there are strong reasons for thinking that it is erroneous. Let us take as an illustration the law of contradiction. This is commonly stated in the form "Nothing can both be and not be," which is intended to express the fact that nothing can at once have and not have a given quality. Thus, for example, if a tree is a beech it cannot also be not a beech; if my table is rectangular it cannot also be not rectangular, and so on.

Now what makes it natural to call this principle a law of *thought* is that it is by thought rather than by outward observation that we persuade ourselves of its necessary truth. When we have seen that a tree is a beech, we do not need to look again in order to ascertain whether it is also not a beech; thought alone makes us know that this is impossible. But the conclusion that the law of contradiction is a law of *thought* is nevertheless erroneous. What we believe, when we believe the law of contradiction, is not that the mind is so made that it must believe the law of contradiction. *This* belief is a subsequent result of psychological reflection, which presupposes the belief in the law of contradiction. The belief in the law of contradiction is a belief about things, not only about thoughts. It is not, e.g., the belief that if we *think* a certain tree is a beech, we cannot at the same time *think* that it is not a beech; it is the belief that if the tree *is* a beech, it cannot at the same time *be* not a beech. Thus the law of contradiction is about things, and not merely about thoughts; and although belief in the law of contradiction is a thought, the law of contradiction itself is not a thought, but a fact concerning the things in the world. If this, which we believe when we believe the law of contradiction, were not true of the things in the world, the fact that we were compelled to *think* it true would not save the law of contradiction from being false; and this shows that the law is not a law of *thought*.

A similar argument applies to any other *a priori* judgement. When we judge that two and two are four, we are not making a judgement about our thoughts, but about all actual or possible couples. The fact that our minds are so constituted as to believe that two and two are four, though it is true, is emphatically not what we assert when we assert that two and two are four. And no fact about the constitution of our minds could make it *true* that two and two are four. Thus our *a priori* knowledge, if it is not erroneous, is not merely knowledge about the constitution of our minds, but is applicable to whatever the world may contain, both what is mental and what is non-mental.

The fact seems to be that all our *a priori* knowledge is concerned with entities which do not, properly speaking, *exist*, either in the mental or in the physical world. These entities are such as can be named by parts of speech which are not substantives; they are such entities as qualities and relations. Suppose, for instance, that I am in my room. I exist, and my room exists; but does "in" exist? Yet obviously the word 'in' has a meaning; it denotes a relation which holds between me and my room. This relation is something, although we cannot say that it exists *in the same sense* in which I and my room exist. The relation "in" is something which we can think about and understand, for, if we could not understand it, we could not understand the sentence "I am in my room." Many philosophers, following Kant, have maintained that relations are the work of the mind, that things in themselves have no relations, but that the mind brings them together in one act of thought and thus produces the relations which it judges them to have.

This view, however, seems open to objections similar to those which we urged before against Kant. It seems plain that it is not thought which produces the truth of the proposition "I am in my room." It may be true that an earwig is in my room, even if neither I nor the earwig nor any one else is aware of this truth; for this truth concerns only the earwig and the room, and does not depend upon anything else. Thus relations, as we shall see more fully in the next chapter, must be placed in a world which is neither mental nor physical. This world is of great importance to philosophy, and in particular to the problems of *a priori* knowledge. In the next chapter we shall proceed to develop its nature and its bearing upon the questions with which we have been dealing.

Chapter IX The world of universals

At the end of the preceding chapter we saw that such entities as relations appear to have a being which is in some way different from that of physical objects, and also different from that of minds and from that of sense-data. In the present chapter we have to consider what is the nature of this kind of being, and also what objects there are that have this kind of being. We will begin with the latter question.

The problem with which we are now concerned is a very old one, since it was brought into philosophy by Plato. Plato's "theory of ideas" is an attempt to solve this very problem, and in my opinion it is one of the most successful attempts hitherto made. The theory to be advocated in what follows is largely Plato's, with merely such modifications as time has shown to be necessary.

The way the problem arose for Plato was more or less as follows. Let us consider, say, such a notion as *justice*. If we ask ourselves what justice is, it is natural to proceed by considering this, that, and the other just act, with a view to discovering what they have in common. They must all, in some sense, partake of a common nature, which will be found in whatever is just and in nothing else. This common nature, in virtue of which they are all just, will be justice itself, the pure essence the admixture of which with facts of ordinary life produces the multiplicity of just acts. Similarly with any other word which may be applicable to common facts, such as 'whiteness' for example. The word will be applicable to a number of particular things because they all participate in a common nature or essence. This pure essence is what Plato calls an "idea" or "form." (It must not be supposed that "ideas," in his sense, exist in minds, though they may be apprehended by minds.) The "idea" *justice* is not identical with anything that is just: it is something other than particular things, which particular things partake of. Not being particular, it cannot itself exist in the world of sense. Moreover it is not fleeting or changeable like the things of sense: it is eternally itself, immutable and indestructible.

Thus Plato is led to a supra-sensible world, more real than the common world of sense, the unchangeable world of ideas, which alone gives to the world of sense whatever pale reflection of reality may belong to it. The truly real world, for Plato, is the world of ideas; for whatever we may attempt to say about things in the world of sense, we can only succeed in saying that they participate in such and such ideas, which, therefore, constitute all their character. Hence it is easy to pass on into a mysticism. We may hope, in a mystic illumination, to *see* the ideas as we see objects of sense; and we may imagine that the ideas exist in heaven. These mystical developments are very natural, but the basis of the theory is in logic, and it is as based in logic that we have to consider it.

The word "idea" has acquired, in the course of time, many associations which are quite misleading when applied to Plato's "ideas." We shall therefore use the word "universal" instead of the word "idea," to describe what Plato meant. The essence of the sort of entity that Plato meant is that it is opposed to the particular things that are given in sensation. We speak of whatever is given in sensation, or is of the same nature as things given in sensation, as a *particular*; by opposition to this, a *universal* will be anything which may be shared by many particulars, and has those characteristics which, as we saw, distinguish justice and whiteness from just acts and white things.

When we examine common words, we find that, broadly speaking, proper names stand for particulars, while other substantives, adjectives, prepositions, and verbs stand for universals. Pronouns stand for particulars, but are ambiguous: it is only by the context or the circumstances that we know what particulars they stand for. The word "now" stands for a particular, namely the present moment; but like pronouns, it stands for an ambiguous particular, because the present is always changing.

It will be seen that no sentence can be made up without at least one word which denotes a universal. The nearest approach would be some such statement as "I like this." But even here the word "like" denotes a universal, for I may like other things, and other people may like things. Thus all truths involve universals, and all knowledge of truths involves acquaintance with universals.

Seeing that nearly all the words to be found in the dictionary stand for universals, it is strange that hardly anybody except students of philosophy ever realizes that there are such entities as universals. We do not naturally dwell upon those words in a sentence which do not stand for particulars; and if we are forced to dwell upon a word which stands for a universal, we naturally think of it as standing for some one of the particulars that come under the universal. When, for example, we hear the sentence, "Charles I's head was cut off," we may naturally enough think of Charles I, of Charles I's head, and of the operation of cutting off *his* head, which are all particulars; but we do not naturally dwell upon what is meant by the word "head" or the word "cut," which is a universal. We feel such words to be incomplete and insubstantial; they seem to demand a context before anything can be done with them. Hence we succeed in avoiding all notice of universals as such, until the study of philosophy forces them upon our attention.

Even among philosophers, we may say, broadly, that only those universals which are named by adjectives or substantives have been much or often recognized, while those named by verbs and prepositions have been usually overlooked. This omission has had a very great effect upon philosophy; it is hardly too much to say that most metaphysics, since Spinoza, has been largely determined by it. The way this has occurred is, in outline, as follows: Speaking generally, adjectives and common nouns express qualities or properties of single things, whereas prepositions and verbs tend to express relations between two or more things. Thus the neglect of prepositions and verbs led to the belief that every proposition can be regarded as attributing a property to a single thing, rather than as expressing a relation between two or more things. Hence it was supposed that, ultimately, there can be no such entities as relations between things. Hence either there can be only one thing in the universe, or, if there are many things, they cannot possibly interact in any way, since any interaction would be a relation, and relations are impossible.

The first of these views, advocated by Spinoza and held in our own day by Bradley and many other philosophers, is called *monism*; the second, advocated by Leibniz but not very common nowadays, is called *monadism*, because each of the isolated things is called a *monad*. Both these opposing philosophies, interesting as they are, result, in my opinion, from an undue attention to one sort of universals, namely the sort represented by adjectives and substantives rather than by verbs and prepositions.

As a matter of fact, if any one were anxious to deny altogether that there are such things as universals, we should find that we cannot strictly prove that there are such entities as *qualities*, i.e. the universals represented by adjectives and substantives, whereas we can prove that there must be *relations*, i.e. the sort of universals generally represented by verbs and prepositions. Let us take in illustration the universal *whiteness*. If we believe that there is such a universal, we shall say that things are white because they have the quality of whiteness. This view, however, was strenuously denied by Berkeley and Hume, who have been followed in this by later empiricists. The form which their denial took was to deny that there are such things as "abstract ideas." When we want to think of whiteness, they said, we form an image of some particular white thing, and reason concerning this particular, taking care not to deduce anything concerning it which we cannot see to be equally true of any other white thing. As an account of our actual mental processes, this is no doubt largely true. In geometry, for example, when we wish to prove something about all triangles, we draw a particular triangle and reason about it, taking care not to use any characteristic which it does not share with other triangles. The beginner, in order to avoid error, often finds it useful to draw several triangles, as unlike each other as possible, in order to make sure that his reasoning is equally applicable to all of them. But a difficulty emerges as soon as we ask ourselves how we know that a thing is white or a triangle. If we wish to avoid the universals *whiteness* and *triangularity*, we shall choose some particular patch of white or some particular triangle, and say that anything is white or a triangle if it has the right sort of resemblance to our chosen particular. But then the resemblance required will have to be a universal. Since there are many white things, the resemblance must hold between many pairs of particular white things; and this is the characteristic of a universal. It will be useless to say that there is a different resemblance for each pair, for then we shall have to say that these resemblances resemble each other, and thus at last we shall be forced to admit resemblance as a universal. The relation of resemblance, therefore, must be a true universal. And having been forced to admit this universal, we find that it is no longer worth while to invent difficult and unplausible theories to avoid the admission of such universals as whiteness and triangularity.

Berkeley and Hume failed to perceive this refutation of their rejection of "abstract ideas," because, like their adversaries, they only thought of *qualities*, and altogether ignored *relations* as universals. We have therefore here another respect in which the rationalists appear to have been in the right as against the empiricists, although, owing to the neglect or denial of relations, the deductions made by rationalists were, if anything, more apt to be mistaken than those made by empiricists.

Having now seen that there must be such entities as universals, the next point to be proved is that their being is not merely mental. By this is meant that whatever being belongs to them is independent of their being thought of or in any way apprehended by minds. We have already touched on this subject at the end of the preceding chapter, but we must now consider more fully what sort of being it is that belongs to universals.

Consider such a proposition as "Edinburgh is north of London." Here we have a relation between two places, and it seems plain that the relation subsists independently of our knowledge of it. When we come to know that Edinburgh is north of London, we come to know something which has to do only with Edinburgh and London: we do not cause the truth of the proposition by coming to know it, on the contrary we merely apprehend a fact which was there before we knew it. The part of the earth's surface where Edinburgh stands would be north of the part where London stands, even if there were no human being to know about north and south, and even if there were no minds at all in the universe. This is, of course, denied by many philosophers, either for Berkeley's reasons or for Kant's. But we have already considered these reasons, and decided that they are inadequate. We may therefore now assume it to be true that nothing mental is presupposed in the fact that Edinburgh is north of London. But this fact involves the relation "north of," which is a universal; and it would be impossible for the whole fact to involve nothing mental if the relation "north of," which is a constituent part of the fact, did involve anything mental. Hence we must admit that the relation, like the terms it relates, is not dependent upon thought, but belongs to the independent world which thought apprehends but does not create.

This conclusion, however, is met by the difficulty that the relation "north of" does not seem to *exist* in the same sense in which Edinburgh and London exist. If we ask "Where and when does this relation exist?" the answer must be "Nowhere and nowhen." There is no place or time where we can find the relation "north of." It does not exist in Edinburgh any more than in London, for it relates the two and is neutral as between them. Nor can we say that it exists at any particular time. Now everything that can be apprehended by the senses or by introspection exists at some particular time. Hence the relation "north of" is radically different from such things. It is neither in space nor in time, neither material nor mental; yet it is something.

It is largely the very peculiar kind of being that belongs to universals which has led many people to suppose that they are really mental. We can think *of* a universal, and our thinking then exists in a perfectly ordinary sense, like any other mental act. Suppose, for example, that we are thinking of whiteness. Then *in one sense* it may be said that whiteness is "in our mind." We have here the same ambiguity as we noted in discussing Berkeley in Chapter IV. In the strict sense, it is not whiteness that is in our mind, but the act of thinking of whiteness. The connected ambiguity in the word "idea," which we noted at the same time, also causes confusion here. In one sense of this word, namely the sense in which it denotes the *object* of an act of thought, whiteness is an "idea." Hence, if the ambiguity is not guarded against, we may come to think that whiteness is an "idea" in the other sense, i.e. an act of thought; and thus we come to think that whiteness is mental. But in so thinking, we rob it of its essential quality of universality. One man's act of thought is necessarily a different thing from another man's; one man's act of thought at one time is necessarily a different thing from the same man's act of thought at another time. Hence, if whiteness were the thought as opposed to its object, no two different men could think of it, and no one man could think of it twice. That which many different thoughts of whiteness have in common is their *object*, and this object is different from all of them. Thus universals are not thoughts, though when known they are the objects of thoughts.

We shall find it convenient only to speak of things *existing* when they are in time, that is to say, when we can point to some time *at* which they exist (not excluding the possibility of their existing at all times). Thus thoughts and feelings, minds and physical objects *exist*. But universals do not exist in this sense; we shall say that they *subsist* or *have being*, where "being" is opposed to "existence" as being timeless. The world of universals, therefore, may also be described as the world of being. The world of being is unchangeable, rigid, exact, delightful to the mathematician, the logician, the builder of metaphysical systems, and all who love perfection more than life. The world of existence is fleeting, vague, without sharp boundaries, without any clear plan or arrangement, but it contains all thoughts and feelings, all the data of sense, and all physical objects, everything that can do either good or harm, everything that makes any difference to the value of life and the world. According to our temperaments, we shall prefer the contemplation of the one or of the other. The one we do not prefer will probably seem to us a pale shadow of the one we prefer, and hardly worthy to be regarded as in any sense real. But the truth is that both have the same claim on our impartial attention, both are real, and both are important to the metaphysician. Indeed no sooner have we distinguished the two worlds than it becomes necessary to consider their relations.

But first of all we must examine our knowledge of universals. This consideration will occupy us in the following chapter, where we shall find that it solves the problem of *a priori* knowledge, from which we were first led to consider universals.

Chapter X On our knowledge of universals

In regard to one man's knowledge at a given time, universals, like particulars, may be divided into those known by acquaintance, those known only by description, and those not known either by acquaintance or by description.

Let us consider first the knowledge of universals by acquaintance. It is obvious, to begin with, that we are acquainted with such universals as white, red, black, sweet, sour, loud, hard, etc., i.e. with qualities which are exemplified in sense-data. When we see a white patch, we are acquainted, in the first instance, with the particular patch; but by seeing many white patches, we easily learn to abstract the whiteness which they all have in common, and in learning to do this we are learning to be acquainted with whiteness. A similar process will make us acquainted with any other universal of the same sort. Universals of this sort may be called "sensible qualities." They can be apprehended with less effort of abstraction than any others, and they seem less removed from particulars than other universals are.

We come next to relations. The easiest relations to apprehend are those which hold between the different parts of a single complex sense-datum. For example, I can see at a glance the whole of the page on which I am writing; thus the whole page is included in one sense-datum. But I perceive that some parts of the page are to the left of other parts, and some parts are above other parts. The process of abstraction in this case seems to proceed somewhat as follows: I see successively a number of sense-data in which one part is to the left of another; I perceive, as in the case of different white patches, that all these sense-data have something in common, and by abstraction I find that what they have in common is a certain relation between their parts, namely the relation which I call "being to the left of." In this way I become acquainted with the universal relation.

In like manner I become aware of the relation of before and after in time. Suppose I hear a chime of bells: when the last bell of the chime sounds, I can retain the whole chime before my mind, and I can perceive that the earlier bells came before the later ones. Also in memory I perceive that what I am remembering came before the present time. From either of these sources I can abstract the universal relation of before and after, just as I abstracted the universal relation "being to the left off." Thus time-relations, like space-relations, are among those with which we are acquainted.

Another relation with which we become acquainted in much the same way is resemblance. If I see simultaneously two shades of green, I can see that they resemble each other; if I also see a shade of red at the same time, I can see that the two greens have more resemblance to each other than either has to the red. In this way I become acquainted with the universal *resemblance* or *similarity*.

Between universals, as between particulars, there are relations of which we may be immediately aware. We have just seen that we can perceive that the resemblance between two shades of green is greater than the resemblance between a shade of red and a shade of green. Here we are dealing with a relation, namely "greater than," between two relations. Our knowledge of such relations, though it requires more power of abstraction than is required for perceiving the qualities of sense-data, appears to be equally immediate, and (at least in some cases) equally indubitable. Thus there is immediate knowledge concerning universals as well as concerning sense-data.

Returning now to the problem of *a priori* knowledge, which we left unsolved when we began the consideration of universals, we find ourselves in a position to deal with it in a much more satisfactory manner than was possible before. Let us revert to the proposition "two and two are four." It is fairly obvious, in view of what has been said, that this proposition states a relation between the universal "two" and the universal "four." This suggests a proposition which we shall now endeavour to establish: namely, *All* a priori *knowledge deals exclusively with the relations of universals*. This proposition is of great importance, and goes a long way towards solving our previous difficulties concerning *a priori* knowledge.

The only case in which it might seem, at first sight, as if our proposition were untrue, is the case in which an *a priori* proposition states that *all* of one class of particulars belong to some other class, or (what comes to the same thing) that *all* particulars having some one property also have some other. In this case it might seem as though we were dealing with the particulars that have the property rather than with the property. The proposition "two and two are four" is really a case in point, for this may be stated in the form "any two and any other two are four," or "any collection formed of two twos is a collection of four." If we can show that such statements as this really deal only with universals, our proposition may be regarded as proved.

One way of discovering what a proposition deals with is to ask ourselves what words we must understand—in other words, what objects we must be acquainted with—in order to see what the proposition means. As soon as we see what the proposition means, even if we do not yet know whether it is true or false, it is evident that we must have acquaintance with whatever is really dealt with by the proposition. By applying this test, it appears that many propositions which might seem to be concerned with particulars are really concerned only with universals. In the special case of "two and two are four," even when we interpret it as meaning "any collection formed of two twos is a collection of four," it is plain that we can *understand* the proposition, i.e. we can see what it is that it asserts, as soon as we know what is meant by "collection" and "two" and "four." It is quite unnecessary to know all the couples in the world: if it were necessary, obviously we could never understand the proposition, since the couples are infinitely numerous and therefore cannot all be known to us. Thus although our general statement *implies* statements about particular couples, *as soon as we know that there are such particular couples*, yet it does not itself assert or imply that there are such particular couples, and thus fails to make any statement whatever about any actual particular couple. The statement made is about "couple," the universal, and not about this or that couple.

Thus the statement "two and two are four" deals exclusively with universals, and therefore may be known by anybody who is acquainted with the universals concerned and can perceive the relation between them which the statement asserts. It must be taken as a fact, discovered by reflecting upon our knowledge, that we have the power of sometimes perceiving such relations between universals, and therefore of sometimes knowing general *a priori* propositions such as those of arithmetic and logic. The thing that seemed mysterious, when we formerly considered such knowledge, was that it seemed to anticipate and control experience. This, however, we can now see to have been an error. *No* fact concerning anything capable of being experienced can be known independently of experience. We know *a priori* that two things and two other things together make four things, but we do *not* know *a priori* that if Brown and Jones are two, and Robinson and Smith are two, then Brown and Jones and Robinson and Smith are four. The reason is that this proposition cannot be understood at all unless we know that there are such people as Brown and Jones and Robinson and Smith, and this we can only know by experience. Hence, although our general proposition is *a priori*, all its applications to actual particulars involve experience and therefore contain an empirical element. In this way what seemed mysterious in our *a priori* knowledge is seen to have been based upon an error.

It will serve to make the point clearer if we contrast our genuine *a priori* judgement with an empirical generalization, such as "all men are mortals." Here as before, we can *understand* what the proposition means as soon as we understand the universals involved, namely *man* and *mortal*. It is obviously unnecessary to have an individual acquaintance with the whole human race in order to understand what our proposition means. Thus the difference between an *a priori* general proposition and an empirical generalization does not come in the *meaning* of the proposition; it comes in the nature of the *evidence* for it. In the empirical case, the evidence consists in the particular instances. We believe that all men are mortal because we know that there are innumerable instances of men dying, and no instances of their living beyond a certain age. We do not believe it because we see a connexion between the universal *man* and the universal *mortal*. It is true that if physiology can prove, assuming the general laws that govern living bodies, that no living organism can last for ever, that gives a connexion between *man* and *mortality* which would enable us to assert our proposition without appealing to the special evidence of *men* dying. But that only means that our generalization has been subsumed under a wider generalization, for which the evidence is still of the same kind, though more extensive. The progress of science is constantly producing such subsumptions, and therefore giving a constantly wider inductive basis for scientific generalizations. But although this gives a greater *degree* of certainty, it does not give a different *kind*: the ultimate ground remains inductive, i.e. derived from instances, and not an *a priori* connexion of universals such as we have in logic and arithmetic.

Two opposite points are to be observed concerning *a priori* general propositions. The first is that, if many particular instances are known, our general proposition may be arrived at in the first instance by induction, and the connexion of universals may be only subsequently perceived. For example, it is known that if we draw perpendiculars to the sides of a triangle from the opposite angles, all three perpendiculars meet in a point. It would be quite possible to be first led to this proposition by actually drawing perpendiculars in many cases, and finding that they always met in a point; this experience might lead us to look for the general proof and find it. Such cases are common in the experience of every mathematician.

The other point is more interesting, and of more philosophical importance. It is, that we may sometimes know a general proposition in cases where we do not know a single instance of it. Take such a case as the following: We know that any two numbers can be multiplied together, and will give a third called their *product*. We know that all pairs of integers the product of which is less than 100 have been actually multiplied together, and the value of the product recorded in the multiplication table. But we also know that the number of integers is infinite, and that only a finite number of pairs of integers ever have been or ever will be thought of by human beings. Hence it follows that there are pairs of integers which never have been and never will be thought of by human beings, and that all of them deal with integers the product of which is over 100. Hence we arrive at the proposition: "All products of two integers, which never have been and never will be thought of by any human being, are over 100." Here is a general proposition of which the truth is undeniable, and yet, from the very nature of the case, we can never give an instance; because any two numbers we may think of are excluded by the terms of the proposition.

This possibility, of knowledge of general propositions of which no instance can be given, is often denied, because it is not perceived that the knowledge of such propositions only requires a knowledge of the relations of universals, and does not require any knowledge of instances of the universals in question. Yet the knowledge of such general propositions is quite vital to a great deal of what is generally admitted to be known. For example, we saw, in our early chapters, that knowledge of physical objects, as opposed to sense-data, is only obtained by an inference, and that they are not things with which we are acquainted. Hence we can never know any proposition of the form "this is a physical object," where "this" is something immediately known. It follows that all our knowledge concerning physical objects is such that no actual instance can be given. We can give instances of the associated sense-data, but we cannot give instances of the actual physical objects. Hence our knowledge as to physical objects depends throughout upon this possibility of general knowledge where no instance can be given. And the same applies to our knowledge of other people's minds, or of any other class of things of which no instance is known to us by acquaintance.

We may now take a survey of the sources of our knowledge, as they have appeared in the course of our analysis. We have first to distinguish knowledge of things and knowledge of truths. In each there are two kinds, one immediate and one derivative. Our immediate knowledge of things, which we called *acquaintance*, consists of two sorts, according as the things known are particulars or universals. Among particulars, we have acquaintance with sense-data and (probably) with ourselves. Among universals, there seems to be no principle by which we can decide which can be known by acquaintance, but it is clear that among those that can be so known are sensible qualities, relations of space and time, similarity, and certain abstract logical universals. Our derivative knowledge of things, which we call knowledge by *description*, always involves both acquaintance with something and knowledge of truths. Our immediate knowledge of *truths* may be called *intuitive* knowledge, and the truths so known may be called *self-evident* truths. Among such truths are included those which merely state what is given in sense, and also certain abstract logical and arithmetical principles, and (though with less certainty) some ethical propositions. Our *derivative* knowledge of truths consists of everything that we can deduce from self-evident truths by the use of self-evident principles of deduction.

If the above account is correct, all our knowledge of truths depends upon our intuitive knowledge. It therefore becomes important to consider the nature and scope of intuitive knowledge, in much the same way as, at an earlier stage, we considered the nature and scope of knowledge by acquaintance. But knowledge of truths raises a further problem, which does not arise in regard to knowledge of things, namely the problem of *error*. Some of our beliefs turn out to be erroneous, and therefore it becomes necessary to consider how, if at all, we can distinguish knowledge from error. This problem does not arise with regard to knowledge by acquaintance, for, whatever may be the object of acquaintance, even in dreams and hallucinations, there is no error involved so long as we do not go beyond the immediate object: error can only arise when we regard the immediate object, i.e. the sense-datum, as the mark of some physical object. Thus the problems connected with knowledge of truths are more difficult than those connected with knowledge of things. As the first of the problems connected with knowledge of truths, let us examine the nature and scope of our intuitive judgements.

Note

1 Kant's "thing in itself" is identical *in definition* with the physical object, namely, it is the cause of sensations. In the properties deduced from the definition it is not identical, since Kant held (in spite of some inconsistency as regards cause) that we can know that none of the categories are applicable to the "thing in itself."

QUESTIONS

1 Russell says that Kant's theory fails to account for the certainty and universality of arithmetic. Why is this?
2 According to Russell, is the law of non-contradiction a law of thought?
3 According to Russell, what sort of things do we have a priori knowledge of?
4 What is the difference between "existence" and "subsistence"? Which one do universals do?
5 What sorts of things does Russell think we have "acquaintance" with?

A.J. Ayer, "The Elimination of Metaphysics"

The traditional disputes of philosophers are, for the most part, as unwarranted as they are unfruitful. The surest way to end them is to establish beyond question what should be the purpose and method of a philosophical enquiry. And this is by no means so difficult a task as the history of philosophy would lead one to suppose. For if there are any questions which science leaves it to philosophy to answer, a straightforward process of elimination must lead to their discovery.

We may begin by criticising the metaphysical thesis that philosophy affords us knowledge of a reality transcending the world of science and common sense. Later on, when we come to define metaphysics and account for its existence, we shall find that it is possible to be a metaphysician without believing in a transcendent reality; for we shall see that many metaphysical utterances are due to the commission of logical errors, rather than to a conscious desire on the part of their authors to go beyond the limits of experience. But it is convenient for us to take the case of those who believe that it is possible to have knowledge of a transcendent reality as a starting-point for our discussion. The arguments which we use to refute them will subsequently be found to apply to the whole of metaphysics.

One way of attacking a metaphysician who claimed to have knowledge of a reality which transcended the phenomenal world would be to enquire from what premises his propositions were deduced. Must he not begin, as other men do, with the evidence of his senses? And if so, what valid process of reasoning can possibly lead him to the conception of a transcendent reality? Surely from empirical premises nothing whatsoever concerning the properties, or even the existence, of anything super-empirical can legitimately be inferred. But this objection would be met by a denial on the part of the metaphysician that his assertions were ultimately based on the evidence of his senses. He would say that he was endowed with a faculty of intellectual intuition which enabled him to know facts that could not be known through sense-experience. And even if it could be shown that he was relying on empirical premises, and that his venture into a non-empirical world was therefore logically unjustified, it would not follow that the assertions which he made concerning this non-empirical world could not be true. For the fact that a conclusion does not follow from its putative premise is not sufficient to show that it is false. Consequently one cannot overthrow a system of transcendent metaphysics merely by criticising the way in which it comes into

A.J. Ayer, *Language, Truth and Logic* (New York: Dover Publications, 1952), pp. 33–45.

being. What is required is rather a criticism of the nature of the actual statements which comprise it. And this is the line of argument which we shall, in fact, pursue. For we shall maintain that no statement which refers to a "reality" transcending the limits of all possible sense-experience can possibly have any literal significance; from which it must follow that the labours of those who have striven to describe such a reality have all been devoted to the production of nonsense.

It may be suggested that this is a proposition which has already been proved by Kant. But although Kant also condemned transcendent metaphysics, he did so on different grounds. For he said that the human understanding was so constituted that it lost itself in contradictions when it ventured out beyond the limits of possible experience and attempted to deal with things in themselves. And thus he made the impossibility of a transcendent metaphysic not, as we do, a matter of logic, but a matter of fact. He asserted, not that our minds could not conceivably have had the power of penetrating beyond the phenomenal world, but merely that they were in fact devoid of it. And this leads the critic to ask how, if it is possible to know only what lies within the bounds of sense-experience, the author can be justified in asserting that real things do exist beyond, and how he can tell what are the boundaries beyond which the human understanding may not venture, unless he succeeds in passing them himself. As Wittgenstein says, "in order to draw a limit to thinking, we should have to think both sides of this limit,"[1] a truth to which Bradley gives a special twist in maintaining that the man who is ready to prove that metaphysics is impossible is a brother metaphysician with a rival theory of his own.[2]

Whatever force these objections may have against the Kantian doctrine, they have none whatsoever against the thesis that I am about to set forth. It cannot here be said that the author is himself overstepping the barrier he maintains to be impassable. For the fruitlessness of attempting to transcend the limits of possible sense-experience will be deduced, not from a psychological hypothesis concerning the actual constitution of the human mind, but from the rule which determines the literal significance of language. Our charge against the metaphysician is not that he attempts to employ the understanding in a field where it cannot profitably venture, but that he produces sentences which fail to conform to the conditions under which alone a sentence can be literally significant. Nor are we ourselves obliged to talk nonsense in order to show that all sentences of a certain type are necessarily devoid of literal significance. We need only formulate the criterion which enables us to test whether a sentence expresses a genuine proposition about a matter of fact, and then point out that the sentences under consideration fail to satisfy it. And this we shall now proceed to do. We shall first of all formulate the criterion in somewhat vague terms, and then give the explanations which are necessary to render it precise.

The criterion which we use to test the genuineness of apparent statements of fact is the criterion of verifiability. We say that a sentence is factually significant to any given person, if, and only if, he knows how to verify the proposition which it purports to express—that is, if he knows what observations would lead him, under certain conditions, to accept the proposition as being true, or reject it as being false. If, on the other hand, the putative proposition is of such a character that the assumption of its truth, or falsehood, is consistent with any assumption whatsoever concerning the nature of his future experience, then, as far as he is concerned, it is, if not a tautology, a mere pseudo-proposition. The sentence expressing it may be emotionally significant to him; but it is not literally significant. And with regard to questions the procedure is the same. We enquire in every case what observations would lead us to answer the question, one way or the other; and, if none can be discovered, we must conclude that the sentence under consideration does not, as far as we are concerned, express a genuine question, however strongly its grammatical appearance may suggest that it does.

As the adoption of this procedure is an essential factor in the argument of this book, it needs to be examined in detail.

In the first place, it is necessary to draw a distinction between practical verifiability, and verifiability in principle. Plainly we all understand, in many cases believe, propositions which we have not in fact taken steps to verify. Many of these are propositions which we could verify if we took enough trouble. But there remain a number of significant propositions, concerning matters of fact, which we could not verify even if we chose; simply because we lack the practical means of placing ourselves in the situation where the relevant observations could be made. A simple and familiar example of such a proposition is the proposition that there are mountains on the farther side of the moon.[3] No rocket has yet been invented which would enable me to go and look at the farther side of the moon, so that I am unable to decide the matter by actual observation. But I do know what observations would decide it for me, if, as is theoretically conceivable, I were once in a position to make them. And therefore I say that the proposition is verifiable in principle, if not in practice, and is accordingly significant. On the other hand, such a metaphysical pseudo-proposition as "the Absolute enters into, but is itself incapable of, evolution and progress,"[4] is not even in principle verifiable. For one cannot conceive of an observation which would enable one to determine whether the Absolute did, or did not, enter into evolution and progress. Of course it is possible that the author of such a remark is using English words in a way in which they are not commonly used by English-speaking people, and that he does, in fact, intend to assert something which could be empirically verified. But until he makes us understand how the proposition that he wishes to express would be verified, he fails to communicate anything to us. And if he admits, as I think the author of the remark in question would have admitted, that his words were not intended to express either a tautology or a proposition which was capable, at least in principle, of being verified, then it follows that he has made an utterance which has no literal significance even for himself.

A further distinction which we must make is the distinction between the "strong" and the "weak" sense of the term "verifiable." A proposition is said to be verifiable, in the strong sense of the term, if, and only if, its truth could be conclusively established in experience. But it is verifiable, in the weak sense, if it is possible for experience to render it probable. In which sense are we using the term when we say that a putative proposition is genuine only if it is verifiable?

It seems to me that if we adopt conclusive verifiability as our criterion of significance, as some positivists have proposed,[5] our argument will prove too much. Consider, for example, the case of general propositions of law—such propositions, namely, as "arsenic is poisonous"; "all men are mortal"; "a body tends to expand when it is heated." It is of the very nature of these propositions that their truth cannot be established with certainty by any finite series of observations. But if it is recognised that such general propositions of law are designed to cover an infinite number of cases, then it must be admitted that they cannot, even in principle, be verified conclusively. And then, if we adopt conclusive verifiability as our criterion of significance, we are logically obliged to treat these general propositions of law in the same fashion as we treat the statements of the metaphysician.

In face of this difficulty, some positivists[6] have adopted the heroic course of saying that these general propositions are indeed pieces of nonsense, albeit an essentially important type of nonsense. But here the introduction of the term "important" is simply an attempt to hedge. It serves only to mark the authors' recognition that their view is somewhat too paradoxical, without in any way removing the paradox. Besides, the difficulty is not confined to the case of general propositions of law, though it is there revealed most plainly. It is hardly less obvious in the case of propositions about the remote past. For it must surely be admitted that, however strong the evidence in favour of historical statements may be, their truth can never become more than highly probable. And to maintain that they also constituted an important, or unimportant, type of nonsense would be unplausible, to say the very least. Indeed, it will be our contention that no proposition, other than a tautology, can possibly be anything more than a probable hypothesis. And if this is correct, the principle that a sentence can be factually significant only if it expresses what is conclusively verifiable is self-stultifying as a criterion of significance. For it leads to the conclusion that it is impossible to make a significant statement of fact at all.

Nor can we accept the suggestion that a sentence should be allowed to be factually significant if, and only if, it expresses something which is definitely confutable by experience.[7] Those who adopt this course assume that, although no finite series of observations is ever sufficient to establish the truth of a hypothesis beyond all possibility of doubt, there are crucial cases in which a single observation, or series of observations, can definitely confute it. But, as we shall show later on, this assumption is false. A hypothesis cannot be conclusively confuted any more than it can be conclusively verified. For when we take the occurrence of certain observations as proof that a given hypothesis is false, we presuppose the existence of certain conditions. And though, in any given case, it may be extremely improbable that this assumption is false, it is not logically impossible. We shall see that there need be no self-contradiction in holding that some of the relevant circumstances are other than we have taken them to be, and consequently that the hypothesis has not really broken down. And if it is not the case that any hypothesis can be definitely confuted, we cannot hold that the genuineness of a proposition depends on the possibility of its definite confutation.

Accordingly, we fall back on the weaker sense of verification. We say that the question that must be asked about any putative statement of fact is not, Would any observations make its truth or falsehood logically certain? but simply, Would any observations be relevant to the determination of its truth or falsehood? And it is only if a negative answer is given to this second question that we conclude that the statement under consideration is nonsensical.

To make our position clearer, we may formulate it in another way. Let us call a proposition which records an actual or possible observation an experiential proposition. Then we may say that it is the mark of a genuine factual proposition, not that it should be equivalent to an experiential proposition, or any finite number of experiential propositions, but simply that some experiential propositions can be deduced from it in conjunction with certain other premises without being deducible from those other premises alone.[8]

This criterion seems liberal enough. In contrast to the principle of conclusive verifiability, it clearly does not deny significance to general propositions or to propositions about the past. Let us see what kinds of assertion it rules out.

A good example of the kind of utterance that is condemned by our criterion as being not even false but nonsensical would be the assertion that the world of sense-experience was altogether unreal. It must, of course, be admitted that our senses do sometimes deceive us. We may, as the result of having certain sensations, expect certain other sensations to be obtainable which are, in fact, not obtainable. But, in all such cases, it is further sense-experience that informs us of the mistakes that arise out of sense-experience. We say that the senses sometimes deceive us, just because the expectations to which our sense-experiences give rise do not always accord with what we subsequently experience. That is, we rely on our senses to substantiate or confute the judgements which are based on our sensations. And therefore the fact that our perceptual judgements are sometimes found to be erroneous has not the slightest tendency to show that the world of sense-experience is unreal. And, indeed, it is plain that no conceivable observation, or series of observations, could have any tendency to show that the world revealed to us by sense-experience was unreal. Consequently, anyone who condemns the sensible world as a world of mere appearance, as opposed to reality, is saying something which, according to our criterion of significance, is literally nonsensical.

An example of a controversy which the application of our criterion obliges us to condemn as fictitious is provided by those who dispute concerning the number of substances that there are in the world. For it is admitted both by monists, who maintain that reality is one substance, and by pluralists, who maintain that reality is many, that it is impossible to imagine any empirical situation which would be relevant to the solution of their dispute. But if we are told that no possible observation could give any probability either to the assertion that reality was one substance or to the assertion that it was many, then we must conclude that neither assertion is significant. We shall see later on[9] that there are genuine logical and empirical questions involved in the dispute between monists and pluralists. But the metaphysical question concerning "substance" is ruled out by our criterion as spurious.

A similar treatment must be accorded to the controversy between realists and idealists, in its metaphysical aspect. A simple illustration, which I have made use of in a similar argument elsewhere,[10] will help to demonstrate this. Let us suppose that a picture is discovered and the suggestion made that it was painted by Goya. There is a definite procedure for dealing with such a question. The experts examine the picture to see in what way it resembles the accredited works of Goya, and to see if it bears any marks which are characteristic of a forgery; they look up contemporary records for evidence of the existence of such a picture, and so on. In the end, they may still disagree, but each one knows what empirical evidence would go to confirm or discredit his opinion. Suppose, now, that these men have studied philosophy, and some of them proceed to maintain that this picture is a set of ideas in the perceiver's mind, or in God's mind, others that it is objectively real. What possible experience could any of them have which would be relevant to the solution of this dispute one way or the other? In the ordinary sense of the term "real," in which it is opposed to "illusory," the reality of the picture is not in doubt. The disputants have satisfied themselves that the picture is real, in this sense, by obtaining a correlated series of sensations of sight and sensations of touch. Is there any similar process by which they could discover whether the picture was real, in the sense in which the term "real" is opposed to "ideal"? Clearly there is none. But, if that is so, the problem is fictitious according to our criterion. This does not mean that the realist-idealist controversy may be dismissed without further ado. For it can legitimately be regarded as a dispute concerning the analysis of existential propositions, and so as involving a logical problem which, as we shall see, can be definitively solved.[11] What we have just shown is that the question at issue between idealists and realists becomes fictitious when, as is often the case, it is given a metaphysical interpretation.

There is no need for us to give further examples of the operation of our criterion of significance. For our object is merely to show that philosophy, as a genuine branch of knowledge, must be distinguished from metaphysics. We are not now concerned with the historical question how much of what has traditionally passed for philosophy is actually metaphysical. We shall, however, point out later on that the majority of the "great philosophers" of the past were not essentially metaphysicians, and thus reassure those who would otherwise be prevented from adopting our criterion by considerations of piety.

As to the validity of the verification principle, in the form in which we have stated it, a demonstration will be given in the course of this book. For it will be shown that all propositions which have factual content are empirical hypotheses; and that the function of an empirical hypothesis is to provide a rule for the anticipation of experience.[12] And this means that every empirical hypothesis must be relevant to some actual, or possible, experience, so that a statement which is not relevant to any experience is not an empirical hypothesis, and accordingly has no factual content. But this is precisely what the principle of verifiability asserts.

It should be mentioned here that the fact that the utterances of the metaphysician are nonsensical does not follow simply from the fact that they are devoid of factual content. It follows from that fact, together with the fact that they are not *a priori* propositions. And in assuming that they are not *a priori* propositions, we are once again anticipating the conclusions of a later chapter in this book.[13] For it will be shown there that *a priori* propositions, which have always been attractive to philosophers on account of their certainty, owe this certainty to the fact that they are tautologies. We may accordingly define a metaphysical sentence as a sentence which purports to express a genuine proposition, but does, in fact, express neither a tautology nor an empirical hypothesis. And as tautologies and empirical hypotheses form the entire class of significant propositions, we are justified in concluding that all metaphysical assertions are nonsensical. Our next task is to show how they come to be made.

The use of the term "substance," to which we have already referred, provides us with a good example of the way in which metaphysics mostly comes to be written. It happens to be the case that we cannot, in our language, refer to the sensible properties of a thing without introducing a word or phrase which appears to stand for the thing itself as opposed to anything which may be said about it. And, as a result of this, those who are infected by the primitive superstition that to every name a single real entity must correspond assume that it is necessary to distinguish logically between the thing itself and any, or all, of its sensible properties. And so they employ the term "substance" to refer to the thing itself. But from the fact that we happen to employ a single word to refer to a thing, and make that word the grammatical subject of the sentences in which we refer to the sensible appearances of the thing, it does not by any means follow that the thing itself is a "simple entity," or that it cannot be defined in terms of the totality of its appearances. It is true that in talking of "its" appearances we appear to distinguish the thing from the appearances, but that is simply an accident of linguistic usage. Logical analysis shows that what makes these "appearances" the "appearances of" the same thing is not their relationship to an entity other than themselves, but their relationship to one another. The metaphysician fails to see this because he is misled by a superficial grammatical feature of his language.

A simpler and clearer instance of the way in which a consideration of grammar leads to metaphysics is the case of the metaphysical concept of Being. The origin of our temptation to raise questions about Being, which no conceivable experience would enable us to answer, lies in the fact that, in our language, sentences which express existential propositions and sentences which express attributive propositions may be of the same grammatical form. For instance, the sentences "Martyrs exist" and "Martyrs suffer" both consist of a noun followed by an intransitive verb, and the fact that they have grammatically the same appearance leads one to assume that they are of the same logical type. It is seen that in the proposition "Martyrs suffer," the members of a certain species are credited with a certain attribute, and it is sometimes assumed that the same thing is true of such a proposition as "Martyrs exist." If this were actually the case, it would, indeed, be as legitimate to speculate about the Being of martyrs as it is to speculate about their suffering. But, as Kant pointed out,[14] existence is not an attribute. For, when we ascribe an attribute to a thing, we covertly assert that it exists: so that if existence were itself an attribute, it would follow that all positive existential propositions were tautologies, and all negative existential propositions self-contradictory; and this is not the case.[15] So that those who raise questions about Being which are based on the assumption that existence is an attribute are guilty of following grammar beyond the boundaries of sense.

A similar mistake has been made in connection with such propositions as "Unicorns are fictitious." Here again the fact that there is a superficial grammatical resemblance between the English sentences "Dogs are faithful" and "Unicorns are fictitious," and between the corresponding sentences in other languages, creates the assumption that they are of the same logical type. Dogs must exist in order to have the property of being faithful, and so it is held that unless unicorns in some way existed they could not have the property of being fictitious. But, as it is plainly self-contradictory to say that fictitious objects exist, the device is adopted of saying that they are real in some non-empirical sense—that they have a mode of real being which is different from the mode of being of existent things. But since there is no way of testing whether an object is real in this sense, as there is for testing whether it is real in the ordinary sense, the assertion that fictitious objects have a special non-empirical mode of real being is devoid of all literal significance. It comes to be made as a result of the assumption that being fictitious is an attribute. And this is a fallacy of the same order as the fallacy of supposing that existence is an attribute, and it can be exposed in the same way.

In general, the postulation of real non-existent entities results from the superstition, just now referred to, that, to every word or phrase that can be the grammatical subject of a sentence, there must somewhere be a real entity corresponding. For as there is no place in the empirical world for many of these "entities," a special non-empirical world is invoked to house them. To this error must be attributed, not only the utterances of a Heidegger, who bases his metaphysics on the assumption that "Nothing" is a name which is used to denote something peculiarly mysterious,[16] but also the prevalence of such problems as those concerning the reality of propositions and universals whose senselessness, though less obvious, is no less complete.

These few examples afford a sufficient indication of the way in which most metaphysical assertions come to be formulated. They show how easy it is to write sentences which are literally nonsensical without seeing that they are nonsensical. And thus we see that the view that a number of the traditional "problems of philosophy" are metaphysical, and consequently fictitious, does not involve any incredible assumptions about the psychology of philosophers.

Among those who recognise that if philosophy is to be accounted a genuine branch of knowledge it must be defined in such a way as to distinguish it from metaphysics, it is fashionable to speak of the metaphysician as a kind of misplaced poet. As his statements have no literal meaning, they are not subject to any criteria of truth or falsehood: but they may still serve to express, or arouse, emotion, and thus be subject to ethical or æsthetic standards. And it is suggested that they may have considerable value, as means of moral inspiration, or even as works of art. In this way, an attempt is made to compensate the metaphysician for his extrusion from philosophy.[17]

I am afraid that this compensation is hardly in accordance with his deserts. The view that the metaphysician is to be reckoned among the poets appears to rest on the assumption that both talk nonsense. But this assumption is false. In the vast majority of cases the sentences which are produced by poets do have literal meaning. The difference between the man who uses language scientifically and the man who uses it emotively is not that the one produces sentences which are incapable of arousing emotion, and the other sentences which have no sense, but that the one is primarily concerned with the expression of true propositions, the other with the creation of a work of art. Thus, if a work of science contains true and important propositions, its value as a work of science will hardly be diminished by the fact that they are inelegantly expressed. And similarly, a work of art is not necessarily the worse for the fact that all the propositions comprising it are literally false. But to say that many literary works are largely composed of falsehoods, is not to say that they are composed of pseudo-propositions. It is, in fact, very rare for a literary artist to produce sentences which have no literal meaning. And where this does occur, the sentences are carefully chosen for their rhythm and balance. If the author writes nonsense, it is because he considers it most suitable for bringing about the effects for which his writing is designed.

The metaphysician, on the other hand, does not intend to write nonsense. He lapses into it through being deceived by grammar, or through committing errors of reasoning, such as that which leads to the view that the sensible world is unreal. But it is not the mark of a poet simply to make mistakes of this sort. There are some, indeed, who would see in the fact that the metaphysician's utterances are senseless a reason against the view that they have æsthetic value. And, without going so far as this, we may safely say that it does not constitute a reason for it.

It is true, however, that although the greater part of metaphysics is merely the embodiment of humdrum errors, there remain a number of metaphysical passages which are the work of genuine mystical feeling; and they may more plausibly be held to have moral or æsthetic value. But, as far as we are concerned, the distinction between the kind of metaphysics that is produced by a philosopher who has been duped by grammar, and the kind that is produced by a mystic who is trying to express the inexpressible, is of no great importance: what is important to us is to realise that even the utterances of the metaphysician who is attempting to expound a vision are literally senseless; so that henceforth we may pursue our philosophical researches with as little regard for them as for the more inglorious kind of metaphysics which comes from a failure to understand the workings of our language.

Notes

1 Ludwig Wittgenstein, *Tractatus Logico-Philosophicus* (London: Routledge & Kegan Paul, 1922), preface.
2 F.H. Bradley, *Appearance and Reality* (Oxford: Clarendon Press, 1962), 2nd ed., p. 1.
3 This example has been used by Professor Schlick to illustrate the same point.
4 A remark taken at random from *Appearance and Reality*, by F.H. Bradley.
5 E.g. M. Schlick, "Positivismus und Realismus," *Erkenntnis* 1 (1930); F. Waisman, "Logische Analyse des Warscheinlichkeitsbegriffs," *Erkenntnis* 1 (1930).
6 E.g. M. Schlick, "Die Kausalität in der gegenwärtigen Physik," *Naturwissenschaft* 19 (1931).
7 This has been proposed by Karl Popper in his *Logik der Forschung*. [English translation: *The Logic of Scientific Discovery* (New York: Harper and Row, 1965).]
8 This is an over-simplified statement, which is not literally correct. I give what I believe to be the correct formulation in the Introduction (*Language, Truth and Logic*), p. 13.
9 In Chapter VIII (*Language, Truth and Logic*).
10 Vide Ayer, "Demonstration of the Impossibility of Metaphysics," *Mind* 43 (1934): 334–45, p. 339.
11 Vide Chapter VIII (*Language, Truth and Logic*).
12 Vide Chapter V (*Language, Truth and Logic*).
13 Chapter IV (*Language, Truth and Logic*).
14 Vide *Critique of Pure Reason* (New York: St. Martin's Press, 1965), "Transcendental Dialectic," Book II, Chapter iii, section 4.

15 This argument is well stated by John Wisdom, *Interpretation and Analysis* (London: K. Paul, Trench, Trubner & Co., 1931), pp. 62, 63.

16 Vide *Was ist Metaphysik?* by Martin Heidegger (Bonn: F. Cohen, 1931): criticized by Rudolf Carnap in his "Überwindung der Metaphysik durch logische Analyse der Sprache," *Erkenntnis* 2 (1932) [English translation: "The Elimination of Metaphysics through Logical Analysis of Language," tr. by Arthur Pap, in *Logical Positivism*, ed. A.J. Ayer (New York: Free Press, 1959)].

17 For a discussion of this point, see also C.A. Mace, "Representation and Expression," *Analysis* 1 (1934): 33–8; and "Metaphysics and Emotive Language," *Analysis* 2 (1934): 6–10.

QUESTIONS

1 What is the criterion of verifiability, and what is it a criterion of?
2 What are the "strong" and "weak" senses of "verifiable"?
3 How does Ayer define a "metaphysical sentence"?
4 Would Ayer say that all systems of metaphysics are false?

W.V. Quine, "Two Dogmas of Empiricism[1]"

Modern empiricism has been conditioned in large part by two dogmas. One is a belief in some fundamental cleavage between truths which are *analytic*, or grounded in meanings independently of matters of fact, and truths which are *synthetic*, or grounded in fact. The other dogma is *reductionism:* the belief that each meaningful statement is equivalent to some logical construct upon terms which refer to immediate experience. Both dogmas, I shall argue, are ill founded. One effect of abandoning them is, as we shall see, a blurring of the supposed boundary between speculative metaphysics and natural science. Another effect is a shift toward pragmatism.

I. Background for analyticity

Kant's cleavage between analytic and synthetic truths was foreshadowed in Hume's distinction between relations of ideas and matters of fact, and in Leibniz's distinction between truths of reason and truths of fact. Leibniz spoke of the truths of reason as true in all possible worlds. Picturesqueness aside, this is to say that the truths of reason are those which could not possibly be false. In the same vein we hear analytic statements defined as statements whose denials are self-contradictory. But this definition has small explanatory value; for the notion of self-contradictoriness, in the quite broad sense needed for this definition of analyticity, stands in exactly the same need of clarification as does the notion of analyticity itself.[2] The two notions are the two sides of a single dubious coin.

Kant conceived of an analytic statement as one that attributes to its subject no more than is already conceptually contained in the subject. This formulation has two shortcomings: it limits itself to statements of subject-predicate form, and it appeals to a notion of containment which is left at a metaphorical level. But Kant's intent, evident more from the use he makes of the notion of analyticity than from his definition of it, can be restated thus: a statement is analytic when it is true by virtue of meanings and independently of fact. Pursuing this line, let us examine the concept of *meaning* which is presupposed.

We must observe to begin with that meaning is not to be identified with naming, or reference. Consider Frege's example of "Evening Star" and "Morning Star." Understood not merely as a recurrent evening apparition but as a body, the Evening Star is the planet Venus, and the Morning Star is the same. The two

W.V. Quine, "Two Dogmas of Empiricism," *Philosophical Review* 60 (1951): 20–43.

singular terms *name* the same thing. But the meanings must be treated as distinct, since the identity "Evening Star = Morning Star" is a statement of fact established by astronomical observation. If "Evening Star" and "Morning Star" were alike in meaning, the identity "Evening Star = Morning Star" would be analytic.

Again there is Russell's example of "Scott" and "the author of *Waverley*." Analysis of the meanings of words was by no means sufficient to reveal to George IV that the person named by these two singular terms was one and the same.

The distinction between meaning and naming is no less important at the level of abstract terms. The terms "9" and "the number of planets" name one and the same abstract entity but presumably must be regarded as unlike in meaning; for astronomical observation was needed, and not mere reflection on meanings, to determine the sameness of the entity in question.

Thus far we have been considering singular terms. With general terms, or predicates, the situation is somewhat different but parallel. Whereas a singular term purports to name an entity, abstract or concrete, a general term does not; but a general term is *true* of an entity, or of each of many, or of none. The class of all entities of which a general term is true is called the *extension* of the term. Now paralleling the contrast between the meaning of a singular term and the entity named, we must distinguish equally between the meaning of a general term and its extension. The general terms "creature with a heart" and "creature with a kidney," e.g., are perhaps alike in extension but unlike in meaning.

Confusion of meaning with extension, in the case of general terms, is less common than confusion of meaning with naming in the case of singular terms. It is indeed a commonplace in philosophy to oppose intension (or meaning) to extension, or, in a variant vocabulary, connotation to denotation.

The Aristotelian notion of essence was the forerunner, no doubt, of the modern notion of intension or meaning. For Aristotle it was essential in men to be rational, accidental to be two-legged. But there is an important difference between this attitude and the doctrine of meaning. From the latter point of view it may indeed be conceded (if only for the sake of argument) that rationality is involved in the meaning of the word "man" while two-leggedness is not; but two-leggedness may at the same time be viewed as involved in the meaning of "biped" while rationality is not. Thus from the point of view of the doctrine of meaning it makes no sense to say of the actual individual; who is at once a man and a biped, that his rationality is essential and his two-leggedness accidental or vice versa. Things had essences, for Aristotle, but only linguistic forms have meanings. Meaning is what essence becomes when it is divorced from the object of reference and wedded to the word.

For the theory of meaning the most conspicuous question is as to the nature of its objects: what sort of things are meanings? They are evidently intended to be ideas, somehow—mental ideas for some semanticists, Platonic ideas for others. Objects of either sort are so elusive, not to say debatable, that there seems little hope of erecting a fruitful science about them. It is not even clear, granted meanings, when we have two and when we have one; it is not clear when linguistic forms should be regarded as *synonymous*, or alike in meaning, and when they should not. If a standard of synonymy should be arrived at, we may reasonably expect that the appeal to meanings as entities will not have played a very useful part in the enterprise.

A felt need for meant entities may derive from an earlier failure to appreciate that meaning and reference are distinct. Once the theory of meaning is sharply separated from the theory of reference, it is a short step to recognizing as the business of the theory of meaning simply the synonymy of linguistic forms and the analyticity of statements; meanings themselves, as obscure intermediary entities, may well be abandoned.

The description of analyticity as truth by virtue of meanings started us off in pursuit of a concept of meaning. But now we have abandoned the thought of any special realm of entities called meanings. So the problem of analyticity confronts us anew.

Statements which are analytic by general philosophical acclaim are not, indeed, far to seek. They fall into two classes. Those of the first class, which may be called *logically true*, are typified by:

(1) No unmarried man is married.

The relevant feature of this example is that it is not merely true as it stands, but remains true under any and all reinterpretations of "man" and "married." If we suppose a prior inventory of *logical* particles, comprising "no," "un-," "not," "if," "then," "and," etc., then in general a logical truth is a statement which is true and remains true under all reinterpretations of its components other than the logical particles.

But there is also a second class of analytic statements, typified by:

(2) No bachelor is married.

The characteristic of such a statement is that it can be turned into a logical truth by putting synonyms for synonyms; thus (2) can be turned into (1) by putting "unmarried man" for its synonym "bachelor." We still lack a proper characterization of this second class of analytic statements, and therewith of analyticity generally, inasmuch as we have had in the above description to lean on a notion of "synonymy" which is no less in need of clarification than analyticity itself.

In recent years Carnap has tended to explain analyticity by appeal to what he calls state-descriptions.[3] A state-description is any exhaustive assignment of truth values to the atomic, or noncompound, statements of the language. All other statements of the language are, Carnap assumes, built up of their component clauses by means of the familiar logical devices, in such a way that the truth value of any complex statement is fixed for each state-description by specifiable logical laws. A statement is then explained as analytic when it comes out true under every state-description. This account is an adaptation of Leibniz's "true in all possible worlds." But note that this version of analyticity serves its purpose only if the atomic statements of the language are, unlike "John is a bachelor" and "John is married," mutually independent. Otherwise there would be a state-description which assigned truth to "John is a bachelor" and falsity to "John is married", and consequently "All bachelors are married" would turn out synthetic rather than analytic under the proposed criterion. Thus the criterion of analyticity in terms of state-descriptions serves only for languages devoid of extralogical synonym-pairs, such as "bachelor" and "unmarried man":

synonym-pairs of the type which give rise to the "second class" of analytic statements. The criterion in terms of state-descriptions is a reconstruction at best of logical truth.

I do not mean to suggest that Carnap is under any illusions on this point. His simplified model language with its state-descriptions is aimed primarily not at the general problem of analyticity but at another purpose, the clarification of probability and induction. Our problem, however, is analyticity; and here the major difficulty lies not in the first class of analytic statements, the logical truths, but rather in the second class, which depends on the notion of synonymy.

II. Definition

There are those who find it soothing to say that the analytic statements of the second class reduce to those of the first class, the logical truths, by *definition*; "bachelor," e.g., is *defined* as "unmarried man." But how do we find that "bachelor" is defined as "unmarried man"? Who defined it thus, and when? Are we to appeal to the nearest dictionary, and accept the lexicographer's formulation as law? Clearly this would be to put the cart before the horse. The lexicographer is an empirical scientist, whose business is the recording of antecedent facts; and if he glosses "bachelor" as "unmarried man" it is because of his belief that there is a relation of synonymy between these forms, implicit in general or preferred usage prior to his own work. The notion of synonymy presupposed here has still to be clarified, presumably in terms relating to linguistic behavior. Certainly the "definition" which is the lexicographer's report of an observed synonymy cannot be taken as the ground of the synonymy.

Definition is not, indeed, an activity exclusively of philologists. Philosophers and scientists frequently have occasion to "define" a recondite term by paraphrasing it into terms of a more familiar vocabulary. But ordinarily such a definition, like the philologist's, is pure lexicography, affirming a relationship of synonymy antecedent to the exposition in hand.

Just what it means to affirm synonymy, just what the interconnections may be which are necessary and sufficient in order that two linguistic forms be properly describable as synonymous, is far from clear; but, whatever these interconnections may be, ordinarily they are grounded in usage. Definitions reporting selected instances of synonymy come then as reports upon usage.

There is also, however, a variant type of definitional activity which does not limit itself to the reporting of pre-existing synonymies. I have in mind what Carnap calls *explication*—an activity to which philosophers are given, and scientists also in their more philosophical moments. In explication the purpose is not merely to paraphrase the definiendum into an outright synonym, but actually to improve upon the definiendum by refining or supplementing its meaning. But even explication, though not merely reporting a pre-existing synonymy between definiendum and definiens, does rest nevertheless on *other* pre-existing synonymies. The matter may be viewed as follows. Any word worth explicating has some contexts which, as wholes, are clear and precise enough to be useful; and the purpose of explication is to preserve the usage of these favored contexts while sharpening the usage of other contexts. In order that a given definition be suitable for purposes of explication, therefore, what is required is not that the definiendum in its antecedent usage be synonymous with the definiens, but just that each of these favored contexts of the definiendum, taken as a whole in its antecedent usage, be synonymous with the corresponding context of the definiens.

Two alternative definientia may be equally appropriate for the purposes of a given task of explication and yet not be synonymous with each other; for they may serve interchangeably within the favored contexts but diverge elsewhere. By cleaving to one of these definientia rather than the other, a definition of explicative kind generates, by fiat, a relationship of synonymy between definiendum and definiens which did not hold before. But such a definition still owes its explicative function, as seen, to pre-existing synonymies.

There does, however, remain still an extreme sort of definition which does not hark back to prior synonymies at all; viz., the explicitly conventional introduction of novel notations for purposes of sheer abbreviation. Here the definiendum becomes synonymous with the definiens simply because it has been created expressly for the purpose of being synonymous with the definiens. Here we have a really transparent case of synonymy created by definition; would that all species of synonymy were as intelligible. For the rest, definition rests on synonymy rather than explaining it.

The word "definition" has come to have a dangerously reassuring sound, due no doubt to its frequent occurrence in logical and mathematical writings. We shall do well to digress now into a brief appraisal of the role of definition in formal work.

In logical and mathematical systems either of two mutually antagonistic types of economy may be striven for, and each has its peculiar practical utility. On the one hand we may seek economy of practical expression: ease and brevity in the statement of multifarious relationships. This sort of economy calls usually for distinctive concise notations for a wealth of concepts. Second, however, and oppositely, we may seek economy in grammar and vocabulary; we may try to find a minimum of basic concepts such that, once a distinctive notation has been appropriated to each of them, it becomes possible to express any desired further concept by mere combination and iteration of our basic notations. This second sort of economy is impractical in one way, since a poverty in basic idioms tends to a necessary lengthening of discourse. But it is practical in another way: it greatly simplifies theoretical discourse *about* the language, through minimizing the terms and the forms of construction wherein the language consists.

Both sorts of economy, though prima facie incompatible, are valuable in their separate ways. The custom has consequently arisen of combining both sorts of economy by forging in effect two languages, the one a part of the other. The inclusive language, though redundant in grammar and vocabulary, is economical in message lengths, while the part, called *primitive notation*, is economical in grammar and vocabulary. Whole and part are correlated by rules of translation whereby each idiom not in primitive notation is equated to some complex built up of primitive notation. These rules of translation are the so-called *definitions* which appear in formalized systems. They are best viewed not as adjuncts to one language but as correlations between two languages, the one a part of the other.

But these correlations are not arbitrary. They are supposed to show how the primitive notations can accomplish all purposes, save brevity and convenience, of the redundant language. Hence the definiendum and its definiens may be expected, in each case, to be related in one or another of the three ways lately noted. The definiens may be a faithful paraphrase of the definiendum into the narrower notation, preserving a direct synonymy as of antecedent usage; or the definiens may, in the spirit of explication, improve upon the antecedent usage of the definiendum; or finally, the definiendum may be a newly created notation, newly endowed with meaning here and now.

In formal and informal work alike, thus, we find that definition—except in the extreme case of the explicitly conventional introduction of new notations—hinges on prior relationships of synonymy. Recognizing then that the notion of definition does not hold the key to synonymy and analyticity, let us look further into synonymy and say no more of definition.

III. Interchangeability

A natural suggestion, deserving close examination, is that the synonymy of two linguistic forms consists simply in their interchangeability in all contexts without change of truth value; interchangeability, in Leibniz's phrase, *salva veritate*. Note that synonyms so conceived need not even be free from vagueness, as long as the vaguenesses match.

But it is not quite true that the synonyms "bachelor" and "unmarried man" are everywhere interchangeable *salva veritate*. Truths which become false under substitution of "unmarried man" for "bachelor" are easily constructed with help of "bachelor of arts" or "bachelor's buttons." Also with help of quotation, thus:

'Bachelor' has less than ten letters.

Such counterinstances can, however, perhaps be set aside by treating the phrases "bachelor of arts" and "bachelor's buttons" and the quotation " 'bachelor' " each as a single indivisible word and then stipulating that the interchangeability *salva veritate* which is to be the touchstone of synonymy is not supposed to apply to fragmentary occurrences inside of a word. This account of synonymy, supposing it acceptable on other counts, has indeed the drawback of appealing to a prior conception of "word" which can be counted on to present difficulties of formulation in its turn. Nevertheless some progress might be claimed in having reduced the problem of synonymy to a problem of wordhood. Let us pursue this line a bit, taking "word" for granted.

The question remains whether interchangeability *salva veritate* (apart from occurrences within words) is a strong enough condition for synonymy, or whether, on the contrary, some nonsynonymous expressions might be thus interchangeable. Now let us be clear that we are not concerned here with synonymy in the sense of complete identity in psychological associations or poetic quality; indeed no two expressions are synonymous in such a sense. We are concerned only with what may be called *cognitive synonymy*. Just what this is cannot be said without successfully finishing the present study; but we know something about it from the need which arose for it in connection with analyticity in Section I. The sort of synonymy needed there was merely such that any analytic statement could be turned into a logical truth by putting synonyms for synonyms. Turning the tables and assuming analyticity, indeed, we could explain cognitive synonymy of terms as follows (keeping to the familiar example): to say that "bachelor" and "unmarried man" are cognitively synonymous is to say no more nor less than that the statement:

(3) All and only bachelors are unmarried men

is analytic.[4]

What we need is an account of cognitive synonymy not presupposing analyticity—if we are to explain analyticity conversely with help of cognitive synonymy as undertaken in Section I. And indeed such an independent account of cognitive synonymy is at present up for consideration, viz., interchangeability *salva veritate* everywhere except within words. The question before us, to resume the thread at last, is whether such interchangeability is a sufficient condition for cognitive synonymy. We can quickly assure ourselves that it is, by examples of the following sort. The statement:

(4) Necessarily all and only bachelors are bachelors

is evidently true, even supposing "necessarily" so narrowly construed as to be truly applicable only to analytic statements. Then, *if* "bachelor" and "unmarried man" are interchangeable *salva veritate*, the result

(5) Necessarily, all and only bachelors are unmarried men

of putting "unmarried man" for an occurrence of "bachelor" in (4) must, like (4), be true. But to say that (5) is true is to say that (3) is analytic, and hence that "bachelor" and "unmarried men" are cognitively synonymous.

Let us see what there is about the above argument that gives it its air of hocus-pocus. The condition of interchangeability *salva veritate* varies in its force with variations in the richness of the language at hand. The above argument supposes we are working with a language rich enough to contain the adverb "necessarily," this adverb being so construed as to yield truth when and only when applied to an analytic statement. But can we condone a language which contains such an adverb? Does the adverb really make sense? To suppose that it does is to suppose that we have already made satisfactory sense of "analytic." Then what are we so hard at work on right now?

Our argument is not flatly circular, but something like it. It has the form, figuratively speaking, of a closed curve in space.

Interchangeability *salva veritate* is meaningless until relativized to a language whose extent is specified in relevant respects. Suppose now we consider a language containing just the following materials. There is an indefinitely large stock of one- and many-place predicates, mostly having to do with extralogical subject matter. The rest of the language is logical. The atomic sentences consist each of a predicate followed by one or more variables; and the complex sentences are built up of atomic ones by truth functions and quantification. In effect such a language enjoys the benefits also of descriptions and class names and indeed singular terms generally, these being contextually definable in known ways.[5] Such a language can be adequate to classical mathematics and indeed to scientific discourse generally, except in so far as the latter involves debatable devices such as modal adverbs and contrary-to-fact conditionals. Now a language of this type is *extensional*, in this sense: any two predicates which *agree extensionally* (i.e., are true of the same objects) are interchangeable *salva veritate*.

In an extensional language, therefore, interchangeability *salva veritate* is no assurance of cognitive synonymy of the desired type. That "bachelor" and "unmarried man" are interchangeable *salva veritate* in an extensional language assures us of no more than that (3) is true. There is no assurance here that the extensional agreement of 'bachelor' and "unmarried man" rests on meaning rather than merely on accidental matters of fact, as does extensional agreement of "creature with a heart" and "creature with a kidney."

For most purposes extensional agreement is the nearest approximation to synonymy we need care about. But the fact remains that extensional agreement falls far short of cognitive synonymy of the type required for explaining analyticity in the manner of Section I. The type of cognitive synonymy required there is such as to equate the synonymy of "bachelor" and "unmarried man" with the analyticity of (3), not merely with the truth of (3).

So we must recognize that interchangeability *salva veritate*, if construed in relation to an extensional language, is not a sufficient condition of cognitive synonymy in the sense needed for deriving analyticity in the manner of Section I. If a language contains an intensional adverb "necessarily" in the sense lately noted, or other particles to the same effect, then interchangeability *salva veritate* in such a language does afford a sufficient condition of cognitive synonymy; but such a language is intelligible only if the notion of analyticity is already clearly understood in advance.

The effort to explain cognitive synonymy first, for the sake of deriving analyticity from it afterward as in Section I, is perhaps the wrong approach. Instead we might try explaining analyticity somehow without appeal to cognitive synonymy. Afterward we could doubtless derive cognitive synonymy from analyticity satisfactorily enough if desired. We have seen that cognitive synonymy of "bachelor" and "unmarried man" can be explained as analyticity of (3). The same explanation works for any pair of one-place predicates, of course, and it can be extended in obvious fashion to many-place predicates. Other syntactical categories can also be accommodated in fairly parallel fashion. Singular terms may be said to be cognitively synonymous when the statement of identity formed by putting "=" between them is analytic. Statements may be said simply to be cognitively synonymous when their biconditional (the result of joining them by "if and only if") is analytic.[6] If we care to lump all categories into a single formulation, at the expense of assuming again the notion of "word" which was appealed to early in this section, we can describe any two linguistic forms as cognitively synonymous when the two forms are interchangeable (apart from occurrences within "words") *salva* (no longer *veritate* but) *analyticitate*. Certain technical questions arise, indeed, over cases of ambiguity or homonymy; let us not pause for them, however, for we are already digressing. Let us rather turn our backs on the problem of synonymy and address ourselves anew to that of analyticity.

IV. Semantical rules

Analyticity at first seemed most naturally definable by appeal to a realm of meanings. On refinement, the appeal to meanings gave way to an appeal to synonymy or definition. But definition turned out to be a will-o'-the-wisp, and synonymy turned out to be best understood only by dint of a prior appeal to analyticity itself. So we are back at the problem of analyticity.

I do not know whether the statement "Everything green is extended" is analytic. Now does my indecision over this example really betray an incomplete understanding, an incomplete grasp of the "meanings", of "green" and "extended"? I think not. The trouble is not with "green" or "extended," but with "analytic."

It is often hinted that the difficulty in separating analytic statements from synthetic ones in ordinary language is due to the vagueness of ordinary language and that the distinction is clear when we have a precise artificial language with explicit "semantical rules." This, however, as I shall now attempt to show, is a confusion.

The notion of analyticity about which we are worrying is a purported relation between statements and languages: a statement *S* is said to be *analytic for* a language *L*, and the problem is to make sense of this relation generally, i.e., for variable "*S*" and "*L*." The point that I want to make is that the gravity of this problem is not perceptibly less for artificial languages than for natural ones. The problem of making sense of the idiom "*S* is analytic for *L*," with variable "*S*" and "*L*," retains its stubbornness even if we limit the range of the variable "*L*" to artificial languages. Let me now try to make this point evident.

For artificial languages and semantical rules we look naturally to the writings of Carnap. His semantical rules take various forms, and to make my point I shall have to distinguish certain of the forms. Let us suppose, to begin with, an artificial language L_o whose semantical rules have the form explicitly of a specification, by recursion or otherwise, of all the analytic statements of L_o. The rules tell us that such and such statements, and only those, are the analytic statements of L_o. Now here the difficulty is simply that the rules contain the word "analytic," which we do not understand! We understand what expressions the rules attribute analyticity to, but we do not understand what the rules attribute to those expressions. In short, before we can understand a rule which begins "A statement *S* is analytic for language L_o if and only if . . . ," we must understand the general relative term "analytic for"; we must understand "*S* is analytic for *L*" where "*S*" and "*L*" are variables.

Alternatively we may, indeed, view the so-called rule as a conventional definition of a new simple symbol "analytic-for-L_o," which might better be written untendentiously as "*K*" so as not to seem to throw light on the interesting word "analytic." Obviously any number of classes *K*, *M*, *N*, etc. of statements of L_o can be specified for various purposes or for no purpose; what does it mean to say that *K*, as against *M*, *N*, etc., is the class of the "analytic" statements of L_o?

By saying what statements are analytic for L_o we explain "analytic-for-L_o" but not "analytic," not "analytic for." We do not begin to explain the idiom "*S* is analytic for *L*" with variable "*S*" and "*L*," even though we be content to limit the range of "*L*" to the realm of artificial languages.

Actually we do know enough about the intended significance of "analytic" to know that analytic statements are supposed to be true. Let us then turn to a second form of semantical rule, which says not that such and such statements are analytic but simply that such and such statements are included among the truths. Such a rule is not subject to the criticism of containing the un-understood word "analytic"; and we may grant for the sake of argument that there is no difficulty over the broader term "true." A semantical rule of this second type, a rule of truth, is not supposed to specify all the truths of the language; it merely stipulates, recursively or otherwise, a certain multitude of statements which, along with others unspecified, are to count as true. Such a rule may be conceded to be quite clear. Derivatively, afterward, analyticity can be demarcated thus: a statement is analytic if it is (not merely true but) true according to the semantical rule.

Still there is really no progress. Instead of appealing to an unexplained word "analytic," we are now appealing to an unexplained phrase "semantical rule." Not every true statement which says that the statements of some class are true can count as a semantical rule—otherwise *all* truths would be "analytic" in the sense of being true according to semantical rules. Semantical rules are distinguishable, apparently, only by the fact of appearing on a page under the heading "Semantical Rules"; and this heading is itself then meaningless.

We can say indeed that a statement is *analytic-for-*L_0 if and only if it is true according to such and such specifically appended "semantical rules," but then we find ourselves back at essentially the same case which was originally discussed: "*S* is analytic-for-L_0 if and only if . . ." Once we seek to explain "*S* is analytic for *L*" generally for variable "*L*" (even allowing limitation of "*L*" to artificial languages), the explanation "true according to the semantical rules of *L*" is unavailing; for the relative term 'semantical rule of' is as much in need of clarification, at least, as "analytic for."

It might conceivably be protested that an artificial language *L* (unlike a natural one) is a language in the ordinary sense *plus* a set of explicit semantical rules—the whole constituting, let us say, an ordered pair; and that the semantical rules of *L* then are specifiable simply as the second component of the pair *L*. But, by the same token and more simply, we might construe an artificial language *L* outright as an ordered pair whose second component is the class of its analytic statements; and then the analytic statements of *L* become specifiable simply as the statements in the second component of *L*. Or better still, we might just stop tugging at our bootstraps altogether.

Not all the explanations of analyticity known to Carnap and his readers have been covered explicitly in the above considerations, but the extension to other forms is not hard to see. Just one additional factor should be mentioned which sometimes enters: sometimes the semantical rules are in effect rules of translation into ordinary language, in which case the analytic statements of the artificial language are in effect recognized as such from the analyticity of their specified translations in ordinary language. Here certainly there can be no thought of an illumination of the problem of analyticity from the side of the artificial language.

From the point of view of the problem of analyticity the notion of an artificial language with semantical rules is a *feu follet par excellence*. Semantical rules determining the analytic statements of an artificial language are of interest only in so far as we already understand the notion of analyticity; they are of no help in gaining this understanding.

Appeal to hypothetical languages of an artificially simple kind could conceivably be useful in clarifying analyticity, if the mental or behavioral or cultural factors relevant to analyticity—whatever they may be—were somehow sketched into the simplified model. But a model which takes analyticity merely as in irreducible character is unlikely to throw light on the problem of explicating analyticity.

It is obvious that truth in general depends on both language and extralinguistic fact. The statement "Brutus killed Caesar" would be false if the world had been different in certain ways, but it would also be false if the word "killed" happened rather to have the sense of "begat." Hence the temptation to suppose in general that the truth of a statement is somehow analyzable into a linguistic component and a factual component. Given this supposition, it next seems reasonable that in some statements the factual component should be null; and these are the analytic statements. But, for all its a priori reasonableness, a boundary between analytic and synthetic statements simply has not been drawn. That there is such a distinction to be drawn at all is an unempirical dogma of empiricists, a metaphysical article of faith.

V. The verification theory and reductionism

In the course of these somber reflections we have taken a dim view first of the notion of meaning, then of the notion of cognitive synonymy, and finally of the notion of analyticity. But what, it may be asked, of the verification theory of meaning? This phrase has established itself so firmly as a catchword of empiricism that we should be very unscientific indeed not to look beneath it for a possible key to the problem of meaning and the associated problems.

The verification theory of meaning, which has been conspicuous in the literature from Peirce onward, is that the meaning of a statement is the method of empirically confirming or infirming it. An analytic statement is that limiting case which is confirmed no matter what.

As urged in Section I, we can as well pass over the question of meanings as entities and move straight to sameness of meaning, or synonymy. Then what the verification theory says is that statements are synonymous if and only if they are alike in point of method of empirical confirmation or infirmation.

This is an account of cognitive synonymy not of linguistic forms generally, but of statements.[7] However, from the concept of synonymy of statements we could derive the concept of synonymy for other linguistic forms, by considerations somewhat similar to those at the end of Section III. Assuming the notion of "word," indeed, we could explain any two forms as synonymous when the putting of the one form for an occurrence of the other in any statement (apart from occurrences within "words") yields a synonymous statement. Finally, given the concept of synonymy thus for linguistic forms generally, we could define analyticity in terms of synonymy and logical truth as in Section I. For that matter, we could define analyticity more simply in terms of just synonymy of statements together with logical truth; it is not necessary to appeal to synonymy of linguistic forms other than statements. For a statement may be described as analytic simply when it is synonymous with a logically true statement.

So, if the verification theory can be accepted as an adequate account of statement synonymy, the notion of analyticity is saved after all. However, let us reflect. Statement synonymy is said to be likeness of method of empirical confirmation or infirmation. Just what are these methods which are to be compared for likeness? What, in other words, is the nature of the relationship between a statement and the experiences which contribute to or detract from its confirmation?

The most naive view of the relationship is that it is one of direct report. This is *radical reductionism*. Every meaningful statement is held to be translatable into a statement (true or false) about immediate experience. Radical reductionism, in one form or another, well antedates the verification theory of meaning explicitly so-called. Thus Locke and Hume held that every idea must either originate directly in sense experience or else be compounded of ideas thus originating; and taking a hint from Tooke[8] we might rephrase this doctrine in semantical jargon by saying that a term, to be significant at all, must be either a name of a sense datum or a compound of such names or an abbreviation of such a compound. So stated, the doctrine remains ambiguous as between sense data as sensory events and sense data as sensory qualities; and it remains vague as to the admissible ways of compounding. Moreover, the doctrine is unnecessarily and intolerably restrictive in the term-by-term critique which it imposes. More reasonably, and without yet exceeding the limits of what I have called radical reductionism, we may take full statements as our significant units—thus demanding that our statements as wholes be translatable into sense-datum language, but not that they be translatable term by term.

This emendation would unquestionably have been welcome to Locke and Hume and Tooke, but historically it had to await two intermediate developments. One of these developments was the increasing emphasis on verification or confirmation, which came with the explicitly so-called verification theory of meaning. The objects of verification or confirmation being statements, this emphasis gave the statement an ascendancy over the word or term as unit of significant discourse. The other development, consequent upon the first, was Russell's discovery of the concept of incomplete symbols defined in use.

Radical reductionism, conceived now with statements as units, sets itself the task of specifying a sense-datum language and showing how to translate the rest of significant discourse, statement by statement, into it. Carnap embarked on this project in the *Aufbau*.[9]

The language which Carnap adopted as his starting point was not a sense-datum language in the narrowest conceivable sense, for it included also the notations of logic, up through higher set theory. In effect in included the whole language of pure mathematics. The ontology implicit in it (i.e., the range of values of its variables) embraced not only sensory events but classes, classes of classes, and so on. Empiricists there are who would boggle at such prodigality. Carnap's starting point is very parsimonious, however, in its extralogical or sensory part. In a series of constructions in which he exploits the resources of modern logic with much ingenuity, he succeeds in defining a wide array of important additional sensory concepts which, but for his constructions, one would not have dreamed were definable on so slender a basis. Carnap was the first empiricist who, not content with asserting the reducibility of science to terms of immediate experience, took serious steps toward carrying out the reduction.

Even supposing Carnap's starting point satisfactory, his constructions were, as he himself stressed, only a fragment of the full program. The construction of even the simplest statements about the physical world was left in a sketchy state. Carnap's suggestions on this subject were, despite their sketchiness, very suggestive. He explained spatio-temporal point-instants as quadruples of real numbers and envisaged assignment of sense qualities to point-instants according to certain canons. Roughly summarized, the plan was that qualities should be assigned to point-instants in such a way as to achieve the laziest world compatible with our experience. The principle of least action was to be our guide in constructing a world from experience.

Carnap did not seem to recognize, however, that his treatment of physical objects fell short of reduction not merely through sketchiness, but in principle. Statements of the form "Quality q is at point-instant x; y; z; t" were, according to his canons, to be apportioned truth values in such a way as to maximize and minimize certain over-all features, and with growth of experience the truth values were to be progressively revised in the same spirit. I think this is a good schematization (deliberately oversimplified, to be sure) of what science really does; but it provides no indication, not even the sketchiest, of how a statement of the form "Quality q is at x; y; z; t" could ever be translated into Carnap's initial language of sense data and logic. The connective "is at" remains an added undefined connective; the canons counsel us in its use but not in its elimination.

Carnap seems to have appreciated this point afterward; for in his later writings he abandoned all notion of the translatability of statements about the physical world into statements about immediate experience. Reductionism in its radical form has long since ceased to figure in Carnap's philosophy.

But the dogma of reductionism has, in a subtler and more tenuous form, continued to influence the thought of empiricists. The notion lingers that to each statement, or each synthetic statement, there is associated a unique range of possible sensory events such that the occurrence of any of them would add to the likelihood of truth of the statement, and that there is associated also another unique range of possible sensory events whose occurrence would detract from that likelihood. This notion is of course implicit in the verification theory of meaning.

The dogma of reductionism survives in the supposition that each statement, taken-in isolation from its fellows, can admit of confirmation or information at all. My countersuggestion, issuing essentially from Carnap's doctrine of the physical world in the *Aufbau*, is that our statements about the external world face the tribunal of sense experience not individually but only as a corporate body.

The dogma of reductionism, even in its attenuated form, is intimately connected with the other dogma: that there is a cleavage between the analytic and the synthetic. We have found ourselves led, indeed, from the latter problem to the former through the verification theory of meaning. More directly, the one dogma clearly supports the other in this way: as long as it is taken to be significant in general to speak of the confirmation and information of a statement, it seems significant to speak also of a limiting kind of statement which is vacuously confirmed, *ipso facto*, come what may; and such a statement is analytic.

The two dogmas are, indeed, at root identical. We lately reflected that in general the truth of statements does obviously depend both upon language and upon extralinguistic fact; and we noted that this obvious circumstance carries in its train, not logically but all too naturally, a feeling that the truth of a statement is somehow analyzable into a linguistic component and a factual component. The factual component must, if we are empiricists, boil down to a range of confirmatory experiences. In the extreme case where the linguistic component is all that matters, a true statement is analytic. But I hope we are now impressed with how stubbornly the distinction between analytic and synthetic has resisted any straightforward drawing. I am impressed also, apart from prefabricated examples of black and white balls in an urn, with how baffling the problem has always been of arriving at any explicit theory of the empirical confirmation of a synthetic statement. My present suggestion is that it is nonsense, and the root of much nonsense, to speak of a linguistic component and a factual component in the truth of any individual statement. Taken collectively, science has its double dependence upon language and experience; but this duality is not significantly traceable into the statements of science taken one by one.

Russell's concept of definition in use was, as remarked, an advance over the impossible term-by-term empiricism of Locke and Hume. The statement, rather than the term, came with Russell to be recognized as the unit accountable to an empiricist critique. But what I am now urging is that even in taking the statement as unit we have drawn our grid too finely. The unit of empirical significance is the whole of science.

VI. Empiricism without the dogmas

The totality of our so-called knowledge or beliefs, from the most casual matters of geography and history to the profoundest laws of atomic physics or even of pure mathematics and logic, is a man-made fabric which impinges on experience only along the edges. Or, to change the figure, total science is like a field of force whose boundary conditions are experience. A conflict with experience at the periphery occasions readjustments in the interior of the field. Truth values have to be redistributed over some of our statements. Re-evaluation of some statements entails re-evaluation of others, because of their logical interconnections—the logical laws being in turn simply certain further statements of the system, certain further elements of the field. Having re-evaluated one statement we must re-evaluate some others, whether they be statements logically connected with the first or whether they be the statements of logical connections themselves. But the total field is so undetermined by its boundary conditions, experience, that there is much latitude of choice as to what statements to re-evaluate in the light of any single contrary experience. No particular experiences are linked with any particular statements in the interior of the field, except indirectly through considerations of equilibrium affecting the field as a whole.

If this view is right, it is misleading to speak of the empirical content of an individual statement—especially if it be a statement at all remote from the experiential periphery of the field. Furthermore it becomes folly to seek a boundary between synthetic statements, which hold contingently on experience, and analytic statements which hold come what may. Any statement can be held true come what may, if we make drastic enough adjustments elsewhere in the system. Even a statement very close to the periphery can be held true in the face of recalcitrant experience by pleading hallucination or by amending certain statements of the kind called logical laws. Conversely, by the same token, no statement is immune to revision. Revision even of the logical law of the excluded middle has been proposed as a means of simplifying quantum mechanics; and what difference is there in principle between such a shift and the shift whereby Kepler superseded Ptolemy, or Einstein Newton, or Darwin Aristotle?

For vividness I have been speaking in terms of varying distances from a sensory periphery. Let me try now to clarify this notion without metaphor. Certain statements, though *about* physical objects and not sense experience, seem peculiarly germane to sense experience—and in a selective way: some statements to some experiences, others to others. Such statements, especially germane to particular experiences, I picture as near the periphery. But in this relation of "germaneness" I envisage nothing more than a loose association reflecting the relative likelihood, in practice, of our choosing one statement rather than another for revision in the event of recalcitrant experience. For example, we can imagine recalcitrant experiences to which we would surely be inclined to accommodate our system by re-evaluating just the statement that there are brick houses on Elm Street, together with related statements on the same topic. We can imagine other recalcitrant experiences to which we would be inclined to accommodate our system by re-evaluating just the statement that there are no centaurs, along with kindred statements. A recalcitrant experience can, I have already urged, be accommodated by any of various alternative re-evaluations in various alternative quarters of the total system; but, in the cases which we are now imagining, our natural tendency to disturb the total system as little as possible would lead us to focus our revisions upon these specific statements concerning brick houses or centaurs. These statements are felt, therefore, to have a sharper empirical reference than highly theoretical statements of physics or logic or ontology. The latter statements may be thought of as relatively centrally located within the total network, meaning merely that little preferential connection with any particular sense data obtrudes itself.

As an empiricist I continue to think of the conceptual scheme of science as a tool, ultimately, for predicting future experience in the light of past experience. Physical objects are conceptually imported into the situation as convenient intermediaries—not by definition in terms of experience, but simply as irreducible posits comparable, epistemologically, to the gods of Homer. Let me interject that for my part I do, qua lay physicist, believe in physical objects and not in Homer's gods; and I consider it a scientific error to believe otherwise. But in point of epistemological footing the physical objects and the gods differ only in degree and not in kind. Both sorts of entities enter our conception only as cultural posits. The myth of physical objects is epistemologically superior to most in that it has proved more efficacious than other myths as a device for working a manageable structure into the flux of experience.

Imagine, for the sake of analogy, that we are given the rational numbers. We develop an algebraic theory for reasoning about them, but we find it inconveniently complex, because certain functions such as square root lack values for some arguments. Then it is discovered that the rules of our algebra can be much simplified by conceptually augmenting our ontology with some mythical entities, to be called irrational numbers. All we continue to be really interested in, first and last, are rational numbers; but we find that we can commonly get from one law about rational numbers to another much more quickly and simply by pretending that the irrational numbers are there too.

I think this a fair account of the introduction of irrational numbers and other extensions of the number system. The fact that the mythical status of irrational numbers eventually gave way to the Dedekind–Russell version of them as certain infinite classes of ratios is irrelevant to my analogy. That version is impossible anyway as long as reality is limited to the rational numbers and not extended to classes of them.

Now I suggest that experience is analogous to the rational numbers and that the physical objects, in analogy to the irrational numbers, are posits which serve merely to simplify our treatment of experience. The physical objects are no more reducible to experience than the irrational numbers to rational numbers, but their incorporation into the theory enables us to get more easily from one statement about experience to another.

The salient differences between the positing of physical objects and the positing of irrational numbers are, I think, just two. First, the factor of simplification is more overwhelming in the case of physical objects than in the numerical case. Second, the positing of physical objects is far more archaic, being indeed coeval, I expect, with language itself. For language is social and so depends for its development upon intersubjective reference.

Positing does not stop with macroscopic physical objects. Objects at the atomic level and beyond are posited to make the laws of macroscopic objects, and ultimately the laws of experience, simpler and more manageable; and we need not expect or demand full definition of atomic and subatomic entities in terms of macroscopic ones, any more than definition of macroscopic things in terms of sense data. Science is a continuation of common sense; and it continues the common-sense expedient of swelling ontology to simplify theory.

Physical objects, small and large, are not the only posits. Forces are another example; and indeed we are told nowadays that the boundary between energy and matter is obsolete. Moreover, the abstract entities which are the substance of mathematics—ultimately classes and classes of classes and so on up—are another posit in the same spirit. Epistemologically these are myths on the same footing with physical objects and gods, neither better nor worse except for differences in the degree to which they expedite our dealings with sense experiences.

The over-all algebra of rational and irrational numbers is underdetermined by the algebra of rational numbers, but is smoother and more convenient; and it includes the algebra of rational numbers as a jagged or gerrymandered part. Total science, mathematical and natural and human, is similarly but more extremely underdetermined by experience. The edge of the system must be kept squared with experience; the rest, with all *its* elaborate myths or fictions, has as its objective the simplicity of laws.

Ontological questions, under this view, are on a par with questions of natural science. Consider the question whether to countenance classes as entities. This, as I have argued elsewhere,[10] is the question whether to quantify with respect to variables which take classes as values. Now Carnap has maintained[11] that this is a question not of matters of fact but of choosing a convenient language form, a convenient conceptual scheme or framework for science. With this I agree; but only on the proviso that the same be conceded regarding scientific hypotheses generally. Carnap has recognized[12] that he is able to preserve a double standard for ontological questions and scientific hypotheses only by assuming an absolute distinction between the analytic and the synthetic; and I need not say again that this is a distinction which I reject.

Some issues do, I grant, seem more a question of convenient conceptual scheme and others more a question of brute fact. The issue over there being classes seems more a question of convenient conceptual scheme; the issue over there being centaurs, or brick houses on Elm Street, seems more a question of fact. But I have been urging that this difference is only one of degree, and that it turns upon our vaguely pragmatic inclination to adjust one strand of the fabric of science rather than another in accommodating some particular recalcitrant experience. Conservatism figures in such choices, and so does the quest for simplicity.

Carnap, Lewis, and others take a pragmatic stand on the question of choosing between language forms, scientific frameworks; but their pragmatism leaves off at the imagined boundary between the analytic and the synthetic. In repudiating such a boundary I espouse a more thorough pragmatism. Each man is given a scientific heritage plus a continuing barrage of sensory stimulation; and the considerations which guide him in warping his scientific heritage to fit his continuing sensory promptings are, where rational, pragmatic.

Notes

1 Much of this paper is devoted to a critique of analyticity which I have been urging orally and in correspondence for years past. My debt to the other participants in those discussions, notably Carnap, Church, Goodman, Tarski, and White, is large and indeterminate. White's excellent essay "The Analytic and the Synthetic: An Untenable Dualism," in *John Dewey: Philosopher of Science and Freedom* (New York: Dial Press, 1950), says much of what needed to be said on the topic; but in the present paper I touch on some further aspects of the problem. I am grateful to Dr. Donald L. Davidson for valuable criticism of the first draft.

2 See White, *op. cit.*, p. 324.

3 R. Carnap, *Meaning and Necessity* (Chicago: University of Chicago Press, 1947), pp. 9ff.; *Logical Foundations of Probability* (Chicago: University of Chicago Press, 1950), pp. 70ff.

4 This is cognitive synonymy in a primary, broad sense. Carnap (*Meaning and Necessity*, pp. 56ff.) and Lewis (*Analysis of Knowledge and Valuation* [La Salle, Ill.: Open Court, 1946], pp. 83ff.) have suggested how, once this notion is at hand, a narrower sense of cognitive synonymy which is preferable for some purposes can in turn be derived. But this special ramification of concept-building lies aside from the present purposes and must not be confused with the broad sort of cognitive synonymy here concerned.

5 See, e.g., my *Mathematical Logic* (New York: W.W. Norton & Company, 1940), sec. 24, 26, 27; or *Methods of Logic* (New York: Holt, 1950), sec. 37ff.

6 The "if and only if" itself is intended in the truth functional sense. See Carnap, *Meaning and Necessity*, p. 14.

7 The doctrine can indeed be formulated with terms rather than statements as the units. Thus C.I. Lewis describes the meaning of a term as "*a criterion in mind*, by reference to which one is able to apply or refuse to apply the expression in question in the case of presented, or imagined, things or situations" (*op. cit.*, p. 133).

8 John Horne Tooke, *The Diversions of Purley* (London, 1776; Boston, 1806), I, ch. ii.

9 R. Carnap, *Der logische Aufbau der Welt* (Berlin, 1928) [English translation: *The Logical Structure of the World* (Berkeley, Calif.: University of California Press, 1967)].

10 E.g., in "Notes on Existence and Necessity," *Journal of Philosophy* 40 (1943): 113–127.

11 Carnap, "Empiricism, Semantics, and Ontology," *Revue internationale de philosophie* 4 (1950): 20–40.

12 *Op. cit.*, p. 32, footnote.

QUESTIONS

1 What are the two "dogmas" Quine alludes to?
2 What sorts of statements does Quine think are subject to revision?
3 In Quine's terminology, what does it mean to say a statement is "close to the periphery" of our beliefs?

Rudolf Carnap, *Philosophical Foundations of Physics*

Non-Euclidean Geometries

In searching for an axiom to put in place of Euclid's parallel axiom, there are two opposite directions in which we can move:

(1) We can say that on a plane, through a point outside a line, there is *no* parallel. (Euclid had said there is exactly one.)
(2) We can say that there are *more than one* parallels. (It turns out that, if there are more than one, there will be an infinite number.)

The first of these deviations from Euclid was explored by the Russian mathematician Nikolai Lobachevski, the second by the German mathematician Georg Friedrich Riemann. In the chart in Table 1, I have placed the two non-Euclidean geometries on opposite sides of the Euclidean to emphasize how they deviate from the Euclidean structure in opposite directions.

Type of geometry	Number of parallels	Sum of angles in triangle	Ratio of circumference to diameter of circle	Measure of curvature
Lobachevski	∞	< 180°	$> \pi$	< 0
Euclid	1	180°	π	0
Riemann	0	> 180°	$< \pi$	> 0

Table 1

Lobachevski's geometry was discovered independently and almost simultaneously by Lobachevski, who published his work in 1835, and by the Hungarian mathematician Johann Bolyai, who published his results three years earlier. Riemann's geometry was not discovered until about twenty years later. If you would like to look further into the subject of non-Euclidean geometries, there are several good books available in English. One is *Non-Euclidean Geometry* by the

Rudolf Carnap, *Philosophical Foundations of Physics: An Introduction to the Philosophy of Science*, ed. Martin Gardner (New York: Basic Books, 1966).

Italian mathematician Roberto Bonola. It contains the two articles by Bolyai and Lobachevski, and it is interesting to read them in their original form. I think the best book that discusses non-Euclidean geometry from the point of view adopted here, namely, its relevance to the philosophy of geometry and space, is Hans Reichenbach's *Philosophie der Raum-Zeit-Lehre*, first published in 1928 but now available in English translation as *The Philosophy of Space and Time*. If you are interested in the historical point of view, there is Max Jammer's book, *Concepts of Space: The History of Theories of Space in Physics*. Sometimes Jammer's discussions are a bit metaphysical. I am not sure whether this is due to his own views or to those of the men he is discussing; in any case, it is one of the few books that takes up in detail the historical development of the philosophy of space.

Let us look more closely at the two non-Euclidean geometries. In the Lobachevski geometry, technically called hyperbolic geometry, there are an infinite number of parallels. In the Riemann geometry, known as elliptic geometry, there are no parallels. How is a geometry that does not contain parallel lines possible? We can understand this by turning to a model that is not exactly the model of an elliptic geometry, but one closely related to it—a model of spherical geometry. The model is simply the surface of a sphere. We view this surface as analogous to a plane. Straight lines on a plane are here represented by the great circles of the sphere. In more general terms, we say that in any non-Euclidean geometry the lines that correspond to straight lines in Euclidean geometry are "geodesic lines". They share with straight lines the property of being the shortest distance between two given points. On our model, the surface of the sphere, the shortest distance between two points, the geodesic, is a portion of a great circle. Great circles are the curves obtained by cutting the sphere with a plane through the sphere's center. The equator and the meridians of the earth are familiar examples.

In Figure 1 two meridians have been drawn perpendicular to the equator. In Euclidean geometry, we expect two lines perpendicular to a given line to be parallel, but on the sphere these lines meet at the North Pole and also at the South Pole. On the sphere there are no two straight lines, or, rather, quasistraight lines, *i.e.*, great circles, that do not meet. We have here, then, an easily imaginable model of a geometry in which there are no parallel lines.

The two non-Euclidean geometries can also be distinguished by the sum of the angles of a triangle. This distinction is important from the standpoint of empirical investigations of the structure of space. Gauss was the first to see clearly that only an empirical investigation of space can disclose the nature of the geometry that best describes it. Once we realize that non-Euclidean geometries can be logically consistent, we can no longer say, without making empirical tests, which geometry holds in nature. In spite of the Kantian prejudice prevailing in his time, Gauss may actually have undertaken an experiment of this sort.

It is easy to see that testing triangles is much easier than testing parallel lines. Lines thought to be parallel might not meet until they had been prolonged for many billions of miles, but measuring the angles of a triangle can be undertaken in a small region of space. In Euclidean geometry the sum of the angles of any triangle is equal to two right angles, or 180 degrees. In Lobachevski's hyperbolic geometry, the sum of the angles of any triangle is less than 180 degrees. In the Riemannian elliptic geometry the sum is greater than 180 degrees.

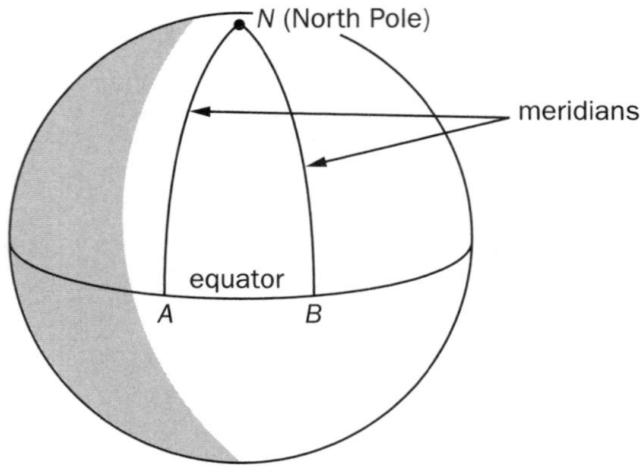

Figure 1

The deviation from 180 degrees, in elliptic geometry, is easily understood with the aid of our model, the surface of a sphere. Consider the triangle NAB in Figure 1; it is formed by segments of two meridians and the equator. The two angles at the equator are 90 degrees, so we already have a total of 180 degrees. Adding the angle at the North Pole will bring the sum to more than 180. If we move the meridians until they cross each other at right angles, each angle of the triangle will be a right angle, and the sum of all three will be 270 degrees.

We know that Gauss thought of making a test of the sum of the angles of an enormous stellar triangle, and there are reports that he actually carried out a similar test, on a terrestrial scale, by triangulating three mountain tops in Germany. He was a professor at Göttingen, so it is said that he chose a hill near the city and two mountain tops that could be seen from the top of this hill. He had already done important work in applying the theory of probability to errors of measurement, and this would have provided an opportunity to make use of such procedures. The first step would have been to measure the angles optically from each summit, repeating the measurement many times. By taking the mean of these observational results, under certain constraints, he could determine the most probable size of each angle and, therefore, the most probable value for their sum. From the dispersion of the results, he could then calculate the probable error; that is, a certain interval around the mean, such that the probability of the true value lying within the interval was equal to the probability of it lying outside the interval. It is said that Gauss did this and that he found the sum of the three angles to be not exactly 180 degrees, but deviating by such a small amount that it was within the interval of probable error. Such a result would indicate either that space is Euclidean or, if non-Euclidean, that its deviation is extremely small—less than the probable error of the measurements.

Even if Gauss did not actually make such a test, as recent scholarship has indicated, the legend itself is an important milestone in the history of scientific methodology. Gauss was certainly the first to ask the revolutionary question, what shall we find if we make an empirical investigation of the geometrical structure of space? No one else had thought of making such an investigation. Indeed, it was considered preposterous, like trying to find by empirical means the product of seven and eight. Imagine that we have here seven baskets, each containing eight balls. We count all the balls many times. Most of the time we get 56, but occasionally we get 57 or 55. We take the mean of these results to discover the true value of seven times eight. The French mathematician P.E.B. Jourdain once jokingly suggested that the best way to do this would be not to do the counting yourself, because you are not an expert in counting. The experts are the headwaiters, who are constantly adding and multiplying numbers. The most experienced head-waiters should be brought together and asked how much seven times eight is. One would not expect much deviation in their answers, but if you use larger numbers, say, 23 times 27, there would be some dispersion. We take the mean of all their answers, weighted according to the number of waiters who gave each answer, and, on this basis, we obtain a scientific estimate of the product of 23 and 27.

Any attempt to investigate empirically a geometrical theorem seemed just as preposterous as this to Gauss's contemporaries. They viewed geometry in the same way they viewed arithmetic. They believed, with Kant, that our intuition does not make geometrical mistakes. When we "see" something in our imagination, it cannot be otherwise. That someone should measure the angles of a triangle—not just for fun or to test the quality of optical instruments, but to find the true value of their sum—seemed entirely absurd. Everyone could see, after a little training in Euclidean geometry, that the sum *must* be 180 degrees. For this reason, it is said, Gauss did not publish the fact that he made such an experiment, nor even that he regarded such an experiment as worth doing. Nevertheless, as a result of continued speculation about non-Euclidean geometries, many mathematicians began to realize that these strange new geometries posed a genuine empirical problem. Gauss himself did not find a conclusive answer; but he provided a strong stimulation for thinking in a non-Kantian way about the whole problem of the structure of space in nature.

To see more clearly how the various non-Euclidean geometries differ from one another, let us again consider the surface of a sphere. As we have seen, this is a convenient model that helps us understand intuitively the geometrical structure of a plane in Riemannian space. (Riemannian space here means what is called elliptical space. The term "Riemannian space" also has a more general meaning that will be clarified later.)

We must be careful not to overextend the analogy between the Riemannian plane and the sphere's surface, because any two straight lines on a plane in Riemannian space have only one point in common, whereas the lines on a sphere that correspond to straight lines—the great circles—always meet at *two* points. Consider, for example, two meridians. They meet at both the North Pole and the South Pole. Strictly speaking, our model corresponds to the Riemannian plane only if we restrict ourselves to a portion of the sphere's surface that does not contain opposite points, like the North and South poles. If the entire sphere is our model, we must assume that each point on the Riemannian plane is represented on the surface of the sphere by a pair of opposite points. Starting from the North Pole and traveling to the South Pole on the earth would correspond to starting from one point on the Riemannian plane, traveling in a straight line on the plane, and returning to that same point. All geodesic lines in Riemannian space have the same finite length and are closed, like the circumference of a circle. The extreme deviation of this fact from our intuition is probably the reason this kind of geometry was discovered later than Lobachevski's geometry.

With the aid of our spherical model, we easily see that, in Riemannian space, the ratio of a circle's circumference to its diameter is always less than pi. Figure 2

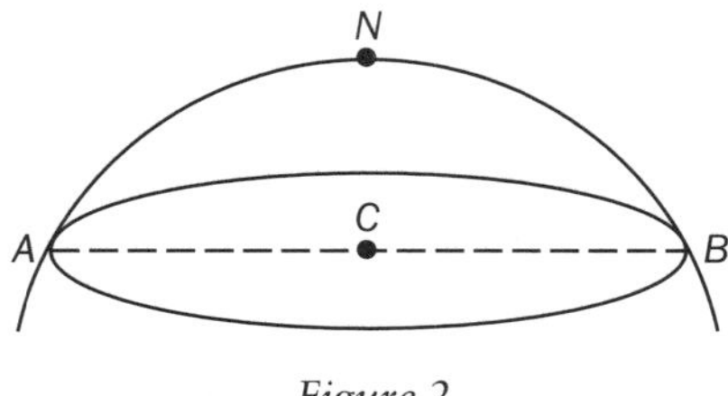

Figure 2

shows a circle on the earth that has the North Pole for its center. This corresponds to a circle in the Riemannian plane. Its radius is not the line *CB*, because that does not lie on the sphere's surface, which is our model. The radius is the arc *NB*, and the diameter is the arc *ANB*. We know that the circumference of this circle has the ratio of pi to the line segment *ACB*. Since the arc *ANB* is longer than the segment *ACB*, it is clear that the ratio of the circle's perimeter to *ANB* (the circle's diameter in the Riemannian plane) must be less than pi.

It is not so easy to see that in the Lobachevski space it is just the other way: the ratio of a circle's circumference to its diameter must be greater than pi. Perhaps we can visualize it with the aid of another model. This model (shown in Figure 3)

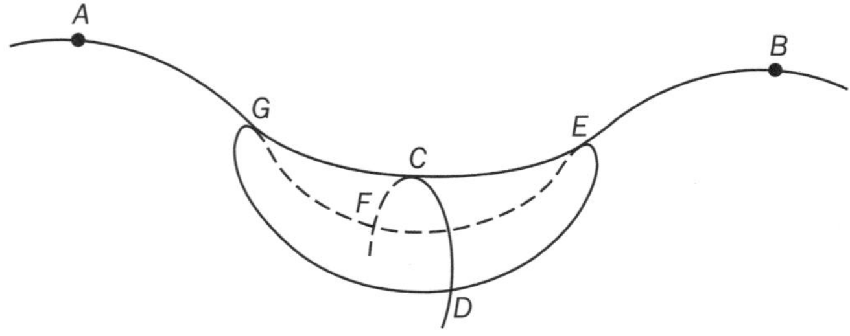

Figure 3

cannot be used for the entire Lobachevski plane—certainly not for three-dimensional Lobachevski space—but it can be used for a limited portion of the Lobachevski plane. The model is a saddle-shaped surface resembling a pass between two mountains. *A* is one mountain top, *C* is the pass, *B* is the other mountain top. Try to visualize this surface. There is a curve, perhaps a path, passing through point *F* on the far side of the pass, rising over the pass through point *C*, then going down on the near side of the pass through point *D*. The saddle-shaped portion of this surface, including points *C*, *D*, *E*, *F*, *G*, can be regarded as a model of the structure in a Lobachevski plane.

What form does a circle have on this model? Assume that the center of a circle is at *C*. The curved line *DEFGD* represents the circumference of a circle that is at all points the same distance from the center *C*. If you stand at point *D*, you find yourself lower than the circle's center; if you walk along the circle to *E*, you find yourself higher than the center. It is not hard to see that this wavy line, which corresponds to a circle in the Lobachevski plane, must be longer than an ordinary circle on a Euclidean plane that has *CD* for its radius. Because it is longer, the ratio of the circumference of this circle to its diameter (arc *FCD* or arc *GCE*) must be greater than pi.

A more exact model, corresponding accurately in all measurements to a part of a Lobachevski plane, can be constructed by taking a certain curve, called a tractrix (arc *AB* in Figure 4), and rotating it around the axis *CD*. The surface gener-

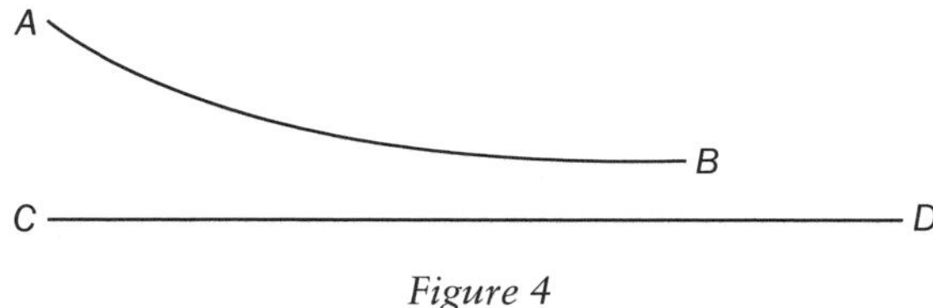

Figure 4

ated by this rotation is called a pseudosphere. Perhaps you have seen a plaster of Paris model of this surface. If you study such a model, you can see that triangles on its surface have three angles totaling less than 180 degrees and that circles have a ratio of circumference to diameter that exceeds pi. The larger the circle on such a surface, the greater will be the ratio's deviation from pi. We must not think of this as meaning that pi is not a constant. Pi is the ratio of the circumference of a circle in a Euclidean plane to its diameter. This fact is not altered by the existence of non-Euclidean geometries in which the ratio of a circle's circumference to its diameter is a variable that may be greater or less than pi.

All surfaces, both Euclidean and non-Euclidean, have at any of their points a measure called the "measure of curvature" of that surface at that point. The Lobachevski geometry is characterized by the fact that, in any plane, at any point, the plane's measure of curvature is negative and constant. There is an infinite number of different Lobachevski geometries. Each is characterized by a certain fixed parameter—a negative number—that is the measure of curvature of a plane in that geometry.

You might object that, if it is a plane, then it cannot have a curvature. But "curvature" is a technical term and is not to be understood here in the ordinary sense. In Euclidean geometry we measure the curvature of a line at any point by taking the reciprocal of its "radius of curvature". "Radius of curvature" means the radius of a certain circle that coincides, so to speak, with an infinitesimal part of the line at the point in question. If a curved line is almost straight, the radius of curvature is long. If the line is strongly curved, the radius is short.

How do we measure the curvature of a surface at a given point? We first measure the curvature of two geodesics that intersect at that point and extend in two directions, called the "principal directions" of the surface at that point. One direction gives the maximum curvature of a geodesic at that point, and the other gives the minimum curvature. We then define the curvature of the surface at that point as the product of the two reciprocals of the two radii of curvature of the two geodesics. For example, consider the mountain pass shown in Figure 3. How do we measure the curvature of this surface at point *C*? We see that one geodesic, the arc *GCE*, curves in a concave manner (looking down on the surface), whereas the geodesic at right angles to it, arc *FCD*, curves in a convex manner. These two geodesics give the maximum and minimum curvatures of the surface at point *C*. Of course, if we look *up* at this surface from the underside, arc *GCE* appears convex, and arc *FCD* appears concave. It does not matter at all from which side we view the surface, which curve we wish to consider convex and which concave. By convention, we call one side positive and the other negative. The product of the reciprocals of these two radii, $\frac{1}{R_1 R_2}$, gives us the measure of curvature of the saddle surface at point *C*. At any point on the saddle surface, one radius of curvature will be positive, the other negative. The product of the two reciprocals of those radii and, consequently, the measure of curvature of the surface, must therefore always be negative.

This is not the case with respect to a surface that is completely convex, such as that of a sphere or an egg. On such a surface, the two geodesics, in the two principal directions, both curve the same way. One geodesic may curve more strongly than the other, but both curve in the same manner. Again, it does not matter whether we view such a surface from one side and call the two radii of curvature positive or from the other and call them negative. The product of their reciprocals will always be positive. Therefore, on any convex surface such as that of a sphere, the measure of curvature at any point will be positive.

The Lobachevski geometry, represented by the saddle-surface model, can be characterized in this way: for any Lobachevski space, there is a certain negative value that is the measure of curvature for any point in any plane in that space. The Riemannian geometry, represented by the spherical surface, can be characterized in a similar way: for any Riemannian space, there is a certain positive value that is the measure of curvature for any point on any plane in that space. Both are spaces of constant curvature. This means that, for any one such space, the measure of curvature at any point, in any plane, is the same.

Let k be the measure of curvature. In Euclidean space, which also has a constant curvature, $k = 0$. In Lobachevski space, $k < 0$. In Riemannian space, $k > 0$. These numerical values are not determined by the axioms of the geometry. Different Riemannian spaces are obtained by choosing different positive value for k and different Lobachevski spaces are obtained by choosing different negative values for k. Aside from the value of the parameter k, all the theorems are entirely alike in all Lobachevski spaces and are entirely alike in all Riemannian spaces. Of course, the theorems of each geometry are quite different from those of the other.

It is important to realize that "curvature," in its original and literal sense, applies only to surfaces of a *Euclidean model* of a non-Euclidean plane. The sphere and the pseudosphere are curved surfaces in this sense. But the term "measure of curvature," as applied to non-Euclidean planes, does not mean that these planes "curve" in the ordinary sense. Generalizing the term "curvature," so that it applies to non-Euclidean planes, is justified, because the internal geometrical structure of a Riemannian plane is the same as the structure of the surface of a Euclidean sphere; the same is true of the structure of the plane in Lobachevski space and the surface of a Euclidean pseudosphere. Scientists often take an old term and give it a more general meaning. This caused no difficulty at all during the nineteenth century, because non-Euclidean geometries were studied only by mathematicians. The trouble began when Einstein made use of non-Euclidean geometry in his general theory of relativity. This took the subject out of the field of pure mathematics and into the field of physics, where it became a description of the actual world. People wanted to understand what Einstein was doing, so books were written explaining these things to the layman. In those books, the authors sometimes discussed "curved planes" and "curved space." That was an extremely unfortunate, misleading way of speaking. They should have said: "There is a certain measure *k*—mathematicians call it 'measure of curvature', but don't pay any attention to that phrase—and this *k* is positive inside the sun but negative in the sun's gravitational field. As we go farther away from the sun, the negative value of *k* approaches zero."

Instead of putting it this way, popular writers said that Einstein had discovered that the planes in our space are curved. That could only confuse the layman. Readers asked what it means to say that planes are curved. If they are curved, they thought, they should not be called planes! Such talk of curved space led people to believe that everything in space is distorted, or bent. Sometimes the writers of books on relativity even talked about how the force of gravitation bends the planes. They described it with real feeling, as if it were analogous to someone bending a metal sheet. This type of thinking led to strange consequences, and some writers objected to Einstein's theory on those grounds. All this could have been avoided if the term "curvature" had been avoided.

On the other hand, to introduce a term entirely different from one already in customary use in mathematics is not easy to do. The best procedure, therefore, is to accept the term "curvature" as a technical term but clearly understand that this term should not be connected with the old associations. Do not think of a non-Euclidean plane as being "bent" into a shape that is no longer a plane. It does not have the internal structure of a Euclidean plane, but it is a plane in the sense that the structure on one side of it is exactly like the structure on the other side. Here we see the danger in saying that the Euclidean sphere is a model of the Riemannian plane, because, if you think of a sphere, you think of the inside as quite different from the outside. From the inside, the surface looks concave; from the outside, it is convex. This is not true of the plane in either the Lobachevski or Riemannian space. In both spaces the two sides of the plane are identical. If we leave the plane on one side, we observe nothing different from what we observe if we leave the plane on the other side. But the inner structure of the plane is such that we can, with the help of the parameter *k*, measure its degree of "curvature." We must remember that this is curvature in a technical sense, and is not quite the same as our intuitive understanding of curvature in Euclidean space.

Another terminological confusion, easily cleared up, concerns the two meanings (we alluded to them earlier in this chapter) of "Riemannian geometry." When Riemann first devised his geometry of constant positive curvature, it was called Riemannian to distinguish it from the earlier space of Lobachevski, in which the constant curvature is negative. Later, Riemann developed a generalized theory of spaces with variable curvature, spaces that have not been dealt with axiomatically. (The axiomatic forms of non-Euclidean geometry, in which all of Euclid's axioms are retained except that the parallel axiom has been replaced by a new axiom, are confined to spaces of constant curvature.) In Riemann's general theory, any number of dimensions can be considered, and, in all cases, the curvature may vary continuously from point to point.

When physicists speak of "Riemannian geometry", they mean the generalized geometry in which the old Riemannian and Lobachevski geometries (today called elliptic and hyperbolic geometries), together with Euclidean geometry, are the simplest special cases. In addition to those special cases, generalized Riemannian geometry contains a great variety of spaces of varying curvature. Among these spaces is the space Einstein adopted for his general theory of relativity.

Chapter 15 Poincaré versus Einstein

Henri Poincaré, a famous French mathematician and physicist and the author of many books on the philosophy of science, most of them before the time of Einstein, devoted much attention to the problem of the geometrical structure of space. One of his important insights is so essential for an understanding of modern physics that it will be worthwhile to discuss it in some detail.[1]

Suppose, Poincaré wrote, that physicists should discover that the structure of actual space deviated from Euclidean geometry. Physicists would then have to choose between two alternatives. They could either accept non-Euclidean geometry as a description of physical space, or they could preserve Euclidean geometry by adopting new laws stating that all solid bodies undergo certain contractions and expansions. As we have seen in earlier chapters, in order to measure accurately with a steel rod, we must make corrections that account for the thermal expansions or contractions of the rod. In a similar way, said Poincaré, if observations suggested that space was non-Euclidean, physicists could retain Euclidean space by introducing into their theories new forces—forces that would, under specified conditions, expand or contract solid bodies.

New laws would also have to be introduced in the field of optics, because we can also study physical geometry by means of light rays. Such rays are assumed to be straight lines. The reader will recall that the three sides of Gauss's triangle, which had mountains for vertices, did not consist of solid rods—the distances were much too great—but of light rays. Suppose, Poincaré said, that the sum of the angles of a large triangle of this sort were found to deviate from 180 degrees. Instead of abandoning Euclidean geometry, we could say that the deviation is due to a bending of light rays. If we introduce new laws for the deflection of light rays, we can always do it in such a way that we keep Euclidean geometry.

This was an extremely important insight. Later, I shall try to explain just how Poincaré meant it and how it can be justified. In addition to this far-reaching insight, Poincaré predicted that physicists would always choose the second way. They will prefer, he said, to keep Euclidean geometry, because it is much simpler than non-Euclidean. He did not know, of course, of the complex non-Euclidean space that Einstein would soon propose. He probably thought only of the simpler non-Euclidean spaces of constant curvature; otherwise, he would no doubt have thought it even *less* likely that physicists would abandon Euclid. To make a few alterations in the laws that concern solid bodies and light rays seemed, to Poincaré, justified on the ground that it would retain the simpler system of Euclid. Ironically, it was just a few years later, in 1915, that Einstein developed his general theory of relativity, in which non-Euclidean geometry was adopted.

It is important to understand Poincaré's point of view; it helps us to understand Einstein's reasons for abandoning it. We will try to make it clear in an intuitive way, rather than by calculations and formulas, so that we can visualize it. To do this, we will use a device employed by Hermann von Helmholtz, the great German physicist, many decades before Poincaré wrote on the topic. Helmholtz wanted to show that Gauss had been right in regarding the geometrical structure of space as an empirical problem. Let us imagine, he said, a two-dimensional world in which two-dimensional beings walk about and push around objects. These beings and all the objects in their world are completely flat, like the two-dimensional creatures in Edwin A. Abbott's amusing fantasy, *Flatland*. They live, not on a plane, but on the surface of a sphere. The sphere is gigantic in relation to their own size; they are the size of ants, and the sphere is as large as the earth. It is so large that they never travel all the way around it. In other words, their movements are confined to a limited domain on the surface of the sphere. The question is, can these creatures, by making internal measurements on their two-dimensional surface, ever discover whether they are on a plane or a sphere or some other kind of surface?

Helmholtz answered that they can. They could make a very large triangle and measure the angles. If the sum of the angles were greater than 180 degrees, they would know they were on a surface with positive curvature; if they found the same positive curvature at every point on their continent, they would know they were on the surface of a sphere or of part of a sphere. (Whether the sphere is complete or not is another question.) The hypothesis that their whole universe was a spherical surface would be reasonable. We, of course, can see at a glance that it is such a surface because we are three-dimensional creatures who stand outside it. But Helmholtz made it clear that the two-dimensional creatures themselves, by measuring the angles of a triangle or the ratio of the circle to its diameter (or various other quantities), could calculate the measure of curvature at each spot on their surface. Gauss was right, therefore, to think he could determine whether our three-dimensional space has a positive or negative curvature by making measurements. If we imagine our space imbedded in a higher-dimensional universe, we can speak of a real bend or curvature of our space, for it would appear curved to four-dimensional creatures.

We must examine this a little more closely. Suppose that the two-dimensional creatures discover that, when they measure triangles with their measuring rods, at every point on their continent there is the same positive curvature for triangles of the same size. Among these creatures are two physicists, P_1 and P_2. Physicist P_1 maintains theory T_1, which says that the region on which he and his fellow-creatures live is part of a spherical surface S_1. His colleague, physicist P_2, maintains theory T_2, which says that the region is a flat surface S_2. In Figure 5 these

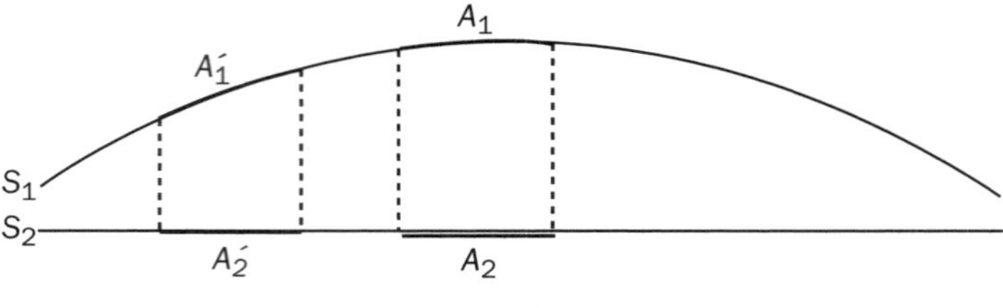

Figure 5

two surfaces are drawn in profile. Let us assume that in S_1 there are rigid two-dimensional bodies, such as creatures and measuring rods, that move about without change of size or shape. For every body in S_1 there is a corresponding flat body in S_2, which is its projection, a projection made by, say, parallel lines perpendicular to the plane S_2 (in the illustration these parallel lines are shown as broken lines). If a body in S_1 moves from position A_1 to A_1', its shadow body in S_2 moves from A_2 to A_2'. We assume that bodies in S_1 are rigid; therefore, the length A_1 is equal to that of A_1'. But this means that A_2' must be shorter than A_2.

Helmholtz pointed out that, when we measure something with a measuring rod, what we actually observe is nothing more than a series of point coincidences. This can easily be seen from our earlier description of the measurement of the edge of a fence, at the beginning of Chapter 9.

Look once more at Figure 1. The projection from S_1 to S_2 is called a one-to-one mapping. (This could not be done if S_1 were an entire sphere, but we have assumed that S_1 is only a limited region on a sphere.) For every point on S_1, there is exactly one corresponding point on S_2. Therefore, as beings move about on S_1, observing point coincidences between their measuring rods and what they are measuring, their shadow beings on S_2 make exactly the same observations on the corresponding shadow bodies. Since the bodies in S_1 are assumed to be rigid, the corresponding bodies in S_2 cannot be rigid. They must suffer certain contractions and expansions such as we have indicated in the illustration.

Let us return to the two physicists, P_1 and P_2 who hold different theories about the nature of their flat world. P_1 says that this world must be part of a sphere. P_2 insists that it is a plane but that bodies expand and contract in certain predictable ways as they move around. For example, they get longer as they move toward the central part of S_2, shorter as they move away from the center. P_1 maintains that light rays are geodesics on the curved surface S_1; that is, they follow the arcs of great circles. These arcs will project to S_2 as the arcs of ellipses. P_2, in order to defend his theory that the world is a plane, must, therefore, devise optical theories in which light rays move in elliptical paths.

How can the two physicists decide which of them is right? The answer is that there is no way of deciding. Physicist P_1 contends that their world is part of the surface of a sphere and that bodies do not suffer contractions and expansions except, of course, for such familiar phenomena (or, rather, the two-dimensional analogs of such phenomena) as thermal expansion, elastic expansion, and so on. Physicist P_2 describes the same world in a different way. He thinks it is a plane but that bodies expand and contract in certain ways as they move over the surface. We, who are in a three-dimensional space, can observe this two-dimensional world and see whether it is a sphere or plane, but the two physicists are restricted to their world. They cannot in principle decide which theory is correct. For this reason, Poincaré said, we should not even raise the question of who is right. The two theories are no more than two different methods of describing the same world.

There is an infinity of different ways that physicists on the sphere could describe their world, and, according to Poincaré, it is entirely a matter of convention which way they choose. A third physicist might hold the fantastic theory that the world had this shape:

He could defend such a theory by introducing still more complicated laws of mechanics and optics, laws that would make all observations compatible with the theory. For practical reasons, no physicist on the sphere would wish to propose such a theory. But, Poincaré insisted, there is no logical reason why he could not do so.

We can imagine a two-dimensional analog of Poincaré saying to the rival physicists: "There is no need to quarrel. You are simply giving different descriptions of the same totality of facts." Leibniz, the reader may recall, had earlier defended a similar point of view. If there is in principle no way of deciding between two statements, Leibniz declared, we should not say they have different meanings. If all bodies in the universe doubled in size overnight, would the world seem strange to us next morning? Leibniz said it would not. The size of our own bodies would double, so there would be no means by which we could detect a change. Similarly, if the entire universe moved to one side by a distance of ten miles, we could not detect it. To assert that such a change had occurred would, therefore, be meaningless. Poincaré adopted this view of Leibniz's and applied it to the geometrical structure of space. We may find experimental evidence suggesting that physical space is non-Euclidean, but we can always keep the simpler Euclidean space if we are willing to pay a price for it. As we have seen, Poincaré did not think that this price would ever be too high.

There are two basic points that our consideration of the flat world was intended to make clear and that we shall apply to our actual world. First, by making use of ordinary measuring procedures to which we are accustomed, we might arrive at the result that space has a non-Euclidean structure. Some recent philosophers (Hugo Dingler, for example) have not been able to see this. They hold that our measuring procedures employ instruments that have been manufactured under the assumption that geometry is Euclidean; therefore, these instruments could not possibly give us anything but Euclidean results. This contention is certainly wrong. Our instruments occupy such tiny parts of space that the question of how our space deviates from Euclidean geometry does not enter into their construction. Consider, for example, a surveyor's instrument for measuring angles. It contains a circle divided into 360 equal parts, but it is such a small circle that, even if space deviated from the Euclidean to a degree that Gauss hoped he could measure (a much greater degree than the deviation in relativity theory), it would still have no effect on the construction of this circle. In small regions of space, Euclidean geometry would still hold with very high approximation. This is sometimes expressed by saying that non-Euclidean space has a Euclidean structure in small environments. From a strict mathematical standpoint, it is a matter of a limit. The smaller the region of space, the closer its structure gets to the Euclidean. But our laboratory instruments occupy such minute portions of space that we can completely disregard any influence non-Euclidean space might have on their construction.

Even if the deviation from Euclidean geometry were so strong that the sum of the angles in a small triangle (say, one drawn on a designer's board) would differ considerably from 180 degrees, that fact could certainly be determined with the help of instruments made in the customary way. Suppose that the beings on the spherical surface S_1 (see Figure 1) construct a protractor by cutting a circular disk and dividing its circumference into 360 equal parts. If this protractor were used for measuring the angles of a triangle formed (as in an earlier example) by two half meridians and a quarter of the equator, it would show each angle to be 90 degrees and, therefore, the sum of the three angles to be 270 degrees.

The second basic point brought out by our consideration of the two-dimensional world is that, if we find empirical evidence of a non-Euclidean space, we can preserve Euclidean geometry provided we are willing to introduce complications into the laws that govern solid bodies and the laws of light rays. When we look at surfaces within our space, such as a surface on which we see an ant crawling, it is meaningful to ask whether the surface is a plane, or part of a sphere, or some other type of surface. On the other hand, if we are dealing with the space of our universe, a space we cannot observe as something imbedded in a universe of higher dimensions, then it is meaningless to ask whether space is non-Euclidean or whether our laws must be modified to preserve Euclidean geometry. The two theories are merely two descriptions of the same facts. We can call them equivalent descriptions because we make exactly the same predictions about observable events in both theories. Perhaps "observationally equivalent" would be a more appropriate phrase. The theories may differ considerably in their logical structure, but if their formulas and laws always lead to the same predictions about observable events, we can say that they are equivalent theories.

At this point, it is well to distinguish clearly between what we mean here by equivalent theories and what is sometimes meant by this phrase. Occasionally two physicists will propose two different theories to account for the same set of facts. Both theories may successfully explain this set of facts, but the theories may not be the same with respect to observations not yet made. That is, they may contain different predictions about what may be observed at some future time. Even though two such theories account completely for known observations, they should be regarded as essentially different physical theories.

Sometimes it is not easy to devise experiments that will distinguish between two rival theories that are not equivalent. A classic example is provided by Newton's theory of gravitation and Einstein's theory of gravitation. Differences in the predictions of these two theories are so small that clever experiments had to be devised and precise measurements made before it could be decided which theory made the best predictions. When Einstein later proposed his unified field theory, he said he was unable to think of any crucial experiment that could decide between this theory and other theories. He made it clear that his theory was not equivalent to any previous theory, but it was so abstractly stated that he was unable to deduce any consequences that could be observed under the present degree of precision of our best instruments. He believed that, if his unified field theory were investigated further or if our instruments improved sufficiently, it might be possible some day to make a decisive observation. It is very important to understand that "equivalent theories," as used here, means something much stronger than the fact that two theories account for all known observations. Equivalence here means that two theories lead in all cases to exactly the same predictions, like the theories of the two physicists in our flatland illustration.

In the next two chapters we will see in detail how Poincaré's insight into the observational equivalence of Euclidean and non-Euclidean theories of space leads to a deeper understanding of the structure of space in relativity theory.

Note

1 Poincaré's view on this matter is brought out most explicitly in his *Science and Hypothesis* (London: 1905); (New York: Dover, 1952).

QUESTIONS

1. What are the three kinds of geometrical system? What does each kind of geometry say about parallel lines?
2. What does each imply about the sum of the interior angles of a triangle?
3. Briefly, how do we know that a non-Euclidean geometry is consistent?
4. In Carnap's example of the physicists with the two different theories: (a) What kind of geometry obtains according to T_1? (b) What kind of geometry obtains according to T_2?
5. Which theory, if any, does Carnap prefer?

Laurence BonJour, "Appendix: Non-Euclidean Geometry and Relativity"

§A.1. Introduction

In this appendix, I will try to say something about the implications of non-Euclidean geometry and especially its role in the theory of General Relativity for a rationalist view of *a priori* knowledge. There can be little doubt that from a historical standpoint, the development of non-Euclidean geometries was a major factor in producing the widespread conviction that a rationalist position is untenable. Euclidean geometry was after all the most striking example of seemingly substantive *a priori* knowledge of independent reality, invoked by Kant as one of the crucial examples of the synthetic *a priori*. But, according to the simplest version of the standard story, within a few years after Kant, the development of non-Euclidean geometry by Lobashevsky and others showed that Euclidean geometry was not necessarily true of physical space, making it an empirical issue which geometry correctly describes the physical world. And eventually, or so the story goes, this empirical question was resolved by General Relativity in favor of a version of Riemannian or elliptical geometry and against Euclid. The suggested further argument, often left fairly implicit, is that if the rationalist view fails in this paradigmatic case, there can be no good reason for thinking that it will in the end be any more acceptable elsewhere.

My view is that this picture is oversimplified and misleading in important ways, which I will try to explain in what follows. But there are two important caveats that must be borne in mind throughout. The first is that there is no space here for anything like a comprehensive discussion of these matters, even if that were within my powers. And the second is that a really complete and authoritative discussion is clearly not within my powers in any case: I am not a mathematician or a physicist, nor even a philosopher of mathematics or physics. But I do not think that general epistemology can afford to leave these important issues entirely to specialists (whose grasp of the general epistemological issues is in any case not always beyond question).

One important point is easily made: even if the standard story were complete and accurate in every respect, it is not at all obvious that it would pose a serious objection to the sort of rationalist position that has been developed in the present book, namely a moderate rationalism that recognizes and indeed insists on the fallibility of rational insight. Even prior to the advent of non-Euclidean

Laurence BonJour, *In Defense of Pure Reason* (Cambridge University Press, 1998).

geometries, geometers and philosophers were worried about the status of the Euclidean parallels postulate: it seemed "less certain" than the others, and it was in fact in the course of attempts to derive it from the other postulates that non-Euclidean geometries were discovered. One further consideration here is that geometry is on any view a very special case. There is no reason to think that the same sort of situation, with different deductive systems covering the same general subject-matter, exists in other areas of alleged *a priori* knowledge: there are no alternative arithmetics, no alternative versions of calculus, etc.; and though some philosophers like to talk about alternative logics, it is far from clear that these are in the end more than purely formal constructions.[1] Thus there is, I submit, no reason why a rationalist could not simply concede that the *a priori* convictions underlying Euclidean geometry were mistaken in just the way the standard story claims, while still insisting that this provides no serious reason for skepticism about *a priori* justification in general. But while I believe that such a guarded response is dialectically adequate as a defense of the rationalist position, I also think that there are other and more interesting responses available, which I will briefly explore here.

§A.2. The mathematical and scientific background

We may begin with a somewhat fuller, though still very compressed description of the development of non-Euclidean geometry, followed by a similarly brief look at the theory of general relativity.[2] Euclid's presentation of his system of geometry relies on five postulates, the fifth of which has become known as the Parallel Postulate:

> If a straight line falling on two straight lines makes the interior angles on the same side together less than two right angles, the two straight lines, if produced indefinitely, meet on that side on which the angles are together less than two right angles.[3]

This postulate is substantially longer and more complicated than the other four. Euclid seems to have regarded it as less intuitively obvious or self-evident than the others and therefore makes as little use of it as possible. In the context of the other postulates it is equivalent to the following more familiar postulate (Playfair's Postulate):

> Through a given point not on a given line there exists exactly one parallel (i.e., line that does not intersect the given line) to the given line.

Note carefully that "parallel" here means precisely that the two lines will never intersect no matter how far they are extended, *not* that they are equidistant; and that a straight line is to be taken, at least initially, as simply one whose length between any two points on it is the shortest distance between those points.

Though Playfair's version is somewhat easier to understand than Euclid's original, it too was regarded as less than fully self-evident, and many attempts were made through the years to derive the Parallel Postulate from the other Euclidean postulates. Eventually, in the nineteenth century, it was discovered that if the

Parallel Postulate is replaced by one of the conflicting postulates (i) that many parallels exist or (ii) that no parallels exist, alternative systems still intuitively recognizable as geometries result. These systems (Lobashevskian or hyperbolic geometry, resulting from the many parallels postulate; Riemannian or elliptic geometry, resulting from the no parallels postulate[4]) can be modeled within Euclidean geometry and hence are formally consistent on the assumption that Euclidean geometry itself is consistent.

This result has by itself been widely regarded, both then and later, as a refutation of the claim that Euclidean geometry provides *a priori* insight into the nature of physical space. It is easy, however, to see that such a conclusion does not follow without an appeal to something like the moderate empiricist view of *a priori* justification, a view that was shown in Chapter 2, to be quite untenable. That non-Euclidean geometries are formally consistent shows indeed that Euclidean geometry is not logically necessary or analytic, that is, not such that its denial results (via merely logical transformations) in a *formal* contradiction. But from Kant's standpoint or that of the traditional rationalist, this is in no way surprising. Their claim, after all, is that geometry represents *synthetic a priori* knowledge, a claim that is *supported* in part, not refuted, by the discovery that competing geometries are formally consistent.

Thus the mere fact that non-Euclidean geometries are formally consistent, and more generally that the mathematics of curved and multi-dimensional spaces is perfectly acceptable as mathematics, does *not*, in and of itself, show that such theories represent *a priori* possible accounts of the structure of actual physical space. A useful issue for comparison here is that of the number of dimensions of space. There is no doubt that the mathematics of n-dimensional spaces is perfectly clear-cut and unproblematic, no matter how large n is taken to be or even indeed whether it remains finite. But it simply does not follow from the mathematics alone that, for example, fifteen-dimensional physical space is a genuine metaphysical possibility.[5] Analogously, the fact that non-Euclidean spaces are mathematically possible and coherent has in itself no tendency to show that the rationalists were wrong to think that we can know *a priori* that the space of the world is Euclidean.[6]

To give even the appearance of a problem for the rationalist, it is therefore necessary to bring in the physical theory somewhat inappropriately referred to as the General Theory of Relativity. General Relativity is fundamentally an attempt to give an account of gravitation that is consistent with Einstein's earlier (and much more strongly confirmed) theory of Special Relativity: one that avoids treating gravitational attraction across space as instantaneous. Einstein accomplishes this goal in part by identifying the structure of the gravitational field with the structure of space itself. Intuitively, the result is a view in which space itself is curved and in which the curvature of space varies with concentration of matter in a particular location, with the curvature being described by a complicated version of elliptical geometry. It is this result that, according to the simple version of the story outlined above, establishes that Euclidean geometry, far from being the *a priori* knowable truth about the physical world that rationalists have claimed, is not true at all.

But, as I have already suggested, this view of the situation is at the very least much too simple. In fact, the classic empirical tests of general relativity do not directly support the identification of the gravitational field with the structure of space. Rather they show such things as that light rays are deflected by the presence of a large gravitational mass. This is why an alternative theory with flat Euclidean space (or rather flat Minkowski space–time) can accommodate the same observations. Such a theory would postulate what Reichenbach referred to as "universal forces," forces that depend on the concentration of matter and that have the power to deflect light rays, distort measuring rods, affect the movement of clocks, and deflect moving particles. According to such an alternative theory, what Einstein discovered was not that Euclid was wrong about the structure of space, but rather that the effects of gravitation are far more complicated and pervasive than Newtonian physicists had realized.[7]

§A.3. Some alternatives

What then is the correct thing to say about the geometry of physical space in light of non-Euclidean geometry and General Relativity? We may approach this issue by considering the set of alternative positions distinguished by Sklar.[8]

(i) Poincaré's conventionalism: the choice between (a) General Relativity (with a non-Euclidean account of the geometry of space as a component) and (b) the view that combines a Euclidean account of space with a physics of universal forces is a matter of convention, with the choice to be decided on the basis of considerations like simplicity. Neither choice is correct in any deep metaphysical or epistemological sense.

(ii) Reichenbach's positivistic empiricism: the fact that both of these alternatives (and indeed others besides) are both logically consistent and compatible with all the evidence shows that there is no metaphysically or epistemologically significant choice to be made; while there may be methodological reasons for preferring one combined view to the other, at bottom they are simply two ways of saying the same thing, not two theories but just two ways of formulating a single theory.

(iii) "Apriorism": the view that Sklar refers to by this label holds that methodological criteria such as "simplicity, systematic power, elegance, etc." (121) provide a rational basis for deciding between empirically indistinguishable theories, where this presumably means one that is relevant to likelihood of truth, rather than to merely methodological or practical virtues (though Sklar is substantially less clear on this point than one would like).

(iv) Skepticism: though the opposed views in question do make genuinely distinct claims about the world, there is no rational basis that is relevant to truth for choosing among them. We are thus forever condemned to ignorance concerning the actual geometry of physical space.

A full consideration of these alternatives would greatly exceed the allowable bounds of the present discussion, but the points that matter for present purposes can be made quite briefly. (Sklar himself does not opt conclusively for any of these views.)

First, it is extremely hard to make clear sense of the conventionalist view. If conventionalism is to be distinct from the empiricist view, it must hold that the combined views in question do indeed make distinct claims about the world. But if this is so, why should it be thought acceptable to adopt one of these distinct views on a merely conventional basis, assuming that such adoption is understood to involve a claim of truth and not merely of practical acceptability? Lacking any good answer to this question, the conventionalist position collapses into skepticism—or else becomes indistinguishable from the empiricist view, if the claim that the two combined views are genuinely distinct is withdrawn.

Second, the empiricist alternative also seems untenable, though in a quite different way. From an intuitive standpoint, it seems obvious that there is a genuine difference between an infinite Euclidean space and a finite (though unbounded) Riemannian one, even if our empirical evidence is unable to distinguish between them. The verificationism that underlies this alternative in effect evades skepticism only by the transparent maneuver of insisting that any question that we are unable to answer must not be meaningful. Such a view has been thoroughly discredited in relation to other epistemological issues, and I can see no reason for taking it any more seriously in this area.

Third, "apriorism" as construed by Sklar represents only a modest improvement over the two positions just discussed. This view concedes, correctly I believe, that the choice between the opposed combined views is genuine and does not try to say that it can somehow be made on a merely conventional basis. But the claim that following methodological criteria like simplicity is conductive to finding the truth of the matter is almost entirely unsupported in Sklar's account and may well be insupportable. More importantly, as Sklar's label recognizes, any argument that could be made with respect to the truth conduciveness of these criteria could only be an *a priori* argument – and, we may add, not one that could be regarded as analytic in any plausible sense.

Thus Sklar's other three views all threaten to collapse into skepticism. Moreover, the most plausible of these purportedly non-skeptical views could be made adequate only by appeal to *a priori* insight of just the sort defended by the rationalist. The specific insights required for this purpose may not in the end be available, in which case the skeptic would prevail. But the fact that there is no apparent non-skeptical alternative to rationalism as an account of how we might have knowledge of the structure of space still seems to constitute a second reason, over and above that offered at the end of the first section above, for thinking that no serious basis for an anti-rationalist argument is to be found in this area.

§A.4. Geometry and rational insight

There is, however, one further point to be made, in some respects the most fundamental of all. One important question that has not been considered so far is whether there is after all any apparent rational insight or set of insights that supports the claim that Euclidean geometry correctly describes the structure of physical space. This question receives very little attention in the existing literature, where it tends to be assumed, without much discussion, that the seeming obviousness of the Euclidean perspective is merely a kind of psychological illusion.

Such a dismissive view may well be correct, but it does not seem to me obviously so. Nonetheless I will make no real effort to resolve this issue here, except to remark that it seems to me to turn in the end on whether or not we have an intuitive grasp of the notion of straightness that is independent of the identification of straight lines with such physical phenomena as the path of a light ray, one that would make it intelligible to say that all such physical phenomena might follow curved paths. If we have such an intuitive conception of straightness, then the usual discussions that turn on a dichotomy between a "pure geometry" that is merely an uninterpreted formal system and an "applied geometry" or "physical geometry" that depends on the identification of straight lines with physical phenomena omit a crucial alternative: a geometry that is neither merely formal nor in this sense physical, but rather reflects our intuitive notion of straightness and its implications. That there is such an alternative, which is obviously the one to which a traditional rationalism in this area would want to appeal, is far from clear; but to simply assume in setting up the issue that the dichotomy between pure and applied geometry is exhaustive, as so many discussions do, obviously begs the entire question.

My point for the moment, with which I will conclude this Appendix, is the more modest one that *if* there is after all an *a priori* insight or apparent insight that such a non-physical and also not merely formal geometry provides a correct account of the necessary features of space (and if this insight survives further reflective scrutiny), we have found *no reason at all* why it should not be accorded fully as much weight as any other such insight. Far from refuting such an insight, as we now see, the existence of consistent non-Euclidean geometries and the empirical case for General Relativity do not count against it in any way, since both of these results are fully compatible with a theory that incorporates the Euclidean view.

To be sure, if there were an *a priori* case to be made along the lines of Sklar's "apriorism" for the truth-conduciveness of some methodological criterion (or criteria) such as simplicity, and if the General Relativistic view that incorporates non-Euclidean geometry were preferable on the basis of this criterion (as it seems likely that it would be), then the apparent rational insight in favor of Euclid might after all be corrected and hence overridden, with experience playing a role in this result. But this would only be an example of the fallibility and corrigibility of apparent rational insight, as discussed above (see §§4.5–4.6), and thus once again would pose no special problem for the moderate rationalist.

Notes

1 An adequate defense of this remark would require a still wider investigation of issues centering around, though not confined to, the philosophy of quantum mechanics, an investigation that is even more obviously impossible here. For present purposes I can only record my conviction that the proposals for quantum logics that have been offered are of no real help in resolving or even understanding the seeming paradoxes that arise there. In a nutshell, what is required to make sense of quantum mechanics, if indeed this is possible, is not a new and better logic, but rather a new and better metaphysics.

2 I rely on many different sources here, but most of all on Lawrence Sklar's wonderful book *Space, Time, and Spacetime* (Berkeley, Calif.: University of California

Press, 1976). Parenthetical references in this Appendix are to the pages of this book. Sklar's own view of these issues will be briefly considered below.

3 Quoted in Sklar, pp. 14–15.

4 Hyperbolic geometry retains the other Euclidean axioms and tacit assumptions unaltered, but elliptic geometry requires changes in some of them as well: in fact the existence of parallels (though not of a unique parallel) can be proved from the other Euclidean axioms and assumptions; in addition, the fact that elliptic straight lines are circular or closed (great circles on the surface of a sphere are the most straightforward example) forces alterations in Euclid's implicit assumptions about the idea of betweenness (as made explicit, e.g., by Hilbert). These niceties can, however, be ignored for our limited purposes here.

5 For an argument, to my mind convincing, that space (as opposed to space–time) could not have more than three dimensions, see Richard Swinburne, *Space and Time*, 2nd ed. (London: Macmillan, 1981), chapter 7.

6 One possible source of confusion here is that mathematicians use the term "space" to refer to any abstract set of relations that has a structure analogous to ordinary space, i.e., roughly one that can be described in terms of locations represented by *n*-tuples of numbers. In this abstract sense, there is no doubt that non-Euclidean "spaces" are perfectly coherent and possible, as are *n*-dimensional spaces for even infinite values of *n* and indeed structures that are even more intuitively bizarre.

7 See Sklar, pp. 98–101, for further discussion.

8 Ibid., pp. 88–146. I have somewhat simplified Sklar's picture by abstracting from his concern with the tenability of the observational/theoretical distinction.

QUESTIONS

1 According to BonJour, is rational insight infallible?

2 According to BonJour, does the fact that non-Euclidean geometries are consistent refute the rationalist conception of our geometrical knowledge? Explain briefly why or why not.

3 Of the two theories discussed by Reichenbach and Carnap, which one would a rationalist be most likely to prefer?

FURTHER READING ON REASON AND THE A PRIORI

Ayer, A.J., "The A Priori," in *Language, Truth, and Logic* (New York: Dover Publications, 1952).

Bealer, George, "A Theory of the A Priori," *Philosophical Perspectives* 13 (1999): 29–55.

Benacerraf, Paul, "Mathematical Truth," *Journal of Philosophy* 70 (1973): 661–79.

BonJour, Laurence, *In Defense of Pure Reason* (Cambridge: Cambridge University Press, 1998).

Carnap, Rudolf, "The Elimination of Metaphysics through Logical Analysis of

Language," pp. 60–81 in *Logical Positivism*, ed. A.J. Ayer (New York: Free Press, 1959).

Field, Hartry, "Realism and Anti-Realism about Mathematics," *Philosophical Topics* 13 (1982): 45–69.

Field, Hartry, "Epistemological Nonfactualism and the A Prioricity of Logic," *Philosophical Studies* 92 (1998): 1–24.

Frege, Gottlob, *The Foundations of Arithmetic* (Evanston, IL: Northwestern University Press, 1980).

Fumerton, Richard, "A Priori Philosophy after an A Posteriori Turn," *Midwest Studies in Philosophy* 23 (1999): 21–33.

Harris, James and Richard Severens (eds) *Analyticity: Selected Readings* (Chicago: Quadrangle Books, 1970).

Irvine, A.D. (ed.) *Physicalism in Mathematics* (Dordrecht: Kluwer, 1990).

Kim, Jaegwon, "The Role of Perception in A Priori Knowledge: Some Remarks," *Philosophical Studies* 40 (1981): 339–54.

Kim, Jaegwon, "What is Naturalized Epistemology?," pp. 216–36 in *Supervenience and Mind* (Cambridge: Cambridge University Press, 1993).

Kitcher, Philip, "A Priori Knowledge," in *Naturalizing Epistemology*, ed. Hilary Kornblith (Cambridge, MA: MIT Press, 1994).

Kripke, Saul, *Naming and Necessity* (Cambridge, MA: Harvard University Press, 1980).

Miscevic, Nenad, "The Rationalist and the Tortoise," *Philosophical Studies* 92 (1998): 175–9.

Moser, Paul (ed.) *A Priori Knowledge* (Oxford: Oxford University Press, 1987).

Quine, W.V., *From a Logical Point of View* (New York: Harper, 1961).

Quine, W.V., *Ontological Relativity and Other Essays* (New York: Columbia University Press, 1969).

Resnik, Michael (ed.) *Mathematical Objects and Mathematical Knowledge* (Brookfield, VT: Dartmouth Publishing Co., 1995).

Schirn, Matthias (ed.) *The Philosophy of Mathematics Today* (Oxford: Clarendon Press, 1998).

4

TESTIMONY

Testimony, like memory, is an extremely pervasive source of knowledge that has traditionally been neglected by epistemologists. Here, I use "testimony" broadly, to include all cases in which a person asserts something, and another person hears, reads, or otherwise witnesses the assertion. In this sense, my beliefs that China is in Asia, that the Earth orbits the sun, and that my friend's birthday is on June 29, are all based on testimony. Testimony also plays a crucial role in science, where scientists' testimony as to their observations is relied upon by other scientists who are constructing theories. Yet, little has been written about the epistemology of testimony.

One reason for this neglect may lie in the traditional views, developed by such thinkers as Locke and Hume, about the probative value of testimony. Locke has particularly disparaging words to say about the practice of relying on testimony. He thinks both that other people are a highly unreliable source of information and that, even when they speak truthfully, one cannot gain true knowledge merely by taking someone else's word. His view was taken up by the Royal Society (a famous scientific organization that started in the 1600s and continues today) which adopted the motto *Nullius in verba* ("On no man's word"). This sort of attitude was largely a reaction to the over-reliance in medieval philosophy on appeals to authority.

David Hume is a bit more conciliatory: he regards testimony as simply one form of inductive evidence among others. In his essay "Of Miracles" (mainly a criticism of the belief in miracles), he lays down the basic principles of inductive evidence, including testimonial evidence: the probability one should assign to a given kind of event happening in given circumstances is proportional to the frequency with which events of that kind have, in one's past experience, happened in such circumstances. The reason that we are often justified in believing the testimony of others is simply that in the past, when we have been able to check, we have usually found the statements made by others to be true. He goes on to use these principles to argue that a belief in miracles cannot be justified on the basis of testimony, because it is always more likely that the testator is lying or mistaken than it is that a miracle has happened, since one has more past experience of people lying or being mistaken than one has of laws of nature being violated.

Here as elsewhere, Thomas Reid rejected the conventional wisdom of his time. Reid noticed that, if one had to rely solely upon induction as Hume proposed, one would have little ground for believing the majority of the things that we in fact believe on the testimony of others. The situation would be particularly difficult for children who, before accepting anything told them by an adult, would first have to acquire extensive experience and construct an inductive argument for the reliability of adults. Many children would probably be run over by cars or poison themselves before they succeeded in collecting all the necessary evidence. Fortunately, Reid observed, human beings have two innate tendencies which enable us much more easily to gain knowledge through testimony: the first is our instinctive tendency to tell the truth (as we see it); the second is the tendency simply to believe what others say. We have the latter tendency even before we have had a chance to test the reliability of others, and Reid thinks it is a good thing that we have it. This is not to deny that we may, after acquiring experience, have reason either to increase or to decrease our degree of trust in the testimony of others in certain circumstances (if you know someone has lied to you many times in the past, your innate tendency to trust his word will be defeated).

C.A.J. Coady similarly criticizes what he calls "the reductionist thesis," which holds that we rely on testimony because we have observed a correlation between what people say and what is true. One way of interpreting this idea is that people in general (or my community in general) have observed such a correlation. But this would lead to a circular argument, because in order to know that people have generally observed such a correlation, I would have to accept the testimony of others that they have observed such a correlation. Another interpretation is that each person *individually* has observed such a correlation. But Coady finds this suggestion "obviously false," in that most of us have never in fact checked on the veracity of the vast majority of reports that we have received from others. It seems that we simply lack a sufficient inductive basis for generalizing as to the reliability of other people.

Coady goes on to argue, furthermore, that it is not even coherent to suppose, as a proponent of the reductionist thesis does, that there could be a society in which people were generally *not* reliable in their testimony. In order for people to have a meaningful language or to count as making statements, there must be some sort of correlation between their utterances and features of reality. If some society regularly used the word "gnos" when in the *absence* of trees, it would not be correct to interpret "gnos" as meaning "tree." Finally, Coady criticizes one argument that Hume seems to make for the reductionist thesis: namely, the argument that since inductive evidence can *undermine* the credibility of testimony, therefore the credibility of testimony depends upon positive inductive evidence in favor of its reliability. Coady finds this argument invalid, comparing it to the (obviously invalid) argument that since testimony can undermine a belief based on observation, therefore the credibility of observation in general depends upon testimony.

John Locke, *Essay Concerning Human Understanding*

(Book I, chapter iv)

§23. What censure, doubting thus of innate Principles, may deserve from Men, who will be apt to call it, pulling up the old foundations of Knowledge and Certainty, I cannot tell: I perswade my self, at least, that the way I have pursued, being conformable to Truth, lays those foundations surer. This I am certain, I have not made it my business, either to quit, or follow any Authority in the ensuing Discourse: Truth has been my only aim; and where-ever that has appeared to lead, my Thoughts have impartially followed, without minding, whether the footsteps of any other lay that way, or no. Not that I want a due respect to other Mens Opinions; but after all, the *greatest reverence is due to Truth*; and, I hope, it will not be thought arrogance, to say, That, perhaps, we should make greater progress in the discovery of rational and contemplative *Knowledge*, if we *sought* it in the Fountain, *in the consideration of Things themselves*; and made use rather of our own Thoughts, than other Mens to find it. For, I think, we may as rationally hope to see with other Mens Eyes, as to know by other Mens Understandings. So much as we our selves consider and comprehend of Truth and Reason, so much we possess of real and true Knowledge. The floating of other Mens Opinions in our brains makes us not one jot the more knowing, though they happen to be true. What in them was Science, is in us but Opiniatrety, whilst we give up our Assent only to reverend Names, and do not, as they did, employ our own Reason to *understand* those *Truths*, which gave them reputation. *Aristotle* was certainly a knowing Man, but no body ever thought him so, because he blindly embraced, and confidently vented the Opinions of another. And if the taking up of another's Principles, without examining them, made not him a Philosopher, I suppose it will hardly make any body else so. In the Sciences, every one has so much, as he really knows and comprehends: What he believes only, and takes upon trust, are but shreads; which however well in the whole piece, make no considerable addition to his stock, who gathers them. Such borrowed Wealth, like Fairy-money, though it were Gold in the hand from which he received it, will be but Leaves and Dust when it comes to use.

John Locke, *Essay Concerning Human Understanding*, ed. P.H. Nidditch (Oxford: Clarendon Press, 1975).

(Book IV, chapter xx)

§17. *Fourthly*, The fourth and last *wrong Measure of Probability* I shall take notice of, and which keeps in Ignorance, or Errour, more People than all the other together, is that which I have mentioned in the fore-going Chapter, I mean, the *giving up our Assent to the common received Opinions*, either of our Friends, or Party; Neighbourhood, or Country. How many Men have no other ground for their Tenets, than the supposed Honesty, or Learning, or Number of those of the same Profession? As if honest, or bookish Men could not err; or Truth were to be established by the Vote of the Multitude: yet this with most Men serves the Turn. The Tenet has had the attestation of reverend Antiquity, it comes to me with the Pass-port of former Ages, and therefore I am secure in the Reception I give it: other Men have been, and are of the same Opinion, (for that is all is said,) and therefore it is reasonable for me to embrace it. A Man may more justifiably throw up Cross and Pile for his Opinions, than take them up by such Measures. All Men are liable to Errour, and most Men are in many Points, by Passion or Interest, under Temptation to it. If we could but see the secret motives, that influenced the Men of Name and Learning in the World, and the Leaders of Parties, we should not always find, that it was the embracing of Truth for its own sake, that made them espouse the Doctrines, they owned and maintained. This at least is certain, there is not an Opinion so absurd, which a Man may not receive upon this ground. There is no Errour to be named, which has not had its Professors: And a Man shall never want crooked Paths to walk in, if he thinks that he is in the right way, where-ever he has the Foot-steps of others to follow.

QUESTIONS

1 According to Locke, is reliance on the authority of learned people a good way to gain knowledge?

David Hume, "Of Miracles"

Part I

There is, in Dr. Tillotson's writings, an argument against the *real presence*, which is as concise, and elegant, and strong as any argument can possibly be supposed against a doctrine, so little worthy of a serious refutation. It is acknowledged on all hands, says that learned prelate, that the authority, either of the scripture or of tradition, is founded merely in the testimony of the apostles, who were eye-witnesses to those miracles of our Saviour, by which he proved his divine mission. Our evidence, then, for the truth of the *Christian* religion is less than the evidence for the truth of our senses; because, even in the first authors of our religion, it was no greater; and it is evident it must diminish in passing from them to their disciples; nor can any one rest such confidence in their testimony, as in the immediate object of his senses. But a weaker evidence can never destroy a stronger; and therefore, were the doctrine of the real presence ever so clearly revealed in scripture, it were directly contrary to the rules of just reasoning to give our assent to it. It contradicts sense, though both the scripture and tradition, on which it is supposed to be built, carry not such evidence with them as sense; when they are considered merely as external evidences, and are not brought home to every one's breast, by the immediate operation of the Holy Spirit.

Nothing is so convenient as a decisive argument of this kind, which must at least *silence* the most arrogant bigotry and superstition, and free us from their impertinent solicitations. I flatter myself, that I have discovered an argument of a like nature, which, if just, will, with the wise and learned, be an everlasting check to all kinds of superstitious delusion, and consequently, will be useful as long as the world endures. For so long, I presume, will the accounts of miracles and prodigies be found in all history, sacred and profane.

Though experience be our only guide in reasoning concerning matters of fact; it must be acknowledged, that this guide is not altogether infallible, but in some cases is apt to lead us into errors. One, who in our climate, should expect better weather in any week of June than in one of December, would reason justly, and conformably to experience; but it is certain, that he may happen, in the event, to find himself mistaken. However, we may observe, that, in such a case, he would have no cause to complain of experience; because it commonly informs us

David Hume, *Enquiry Concerning Human Understanding* (in *Enquiries*, ed. L.A. Selby-Bigge, Oxford: Clarendon Press, 1902).

beforehand of the uncertainty, by that contrariety of events, which we may learn from a diligent observation. All effects follow not with like certainty from their supposed causes. Some events are found, in all countries and all ages, to have been constantly conjoined together: Others are found to have been more variable, and sometimes to disappoint our expectations; so that, in our reasonings concerning matter of fact, there are all imaginable degrees of assurance, from the highest certainty to the lowest species of moral evidence.

A wise man, therefore, proportions his belief to the evidence. In such conclusions as are founded on an infallible experience, he expects the event with the last degree of assurance, and regards his past experience as a full *proof* of the future existence of that event. In other cases, he proceeds with more caution: He weighs the opposite experiments: He considers which side is supported by the greater number of experiments: to that side he inclines, with doubt and hesitation; and when at last he fixes his judgement, the evidence exceeds not what we properly call *probability*. All probability, then, supposes an opposition of experiments and observations, where the one side is found to overbalance the other, and to produce a degree of evidence, proportioned to the superiority. A hundred instances or experiments on one side, and fifty on another, afford a doubtful expectation of any event; though a hundred uniform experiments, with only one that is contradictory, reasonably beget a pretty strong degree of assurance. In all cases, we must balance the opposite experiments, where they are opposite, and deduct the smaller number from the greater, in order to know the exact force of the superior evidence.

To apply these principles to a particular instance; we may observe, that there is no species of reasoning more common, more useful, and even necessary to human life, than that which is derived from the testimony of men, and the reports of eye-witnesses and spectators. This species of reasoning, perhaps, one may deny to be founded on the relation of cause and effect. I shall not dispute about a word. It will be sufficient to observe that our assurance in any argument of this kind is derived from no other principle than our observation of the veracity of human testimony, and of the usual conformity of facts to the reports of witnesses. It being a general maxim, that no objects have any discoverable connexion together, and that all the inferences, which we can draw from one to another, are founded merely on our experience of their constant and regular conjunction; it is evident, that we ought not to make an exception to this maxim in favour of human testimony, whose connexion with any event seems, in itself, as little necessary as any other. Were not the memory tenacious to a certain degree, had not men commonly an inclination to truth and a principle of probity; were they not sensible to shame, when detected in a falsehood; Were not these, I say, discovered by *experience* to be qualities, inherent in human nature, we should never repose the least confidence in human testimony. A man delirious, or noted for falsehood and villany, has no manner of authority with us.

And as the evidence, derived from witnesses and human testimony, is founded on past experience, so it varies with the experience, and is regarded either as a *proof* or a *probability*, according as the conjunction between any particular kind of report and any kind of object has been found to be constant or variable. There are a number of circumstances to be taken into consideration in all judgements of this kind; and the ultimate standard, by which we determine all disputes, that may arise concerning them, is always derived from experience and observation. Where this experience is not entirely uniform on any side, it is attended with an unavoidable contrariety in our judgements, and with the same opposition and mutual destruction of argument as in every other kind of evidence. We frequently hesitate concerning the reports of others. We balance the opposite circumstances, which cause any doubt or uncertainty; and when we discover a superiority on any side, we incline to it; but still with a diminution of assurance, in proportion to the force of its antagonist.

This contrariety of evidence, in the present case, may be derived from several different causes; from the opposition of contrary testimony; from the character or number of the witnesses; from the manner of their delivering their testimony; or from the union of all these circumstances. We entertain a suspicion concerning any matter of fact, when the witnesses contradict each other; when they are but few, or of a doubtful character; when they have an interest in what they affirm; when they deliver their testimony with hesitation, or on the contrary, with too violent asseverations. There are many other particulars of the same kind, which may diminish or destroy the force of any argument, derived from human testimony.

Suppose, for instance, that the fact, which the testimony endeavours to establish, partakes of the extraordinary and the marvellous; in that case, the evidence, resulting from the testimony, admits of a diminution, greater or less, in proportion as the fact is more or less unusual. The reason why we place any credit in witnesses and historians, is not derived from any *connexion*, which we perceive *a priori*, between testimony and reality, but because we are accustomed to find a conformity between them. But when the fact attested is such a one as has seldom fallen under our observation, here is a contest of two opposite experiences; of which the one destroys the other, as far as its force goes, and the superior can only operate on the mind by the force, which remains. The very same principle of experience, which gives us a certain degree of assurance in the testimony of witnesses, gives us also, in this case, another degree of assurance against the fact, which they endeavour to establish; from which contradition there necessarily arises a counterpoize, and mutual destruction of belief and authority.

I should not believe such a story were it told me by Cato, was a proverbial saying in Rome, even during the lifetime of that philosophical patriot.[1] The incredibility of a fact, it was allowed, might invalidate so great an authority.

The Indian prince, who refused to believe the first relations concerning the effects of frost, reasoned justly; and it naturally required very strong testimony to engage his assent to facts, that arose from a state of nature, with which he was unacquainted, and which bore so little analogy to those events, of which he had had constant and uniform experience. Though they were not contrary to his experience, they were not conformable to it.[2]

But in order to encrease the probability against the testimony of witnesses, let us suppose, that the fact, which they affirm, instead of being only marvellous, is really miraculous; and suppose also, that the testimony considered apart and in itself, amounts to an entire proof; in that case, there is proof against proof, of which the strongest must prevail, but still with a diminution of its force, in proportion to that of its antagonist.

A miracle is a violation of the laws of nature; and as a firm and unalterable experience has established these laws, the proof against a miracle, from the very nature of the fact, is as entire as any argument from experience can possibly be imagined. Why is it more than probable, that all men must die; that lead cannot, of itself, remain suspended in the air; that fire consumes wood, and is extinguished by water; unless it be, that these events are found agreeable to the laws of nature, and there is required a violation of these laws, or in other words, a miracle to prevent them? Nothing is esteemed a miracle, if it ever happen in the common course of nature. It is no miracle that a man, seemingly in good health, should die on a sudden: because such a kind of death, though more unusual than any other, has yet been frequently observed to happen. But it is a miracle, that a dead man should come to life; because that has never been observed in any age or country. There must, therefore, be a uniform experience against every miraculous event, otherwise the event would not merit that appellation. And as a uniform experience amounts to a proof, there is here a direct and full *proof*, from the nature of the fact, against the existence of any miracle; nor can such a proof be destroyed, or the miracle rendered credible, but by an opposite proof, which is superior.[3]

The plain consequence is (and it is a general maxim worthy of our attention), "That no testimony is sufficient to establish a miracle, unless the testimony be of such a kind, that its falsehood would be more miraculous, than the fact, which it endeavours to establish; and even in that case there is a mutual destruction of arguments, and the superior only gives us an assurance suitable to that degree of force, which remains, after deducting the inferior." When anyone tells me, that he saw a dead man restored to life, I immediately consider with myself, whether it be more probable, that this person should either deceive or be deceived, or that the fact, which he relates, should really have happened. I weigh the one miracle against the other; and according to the superiority, which I discover, I pronounce my decision, and always reject the greater miracle If the falsehood of his testimony would be more miraculous, than the event which he relates; then, and not till then, can he pretend to command my belief or opinion.

Part II

In the foregoing reasoning we have supposed, that the testimony, upon which a miracle is founded, may possibly amount to an entire proof, and that the falsehood of that testimony would be a real prodigy: But it is easy to shew, that we have been a great deal too liberal in our concession, and that there never was a miraculous event established on so full an evidence.

For *first*, there is not to be found, in all history, any miracle attested by a sufficient number of men, of such unquestioned good-sense, education, and learning, as to secure us against all delusion in themselves; of such undoubted integrity, as to place them beyond all suspicion of any design to deceive others; of such credit and reputation in the eyes of mankind, as to have a great deal to lose in case of their being detected in any falsehood; and at the same time, attesting facts performed in such a public manner and in so celebrated a part of the world, as to render the detection unavoidable: All which circumstances are requisite to give us a full assurance in the testimony of men.

Secondly. We may observe in human nature a principle which, if strictly examined, will be found to diminish extremely the assurance, which we might, from human testimony, have, in any kind of prodigy. The maxim, by which we commonly conduct ourselves in our reasonings, is, that the objects, of which we have no experience, resembles those, of which we have; that what we have found to be most usual is always most probable; and that where there is an opposition of arguments, we ought to give the preference to such as are founded on the greatest number of past observations. But though, in proceeding by this rule, we readily reject any fact which is unusual and incredible in an ordinary degree; yet in advancing farther, the mind observes not always the same rule; but when anything is affirmed utterly absurd and miraculous, it rather the more readily admits of such a fact, upon account of that very circumstance, which ought to destroy all its authority. The passion of *surprise* and *wonder*, arising from miracles; being an agreeable emotion, gives a sensible tendency towards the belief of those events, from which it is derived. And this goes so far, that even those who cannot enjoy this pleasure immediately, nor can believe those miraculous events, of which they are informed, yet love to partake of the satisfaction at second-hand or by rebound, and place a pride and delight in exciting the admiration of others.

With what greediness are the miraculous accounts of travellers received, their descriptions of sea and land monsters, their relations of wonderful adventures, strange men, and uncouth manners? But if the spirit of religion join itself to the love of wonder, there is an end of common sense; and human testimony, in these circumstances, loses all pretensions to authority. A religionist may be an enthusiast, and imagine he sees what has no reality: he may know his narrative to be false, and yet persevere in it, with the best intentions in the world, for the sake of promoting so holy a cause: or even where this delusion has not place, vanity, excited by so strong a temptation, operates on him more powerfully than on the rest of mankind in any other circumstances; and self-interest with equal force. His auditors may not have, and commonly have not, sufficient judgement to canvass his evidence: what judgement they have, they renounce by principle, in these sublime and mysterious subjects: or if they were ever so willing to employ it, passion and a heated imagination disturb the regularity of its operations. Their credulity increases his impudence: and his impudence overpowers their credulity.

Eloquence, when at its highest pitch, leaves little room for reason or reflection; but addressing itself entirely to the fancy or the affections, captivates the willing hearers, and subdues their understanding. Happily, this pitch it seldom attains. But what a Tully or a Demosthenes could scarcely effect over a Roman or Athenian audience, every *Capuchin*, every itinerant or stationary teacher can perform over the generality of mankind, and in a higher degree, by touching such gross and vulgar passions.

The many instances of forged miracles, and prophecies, and supernatural events, which, in all ages, have either been detected by contrary evidence, or which detect themselves by their absurdity, prove sufficiently the strong propensity of mankind to the extraordinary and the marvellous, and ought reasonably to beget a suspicion against all relations of this kind. This is our natural way of thinking, even with regard to the most common and most credible events. For instance: There is no kind of report which rises so easily, and spreads so quickly, especially in country places and provincial towns, as those concerning marriages; insomuch that two young persons of equal condition never see each other twice, but the whole neighbourhood immediately join them together. The pleasure of telling a piece of news so interesting, of propagating it, and of being the first reporters of it, spreads the intelligence. And this is so well known, that no man of sense gives attention to these reports, till he find them confirmed by some greater evidence. Do not the same passions, and others still stronger, incline the generality of mankind to believe and report, with the greatest vehemence and assurance, all religious miracles?

Thirdly. It forms a strong presumption against all supernatural and miraculous relations, that they are observed chiefly to abound among ignorant and barbarous nations; or if a civilized people has ever given admission to any of them, that people will be found to have received them from ignorant and barbarous ancestors, who transmitted them with that inviolable sanction and authority, which always attend received opinions. When we peruse the first histories of all nations, we are apt to imagine ourselves transported into some new world; where the whole frame of nature is disjointed, and every element performs its operations in a different manner, from what it does at present. Battles, revolutions, pestilence, famine and death, are never the effect of those natural causes, which we experience. Prodigies, omens, oracles, judgements, quite obscure the few natural events, that are intermingled with them. But as the former grow thinner every page, in proportion as we advance nearer the enlightened ages, we soon learn, that there is nothing mysterious or supernatural in the case, but that all proceeds from the usual propensity of mankind towards the marvellous, and that, though this inclination may at intervals receive a check from sense and learning, it can never be thoroughly extirpated from human nature.

It is strange, a judicious reader is apt to say, upon the perusal of these wonderful historians, *that such prodigious events never happen in our days*. But it is nothing strange, I hope, that men should lie in all ages. You must surely have seen instances enough of that frailty. You have yourself heard many such marvellous relations started, which, being treated with scorn by all the wise and judicious, have at last been abandoned even by the vulgar. Be assured, that those renowned lies, which have spread and flourished to such a monstrous height, arose from like beginnings; but being sown in a more proper soil, shot up at last into prodigies almost equal to those which they relate.

It was a wise policy in that false prophet, Alexander, who though now forgotten, was once so famous, to lay the first scene of his impostures in Paphlagonia, where, as Lucian tells us, the people were extremely ignorant and stupid, and ready to swallow even the grossest delusion. People at a distance, who are weak enough to think the matter at all worth enquiry, have no opportunity of receiving better information. The stories come magnified to them by a hundred circumstances. Fools are industrious in propagating the imposture; while the wise and learned are contented, in general, to deride its absurdity, without informing themselves of the particular facts, by which it may be distinctly refuted. And thus the impostor above mentioned was enabled to proceed, from his ignorant Paphlagonians, to the enlisting of votaries, even among the Grecian philosophers, and men of the most eminent rank and distinction in Rome: nay, could engage the attention of that sage emperor Marcus Aurelius; so far as to make him trust the success of a military expedition to his delusive prophecies.

The advantages are so great, of starting an imposture among an ignorant people, that, even though the delusion should be too gross to impose on the generality of them (*which, though seldom, is sometimes the case*) it has a much better chance for succeeding in remote countries, than if the first scene had been laid in a city renowned for arts and knowledge. The most ignorant and barbarous of these barbarians carry the report abroad. None of their countrymen have a large correspondence, or sufficient credit and authority to contradict and beat down the delusion. Men's inclination to the marvellous has full opportunity to display itself. And thus a story, which is universally exploded in the place where it was first started, shall pass for certain at a thousand miles distance. But had Alexander fixed his residence at Athens, the philosophers of that renowned mart of learning had immediately spread, throughout the whole Roman empire, their sense of the matter; which, being supported by so great authority, and displayed by all the force of reason and eloquence, had entirely opened the eyes of mankind. It is true; Lucian, passing by chance through Paphlagonia, had an opportunity of performing this good office. But, though much to be wished, it does not always happen, that every Alexander meets with a Lucian, ready to expose and detect his impostures.

I may add as a *fourth* reason, which diminishes the authority of prodigies, that there is no testimony for any, even those which have not been expressly detected, that is not opposed by an infinite number of witnesses; so that not only the miracle destroys the credit of testimony, but the testimony destroys itself. To make this the better understood, let us consider, that, in matters of religion, whatever is different is contrary; and that it is impossible the religions of ancient Rome, of Turkey, of Siam, and of China should, all of them, be established on any solid foundation. Every miracle, therefore, pretended to have been wrought in any of these religions (and all of them abound in miracles), as its direct scope is to establish the particular system to which it is attributed; so has it the same force, though more indirectly, to overthrow every other system. In destroying a rival system, it likewise destroys the credit of those miracles, on which that system was established; so that all the prodigies of different religions are to be regarded as contrary facts, and the evidences of these prodigies, whether weak or strong, as opposite to each other. According to this method of reasoning, when we believe any miracle of Mahomet or his successors, we have for our warrant the testimony of a few barbarous Arabians: And on the other hand, we are to regard the authority of Titus Livius, Plutarch, Tacitus, and, in short, of all the authors and witnesses, Grecian, Chinese, and Roman Catholic, who have related any miracle in their particular religion; I say, we are to regard their testimony in the same light as if they had mentioned that Mahometan miracle, and had in express terms contradicted it, with the same certainty as they have for the miracle they relate. This argument may appear over subtile and refined; but is not in reality different from the reasoning of a judge, who supposes, that the credit of two witnesses, maintaining a crime against any one, is destroyed by the testimony of two others, who affirm him to have been two hundred leagues distant, at the same instant when the crime is said to have been committed.

One of the best attested miracles in all profane history, is that which Tacitus reports of Vespasian, who cured a blind man in Alexandria, by means of his spittle, and a lame man by the mere touch of his foot; in obedience to a vision of the god Serapis, who had enjoined them to have recourse to the Emperor, for these miraculous cures. The story may be seen in that fine historian;[4] where every circumstance seems to add weight to the testimony, and might be displayed at large with all the force of argument and eloquence, if any one were now concerned to enforce the evidence of that exploded and idolatrous superstition. The gravity, solidity, age, and probity of so great an emperor, who, through the whole course of his life, conversed in a familiar manner with his friends and courtiers, and never affected those extraordinary airs of divinity assumed by Alexander and Demetrius. The historian, a cotemporary writer, noted for candour and veracity, and withal, the greatest and most penetrating genius, perhaps, of all antiquity; and so free from any tendency to credulity, that he even lies under the contrary imputation, of atheism and profaneness: The persons, from whose authority he related the miracle, of established character for judgement and veracity, as we may well presume; eye-witnesses of the fact, and confirming their testimony, after the Flavian family was despoiled of the empire, and could no longer give any reward, as the price of a lie. *Utrumque, qui interfuere, nunc quoque memorant, postquam nullum mendacio pretium.* To which if we add the public nature of the facts, as related, it will appear, that no evidence can well be supposed stronger for so gross and so palpable a falsehood.

There is also a memorable story related by Cardinal de Retz, which may well deserve our consideration. When that intriguing politician fled into Spain, to avoid the persecution of his enemies, he passed through Saragossa, the capital of Arragon, where he was shewn, in the cathedral, a man, who had served seven years as a door-keeper, and was well known to every body in town, that had ever paid his devotions at that church. He had been seen, for so long a time, wanting a leg; but recovered that limb by the rubbing of holy oil upon the stump; and the cardinal assures us that he saw him with two legs. This miracle was vouched by all the canons of the church; and the whole company in town were appealed to for a confirmation of the fact; whom the cardinal found, by their zealous devotion, to be thorough believers of the miracle. Here the relater was also contemporary to the supposed prodigy, of an incredulous and libertine character, as well as of great genius; the miracle of so *singular* a nature as could scarcely admit of a counterfeit, and the witnesses very numerous, and all of them, in a manner, spectators of the fact, to which they gave their testimony. And what adds mightily to the force of the evidence, and may double our surprise on this occasion, is, that the cardinal himself, who relates the story, seems not to give any credit to it, and consequently cannot be suspected of any concurrence in the holy fraud. He considered justly, that it was not requisite, in order to reject a fact of this nature, to be able accurately to disprove the testimony, and to trace its falsehood, through all the circumstances of knavery and credulity which produced it. He knew, that, as this was commonly altogether impossible at any small distance of time and place; so was it extremely difficult, even where one was immediately present, by reason of the bigotry, ignorance, cunning, and roguery of a great part of mankind. He therefore concluded, like a just reasoner, that such an evidence carried falsehood upon the very face of it, and that a miracle, supported by any human testimony, was more properly a subject of derision than of argument.

There surely never was a greater number of miracles ascribed to one person, than those, which were lately said to have been wrought in France upon the tomb of Abbé Paris, the famous Jansenist, with whose sanctity the people were so long deluded. The curing of the sick, giving hearing to the deaf, and sight to the blind, were every where talked of as the usual effects of that holy sepulchre. But what is more extraordinary; many of the miracles were immediately proved upon the spot, before judges of unquestioned integrity, attested by witnesses of credit and distinction, in a learned age, and on the most eminent theatre that is now in the world. Nor is this all: a relation of them was published and dispersed every where; nor were the *Jesuits*, though a learned body, supported by the civil magistrate, and determined enemies to those opinions, in whose favour the miracles were said to have been wrought, ever able distinctly to refute or detect them. Where shall we find such a number of circumstances, agreeing to the corroboration of one fact? And what have we to oppose to such a cloud of witnesses, but the absolute impossibility or miraculous nature of the events, which they relate? And this surely, in the eyes of all reasonable people, will alone be regarded as a sufficient refutation.

Is the consequence just, because some human testimony has the utmost force and authority in some cases, when it relates the battle of Philippi or Pharsalia for instance; that therefore all kinds of testimony must, in all cases, have equal force and authority? Suppose that the Cæsarean and Pompeian factions had, each of them, claimed the victory in these battles, and that the historians of each party had uniformly ascribed the advantage to their own side; how could mankind, at this distance, have been able to determine between them? The contrariety is equally strong between the miracles related by Herodotus or Plutarch, and those delivered by Mariana, Bede, or any monkish historian.

The wise lend a very academic faith to every report which favours the passion of the reporter; whether it magnifies his country, his family, or himself, or in any other way strikes in with his natural inclinations and propensities. But what greater temptation than to appear a missionary, a prophet, an ambassador from heaven? Who would not encounter many dangers and difficulties, in order to attain so sublime a character? Or if, by the help of vanity and a heated imagination, a man has first made a convert of himself, and entered seriously into the delusion; who ever scruples to make use of pious frauds, in support of so holy and meritorious a cause?

The smallest spark may here kindle into the greatest flame; because the materials are always prepared for it. The *avidum genus auricularum*,[5] the gazing populace, receive greedily, without examination, whatever sooths superstition, and promotes wonder.

How many stories of this nature have, in all ages, been detected and exploded in their infancy? How many more have been celebrated for a time, and have afterwards sunk into neglect and oblivion? Where such reports, therefore, fly about, the solution of the phenomenon is obvious; and we judge in conformity to regular experience and observation, when we account for it by the known and natural principles of credulity and delusion. And shall we, rather than have a recourse to so natural a solution, allow of a miraculous violation of the most established laws of nature?

I need not mention the difficulty of detecting a falsehood in any private or even public history, at the place, where it is said to happen; much more when the scene is removed to ever so small a distance. Even a court of judicature, with all the authority, accuracy, and judgement, which they can employ, find themselves often at a loss to distinguish between truth and falsehood in the most recent actions. But the matter never comes to any issue, if trusted to the common method of altercations and debate and flying rumours; especially when men's passions have taken part on either side.

In the infancy of new religions, the wise and learned commonly esteem the matter too inconsiderable to deserve their attention or regard. And when afterwards they would willingly detect the cheat, in order to undeceive the deluded multitude, the season is now past, and the records and witnesses, which might clear up the matter, have perished beyond recovery.

No means of detection remain, but those which must be drawn from the very testimony itself of the reporters: and these, though always sufficient with the judicious and knowing, are commonly too fine to fall under the comprehension of the vulgar.

Upon the whole, then, it appears, that no testimony for any kind of miracle has ever amounted to a probability, much less to a proof; and that, even supposing it amounted to a proof, it would be opposed by another proof; derived from the very nature of the fact, which it would endeavour to establish. It is experience only, which gives authority to human testimony; and it is the same experience, which assures us of the laws of nature. When, therefore, these two kinds of experience are contrary, we have nothing to do but substract the one from the other, and embrace an opinion, either on one side or the other, with that assurance which arises from the remainder. But according to the principle here explained, this substraction, with regard to all popular religions, amounts to an entire annihilation; and therefore we may establish it as a maxim, that no human testimony can have such force as to prove a miracle, and make it a just foundation for any such system of religion.

I beg the limitations here made may be remarked, when I say, that a miracle can never be proved, so as to be the foundation of a system of religion. For I own, that otherwise, there may possibly be miracles, or violations of the usual course of nature, of such a kind as to admit of proof from human testimony; though, perhaps, it will be impossible to find any such in all the records of history. Thus, suppose, all authors, in all languages, agree, that, from the first of January 1600, there was a total darkness over the whole earth for eight days: suppose that the tradition of this extraordinary event is still strong and lively among the people: that all travellers, who return from foreign countries, bring us accounts of the same tradition, without the least variation or contradiction: it is evident, that our present philosophers, instead of doubting the fact, ought to receive it as certain, and ought to search for the causes whence it might be derived. The decay, corruption, and dissolution of nature, is an event rendered probable by so many analogies, that any phenomenon, which seems to have a tendency towards that catastrophe, comes within the reach of human testimony, if that testimony be very extensive and uniform.

But suppose, that all the historians who treat of England, should agree, that, on the first of January 1600, Queen Elizabeth died; that both before and after her death she was seen by her physicians and the whole court, as is usual with persons of her rank; that her successor was acknowledged and proclaimed by the parliament; and that, after being interred a month, she again appeared, resumed the throne, and governed England for three years: I must confess that I should be surprised at the concurrence of so many odd circumstances, but should not have the least inclination to believe so miraculous an event. I should not doubt of her pretended death, and of those other public circumstances that followed it: I should only assert it to have been pretended, and that it neither was, nor possibly could be real. You would in vain object to me the difficulty, and almost impossibility of deceiving the world in an affair of such consequence; the wisdom and solid judgement of that renowned queen; with the little or no advantage which she could reap from so poor an artifice: All this might astonish me; but I would still reply, that the knavery and folly of men are such common phenomena, that I should rather believe the most extraordinary events to arise from their concurrence, than admit of so signal a violation of the laws of nature.

But should this miracle be ascribed to any new system of religion; men, in all ages, have been so much imposed on by ridiculous stories of that kind, that this very circumstance would be a full proof of a cheat, and sufficient, with all men of sense, not only to make them reject the fact, but even reject it without farther examination. Though the Being to whom the miracle is ascribed, be, in this case, Almighty, it does not, upon that account, become a whit more probable; since it is impossible for us to know the attributes or actions of such a Being, otherwise than from the experience which we have of his productions, in the usual course of nature. This still reduces us to past observation, and obliges us to compare the instances of the violation of truth in the testimony of men, with those of the violation of the laws of nature by miracles, in order to judge which of them is most likely and probable. As the violations of truth are more common in the testimony concerning religious miracles, than in that concerning any other matter of fact; this must diminish very much the authority of the former testimony, and make us form a general resolution, never to lend any attention to it, with whatever specious pretence it may be covered.

Lord Bacon seems to have embraced the same principles of reasoning. "We ought," says he, "to make a collection or particular history of all monsters and prodigious births or productions, and in a word of every thing new, rare, and extraordinary in nature. But this must be done with the most severe scrutiny, lest we depart from truth. Above all, every relation must be considered as suspicious, which depends in any degree upon religion, as the prodigies of Livy: And no less so, every thing that is to be found in the writers of natural magic or alchimy, or such authors, who seem, all of them, to have an unconquerable appetite for falsehood and fable."[6]

I am the better pleased with the method of reasoning here delivered, as I think it may serve to confound those dangerous friends or disguised enemies to the *Christian Religion*, who have undertaken to defend it by the principles of human reason. Our most holy religion is founded on *Faith*, not on reason; and it is a sure method of exposing it to put it to such a trial as it is, by no means, fitted to endure. To make this more evident, let us examine those miracles, related in scripture; and not to lose ourselves in too wide a field, let us confine ourselves to such as we find in the *Pentateuch*, which we shall examine, according to the principles of these pretended Christians, not as the word or testimony of God himself, but as the production of a mere human writer and historian. Here then we are first to consider a book, presented to us by a barbarous and ignorant people, written in an age when they were still more barbarous, and in all probability long after the facts which it relates, corroborated by no concurring testimony, and resembling those fabulous accounts, which every nation gives of its origin. Upon reading this book, we find it full of prodigies and miracles. It gives an account of a state of the world and of human nature entirely different from the present: Of our fall from that state: Of the age of man, extended to near a thousand years: Of the destruction of the world by a deluge: Of the arbitrary choice of one people, as the favourites of heaven; and that people the countrymen of the author: Of their deliverance from bondage by prodigies the most astonishing imaginable: I desire any one to lay his hand upon his heart, and after a serious consideration declare, whether he thinks that the falsehood of such a book, supported by such a testimony, would be more extraordinary and miraculous than all the miracles it relates; which is, however, necessary to make it be received, according to the measures of probability above established.

What we have said of miracles may be applied, without any variation, to prophecies; and indeed, all prophecies are real miracles, and as such only, can be admitted as proofs of any revelation. If it did not exceed the capacity of human nature to foretell future events, it would be absurd to employ any prophecy as an argument for a divine mission or authority from heaven. So that, upon the whole, we may conclude, that the *Christian Religion* not only was at first attended with miracles, but even at this day cannot be believed by any reasonable person without one. Mere reason is insufficient to convince us of its veracity: And whoever is moved by *Faith* to assent to it, is conscious of a continued miracle in his own person, which subverts all the principles of his understanding, and gives him a determination to believe what is most contrary to custom and experience.

Notes

1 Plutarch, in vita Catonis.

2 No Indian, it is evident, could have experience that water did not freeze in cold climates. This is placing nature in a situation quite unknown to him; and it is impossible for him to tell *a priori* what will result from it. It is making a new experiment, the consequence of which is always uncertain. One may sometimes conjecture from analogy what will follow; but still this is but conjecture. And it must be confessed, that, in the present case of freezing, the event follows contrary to the rules of analogy, and is such as a rational Indian would not look for. The operations of cold upon water are not gradual, according to the degrees of cold; but whenever it comes to the freezing point, the water passes in a moment, from the utmost liquidity to perfect hardness. Such an event, therefore, may be denominated *extraordinary*, and requires a pretty strong testimony, to render it credible to people in a warm climate; But still it is not *miraculous*, nor contrary to uniform experience of the course of nature in cases where all the circumstances are the same. The inhabitants of Sumatra have always seen water fluid in their own climate, and the freezing of their rivers ought to be deemed a prodigy: But they never saw water in Muscovy during the winter; and therefore they cannot reasonably be positive what would there be the consequence.

3 Sometimes an event may not, *in itself, seem* to be contrary to the laws of nature, and yet, if it were real, it might, by reason of some circumstances, be

denominated a miracle; because, in *fact*, it is contrary to these laws. Thus if a person, claiming a divine authority, should command a sick person to be well, a healthful man to fall down dead, the clouds to pour rain, the winds to blow, in short, should order many natural events, which immediately follow upon his command; these might justly be esteemed miracles, because they are really, in this case, contrary to the laws of nature. For if any suspicion remain, that the event and command concurred by accident, there is no miracle and no transgression of the laws of nature. If this suspicion be removed, there is evidently a miracle, and a transgression of these laws; because nothing can be more contrary to nature than that the voice or command of a man should have such an influence. A miracle may be accurately defined, *a transgression of a law of nature by a particular volition of the Deity, or by the interposition of some invisible agent*. A miracle may either be discoverable by men or not. This alters not its nature and essence. The raising of a house or ship into the air is a visible miracle. The raising of a feather, when the wind wants ever so little of a force requisite for that purpose, is as real a miracle, though not so sensible with regard to us.

4 Hist. lib. iv. cap. 81. Suetonius gives nearly the same account *in vita* Vesp.

5 Lucret.

6 Nov. Org. lib. ii. aph. 29.

QUESTIONS

1 According to Hume, what is a miracle?

2 What is the difference between the sort of experience that provides a "proof" of a generalization, and the sort of experience that provides "probability"?

3 (Referring to question 3) According to Hume, which sort of evidence do we have for the laws of nature?

4 According to Hume, which sort of evidence do we have for the veracity of human testimony?

Thomas Reid, *Inquiry into the Human Mind*

Of the analogy between perception and the credit we give to human testimony

The objects of human knowledge are innumerable; but the channels by which it is conveyed to the mind are few. Among these, the perception of external things by our senses, and the informations which we receive upon human testimony, are not the least considerable; and so remarkable is the analogy between these two, and the analogy between the principles of the mind which are subservient to the one and those which are subservient to the other, that, without further apology, we shall consider them together.

In the testimony of Nature given by the senses, as well as in human testimony given by language, things are signified to us by signs: and in one as well as the other, the mind, either by original principles or by custom, passes from the sign to the conception and belief of the things signified.

We have distinguished our perceptions into original and acquired; and language, into natural and artificial. Between acquired perception and artificial language, there is a great analogy; but still a greater between original perception and natural language.

The signs in original perception are sensations, of which Nature hath given us a great variety, suited to the variety of the things signified by them. Nature hath established a real connection between the signs and the things signified; and Nature hath also taught us the interpretation of the signs—so that, previous to experience, the sign suggests the thing signified, and create the belief of it.

The signs in natural language are features of the face, gestures of the body, and modulations of the voice; the variety of which is suited to the variety of the things signified by them. Nature hath established a real connection between these signs, and the thoughts and dispositions of the mind which are signified by them; and Nature hath taught us the interpretation of these signs; so that, previous to experience, the signs suggest the thing signified, and create the belief of it.

A man in company, without doing good or evil, without uttering an articulate sound, may behave himself gracefully, civilly, politely; or, on the contrary, meanly, rudely, and impertinently. We see the dispositions of his mind by their natural signs in his countenance and behaviour, in the same manner as we

Thomas Reid, *Inquiry into the Human Mind*, from *Inquiry and Essays*, ed. R.E. Beanblossom and K. Lehrer (Indianapolis, Ind.: Hackett, 1983).

perceive the figure and other qualities of bodies by the sensations which nature hath connected with them.

The signs in the natural language of the human countenance and behaviour, as well as the signs in our original perceptions, have the same signification in all climates and in all nations; and the skill of interpreting them is not acquired, but innate.

In acquired perception, the signs are either sensations, or things which we perceive by means of sensations. The connection between the sign and the thing signified, is established by nature; and we discover this connection by experience; but not without the aid of our original perceptions, or of those which we have already acquired. After this connection is discovered, the sign, in like manner as in original perception, always suggests the things signified, and creates the belief of it.

In artificial language, the signs are articulate sounds, whose connection with the things signified by them, is established by the will of men; and, in learning our mother tongue, we discover this connection by experience; but not without the aid of natural language, or of what we had before attained of artificial language. And, after this connection is discovered, the sign, as in natural language, always suggests the thing signified, and creates the belief of it.

Our original perceptions are few, compared with the acquired; but, without the former, we could not possibly attain the latter. In like manner, natural language is scanty, compared with artificial; but, without the former, we could not possibly attain the latter.

Our original perceptions, as well as the natural language of human features and gestures, must be resolved into particular principles of the human constitution. Thus, it is by one particular principle of our constitution that certain features express anger; and, by another particular principle, that certain features express benevolence. It is, in like manner, by one particular principle of our constitution that a certain sensation signifies hardness in the body which I handle; and it is by another particular principle that a certain sensation signifies motion in that body.

But our acquired perceptions, and the information we receive by means of artificial language, must be resolved into general principles of the human constitution. When a painter perceives that this picture is the work of Raphael, that the work of Titian; a jeweller, that this is a true diamond, that a counterfeit; a sailor, that this is a ship of five hundred ton, that of four hundred; these different acquired perceptions are produced by the same general principles of the human mind, which have a different operation in the same person according as they are variously applied, and in different persons according to the diversity of their education and manner of life. In like manner, when certain articulate sounds convey to my mind the knowledge of the battle of Pharsalia, and others, the knowledge of the battle of Poltowa—when a Frenchman and an Englishman receive the same information by different articulate sounds—the signs used in these different cases, produce the knowledge and belief of the things signified, by means of the same general principles of the human constitution.

Now, if we compare the general principles of our constitution, which fit us for receiving information from our fellow-creatures by language, with the general principles which fit us for acquiring the perception of things by our senses, we shall find them to be very similar in their nature and manner of operation.

When we begin to learn our mother tongue, we perceive, by the help of natural language, that they who speak to us use certain sounds to express certain things we imitate the same sounds when we would express the same things; and find that we are understood.

But here a difficulty occurs which merits our attention, because the solution of it leads to some original principles of the human mind, which are of great importance, and of very extensive influence. We know by experience that men *have* used such words to express such things; but all experience is of the *past*, and can, of itself, give no notion or belief of what is *future*. How come we, then, to believe, and to rely upon it with assurance, that men, who have it in their power to do otherwise, will continue to use the same words when they think the same things? Whence comes this knowledge and belief—this foresight, we ought rather to call it—of the future and voluntary actions of our fellow-creatures? Have they promised that they will never impose upon us by equivocation or falsehood? No, they have not. And, if they had, this would not solve the difficulty; for such promise must be expressed by words or by other signs; and, before we can rely upon it, we must be assured that they put the usual meaning upon the signs which express that promise. No man of common sense ever thought of taking a man's own word for his honesty; and it is evident that we take his veracity for granted when we lay any stress upon his word or promise. I might add, that this reliance upon the declarations and testimony of men is found in children long before they know what a promise is.

There is, therefore, in the human mind an early anticipation, neither derived from experience, nor from reason, nor from any compact or promise, that our fellow-creatures will use the same signs in language, when they have the same sentiments.

This is, in reality, a kind of prescience of human actions; and it seems to me to be an original principle of the human constitution, without which we should be incapable of language, and consequently incapable of instruction.

The wise and beneficent Author of Nature, who intended that we should be social creatures, and that we should receive the greatest and most important part of our knowledge by the information of others, hath, for these purposes, implanted in our natures two principles that tally with each other.

The first of these principles is, a propensity to speak truth, and to use the signs of language so as to convey our real sentiments. This principle has a powerful operation, even in the greatest liars; for where they lie once, they speak truth a hundred times. Truth is always uppermost, and is the natural issue of the mind. It requires no art or training, no inducement or temptation, but only that we yield to a natural impulse. Lying, on the contrary, is doing violence to our nature; and is never practised, even by the worst men, without some temptation. Speaking truth is like using our natural food, which we would do from appetite, although it answered no end; but lying is like taking physic, which is nauseous to the taste, and which no man takes but for some end which he cannot otherwise attain.

If it should be objected, That men may be influenced by moral or political considerations to speak truth, and, therefore, that their doing so is no proof of such an original principle as we have mentioned—I answer, First, That moral or political considerations can have no influence until we arrive at years of understanding and reflection; and it is certain, from experience, that children keep to truth invariably, before they are capable of being influenced by such considerations. Secondly, When we are influenced by moral or political considerations, we must be conscious of that influence, and capable of perceiving it upon reflection. Now, when I reflect upon my actions most attentively, I am not conscious that, in speaking truth, I am influenced on ordinary occasions by any motive, moral or political. I find that truth is always at the door of my lips, and goes forth spontaneously, if not held back. It requires neither good nor bad intention to bring it forth, but only that I be artless and undesigning. There may indeed be temptations to falsehood, which would be too strong for the natural principle of veracity, unaided by principles of honour or virtue; but where there is no such temptation, we speak truth by instinct—and this instinct is the principle I have been explaining.

By this instinct, a real connection is formed between our words and our thoughts, and thereby the former become fit to be signs of the latter, which they could not otherwise be. And although this connection is broken in every instance of lying and equivocation, yet these instances being comparatively few, the authority of human testimony is only weakened by them, but not destroyed.

Another original principle implanted in us by the Supreme Being, is a disposition to confide in the veracity of others, and to believe what they tell us. This is the counterpart to the former; and, as that may be called *the principle of veracity*, we shall, for want of a more proper name, call this *the principle of credulity*. It is unlimited in children, until they meet with instances of deceit and falsehood; and it retains a very considerable degree of strength through life.

If Nature had left the mind of the speaker *in aequilibrio*, without any inclination to the side of truth more than to that of falsehood, children would lie as often as they speak truth, until reason was so far ripened as to suggest the imprudence of lying, or conscience, as to suggest its immorality. And if Nature had left the mind of the hearer *in aequilibrio*, without any inclination to the side of belief more than to that of disbelief, we should take no man's word until we had positive evidence that he spoke truth. His testimony would, in this case, have no more authority than his dreams; which may be true or false, but no man is disposed to believe them, on this account, that they were dreamed. It is evident that, in the matter of testimony, the balance of human judgment is by nature inclined to the side of belief; and turns to that side of itself, when there is nothing put into the opposite scale. If it was not so, no proposition that is uttered in discourse would be believed, until it was examined and tried by reason; and most men would be unable to find reasons for believing the thousandth part of what is told them. Such distrust and incredulity would deprive us of the greatest benefits of society, and place us in a worse condition than that of savages.

Children, on this supposition, would be absolutely incredulous, and, therefore, absolutely incapable of instruction: those who had little knowledge of human life, and of the manners and characters of men, would be in the next degree incredulous: and the most credulous men would be those of greatest experience, and of the deepest penetration; because, in many cases, they would be able to find good reasons for believing testimony, which the weak and the ignorant could not discover.

In a word, if credulity were the effect of reasoning and experience, it must grow up and gather strength, in the same proportion as reason and experience do. But, if it is the gift of Nature, it will be strongest in childhood, and limited and restrained by experience; and the most superficial view of human life shews, that the last is really the case, and not the first.

It is the intention of Nature, that we should be carried in arms before we are able to walk upon our legs; and it is likewise the intention of Nature, that our belief should be guided by the authority and reason of others, before it can be guided by our own reason. The weakness of the infant, and the natural affection of the mother, plainly indicate the former; and the natural credulity of youth, and authority of age, as plainly indicate the latter. The infant, by proper nursing, and care, acquires strength to walk without support. Reason hath likewise her infancy, when she must be carried in arms: then she leans entirely upon authority, by natural instinct, as if she was conscious of her own weakness; and, without this support, she becomes vertiginous. When brought to maturity by proper culture, she begins to feel her own strength, and leans less upon the reason of others; she learns to suspect testimony in some cases, and to disbelieve it in others; and sets bounds to that authority to which she was at first entirely subject. But still, to the end of life, she finds a necessity of borrowing light from testimony, where she has none within herself, and of leaning, in some degree, upon the reason of others, where she is conscious of her own imbecility.

And as, in many instances, Reason, even in her maturity, borrows aid from testimony, so in others she mutually gives aid to it, and strengthens its authority. For, as we find good reason to reject testimony in some cases, so in others we find good reason to rely upon it with perfect security, in our most important concerns. The character, the number, and the disinterestedness of witnesses, the impossibility of collusion, and the incredibility of their concurring in their testimony without collusion, may give an irresistible strength to testimony, compared to which its native and intrinsic authority is very inconsiderable.

QUESTIONS

1. What does Reid mean by "natural language"?
2. Give an example of "acquired perception."
3. According to Reid, the "Author of Nature" has implanted two principles in us to enable the sharing of knowledge. What are those two principles?
4. According to Reid, is reliance on testimony a good way to gain knowledge?

C.A.J. Coady, "Testimony and Observation"

In answer to the question "Why do you believe that?" or "How do you know that?" it is proper to make such replies as "I saw it" or "It follows from this" or "It usually happens like that" or "Jones told me so." There may be more than these four kinds of reply possible (e.g., "It's a matter of insight," "I remember it," "I intuited it") and there may be more than one way of interpreting or taking any of them. Nonetheless there are *at least* these four kinds of reply possible and there are at least four standard ways of interpreting them which give rise to four prima facie categories of evidence: observation, deductive inference, inductive inference, and testimony. The first three have had a great deal of attention paid to them in philosophy but the fourth has been relatively neglected.[1] I hope to do something toward repairing that neglect; a neglect which certainly cannot have arisen from the insignificance of the role played by testimony in the forming of beliefs in the community since as Hume notes: ". . . there is no species of reasoning more common, more useful, and even necessary to human life, than that which is derived from the testimony of men and the reports of eye-witnesses and spectators."[2]

Hume is, indeed, one of the few philosophers I have read who has offered anything like a sustained account of testimony and if any view has a claim to the title of "the received view" it is his. In what follows I shall examine and criticize Hume's position in the hope of throwing light on more general issues concerning the nature and status of testimony. Hume's account of the matter is offered in his essay on Miracles which is Sect. 10 of *An Enquiry Concerning Human Understanding*. Essentially his theory constitutes a reduction of testimony as a form of evidence or support to the status of a species (one might almost say, a mutation) of inductive inference. And, again, insofar as inductive inference is reduced by Hume to a species of observation and consequences attendant upon observations then in a like fashion testimony meets the same fate. So we find him saying immediately after the piece quoted above:

> This species of reasoning, perhaps, one may deny to be founded on the relation of cause and effect. I shall not dispute about a word. It will be sufficient to observe that our assurance in any argument of this kind is derived from no other principle than our observation of the veracity of

C.A.J. Coady, "Testimony and Observation," *American Philosophical Quarterly* 10 (1973): 149–55.

> human testimony, and of the usual conformity of facts to the reports of witnesses. It being a general maxim, that no objects have any discoverable connexion together, and that all the inferences, which we can draw from one to another, are founded merely on our experience of their constant and regular conjunction; it is evident that we ought not to make an exception to this maxim in favour of human testimony, whose connexion with any event seems, in itself, as little necessary as any other. (p. 111.)

And elsewhere in the same essay he says:

> The reason why we place any credit in witnesses and historians, is not derived from any *connexion*, which we perceive *a priori*, between testimony and reality, but because we are accustomed to find a conformity between them." (p. 113.)

This is the view that I want to contest and, as it is convenient to have a label, I shall call it the Reductionist Thesis and shall employ the abbreviation R.T. to refer to it. My criticism begins by calling attention to a fatal ambiguity in the use of terms like "experience" and "observation" in the Humean statement of R.T. We are told by Hume that we only trust in testimony because experience has shown it to be reliable but where experience means individual observation and the expectations it gives rise to, this seems plainly false and, on the other hand, where it means common experience (i.e., the reliance upon the observations of others) it is surely question-begging. To take the second horn of the dilemma first—let us call it R.T.[2]—we find Hume speaking of "*our* observation of the veracity of human testimony" and "*our* experience of their constant and regular conjunction." And it is clear enough that Hume often means to refer by such phrases to the common experience of mankind and not to the mere solitary observations of David Hume. Our reliance upon testimony as an institution, so to speak, is supposed to be based on the same kind of footing as our reliance upon laws of nature (Hume thinks of this as an important premiss in his critique of miracles) and he speaks of the "firm and unalterable experience" which has established these laws. It is an important part of his argument that a miracle must be a violation of the laws of nature and so he says:

> It is no miracle that a man, seemingly in good health, should die on a sudden: because such a kind of death, though more unusual than any other, has yet been frequently observed to happen. But it is a miracle that a dead man should come to life; because that has *never* been observed in any age or country. There must therefore be a uniform experience against every miraculous event, otherwise the event would not merit that appellation. (p. 115.)

We may ignore, for our purposes here, the validity of this highly debatable account of a law of nature and the blatant question-begging of his "*never* been observed in any age or country" and yet gather from this extract the need Hume has to mean by "experience," "observation," and the like, the common experience of mankind. Clearly his argument does not turn on the fact, for instance, that *he* has "frequently observed" the sudden death of a man "seemingly in good health"—it is quite likely that Hume (like most of us) never had occasion to observe personally anything of the kind. And the point is surely clinched by his reference to "uniform experience" and his use of the phrase "observed in any age or country."

Evidently then, R.T., as actually argued by Hume, is involved in vicious circularity since the experience upon which our reliance upon testimony as a form of evidence is supposed to rest is itself reliant upon testimony which cannot itself be reduced in the same way. The idea of taking seriously someone else's observations, someone else's experience, already requires us to take their testimony (in this case, reports of what they observe) equally seriously. It is ludicrous to talk of their observations being the major part of our justification in taking their reports seriously when we have to take their reports seriously in order to know what their observations are.

Hume's conflation of personal and communal observation can be further illustrated by a passage from the *Treatise of Human Nature* (Bk. I, Pt. IV, Sect. II). Discussing our reasons for believing in the continued, independent existence of material things, he says:

> I receive a letter, which, upon opening it, I perceive by the handwriting and subscription to have come from a friend, who says he is two hundred leagues distant. It is evident I can never account for this phenomenon, conformable to my experience in other instances, without spreading out in my mind the whole sea and continent between us, and supposing the effects and continued existence of posts and ferries, according to my memory and observation. (p. 196, Selby-Bigge edition.)

Here we have Hume using "my" observation when he is clearly not entitled to do so since there is probably no single person who has personally observed the complete path of even *one* letter from the moment it leaves the sender's hand to the moment it reaches its destination. Hume might have observed postmen, posts, ferries, etc., but his beliefs about what they do (his belief in the postal system) is dependent upon a complicated web of testimony, a highlight among which would no doubt be what he was told by his teachers or parents. And yet, "my memory and observation." How easy it is to appropriate at a very fundamental level what is known by report and what is known by personal observation. Similarly, that babies are born of women in a certain way is known to all of us and it is a fact of observation but very few of us have ever observed it for ourselves.

So much for the second part of the dilemma but what of the first part—let us call it R.T.[1] Surely we can, on Hume's behalf, retract his incautious commitment to common experience and state the R.T. in terms of personal observations alone. My claim was that so stated R.T.[1] is plainly false but this has yet to be shown. R.T.[1] would run something like this:

> We rely upon testimony as a species of evidence *because* each of us observes for himself a constant and regular conjunction between what people report and the way the world is. More particularly, we each observe for ourselves

> a constant conjunction between kinds of report and kinds of situation so that we have good inductive grounds for expecting this conjunction to continue in the future.

My justification for bringing in the idea of a kind of report correlating with a kind of situation is Hume himself:

> And as the evidence, derived from witnesses and human testimony, is founded on past experience, so it varies with the experience, and is regarded either as a *proof* or a *probability* according as the conjunction between any particular kind of report and any kind of object has been found to be constant or variable. (p. 112.)

Now I characterized this sort of position as "plainly false" because it seems absurd to suggest that, individually, we have done anything like the amount of fieldwork that R.T.[1] requires. As mentioned earlier, most of us have never seen a baby born nor have we examined the circulation of the blood nor the actual geography of the world nor any fair sample of the laws of the land nor have we made the observations that lie behind our knowledge that the lights in the sky are heavenly bodies immensely distant nor a vast number of other observations that R.T.[1] would seem to require. Some people have of course made them *for us* but we are precluded from taking any solace from this fact under the present interpretation of R.T. So it was this general situation that made me speak of R.T.[1] as plainly false.

But the matter is perhaps more complex than such a characterization would indicate as can be seen by considering a possible rejoinder by the defenders of R.T.[1]. This rejoinder might run as follows: "You are ignoring the very important provision, made by Hume, that the conjunction in individual experience is between kinds of report and kinds of object. This cuts down the amount of observing that has to be done and makes the project a manageable one for an individual." I think I may reasonably plead "not guilty" to this accusation inasmuch as I intended the list above (of conjunctions never checked personally by most of us) to be more than a recital of particular conjunctions that R.T.[1] requires us to have personally checked. The list was supposed to be typical in the sense that it indicated *areas* in which we rightly accept testimony without ever having engaged in the sort of checking of reports against personal observation that R.T.[1] demands.

But quite apart from this, there seem to me to be serious difficulties in the very idea of finding constant conjunctions between (in Hume's words) "any particular kind of report and any kind of object." Hume wants these conjunctions to be something like the kinds of conjunctions he thinks are required to establish causal laws and even laws of nature. In such matters the decisive constant conjunctions are between one kind of object and another kind of object. But whatever we think about the idea of a kind of object, the notion of a kind of report surely requires some explanation in this context. Unfortunately Hume does nothing to provide such an explanation and since the matter is also of interest in its own right I shall risk a digression to consider some possible interpretations and their implications before turning to a different, and perhaps more decisive, difficulty for the type of approach represented by R.T.[1].

It seems to me that "kind of report" may be meant to refer either to the kind of speaker who gives the report or to the kind of content the report contains. If it is the former that is intended (and some of Hume's remarks *seem* to indicate this) then presumably the kind of speaker will not be determined by such considerations as color of skin or nationality or hair-style or height, rather, the relevant kind will have something to do with authority or expertise or credentials to say. So the R.T.[1] would go something like: We rely upon testimony because we have each personally observed a correlation between expert (or authoritative) reports and the kinds of situations reported in a large number of cases.

But the major difficulty for this interpretation is that a man's being an expert or an authority on some matter cannot be a matter of mere inspection in the way that his being white or tall is. That some man is an expert on, say, geography or South East Asian politics, is either known on the testimony of others (by far the most usual case) or it has to be established by observing some high correlation between his reports and the relevant situations in the world. If the former then we are no further advanced upon the R.T. program of justification since the same problem of establishing expertise must arise again and again. But if the latter, then the notion of an authority or an expert no longer provides us with any specification of a *kind of report*. That is to say, we cannot use the idea of *a kind of report* as equivalent to *report of a kind of speaker* and then proceed to validate testimony along the lines of R.T.[1] because the kind of correlation situation *the existence of which we would supposedly be investigating* would have to be known by us to exist already before we could set up the terms of the investigation.[3]

This indicates that the business of establishing constant conjunctions between kinds of report and kinds of situation must begin with the interpretation of "kinds of report" as "reports of kinds of situation." And certainly this seems to be a natural way of interpreting Hume's intentions at this point. An initial problem for this interpretation concerns the degree of generality that should attach to the content of a report before it qualifies as a kind of report. That is to say, some sort of decision would presumably be required as to whether or not the report "There is a sick lion in Taronga Park Zoo" belonged to the kind medical report or geographical report or empirical report or existence report. Perhaps it could be said to belong to all of them or to some and not to others but whatever was said it would be of considerable importance to the establishing of conjunctions, since a decision here is a decision about the actual identity of the conjunctions and hence, in consequence, about the degree of correlation likely to be established. For instance, if the report were treated as belonging to the kind "existence report" then it might be that Jones had personally established quite a large number of conjunctions between existence reports and the relevant existence situations without this being any real reason for accepting the report in question. (Compare with: "There is a Martian in my study" which is equally well supported by Jones's personal experience of existence reports.) On the other hand, if it were treated as a medical report then Jones may have had very little personal experience of correlations between medical reports and medical facts yet this would hardly be a real reason for not accepting the report. In addition, Jones would, on Hume's hypothesis, now have a strong reason for accepting the report if he classifies it one way and no reason for accepting it if he classifies it another way. Since either classification is logically permissible then it seems to be purely a matter of whim whether Jones has or has not good reason for accepting the report. Clearly some sort of non-arbitrary restriction on the scope of "report of a kind of situation" is required to make this notion of any real value in the elaboration of R.T.[1]. Here, however, I shall pursue no further the interpretation of "kind of report" and the difficulties involved in specifying clearly the sort of correlations required by R.T.[1] because, on the perhaps dubious assumption that the difficulties are soluble, I want to raise what seems to me to be a more fundamental problem.

This difficulty consists in the fact that the whole enterprise of R.T.[1] in its present form requires that we understand what testimony is independently of knowing that it is, in general, a reliable form of evidence about the way the world is. This is, of course, the point of Hume's saying:

> The reason why we place any credit in witnesses and historians, is not derived from any *connexion*, which we perceive *a priori*, between testimony and reality, but because we are accustomed to find a conformity between them. (p. 113.)

It is a clear implication from this that we might have discovered (though in fact we did not) that there was no conformity at all between testimony and reality. Hume's position requires the possibility that we clearly isolate the reports that people make about the world for comparison by personal observation with the actual state of the world and find a high, low, or no correlation between them. But it is by no means clear that we can understand this suggestion. To take the most extreme discovery: imagine a world in which an extensive survey yields no correlation between reports and (individually observed) facts. In such a colossally topsy-turvy world what evidence would there possibly be for the existence of reports at all? Imagine a community of Martians who are in the mess that R.T.[1] allows as a possibility. Let us suppose for the moment that they have a language which we can translate (there are difficulties in this supposition as we shall see shortly) with names for distinguishable things in their environment and suitable predicative equipment. We find, however, to our astonishment, that whenever they construct sentences addressed to each other in the absence (from their vicinity) of the things designated by the names but when they are, as we should think, in a position to *report* then they seem to say what we (more synoptically placed) can observe to be false. But in such a situation there would be no reason to believe that they even had the practice of reporting. There would be no behavior or setting for what we know as reporting. There would, for instance, be no reliance upon the utterances of others; just this curious fantasy practice rather like the fantasy games of children ("Mummy, there's a burglar in the house") but generalized to the stage where we can discern no point in the activity at all, even a parasitic point. The supposition that reports could be divorced from reality in this way is like the supposition that orders might never be obeyed. If there were Martians who uttered certain sounds in a tone of voice like the tone we use in ordering we might initially conjecture that they were issuing orders in making these sounds but this conjecture would just be refuted if it were found that these sounds never had any effect that might be described as obedience upon any audience.

But actually the situation with reporting and testifying is even worse than this because the supposed Martian community seem to be in trouble even about the content of the utterances that are alleged to be non-correlated reports. The question of the meaning or content of what they say in their alleged reports is of great importance because the task of looking for a correlation or conjunction of the Humean type is dependent upon knowing what state of affairs is supposed to correlate with the utterance. The principle of correlation has to be given by the meaning of the utterances because, after all, *any* utterance is correlated with or conjoined to *any* situation according to *some* principle of matching. So, even if we allow, for the sake of argument, that we can understand what it is for the Martians to engage in reporting, we cannot accept the coherence of the no-correlation story unless we can understand what Martian reports actually say. But it is precisely here that serious difficulties arise and to see how they arise we must look more closely at the supposed Martian situation.

Although I have not tried to define testimony (and there are problems facing any such attempt) it should be clear that, on any plausible definition, a very high proportion of the statements made by a community over a sample period will have to be testimony statements. These utterances will contrast with such speech episodes as soliloquies, musings, and conjectures. In the Martian community a common vocabulary is employed across different speech acts so that, as with us, the same form of words may be used for either conjecture or testimony (e.g., "He pushed her in") although there may also be speech-act indicators available of an Austinian or Searlean form ("I testify that . . . ," "I conjecture that . . ."). Suppose then that we encounter a Martian who uses the utterance "Kar do gnos u grin" in the presence of a tree in a garden. Perhaps he waves a languid hand at the tree as he does so. We speculate that this utterance means, can be translated as, "There is a tree in the garden" and, in particular, that "gnos" means "tree."[4] We then find, however, that the Martian frequently uses "gnos" in remarks in situations not involving the presence of a tree in his observational vicinity. Some few of these remarks we assess as mere conjectures (and I shall ignore the problems raised by the question of how this assessment is made) but the majority we decide to be testimony. So we find the Martian saying things of the form: "Kar do gnos u grin," "Kar do gnos u bilt," "Kar do gnos u tonk" and we guess that these mean "There is a tree in the garden," "There is a tree in the study," "There is a tree in the field," or whatever. But then we find that there never is a tree in the garden or in the study or in the field and that in fact this Martian never uses "gnos" to make a true statement when he is talking (non-conjecturely) to others about, as it seems, absent trees. Furthermore, *no* Martian ever uses "gnos" to make a true report about absent trees though they make, as we surmise, constant attempts to do so. Furthermore, no Martian ever contradicts or corrects another Martian about absent trees on the basis of his own observation or the "testimony" of others *since* by hypothesis no testimony ever matches the facts. Surely in this sort of set-up we would have to conclude that "gnos" did not mean "tree" or that it did not mean it unambiguously or possibly that the Martians have a device for negation which we have not yet uncovered (so that "Kar do gnos u grin" really means "There isn't a tree in the garden") or perhaps that the Martians are totally incomprehensible to us. Indeed this last conclusion would be considerably fortified by the fact that the linguistic chaos described above is generated on behalf of not just one sound "gnos" that the Martians utter but by every sound which is supposed to be a word and upon the reference of which the truth or falsity of an alleged report could turn!

It might be complained at this point that I have not described the Martian community in sufficient detail and I readily concede that my account of their circumstances is somewhat sketchy. Possibly an attempt could be made to fill out such details as whether their non-veridical testimony has the form of a massive mistake or a massive deception but any such attempt would, I believe, only add support to my conclusion that their supposed situation is eventually unintelligible to us. I am content if enough has been said of their plight to raise serious doubts about the task of identifying the contents of Martian-type reports and hence of establishing Humean correlations in such a world. The general point here is that although making true reports with words is not the same thing as using the words correctly, nonetheless the ability to make true reports with words *is* connected with using the words correctly and this ability is something that can only be exhibited (even to the persons themselves) in the consistent making of true reports.

There is a further point to be made about the connection of testimony with meaning. If we take it that teaching someone the meaning of words involves the giving of reports and testimony then the present form of $R.T.^1$ is in even hotter water than before since the suggestion that no reports in fact conform to reality involves the claim that our imagined Martians never report to the Martian children the actual use of their words. Here the idea that the Martians have a public language gets no grip at all.[5] I do not intend exploring this difficulty any further, however, since I am not clear whether Hume would regard such remarks as "'Cat' means one of these" or "'Cat' is the word for a four-legged etc." as pieces of testimony. I think it quite likely that he would insofar as he would probably regard them as reports upon the empirical fact that such terms are used in a certain way in a certain community. I do not want to prejudge the question of whether they are such reports but if they are or if the proponent of R.T. believes that they are then he has no way at all of setting up the possibility upon which his theory rests.

Let us summarize our progress to date. From Hume's account of testimony I extracted a reductionist thesis which had two forms. I argued that the second form, $R.T.^2$, which justified testimony in terms of common experience was circular and that the first form, $R.T.^1$, which justified testimony in terms of individual observation was simply false since our reliance upon testimony rightly goes beyond anything that could be justified by personal observations. I then considered the rejoinder that $R.T.^1$ might be more plausible if great weight were put upon the observation of constant conjunction between kinds of report and kinds of object and I argued that much was unclear about what was to count as a kind of report, and hence what was to count as a correlation, for the purposes of $R.T.^1$. In any case $R.T.^1$ surely requires that any such investigation into conjunctions of reports with states of affairs might conclude that there were no such correlations between the two. The supposition that such a situation obtained was pursued for the purpose of reductio ad absurdum and I argued that in such a situation, (a) there could be no such things as reports, (b) even if there were reports, there could be no way of establishing Humean correlations or non-correlations since there could be no way of determining the contents of the alleged reports in order to correlate them, and (c) the idea of a public language seems undermined.

Am I then saying, in opposition to Hume, that there *is* an a priori connection between testimony and reality? An answer to this question would have to rely on a comprehensive theory of knowledge which could determine the conditions under which an a priori connection holds between some x and reality and hence not only whether there is such a connection between testimony and reality but also whether such a connection holds, say, between perception and reality. I cannot provide such a theory here but I do not understand the idea that testimony could exist in a community and yet it be possible to discover empirically that it had no "connection with reality." Hence, I suspect that the problem of justifying testimony is a pseudo-problem and that the evidence of testimony constitutes a fundamental category of evidence which is not reducible to, or justifiable in terms of, such other basic categories as observation or deductive inference. This opinion I have not proved but if my argument so far is correct then there is no sense to the idea of justifying testimony by observation, at least where this involves anything like a search for Humean correlations.[6]

Now, of course, none of this sloganizing means that there is no such thing as mistaken or lying testimony and it is, I think, the fact that there are conditions and circumstances under which we disregard the reports of witnesses which Hume sees as providing support for R.T. independently of his methodological doctrine that there can be no necessary connection between any one object (or kind of object) and any other object (or kind of object).

> Were not the memory tenacious to a certain degree, had not men commonly an inclination to truth and a principle of probity; were they not sensible to shame, when detected in a falsehood: Were not these, I say, discovered by *experience* to be qualities, inherent in human nature, we should never repose the least confidence in human testimony. A man delirious, or noted for falsehood and villany, has no manner of authority with us. (p. 112.)

Hume's argument is not fully explicit here but he seems to be claiming that since we sometimes discover by observation and experience that some testimony is *unreliable* (i.e., "A man delirious or noted for falsehood or villainy has no manner of authority with us") then we must discover the general *reliability* of testimony by the same method. But this surely has only to be stated to be seen to be invalid for the fact that observation can sometimes uncover false testimony does nothing toward showing that the general reliability of testimony depends upon observation in the way R.T. requires.

Furthermore, the fact that observation will sometimes lead us to reject some piece of testimony needs to be set against two other facts, namely—

(a) That other testimony sometimes leads us to reject some piece of testimony without personal observation entering into the matter. Consider, for instance, Hume's *very* example of the man noted for delirium or falsehood or villainy.

(b) That testimony sometimes leads us to reject some piece of observation. There are many different sorts of cases here. In philosophical discussions about people who "see" a table in front of them in optimum observational conditions but become convinced that there is no table there because everyone around them says there isn't. Less fancifully, this case springs from those in which the testimony of others assures us that we are or are not hallucinating. Furthermore, there are often situations where we accept correction of our ordinary mis-observations from the reports of others:—"Look at that herd of cows," "They're not cows they're rock formations." Or we observe a scuffle between three men and the upshot is that one of them is stabbed. There were four of us observing it and I hold that the man stabbed himself but the others maintain stoutly that one of the other two, namely Smith, delivered the blow. I capitulate. Surely this could be the reasonable thing to do in some circumstances. Indeed, it would seem equally as valid, on Hume's line of argument, to claim that since testimony sometimes leads us to abandon an observation then we rely upon observation in general only because we have established its reliability on the basis of testimony. But I think Hume would hardly be happy with *this* employment of his mode of argument.

Notes

1 A notable non-neglector is Professor H.H. Price who has discussed the issue in his recent book, *Belief* (London: Allen & Unwin, 1969). His chapter on this ("The Evidence of Testimony") has a quite different orientation to my discussion although he shows himself to be well aware of some of those defects in the traditional approach to which I shall be directing attention. Sydney Shoemaker also touches upon some of the issues discussed here in ch. 6 of his book *Self-Knowledge and Self-Identity* (Ithaca: N.Y.: Cornell University Press, 1963). Although Shoemaker is not primarily concerned with testimony he does, as I do, reject the idea that the validity of testimony could be established by observation. His arguments, however, are very different from mine and reflect his basic concern with certain problems of self-knowledge and memory. They also reflect certain Wittgensteinian assumptions about memory, language, and philosophy which I do not wish either to discuss or employ in what follows.

2 Sect. 88, David Hume, *An Enquiry Concerning Human Understanding* (Oxford: Clarendon, 1957). All quotations hereafter from this work are taken from L. A. Selby-Bigge's Second Edition of the *Enquiries* published by Clarendon Press, Oxford. Bracketed page references in my text are to that edition.

3 It may appear that part of this difficulty could be met by recourse to the qualification "report of a so-called expert" but this is mere appearance since we require some assurance that we are checking the reports of those who are not merely self-styled experts but widely acknowledged as such and this sort of assurance could only be had by reliance upon testimony.

4 There is perhaps a problem in working out what he is up to and hence a puzzle as to how we are even entitled to speculate that his utterance means *this* but suppose that there is enough about his behavior to permit us to conclude that he is soliloquizing in the fashion of one who is struck by the existence of that particular tree in that particular garden.

5 The problem arises dramatically in the teaching situation but it might be objected that it is a merely contingent fact that languages are acquired by teaching. I am not altogether clear about the import here of the phrase "a merely contingent fact" but in any event essentially the same difficulty arises in the correction situation. It is surely unimaginable that a community could operate a

common language without the resources for correcting the inevitable divergences from correct use.

6 I have not of course proved that our reliance on testimony may not be "justified" in some other manner. Russell, for one, has attempted (in *Human Knowledge Its Scope and Limits* [New York: Simon and Schuster, 1948]) to justify testimony by recourse to a principle of analogy and Price (*op. cit.*) by recourse to a methodological rule. I hope it is clear from what has been said in this paper, however, that such attempts face very serious difficulties, some of which are simple extensions of the difficulties faced by Hume.

QUESTIONS

1 What is R.T.?
2 What are $R.T.^1$ and $R.T.^2$?
3 According to Coady, what is the basic problem with $R.T.^2$?
4 What is the basic problem with $R.T.^1$?
5 Does Coady think there could be a society in which people's reports are generally false?

FURTHER READING ON TESTIMONY

Audi, Robert, "The Place of Testimony in the Fabric of Knowledge and Justification," *American Philosophical Quarterly* 34 (1997): 405–22.

Burge, Tyler, "Content Preservation," *Philosophical Review* 102 (1993): 457–88.

Christensen, David and Hilary Kornblith, "Testimony, Memory and the Limits of the 'A Priori,'" *Philosophical Studies* 86 (1997): 1–20.

Coady, C.A.J., *Testimony: A Philosophical Study* (Oxford: Clarendon Press, 1992).

Graham, Peter, "The Reliability of Testimony," *Philosophy and Phenomenological Research* 61 (2000): 695–709.

Holder, Rodney, "Hume on Miracles: Bayesian Interpretation, Multiple Testimony, and the Existence of God," *British Journal for the Philosophy of Science* 49 (1998): 49–65.

Lyons, Jack, "Testimony, Induction and Folk Psychology," *Australasian Journal of Philosophy* 75 (1997): 163–78.

Owens, David, *Reason without Freedom* (London: Routledge, 2000).

Sobel, Jordan-Howard, "Hume's Theorem on Testimony Sufficient to Establish a Miracle," *Philosophical Quarterly* 41 (1991): 229–37.

PART II

THE STRUCTURE AND GROWTH OF JUSTIFICATION AND KNOWLEDGE

5

INFERENCE IN GENERAL

The readings in this chapter discuss some miscellaneous issues about the nature of reasoning.

Lewis Carroll's well-known (to philosophers) story about Achilles and the Tortoise implicitly illustrates the distinction between *premises* in an argument and *rules of inference*. When a person makes an inference, say, from premises *A* and *B* to conclusion *Z*, it seems that they must be aware of the logical relationship between the premises and the conclusion—that is, it seems that they must know that if *A* and *B* are true, *Z* is; otherwise, they would not accept the inference. Lewis Carroll's story shows, however, that if we think of this knowledge as an additional premise the person must accept, then an infinite regress ensues.

Richard Fumerton's article addresses the question of the conditions under which a person is justified in believing one thing on the basis of another. He comes to this question from the consideration of a particular problem facing indirect realist theories of perceptual knowledge. Indirect realism (which Fumerton calls "empiricism," but note that he is using this term in a different sense from that used in Chapter 3 of this volume) holds that we are justified in believing claims about the physical world *on the basis of* facts about the character of our own sensory experiences, where experiences are understood as states or events going on in our own minds (see Chapter 1). The problem is that people do not typically even entertain propositions about the character of their sensory experiences as they go about the world; they just think about the physical objects around them. It is unclear how one can say their physical object beliefs are justified by propositions that they do not even consider.

Fumerton offers two possible solutions to this. The first solution is to maintain that *dispositional beliefs* may provide inferential justification for other beliefs. A dispositional belief (as opposed to an *occurrent* belief) is a belief that one is not presently consciously entertaining. For example, you undoubtedly believe that six is less than ten, although you were not consciously thinking of that proposition until I just mentioned it. Before I mentioned the proposition, then, you dispositionally believed that six is less than ten. Fumerton suggests that a person dispositionally believes something if they *would* believe it (occurrently) if they considered it. This helps with the indirect realist's problem, since the indirect realist may maintain that people dispositionally believe many propositions about their experiences, even though we do not consciously entertain these propositions, and that these dispositional beliefs (or dispositions to believe) cause us to accept propositions about the physical world. Fumerton's second proposed solution is to maintain that our beliefs about the physical world are based on facts about sensory experiences only in the sense that facts about sensory experiences *cause* us to accept physical-object propositions and are in fact good evidence for physical-object propositions. Fumerton's definitions D1 and D2 provide two possible accounts of the nature of inferential justification.

David Hume, characteristically, provides a skeptical perspective on inferential justification. He seems to argue that a person can never be justified in believing anything on the basis of argument. The major stages of his argument are as follows. First, he argues that any piece of reasoning is fallible; there is always at least some chance of our making a mistake. To see this, note (a) that if you have just completed a complicated, 50-page proof, it would not be rational to believe the conclusion with complete certainty, without at least checking it over and perhaps showing it to others; and (b) that a long and complicated proof just consists of a series of short, simple steps—or in other words, it is equivalent to a series of short proofs. Therefore, if a complicated proof is prone to error, then short proofs are also subject to error (the probability of error increases with the length of the proof).

Second, Hume argues that because of this, one should always lower one's level of confidence in the conclusion of any argument, according to one's estimate of the probability that one made a mistake in the argument. However, Hume says, one's estimate of the probability of error may itself be in error. So one should estimate the probability of an error in one's first estimate of the probability of error. But one's second estimate may be in error . . . This leads to an infinite series of corrections. At each stage, Hume thinks, we should lower our confidence in our original conclusion, until eventually it is "reduc'd to nothing."

Hume's argument seems to be self-defeating, since it concludes that no argument, including itself, can justify anything. But note that Hume is not trying to convince us to give up accepting conclusions of arguments. He is trying to show that the causes of our beliefs—even when we are convinced by arguments—are not rational, but (as we remarked in the introduction to Chapter 1) he did not consider this a problem.

Lastly, Hilary Kornblith considers a more practically oriented kind of skepticism. Although he does not endorse the argument, Kornblith considers an argument for the conclusion that, in some areas at least, one should avoid reasoning things through. The reason is that human reasoning may be strongly infected by bias, with the result that clever reasoners succeed only in providing themselves with rationalizations for holding onto beliefs that they are attracted to for non-rational reasons. Much of this is unconscious; most people do not think they are rationalizing when they are.

For instance, a person who has a pro-capital punishment bias and is intelligent will likely be able to come up with reasons for doubting the validity of the studies that tend to show that capital punishment has no deterrent effect, and will also likely be able to come up with arguments to counter any criticisms of the studies that tend to show that it has a significant deterrent effect. When evidence is ambiguous or very complex, an intelligent person can generally construct a seemingly logical case for whichever side he wants to defend; thus, the practice of reasoning may prove to be useless, or even harmful, from the standpoint of the goal of getting to the truth. But while Kornblith recognizes this as a significant problem, he does not believe that we should therefore give up reasoning. Instead, he thinks that we can to a large extent counter the effects of bias through the practice of engaging in public debate with people with a variety of viewpoints, in the hopes that the various biases of different people will in effect cancel each other out. Kornblith notes that whether this works or not is an empirical question (it depends upon the characteristics of our present intellectual community), so that the question of to what extent we should trust reasoning is also empirical.

Lewis Carroll, "What the Tortoise said to Achilles"

Achilles had overtaken the Tortoise, and had seated himself comfortably on its back.

"So you've got to the end of our race-course?" said the Tortoise. "Even though it *does* consist of an infinite series of distances? I thought some wiseacre or other had proved that the thing couldn't be done?"

"It *can* be done," said Achilles. "It *has* been done! *Solvitur ambulando*. You see the distances were constantly *diminishing*; and so—"

"But if they had been constantly *increasing*?" the Tortoise interrupted. "How then?"

"Then I shouldn't be *here*," Achilles modestly replied; "and *you* would have got several times round the world, by this time!"

"You flatter me—*flatten*, I mean," said the Tortoise; "for you *are* a heavy weight, and *no* mistake! Well now, would you like to hear of a race-course, that most people fancy they can get to the end of in two or three steps, while it *really* consists of an infinite number of distances, each one longer than the previous one?"

"Very much indeed!" said the Grecian warrior, as he drew from his helmet (few Grecian warriors possessed *pockets* in those days) an enormous note-book and a pencil. "Proceed! And speak *slowly*, please! *Shorthand* isn't invented yet!"

"That beautiful First Proposition of Euclid!" the Tortoise murmured dreamily. "You admire Euclid?"

"Passionately! So far, at least, as one *can* admire a treatise that wo'n't be published for some centuries to come!"

"Well, now, let's take a little bit of the argument in that First Proposition—just *two* steps, and the conclusion drawn from them. Kindly enter them in your note-book. And in order to refer to them conveniently, let's call them *A*, *B*, and *Z*:—

(*A*) Things that are equal to the same are equal to each other.

(*B*) The two sides of this Triangle are things that are equal to the same.

(*Z*) The two sides of this Triangle are equal to each other.

Readers of Euclid will grant, I suppose, that *Z* follows logically from *A* and *B*, so that any one who accepts *A* and *B* as true, *must* accept *Z* as true?"

"Undoubtedly! The youngest child in a High School—as soon as High Schools are invented, which will not be till some two thousand years later—will grant *that*."

Lewis Carroll, "What the Tortoise said to Achilles," *Mind* 4 (1895): 278–80.

"And if some reader had *not* yet accepted *A* and *B* as true, he might still accept the *sequence* as a *valid* one, I suppose?"

"No doubt such a reader might exist. He might say 'I accept as true the Hypothetical Proposition that, if *A* and *B* be true, *Z must* be true; but, I *don't* accept *A* and *B* as true.' Such a reader would do wisely in abandoning Euclid, and taking to football."

"And might there not *also* be some reader who would say 'I accept *A* and *B* as true, but I *don't* accept the Hypothetical'?"

"Certainly there might. *He*, also, had better take to football."

"And *neither* of these readers," the Tortoise continued, "is *as yet* under any logical necessity to accept *Z* as true?"

"Quite so," Achilles assented.

"Well, now, I want you to consider *me* as a reader of the *second* kind, and to force me, logically, to accept *Z* as true."

"A tortoise playing football would be—" Achilles was beginning

"—an anomaly, of course," the Tortoise hastily interrupted. "Don't wander from the point. Let's have *Z* first, and football afterwards!"

"I'm to force you to accept *Z*, am I?" Achilles said musingly. "And your present position is that you accept *A* and *B*, but you *don't* accept the Hypothetical—"

"Let's call it *C*," said the Tortoise.

"—but you *don't* accept

(*C*) If *A* and *B* are true, *Z* must be true."

"That is my present position," said the Tortoise.

"Then I must ask you to accept *C*."

"I'll do so," said the Tortoise, "as soon as you've entered it in that note-book of yours. What else have you got in it?"

"Only a few memoranda," said Achilles, nervously fluttering the leaves: "a few memoranda of—of the battles in which I have distinguished myself!"

"Plenty of blank leaves, I see!" the Tortoise cheerily remarked. "We shall need them *all*!" (Achilles shuddered.) "Now write as I dictate:—

(*A*) Things that are equal to the same are equal to each other.

(*B*) The two sides of this Triangle are things that are equal to the same.

(*C*) If *A* and *B* are true, *Z* must be true.

(*Z*) The two sides of this Triangle are equal to each other."

"You should call it *D*, not *Z*," said Achilles. "It comes *next* to the other three. If you accept *A* and *B* and *C*, you *must* accept *Z*."

"And why *must* I?"

"Because it follows *logically* from them. If *A* and *B* and *C* are true, *Z must* be true. You don't dispute *that*, I imagine?"

"If *A* and *B* and *C* are true, *Z* must be true," the Tortoise thoughtfully repeated. "That's *another* Hypothetical, isn't it? And, if I failed to see its truth, I might accept *A* and *B* and *C*, and *still* not accept *Z*, mightn't I?"

"You might," the candid hero admitted; "though such obtuseness would certainly be phenomenal. Still, the event is *possible*. So I must ask you to grant *one* more Hypothetical."

"Very good. I'm quite willing to grant it, as soon as you've written it down. We will call it

(*D*) If *A* and *B* and *C* are true, *Z* must be true.

Have you entered that in your note-book?"

"I *have*!" Achilles joyfully exclaimed, as he ran the pencil into its sheath. "And at last we've got to the end of this ideal race-course! Now that you accept *A* and *B* and *C* and *D*, *of course* you accept *Z*."

"Do I?" said the Tortoise innocently. "Let's make that quite clear. I accept *A* and *B* and *C* and *D*. Suppose I *still* refused to accept *Z*?"

"Then Logic would take you by the throat, and *force* you to do it!" Achilles triumphantly replied. "Logic would tell you 'You ca'n't help yourself. Now that you've accepted *A* and *B* and *C* and *D*, you *must* accept *Z*!' So you've no choice, you see."

"Whatever *Logic* is good enough to tell me is worth *writing down*," said the Tortoise. "So enter it in your book, please. We will call it

(*E*) If *A* and *B* and *C* and *D* are true, *Z* must be true. Until I've granted *that*, of course I needn't grant *Z*. So it's quite a *necessary* step, you see?"

"I see," said Achilles; and there was a touch of sadness in his tone.

Here the narrator, having pressing business at the Bank, was obliged to leave the happy pair, and did not again pass the spot until some months afterwards. When he did so, Achilles was still seated on the back of the much-enduring Tortoise, and was writing in his note-book, which appeared to be nearly full. The Tortoise was saying "Have you got that last step written down? Unless I've lost count, that makes a thousand and one. There are several millions more to come. And *would* you mind; as a personal favour, considering what a lot of instruction this colloquy of ours will provide for the Logicians of the Nineteenth Century—*would* you mind adopting a pun that my cousin the Mock-Turtle will then make, and allowing yourself to be re-named *Taught-Us?*"

"As you please!" replied the weary warrior, in the hollow tones of despair, as he buried his face in his hands. "Provided that *you*, for *your* part, will adopt a pun the Mock-Turtle never made, and allow yourself to be re-named *A Kill-Ease*!"

QUESTIONS

1 What would step F in Achilles' argument be?

2 How many steps does Achilles have to go through in order to reach his conclusion Z?

Richard Fumerton, "Inferential Justification and Empiricism"

In this paper I shall attempt to draw certain important distinctions between the senses in which one can be said to have an inferentially justified belief. Making these distinctions would lead one rather naturally, I think, to make corresponding distinctions between different senses in which one can be said to have propositional knowledge. My point in making these distinctions is not simply to indicate that they do exist, but, more importantly, to defend what I shall call the *empiricist's version of foundationalism* against an increasingly popular argument, an argument which proceeds from observations about what we do and do not infer.

Given what is usually called the "traditional" analysis of knowledge, in order for an individual *S* to know a proposition *P*, *P* must be true, *S* must believe *P*, and *S* must be justified in believing *P*.[1] Anyone who attempts to explicate knowledge fully or partially in terms of the having of a justified true belief is obviously faced with the problem of explicating the concept of justification. What precisely are those conditions under which one may be correctly described as having a justified belief in some proposition *P*?

In answering this question, we might begin by observing that we often try to justify a belief in one proposition *P* by appealing to the truth of another proposition (or set of propositions) *E*, and by either explicitly or implicitly appealing to a third proposition, namely that *E* confirms or makes *P* probable. It seems obvious that one can challenge such a claim to have justification by challenging the truth of one of two propositions:

(1) That we are justified in believing *E*.
(2) That we are justified in believing that *E* confirms *P*.

This fact has led to the now familiar argument for the thesis of foundationalism. If, in order to justify every belief we have, we must appeal to the truth of some other proposition, we could never justify any belief, for we would have to complete an infinite regress of justification. To claim that we have no justification for believing anything is absurd, the argument continues, and so we must be justified in believing some propositions without having to appeal to the truth of any other

Richard Fumerton, "Inferential Justification and Empiricism," *The Journal of Philosophy* 73 (1976): 557–69.

proposition. I shall call a belief that is justified without being justified through the justification of other beliefs a *noninferentially justified belief*. A belief that must be justified through the justification of other beliefs, I shall call an *inferentially justified belief*. The thesis of foundationalism is the thesis that there are noninferentially justified beliefs. One gets different versions of foundationalism, depending on what one takes to be the objects of noninferentially justified beliefs and how one thinks these beliefs can be used to justify other beliefs. Anyone who claims that one can have a noninferentially justified belief in some proposition asserting the existence of a physical object, I shall call an *epistemological direct realist*. The empiricist's version of foundationalism, to which I alluded in my introduction and which I shall be defending later in this paper, maintains that one can never have a noninferentially justified belief in a physical-object proposition, but that one must always justify one's beliefs in propositions about the physical world in part by appealing to noninferentially justified beliefs in propositions about experience.[2]

Now the argument purporting to show the necessity of some version of foundationalism is, I think, persuasive, though considerations I shall raise in this paper now make it seem less conclusive than it once seemed to me. I am convinced in any event that those who seek to escape the need for foundations by appealing to the concept of circular justification (big circles are all right—only the little ones are fallacious) usually coupled with the so-called "coherence theory of truth," are in error. Circular reasoning is fallacious, and it remains fallacious no matter how pedantic one cares to be in traversing the circumference of the circle. Although the coherence theory of truth might seem to lend some credence to a kind of circular justification, I cannot believe that it will ever overcome the most obvious difficulty: the possibility of mutually exclusive but internally consistent sets of propositions.

In this paper I do not intend to attack the thesis of epistemological direct realism (which I think can be attacked using the well-worn but, I believe, sound argument from the possibility of hallucination) or to consider the reasons that might be held for accepting the empiricist's version of foundationalism. Rather, I want to focus on one very specific objection that has been raised against empiricism (or more generally against any thesis that contradicts epistemological direct realism) most clearly, I think, by Anthony Quinton, in his well-known article, "The Problem of Perception" and more recently in his book, *The Nature of Things*.[3]

Quinton tries to assess the claim that justification of our beliefs in propositions describing physical objects is always inferential and that it is always from propositions about the nature of our experiences that such inferences are made, by noting that for the claim to be correct two conditions must be satisfied:

(1) Statements about experience must count as reasons or evidence for statements about objects.
(2) Statements about experience must in some, no doubt rather obscure, sense be accepted by those who make statements about objects ("The Problem of Perception," 519).

Quinton attempts to cast (1) and (2) in doubt by arguing, rather persuasively, that it is surely not true that most people (who, we assume, have justified beliefs in the existence of physical objects) are always in the "appropriate, sophisticated, phenomenological frame of mind" (507) even to *isolate in thought* that element of experience which C.I. Lewis called the "momentary given." The very existence of what the empiricist calls "sensation" or "experience" (i.e., understood as a state of affairs the occurrence of which entails the existence of no physical object) is a subject of great philosophical dispute, and for many philosophers it is only after long, considered argument that such events are recognized or abstracted from our everyday conception of the world. If most people do not even entertain propositions about their experiences it is surely implausible to suggest that the truth of such propositions constitutes their evidence justifying their beliefs in propositions about the external world.

There are actually three different facts to which one might appeal in presenting this kind of objection to empiricism. These are:

(A) That we seldom if ever consciously infer propositions about objects from propositions about experiences.
(B) That most people, certainly most nonphilosophers, if challenged as to their justification for believing propositions about the external world, would seldom if ever offer as their reasons or evidence propositions about experiences.
(C) That it is quite *meaningless*, that it makes no *sense* to search for evidence justifying a belief in the existence of a physical object that is before one under optimum conditions of perception.

I shall argue that (A) is probably true, but is quite irrelevant to the truth of empiricism; that (B) may well be false, but would be irrelevant to the truth of empiricism even if it were true; and that (C), unsupported by either (A) or (B), remains as simply an unargued denial of the empiricist's version of foundationalism.

(A) is the least controversial claim, but, as I have indicated, it seems to have the least amount of force as an objection to the empiricist's version of foundationalism. Most empiricists would probably admit that we do not entertain propositions describing solely the phenomenological character of our experience before we accept the fact that we are surrounded by physical objects of various kinds. The man who consciously makes inferences from the nature of his present and past experiences to the truth of the proposition that there is a truck headed toward him will spend most of his life in the hospital. It is important to note, however, that Quinton himself places no weight on (A) as an objection to empiricism. Though he does claim that "The best proof that statements about experiences were reasons or evidence for statements about objects would be that we did in fact commonly infer from the one to the other" (519/20) and does note that it is simply not the case that this is so, he immediately discounts the significance of this observation in determining whether or not beliefs in physical object propositions are inferentially justified:

> Furthermore, there are many cases of knowledge by inference, where it is not the least likely that any conscious process of reasoning has

> occurred. . . . We only infer consciously in situations that are unfamiliar or complex (520).

In *The Nature of Things* Quinton, in talking about the epistemological task of reconstructing knowledge, cautions us that: "Such a reconstruction will, as Reichenbach puts it, be concerned with the logical order of justification of beliefs rather than with the psychological or historical order of their discovery" (115). Again, he insists that "Theory of Knowledge as a critical account of the logical order of justification, must be governed by Frege's maxim that the logical and the psychological should always be clearly distinguished from one another" (115).

The most obvious example of beliefs which would have to be inferentially justified if they are to be justified at all, but which nevertheless are not usually *if ever* consciously inferred from that which would constitute our evidence, are beliefs about the future or about subjunctive conditionals. My belief that this glass of water before me now would quench my thirst if I were to drink it is hardly a belief that I form as a result of careful consideration of past instances of water quenching thirst coupled with an application of a synthetic a priori principle of induction. I had formed similar beliefs long before I knew what a principle of induction would be.[4]

Well, if (A) leaves empiricism unscathed, perhaps (B) does not. Though I may never have entertained a proposition asserting a correlation of past instances of water quenching thirst, I would no doubt hit upon such a proposition eventually if I were the least bit cooperative and were challenged to justify my belief that if I were to drink water now it would quench my thirst. Perhaps Quinton is afraid that people would not come up with propositions describing the phenomenological character of their experience, upon being asked to justify their belief in the existence of a physical object before them under optimum conditions of perception. But why should Quinton believe this? No doubt most people would have a difficult time *linguistically* expressing the evidence the empiricist says they have—the language of appearing[5] or the sense-datum language (depending on what one takes the correct analysis of sensations to be) is not the language of the ordinary man—but if they are helped by a friendly philosopher and are coaxed into the appropriate sophisticated frame of mind, why should we think that most people would not come up with the answer the empiricist thinks is the right one?

Furthermore, even if it were not the case that people would respond to a challenge of their beliefs in the way the empiricist thinks they should, it is not clear that Quinton himself believes this would be a decisive objection to the empiricist's position about the nature of the evidence required for the justification of beliefs in an external world. In "The Problem of Perception" Quinton asks us to consider five cases of belief:

(1) I can at once reproduce the course of reasoning that led me to say that it is mother's hat on top of the garage. This is conscious inference, where the reason given is a premise already consciously affirmed.
(2) I can, without hesitation, answer 'by the way he sways about' when asked how I can tell someone is drunk, although I recollect no process of inferring.
(3) I may take some time over or require assistance in accounting for my claim that Towzer is ill by the glazed look in his eye.

(4) I may be unable to give any reason of my own and unwilling to accept any reason offered by another for my assertion that *X* dislikes *Y*. Yet commonly in this type of case I may be extremely confident of the truth of my belief and turn out, in the end, to be quite right.
(5) Finally, consider standing in broad daylight three feet away from a large and perfectly normal chestnut cart-horse and saying "that is a horse" or, more adventurously, "that horse is brown" (520).

Now I take Quinton to be implying that the first four cases are examples of beliefs that might be inferentially justified. The fourth case is more controversial, but let us expand it as follows: I not only correctly decide that *X* dislikes *Y*, but in other situations I have this uncanny ability to judge that one person dislikes another—I am always *caused* to hold this belief by a similar feature of each situation, I am always sure that a reason exists; that is, I am always quite sure that *something* about the situation leads me to this belief, but I am quite unable to pick out that something and offer it as evidence. This fourth case is particularly interesting, for if one can have inferential beliefs of this kind, a failure to *identify* sensation as evidence for the existence of physical objects should not count against the claim that propositions about sensations are always the evidence from which we must ultimately infer the truth of assertions about physical objects. That Quinton himself recognizes that he must distinguish case (5) from case (4) in order to press home his attack on empiricism is, of course, supported by the fact that he does so:

> This (case 5) resembles the previous case (case 4) in that one would be quite unable to give or accept any reason whatever for one's assertion. It differs from it in that one would not be in the very least abashed or apologetic about this. For, in these conditions, the challenge 'how can you tell?' is simply devoid of sense (521).

And here, I think, we finally have the "argument" against empiricism, or at least that part of empiricism which insists that justification of physical-object propositions always involves an inference from evidence concerning the nature of our sensation, namely, the quite dogmatic, unargued assertion, introduced by Austin (the animal in question has changed from a pig to a horse), that it does not always make sense to ask for evidence justifying a belief in a physical-object proposition. Surely one can hardly expect the empiricist to consider such an assertion seriously as a criticism of his position unless it is supported by an argument. He, after all, offers reasons for insisting upon his position (again the best, I think, is the argument from the possibility of hallucination), and it might be appropriate to note in passing that philosophers began to conclude that the question of justifying beliefs in physical-object propositions through evidence was on some occasions *senseless* only after a few frustrating hundreds of years spent in attempting to solve the problems that ensue in trying to answer that question. The epistemological problems concerning perception are enormous, the fight to stave off skepticism uphill, if one accepts the empiricist's version of foundationalism, but one does not make go away a philosophical problem by ignoring it or by arbitrarily inventing a more convenient epistemological starting point devoid of any epistemological significance (the observation statements of W.V. Quine might serve as an example here).

Let us see if we can draw from the above discussion more precise conclusions concerning the nature of the claim that a belief is inferentially justified. Based very roughly on the distinctions Quinton makes through specific examples, let us try to distinguish more formally at least two senses in which one might be said to have an inferentially justified belief. Our task is not to define the notions of justification and confirmation themselves—if it were, the following definitions would, of course, be circular—our task is, rather, to explicate the different senses in which one might be said to have *inferential* justification. Let me offer the definitions first, discuss an important distinction that can be made within those definitions, and evaluate the empiricist's foundationalism and Quinton's objections to that thesis in the light of these distinctions:

D1 *S* has an inferentially justified belief in *P* on the basis of *E*. = Df

(1) *S* believes *P*.

(2) *S* justifiably believes both *E* and the proposition that *E* confirms *P*.

(3) *S* believes *P* because he believes both *E* and the proposition that *E* confirms *P*.

(4) There is no proposition *X* such that *S* is justified in believing both *X* and that *E* & *X* does not confirm *P*.

D2 *S* has an inferentially justified belief in *P* on the basis of *E*. = Df

(1) *S* believes *P*.

(2) *E* confirms *P*.

(3) The *fact* that *E* causes *S* to believe *P*.

(4) There is no proposition *X* such that *S* is justified in believing both *X* and that *E* & *X* does not confirm *P*.

It is important to note that the above distinctions can be compounded by recognizing a distinction between occurrent and dispositional belief. Each of you believes or accepts many propositions that you are not now entertaining, about which you are not now thinking. Five minutes ago, for example, you all believed that 7 + 5 = 12 even though none of you were thinking about that proposition. If an occurrent belief in a proposition can be thought of as a psychological state attending the consideration of that proposition,[6] then the most straightforward analysis of a dispositional belief would employ a subjunctive conditional:

D3 *S* dispositionally believes *P*. = Df *S* would believe (occurrently) *P* if he were to consider it.

Now there seems to be no a priori reason why a person may not have an infinite number of dispositional beliefs, understood this way. Five minutes ago, for example, you presumably believed dispositionally that the number 2 is greater than the number 1, that the number 3 is greater than the number 1, that the number 4 is greater than the number 1, etc. *ad infinitum*. There also seems no reason why one might not have both *inferentially justified* and *noninferentially justified* dispositional beliefs. Thus five minutes ago you had the inferentially justified dispositional belief that fire is hot, a belief which is justified by virtue of the fact that you hold other justified dispositional beliefs, for example, that every time you approached fire in the past it was hot. Again, it may be the case that five minutes ago you had the noninferentially justified dispositional belief that you were appeared to redly, a belief which, perhaps, was not actualized at that time simply because you were not entertaining such an unusual proposition (unusual in the sense that one normally thinks about the world, not about experience). Nevertheless, the proposition in question, one about which you were not thinking, and, let us suppose, one about which you have never thought, may have been one which you would have accepted were you to think about it, and may have been one the truth of which would have been simply given or self-evident were you to consider it; i.e., it may have been the kind of proposition that is such that, when you are acquainted with it through thought, you are also on some occasions given or acquainted with the fact to which it corresponds, as well as the fact that it does so correspond. That one might be able to have an infinite number of justified dispositional beliefs, all of which can play a part in the justification of other beliefs, is the source of my aforementioned concern over the soundness of the argument for foundations. That argument rested on the assertion that an infinite regress of justification was vicious, an assertion which seems quite uncontroversial as long as one thinks of justification as involving a *conscious* process of reasoning. We need not concern ourselves with further discussion of this issue now, for in this paper we are concerned only with that part of empiricism which insists that justification of beliefs in physical-object propositions always involves appeal to propositions about sensations. We can leave open the second part of that thesis, namely that beliefs in some propositions about experience are on some occasions noninferentially justified.

Let us allow, for the moment at least, the beliefs referred to in the above definitions to be either occurrent or dispositional in the sense outlined by D3. If one were to restrict one's attention to *occurrent* beliefs, I suspect the cases of inferential justification as defined by D1 would be extremely unusual indeed. For one thing, the evidence essential to the justification of almost all our everyday beliefs is, quite simply, enormously complex. I come home, find my window broken, footsteps outside my window, my valuables missing, and I immediately conclude that a thief has broken into my house. If asked to justify my belief I would no doubt appeal to the aforementioned truths. But those facts *by themselves* do *not* confirm the proposition that a thief broke into my house—it is only those facts *conjoined with* a vast array of background knowledge *essential* to the justification of this and other similar beliefs: the fact that windows do not break unless acted upon by some force, the fact that physical objects (such as the valuables) do not customarily disappear *in nihilo*, the fact that physical objects do not move by themselves, the fact that it is not a perfectly acceptable custom for one's friends to borrow one's valuables by breaking into one's house and taking them. . . . All this, and, of course, much more, is part of the edifice supporting almost all our empirical beliefs, an edifice which has been built up through years of experiences, experiences which can legitimately be described and employed in the premises of countless inductive arguments. That we actually entertain and accept *all* the relevant propositions that constitute part of our evidence justifying a belief in, for example, the proposition that a thief broke into a house, would be virtually impossible. If we allow dispositional justified beliefs to justify other beliefs and to be, perhaps, justified themselves by noninferentially justified dispositional beliefs, it may well turn out that many of our beliefs are, in fact, justified in just the sense outlined by D1; for it may turn out that we have not only justified dispositional beliefs in all the propositions that constitute our total body of evidence, but also justified dispositional beliefs, presumably noninferentially justified dispositional beliefs, in the relevant epistemic principles, again, principles about which we may never have thought. Indeed, *if* we understand dispositional belief in the way suggested by D3, it is not clear that one would have to appeal to any sense other than D1 in which one might have an inferentially justified belief in order to save empiricism from what seemed to be an initially plausible objection based on observations about what we do and do not infer. For all Quinton has reasonably argued is that most people seldom if ever actually consider propositions describing solely the phenomenological character of their experiences, seldom if ever employ such propositions as premises in a process of conscious inference, and seldom if ever actually offer propositions about the nature of experience as evidence upon being challenged as to their justification for a belief in a physical-object proposition. But, of course, none of this would tell against the possibility that we all have justified dispositional beliefs in propositions describing experience, that we all have justified dispositional beliefs in the relevant epistemic principles asserting a connection between the occurrence of these experiences and the existence of physical objects, and that we are so constituted that the having of these dispositional beliefs leads us to hold appropriate beliefs about the external world.

Suppose, for a moment, however, that D3 as an analysis of dispositional belief is too naive. Suppose that there really is something wrong about attributing to someone a belief in a proposition he has never considered and, perhaps, lacks the sophistication to consider. Would that part of the empiricist's position which contradicts epistemological direct realism fall apart? I think not, for I think we would then reasonably turn to D2 by way of accepting another sense in which one might be said to have inferential justification. Unless dispositional beliefs will do the job (as I suggested they might) in providing us with justification, I think the vast majority of the beliefs we think are justified are quite simply unjustified *in the sense defined by D1*, again, if for no other reason than that the edifice supporting the vast majority of our beliefs (whether or not the empiricist is correct) would have to be so enormously complex as to preclude examination and acceptance. What is more, most people have simply never thought about, let alone tried to justify their beliefs about, the connection between what they take as their evidence and what they conclude from that evidence.

Insofar as reasoning involves a conscious process of inference, most of our beliefs are quite *a-rational*. Even in those cases where we do consciously consider and evaluate the truth of *some* propositions before accepting another proposition on the basis of those propositions, it is simply not the case that we consciously consider and accept *all* of that which is quite essential to our justification. Indeed, many of our beliefs, expectations, and behavior are largely on the level of the lower animals, in that, much of the time, we simply react in certain ways to certain stimuli.

Now one can call beliefs, expectations, and behavior that arise as a causal consequence of given stimuli, without the mediation of any process of conscious inference or reasoning, a-rational if one wants—nothing hinges on the application of a label—but perhaps it would be more useful to characterize justification in such a way that some such beliefs will count as rational and some as irrational. And that is precisely what D2 does. The crucial condition for having an inferentially justified belief in the sense defined by D2, the condition that will still allow us to distinguish between rational and irrational belief, is that condition which is of primary concern when we search for the more idealized kind of inferential justification defined by D1, namely condition 2, that the proposition describing that which causes us to accept a given proposition *P* does indeed confirm or lend support to *P*.

It might seem that, if both D1 and D2 were employed in analyzing two different senses in which one could know a proposition, that concept of knowledge which employs D2 would be approaching the so-called "causal" theory of knowing. But the crucial thing to remember is that the philosophical problems of determining what we know and how we know it will not rest simply on questions of what causes what, but will rest on what they have always rested on, questions of what confirms what or makes what probable. In examining the question of whether we have knowledge of propositions asserting the existence of physical objects, we still must ask ourselves whether the truth of such propositions is ever simply given, i.e., if we are ever immediately acquainted with a physical-object proposition, the fact to which it corresponds, and the fact that it does so correspond. If we decide that the truth of such a proposition is never simply given, if we decide that we must always consciously infer such propositions from other propositions, e.g., propositions describing the nature of our experiences, or that we are always caused to believe such proposition by some other fact, e.g., the fact that we have certain sensations or experiences, we are then faced with the old philosophical problem of determining whether and how propositions about experiences do confirm propositions about the physical world.

Let us note finally that, if what I have said above is true, Quinton in "The Problem of Perception" and in *The Nature of Things* is really an empiricist. Quinton does not deny that experiences (as the empiricist understands experience) exist; he does not deny that we *can* form beliefs about and descriptions of experience; *and he does not deny that the occurrence of sensations plays a crucial role in the formation of our beliefs about the world*, for he claims that they are, in fact, what cause us to believe things about the external world and what in this sense can be thought of as the reasons for our beliefs in physical object propositions:

> The relation between experiences and objects, then, neither is nor should be logical. On the contrary it is causal, a matter of psychological fact. Our beliefs about objects are based on experience in a way that requires not justification but explanation. Experiences are not *my* reasons for my beliefs about objects—to have an experience is not to know or believe anything

> which could be a reason in this sense—though they may be *the* reasons for my believing what I do from the point of view of the psychologist. They may, that is, be the causes of my beliefs and explain them. But they could only be my reasons for my beliefs about objects if I already knew something independently about the relations between experiences and objects ("The Problem of Perception," 525).

Quinton's mistake is in thinking that, if he is correct in concluding that sensations *cause* us to hold beliefs about the world without serving as facts described in premises that are employed in a conscious process of inference, he has bypassed the old philosophical problem raised by empiricism. For, after concluding that sensations cause us to have beliefs about the external world, we as epistemologists must still determine whether what *causes* us to have such beliefs has any connection with the truth of that which we believe; that is, we must determine whether and how propositions describing the occurrence of certain sensations can confirm or make probable propositions asserting the existence of a physical object. Recognizing that there is no conscious process of inference from propositions describing experience to propositions about the external world, recognizing that our beliefs about the world are simply caused by the occurrence of certain sensations, in no way eliminates this problem. We want to know and be able to explicate how we can have inferentially justified beliefs about the world either in the sense defined by D1, allowing for the possibility of having a belief that is both justified and dispositional, or in the sense defined by D2. To do so we must understand the epistemological relationship of experience to the world.

Notes

1 The well-known Gettier problem has convinced many philosophers to search for a fourth condition to an analysis of knowledge. The approaches taken by Ernest Sosa in "The Concept of Knowledge: How Do You Know?," *American Philosophical Quarterly* (April 1974): 113–122, and by Roderick M. Chisholm in a second edition of *Theory of Knowledge* (Prentice Hall, soon to be published) seem to me to be, if not right, at least on the right track.

2 One will presumably need, in addition, noninferentially justified beliefs in the "bridge" principles (at least memory and induction) which enable one to get beyond the content of one's present experience. Throughout this paper I shall be using the terms "experience" (a general term referring to the occurrence of any mental process, e.g., believing, remembering, being in pain, etc.) and "sensation" (referring to a subclass of experience, e.g., visual, tactile, auditory, olfactory, kinesthetic experiences) in the most neutral way possible. You may, for my present purposes, understand a sensation as the sensing of a sense-datum or a way of being appeared to. With all empiricists, however, I am using the terms in such a way that the having of an experience entails no proposition asserting the existence of a physical object.

3 "The Problem of Perception," *Mind* 54 (January 1955): 26–51, reprinted in Robert Swartz, ed., *Perceiving, Sensing, and Knowing* (Garden City: Doubleday, 1965), pp. 491–526 (page references to this article are to the reprinted version); *The Nature of Things* (London: Routledge & Kegan Paul, 1973). Though I

believe Quinton's exposition of this position is the clearest, I think similar arguments can be found in the writings of J.L. Austin and the later Wittgenstein.

4 Quinton would concede the point: *ibid.*, p. 116.

5 Used in what Chisholm called the "noncomparative" sense—see Chisholm, *Perceiving* (Ithaca, N.Y.: Cornell, 1957), pp. 50–53—or what Lewis called the "expressive" sense—see C.I. Lewis, *An Analysis of Knowledge and Valuation* (LaSalle, Ill.: Open Court, 1946), p. 179. Note that Quinton allows that appearing language *can* be used in this way—see "The Problem of Perception," p. 506.

6 This is not, of course, uncontroversial, but I would be prepared to defend this thesis at length in another context.

QUESTIONS

1 What does Fumerton's version of "empiricism" hold?

2 What is the difference between occurrent beliefs and dispositional beliefs?

3 According to Fumerton, does the fact that people do not normally consciously entertain propositions about their experiences refute empiricism? Explain briefly why or why not.

David Hume, "Of Scepticism with Regard to Reason"

In all demonstrative sciences the rules are certain and infallible; but when we apply them, our fallible and uncertain faculties are very apt to depart from them, and fall into error. We must, therefore, in every reasoning form a new judgment, as a check or controul on our first judgment or belief; and must enlarge our view to comprehend a kind of history of all the instances, wherein our understanding has deceiv'd us, compar'd with those, wherein its testimony was just and true. Our reason must be consider'd as a kind of cause, of which truth is the natural effect; but such-a-one as by the irruption of other causes, and by the inconstancy of our mental powers, may frequently be prevented. By this means all knowledge degenerates into probability; and this probability is greater or less, according to our experience of the veracity or deceitfulness of our understanding, and according to the simplicity or intricacy of the question.

There is no Algebraist nor Mathematician so expert in his science, as to place entire confidence in any truth immediately upon his discovery of it, or regard it as anything, but a mere probability. Every time he runs over his proofs, his confidence encreases; but still more by the approbation of his friends; and is rais'd to its utmost perfection by the universal assent and applauses of the learned world. Now 'tis evident, that this gradual encrease of assurance is nothing but the addition of new probabilities, and is deriv'd from the constant union of causes and effects, according to past experience and observation.

In accompts of any length or importance, Merchants seldom trust to the infallible certainty of numbers for their security; but by the artificial structure of the accompts, produce a probability beyond what is deriv'd from the skill and experience of the accomptant. For that is plainly of itself some degree of probability; tho' uncertain and variable, according to the degrees of his experience and length of the accompt. Now as none will maintain, that our assurance in a long numeration exceeds probability, I may safely affirm, that there scarce is any proposition concerning numbers, of which we can have a fuller security. For 'tis easily possible, by gradually diminishing the numbers, to reduce the longest series of addition to the most simple question, which can be form'd, to an addition of two single numbers; and upon this supposition we shall find it impracticable to shew the precise limits of knowledge and of probability, or discover that particular number, at which the one ends and the other begins. But knowledge and

David Hume, *A Treatise of Human Nature* in *The Philosophical Works*, ed. T.H. Green and T.H. Grose, vol. 1 (London, 1886).

probability are of such contrary and disagreeing natures, that they cannot well run insensibly into each other, and that because they will not divide, but must be either entirely present, or entirely absent. Besides, if any single addition were certain, every one wou'd be so, and consequently the whole or total sum; unless the whole can be different from all its parts. I had almost said, that this was certain; but I reflect that it must reduce *itself*, as well as every other reasoning, and from knowledge degenerate into probability.

Since therefore all knowledge resolves itself into probability, and becomes at last of the same nature with that evidence, which we employ in common life, we must now examine this latterspecies of reasoning, and see on what foundation it stands.

In every judgment, which we can form concerning probability, as well as concerning knowledge, we ought always to correct the first judgment, deriv'd from the nature of the object, by another judgment, deriv'd from the nature of the understanding. 'Tis certain a man of solid sense and long experience ought to have, and usually has, a greater assurance in his opinions, than one that is foolish and ignorant, and that our sentiments have different degrees of authority, even with ourselves, in proportion to the degrees of our reason and experience. In the man of the best sense and lougest experience, this authority is never entire; since even such-a-one must be conscious of many errors in the past, and must still dread the like for the future. Here then arises a new species of probability to correct and regulate the first, and fix its just standard and proportion. As demonstration is subject to the controul of probability, so is probability liable to a new correction by a reflex act of the mind, wherein the nature of our understanding, and our reasoning from the first probability become our objects.

Having thus found in every probability, beside the original uncertainty inherent in the subject, a new uncertainty deriv'd from the weakness of that faculty, which judges, and having adjusted these two together, we are oblig'd by our reason to add a new doubt deriv'd from the possibility of error in the estimation we make of the truth and fidelity of our faculties. This is a doubt, which immediately occurs to us, and of which, if we wou'd closely pursue our reason, we cannot avoid giving a decision. But this decision, tho' it shou'd be favourable to our preceding judgment, being founded only on probability, must weaken still further our first evidence, and must itself be weaken'd by a fourth doubt of the same kind, and so on *in infinitum*; till at last there remain nothing of the original probability, however great we may suppose it to have been, and however small the diminution by every new uncertainty. No finite object can subsist under a decrease repeated *in infinitum*; and even the vastest quantity, which can enter into human imagination, must in this manner be reduc'd to nothing. Let our first belief be never so strong, it must infallibly perish by passing thro' so many new examinations, of which each diminishes somewhat of its force and vigour. When I reflect on the natural fallibility of my judgment, I have less confidence in my opinions, than when I only consider the objects concerning which I reason; and when I proceed still farther, to turn the scrutiny against every successive estimation I make of my faculties, all the rules of logic require a continual diminution, and at last a total extinction of belief and evidence.

Shou'd it here be ask'd me, whether I sincerely assent to this argument, which I seem to take such pains to inculcate, and whether I be really one of those sceptics, who hold that all is uncertain, and that our judgment is not in *any* thing possest of *any* measures of truth and falshood; I shou'd reply, that this question is entirely superfluous, and that neither I, nor any other person was ever sincerely and constantly of that opinion. Nature, by an absolute and uncontroulable necessity has determin'd us to judge as well as to breathe and feel; nor can we any more forbear viewing certain objects in a stronger and fuller light, upon account of their customary connexion with a present impression, than we can hinder ourselves from thinking as long as we are awake, or seeing the surrounding bodies, when we turn our eyes towards them in broad sunshine. Whoever has taken the pains to refute the cavils of this *total* scepticism, has really disputed without an antagonist, and endeavour'd by arguments to establish a faculty, which nature has antecedently implanted in the mind, and render'd unavoidable.

My intention then in displaying so carefully the arguments of that fantastic sect, is only to make the reader sensible of the truth of my hypothesis, *that all our reasonings concerning causes and effects are deriv'd from nothing but custom; and that belief is more properly an act of the sensitive, than of the cogitative part of our natures*. I have here prov'd, that the very same principles, which make us form a decision upon any subject, and correct that decision by the consideration of our genius and capacity, and of the situation of our mind, when we examin'd that subject; I say, I have prov'd, that these same principles, when carry'd farther, and apply'd to every new reflex judgment, must, by continually diminishing the original evidence, at last reduce it to nothing, and utterly subvert all belief and opinion. If belief, therefore, were a simple act of the thought, without any peculiar manner of conception, or the addition of a force and vivacity, it must infallibly destroy itself, and in every ease terminate in a total suspense of judgment. But as experience will sufficiently convince any one, who thinks it worth while to try, that tho' he can find no error in the foregoing arguments, yet he still continues to believe, and think, and reason as usual, he may safely conclude, that his reasoning and belief is some sensation or peculiar manner of conception, which 'tis impossible for mere ideas and reflections to destroy.

But here, perhaps, it may be demanded, how it happens, even upon my hypothesis, that these arguments above-explain'd produce not a total suspense of judgment, and after what manner the mind ever retains a degree of assurance in any subject? For as these new probabilities, which by their repetition perpetually diminish the original evidence, are founded on the very same principles, whether of thought or sensation, as the primary judgment, it may seem unavoidable, that in either case they must equally subvert it, and by the opposition, either of contrary thoughts or sensations, reduce the mind to a total uncertainty. I suppose, there is some question propos'd to me, and that after revolving over the impressions of my memory and senses, and carrying my thoughts from them to such objects, as are commonly conjoin'd with them, I feel a stronger and more forcible conception on the one side, than on the other. This strong conception forms my first decision. I suppose, that afterwards I examine my judgment itself, and observing from experience, that 'tis sometimes just and sometimes erroneous, I consider it as regulated by contrary principles or causes, of which some lead to truth, and some to error; and in ballancing these contrary causes, I diminish by a new probability the assurance of my first decision. This new probability is liable to the same diminution as the foregoing, and so on, *in infinitum*. 'Tis therefore demanded, *how it happens, that even after all we retain a degree of belief, which is sufficient for our purpose, either in philosophy or common life.*

I answer, that after the first and second decision; as the action of the mind becomes forc'd and unnatural, and the ideas faint and obscure; tho' the principles of judgment, and the ballancing of opposite causes be the same as at the very beginning; yet their influence on the imagination, and the vigour they add to, or diminish from the thought, is by no means equal. Where the mind reaches not its objects with easiness and facility, the same principles have not the same effect as in a more natural conception of the ideas; nor does the imagination feel a sensation, which holds any proportion with that which arises from its common judgments and opinions. The attention is on the stretch: The posture of the mind is uneasy; and the spirits being diverted from their natural course, are not govern'd in their movements by the same laws, at least not to the same degree, as when they flow in their usual channel.

If we desire similar instances, 'twill not be very difficult to find them. The present subject of metaphysics will supply us abundantly. The same argument, which wou'd have been esteem'd convincing in a reasoning concerning history or politics, has little or no influence in these abstruser subjects, even tho' it be perfectly comprehended; and that because there is requir'd a study and an effort of thought, in order to its being comprehended: And this effort of thought disturbs the operation of our sentiments, on which the belief depends. The case is the same in other subjects. The straining of the imagination always hinders the regular flowing of the passions and sentiments. A tragic poet, that wou'd represent his heroes as very ingenious and witty in their misfortunes, wou'd never touch the passions. As the emotions of the soul prevent any subtile reasoning and reflection, so these latter actions of the mind are equally prejudicial to the former. The mind, as well as the body, seems to be endow'd with a certain precise degree of force and activity, which it never employs in one action, but at the expense of all the rest. This is more evidently true, where the actions are of quite different natures; since in that case the force of the mind is not only diverted, but even the disposition chang'd, so as to render us incapable of a sudden transition from one action to the other, and still more of performing both at once. No wonder, then, the conviction, which arises from a subtile reasoning, diminishes in proportion to the efforts, which the imagination makes to enter into the reasoning, and to conceive it in all its parts. Belief, being a lively conception, can never be entire, where it is not founded on something natural and easy.

This I take to be the true state of the question, and cannot approve of that expeditious way, which some take with the sceptics, to reject at once all their arguments without enquiry or examination. If the sceptical reasonings be strong, say they, 'tis a proof, that reason may have some force and authority: if weak, they can never be sufficient to invalidate all the conclusions of our understanding. This argument is not just; because the sceptical reasonings, were it possible for them to exist, and were they not destroy'd by their subtility, wou'd be successively both strong and weak, according to the successive dispositions of the mind. Reason first appears in possession of the throne, prescribing laws, and imposing maxims, with an absolute sway and authority. Her enemy, therefore, is oblig'd to take shelter under her protection, and by making use of rational arguments to prove the fallaciousness and imbecility of reason, produces, in a manner, a patent under her hand and seal. This patent has at first an authority, proportion'd to the present and immediate authority of reason, from which it is deriv'd. But as it is suppos'd to be contradictory to reason, it gradually diminishes the force of that governing power and its own at the same time; till at last they both vanish away into nothing, by a regular and just diminution. The sceptical and dogmatical reasons are of the same kind, tho' contrary in their operation and tendency; so that where the latter is strong, it has an enemy of equal force in the former to encounter; and as their forces were at first equal, they still continue so, as long as either of them subsists; nor does one of them lose any force in the contest, without taking as much from its antagonist. 'Tis happy, therefore, that nature breaks the force of all sceptical arguments in time, and keeps them from having any considerable influence on the understanding. Were we to trust entirely to their self-destruction, that can never take place, 'till they have first subverted all conviction, and have totally destroy'd human reason.

QUESTIONS

1 Hume says that, when a mathematician runs over a proof again, his confidence in the conclusion increases. What does this show (according to Hume)?
2 According to Hume, if the conclusion of a lengthy proof is uncertain, must the conclusion of a short proof also be uncertain? Why?
3 What main conclusion is Hume trying to establish?

Hilary Kornblith, "Distrusting Reason"

The activity of reason-giving is an important part of our intellectual lives. At times, we offer reasons to justify our actions or our beliefs, both to others and to ourselves. Moreover, most of us take reason-giving to have normative force: if we are presented with good reasons in favor of a belief or a course of action, we take this to provide us with a presumption in favor of forming that belief or performing that action. This is, after all, why reason is so important: it serves, and rightly so, as a guide to both belief and action.

But there are some who are distrustful of reason, who do not take the activity of reason-giving at face value. Reason-giving may be viewed with suspicion as yet one more instrument for wielding power over the oppressed. Views of this sort have been articulated and defended by some feminists, Freudians, Marxists, and deconstructionists, and some such inchoate view may be behind a certain climate of anti-intellectualism that is currently a potent force in public debate on many issues of real import.[1]

This distrust of reason needs to be taken more seriously than it has, to my mind, not only as a political force, but as an intellectual position. In this paper, I try to show that a certain skepticism about reason-giving deserves a hearing. In coming to understand why someone might rationally be suspicious of the practice of reason-giving, those of us who place our trust in this practice may come to understand better what its presuppositions are and what it would take to ground that trust. This paper thus attempts to make a contribution to the field of social epistemology: it attempts to spell out some of the social prerequisites for the proper function of the activity of reason giving.[2]

I

Let us begin by examining a case of rationalization. Andrew has beliefs about the effectiveness of the death penalty in reducing the murder rate which are, at bottom, a product of wishful thinking. Andrew has certain views about the morality of the death penalty, views which he holds on grounds independent of his views about its deterrent effect. His views about the effectiveness of the death penalty as a deterrent are not a product of his understanding of the relevant data. Instead, it is his view about the morality of the death penalty that is driving his view about

Hilary Kornblith, "Distrusting Reason," *Midwest Studies in Philosophy* 23, ed. Peter A. French and Howard K. Wettstein (Boston, Mass.: Blackwell, 1999).

its effects. Conveniently, he has come to believe that the policy he judges to be morally correct also happens to have the best consequences. Andrew's reason for his belief about the deterrent effect of the death penalty is not a good reason. It would not withstand public, or even private, scrutiny. But Andrew is unaware that this is why he believes as he does. He sincerely believes that his reasons for belief are quite different.

Andrew is not entirely uninformed about the various empirical studies that have been done on the deterrent effect of the death penalty. Indeed, when such studies are reported in the newspapers, Andrew is extremely attentive to the details of the news story. The studies that Andrew has seen reported are mixed: some present prima facie evidence of the effectiveness of the death penalty in reducing the murder rate, whereas others present prima facie evidence of its ineffectiveness. Andrew has latched on to the stories that fit with his antecedent view. He remembers them better than the others, and when asked about the death penalty, he is often able to cite relevant statistics from them. He has less vivid memories of the other studies, those that run counter to his belief about the death penalty's effectiveness, and when he reads about these studies he is typically able to mount some perfectly plausible methodological challenge to them: some important variable was not controlled for, the number of cases involved is not statistically significant, and so on. Andrew is intelligent and articulate. He is very good at constructing reasons for his belief from the mixed evidence with which he is confronted, and he is very good at presenting these reasons to others in discussion about the issue. He believes that the reasons that he presents are the reasons for which he holds his belief. But he is wrong about this. The reasons for his belief are quite different. Thus, when Andrew offers reasons for his belief, he is offering a rationalization.[3]

Andrew's intelligence and articulateness are aids to the process of rationalization. Andrew's ability to construct and deploy arguments can be extremely convincing, both to others and to himself. Someone less sophisticated than Andrew would not be able to construct such convincing rationalizations, and opinions of such a person that were the product of wishful thinking would be more easily exposed, both to others and to the person himself. When Andrew offers rationalizations for his badly grounded opinions, his intelligence works against him.

Ordinarily, when we reflect on our reasons for one of our beliefs, we are motivated by a desire to have our beliefs conform to the truth. By scrutinizing our reasons, we hope to be able to recognize cases where our beliefs have outstripped our reasons and thus, where we should not be confident that our beliefs do indeed conform to the truth. When we consider what to believe in prospect, we reflect on our evidence, and this process of reflection is designed to guide belief fixation so as to make it likely that the beliefs we come to have also conform to the truth. Both in the case of reflection on already existing beliefs and in the case of reflection on beliefs we might come to have, our motivation for thinking about reasons is to get at the truth.

Now in the case of rationalization, our motivation for reflecting on reasons is different. Our motivation in these cases may be to make ourselves feel better, to avoid cognitive dissonance, or the like. But if our motivations in these cases are different from those in the typical case, such motivations are not transparent to us. When we rationalize, at least when we do it sincerely, we are not aware of doing so; we are not aware of being motivated by anything other than a desire to get at the truth. And it is precisely because of this that the process of scrutinizing our reasons for belief may, at times, be terribly counterproductive from an epistemological point of view. Scrutinizing our reasons, when we are engaged in sincere rationalizing, will get in the way of the goal of believing truths.

Let us return to Andrew. When Andrew reflects on his reasons for believing as he does about the effects of the death penalty, he is able to devise reasons for his belief that give the appearance of supporting it. Indeed, the reasons he is able to offer are prima facie good reasons for believing as he does. Thus, when Andrew offers these reasons to others, if they are not independently well informed on this matter, they may come, quite reasonably, to believe as Andrew does; and when others do this, their believings, unlike Andrew's, may be motivated by nothing more than a desire to believe the truth. They, unlike Andrew, are being fully responsive to the evidence, it seems. The only problem for Andrew's interlocutors is that Andrew has selectively presented the evidence; but this, of course, is not something that they are in a position to know or even have any reason to suspect. The reasons Andrew presents are, on their face, good reasons. Rational interlocutors who lack independent evidence on the questions about which Andrew speaks should come to believe as he does.

This fact about the interpersonal case of reason-giving is particularly important because it helps to explain why it is that the process of rationalization is so easy to engage in. When we scrutinize our own reasons for belief, we, like Andrew's interlocutors, take the evidence that is available to us at face value.[4] Because the biasing processes that selectively filter our evidence take place behind the scenes, as it were, unavailable to introspection, we are able to produce perfectly good reasons for belief, reasons that not only survive our private scrutiny, but would survive public scrutiny as well. The process of scrutinizing our reasons, in the case of sincere rationalization, gives the illusion of being responsive to available evidence. And the more intelligent one is and the better one is at the skills of presenting and defending arguments, the more powerful the illusion will be, if one engages in rationalizing, that one is forming beliefs in ways that are appropriately responsive to evidence.

These facts about rationalization, I believe, go some distance toward making sense of the phenomenon of distrusting reason. There are certain people who have a deep skepticism about the significance of rational argument. These people are often unmoved by rational argument, and, indeed, seem to find the activity of reason-giving less persuasive the more careful and detailed the argument given. Such people often say things like this: "I know that's a perfectly good argument for *p*, but I don't know whether I should believe *p*"; and this, on its face, seems deeply irrational. What should determine whether one should believe *p*, after all, if not the arguments available for and against it?[5]

But I don't think that this attitude need be irrational at all. First, the ability to form one's beliefs in a way that is responsive to evidence is not at all the same as the ability to present reasons for one's beliefs, either to others or to oneself. Reason-giving requires a wide range of skills that need not be present in the reasons-responsive person. One thing the skeptic about reason-giving may be responding to is the recognition that some people are terrifically adept at providing prima facie reasonable arguments for their beliefs, quite apart from whether those beliefs are correct. Just as a reasonable person might willfully ignore the appeals of a gifted speaker in order to avoid being misled, an intelligent person who recognizes his own weakness in distinguishing apparently good but mistaken reasoning from the genuine item might also willfully ignore detailed and subtle appeals to reason.[6]

But the second reason for thinking that skepticism about reason-giving may often be quite reasonable ties in directly with the points we have made about rationalization.[7] People who are especially intelligent and articulate and who are adept at providing reasons for their beliefs are also, in virtue of that very fact, especially well equipped at providing rationalizations for their beliefs, rationalizations that possess all of the hallmarks of good reasoning. It is not that devising a convincing rationalization for a belief is easy, even for those gifted at argument. But rationalization is often the product of very powerful motivating forces, and thus a great deal of intellectual energy may be brought to the task; the result of this is often a subtle and prima facie rational argument. This provides fuel for skepticism about rational argument, and it is precisely for this reason that the skeptic is especially wary of detailed and elaborate argument. Intricacy of argument, on this view, raises a red flag, for it raises the possibility of rationalization as the underlying source of the argument given rather than truth-responsive reason-giving. Inspection of the details of the argument would be pointless in trying to distinguish these two, for the subtle rationalizer is in a fine position to offer arguments that, on their face, are impeccable. The difference between truth-responsive reason-giving and subtle rationalization does not lie in features intrinsic to the arguments given. A reasonable person who is worried about the possibility of rationalization as a source of a particular act of reason-giving will thus not allow herself to be pulled into the intellectual task of examining the quality of reasoning offered, for this is the wrong place to look to see whether the conclusion is to be trusted. What needs to be examined is the source of the argument—its motivation—rather than its logical credentials. One needs to know whether the person offering the argument is motivated by a desire to believe truths or by something else instead.

One might object at this point that the motivation of the person offering the argument is simply irrelevant when we are trying to figure out what to believe. If the argument offered is a good one, then it doesn't matter whether it reflects the reasons for which the person offering it believes the conclusion. We shouldn't care whether the argument offered is a reflection of the arguer's reasons for belief; all we should care about is whether the argument offered is a reflection of good reasons for us to believe.

There is something right about this objection. The mere fact that an argument offered does not reflect the reasons for which the arguer believes a conclusion does not by itself undermine the value of the reasons offered. Nevertheless, as a matter of empirical fact, the phenomenon of rationalization is typically accompanied by a number of factors that do tend to undermine the value of the reasons offered by the rationalizer. As the case of Andrew illustrates, there is a tremendous selectivity in the way in which rationalizers deal with evidence: they do not present the evidence fairly, either to themselves, in memory, or to others. This point, by itself, is sufficient to show that we must be on the lookout for rationalization.

In addition, many arguments involve subtle appeals to plausibility. There can be little doubt that the rationalizer's sense of plausibility is affected in important ways by the motivation he has for rationalizing, and this does not aid in the project of coming to believe truths. Thus, if an agent suspects that he himself is rationalizing, he has reason to worry about his overall evaluations of plausibility. That an argument is born of rationalization is importantly relevant in determining what one should believe.

More than this, the extent to which inchoate judgments of plausibility come into play in evaluating arguments should be a source of concern even apart from concerns about rationalization. Our sense of plausibility is a fragile reed. There can be little doubt that it is socially conditioned. Being surrounded by people who take a particular view seriously, or, alternatively, simply dismiss a view as unworthy of serious consideration, is likely to have some effect on one's own assessments of plausibility. If those around one are well attuned to the truth, this may be a fine thing. But in less optimal circumstances, where one's epistemic community is badly misguided, one's own sense of plausibility may be distorted as a result. What passes for good reasoning in such communities may have very little connection to the truth.

In the end, the difference between the person who places his full confidence in rational argument and the person who is skeptical of it may come down, in part, to a disagreement about the frequency with which rationalization occurs and the extent to which our sense of plausibility can be distorted. If one believes that rationalization is extremely widespread and that plausibility judgments are extremely malleable, then one may be well advised to be skeptical of rational argument. Under these conditions, attending to the logical niceties of argument would be no more useful in attaining one's epistemic goals than attending to the eye color of the person offering the argument. If, on the other hand, rationalization is rare, and plausibility judgments are firmly fixed in ways that track the truth, then focusing on the logical features of reason-giving may serve as an effective guide to true belief. What divides these two views, to the extent that each is rationally held, is a disagreement about human psychology.

Let me spell out this disagreement in greater detail. The skeptic about reason-giving may view the very activity of giving reasons as far more disconnected from the truth, and indeed, in some cases, from the activity of belief fixation, than we are ordinarily accustomed to thinking. I take the traditional view to be as follows. Human beings often form their beliefs as a result of self-consciously considering reasons. When they do this, they are typically led to beliefs that are likely to be true, at least relative to the evidence available to them. Even when self-conscious consideration of reasons does not occur prior to forming a belief, we often scrutinize our reasons for belief after the fact. When we do this, we begin by determining what our reasons for holding a belief come to, and we then consider the logical credentials of our reasons. When they are good reasons, we continue to hold the belief, and when they are not good reasons, we come to give up the belief. Our reasons are, for the most part, easily available to introspection, and the activity of considering our reasons is thus deeply implicated in the fixation of belief in a way that guides it toward the truth.

But the skeptic about reason-giving may have a very different picture about the relationship among the giving of reasons, belief fixation, and the truth. On this view, belief fixation often occurs independent of self-conscious consideration of reasons. This need not make belief fixation irrational or unrelated to the truth, for we may in many cases be responsive to good reasons even without self-consciously considering them. When we do turn to self-conscious consideration of reasons, on the skeptic's view, the activity of reason-giving may often have little effect on belief fixation. Far from reasons determining which beliefs are formed, as on the traditional view, it is the beliefs we antecedently hold that largely determine the reasons we will come to find. Reason-giving, on this view, is often a matter of rationalization. From the point of view of belief fixation, reason-giving is frequently epiphenomenal.[8]

Even when reason giving is not epiphenomenal, on the skeptic's view, it may have little connection with the truth. Since our sense of plausibility is so easily affected by the standards of our community, a community whose standards have been distorted by external factors will come to taint even the judgments of those otherwise unaffected by those distorting factors prevalent elsewhere in the community. When what passes for good reason really does play a role in belief fixation, then, it does not guide the self-conscious believer toward the truth, but instead serves only to further distort that person's judgment.

The issue between the skeptic about reason-giving and the person who places his trust in it is, I believe, an important one, and I would like to examine it in more detail. But before we try to figure out who is in the right here, we need to consider an objection to the skeptic's position, an objection that challenges its internal coherence. The skeptic's position is worthy of serious consideration only if it can avoid this particular challenge.

II

The challenge I have in mind is that the skeptic's view is self-undermining, for the skeptic on the one hand proclaims that the activity of reason-giving is not connected to the truth and that we should therefore be unmoved by it, and yet, on the other hand, in order to convince us of this particular view, the skeptic offers us reasons. If the skeptic is right about the activity of reason-giving, then her argument would not, and should not, convince us. According to the challenger, skepticism about reason-giving is thus self-undermining.[9]

This challenge fails, I believe, and it fails in two different ways. First, the skeptic's argument may be seen as a simple *reductio*.[10] The skeptic about reason-giving need not be seen as endorsing the argument she gives; instead she may be seen as merely showing that the position of the person who puts his trust in reason-giving is internally inconsistent; that is, it fails to meet that person's own standards. The skeptic, on this view, demonstrates an internal tension in the view of the person who places his trust in rational argument, a tension which that person is in no position to resolve. This is sufficient to undermine the trust in rational argument.

Although this particular way of construing the skeptic's argument absolves her of the charge of undermining her own position, I think that there is a better way to represent what the skeptic is up to. I thus turn to a second response to our challenger.

As I see it, the skeptic does not mean merely to offer a *reductio* in the manner just explained. Instead, the skeptic wishes to endorse the position that reason-giving is so frequently a matter of mere rationalization, and our plausibility judgments so frequently off the mark, that reason should not be taken at face value. Indeed, this particular view of reason-giving is offered as the best available explanation of the social phenomenon of inquiring about and presenting reasons for belief. On this account of the skeptic's position, the charge of internal inconsistency, of self-defeat, is more acute. For on this account, the skeptic is presenting a rational argument *that she endorses* for the view that rational arguments should not produce conviction. How could such a position fail to be self-defeating?

The answer to this question lies in the recognition that our skeptic about reason giving is not a *total* skeptic; indeed, she is very far from it. She is not a skeptic about the possibility of rational belief. She merely denies that a certain activity, an activity that many see as paradigmatically rational, is, indeed, genuinely rational, at least in the typical case. On the skeptic's view, rational belief is not only possible, it is often actual. Beliefs that are not self-consciously arrived at are frequently responsive to reason. Moreover, although the skeptic does not accept the practice of reason-giving at face value, this does not mean that the skeptic is forced to reject every case of reason-giving as bogus. Rather, her view about the frequency of reason-giving as reason-responsive, and reason-giving as mere rationalization, is just the reverse of the person who places his trust in the practice of giving reasons.

Consider the attitude of a rational and cautious person when buying a used car. Such a person will be faced with a good deal of reason-giving on the part of the used car salesman, and it may well be that, if taken at face value, the reasons offered for various purchases are wholly convincing. From the point of view of logic alone, the used car salesman's reasoning is impeccable. But the rational and cautious person does not take the used car salesman's arguments at face value.[11] Rather, in this situation, although one does not simply ignore everything which is said, one does not simply evaluate the logical cogency of the arguments offered either. One may certainly approach argument in this way at the used car lot, while forming beliefs on the basis of argument on other occasions.

Now the skeptic about reason-giving sees the practice of reason-giving generally in much the way that we all regard the arguments of the used car salesman. The skeptic is not concerned about dishonesty or insincerity; rather, she is concerned about sincere rationalization and a distorted sense of plausibility. But just as we all regard the used car salesman's utterances and arguments with a great deal of suspicion, the skeptic sees the default situation almost everywhere as one in which rational argument should not be taken at face value. By the same token, there are situations in which we will come to believe at least some of what the used car salesman tells us because we have independent grounds for overcoming our prima facie distrust. Similarly, the skeptic will insist that the prima facie concern about rationalization and distorted judgment is one that is not only in principle but in practice surmountable, and that when these concerns are properly defeated, we should follow the arguments where they lead. Reason-giving is not automatically irrelevant epistemically, on the skeptic's view; it should simply be regarded as irrelevant until proven otherwise.

Now it is important to recognize that the skeptic does not simply apply this approach to others, assuming that she herself is immune to rationalization or distorted judgment. Rather, she approaches her own explicit reasoning with the same degree of suspicion with which she approaches that of others. After all, her reason for concern about others has to do with rationalization and misguided judgment, not lack of sincerity, and the person who offers sincere rationalizations or whose judgment is somehow misguided is not only a purveyor of misleading arguments but a consumer of them as well. Thus, on the skeptic's view, we should approach all argument, even our own, with the default understanding that it reflects rationalization or misguided judgment, a mere cover for reasons that could not pass rational scrutiny if fully exposed. If an argument is to be taken at face value, then, there must be reason for supposing that the default condition does not apply.

There is no question that it is more difficult to do this in the first-person case than it is in the third-person case. If I can take my own reasoning at face value, then when I consider the reasoning of others of whom I have reason to be suspicious, I have considerable resources on which to draw. In particular, I may reason self-consciously and explicitly about their motivations, their interests and so on, in order to try to figure out when they are most likely to offer mere rationalizations and when it is that their reasoning can be accepted on its face. But if I cannot yet trust myself, or at least cannot yet trust my own explicit reasoning, then my resources are considerably thinner. Nevertheless, I believe that we can make perfectly good sense of the project to which the skeptic is committed.

After all, even those who are not skeptics about reason-giving in general will, on occasion, have reason to treat their own reason-giving with a certain measure of skepticism. We are all familiar with factors that may frequently interfere with the operation of good reasoning, and in ways that are typically invisible to the agent who is subject to them. We not only worry that judges who have a financial stake in the outcome of a certain decision might be biased by recognition of that fact; we worry that we ourselves might also be biased when put in such a situation. Now it just won't do in such a case to introspect and ask oneself whether one is subject to any untoward influence, and then, if one passes the test, go ahead and offer a decision. This won't do simply because we know that such biases work in ways that are not typically available to introspection. No doubt the best thing to do in this kind of case is simply to opt out; one should insist that one is not in a position to make the decision. But this is not to say that the only two options here are either to opt out or to follow the casual deliverances of introspection. And if opting out is not a possibility, then one may attempt systematically to eliminate, to the best of one's ability, the various factors that might serve as a source of bias.

Any such attempt will leave open the possibility of failure. One may, in spite of sincere and responsible attempts to eliminate all possible bias, nevertheless fall victim to it. But to say that there are no guarantees of getting things right here is not to distinguish this situation, epistemically, from any other. Evidence may be gathered here that is relevant to the question of one's own bias, and one may, in some cases, gain sufficient reason to believe that one is not biased in the particular case. At least I see no reason in principle or in practice why this should not be so.[12] But if in this sort of case one may reasonably eliminate the hypothesis that one is moved by rationalization, then the skeptic may do the same. And once the skeptic can eliminate the likelihood of her own bias, in some particular case, then she may approach others in the way we all approach used car dealers. The task of evaluating reasoning for the skeptic is thus much more elaborate than it is for the person who takes reason-giving at face value, but it is not in principle impossible.[13]

In addition, it is important to point out that the skeptic about reason-giving is likely to be, as I mentioned briefly above, suspicious about pieces of reasoning in direct proportion to their logical perspicuity: the more detailed and carefully crafted the argument, the greater the suspicion that rationalization is at work.[14] Reason-giving of a more discursive sort will thus evoke little suspicion. The late Supreme Court Justice William Brennan Jr. described his own style of judicial decision making, very much in this spirit, as seeking a "range of emotional and intuitive responses" rather than "lumbering syllogisms of reason."[15] The skeptic about reason-giving will thus have substantial resources with which to address and resolve, in many cases, her concerns about rationalization. Where she cannot turn back these concerns, she will simply ignore the arguments given.

The skeptic's view is not self-undermining. More than this, I believe, it is a view that needs to be taken quite seriously. So let us do that.

III

The skeptic's view may at first sound like the mirror image of some well-known epistemic principles, principles that, though controversial, have a long history. I have in mind, for example, Thomas Reid's Principle of Credulity,[16] the idea that one should take other people's utterances to be true unless one has specific reason to believe otherwise, and Roderick Chisholm's various principles of evidence,[17] which involve accepting the "testimony of the senses" at face value, unless one has specific counterevidence. These principles are often explained by way of an analogy with the legal doctrine that one should assume a defendant innocent until proven guilty. In the case of Reid and of Chisholm, various sources of evidence are taken at face value unless there is some reason on the other side. Special reason is required to dismiss these sources of evidence; none is required if we are to follow where they seem to lead. The skeptic seems to have exactly the opposite presumption: reason-giving is to be distrusted until there is special reason to believe otherwise.

Chisholm defends his principles of evidence, however, as justified a priori, and it is important to recognize that the skeptic about reason-giving does not see her approach to reason-giving as having any such status. Rather, her presumption about reasoning is seen as an empirical hypothesis that, on her view, is well supported by available evidence. We may understand the skeptic's position only if we see it in that light.

We all recognize that sincere rationalization sometimes occurs, and that on such occasions, we would do well not to take the rationalizer's arguments, however logically impeccable, at face value. What the skeptic believes is that there is a fairly strong correlation between the logical perspicuity with which arguments tend to be offered and the amount of rationalization that underlies them. There is nothing intrinsically wrong with logic or good reasoning itself on this view; any such view would be absurd. Rather, as a matter of empirical fact, it is argued, those who tend to present their arguments with the greatest logical perspicuity are also, on those occasions, most frequently offering rationalizations, or at least so frequently offering rationalizations as to make the best epistemic policy the one of adopting the skeptic's presumption.

Consider the contemporary practice of philosophy, in which a very high premium is attached to giving detailed and logically perspicuous arguments. Surely philosophy is one of the natural homes of logical perspicuity. Is there reason to think that philosophers ought to be especially concerned about the possibility of rationalization? I think that there is. In ethics, for example, there is more than a little reason to think that a philosopher's views about right and wrong may often derive from features of that philosopher's upbringing that would do nothing at all to confer any justification on the views that result. For example, in many cases, a person's views about right and wrong are deeply influenced by that person's religious upbringing, even when that person would not appeal to any religious doctrine in support of those views. Now I do not mean to suggest that a religious origin for a view is automatically a source of distortion; but we all believe that some religious origins of moral views are an important source of distortion. When a person's view is due to some such distorting influence, and that person is able to offer detailed and logically perspicuous arguments that somehow sidestep the real source of the person's view, the worry about rationalization and its influence is particularly acute.

Nor is this peculiar to ethics. In social and political philosophy, there is also special reason to worry about the influence of distorting factors. We each have financial and personal interests that are at stake in any social and political arrangement. The idea that we might be subject to rationalization when considering which arrangements are most just is hardly a paranoid fantasy. It would, indeed, be quite remarkable if such factors rarely came to influence our views about justice, equality, and the like.

Nor do I think that this concern is rightly limited to moral philosophy broadly construed. Although the potential sources of distortion and subsequent rationalization are, I think, both most obvious and most pressing in the moral sphere, I would not wholly exempt other areas of philosophy from these concerns. Moreover, when we consider the extent to which our philosophical views are ripe for biasing influences and subsequent rationalization, it seems that, at a minimum, the responsible philosopher ought to be especially concerned about the possibility of rationalization's playing a large role in the adoption and defense of philosophical views. Here, as elsewhere, merely introspecting to see whether one's own views might have such a source is not a responsible reaction to the problem. Something much more nearly akin to the difficult project the skeptic about reason-giving is forced into may be forced on responsible philosophers as well.

Many will find this suggestion distasteful and, more to the point, epistemically counterproductive. It seems distasteful because in place of the rational discussion of substantive issues in ethics, for example, the skeptic seems to be endorsing the suggestion that when someone offers an argument for some moral view, the first thing we should think about, rather than the issue in moral philosophy that our interlocutor has attempted to raise, is the psychology of our discussant. Only by first analyzing our interlocutor's motivations may we determine whether the argument offered, and indeed, the person offering it, are to be taken seriously. It is surely distasteful to entertain such a suggestion, and it would surely be rude to behave in such a way. A person's motivations for offering an argument do sometimes need to be considered, but surely we entertain such thoughts only when the arguments offered fall very far short of logical standards. Entertaining questions about a person's motivations in offering an argument should be a last resort, not the first.

Leaving issues of etiquette aside, this strategy will also surely strike many as epistemically counterproductive, and for more than one reason. First, it will erode the quality of debate by distracting people from the issues we care most about—the moral issues, say—and focusing discussion on issues that are irrelevant to our real concerns: our interlocutors' motivations. In addition, raising these kinds of issues about people is not likely to be met with equanimity. Raising such personal issues as a subject's motivation in offering an argument, and, in effect, challenging that person's intellectual integrity, are not likely to allow for any issues at all to be discussed in ways that will allow for their resolution. But finally, and most importantly, the issue of a person's motivation in offering arguments is likely to be far more difficult to resolve than the substantive issue under investigation in, say, ethics. We have little access to the information we would need to understand fully a person's motivations, at least unless we know the individual extremely well. Moreover, there is more reason to be concerned about the possibility of rationalization in discussion of these personal issues of character than there is most any of the issues that might be under discussion in the first place. Someone who is genuinely worried about the effects of rationalization in others and in himself should recognize that even so much as entertaining the issue of a person's motivation in offering an argument dramatically increases the likelihood that rationalization will come into play. Focusing on arguments themselves does not assure that rationalization will not play a role, but it is a better strategy than our skeptic is offering, the strategy of examining people's motivations directly.

There is, I believe, a great deal of good sense in this response to the skeptic's suggestions, but before I reply on behalf of the skeptic, I wish to point out how much of the skeptic's position is already granted in this response. This response grants that the concern about rationalization and misguided judgment is a legitimate one and, indeed, does not even insist that the skeptic's assessment of the situation is terribly wide of the mark. There is a need to get around the problem with which a tendency to rationalization and bad judgment presents us, and whereas the skeptic proposes one solution to that—involving an assessment of people's motivations—our respondent has in mind a different solution: simply focusing on argument unless, in the final resort, the arguments themselves are so bad that some view about a person's motivations is rationally forced on us. Focusing on the quality of argument here is seen as a pragmatic strategy for dealing with the very problem the skeptic raises, and the skeptic's strategy, it is argued, merely exacerbates the very real problem about which she is herself concerned.

In considering this response to the skeptic, we may therefore, at least temporarily, accept the skeptic's account of the problem—that apparently rational argument is often deeply infected by rationalization—and focus on the merits of the two solutions being offered. What I wish to suggest is that neither of these two solutions is correct across the board; any reasonable response to the problem will, I believe, require a mixture of these two strategies. How much of each strategy should be used will depend, to a very large extent, on one's assessment of the ultimate source of the problem about rationalization.

Consider our respondent's suggestion that issues about a person's motivation in offering an argument are more difficult, epistemically, than the issues addressed by the argument itself; better then to focus on the issue at hand than to try to clear up questions about the person's motivation before turning to the issue he attempted to raise. This is simply not true in all cases. There are, without a doubt, cases in which a person's motivation in offering an argument is entirely transparent, and what is transparent is that the person is offering a rationalization for something believed on other grounds. Moreover, in some cases of this sort, we are in no position to address the issue that the rationalizer attempted to raise; we simply do not know enough about the issue to enter into discussion with him. In such cases, we should not take the arguments offered by the rationalizer at face value. We should adopt the skeptic's strategy and opt out of the discussion. So we do not want to adopt the respondent's strategy across the board.

But how often do situations like this occur? How often are we in a position to attribute a rationalization to someone, or at least have a strong prima facie concern about it? How often is the question about an interlocutor's motivation more easily resolved than the question the interlocutor wishes to raise? This is where, I believe, a particularly interesting difference between the skeptic and her respondent comes out.

Here is one possibility. Rationalization may well occur quite frequently, but the sources of rationalization may be many and idiosyncratic. Thus, when I offer arguments, they are distorted by my peculiar concerns and irrationalities; when others offer arguments, concerns and irrationalities peculiar to them go to work. If this is the case, then figuring out the kind of rationalization that is operative in a particular argument, or whether rationalization is operative, will require a great deal of knowledge of the particular individual involved. We will rarely have such knowledge, and thus the epistemic task of determining the extent and kind of rationalizations involved in particular arguments will typically be quite difficult. This will make the skeptic's project of examining the motivations behind individual arguments practically infeasible. At the same time, it may also make the skeptic's project unnecessary. For if the sources of distortion vary a great deal, then merely focusing on the arguments themselves may be a very good strategy. My biased recall of relevant information may be salient to others who lack my particular bias, and they will bring this into the open, not by attending to the possible sources of my bias, but simply by focusing on the issue under discussion. The public discussion of reasons here, although it brackets discussion of sources of distortion, will thereby help to overcome the problem that the distorting influences present. This, of course, is just what the respondent to the skeptic suggested.[18]

But there is another possibility, and this involves a very different picture of the sources of distortion and rationalization. Thus, suppose that instead of these sources' being varied and idiosyncratic, there are a very small number of sources of significant distortion and rationalization. Let us suppose, indeed, that there is a single major sources of distortion and rationalization that is very widespread. Thus, for example, Marxists have suggested that class interests form just such a source of distortion and rationalization; some feminists have suggested that the interests of male domination play such a role.[19] If some such hypothesis is correct, then the situation is exactly the reverse of the one described above. First, we need not know much about the particular individual offering an argument to have some sense of the extent or source of rationalization likely to be playing a role; our epistemic task here, once we have come to understand the social factors at work in society at large, is easy. And second, the idea that merely focusing on argument will allow the sources of distortion to come out into the open would, on this view, be mistaken. Because the ideas that tend to be discussed, on this scenario, are all shaped by a common bias, the hope that idiosyncratic biases will cancel one another out misses the point.[20] On this view, the skeptic's strategy is not only epistemically feasible, it is the only strategy that is likely to address the problem of bias and rationalization adequately.

Note too that if the skeptic is right in thinking that public debate is largely shaped by a single source of bias, and that this bias is extremely likely to come into play and overwhelm discussion when certain members of the epistemic community are part of the debate, then a policy of isolation or exclusion will be appropriate. This is just the opposite of the policy of including as many members of the community as possible in discussion in the hope of having the various biases cancel one another out. The policy of isolation or exclusion comes with dangers of its own, of course. But which of these policies best gets at the truth is very much dependent on features of the epistemic community, and the skeptic about reason and the person confident about reason simply have differing views about the nature of that community.

Those who have placed their trust in reason and public discussion of argument are thus betting that the second of these possibilities governing the nature and distribution of bias—a small number of distorting influences affecting the entire tenor of debate—is not the case. The skeptic, on the other hand, suspects that it is precisely this problem that is responsible for our current situation. The skeptic's hypothesis, I believe, is one that we need to take seriously, and the bet that we make when we place our trust in the public discussion of reason is one of which we need to be aware. It is only by taking the skeptic's hypothesis seriously and, if possible, laying it to rest, that our trust in public reason may be fully rational. Moreover, insofar as the rational commitment to the public discussion of reasons presupposes a certain social structure—one in which the effects of bias and rationalization are canceled out—those who are committed to the public discussion of reason should also be committed to ensuring that such a social structure is more than just an ideal; we should be committed to making sure that it is realized and sustained.[21]

Notes

1 A different, though complementary, source of distrust in reason comes from some evolutionary psychologists, who suggest that the kinds of circumstances with which our reasoning faculties are designed to deal are far narrower than the ones to which they are currently applied. For a particularly interesting application

of such a view, see Colin McGinn, *Problems in Philosophy: The Limits of Inquiry* (Oxford: Blackwell, 1993).

2 I approach the practice of reason-giving as one contingent social practice among many that, like any other, may be called into question. In this, I contrast with those who see reason-giving as different, somehow constitutive of rationality. Thus, for example, Thomas Nagel claims that the practice of reason-giving is not "merely another socially conditioned practice" ("Kolakowski: Modernity and the Devil," in his *Other Minds: Critical Essays 1969–1994* [Oxford: Oxford University Press, 1995], 212). And he goes on:

> A defender of the Kantian method must claim that it is legitimate to ask for justifying reasons for a contingent social practice in a way in which it is not legitimate to turn the tables and call reason itself into question by appealing to such a practice. The asymmetry arises because any claim to the rightness of what one is doing is automatically an appeal to its justifiability, and therefore subject to rational criticism. All roads lead to the same court of appeal, a court to which all of us are assumed to have access. Reason is universal because no attempted challenge to its results can avoid appealing to reason in the end—by claiming, for example, that what was presented as an argument is really a rationalization. This can undermine our confidence in the original method or practice only by giving us reasons to believe something else, so that finally we have to think about the arguments to make up our minds. (Ibid., 212–13. A large part of this passage is quoted, with hearty approval, by Daniel Dennett in his review of *Other Minds* in *Journal of Philosophy* 93 [1996]: 428.)

I will not respond to this argument point by point. Instead, this paper may be viewed as presenting an alternative to Nagel's Kantian defense of reason-giving, a position that Nagel has further developed in *The Last Word* (Oxford: Oxford University Press, 1997). As will become clear presently, I believe that the point about rationalization that Nagel mentions in passing has a much deeper significance than he attaches to it and that it may be used to challenge the entire practice of reason-giving. By the same token, if this challenge can be adequately responded to, as I believe it can, then we are presented with a substantive, rather than a transcendental, defense of the practice of reason-giving. For those who are suspicious of transcendental arguments, this is an important result.

3 Andrew's resourcefulness in handling data and the convenient asymmetries in his forgetfulness are not unusual. Indeed, this example is simply adapted from the results of a study on the effects of mixed data on prior opinion: C. Lord, L. Ross, and M.R. Lepper, "Biased Assimilation and Attitude Polarization: The Effects of Prior Theories on Subsequently Considered Evidence," *Journal of Personality and Social Psychology* 37 (1979): 2098–2110.

4 See the discussion of the availability heuristic in Richard Nisbett and Lee Ross, *Inductive Inference: Strategies and Shortcomings of Social Judgment* (Englewood Cliffs, N.J.: Prentice Hall, 1980).

5 Consider, for example, these comments of Jerry Fodor and Ernest Lepore: "It seems to us that what there is no argument for, there is no reason to believe. And what there *is* no reason to believe, one *has* no reason to believe." *Holism: A Shopper's Guide* (Oxford: Blackwell, 1992), p. xiii.

6 By the same token, a person who is particularly good at presenting arguments and recognizes the high regard in which such detailed reason-giving is typically held may use his ability to present detailed arguments in a coercive or oppressive manner. In such cases, it is not the logical features of the argument that are at fault, nor is it irrational that many should fail to attend to such logical features and simply dismiss arguments of this sort out of hand. This kind of concern has been raised in some of the feminist literature.

7 This concern as well has been a focus of some feminist discussions of reason-giving and the objection to what some have called "logocentrism." Although I am quite unsympathetic with most of what has been said under this label, the skeptic about reason giving of this paper may be seen as my own reconstruction of what I take to be the most reasonable objection to so-called logocentrism. But I would not attribute the details of the position developed here to any particular feminist philosopher. For feminist philosophers who have developed such views, see, e.g., Lorraine Code, *Rhetorical Spaces: Essays on Gendered Locations*. (New York: Routledge, 1995) and Andrea Nye, *Words of Power: A Feminist Reading of the History of Logic* (New York: Routledge, 1990).

8 I defend a qualified version of this view in "Introspection and Misdirection," *Australasian Journal of Philosophy* 67 (1989): 410–22.

9 The objection is similar to an objection frequently presented to total skepticism: that the total skeptic undermines his own position in arguing for it because the presentation of any such argument implicitly commits the skeptic to the existence some sort of knowledge whose existence he explicitly denies.

10 This follows the standard response to the claim that total skepticism is self-defeating. See, e.g., Robert Fogelin, *Pyrrhonian Reflections on Knowledge and Justification* (Oxford: Oxford University Press, 1994); Michael Frede, "The Skeptic's Two Kinds of Assent and the Question of the Possibility of Knowledge," in *Essays in Ancient Philosophy* (Minneapolis: University of Minnesota Press, 1987); and Michael Williams, "Skepticism without Theory," *Review of Metaphysics* 41 (1988): 547–88.

11 When I speak of taking an argument at face value, I do not mean to exclude all critical evaluation; taking an argument at face value is not to be identified with gullibility. There is, however, an important difference between focusing on the subject matter of the argument given, however critically, and turning one's attention to the motivations of the person giving it. I see the first as taking the argument at face value, whereas the second is what the skeptic has in mind instead.

12 This is not to deny that individual cases may arrive in which one is not in a position to resolve the question of one's own bias. Cases must, however, be dealt with individually. There is no all-purpose argument to show either that one cannot have good evidence that one is bias-free or that one must always be able to determine whether one is influenced by bias.

13 I do not believe that this is the only way in which one might extricate oneself from the concern about rationalization. In particular, I believe that there may well be cases in which one might rationally eliminate concern about rationalization in particular others while still harboring reasonable concern about one's own propensity to rationalize. But I need not insist on this in order to extricate the skeptic about rational argument from the charge of undermining herself.

14 Even as great a champion of rational argument as W.V. Quine has expressed a sentiment that is similar in important ways to that of the skeptic. Consider Quine's account of attending the American Philosophical Association convention with Carnap:

> We moved with Carnap as henchmen through the metaphysicians' camp. We beamed with partisan pride when he countered a diatribe of Arthur Lovejoy's in his characteristically reasonable way, explaining that if Lovejoy means *A* then *p*, and if he means *B* then *q*. I had yet to learn how unsatisfying this way of Carnap's could sometimes be. ("Homage to Carnap," in *The Ways of Paradox and Other Essays*, revised and enlarged edition [Cambridge: Harvard University Press, 1976], p. 42.)

See also Robert Nozick's remarks about what he calls "coercive philosophy" in *Philosophical Explanations* (Cambridge: Harvard University Press, 1981), pp. 4–8, in which he rejects the method of doing philosophy by way of "knock-down arguments" in favor of the more discursive "philosophical explanations."

15 Quoted by Alex Kozinski in "The Great Dissenter," *New York Times Book Review*, July 6, 1997, p. 15.

16 *Essays on the Intellectual Powers of Man* (Cambridge: MIT Press, 1969).

17 *Theory of Knowledge*, 3rd ed. (Englewood Cliffs, N.J.: Prentice Hall, 1989).

18 This is just a special case of the point that by using different measuring instruments to detect a given phenomenon, we may dramatically decrease the likelihood that our results are mere artifacts of the instruments themselves. The person who places his trust in argument sees individuals as roughly reliable detectors; their individual biases are features of the detectors that lead to experimental artifacts; and these artifacts are revealed as such by using other individuals, that is, other roughly good detectors, who are likely to exhibit a different pattern of experimental artifacts. The extent to which this method works in practice depends on the extent to which the different detectors used are both roughly reliable and exhibit the presupposed difference in experimental artifacts.

19 Notice that these are, in effect, socialized versions of the kinds of problems suggested in the "heuristics and biases" literature of Tversky and Kahneman and Nisbett and Ross. (See Daniel Kahneman, Paul Slovic, and Amos Tversky, eds., *Judgment under Uncertainty: Heuristics and Biases* [Cambridge: Cambridge University Press, 1982]; and Nisbett and Ross, op. cit.) The social fixation of the reasoning strategies that concern the skeptic is of special concern because such a process works far faster than Darwinian methods for fixing inferential strategies. Social fixation of reasoning strategies is Lamarckian.

20 Note that Nagel's assumption in the passage quoted in note 2 that there is "equal access to the court of reason" is thus denied by many Marxists and certain feminists. Consider also Frank Sulloway's claim (*Born to Rebel: Birth Order, Family Dynamics, and Creative Lives* [New York: Pantheon Books, 1996]) that firstborns are strongly disposed to resist conceptually innovative ideas and that later-borns are strongly disposed to accept them. Add to this Sulloway's contention that firstborns tend to be disproportionately successful in their careers. Sulloway notes:

> [This] has practical implications for the selection of scientific commissions

> and the evaluation of their conclusions. Because commission[s] tend to be packed with eminent individuals (and hence firstborns), their votes should perhaps be "weighted" to adjust for individual biases in attitudes toward innovation. (p. 537, n. 43)

This suggestion of Sulloway's, which I take to be eminently sensible, is just an instance of the strategy recommended by the skeptic about reason-giving.

21 I want to thank Louise Antony, David Christensen, Mark Kaplan, William Mann, Derk Pereboom, Joel Pust, Nishi Shah, Miriam Solomon, and William Talbott for especially helpful comments on drafts of this paper, often by way of vigorous disagreement. Versions of the paper were read at Middlebury College, Brigham Young University, Rutgers University, the University of Michigan, Universidad Nacional Autónoma de México, and Dalhousie University, where helpful discussions resulted in numerous changes.

QUESTIONS

1 In Kornblith's example, what is the cause of Andrew's belief that capital punishment has a deterrent effect?
2 Instead of reasoning directly about, say, controversial political issues, what does the skeptic suggest we should do?
3 According to Kornblith, what assumption about the nature of our community are the people who place trust in public reason relying on?

FURTHER READING ON INFERENCE IN GENERAL

Audi, Robert, "Belief, Reason, and Inference," *Philosophical Topics* 14 (1986): 27–65.

Fumerton, Richard, *Metaepistemology and Skepticism* (Lanham, Md.: Rowman & Littlefield, 1995).

Greco, John, "Scepticism and Epistemic Kinds," in *Skepticism*, ed. Ernest Sosa and Enrique Villanueva (Boston: Blackwell, 2000).

Huemer, Michael, "Fumerton's Principle of Inferential Justification," *Journal of Philosophical Research*, forthcoming (2002).

Kornblith, Hilary, "The Laws of Thought," *Philosophy and Phenomenological Research* 52 (1992): 895–911.

Kyburg, Henry, *Epistemology and Inference*, (Minneapolis, Minn.: University of Minnesota Press, 1983).

Miscevic, Nenad, "The Rationalist and the Tortoise," *Philosophical Studies* 92 (1998): 175–9.

Pollock, John and Joseph Cruz, *Contemporary Theories of Knowledge*, 2nd edn (Lanham, Md.: Rowman & Littlefield, 1999).

6

INDUCTIVE INFERENCE

Traditionally, there are said to be two kinds of inference, deductive and inductive. Unfortunately, there are at least two uses of "induction" which are commonly confused with each other. To avoid confusion, it is best to adopt the following definitions:

- *Deductive inference:* A kind of reasoning in which the premises purportedly entail the conclusion; that is, support the conclusion in such a way that it would be impossible for the premises to be true and the conclusion to be false.
- *Non-deductive inference:* A kind of reasoning in which the premises purportedly support the conclusion without entailing it; that is, support the conclusion in such a way that if the premises are true, it is more likely (but not necessary) that the conclusion is true.
- *Inductive inference:* A species of non-deductive reasoning in which the conclusion generalizes on the information given in the premises. Example: the inference from "All observed ravens have been black" to "All ravens are black" is inductive. Likewise for the inference, "The sun has risen every day in the past; therefore, the sun will rise tomorrow."

"Inductive inference" is also sometimes used to mean merely "non-deductive inference," but that is not how I use it here.

Philosophically, the major questions concerning induction are the questions of whether and how inductive inferences are justified—that is, whether and how the premises of an inductive argument provide a reason for believing the conclusion. This issue originates with David Hume's famous argument in section IV of his *Enquiry Concerning Human Understanding*. According to the standard interpretation, Hume there puts forward the thesis of *inductive skepticism:* the thesis that inductive inferences are never justified, that is, that the premises of an inductive argument provide *no reason at all* for believing the conclusion.

This radical conclusion is supported by the following argument, the premises of which Hume seems to endorse (though not in exactly this form) in the included reading:

1. Our beliefs can be divided into three categories:
    (a) *Beliefs about relations of ideas:* These are beliefs that are true by definition and can be known independent of observation, including (Hume thinks) such examples as "All bachelors are unmarried" and "2 + 2 = 4." In modern terminology, these would be called "analytic a priori" beliefs.

(b) *Beliefs about observed matters of fact:* These would be things one is actually observing or has observed. (Matters of fact include all things that are not relations of ideas.) For example, my belief that there is a desk here (while I am looking at it and touching it) is an observed matter of fact.

(c) *Beliefs about unobserved matters of fact:* These include all matters of fact that I am not observing and have not observed. For instance, my belief that there are people living in China is an unobserved (for me) matter of fact, as is my belief that the sun will rise tomorrow. (Tomorrow, assuming I witness the sunrise, it will become an observed matter of fact.)

2. All unobserved matter-of-fact beliefs depend upon inductive inference for their justification. For instance, I think the sun will rise tomorrow because it has risen in the past, and I am generalizing on that experience. I think there are people in China because I have heard things about the people in China and I believe the testimony of others; but I believe the testimony of others because I have formed an (inductive) generalization that people usually tell the truth (in this sort of circumstance, about this sort of thing).
3. All inductive inferences presuppose some such premise as "The course of nature is uniform" or "Unobserved things will resemble observed things." Call this "the Uniformity Principle."
4. The Uniformity Principle is not a relation of ideas proposition, since it is not analytically true. It is logically consistent to hypothesize that the course of nature may not be uniform.
5. The Uniformity Principle is not an observed matter of fact, since it makes a claim about unobserved objects.
6. The Uniformity Principle is an unobserved matter of fact belief. (From 1, 4, 5.)
7. The Uniformity Principle depends for its justification on induction. (From 2, 6.)
8. But the Uniformity Principle cannot be justified by induction, since all inductive inferences presuppose the Uniformity Principle (premise 3), and circular reasoning is not acceptable.
9. The Uniformity Principle cannot be justified. (From 7, 8.)
10. No inductive inference can be justified. (From 3, 9.)

What has come to be known as "the problem of induction" is the problem of showing what is wrong with the above argument and/or showing how inductive inference can be justified.

Many people, upon first encountering Hume's discussion of induction, mistakenly think that Hume's central epistemological point is that the conclusions of induction are fallible—sometimes unobserved objects turn out to be different from observed objects, and so we cannot be absolutely certain, in any given case, that the conclusion of an inductive argument is correct. Nevertheless, they think, the conclusions of inductive arguments may still be *highly probable*.

This appears to be the view of Paul Edwards. Edwards is responding directly to a discussion by Bertrand Russell, but Russell's argument (Russell did not *endorse* inductive skepticism, but he discusses the argument for it) is similar enough to Hume's that we may treat Edwards' paper as a response to Hume as well. Edwards thinks that Russell/Hume, in claiming that there is *no reason* for believing the conclusion of an inductive argument, was simply using the term "reason" in an unusually (and absurdly) strong sense, namely, to mean "deductively conclusive reason."

Unfortunately, this is mistaken—Hume was not claiming merely that the conclusions of inductive arguments are not absolutely certain, but rather that they are not justified at all (see the above argument). Nevertheless, Edwards' paper suggests one possible way of responding to the argument for inductive skepticism: one might reject premise 3, on the grounds that it assumes that all justification must be deductive. One might say instead that "All observed ravens are black" just is, by itself, a (non-demonstrative) reason for believing "All ravens are black." To insist that we must add "Unobserved ravens resemble observed ravens" as a second premise is to insist that we must turn the argument into a deductive one. ("All observed ravens are black. Unobserved ravens resemble observed ravens (in respect of color). Therefore, all ravens are black." is a deductive inference.) Therefore, it might be held that premise 3 begs the question.

Nelson Goodman argues for a "dissolution" of the traditional problem of induction. In his view, in order to show that an inductive argument is justified, all we have to do is show how that inference accords with our accepted argumentative practices. (He compares this to how we find a correct definition, by finding the definition that corresponds to our actual use of the term that is to be defined.) However, Goodman identifies another, "new" problem of induction, which is the problem of stating the actual rules of inductive inference that we accept. Traditionally, it was thought, roughly, that an inductive inference was simply any inference of the form,

All observed As have been B.
Therefore (probably), all As are B.

Goodman gives some counter-examples to this—that is, examples of inferences that have that form, but that would generally *not* be accepted by ordinary people as reasonable inductive inferences. Goodman's most famous example is the inference:

All observed emeralds have been *grue*.
Therefore (probably), all emeralds are grue.

where

x is grue $=_{df}$ [(*x* is first observed before the year 2100 and *x* is green) or (*x* not first observed before the year 2100 and *x* is blue)].

In fact, all emeralds that have ever been observed have been grue, but we do not infer, inductively or otherwise, that all emeralds are grue (for that would mean inferring that the emeralds we dig out of the ground after 2100 will be blue). We think future emeralds will *not* be grue. Since the traditional characterization of what induction is has been refuted by this example, we have a new problem of how to define induction correctly.

Pace Goodman, most epistemologists still believe the old problem of induction—the problem of how to justify inductive inferences—is a problem, so work has continued on diagnosing the problem in Hume's argument. John Foster would probably reject premise 2 in the argument. That premise assumes that all non-deductive inferences must be inductive, but in fact there is another kind of non-deductive inference, namely, *inference to the best explanation*. This is the kind of inference in which one starts from some observations that call for explanation (would be improbable to occur by chance) and one infers the truth of the hypothesis that best explains them. To see how this helps us, suppose that we have observed a certain regularity in nature—say, the fact that massive objects when unsupported have always fallen to the ground. According to Foster, the best explanation for this fact is that there is a law of nature (the law of gravity) which makes it *necessary* for objects to behave in that manner. If there were no law, so the bodies were acting randomly, then it would be extremely improbable that the regularity would have been observed. But if there is a law of nature, then that also implies that in the *future* we should expect to see bodies fall to the ground when dropped. Thus, the inductive conclusion is justified by means of an inference to the best explanation, followed by a prediction deduced from that explanation. Foster goes on to consider other possible (skeptic-friendly) explanations one might offer for the observed regularity but finds the hypothesis of a law of gravity to be the best.

Another recent approach to the problem of induction is the Bayesian approach. Broadly speaking, Bayesians (named after Bayes' Theorem, a theorem in probability theory to which they attribute great import) think that all non-deductive reasoning is reasoning in accordance with the principles of probability and that therefore the mathematical theory of probability should provide an explanation for why induction is justified. The selection from Howson and Urbach's book on the subject is intended to familiarize the reader with some of the basic principles of probability, including the four axioms of probability theory and Bayes' Theorem. This should help to prepare the student for the following selection by David Stove.

Stove treats probabilities as something like degrees of justification—that is, the more probable a proposition is, the more one is justified in accepting it (so a probability of 1 would correspond to conclusive reason for accepting a proposition; a probability of 0 would correspond to conclusive reason for *rejecting* it). He then argues, on the basis of the principles of probability theory, that the conclusion of an inductive argument can indeed be strongly justified by its premises. Suppose we have taken a large sample of ravens from around the world, and found 95% of them to be black. (The other 5% might be albino ravens, dark grey ravens, etc.) We would ordinarily conclude, inductively, that the next raven we look at will probably be black. Essentially, Stove thinks this is justified because (this is a simplified form of the argument):

1. Almost all large samples taken from the population are *representative* (that is, have a proportion of black ravens that is close to the proportion in the total population). This is a necessary mathematical truth (Stove calls it "the arithmetical form of the law of large numbers").
2. Therefore, other things being equal (that is, absent any special reasons for thinking this sample is unusual), this sample is probably representative. (From 1.)
3. This sample contains 95% black ravens.
4. Therefore, the total population probably contains about 95% black ravens. (From 2, 3.)
5. Therefore, other things being equal, the next raven I select will probably be black. (From 4.)

Thus, Stove thinks he has proven that induction is rational. The "other things being equal" clauses in steps (2) and (5) seem to give some leeway for a skeptic, but, arguably, they shift the burden of proof, since a skeptic would have to show reason for thinking this particular sample is special; moreover, it cannot be the case in general that the samples we take are always special. Thus, it does not seem possible to defend a *general* skeptical thesis about induction, although of course some particular inductive arguments can be criticized.

David Hume, *An Enquiry Concerning Human Understanding*

Section IV Sceptical doubts concerning the operations of the understanding

Part I

All the objects of human reason or enquiry may naturally be divided into two kinds, to wit, Relations of Ideas, and Matters of Fact. Of the first kind are the sciences of Geometry, Algebra, and Arithmetic; and in short, every affirmation which is either intuitively or demonstratively certain. *That the square of the hypothenuse is equal to the square of the two sides*, is a proposition which expresses a relation between these figures. *That three times five is equal to the half of thirty*, expresses a relation between these numbers. Propositions of this kind are discoverable by the mere operation of thought, without dependence on what is anywhere existent in the universe. Though there never were a circle or triangle in nature, the truths demonstrated by Euclid would for ever retain their certainty and evidence.

Matters of fact, which are the second objects of human reason, are not ascertained in the same manner; nor is our evidence of their truth, however great, of a like nature with the foregoing. The contrary of every matter of fact is still possible; because it can never imply a contradiction, and is conceived by the mind with the same facility and distinctness, as if ever so conformable to reality. *That the sun will not rise to-morrow* is no less intelligible a proposition, and implies no more contradiction, than the affirmation, *that it will rise*. We should in vain, therefore, attempt to demonstrate its falsehood. Were it demonstratively false, it would imply a contradiction, and could never be distinctly conceived by the mind.

It may, therefore, be a subject worthy of curiosity, to enquire what is the nature of that evidence which assures us of any real existence and matter of fact, beyond the present testimony of our senses, or the records of our memory. This part of philosophy, it is observable, has been little cultivated, either by the

David Hume, "Sceptical Doubts Concerning the Operations of the Understanding," *An Enquiry Concerning Human Understanding*, in *Enquiries Concerning Human Understanding and Concerning the Principles of Morals*, 2nd edn, ed. L.A. Selby-Bigge (Oxford: Clarendon Press, 1902).

ancients or moderns; and therefore our doubts and errors, in the prosecution of so important an enquiry, may be the more excusable; while we march through such difficult paths without any guide or direction. They may even prove useful, by exciting curiosity, and destroying that implicit faith and security, which is the bane of all reasoning and free enquiry. The discovery of defects in the common philosophy, if any such there be, will not, I presume, be a discouragement, but rather an incitement, as is usual, to attempt something more full and satisfactory than has yet been proposed to the public.

All reasonings concerning matter of fact seem to be founded on the relation of Cause and Effect. By means of that relation alone we can go beyond the evidence of our memory and senses. If you were to ask a man, why he believes any matter of fact, which is absent; for instance, that his friend is in the country, or in France; he would give you a reason; and this reason would be some other fact; as a letter received from him, or the knowledge of his former resolutions and promises. A man finding a watch or any other machine in a desert island, would conclude that there had once been men in that island. All our reasonings concerning fact are of the same nature. And here it is constantly supposed that there is a connexion between the present fact and that which is inferred from it. Were there nothing to bind them together, the inference would be entirely precarious. The hearing of an articulate voice and rational discourse in the dark assures us of the presence of some person: Why? because these are the effects of the human make and fabric, and closely connected with it. If we anatomize all the other reasonings of this nature, we shall find that they are founded on the relation of cause and effect, and that this relation is either near or remote, direct or collateral. Heat and light are collateral effects of fire, and the one effect may justly be inferred from the other.

If we would satisfy ourselves, therefore, concerning the nature of that evidence, which assures us of matters of fact, we must enquire how we arrive at the knowledge of cause and effect.

I shall venture to affirm, as a general proposition, which admits of no exception, that the knowledge of this relation is not, in any instance, attained by reasonings *a priori*; but arises entirely from experience, when we find that any particular objects are constantly conjoined with each other. Let an object be presented to a man of ever so strong natural reason and abilities; if that object be entirely new to him, he will not be able, by the most accurate examination of its sensible qualities, to discover any of its causes or effects. Adam, though his rational faculties be supposed, at the very first, entirely perfect, could not have inferred from the fluidity and transparency of water that it would suffocate him, or from the light and warmth of fire that it would consume him. No object ever discovers, by the qualities which appear to the senses, either the causes which produced it, or the effects which will arise from it; nor can our reason, unassisted by experience, ever draw any inference concerning real existence and matter of fact.

This proposition, *that causes and effects are discoverable, not by reason but by experience*, will readily be admitted with regard to such objects, as we remember to have once been altogether unknown to us; since we must be conscious of the utter inability, which we then lay under, of foretelling what would arise from them. Present two smooth pieces of marble to a man who has no tincture of natural philosophy; he will never discover that they will adhere together in such a manner as to require great force to separate them in a direct line, while they make so small a resistance to a lateral pressure. Such events, as bear little analogy to the common course of nature, are also readily confessed to be known only by experience; nor does any man imagine that the explosion of gunpowder, or the attraction of a loadstone, could ever be discovered by arguments *a priori*. In like manner, when an effect is supposed to depend upon an intricate machinery or secret structure of parts, we make no difficulty in attributing all our knowledge of it to experience. Who will assert that he can give the ultimate reason, why milk or bread is proper nourishment for a man, not for a lion or a tiger?

But the same truth may not appear, at first sight, to have the same evidence with regard to events, which have become familiar to us from our first appearance in the world, which bear a close analogy to the whole course of nature, and which are supposed to depend on the simple qualities of objects, without any secret structure of parts. We are apt to imagine that we could discover these effects by the mere operation of our reason, without experience. We fancy, that were we brought on a sudden into this world, we could at first have inferred that one Billiard-ball would communicate motion to another upon impulse; and that we needed not to have waited for the event, in order to pronounce with certainty concerning it. Such is the influence of custom, that, where it is strongest, it not only covers our natural ignorance, but even conceals itself, and seems not to take place, merely because it is found in the highest degree.

But to convince us that all the laws of nature, and all the operations of bodies without exception, are known only by experience, the following reflections may, perhaps, suffice. Were any object presented to us, and were we required to pronounce concerning the effect, which will result from it, without consulting past observation; after what manner, I beseech you, must the mind proceed in this operation? It must invent or imagine some event, which it ascribes to the object as its effect; and it is plain that this invention must be entirely arbitrary. The mind can never possibly find the effect in the supposed cause, by the most accurate scrutiny and examination. For the effect is totally different from the cause, and consequently can never be discovered in it. Motion in the second Billiard-ball is a quite distinct event from motion in the first; nor is there anything in the one to suggest the smallest hint of the other. A stone or piece of metal raised into the air, and left without any support, immediately falls: but to consider the matter *a priori*, is there anything we discover in this situation which can beget the idea of a downward, rather than an upward, or any other motion, in the stone or metal?

And as the first imagination or invention of a particular effect, in all natural operations, is arbitrary, where we consult not experience; so must we also esteem the supposed tie or connexion between the cause and effect, which binds them together, and renders it impossible that any other effect could result from the operation of that cause. When I see, for instance, a Billiard-ball moving in a straight line towards another; even suppose motion in the second ball should by accident be suggested to me, as the result of their contact or impulse; may I not conceive, that a hundred different events might as well follow from that cause? May not both these balls remain at absolute rest? May not the first ball return in a straight line, or leap off from the second in any line or direction? All these suppositions are consistent and conceivable. Why then should we give the preference to one, which is no more consistent or conceivable than the rest? All our reasonings *a priori* will never be able to show us any foundation for this preference.

In a word, then, every effect is a distinct event from its cause. It could not, therefore, be discovered in the cause, and the first invention or conception of it, *a priori*, must be entirely arbitrary. And even after it is suggested, the conjunction of it with the cause must appear equally arbitrary; since there are always many other effects, which, to reason, must seem fully as consistent and natural. In vain, therefore, should we pretend to determine any single event, or infer any cause or effect, without the assistance of observation and experience.

Hence we may discover the reason why no philosopher, who is rational and modest, has ever pretended to assign the ultimate cause of any natural operation, or to show distinctly the action of that power, which produces any single effect in the universe. It is confessed, that the utmost effort of human reason is to reduce the principles, productive of natural phenomena, to a greater simplicity, and to resolve the many particular effects into a few general causes, by means of reasonings from analogy, experience, and observation. But as to the causes of these general causes, we should in vain attempt their discovery; nor shall we ever be able to satisfy ourselves, by any particular explication of them. These ultimate springs and principles are totally shut up from human curiosity and enquiry. Elasticity, gravity, cohesion of parts, communication of motion by impulse; these are probably the ultimate causes and principles which we shall ever discover in nature; and we may esteem ourselves sufficiently happy, if, by accurate enquiry and reasoning, we can trace up the particular phenomena to, or near to, these general principles. The most perfect philosophy of the natural kind only staves off our ignorance a little longer: as perhaps the most perfect philosophy of the moral or metaphysical kind serves only to discover larger portions of it. Thus the observation of human blindness and weakness is the result of all philosophy, and meets us at every turn, in spite of our endeavours to elude or avoid it.

Nor is geometry, when taken into the assistance of natural philosophy, ever able to remedy this defect, or lead us into the knowledge of ultimate causes, by all that accuracy of reasoning for which it is so justly celebrated. Every part of mixed mathematics proceeds upon the supposition that certain laws are established by nature in her operations; and abstract reasonings are employed, either to assist experience in the discovery of these laws, or to determine their influence in particular instances, where it depends upon any precise degree of distance and quantity. Thus, it is a law of motion, discovered by experience, that the moment or force of any body in motion is in the compound ratio or proportion of its solid contents and its velocity; and consequently, that a small force may remove the greatest obstacle or raise the greatest weight, if, by any contrivance or machinery, we can increase the velocity of that force, so as to make it an overmatch for its antagonist. Geometry assists us in the application of this law, by giving us the just dimensions of all the parts and figures which can enter into any species of machine; but still the discovery of the law itself is owing merely to experience, and all the abstract reasonings in the world could never lead us one step towards the knowledge of it. When we reason *a priori*, and consider merely any object or cause, as it appears to the mind, independent of all observation, it never could suggest to us the notion of any distinct object, such as its effect; much less, show us the inseparable and inviolable connexion between them. A man must be very sagacious who could discover by reasoning that crystal is the effect of heat, and ice of cold, without being previously acquainted with the operation of these qualities.

Part II

But we have not yet attained any tolerable satisfaction with regard to the question first proposed. Each solution still gives rise to a new question as difficult as the foregoing, and leads us on to farther enquiries. When it is asked, *What is the nature of all our reasonings concerning matter of fact?* the proper answer seems to be, that they are founded on the relation of cause and effect. When again it is asked, *What is the foundation of all our reasonings and conclusions concerning that relation?* it may be replied in one word, Experience. But if we still carry on our sifting humour, and ask, *What is the foundation of all conclusions from experience?* this implies a new question, which may be of more difficult solution and explication. Philosophers, that give themselves airs of superior wisdom and sufficiency, have a hard task when they encounter persons of inquisitive dispositions, who push them from every corner to which they retreat, and who are sure at last to bring them to some dangerous dilemma. The best expedient to prevent this confusion, is to be modest in our pretensions; and even to discover the difficulty ourselves before it is objected to us. By this means, we may make a kind of merit of our very ignorance.

I shall content myself, in this section, with an easy task, and shall pretend only to give a negative answer to the question here proposed. I say then, that, even after we have experience of the operations of cause and effect, our conclusions from that experience are *not* founded on reasoning, or any process of the understanding. This answer we must endeavour both to explain and to defend.

It must certainly be allowed, that nature has kept us at a great distance from all her secrets, and has afforded us only the knowledge of a few superficial qualities of objects; while she conceals from us those powers and principles on which the influence of these objects entirely depends. Our senses inform us of the colour, weight, and consistence of bread; but neither sense nor reason can ever inform us of those qualities which fit it for the nourishment and support of a human body. Sight or feeling conveys an idea of the actual motion of bodies; but as to that wonderful force or power, which would carry on a moving body for ever in a continued change of place, and which bodies never lose but by communicating it to others; of this we cannot form the most distant conception. But notwithstanding this ignorance of natural powers[1] and principles, we always presume, when we see like sensible qualities, that they have like secret powers, and expect that effects, similar to those which we have experienced, will follow from them. If a body of like colour and consistence with that bread, which we have formerly eat, be presented to us, we make no scruple of repeating the experiment, and foresee, with certainty, like nourishment and support. Now this is a process of the mind or thought, of which I would willingly know the foundation. It is allowed on all hands that there is no known connexion between the sensible qualities and the secret powers; and consequently, that the mind is not led to form such a conclusion concerning their constant and regular conjunction, by anything which it knows of their nature. As to past *Experience*, it can be allowed to give *direct* and *certain* information of those precise objects only, and that precise period of time, which fell under its cognizance: but why this experience should be extended to future times, and to other objects, which for aught we know, may be only in appearance similar; this is the main question on which I would insist. The bread, which I formerly eat, nourished me; that is, a body of such sensible qualities was, at that time, endued with such secret powers: but does it follow, that other bread must also nourish me at another time, and that like sensible qualities must always be attended with like secret powers? The consequence seems nowise necessary. At least, it must be acknowledged that there is here a consequence drawn by the mind; that there is a certain step taken; a process of thought, and an inference, which wants to be explained. These two propositions are far from being the same, *I have found that such an object has always been attended with such an effect*, and *I foresee, that other objects, which are, in appearance, similar, will be attended with similar effects*. I shall allow, if you please, that the one proposition may justly be inferred from the other: I know, in fact, that it always is inferred. But if you insist that the inference is made by a chain of reasoning, I desire you to produce that reasoning. The connexion between these propositions is not intuitive. There is required a medium, which may enable the mind to draw such an inference, if indeed it be drawn by reasoning and argument. What that medium is, I must confess, passes my comprehension; and it is incumbent on those to produce it, who assert that it really exists, and is the origin of all our conclusions concerning matter of fact.

This negative argument must certainly, in process of time, become altogether convincing, if many penetrating and able philosophers shall turn their enquiries this way and no one be ever able to discover any connecting proposition or intermediate step, which supports the understanding in this conclusion. But as the question is yet new, every reader may not trust so far to his own penetration, as to conclude, because an argument escapes his enquiry, that therefore it does not really exist. For this reason it may be requisite to venture upon a more difficult task; and enumerating all the branches of human knowledge, endeavour to show that none of them can afford such an argument.

All reasonings may be divided into two kinds, namely, demonstrative reasoning, or that concerning relations of ideas, and moral reasoning, or that concerning matter of fact and existence. That there are no demonstrative arguments in the case seems evident; since it implies no contradiction that the course of nature may change, and that an object, seemingly like those which we have experienced, may be attended with different or contrary effects. May I not clearly and distinctly conceive that a body, falling from the clouds, and which, in all other respects, resembles snow, has yet the taste of salt or feeling of fire? Is there any more intelligible proposition than to affirm, that all the trees will flourish in December and January, and decay in May and June? Now whatever is intelligible, and can be distinctly conceived, implies no contradiction, and can never be proved false by any demonstrative argument or abstract reasoning *à priori*.

If we be, therefore, engaged by arguments to put trust in past experience, and make it the standard of our future judgement, these arguments must be probable only, or such as regard matter of fact and real existence, according to the division above mentioned. But that there is no argument of this kind, must appear, if our explication of that species of reasoning be admitted as solid and satisfactory. We have said that all arguments concerning existence are founded on the relation of cause and effect; that our knowledge of that relation is derived entirely from experience; and that all our experimental conclusions proceed upon the supposition that the future will be conformable to the past. To endeavour, therefore, the proof of this last supposition by probable arguments, or arguments regarding existence, must be evidently going in a circle, and taking that for granted, which is the very point in question.

In reality, all arguments from experience are founded on the similarity which we discover among natural objects, and by which we are induced to expect effects similar to those which we have found to follow from such objects. And though none but a fool or madman will ever pretend to dispute the authority of experience, or to reject that great guide of human life, it may surely be allowed a philosopher to have so much curiosity at least as to examine the principle of human nature, which gives this mighty authority to experience, and makes us draw advantage from that similarity which nature has placed among different objects. From causes which appear *similar* we expect similar effects. This is the sum of all our experimental conclusions. Now it seems evident that, if this conclusion were formed by reason, it would be as perfect at first, and upon one instance, as after ever so long a course of experience. But the case is far otherwise. Nothing so like as eggs; yet no one, on account of this appearing similarity, expects the same taste and relish in all of them. It is only after a long course of uniform experiments in any kind, that we attain a firm reliance and security with regard to a particular event. Now where is that process of reasoning which, from one instance, draws a conclusion, so different from that which it infers from a hundred instances that are nowise different from that single one? This question I propose as much for the sake of information, as with an intention of raising difficulties. I cannot find, I cannot imagine any such reasoning. But I keep my mind still open to instruction, if any one will vouchsafe to bestow it on me.

Should it be said that, from a number of uniform experiments, we *infer* a connexion between the sensible qualities and the secret powers; this, I must confess, seems the same difficulty, couched in different terms. The question still recurs, on what process of argument this *inference* is founded? Where is the medium, the interposing ideas, which join propositions so very wide of each other? It is confessed that the colour, consistence, and other sensible qualities of bread appear not, of themselves, to have any connexion with the secret powers of nourishment and support. For otherwise we could infer these secret powers from the first appearance of these sensible qualities, without the aid of experience; contrary to the sentiment of all philosophers, and contrary to plain matter of fact. Here, then, is our natural state of ignorance with regard to the powers and influence of all objects. How is this remedied by experience? It only shows us a number of uniform effects, resulting from certain objects, and teaches us that those particular objects, at that particular time, were endowed with such powers and forces. When a new object, endowed with similar sensible qualities, is produced, we expect similar powers and forces, and look for a like effect. From a body of like colour and consistence with bread we expect like nourishment and support. But this surely is a step or progress of the mind, which wants to be explained. When a man says, *I have found, in all past instances, such sensible qualities conjoined with such secret powers*: And when he says, *Similar sensible qualities will always be conjoined with similar secret powers*, he is not guilty of a tautology, nor are these propositions in any respect the same. You say that the one proposition is an inference from the other. But you must confess that the inference is not intuitive; neither is it demonstrative: Of what nature is it, then? To say it is experimental, is begging the question. For all inferences from experience suppose, as their foundation, that the future will resemble the past, and that similar powers will be conjoined with similar sensible qualities. If there be any suspicion that the course of nature may change, and that the past may be no rule for the future, all experience becomes useless, and can give rise to no inference or conclusion. It is impossible, therefore, that any arguments from experience can prove this resemblance of the past to the future; since all these arguments are founded on the supposition of that resemblance. Let the course of things be allowed hitherto ever so regular; that alone, without some new argument or inference, proves not that, for the future, it will continue so. In vain do you pretend to have learned the nature of bodies from your past experience. Their secret nature, and consequently all their effects and influence, may change, without any change in their sensible qualities. This happens sometimes, and with regard to some objects: Why may it not happen always, and with regard to all objects? What logic, what process of argument secures you against this supposition? My practice, you say, refutes my doubts. But you mistake the purport of my question. As an agent, I am quite satisfied in the point; but as a philosopher, who has some share of curiosity, I will not say scepticism, I want to learn the foundation of this inference. No reading, no enquiry has yet been able to remove my difficulty, or give me satisfaction in a matter of such importance. Can I do better than propose the difficulty to the public, even though, perhaps, I have small hopes of obtaining a solution? We shall at least, by this means, be sensible of our ignorance, if we do not augment our knowledge.

I must confess that a man is guilty of unpardonable arrogance who concludes, because an argument has escaped his own investigation, that therefore it does not really exist. I must also confess that, though all the learned, for several ages, should have employed themselves in fruitless search upon any subject, it may still, perhaps, be rash to conclude positively that the subject must, therefore, pass all human comprehension. Even though we examine all the sources of our knowledge, and conclude them unfit for such a subject, there may still remain a suspicion, that the enumeration is not complete, or the examination not accurate. But with regard to the present subject, there are some considerations which seem to remove all this accusation of arrogance or suspicion of mistake.

It is certain that the most ignorant and stupid peasants—nay infants, nay even brute beasts—improve by experience, and learn the qualities of natural objects, by observing the effects which result from them. When a child has felt the sensation of pain from touching the flame of a candle, he will be careful not to put his hand near any candle; but will expect a similar effect from a cause which is similar in its sensible qualities and appearance. If you assert, therefore, that the understanding of the child is led into this conclusion by any process of argument or ratiocination, I may justly require you to produce that argument; nor have you any pretence to refuse so equitable a demand. You cannot say that the argument is abstruse, and may possibly escape your enquiry; since you confess that it is obvious to the capacity of a mere infant. If you hesitate, therefore, a moment, or if, after reflection, you produce any intricate or profound argument, you, in a manner, give up the question, and confess that it is not reasoning which engages us to suppose the past resembling the future, and to expect similar effects from causes which are, to appearance, similar. This is the proposition which I intended to enforce in the present section. If I be right, I pretend not to have made any mighty discovery. And if I be wrong, I must acknowledge myself to be indeed a very backward scholar; since I cannot now discover an argument which, it seems, was perfectly familiar to me long before I was out of my cradle.

Section V Sceptical solution of these doubts

Part I

The passion for philosophy, like that for religion, seems liable to this inconvenience, that, though it aims at the correction of our manners, and extirpation of our vices, it may only serve, by imprudent management, to foster a predominant inclination, and push the mind, with more determined resolution, towards that side which already *draws* too much, by the bias and propensity of the natural temper. It is certain that, while we aspire to the magnanimous firmness of the philosophic sage, and endeavour to confine our pleasures altogether within our own minds, we may, at last, render our philosophy like that of Epictetus, and other *Stoics*, only a more refined system of selfishness, and reason ourselves out of all virtue as well as social enjoyment. While we study with attention the vanity of human life, and turn all our thoughts towards the empty and transitory nature of riches and honours, we are, perhaps, all the while flattering our natural indolence, which, hating the bustle of the world, and drudgery of business, seeks a pretence of reason to give itself a full and uncontrolled indulgence. There is, however, one species of philosophy which seems little liable to this inconvenience, and that because it strikes in with no disorderly passion of the human mind, nor can mingle itself with any natural affection or propensity; and that is the Academic or Sceptical philosophy. The academics always talk of doubt and suspense of judgement, of danger in hasty determinations, of confining to very narrow bounds the enquiries of the understanding, and of renouncing all speculations which lie not within the limits of common life and practice. Nothing, therefore, can be more contrary than such a philosophy to the supine indolence of the mind, its rash arrogance, its lofty pretensions, and its superstitious credulity. Every passion is mortified by it, except the love of truth; and that passion never is, nor can be, carried to too high a degree. It is surprising, therefore, that this philosophy, which, in almost every instance, must be harmless and innocent, should be the subject of so much groundless reproach and obloquy. But, perhaps, the very circumstance which renders it so innocent is what chiefly exposes it to the public hatred and resentment. By flattering no irregular passion, it gains few partizans: By opposing so many vices and follies, it raises to itself abundance of enemies, who stigmatize it as libertine, profane, and irreligious.

Nor need we fear that this philosophy, while it endeavours to limit our enquiries to common life, should ever undermine the reasonings of common life, and carry its doubts so far as to destroy all action, as well as speculation. Nature will always maintain her rights, and prevail in the end over any abstract reasoning whatsoever. Though we should conclude, for instance, as in the foregoing section, that, in all reasonings from experience, there is a step taken by the mind which is not supported by any argument or process of the understanding; there is no danger that these reasonings, on which almost all knowledge depends, will ever be affected by such a discovery. If the mind be not engaged by argument to make this step, it must be induced by some other principle of equal weight and authority; and that principle will preserve its influence as long as human nature remains the same. What that principle is may well be worth the pains of enquiry.

Suppose a person, though endowed with the strongest faculties of reason and reflection, to be brought on a sudden into this world; he would, indeed, immediately observe a continual succession of objects, and one event following another; but he would not be able to discover anything farther. He would not, at first, by any reasoning, be able to reach the idea of cause and effect; since the particular powers, by which all natural operations are performed, never appear to the senses; nor is it reasonable to conclude, merely because one event, in one instance, precedes another, that therefore the one is the cause, the other the effect. Their conjunction may be arbitrary and casual. There may be no reason to infer the existence of one from the appearance of the other. And in a word, such a person, without more experience, could never employ his conjecture or reasoning concerning any matter of fact, or be assured of anything beyond what was immediately present to his memory and senses.

Suppose, again, that he has acquired more experience, and has lived so long in the world as to have observed familiar objects or events to be constantly conjoined together; what is the consequence of this experience? He immediately infers the existence of one object from the appearance of the other. Yet he has not, by all his experience, acquired any idea or knowledge of the secret power by which the one object produces the other; nor is it, by any process of reasoning, he is engaged to draw this inference. But still he finds himself determined to draw it: And though he should be convinced that his understanding has no part in the operation, he would nevertheless continue in the same course of thinking. There is some other principle which determines him to form such a conclusion.

This principle is Custom or Habit. For wherever the repetition of any particular act or operation produces a propensity to renew the same act or operation, without being impelled by any reasoning or process of the understanding, we always say, that this propensity is the effect of *Custom*. By employing that word, we pretend not to have given the ultimate reason of such a propensity. We only point out a principle of human nature, which is universally acknowledged, and which is well known by its effects. Perhaps we can push our enquiries no farther, or pretend to give the cause of this cause; but must rest contented with it as the ultimate principle, which we can assign, of all our conclusions from experience. It is sufficient satisfaction, that we can go so far, without repining at the narrowness of our faculties because they will carry us no farther. And it is certain we here advance a very intelligible proposition at least, if not a true one, when we assert that, after the constant conjunction of two objects—heat and flame, for instance, weight and solidity—we are determined by custom alone to expect the one from the appearance of the other. This hypothesis seems even the only one which explains the difficulty, why we draw, from a thousand instances, an inference which we are not able to draw from one instance, that is, in no respect, different from them. Reason is incapable of any such variation. The conclusions which it draws from considering one circle are the same which it would form upon surveying all the circles in the universe. But no man, having seen only one body move after being impelled by another, could infer that every other body will move after a like impulse. All inferences from experience, therefore, are effects of custom, not of reasoning.[2]

Custom, then, is the great guide of human life. It is that principle alone which renders our experience useful to us, and makes us expect, for the future, a similar train of events with those which have appeared in the past, Without the influence of custom, we should be entirely ignorant of every matter of fact beyond what is immediately present to the memory and senses. We should never know how to adjust means to ends, or to employ our natural powers in the production of any effect. There would be an end at once of all action, as well as of the chief part of speculation.

But here it may be proper to remark, that though our conclusions from experience carry us beyond our memory and senses, and assure us of matters of fact which happened in the most distant places and most remote ages, yet some fact must always be present to the senses or memory, from which we may first proceed in drawing these conclusions. A man, who should find in a desert country the remains of pompous buildings, would conclude that the country had, in ancient times, been cultivated by civilized inhabitants; but did nothing of this nature occur to him, he could never form such an inference. We learn the events of former ages from history; but then we must peruse the volumes in which this instruction is contained, and thence carry up our inferences from one testimony to another, till we arrive at the eyewitnesses and spectators of these distant events. In a word, if we proceed not upon some fact, present to the memory or senses, our reasonings would be merely hypothetical; and however the particular links might be connected with each other, the whole chain of inferences would have nothing to support it, nor could we ever, by its means, arrive at the knowledge of any real existence. If I ask why you believe any particular matter of fact, which you relate, you must tell me some reason; and this reason will be some other fact, connected with it. But as you cannot proceed after this manner, *in infinitum*, you must at last terminate in some fact, which is present to your memory or senses; or must allow that your belief is entirely without foundation.

What, then, is the conclusion of the whole matter? A simple one; though, it must be confessed, pretty remote from the common theories of philosophy. All belief of matter of fact or real existence is derived merely from some object, present to the memory or senses, and a customary conjunction between that and some other object. Or in other words; having found, in many instances, that any two kinds of objects—flame and heat, snow and cold—have always been conjoined together; if flame or snow be presented anew to the senses, the mind is carried by custom to expect heat or cold, and to *believe* that such a quality does exist, and will discover itself upon a nearer approach. This belief is the necessary result of placing the mind in such circumstances. It is an operation of the soul, when we are so situated, as unavoidable as to feel the passion of love, when we receive benefits; or hatred, when we meet with injuries. All these operations are a species of natural instincts, which no reasoning or process of the thought and understanding is able either to produce or to prevent.

At this point, it would be very allowable for us to stop our philosophical researches. In most questions we can never make a single step farther; and in all questions we must terminate here at last, after our most restless and curious enquiries. But still our curiosity will be pardonable, perhaps commendable, if it carry us on to still farther researches, and make us examine more accurately the nature of this *belief*, and of the *customary conjunction*, whence it is derived. By this means we may meet with some explications and analogies that will give satisfaction; at least to such as love the abstract sciences, and can be entertained with speculations, which, however accurate, may still retain a degree of doubt and uncertainty. As to readers of a different taste; the remaining part of this section is not calculated for them, and the following enquiries may well be understood, though it be neglected.

Notes

1 The word, Power, is here used in a loose and popular sense. The more accurate explication of it would give additional evidence to this argument.

2 Nothing is more useful than for writers, even, on *moral, political*, or *physical* subjects, to distinguish between *reason* and *experience*, and to suppose, that these species of argumentation are entirely different from each other. The former are taken for the mere result of our intellectual faculties, which, by considering *à priori* the nature of things, and examining the effects, that must follow from their operation, establish particular principles of science and philosophy. The latter are supposed to be derived entirely from sense and observation, by which we learn what has actually resulted from the operation of particular objects, and are thence able to infer, what will, for the future, result from them. Thus, for instance, the limitations and restraints of civil government, and a legal constitution, may be defended, either from *reason*, which reflecting on the great frailty and corruption of human nature, teaches, that no man can safely be trusted with unlimited authority; or from *experience* and history, which inform us of the enormous abuses, that ambition, in every age and country, has been found to make of so imprudent a confidence.

The same distinction between reason and experience is maintained in all our deliberations concerning the conduct of life; while the experienced statesman, general physician, or merchant is trusted and followed; and the unpractised novice, with whatever natural talents endowed, neglected and despised. Though it be allowed, that reason may form very plausible conjectures with regard to the consequences of such a particular conduct in such particular circumstances; it is still supposed imperfect, without the assistance of experience, which is alone able to give stability and certainty to the maxims, derived from study and reflection.

But notwithstanding that this distinction be thus universally received, both in the active speculative scenes of life, I shall not scruple to pronounce, that it is, at bottom, erroneous, at least, superficial.

If we examine those arguments, which, in any of the sciences above mentioned, are supposed to be the mere effects of reasoning and reflection, they will be found to terminate, at last, in some general principle or conclusion, for which we can assign no reason but observation and experience. The only difference een them and those maxims, which are vulgarly esteemed the result of pure rience, is, that the former cannot be established without some process of ught, and some reflection on what we have observed, in order to distinguish circumstances, and trace its consequences: Whereas in the latter, the experienced event is exactly and fully familiar to that which we infer as the result of any particular situation. The history of a Tiberius or a Nero makes us dread a like tyranny, were our monarchs freed from the restraints of laws and senates: But the observation of any fraud or cruelty in private life is sufficient, with the aid of a little thought, to give us the same apprehension; while it serves as an instance of the general corruption of human nature, and shows us the danger which we must incur by reposing an entire confidence in mankind. In both cases, it is experience which is ultimately the foundation of our inference and conclusion.

There is no man so young and unexperienced, as not to have formed, from observation, many general and just maxims concerning human affairs and the conduct of life; but it must be confessed, that, when a man comes to put these in practice, he will be extremely liable to error, till time and farther experience both enlarge these maxims, and teach him their proper use and application. In every situation or incident, there are many particular and seemingly minute circumstances, which the man of greatest talent is, at first, apt to overlook, though on them the justness of his conclusions, and consequently the prudence of his conduct, entirely depend. Not to mention, that, to a young beginner, the general observations and maxims occur not always on the proper occasions, nor can be immediately applied with due calmness and distinction. The truth is, an unexperienced reasoner could be no reasoner at all, were he absolutely unexperienced; and when we assign that character to any one, we mean it only in a comparative sense, and suppose him possessed of experience, in a smaller and more imperfect degree.

QUESTIONS

1. What is a "relation of ideas" proposition?
2. According to Hume, how does one discover cause-and-effect relationships?
3. What is the main conclusion of section IV?
4. According to Hume, why can't arguments from experience prove that the future will resemble the past?
5. According to Hume, what causes people to accept inductive reasoning?

Paul Edwards, "Russell's Doubts about Induction"

I.

A. In the celebrated chapter on induction in his *Problems of Philosophy*, Bertrand Russell asks the question: "Have we any reason, assuming that they (laws like the law of gravitation) have always held in the past, to suppose that these laws will hold in the future?"[1] Earlier in the same chapter he raises the more specific question: "Do *any* number of cases of a law being fulfilled in the past afford evidence that it will be fulfilled in the future?"[2] We may reformulate these questions in a way which lends itself more easily to critical discussion as follows:

(1) Assuming that we possess *n* positive instances of a phenomenon, observed in extensively varied circumstances, and that we have not observed a single negative instance (where *n* is a large number), have we any reason to suppose that the *n* + 1st instance will also be positive?
(2) Is there any number *n* of observed positive instances of a phenomenon which affords evidence that the *n* + 1st instance will also be positive?

It is clear that Russell uses "reason" synonymously with "good reason" and "evidence" with "sufficient evidence". I shall follow the same procedure throughout this article.

Russell asserts that unless we appeal to a non-empirical principle which he calls the "principle of induction", both of his questions must be answered in the negative. "Those who emphasised the scope of induction", he writes, "wished to maintain that all logic is empirical, and therefore could not be expected to realise that induction itself, their own darling, required a logical principle which obviously could not be proved inductively, and must therefore be *a priori* if it could be known at all".[3] "We must either accept the inductive principle on the ground of its intrinsic evidence or forgo all justification of our expectations about the future".[4]

In conjunction with the inductive principle, on the other hand, question (1) at least, he contends, can be answered in the affirmative. "Whether inferences from past to future are valid depends wholly, if our discussion has been sound, upon the inductive principle: if it is true, such inferences are valid."[5] Unfortunately

Paul Edwards, "Russell's Doubts about Induction," *Mind* 58 (1949): 141–63.

Russell does not make it clear whether in his opinion the same is true about question (2).

As against Russell, I shall try to show in this article that question (1) can be answered in the affirmative without in any way appealing to a non-empirical principle. I shall also attempt to show that, without in any way invoking a non-empirical principle, numbers of observed positive instances do frequently afford us evidence that unobserved instances of the same phenomenon are also positive. At the outset, I shall concentrate on question (1) since this is the more general question. Once we have answered question (1) it will require little further effort to answer question (2).

I want to emphasise here that, to keep this paper within manageable bounds, I shall refrain from discussing, at any rate explicitly, the questions "Are any inductive conclusions probable?" and "Are any inductive conclusions certain?" I hope to fill in this gap on another occasion.

It will be well to conduct our discussion in terms of a concrete example. Supposing a man jumps from a window on the fiftieth floor of the Empire State Building. Is there any reason to suppose that his body will move in the direction of the street rather than say in the direction of the sky or in a flat plane? There can be no doubt that any ordinary person and any philosophically unsophisticated scientist, would answer this question in the affirmative without in any way appealing to a non-empirical principle. He would say that there is an excellent reason to suppose that the man's body will move towards the street. This excellent reason, he would say, consists in the fact that whenever in the past a human being jumped out of a window of the Empire State Building his body moved in a downward direction; that whenever any human being anywhere jumped out of a house he moved in the direction of the ground; that, more generally, whenever a human body jumped or was thrown off an elevated locality in the neighbourhood of the earth, it moved downwards and not either upwards or at an angle of 180°; that the only objects which have been observed to be capable of moving upwards by themselves possess certain special characteristics which human beings lack; and finally in all the other observed confirmations of the theory of gravitation.

B. The philosophers who reject commonsense answers like the one just described, have relied mainly on three arguments. Russell himself explicitly employs two of them and some of his remarks make it clear that he also approves of the third. These three arguments are as follows: (*a*) Defenders of commonsense point to the fact that many inferences to unobserved events were subsequently, by means of direct observation, found to have resulted in true conclusions. However, any such appeal to observed results of inductive inferences is irrelevant. For the question at stake is: Have we ever a reason, assuming that all the large number of observed instances of a phenomenon are positive, to suppose that an instance which is still unobserved is also positive? The question is not: Have we ever a reason for supposing that instances which have by now been observed but were at one time unobserved are positive? In Russell's own words: "We have experience of past futures, but not of future futures, and the question is: Will future futures resemble past futures? This question is not to be answered by an argument which starts from past futures alone."[6]

(*b*) Cases are known where at a certain time a large number of positive instances and not a single negative instance had been observed and where the next instance nevertheless turned out to be negative. "We know that in spite of frequent repetitions there sometimes is a failure at the last."[7] The man, for instance, "who has fed the chicken every day throughout its life at last wrings its neck instead."[8] Even in the case of the human being who is jumping out of the Empire State Building, "we may be in no better position than the chicken which unexpectedly has its neck wrung."[9]

(*c*) The number of positive and negative necessary conditions for the occurrence of any event is infinite or at any rate too large to be directly observed by a human being or indeed by all human beings put together. None of us, for example, has explored every corner of the universe to make sure that there nowhere exists a malicious but powerful individual who controls the movements of the sun by means of wires which are too fine to be detected by any of our microscopes. None of us can be sure that there is no such Controller who, in order to play a joke with the human race, will prevent the sun from rising tomorrow. Equally, none of us can be sure that there is nowhere a powerful individual who can, if he wishes, regulate the movement of human bodies by means of ropes which are too thin to be detected by any of our present instruments. None of us therefore can be sure than when a man jumps out of the Empire State Building he will not be drawn skyward by the Controller of Motion. Hence we have no reason to suppose that the man's body will move in the direction of the street and not in the direction of the sky.

In connexion with the last of these three arguments attention ought to be drawn to a distinction which Russell makes between what he calls the "interesting" and the "uninteresting" doubt about induction.[10] The uninteresting doubt is doubt about the occurrence of a given event on the ground that not all the conditions which are known to be necessary are in fact known to be present. What Russell calls the interesting doubt is the doubt whether an event will take place although all the conditions known to be necessary are known to obtain. Russell's "interesting doubt", if I am not mistaken, is identical with Donald Williams's "tragic problem of induction".[11]

II.

As I indicated above, it is my object in this article to defend the commonsense answers to both of Russell's questions. I propose to show, in other words, that, without in any way calling upon a non-empirical principle for assistance, we often have a reason for supposing that a generalisation will be confirmed in the future as it has been confirmed in the past. I also propose to show that numbers "of cases of a law being fulfilled in the past" do often afford evidence that it will be fulfilled in the future.

However, what I have to say in support of these answers is so exceedingly simple that I am afraid it will not impress the philosophers who are looking for elaborate and complicated theories to answer these questions. But I think I can make my case appear plausible even in the eyes of some of these philosophers if I describe at some length the general method of resolving philosophical puzzles which I shall apply to the problem of induction.

Let us consider a simple statement like "there are several thousand physicians in New York". We may call this a statement of commonsense, meaning thereby no more than that anybody above a certain very moderate level of instruction and intelligence would confidently give his assent to it.

The word "physician", as ordinarily used, is not entirely free from ambiguity. At times it simply means "person who possesses a medical degree from a recognised academic institution". At other times, though less often, it means the same as "person who possesses what is by ordinary standards a considerable skill in curing diseases". On yet other occasions when people say about somebody that he is a physician they mean both that he has a medical degree and that he possesses a skill in curing diseases which considerably exceeds that of the average layman.

Let us suppose that in the commonsense statement "there are several thousand physicians in New York" the word "physician" is used exclusively in the last-mentioned sense. This assumption will simplify our discussion, but it is not at all essential to any of the points I am about to make. It is essential, however, to realise that when somebody asserts in ordinary life that there are several thousand physicians in New York, he is using the word "physician" in one or other of the ordinary senses just listed. By "physician" he does not mean for example "person who can speedily repair bicycles" or "person who can cure any conceivable illness in less than two minutes".

Now, supposing somebody were to say "Really, there are no physicians at all in New York", in the belief that he was contradicting and refuting commonsense. Supposing that on investigation it turns out that by "physician" he does not mean "person who has a medical degree and who has considerably more skill in curing disease than the average layman". It turns out that by "physician" he means "person who has a medical degree and who can cure any conceivable illness in less than two minutes".

What would be an adequate reply to such an "enemy of commonsense"? Clearly it would be along the following lines: "What you say is true. There are no physicians in New York—in *your* sense of the word. There are no persons in New York who can cure any conceivable disease in less than two minutes. But this in no way contradicts the commonsense view expressed by "there are several thousand physicians in New York". For the latter asserts no more than that there are several thousand people in New York who have a medical degree and who possess a skill in curing disease which considerably exceeds that of the average layman. You are guilty of *ignoratio elenchi* since the proposition you refute is different from the proposition you set out to refute."

Our discussion from here on will be greatly simplified by introducing a few technical terms. Let us, firstly, call "*ignoratio elenchi* by *redefinition*" any instance of *ignoratio elenchi* in which (i) the same sentence expresses both the proposition which ought to be proved and the proposition which is confused with it and where (ii) in the latter employment of the sentence one or more of its parts are used in a sense which is different from their ordinary sense or senses. Secondly, let us refer to any redefinition of a word which includes all that the ordinary definition of the word includes but which includes something else as well as a "*high* redefinition"; and to the sense which is defined by a high redefinition we shall refer as a high sense of the word. Thus "person who has a medical degree and who is capable of curing any conceivable disease in less than two minutes" is a high redefinition of "physician" and anybody using the word in that fashion is using it in a high sense. Thirdly, we shall refer to a redefinition of a word which includes something but not all of what the ordinary definition includes and which includes nothing else as a "*low* redefinition"; and the sense which is defined by a low redefinition we shall call a low sense of the word. "Person capable of giving first aid" or "person who knows means of alleviating pain" would be low redefinitions of "physician". Finally, it will be convenient to call a statement in which a word is used in a high or in a low sense a *redefinitional statement*. If the word is used in a high sense we shall speak of a highdefinitional statement; if it is used in a low sense we shall speak of a lowdefinitional statement.

A short while ago, I pointed out that the man who says "there are no physicians in New York", meaning that there are no people in New York who have a medical degree and who can cure any conceivable illness in less than two minutes, is not really contradicting the commonsense view that there are physicians in New York. I pointed out that he would be guilty of what in our technical language is called an *ignoratio elenchi* by redefinition. Now, it seems to me that the relation between the assertion of various philosophers that past experience never constitutes a reason for prediction or generalisation except perhaps in conjunction with a non-empirical principle and the commonsense view that past experience does often by itself constitute a reason for inferences to unobserved events has some striking resemblances to the relation between the redefinitional statement about physicians in New York and the commonsense view which this redefinitional statement fails to refute. And more generally, it strongly seems to me that almost all the bizarre pronouncements of philosophers—their "paradoxes", their "silly" theories—are in certain respects strikingly like the statement that there are no physicians in New York, made by one who means to assert that there are no people in New York who have medical degrees and who are capable of curing any conceivable disease in less than two minutes.

In making the last statement I do not mean to deny that there are also important differences between philosophical paradoxes and the highdefinitional statement about physicians. There are three differences in particular which have to be mentioned if my subsequent remarks are not to be seriously misleading. Firstly, many of the philosophical paradoxes are not without some point; they do often draw attention to likenesses and differences which ordinary usage obscures. Secondly, the redefinitions which are implicit in philosophical paradoxes do quite often, though by no means always, receive a certain backing from ordinary usage. Frequently, that is to say, there is a secondary sense or trend in ordinary usage which corresponds to the philosophical redefinition, the "real" sense of the word.[12] Thirdly, philosophical paradoxes are invariably ambiguous in a sense in which the highdefinitional statement about the physicians is not ambiguous. . . .[13]

A. Supposing a man, let us call him M, said to us "I have not yet found any physicians in New York". Suppose we take him to Park Avenue and introduce him to Brown, a man who has a medical degree and who has cured many people suffering from diseases of the ear. Brown admits, however, that he has not been able to cure *all* the patients who ever consulted him. He also admits that many of his cures took a long time, some as long as eight years. On hearing this, M says "Brown certainly isn't a physician".

Supposing we next take M to meet Black who has a medical degree and who can prove to M's and to our satisfaction that he has cured every patient who ever consulted him. Moreover, none of Black's cures took more than three years. However, on hearing that some of Black's cures took as long as two years and ten months, M says "Black certainly isn't a physician either".

Finally we introduce M to White who has a medical degree and who has cured every one of his patients in less than six months. When M hears that some of White's cures took as long as-five and a half months, he is adamant and exclaims "White—what a ridiculous error to call him a physician!"

At this stage, if not much sooner, all of us would impatiently ask M: What on earth do you mean by "physician"? And we would plainly be justified in adding: Whatever you may mean by "physician", in any sense in which we ever use the word, Black and Brown and White are physicians and very excellent ones at that.

Let us return now to Russell's doubt about the sun's rising to-morrow or about what would happen to a man who jumps out of the Empire State Building. Let us consider what Russell would say in reply to the following question: Supposing that the observed confirmatory instances for the theory of gravitation were a million or ten million times as extensive as they now are and that they were drawn from a very much wider field; would we then have a reason to suppose that the man will fall into the street and not move up into the sky? It is obvious that Russell and anybody taking his view would say "No". He would reply that though our *expectation* that the man's body will move in the direction of the street would be even stronger then than it is at present, we would still be without a *reason*.

Next, let us imagine ourselves to be putting the following question to Russell: Supposing the world were such that no accumulation of more than five hundred observed positive instances of a phenomenon has ever been found to be followed by a negative instance; supposing, for instance, that all the chickens who have ever been fed by the same man for 501 days in succession or more are still alive and that all the men too are still alive feeding the chickens every day—would the observed confirmations of the law of gravity in that case be a reason to suppose that the man jumping out of the Empire State Building will move in the direction of the street and not in the direction of the sky? I am not quite sure what Russell would say in reply to this question. Let us assume he would once again answer "No—past experience would not even then ever be a *reason*".

Thirdly and finally, we have to consider what Russell would say to the following question: Supposing we had explored every corner of the universe with instruments millions of times as fine and accurate as any we now possess and that we had yet failed to discover any Controller of the movements of human bodies—would we then in our predictions about the man jumping out of the Empire State Building be in a better position than the chicken is in predicting its meals? Would our past observations then be a reason for our prediction? Whatever Russell would in fact say to this, it is clear that his remarks concerning the "interesting" doubt about induction require him to answer our question in the negative. He would have to say something like this: "Our *expectation* that the man's body will move in a downward direction will be even stronger than it is now. However, without invoking a non-empirical principle, we shall not *really* be in a better position than the chicken. We should still fail to possess a *reason*."

As in the case of the man who refused to say that Brown, Black, and White were doctors, our natural response to all this will be to turn to Russell and say: What do you mean by "being in a better position"? What on earth do you mean by "a reason"? And, furthermore, why should anybody be interested in a reason in your sense of the word?

Russell's remarks about the need for a general principle like his principle of induction to serve as major premiss in every inductive argument make it clear what he means by a reason: like the Rationalists and Hume (in most places), he means by "reason" a *logically conclusive* reason and by "evidence" *deductively conclusive* evidence. When "reason" is used in this sense, it must be admitted that past observations can never by themselves be a reason for any prediction whatsoever. But "reason" is not used in this sense when, in science or in ordinary life, people claim to have a reason for a prediction.

So far as I can see, there are three different trends in the ordinary usage of "reason for an inductive conclusion" and according to none of them does the word mean "logically conclusive reason". Among the three trends one is much more prominent than the others. It may fitly be called the main sense of the word. According to this main sense, what we mean when we claim that we have a reason for a prediction is that the past observations of this phenomenon or of analogical phenomena are of a certain kind: they are exclusively or predominantly positive, the number of the positive observations is at least fairly large, and they come from extensively varied sets of circumstances. This is of course a very crude formulation. But for the purposes of this article it is, I think, sufficient.[14]

Next, there is a number of trends according to which we mean very much less than this. Occasionally, for instance, we simply mean that it is *reasonable* to infer the inductive conclusion. And clearly it may be reasonable to infer an inductive conclusion for which we have no reason in the main sense. Thus let us suppose I know that Parker will meet Schroeder in a game in the near future and that it is imperative for me not to suspend my judgment but to come to a conclusion as to who will win. Supposing I know nothing about their present form and nothing also about the type of court on which the match is to be played. All I know is that Parker and Schroeder have in the previous two seasons met six times, Parker scoring four victories to Schroeder's two. In these circumstances it would be reasonable for me to predict that Parker will win and unreasonable to predict that Schroeder will win. Clearly however, in the main sense of the word I have no reason for either prediction.

Again there is a trend according to which any positive instance of a phenomenon is *a* reason for concluding that the next instance of the phenomenon will be positive. Thus in the circumstances described in the preceding paragraph, it would be quite proper to say we have *more reason* for supposing that Parker will win than for predicting Schroeder's victory. It would be quite proper also to say that we have *some reason* for supposing that Schroeder will win. It would be proper to say this even if Schroeder had won only one of the six matches. To all these and similar trends in the ordinary usage of "reason for an inductive conclusion" I shall from now on refer as the second ordinary sense of the word.

There can be no doubt that in both these ordinary senses of the word, we frequently have a reason for an inductive conclusion. In these senses we have an excellent reason for supposing that the man jumping out of the Empire State

Building will move in the direction of the street, that the sun will rise to-morrow and that Stalin will die before the year 2000. The answer to question (1) is therefore a firm and clear "Yes": in many domains we have a multitude of exclusively positive instances coming from extensively different circumstances.

The same is true if "reason" is used in the third ordinary sense. . . . For the time being it will be convenient and, I think, not at all misleading to speak as if what I have called the main sense is the *only* ordinary sense of "reason for an inductive conclusion".

It should now be clear that, when Russell says that observed instances are never by themselves a reason for an inductive conclusion, he is guilty of an *ignoratio elenchi* by redefinition. His assertion that the premisses of an inductive argument never by themselves constitute a *logically conclusive* reason for an inductive conclusion in no way contradicts the commonsense assertion that they frequently constitute a reason *in the ordinary sense of the word*. Russell's definition of "reason" is indeed in one respect not a redefinition since in certain contexts we do use "reason" to mean "deductively conclusive reason". However, it is a redefinition in that we never in ordinary life use "reason" in Russell's sense when we are talking about inductive arguments.

Moreover, if "reason" means "deductively conclusive reason", Russell's questions are no more genuinely questions than *e.g.*, the sentence "Is a father a female parent?" For, since part of the definition of "inductive inference" is inference from something observed to something unobserved, it is a *contradiction* to say that an inference is both inductive and at the same time in the same respect deductively conclusive. Russell's "interesting" doubt, then, is no more sensible or interesting than the "doubt" whether we shall ever see something invisible or find an object which is a father and also female or an object which is a man but not a human being.

Notes

1 New York: Oxford University Press, 1997, p. 64.
2 p. 62.
3 *Our Knowledge of the External World* (London: Allen & Unwin, 1926), p. 226.
4 *Problems of Philosophy*, p. 68.
5 *External World*, p. 226.
6 *Problems of Philosophy*, p. 65.
7 *loc. cit.*, p. 66.
8 *loc. cit.*, p. 63.
9 *Ibid.*
10 *loc. cit.*, p. 61.
11 "Induction and the Future," *Mind* 57 (1948): p. 227.
12 Prominent instances of this phenomenon are "real certainty," "real knowledge," "real sameness," "real freedom," and "really contemporaneous events."
13 The last of these points seems to me to be of enormous importance for understanding the phenomenon of philosophical paradoxes.
14 I have so far left out one important element in the main sense of "reason for an inductive conclusion". . . . this omission will not affect any of my points.

QUESTIONS

1 Does Edwards think that we have good reason to accept inductive conclusions?
2 In Edwards' example of the man who says there are no physicians in New York, what does the man mean by "physician"?
3 According to Edwards, what does Russell mean by "reason"?

Nelson Goodman, "The New Riddle of Induction"

1. The old problem of induction

At the close of the preceding lecture, I said that today I should examine how matters stand with respect to the problem of induction. In a word, I think they stand ill. But the real difficulties that confront us today are not the traditional ones. What is commonly thought of as the Problem of Induction has been solved, or dissolved; and we face new problems that are not as yet very widely understood. To approach them, I shall have to run as quickly as possible over some very familiar ground.

The problem of the validity of judgments about future or unknown cases arises, as Hume pointed out, because such judgments are neither reports of experience nor logical consequences of it. Predictions, of course, pertain to what has not yet been observed. And they cannot be logically inferred from what has been observed; for what *has* happened imposes no logical restrictions on what *will* happen. Although Hume's dictum that there are no necessary connections of matters of fact has been challenged at times, it has withstood all attacks. Indeed, I should be inclined not merely to agree that there are no necessary connections of matters of fact, but to ask whether there are any necessary connections at all[1]—but that is another story.

Hume's answer to the question how predictions are related to past experience is refreshingly non-cosmic. When an event of one kind frequently follows upon an event of another kind in experience, a habit is formed that leads the mind, when confronted with a new event of the first kind, to pass to the idea of an event of the second kind. The idea of necessary connection arises from the felt impulse of the mind in making this transition.

Now if we strip this account of all extraneous features, the central point is that to the question "Why one prediction rather than another?", Hume answers that the elect prediction is one that accords with a past regularity, because this regularity has established a habit. Thus among alternative statements about a future moment, one statement is distinguished by its consonance with habit and thus with regularities observed in the past. Prediction according to any other alternative is errant.

How satisfactory is this answer? The heaviest criticism has taken the righteous

Nelson Goodman, "The New Riddle of Induction," *Fact, Fiction, and Forecast* (Indianapolis, Ind.: Bobbs-Merrill, 1973).

position that Hume's account at best pertains only to the source of predictions, not their legitimacy; that he sets forth the circumstances under which we make given predictions—and in this sense explains why we make them—but leaves untouched the question of our license for making them. To trace origins, runs the old complaint, is not to establish validity: the real question is not why a prediction is in fact made but how it can be justified. Since this seems to point to the awkward conclusion that the greatest of modern philosophers completely missed the point of his own problem, the idea has developed that he did not really take his solution very seriously, but regarded the main problem as unsolved and perhaps as insoluble. Thus we come to speak of "Hume's problem" as though he propounded it as a question without answer.

All this seems to me quite wrong. I think Hume grasped the central question and considered his answer to be passably effective. And I think his answer is reasonable and relevant, even if it is not entirely satisfactory. I shall explain presently. At the moment, I merely want to record a protest against the prevalent notion that the problem of justifying induction, when it is so sharply dissociated from the problem of describing how induction takes place, can fairly be called Hume's problem.

I suppose that the problem of justifying induction has called forth as much fruitless discussion as has any half-way respectable problem of modern philosophy. The typical writer begins by insisting that some way of justifying predictions must be found; proceeds to argue that for this purpose we need some resounding universal law of the Uniformity of Nature, and then inquires how this universal principle itself can be justified. At this point, if he is tired, he concludes that the principle must be accepted as an indispensable assumption; or if he is energetic and ingenious, he goes on to devise some subtle justification for it. Such an invention, however, seldom satisfies anyone else; and the easier course of accepting an unsubstantiated and even dubious assumption much more sweeping than any actual predictions we make seems an odd and expensive way of justifying them.

2. Dissolution of the old problem

Understandably, then, more critical thinkers have suspected that there might be something awry with the problem we are trying to solve. Come to think of it, what precisely would constitute the justification we seek? If the problem is to explain how we know that certain predictions will turn out to be correct, the sufficient answer is that we don't know any such thing. If the problem is to *find* some way of distinguishing antecedently between true and false predictions, we are asking for prevision rather than for philosophical explanation. Nor does it help matters much to say that we are merely trying to show that or why certain predictions are *probable*. Often it is said that while we cannot tell in advance whether a prediction concerning a given throw of a die is true, we can decide whether the prediction is a probable one. But if this means determining how the prediction is related to actual frequency distributions of future throws of the die, surely there is no way of knowing or proving this in advance. On the other hand, if the judgment that the prediction is probable has nothing to do with subsequent occurrences, then the question remains in what sense a probable prediction is any better justified than an improbable one.

Now obviously the genuine problem cannot be one of attaining unattainable knowledge or of accounting for knowledge that we do not in fact have. A better understanding standing of our problem can be gained by looking for a moment at what is involved in justifying non-inductive inferences. How do we justify a *de*duction? Plainly, by showing that it conforms to the general rules of deductive inference. An argument that so conforms is justified or valid, even if its conclusion happens to be false. An argument that violates a rule is fallacious even if its conclusion happens to be true. To justify a deductive conclusion therefore requires no knowledge of the facts it pertains to. Moreover, when a deductive argument has been shown to conform to the rules of logical inference, we usually consider it justified without going on to ask what justifies the rules. Analogously, the basic task in justifying an inductive inference is to show that it conforms to the general rules of *in*duction. Once we have recognized this, we have gone a long way towards clarifying our problem.

Yet, of course, the rules themselves must eventually be justified. The validity of a deduction depends not upon conformity to any purely arbitrary rules we may contrive, but upon conformity to valid rules. When we speak of *the* rules of inference we mean the valid rules—or better, *some* valid rules, since there may be alternative sets of equally valid rules. But how is the validity of rules to be determined? Here again we encounter philosophers who insist that these rules follow from some self-evident axiom, and others who try to show that the rules are grounded in the very nature of the human mind. I think the answer lies much nearer the surface. Principles of deductive inference are justified by their conformity with accepted deductive practice. Their validity depends upon accordance with the particular deductive inferences we actually make and sanction. If a rule yields inacceptable inferences, we drop it as invalid. Justification of general rules thus derives from judgments rejecting or accepting particular deductive inferences.

This looks flagrantly circular. I have said that deductive inferences are justified by their conformity to valid general rules, and that general rules are justified by their conformity to valid inferences. But this circle is a virtuous one. The point is that rules and particular inferences alike are justified by being brought into agreement with each other. *A rule is amended if it yields an inference we are unwilling to accept; an inference is rejected if it violates a rule we are unwilling to amend*. The process of justification is the delicate one of making mutual adjustments between rules and accepted inferences; and in the agreement achieved lies the only justification needed for either.

All this applies equally well to induction. An inductive inference, too, is justified by conformity to general rules, and a general rule by conformity to accepted inductive inferences. Predictions are justified if they conform to valid canons of induction; and the canons are valid if they accurately codify accepted inductive practice.

A result of such analysis is that we can stop plaguing ourselves with certain spurious questions about induction. We no longer demand an explanation for guarantees that we do not have, or seek keys to knowledge that we cannot obtain. It dawns upon us that the traditional smug insistence upon a hard-and-fast line between justifying induction and describing ordinary inductive practice distorts the problem. And we owe belated apologies to Hume. For in dealing with the question how normally accepted inductive judgments are made, he was in fact dealing with the question of inductive validity.[2] The validity of a prediction consisted for him in its arising from habit, and thus in its exemplifying some past regularity. His answer was incomplete and perhaps not entirely correct; but it was not beside the point. The problem of induction is not a problem of demonstration but a problem of defining the difference between valid and invalid predictions.

This clears the air but leaves a lot to be done. As principles of *de*ductive inference, we have the familiar and highly developed laws of logic; but there are available no such precisely stated and well-recognized principles of inductive inference. Mill's canons hardly rank with Aristotle's rules of the syllogism, let alone with *Principia Mathematica*. Elaborate and valuable treatises on probability usually leave certain fundamental questions untouched. Only in very recent years has there been any explicit and systematic work upon what I call the constructive task of confirmation theory.

3. The constructive task of confirmation theory

The task of formulating rules that define the difference between valid and invalid inductive inferences is much like the task of defining any term with an established usage. If we set out to define the term "tree", we try to compose out of already understood words an expression that will apply to the familiar objects that standard usage calls trees, and that will not apply to objects that standard usage refuses to call trees. A proposal that plainly violates either condition is rejected; while a definition that meets these tests may be adopted and used to decide cases that are not already settled by actual usage. Thus the interplay we observed between rules of induction and particular inductive inferences is simply an instance of this characteristic dual adjustment between definition and usage, whereby the usage informs the definition, which in turn guides extension of the usage.

Of course this adjustment is a more complex matter than I have indicated. Sometimes, in the interest of convenience or theoretical utility, we deliberately permit a definition to run counter to clear mandates of common usage. We accept a definition of "fish" that excludes whales. Similarly we may decide to deny the term "valid induction" to some inductive inferences that are commonly considered valid, or apply the term to others not usually so considered. A definition may modify as well as extend ordinary usage.[3]

Some pioneer work on the problem of defining confirmation or valid induction has been done by Professor Hempel.[4] Let me remind you briefly of a few of his results. Just as deductive logic is concerned primarily with a relation between statements—namely the consequence relation—that is independent of their truth or falsity, so inductive logic as Hempel conceives it is concerned primarily with a comparable relation of confirmation between statements. Thus the problem is to define the relation that obtains between any statement S_1 and another S_2 if and only if S_1 may properly be said to confirm S_2 in any degree.

With the question so stated, the first step seems obvious. Does not induction proceed in just the opposite direction from deduction? Surely some of the evidence-statements that inductively support a general hypothesis are consequences of it. Since the consequence relation is already well defined by deductive logic, will not be on firm ground in saying that confirmation embraces the converse relation? The laws of deduction in reverse will then be among the laws of induction.

Let's see where this leads us. We naturally assume further that whatever confirms a given statement confirms also whatever follows from that statement.[5] But if we combine this assumption with our proposed principle, we get the embarrassing result that every statement confirms every other. Surprising as it may be that such innocent beginnings lead to such an intolerable conclusion, the proof is very easy. Start with any statement S_1. It is a consequence of, and so by our present criterion confirms, the conjunction of S_1 and any statement whatsoever—call it S_2. But the confirmed conjunction, $S_1 \cdot S_2$, of course has S_2 as a consequence. Thus every statement confirms all statements.

The fault lies in careless formulation of our first proposal. While some statements that confirm a general hypothesis are consequences of it, not all its consequences confirm it. This may not be immediately evident; for indeed we do in some sense furnish support for a statement when we establish one of its consequences. We settle one of the questions about it. Consider the heterogeneous conjunction:

> 8497 is a prime number and the other side of the moon is flat and Elizabeth the First was crowned on a Tuesday.

To show that any one of the three component statements is true is to support the conjunction by reducing the net undetermined claim. But support[6] of this kind is not confirmation; for establishment of one component endows the whole statement with no credibility that is transmitted to other component statements. Confirmation of a hypothesis occurs only when an instance imparts to the hypothesis some credibility that is conveyed to other instances. Appraisal of hypotheses, indeed, is incidental to prediction, to the judgment of new cases on the basis of old ones.

Our formula thus needs tightening. This is readily accomplished, as Hempel points out, if we observe that a hypothesis is genuinely confirmed only by a statement that is an instance of it in the special sense of entailing not the hypothesis itself but its relativization or restriction to the class of entities mentioned by that statement. The relativization of a general hypothesis to a class results from restricting the range of its universal and existential quantifiers to the members of that class. Less technically, what the hypothesis says of all things the evidence statement says of one thing (or of one pair or other *n*-ad of things). This obviously covers the confirmation of the conductivity of all copper by the conductivity of a given piece; and it excludes confirmation of our heterogeneous conjunction by any of its components. And, when taken together with the principle that what confirms a statement confirms all its consequences, this criterion does not yield the untoward conclusion that every statement confirms every other.

New difficulties promptly appear from other directions, however. One is the infamous paradox of the ravens. The statement that a given object, say this piece of paper, is neither black nor a raven confirms the hypothesis that all non-black things are non-ravens. But this hypothesis is logically equivalent to the hypothesis that all ravens are black. Hence we arrive at the unexpected conclusion that the statement that a given object is neither black nor a raven confirms the hypothesis that all ravens are black. The prospect of being able to investigate ornithological theories without going out in the rain is so attractive that we know there must be a catch in it. The trouble this time, however, lies not in faulty definition, but in tacit and illicit reference to evidence not stated in our example. Taken by itself, the statement that the given object is neither black nor a raven confirms the hypothesis that everything that is not a raven is not black as well as the hypothesis that everything that is not black is not a raven. We tend to ignore the former hypothesis because we know it to be false from abundant other evidence—from all the familiar things that are not ravens but are black. But we are required to assume that no such evidence is available. Under this circumstance, even a much stronger hypothesis is also obviously confirmed: that nothing is either black or a raven. In the light of this confirmation of the hypothesis that there are no ravens, it is no longer surprising that under the artificial restrictions of the example, the hypothesis that all ravens are black is also confirmed. And the prospects for indoor ornithology vanish when we notice that under these same conditions, the contrary hypothesis that no ravens are black is equally well confirmed.[7]

On the other hand, our definition does err in not forcing us to take into account all the *stated* evidence. The unhappy results are readily illustrated. If two compatible evidence statements confirm two hypotheses, then naturally the conjunction of the evidence statements should confirm the conjunction of the hypotheses.[8] Suppose our evidence consists of the statements E_1 saying that a given thing b is black, and E_2 saying that a second thing c is not black. By our present definition, E_1 confirms the hypothesis that everything is black, and E_2 the hypothesis that everything is non-black. The conjunction of these perfectly compatible evidence statements will then confirm the self-contradictory hypothesis that everything is both black and non-black. Simple as this anomaly is, it requires drastic modification of our definition. What given evidence confirms is not what we arrive at by generalizing from separate items of it, but—roughly speaking—what we arrive at by generalizing from the total stated evidence. The central idea for an improved definition is that, within certain limitations, what is asserted to be true for the narrow universe of the evidence statements is confirmed for the whole universe of discourse. Thus if our evidence is E_1 and E_2, neither the hypothesis that all things are black nor the hypothesis that all things are non-black is confirmed; for neither is true for the evidence-universe consisting of b and c. Of course, much more careful formulation is needed, since some statements that are true of the evidence-universe—such as that there is only one black thing—are obviously not confirmed for the whole universe. These matters are taken care of by the studied formal definition that Hempel develops on this basis; but we cannot and need not go into further detail here.

No one supposes that the task of confirmation-theory has been completed. But the few steps I have reviewed—chosen partly for their bearing on what is to follow—show how things move along once the problem of definition displaces the problem of justification. Important and long-unnoticed questions are brought to light and answered; and we are encouraged to expect that the many remaining questions will in time yield to similar treatment.

But our satisfaction is shortlived. New and serious trouble begins to appear.

4. The new riddle of induction

Confirmation of a hypothesis by an instance depends rather heavily upon features of the hypothesis other than its syntactical form. That a given piece of copper conducts electricity increases the credibility of statements asserting that other pieces of copper conduct electricity, and thus confirms the hypothesis that all copper conducts electricity. But the fact that a given man now in this room is a third son does not increase the credibility of statements asserting that other men now in this room are third sons, and so does not confirm the hypothesis that all men now in this room are third sons. Yet in both cases our hypothesis is a generalization of the evidence statement. The difference is that in the former case the hypothesis is a *lawlike* statement; while in the latter case, the hypothesis is a merely contingent or accidental generality. Only a statement that is *lawlike*—regardless of its truth or falsity or its scientific importance—is capable of receiving confirmation from an instance of it; accidental statements are not. Plainly, then, we must look for a way of distinguishing lawlike from accidental statements.

So long as what seems to be needed is merely a way of excluding a few odd and unwanted cases that are inadvertently admitted by our definition of confirmation, the problem may not seem very hard or very pressing. We fully expect that minor defects will be found in our definition and that the necessary refinements will have to be worked out patiently one after another. But some further examples will show that our present difficulty is of a much graver kind.

Suppose that all emeralds examined before a certain time *t* are green.[9] At time *t*, then, our observations support the hypothesis that all emeralds are green; and this is in accord with our definition of confirmation. Our evidence statements assert that emerald *a* is green, that emerald *b* is green, and so on; and each confirms the general hypothesis that all emeralds are green. So far, so good.

Now let me introduce another predicate less familiar than "green". It is the predicate "grue" and it applies to all things examined before *t* just in case they are green but to other things just in case they are blue. Then at time *t* we have, for each evidence statement asserting that a given emerald is green, a parallel evidence statement asserting that that emerald is grue. And the statements that emerald *a* is grue, that emerald *b* is grue, and so on, will each confirm the general hypothesis that all emeralds are grue. Thus according to our definition, the prediction that all emeralds subsequently examined will be green and the prediction that all will be grue are alike confirmed by evidence statements describing the same observations. But if an emerald subsequently examined is grue, it is blue and hence not green. Thus although we are well aware which of the two incompatible predictions is genuinely confirmed, they are equally well confirmed according to our present definition. Moreover, it is clear that if we simply choose an appropriate predicate, then on the basis of these same observations we shall have equal confirmation, by our definition, for any prediction whatever about other emeralds—or indeed about anything else.[10] As in our earlier example, only the predictions subsumed under lawlike hypotheses are genuinely confirmed; but we have no criterion as yet for determining lawlikeness. And now we see that without some such criterion, our definition not merely includes a few unwanted cases, but is so completely ineffectual that it virtually excludes nothing. We are left once again with the intolerable result that anything confirms anything. This difficulty cannot be set aside as an annoying detail to be taken care of in due course. It has to be met before our definition will work at all.

Nevertheless, the difficulty is often slighted because on the surface there seem to be easy ways of dealing with it. Sometimes, for example, the problem is thought to be much like the paradox of the ravens. We are here again, it is pointed out, making tacit and illegitimate use of information outside the stated evidence: the information, for example, that different samples of one material are usually alike in conductivity, and the information that different men in a lecture audience are usually not alike in the number of their older brothers. But while it is true that such information is being smuggled in, this does not by itself settle the matter as it settles the matter of the ravens. There the point was that when the smuggled information is forthrightly declared, its effect upon the confirmation of the hypothesis in question is immediately and properly registered by the definition we are using. On the other hand, if to our initial evidence we add statements concerning the conductivity of pieces of other materials or concerning the number of older brothers of members of other lecture audiences, this will not in the least affect the confirmation, according to our definition, of the hypothesis concerning copper or of that concerning this lecture audience. Since our definition is insensitive to the bearing upon hypotheses of evidence so related to them, even when the evidence is fully declared, the difficulty about accidental hypotheses cannot be explained away on the ground that such evidence is being surreptitiously taken into account.

A more promising suggestion is to explain the matter in terms of the effect of this other evidence not directly upon the hypothesis in question but *in*directly through other hypotheses that *are* confirmed, according to our definition, by such evidence. Our information about other materials does by our definition confirm such hypotheses as that all pieces of iron conduct electricity, that no pieces of rubber do, and so on; and these hypotheses, the explanation runs, impart to the hypothesis that all pieces of copper conduct electricity (and also to the hypothesis that none do) the character of lawlikeness—that is, amenability to confirmation by direct positive instances when found. On the other hand, our information about other lecture audiences *dis*confirms many hypotheses to the effect that all the men in one audience are third sons, or that none are; and this strips any character of lawlikeness from the hypothesis that all (or the hypothesis that none) of the men in *this* audience are third sons. But clearly if this course is to be followed, the circumstances under which hypotheses are thus related to one another will have to be precisely articulated.

The problem, then, is to define the relevant way in which such hypotheses must be alike. Evidence for the hypothesis that all iron conducts electricity enhances the lawlikeness of the hypothesis that all zirconium conducts electricity, but does not similarly affect the hypothesis that all the objects on my desk conduct electricity. Wherein lies the difference? The first two hypotheses fall under the broader hypothesis—call it "*H*"—that every class of things of the same material is uniform in conductivity; the first and third fall only under some such hypothesis as—call it "*K*"—that every class of things that are either all of the same material or all on a desk is uniform in conductivity. Clearly the important difference here is that evidence for a statement affirming that one of the classes covered by *H* has the property in question increases the credibility of any statement affirming that another such class has this property; while nothing of the sort holds true with respect to *K*. But this is only to say that *H* is lawlike and *K* is not. We are faced anew with the very problem we are trying to solve: the problem of distinguishing between lawlike and accidental hypotheses.

The most popular way of attacking the problem takes its cue from the fact that accidental hypotheses seem typically to involve some spatial or temporal restriction, or reference to some particular individual. They seem to concern the people in some particular room, or the objects on some particular person's desk; while lawlike hypotheses characteristically concern all ravens or all pieces of copper whatsoever. Complete generality is thus very often supposed to be a sufficient condition of lawlikeness; but to define this complete generality is by no means easy. Merely to require that the hypothesis contain no term naming, describing, or indicating a particular thing or location will obviously not be enough. The troublesome hypothesis that all emeralds are grue contains no such term; and where such a term does occur, as in hypotheses about men in *this room*, it can be suppressed in favor of some predicate (short or long, new or old) that contains no such term but applies only to exactly the same things. One might think, then, of excluding not only hypotheses that actually contain terms for specific individuals but also all hypotheses that are equivalent to others that do contain such terms. But, as we have just seen, to exclude only hypotheses of which *all* equivalents contain such terms is to exclude nothing. On the other hand, to exclude all hypotheses that have *some* equivalent containing such a term is to exclude everything; for even the hypothesis

All grass is green

has as an equivalent

All grass in London or elsewhere is green.

The next step, therefore, has been to consider ruling out predicates of certain kinds. A syntactically universal hypothesis is lawlike, the proposal runs, if its predicates are "purely qualitative" or "non-positional."[11] This will obviously accomplish nothing if a purely qualitative predicate is then conceived either as one that is equivalent to some expression free of terms for specific individuals, or as one that is equivalent to no expression that contains such a term; for this only raises again the difficulties just pointed out. The claim appears to be rather that at least in the case of a simple enough predicate we can readily determine by direct inspection of its meaning whether or not it is purely qualitative. But even aside from obscurities in the notion of "the meaning" of a predicate, this claim seems to me wrong. I simply do not know how to tell whether a predicate is qualitative or positional, except perhaps by completely begging the question at issue and asking whether the predicate is "well-behaved"—that is, whether simple syntactically universal hypotheses applying it are lawlike.

This statement will not go unprotested. "Consider", it will be argued, "the predicates 'blue' and 'green' and the predicate 'grue' introduced earlier, and also the predicate 'bleen' that applies to emeralds examined before time *t* just in case they are blue and to other emeralds just in case they are green. Surely it is clear", the argument runs, "that the first two are purely qualitative and the second two are not; for the meaning of each of the latter two plainly involves reference to a specific temporal position." To this I reply that indeed I do recognize the first two as well-behaved predicates admissible in lawlike hypotheses, and the second two as ill-behaved predicates. But the argument that the former but not the latter are purely qualitative seems to me quite unsound. True enough, if we start with "blue" and "green", then "grue" and "bleen" will be explained in terms of "blue" and "green" and a temporal term. But equally truly, if we start with "grue" and "bleen", then "blue" and "green" will be explained in terms of "grue" and "bleen" and a temporal term; "green", for example, applies to emeralds examined before time *t* just in case they are grue, and to other emeralds just in case they are bleen. Thus qualitativeness is an entirely relative matter and does not by itself establish any dichotomy of predicates. This relativity seems to be completely overlooked by those who contend that the qualitative character of a predicate is a criterion for its good behavior.

Of course, one may ask why we need worry about such unfamiliar predicates as "grue" or about accidental hypotheses in general, since we are unlikely to use them in making predictions. If our definition works for such hypotheses as are normally employed, isn't that all we need? In a sense, yes; but only in the sense that we need no definition, no theory of induction, and no philosophy of knowledge at all. We get along well enough without them in daily life and in scientific research. But if we seek a theory at all, we cannot excuse gross anomalies resulting from a proposed theory by pleading that we can avoid them in practice. The odd cases we have been considering are clinically pure cases that, though seldom encountered in practice, nevertheless display to best advantage the symptoms of a widespread and destructive malady.

We have so far neither any answer nor any promising clue to an answer to the question what distinguishes lawlike or confirmable hypotheses from accidental or non-confirmable ones; and what may at first have seemed a minor technical difficulty has taken on the stature of a major obstacle to the development of a satisfactory theory of confirmation. It is this problem that I call the new riddle of induction.

5. The pervasive problem of projection

At the beginning of this lecture, I expressed the opinion that the problem of induction is still unsolved, but that the difficulties that face us today are not the old ones; and I have tried to outline the changes that have taken place. The problem of justifying induction has been displaced by the problem of defining confirmation, and our work upon this has left us with the residual problem of distinguishing between confirmable and non-confirmable hypotheses. One might say roughly that the first question was "Why does a positive instance of a hypothesis give any grounds for predicting further instances?"; that the newer question was "What is a positive instance of a hypothesis?"; and that the crucial remaining question is "What hypotheses are confirmed by their positive instances?"

The vast amount of effort expended on the problem of induction in modern times has thus altered our afflictions but hardly relieved them. The original difficulty about induction arose from the recognition that anything may follow upon anything. Then, in attempting to define confirmation in terms of the converse of the consequence relation, we found ourselves with the distressingly similar difficulty that our definition would make any statement confirm any other. And now, after modifying our definition drastically, we still get the old devastating result that any statement will confirm any statement. Until we find a way of exercising some control over the hypotheses to be admitted, our definition makes no distinction whatsoever between valid and invalid inductive inferences.

The real inadequacy of Hume's account lay not in his descriptive approach but in the imprecision of his description. Regularities in experience, according to him, give rise to habits of expectation; and thus it is predictions conforming to past regularities that are normal or valid. But Hume overlooks the fact that some regularities do and some do not establish such habits; that predictions based on some regularities are valid while predictions based on other regularities are not. Every word you have heard me say has occurred prior to the final sentence of this lecture; but that does not, I hope, create any expectation that every word you will hear me say will be prior to that sentence. Again, consider our case of emeralds. All those examined before time *t* are green; and this leads us to expect, and confirms the prediction, that the next one will be green. But also, all those examined are grue; and this does not lead us to expect, and does not confirm the prediction, that the next one will be grue. Regularity in greenness confirms the prediction of further cases; regularity in grueness does not. To say that valid predictions are those based on past regularities, without being able to say *which* regularities, is thus quite pointless. Regularities are where you find them, and you can find them anywhere. As we have seen, Hume's failure to recognize and deal with this problem has been shared even by his most recent successors.

As a result, what we have in current confirmation theory is a definition that is adequate for certain cases that so far can be described only as those for which it is adequate. The theory works where it works. A hypothesis is confirmed by statements related to it in the prescribed way provided it is so confirmed. This is a good deal like having a theory that tells us that the area of a plane figure is one-half the base times the altitude, without telling us for what figures this holds. We must somehow find a way of distinguishing lawlike hypotheses, to which our definition of confirmation applies, from accidental hypotheses, to which it does not.

Today I have been speaking solely of the problem of induction, but what has been said applies equally to the more general problem of projection. As pointed out earlier, the problem of prediction from past to future cases is but a narrower version of the problem of projecting from any set of cases to others. We saw that a whole cluster of troublesome problems concerning dispositions and possibility can be reduced to this problem of projection. That is why the new riddle of induction, which is more broadly the problem of distinguishing between projectible and non-projectible hypotheses, is as important as it is exasperating.

Our failures teach us, I think, that lawlike or projectible hypotheses cannot be distinguished on any merely syntactical grounds or even on the ground that these hypotheses are somehow purely general in meaning. Our only hope lies in re-examining the problem once more and looking for some new approach. This will be my course in the final lecture.

Notes

1 Although this remark is merely an aside, perhaps I should explain for the sake of some unusually sheltered reader that the notion of a necessary connection of ideas, or of an absolutely analytic statement, is no longer sacrosanct. Some, like Quine and White, have forthrightly attacked the notion; others, like myself, have simply discarded it; and still others have begun to feel acutely uncomfortable about it.

2 A hasty reader might suppose that my insistence here upon identifying the problem of justification with a problem of description is out of keeping with my parenthetical insistence in the preceding lecture that the goal of philosophy is something quite different from the mere description of ordinary or scientific procedure. Let me repeat that the point urged there was that the organization of the explanatory account need not reflect the manner or order in which predicates are adopted in practice. It surely must describe practice, however, in the sense that the extensions of predicates as explicated must conform in certain ways to the extensions of the same predicates as applied in practice. Hume's account is a description in just this sense. For it is an attempt to set forth the circumstances under which those inductive judgments are made that are normally accepted as valid; and to do that is to state necessary and sufficient conditions for, and thus to define, valid induction. What I am maintaining above is that the problem of justifying induction is not something over and above the problem of describing or defining valid induction.

3 For a fuller discussion of definition in general see Chapter I of Nelson Goodman, *The Structure of Appearance* (Indianapolis, Ind.: Bobbs-Merrill, 1966).

4 The basic article is 'A Purely Syntactical Definition of Confirmation', *Journal of Symbolic Logic* 8 (1943): 122–43. A much less technical account is given in 'Studies in the Logic of Confirmation', *Mind* 54 (1945), pp. 1–26 and 97–121. Later work by Hempel and others on defining *degree* of confirmation does not concern us here.

5 I am not here asserting that this is an indispensable requirement upon a definition of confirmation. Since our commonsense assumptions taken in combination quickly lead us to absurd conclusions, some of these assumptions have to be dropped; and different theorists may make different decisions about which to drop and which to preserve. Hempel gives up the converse consequence condition, while Carnap (*Logical Foundations of Probability*, Chicago: University of Chicago Press, 1962, pp. 474–6) drops both the consequence condition and the converse consequence condition. Such differences of detail between different treatments of confirmation do not affect the central points I am making in this lecture.

6 Any hypothesis is 'supported' by its own positive instances; but support—or better, direct factual support—is only one factor in confirmation. This factor has been separately studied by John G. Kemeny and Paul Oppenheim in 'Degree of Factual Support', *Philosophy of Science*, vol. 19 (1952), pp. 307–24. As will appear presently, my concern in these lectures is primarily with certain other important factors in confirmation, some of them quite generally neglected.

7 An able and thorough exposition of this paragraph is given by Israel Scheffler in his *Anatomy of Inquiry* (New York: Alfred A. Knopf, 1963), pp. 286–91.

8 The status of the conjunction condition is much like that of the consequence condition—see note 5. Although Carnap drops the conjunction condition also (p. 394), he adopts for different reasons the requirement we find needed above: that the total available evidence must always be taken into account (pp. 211–13).

9 Although the example used is different, the argument to follow is substantially the same as that set forth in my note 'A Query on Confirmation', *Journal of Philosophy* 43 (1946): 383–5.

10 For instance, we shall have equal confirmation, by our present definition, for the prediction that roses subsequently examined will be blue. Let "emerose" apply just to emeralds examined before time *t*, and to roses examined later. Then all emeroses so far examined are grue, and this confirms the hypothesis that all emeroses are grue and hence the prediction that roses subsequently examined will be blue. The problem raised by such antecedents has been little noticed, but is no easier to meet than that raised by similarly perverse consequents.

11 Carnap took this course in his paper 'On the Application of Inductive Logic', *Philosophy and Phenomenological Research* 8 (1947), pp. 133–47, which is in part a reply to my 'A Query on Confirmation'. The discussion was continued in my note 'On Infirmities of Confirmation Theory', *Philosophy and Phenomenological Research* 8 (1947), pp. 149–51; and in Carnap's 'Reply to Nelson Goodman', same journal, same volume, pp. 461–2.

QUESTIONS

1 What is the "old problem" of induction?
2 According to Goodman, how can one show that a rule of inference is justified?
3 What is the "new problem" of induction?
4 Define "x is grue."
5 According to Goodman, is the sentence "All emeralds are grue" projectible? What about the sentence "All emeralds are green"?

John Foster, "Induction, Explanation and Natural Necessity"

I want to examine a possible solution to the problem of induction—one which, as far as I know, has not been discussed elsewhere. The solution makes crucial use of the notion of objective natural necessity. For the purposes of this discussion, I shall assume that this notion is coherent. I am aware that this assumption is controversial, but I do not have space to examine the issue here.

I

Ayer is one philosopher who denies that the notion is coherent. But he also claims that even if it were, it would not help in meeting the problem of induction. "If on the basis of the fact that all the A's hitherto observed have been B's we are seeking for an assurance that the next A we come upon will be a B, the knowledge, if we could have it, that all A's are B's would be quite sufficient; to strengthen the premise by saying that they not only are but must be B's adds nothing to the validity of the inference. The only way in which this move could be helpful would be if it were somehow easier to discover that all A's must be B's than that they merely were so."[1] And this, Ayer thinks, is clearly impossible. "It must be easier to discover, or at least find some good reason for believing, that such and such an association of properties always does obtain, than that it must obtain; for it requires less for the evidence to establish."[2]

Despite its initial plausibility, Ayer's reasoning is fallacious. The first point to notice is that there is a form of empirical inference which is rational, but not inductive in the relevant sense. In the relevant sense, we make an inductive inference when, from our knowledge that all the examined *A*s are *B*s, we infer that all *A*s are *B*s or that some particular unexamined *A* is *B*. In such cases the inductive inference is just an extrapolation from the evidence—an extension to all or some of the unexamined cases of what we have found to hold for the examined cases. Not all rational empirical inferences are of this kind. Thus consider the way in which chemists have established that water is H_2O. No doubt there is a step of extrapolative induction, from the chemical composition of the samples examined to the composition of water in general.[3] But this is not the only step of inference. For the composition of the samples is not directly observed: it is detected by

John Foster, "Induction, Explanation and Natural Necessity," *Proceedings of the Aristotelian Society* 83 (1982–83): 87–101.

inference from how the samples respond to certain tests. The rationale for such inference is the explanatory power of the conclusion it yields. The conclusion is accepted because it best explains the experimental findings—at least it does so in the framework of a more comprehensive chemical theory which is itself accepted largely on explanatory grounds. Thus the conclusion is reached not by extrapolation, but by an inference to the best explanation.

Now look again at Ayer's argument. Ayer is assuming that since "All *A*s must be *B*s" makes a stronger claim than "All *A*s are *B*s," it is no good, in the face of the sceptic's challenge, trying to justify an acceptance of the second via an inference to the first. Now if extrapolative induction is the only form of inference available, Ayer is clearly right. An extrapolation to the stronger conclusion (which associates *A* and *B* across all nomologically possible worlds) already includes an extrapolation to the weaker (which associates *A* and *B* in the actual world) and hence cannot serve to mediate it: any sceptical objection to the smaller extrapolation is automatically an objection to the larger. But suppose we could reach the stronger conclusion by an inference to the best explanation. This would allow an inference to the stronger conclusion to be what justifies an acceptance of the weaker. For it might be precisely because the stronger conclusion is stronger that it has the explanatory power required to make it worthy of acceptance, and thus precisely because we are justified in accepting the stronger conclusion on explanatory grounds that we are justified in accepting the weaker conclusion it entails. This is the possibility which Ayer has missed and which I want to examine in the subsequent sections.

II

Let us focus on a particular case. Hitherto (or so I shall assume), as far as our observations reveal, bodies have always behaved gravitationally—and here I use 'gravitational behaviour' to cover all the various kinds of behaviour, such as stones falling and planets following elliptical orbits, which are normally taken as manifestations of gravitational force. On this basis we are confident that bodies will continue to behave gravitationally in future. But is such confidence well-founded? Does the past regularity afford rational grounds for expecting its future continuation? Here is what strikes me as a natural response. The past consistency of gravitational behaviour calls for some explanation. For given the infinite variety of ways in which bodies might have behaved non-gravitationally and, more importantly, the innumerable occasions on which some form of non-gravitational behaviour might have occurred and been detected, the consistency would be an astonishing coincidence if it were merely accidental—so astonishing as to make the accident-hypothesis quite literally incredible. But if the past consistency calls for some explanation, what is that explanation to be? Surely it must be that gravitational behaviour is the product of natural necessity: bodies have hitherto always behaved gravitationally because it is a law of nature that bodies behave in that way. But if we are justified in postulating a law of gravity to explain the past consistency, then we are justified, to at least the same degree, in expecting gravitational behaviour in future. For the claim that bodies have to behave gravitationally entails the weaker claim that they always do. Consequently, our confidence that bodies will continue to behave in this way is well-founded. The past regularity does indeed, by means of an explanatory inference, afford rational grounds for expecting its future continuation.

This is just one case. But it illustrates what is arguably a quite general solution to the problem of induction—a solution which is summarized by the following three claims:

(1) The only primitive rational form of empirical inference is inference to the best explanation.
(2) When rational, an extrapolative inference can be justified by being recast as the product of two further steps of inference, neither of which is, as such, extrapolative. The first step is an inference to the best explanation—an explanation of the past regularity whose extrapolation is at issue. The second is a deduction from this explanation that the regularity will continue or that it will do so subject to the continued obtaining of certain conditions.
(3) A crucial part of the inferred explanation, and sometimes the whole of it, is the postulation of certain laws of nature—laws which are not mere generalizations of fact, but forms of (objective) natural necessity.

How this solution works out in detail will, of course, vary from case to case. Sometimes the nomological postulates will form the whole explanation (when the past regularity is a consequence of the laws alone) and sometimes only part (when the past regularity is only a consequence of the laws together with the obtaining of certain specific conditions). Sometimes the predictive conclusion deduced from the explanation will be categorical ("the regularity will continue") and sometimes hypothetical ("the regularity will continue if such and such conditions continue to obtain"). And most importantly, in any particular case, our choice of the *best* explanation will depend to a large extent on what other explanatory theories we have already established or have good reason to accept.

To gain a better understanding of the proposed solution—let us call it the *nomological-explanatory solution* (NES)—three points must now be noted.

(i) Some philosophers hold, contrary to claim (1), that extrapolative induction is a primitive form of rational inference (i.e. *inherently* rational) and that consequently any attempt to justify it by its reduction to other forms of inference is misconceived. I cannot accept this view. Suppose (perhaps *per impossible*) we knew that there were no laws or other kinds of objective constraint governing the motions of bodies and thus had to interpret the past consistency of gravitational behaviour as purely accidental. Such knowledge is logically compatible with the belief that the regularity will continue. But clearly we would have no grounds for thinking that it will. For in knowing that there were no constraints, we would know that on any future occasion any form of behaviour was as objectively likely as any other, and this would deprive the past consistency of any predictive value. This result is in line with NES, since the envisaged knowledge explicitly blocks the explanatory inference: if we know there are no laws, we cannot offer a nomological explanation of the past regularity. But how can the result be explained by those who hold induction to be inherently rational? Why should the envisaged knowledge undermine the extrapolative inference unless the rationality of that inference depends on some further inference with whose conclusion the knowledge logically conflicts? I can see no answer to this.

(ii) As indicated in (3), the postulated laws are forms of objective natural necessity. This is crucial. If the laws were mere factual generalizations, or such generalizations set in the perspective of some attitude we have towards them,[4] they would not be explanatory in the relevant sense. In particular, their postulation could not be justified by an inference of a non-extrapolative kind. Thus suppose we construed the law of gravity as merely the fact that bodies always behave gravitationally. There is, I suppose, a sense in which the postulation of this 'law' might be taken to explain the past consistency of gravitational behaviour—the sense in which to explain a fact is to subsume it under something more general. But it cannot be this sort of explanation which is involved in NES. For if it were, the inference to it would be an ordinary step of extrapolative induction and hence vulnerable to the sceptic's attack. In subsuming the past regularity under a universal regularity we would not be diminishing its coincidental character, but merely extending the scope of the coincidence to cover a larger domain. And it is just this kind of extension which the sceptic calls in question. The reason we can hope to do better with laws of a genuinely necessitational kind is that, arguably, their postulation can be justified by reasoning of a quite different sort. Thus, arguably, we are justified in postulating a law of gravity, as a form of objective natural necessity, because it eliminates what would otherwise be an astonishing coincidence: it enables us to avoid the incredible hypothesis that the past consistency of gravitational behaviour, over such a vast range of bodies, occasions and circumstances, is merely accidental.

(iii) It may be wondered whether past regularities really do call for explanation. Suppose I toss a coin 1000 times, randomizing the method and circumstances of the tossing from occasion to occasion, and each time it comes down heads. Let *H* be the hypothesis that the coin is unbiased, i.e. (in effect) that, for an arbitrary toss, its chances of heads and tails are equal. On the supposition of *H*, the antecedent probability of the run of heads was astronomically small: $(\frac{1}{2})^{1000}$. But while astronomically small, it was no less than the antecedent probability of any other of the possible sequences of outcomes: for 1000 tosses, there are 2^{1000} possible sequences and on the hypothesis of no bias each has the same probability. This may lead us to suppose that the occurrence of the run does not count as evidence against *H* and hence does not call for any explanation. For it seems that on the supposition of *H* we should be no more surprised at the run of heads than at any other sequence which might have occurred. In the same way we may be led to suppose that the past consistency of gravitational behaviour calls for no explanation—that on the supposition of no laws or constraints this consistency should seem, in retrospect, no more astonishing than any other determinate sequence of behavioural outcomes.

However, this reasoning is fallacious. Suppose I selected the coin at random from a bag of coins, knowing that half are unbiased and half are very strongly biased in favour of heads. Prior to the series of tosses, I could assign equal epistemic probabilities to *H* and to the alternative hypothesis (*H′*) that the coin is heads-biased. If the reasoning above were sound, the subsequent run would not alter these probabilities: that is, even after the run I should have no more reason to accept *H′* than *H*, since on the supposition of *H* the antecedent probability of the run was no smaller than that of any other possible sequence. But this is clearly wrong. Obviously I have very strong grounds for accepting *H′*. If I were to make a habit of betting on *H′* in such circumstances, I could expect to win almost every time. For what matter here are not the relative antecedent probabilities of alternative sequences on the supposition of *H*, but the relative antecedent probabilities of the run on the alternative hypotheses. What makes *H′* overwhelmingly more credible given the evidence of the run is that, antecedently, the run was overwhelmingly more probable on the supposition of *H′* than of *H*. Another relevant factor, of course, are the relative epistemic probabilities of *H* and *H′* prior to the evidence of the run. Had we set the initial probability of *H* higher than *H′*, this would have reduced the strength of the subsequent grounds for accepting *H′* on the evidence. But to make any practical difference, we would have had to set the initial probability of *H′* astronomically low, simply because of the extreme difference in the antecedent probabilities of the run on the two hypotheses.

Let us now apply these considerations to the gravitational case. One hypothesis (H_1) is that, in the respects which concern us, the behaviour of bodies is not subject to any laws or constraints, so that any consistent pursuit of gravitational behaviour would be purely accidental. What makes the past consistency count so strongly against H_1 is not just that its antecedent probability would be astronomically small on the supposition of H_1 (for this would be true of each possible sequence of behavioural outcomes), but that there are alternative hypotheses on which this probability would be substantially higher and which do not, on the face of it, have a sufficiently lower initial probability to balance this difference. In particular, there is the hypothesis (H_2) that it is a law of nature that bodies behave gravitationally. On this hypothesis, which has been proposed as the best explanation of the consistency, the consistency would be antecedently inevitable. As far as I can see, the only way in which one could rationally retain H_1 in the face of the evidence would be by maintaining that the very notion of natural necessity is incoherent. This is an arguable position (though I think it is mistaken), but, as I said at the outset, I am discounting it for the purposes of the present discussion.

III

NES is beginning to look very plausible. However, there are two major objections to it—in effect, two versions of a single objection. I shall consider one in this section and the other in the next.

The past consistency of gravitational behaviour would indeed be an astonishing coincidence if it were merely accidental. Let us agree, then, that we are justified in taking it to be the product of natural necessity: bodies have always behaved gravitationally, within the scope of our observations, because they had to. But why should we suppose that this natural necessity holds constant over *all* bodies, *all* places and *all* times? Why should we suppose that there is a *universal* law of gravity rather than one which, while covering our data, is restricted in scope to some particular set of bodies or some particular portion of the space–time continuum? For example, with *t* as the present moment, consider the following three nomological hypotheses:

(A) It is a law *for all times* that (alternatively,[5] it is a law that *at all times*) bodies behave gravitationally.

(B) It is a law *for all times before t* that (alternatively,[5] it is a law that *at all times before t*) bodies behave gravitationally.
(C) (B) and there is no more comprehensive gravitational law.

To justify our belief that bodies will continue to behave gravitationally in future, we have to justify an acceptance of (A) in preference to (C). But how can this be done by an explanatory inference? For both (A) and (C), by including (B), account for the gravitational regularity so far. It seems that to justify an acceptance of (A) we have to fall back on extrapolative induction, arguing that because gravitational behaviour has been necessary hitherto, it is likely to be necessary in future. But if so, we have not answered the sceptical problem. Nor, indeed, do we seem to have made any progress at all. For if we have to resort to induction at this point, we might just as well apply it directly to the past regularity without bringing in nomological explanation at all.

Is this objection decisive? Well it is certainly true that (B), and hence both (A) and (C), offer explanations, in the relevant sense, of the past regularity. But this alone is not enough to sustain the objection. What the objector must show is that, as explanations, (C) is not inferior to (A); or put another way, that (B) is not inferior to (A) as a terminus of explanation. And it is on this point, I think, that the defender of NES has a reasonable case. For it seems to me that a law whose scope is restricted to some particular period is more mysterious, inherently more puzzling, than one which is temporally universal. Thus if someone were to propose (C), our response would be to ask why the fundamental law should be time-discriminatory in that way. Why should *t* have this unique significance in the structure of the universe that bodies are gravitationally constrained in the period up to *t* but not thereafter? Barring the postulation of a malicious demon, these questions are unanswerable: any answer we could receive would only serve to show that the fundamental laws were not as suggested—that there was a deeper explanation in terms of time-impartial laws and a difference, relevant to the operation of these laws, in the conditions which obtain in the two periods. It is because these questions seem pertinent and yet are *ex hypothesi* unanswerable that we are left feeling that, as hypothesized, nature is inherently puzzling and precludes an explanation of our empirical data which is both correct and, from the standpoint of our rational concerns, fully satisfactory. And it is for this reason that, presented with the data (the past gravitational consistency) and the alternatives (A) and (C), we are justified in preferring (A). We are justified in preferring (A) because it is the *better* explanation, and it is the better explanation because, unlike (C), it dispels one mystery without creating another: it dispels the mystery of past regularity without creating the mystery of capricious necessity. For the same reason we are justified in preferring (A) to other hypotheses of a similar kind to (C) such as those which restrict the scope of the gravitational law to some particular set of bodies or some particular region of space.

The objector might reply that I am guilty of double standards. I am claiming that in the case of behaviour we should avoid unexplained regularity, while in the case of necessity we should avoid unexplained caprice. What I hold to be problematic is, in the one case, a behavioural uniformity not explained by laws and, in the other, a variation in behavioural constraints not explained by a difference in the relevant conditions. But why should our expectations for behaviour and necessity be so strikingly different? If there is no problem in expecting irregular behaviour when there are no laws to forbid it, why should there be a problem in building a measure of irregularity into the laws themselves? Conversely, if it is reasonable to expect the laws to be uniform over bodies, space and time, given no positive evidence against it, why should it not also be reasonable to expect uniformities of behaviour without the backing of laws? It seems that I am relying on opposite standards of rationality in the two cases.

Well in a sense I am. But that is just because the cases are quite different. What makes them quite different is that, unlike the concept of behaviour, the concept of necessity has some notion of generality built into it. Thus try to imagine a world in which there are no conspicuous uniformities, but in which for each object *x* and time *y* there is a separate law prescribing how *x* is to behave at *y*. In such a world everything that happens has to happen, by natural necessity, but there is no uniform system of necessity, or anything remotely resembling one, which imposes the same constraints on situations of the same kind. Each law is concerned with the behaviour of a unique object at a unique time. Now it seems to me that such a world is not possible, not because we cannot conceive of such randomness in behaviour, but because we cannot conceive of such singularity in the scope of the laws. And this is not just a trivial point about the meaning of the word "law"—a point which we could avoid by choosing another term. Rather, we cannot make sense of the claim that it is naturally necessary for a particular object to behave in a certain way at a particular time except as a claim which is implicitly more general, concerning how it is naturally necessary for objects of a certain type to behave in situations of a certain kind. This is not to say that we cannot conceive of laws (i.e. natural necessities) which are to some degree restricted by some singular reference. We can, I think, conceive of the law postulated by (C), whose scope is restricted to a certain period. But this is only because the restriction leaves room for enough generality of scope for the notion of law to gain purchase. In itself a singular restriction is something which runs counter to the direction of nomological explanation. This is why we serve the purposes of explanation better, if there is a need for explanation at all, by postulating laws without such restrictions, if we can do so compatibly with our data. And in particular, this is why, given the past consistency of gravitational behaviour, we rightly regard (A) as a more satisfactory explanation than (C) or any other explanation of a similarly restricted kind, whether the restriction is to a period, to a region or to a sample of bodies. None of these considerations which apply to our concept of natural necessity carry over to our concept of behaviour. There is no implicit notion of generality in our concept of an object's behaving in a certain way at a certain time. Indeed, our rational expectation is that without the backing of laws the total pattern of behaviour will be more or less random, not because there is anything to ensure this, but because there is nothing to ensure regularity and because, if it is left to chance, the probability of any significant regularity is exceedingly small. In short, there is something *a priori* perplexing about an arbitrary restriction in the laws and something *a priori* surprising about a coincidental regularity in behaviour.

IV

We must now consider the second major objection to NES. Here again I shall continue to focus on the case of gravity.

Let us agree that the past consistency of gravitational behaviour calls for nomological explanation and that, since there is no special reason to impose a singular restriction, this explanation should be in terms of laws which are universal in scope. Even so the sceptic has ample room for manoeuvre. All he needs is some general description "φ," not involving, explicitly or implicitly, any singular reference, such that "φ" applies to the circumstances of the past regularity but not, as far as we know, to other circumstances or to those particular circumstances with which we are predictively concerned. He can then claim that the past regularity is adequately explained by the hypothesis:

(D) It is a law that in φ-circumstances bodies behave gravitationally.

This postulates a universal law, covering all bodies, places and times. But it does not entail anything about the behaviour of bodies in non-φ circumstances, i.e. in precisely those circumstances with which, given the evidence of the past regularity, we are predictively concerned. The sceptic will argue that because (D) adequately explains the past regularity, then, to the extent that (A) goes beyond (D), we have no grounds for accepting (A)—in other words, that we have no grounds, other than inductive, for preferring (A) to the alternative hypothesis, (E), which conjoins (D) with the denial that there is a more comprehensive gravitational law. Obviously, the same objection could be applied to any case in which NES was invoked to justify an inductive inference.

It is not easy to evaluate this objection. One difficulty is that we need some general but reasonably detailed account of what makes one explanation better than another. Clearly there is at least one factor on the side of the sceptic: if two hypotheses both explain the data and one hypothesis is stronger than the other (i.e. entails but is not entailed by it), then, other things being equal, the weaker hypothesis is to be preferred (thus if other things were equal, (D) would be preferable both to (A) and to (E)). What is far from clear is how we are to determine whether other things are equal. It is easy enough to say something very general and non-committal: e.g. other things are not equal just in case the weaker hypothesis, while explaining the data, postulates some state of affairs which itself calls for further explanation of a kind which the stronger hypothesis supplies, or the conjunction of the weaker hypothesis and the negation of the stronger postulates a state of affairs which is inherently more puzzling than the state of affairs which the stronger hypothesis postulates. But what we need, to evaluate the objection, is a set of more specific principles, justified independently of induction, which will enable us to decide case by case whether a state of affairs does call for explanation or is inherently puzzling. And the formulation of such principles would be a large and difficult task, if it is possible at all. A further difficulty, at least for a defender of NES, is that there is an infinite range of non-equivalent descriptions which could play the role of "φ." To rebut the objection entirely, it would be necessary to divide this range into a finite number of categories, show that the differences within each category were, relative to the present issue, irrelevant and then rebut the objection for each category. This too promises to be a difficult and perhaps impossible task, even if, for each separate description, the objection could be shown to fail.

All I can do here is to examine some of the more obvious cases on their own merits. One such case would be to model (D) and (E) on the cases of (B) and (C) considered earlier. Thus suppose "S" is a state-description of the universe at *t* (i.e. the present moment) and "*Fx*" is defined as "the universe is in state S at time *x*." Then we have as examples of (D) and (E):

(D^1) It is a law that at any time before an F-time bodies behave gravitationally.
(E^1) (D^1) and there is no more comprehensive gravitational law.

For all we know, an F-time will not occur in the future. So explaining the regularity by (D^1) provides no basis for extrapolation. The question is: are there non-inductive grounds for claiming that (A) serves better than (D^1) as a terminus of explanation? And this question becomes: is the state of affairs postulated by (E^1) inherently more puzzling than that postulated by (A)? I think the answer is "Yes," for two reasons. Firstly, in effect (E^1) involves action at a temporal distance. For if (E^1) were true, then (and here I assume, for simplicity, that *t* is the only F-time) each past instance of gravitational behaviour would directly causally depend, in part, on the intrinsic state of the universe at *t*, there being no continuous causal chain mediating this causal dependence and spanning the temporal interval between *t* and time of the behaviour. Secondly, since *t* is subsequent to the past instances of gravitational behaviour, the direction of the causal influence involved would be from later to earlier: the occurrence of gravitational behaviour in the past would be partly the causal result of the state of the universe now. In both these respects, and especially the second, what (E^1) postulates is inherently more puzzling than what (A) postulates, and consequently (A) is a better explanation than (E^1) and better, as a terminus of explanation, than (D^1).

One way for the sceptic to eliminate both these defects would be as follows. Take each occasion *i* of observed gravitational behaviour and form a very detailed description "F^1" of the intrinsic conditions obtaining immediately prior to this behaviour—a description sufficiently detailed to distinguish it, as far as we know, from the conditions which will obtain on any future occasion or on those future occasions with which we are predictively concerned. We then let "φ" be the disjunction of these descriptions, so that "in φ-circumstances" means "either in F^1-circumstances or in F^2-circumstances or . . ." where the disjunctive list exactly covers all the specific conditions in which gravitational behaviour has occurred and been detected so far. Let us call (D) and (E) thus interpreted (D^2) and (E^2). Then (E^2) avoids the two mentioned defects of (E^1). It does not postulate any backwards causation or any direct causation at a temporal distance. If (E^2) were true, each past instance of gravitational behaviour would causally depend solely on the intrinsic conditions obtaining on that occasion.

Are there any other grounds for claiming that (A) is a better explanation than (E^2) and better, as a terminus of explanation, than (D^2)? I think there are. The first point to notice is that, in effect, (D^2) explains the past regularity of gravitational behaviour by providing a separate explanation of each past instance. Because "φ"

does not signify a natural generic property, but rather a disjunctive list of the complex properties separately drawn from the separate instances, it would be less misleading to reformulate (D^2) as a long list of separate hypotheses: "It is a law that in F^1-circumstances bodies behave gravitationally; it is a law that in F^2-circumstances bodies behave gravitationally; . . .". The whole list would provide an explanation of the past consistency only in the sense that each hypothesis provided an *ad hoc* explanation of one behavioural instance. How then should we respond to someone who offers (D^2) as a terminus of explanation, i.e. asserts (E^2)? Well, we are likely to find the state of affairs he postulates inherently puzzling, since the way the laws discriminate between φ and non-φ circumstances is not based on any natural mode of classification: it seems peculiar that just the listed circumstances should be gravitationally efficacious when they are no more similar to each other than they are to other circumstances. Still, it may be hard to establish that the grounds for this puzzlement are non-inductive, and for this reason I would put the stress on a different point. Even though in a sense (D^2) explains the past consistency of gravitational behaviour (by separately explaining each instance), it leaves us with another consistency which calls for explanation and which would be very hard to explain if we accepted (E^2): for although there are infinitely many types of circumstances (all those that are non-φ) to which the (D^2)-law does not apply, whenever we have checked for gravitational behaviour the circumstances have always been of a type (φ) to which the law does apply. This would be an astonishing coincidence if it were purely accidental, and, on the face of it, it would be purely accidental on the supposition of (E^2).[6] No such coincidence arises on the supposition of (A), and for this reason, if no other, (A) is the preferable hypothesis.

These are, of course, only two examples of the way in which the sceptic might pose the objection and the fact that we can rebut them does not mean that he cannot turn to others. But the onus is now on him to produce a convincing case. My guess is that whatever he chooses for "φ," there will be some way of vindicating our preference for (A).

V

It goes without saying that this discussion has been sketchy and inconclusive. I have concentrated throughout on a single example of inductive inference (that concerning gravity) and even with respect to this example I have not had space to deal adequately with the issues raised in the last section. Moreover, I have carried throughout the controversial assumption that we can make sense of the notion of objective natural necessity. What I hope I have shown is that, if we can make sense of this notion, the nomological-explanatory solution is worth considering. I, for one, find it quite plausible.

Notes

1 Ayer, *The Central Questions of Philosophy* (London: Weidenfeld and Nicolson, 1973), pp. 149–50.

2 Ibid. p. 150.

3 I.e. to what *pre-theoretically* qualifies as water.

4 For an attitudinal account, see Ayer, *The Concept of a Person* (New York: St. Martin's Press, 1963), ch. 8.

5 I shall not inquire as to whether these are merely alternative formulations or differ in substance. As far as I can see, if there is a difference in substance, it does not affect my argument.

6 Of course it was not accidental that the sceptic chose to postulate a law which exactly covered the examined cases. But that is beside the point.

QUESTIONS

1. According to Foster, how does a "law" differ from a mere factual generalization?
2. According to Foster, what is the best explanation for the fact that we have always observed bodies to "behave gravitationally"?
3. Consider the hypothesis that it is a law of nature that all bodies behave gravitationally until time *t*, but not thereafter. Why, according to Foster, would this not be a good explanation of our evidence?

Colin Howson and Peter Urbach, *Scientific Reasoning: The Bayesian Approach*

Some logical preliminaries

We shall be employing some, but not many, of the notions of elementary logic—principally just the so-called logical connectives, or truth-functional operations, "and," "or," and "not." We shall use a fairly standard notation here, symbolising "and" by "&", "or" by "**v**", and "not" by "~". Thus *a* & *b* is the conjunction of the sentences *a* and *b*, and it will be taken to be true just when *a* and *b* are both true (we should strictly put "*a* & *b*" in quotation marks, but the text would look awful and where no confusion is likely to arise we shall omit them). "**v**" is inclusive "or", that is, *a* **v** *b* will be false just when *a* and *b* are both false. Every sentence will be taken to be true or false when all its referring terms are assigned a specific reference (this is called the condition of bivalence). ~*a*, of course, will be true just when *a* is false. Occasionally we shall make use of the biconditional "$\leftrightarrow$": $a \leftrightarrow b$ is true just in case *a* and *b* are both true or both false.

We shall use the notation $a \vdash b$ to signify that *a* entails *b* deductively; and to say that *a* entails *b* deductively is simply to say that it is impossible, independently of the state of the world, for *a* to be true and *b* false. $a \vdash a$, $a \vdash {\sim}{\sim} a$, $a \,\&\, b \vdash a$, $a \vdash a$ **v** *b*, are some simple examples of entailment.

The notation *a* <=> *b* will signify that *a* is equivalent to *b*; that is to say, it is impossible, independently of the state of the world, for *a* and *b* to possess different truth values (i.e. *true*, *false*). *a* <=> *a*, *a* <=> ~ ~*a*, *a* & *b* <=> *b* & *a*, *a* **v** *b* <=> *b* **v** *a* are some simple examples of equivalence. It is not difficult to infer that *a* <=> *b* just in case $a \vdash b$ and $b \vdash a$, and that *a* <=> *b* just in case $a \leftrightarrow b$ is a tautology.

A *tautology* is a sentence, like "if it is not the case that it is not raining here now, then it is raining here now", which is true independently of the state of the world, and a *contradiction* is a statement, like "Socrates is a man and it is not the case that Socrates is a man", which is false independently of the state of the world. Both types of statement are easy to generate using the connectives: thus, *a* **v** ~ *a*, ~(*a* & ~ *a*) are examples of tautologies so generated, and it is fairly obvious that once one has a tautology, one can obtain a contradiction (or vice versa) by simply negating it. Moreover, it is also a simple inference from the definitions of tautology and contradiction that any statement deductively entails a tautology and is entailed by a contradiction.

Colin Howson and Peter Urbach, *Scientific Reasoning: The Bayesian Approach* (La Salle, Ill.: Open Court, 1989).

Our notions of entailment and equivalence are stronger than the purely logical ones, as they are to be understood as incorporating all of contemporary mathematics. Thus, for example, if x is any individual, and A and B any two sets, then "$x \in A$ & $x \in B$" will be regarded as deductively entailing "$x \in A \cap B$". $\in$ as usual signifies the membership relation, and $\cap$ the intersection of the two sets A and B, that is to say, the set whose members are common to A and B. The union $A \cup B$ of two sets A and B is the set whose members are in A or in B or in both A and B. The complement $B - A$ of a set A with respect to some set B is the set whose members are the members of B excluding all those which are also members of A. "$A \subseteq B$" signifies that A is a subset of B; that is, every member of A is also a member of B. It follows immediately that every set is a subset of itself. A *singleton* set is a set with one member only. The empty set is, as usual, denoted by the symbol $\varnothing$.

The probability calculus

The axioms

Let us assume that we are given a class S of sentences $a, b, c, \ldots$, which may also contain conjunctions, disjunctions, and negations of any given sentences which it contains. At the extreme, S may be *closed* under these truth-functional operations; that is to say, S may be such that it contains a & b, $a \vee b$, $\sim a$, and $\sim b$, whenever it contains a and b. We shall not assume this to be the case, though we shall assume that S is non-empty, and also that it contains at least one tautology. A probability function on S is a function which assigns non-negative real numbers to the sentences in S, in such a way that every tautology is assigned the value 1, and the sum of the probabilities of two mutually inconsistent sentences is equal to the probability of their disjunction; in other words, the following three conditions, or axioms, are satisfied:

(1) $P(a) \geq 0$ for all a in S
(2) $P(t) = 1$ if t is a tautology
(3) $P(a \vee b) = P(a) + P(b)$ if a and b and $a \vee b$ are all in S, and a and b are mutually inconsistent; i.e., such that one entails the negation of the other.

These three conditions suffice to generate that part of the probability calculus dealing with so-called *absolute*, or *unconditional*, *probabilities*. (3) is often called the *Additivity Principle*, since it states that P adds over disjunctions of pairs of mutually inconsistent statements. As we shall show shortly, (3) together with the other axioms implies that P adds over all finite disjunctions of mutually exclusive statements.

So-called *conditional probabilities* are given as a function $P(\cdot \mid \cdot)$ of two variables, called the conditional probability function based on P, which satisfies the condition

$$(4)\ P(a \mid b) = \frac{P(a \,\&\, b)}{P(b)},$$

where a, b, and $a \& b$ are in S, and where $P(b) \neq 0$. Many authors take $P(a \mid b)$ to be defined by this condition; we prefer to regard (4), however, as a postulate on a par with (1)–(3). (This means that "$P(a \mid b)$" is in effect a primitive of the theory in the same way as $P(a)$.) The reason for this is that in some interpretations of the calculus, independent meanings are given conditional and unconditional probabilities, and equation (4) becomes a synthetic, not an analytic, truth.

In what follows, any result involving $P(a \mid b)$, for any a, b, will be taken to have satisfied the conditions stated in (4), that $P(b) > 0$, and that the statements b and $a \& b$ are in S. . . .

Two different interpretations of the probability calculus

We have presented the fundamental principles of the probability calculus in a rather unmotivated and abstract way because, as has been remarked since the beginning of the nineteenth century, there are at least two quite distinct notions of probability, both of which appear to satisfy the formal conditions 1–4 above. According to one of these, the probability calculus expresses the fundamental laws regulating the assignment of objective physical probabilities to events defined in the outcome spaces of stochastic experiments (a classical example of a stochastic trial, and, because of its simplicity, one we shall make much use of subsequently, is that of tossing a coin and noting which face falls uppermost).

The other notion of probability is epistemic. This type of probability is, to use Laplace's famous words, "relative in part to [our] ignorance, in part to [our] knowledge"[1]: it expresses numerically degrees of uncertainty in the light of data. We shall be discussing these two notions in considerable detail in the following chapters; we mention them here not only because they involve distinct interpretations of the probability-values themselves, but also because the statements to which they assign probabilities are of quite distinct types. In the latter, epistemic, interpretation, the statements to which the probabilities are assigned are specific hypotheses, like "the Labour Party will not win the next General Election in the UK". As we shall see, however, there is more than one epistemic interpretation, an ostensibly person-independent one, and a frankly subjective one.

There is also more than one objectivist interpretation of the probability function, and in at least one of these, the statements describe *generic* events which can arise as possible outcomes of a stochastic trial or experiment. But here we are faced with an apparent difficulty: "the coin lands heads" is true or false relative to specific tosses of specific coins. How can a sentence describe the generic event of landing heads? The answer is, in brief, that it does so by leaving the referents of the appropriate singular terms in the sentence unspecified within the type, or class, from which they come. In a natural language such as English, we are not accustomed to the notion of a syntactically well-formed but partially uninterpreted sentence. Within the notation of formal logic, however, the notion is easily characterised. Thus, $B(a)$, where a is an individual name, or constant, and B a predicate symbol, describes a *specific* individual event when a and B are both fixed (a might, for example, be made to refer to the next toss of this coin, and B be the predicate, *lands heads*). The same formal sentence $B(a)$ will be said to describe the *generic* event of this coin's landing heads, when a is not specified as any one of the tosses of this coin, but B remains fixed as the predicate *lands heads*, referred to the class of tosses of this coin. It might seem more appropriate to employ a free-variable formula $B(x)$ to refer to the generic event, and some authors do. Nothing is wrong with this in principle, but choosing that expression would deny us the use of ordinary vernacular sentences, where there is no syntactical distinction between terms which have definite as opposed to indefinite reference. As probabilities are characteristically assigned to vernacular sentences and not to the formulas of formal languages, we shall accordingly use one and the same sentence for both specific and generic reference, distinguishing those uses by appropriate contextual stipulation.

The reader should note that even a sentence like "This coin lands heads on the *i*th toss" is as ambiguous between specific and generic reference as "this coin lands heads". The term "the *i*th toss" refers implicitly to a finite or infinite sequence of tosses of this coin, but again, we may choose to make that reference generic or specific. The motive, speaking for objective-probability theorists of a certain stripe, for attaching probabilities to generic events, or rather to the sentences characterising those generic events, is, as we shall see in Chapter 9, that the associated probability numbers are not intended to describe features of the outcome of any particular performance of the experiment, but, on the contrary, to express the frequency with which the event in question occurs in long sequences of performances of that experiment. But some people have also tried to construct theories of objective probability in which these probabilities are attached to predictions about the outcome of a specific performance of some stochastic trial. We shall defer all discussion of these attempts to the appropriate chapter, however, and proceed now to derive the familiar "laws" of the probability calculus from the axioms 1–4.

Useful theorems of the calculus

. . . The first result states the well-known fact that the probability of a sentence and that of its negation sum to 1:

(5) $P(\sim a) = 1 - P(a)$

Proof.

$a \vdash \sim\sim a$. Hence by (3) $P(a \vee \sim a) = P(a) + P(\sim a)$. But by (2) $P(a \vee \sim a) = 1$, whence (5).

Next, it is simple to show that contradictions have zero probability:

(6) $P(f) = 0$, where f is any contradiction.

Proof.

$\sim f$ is a tautology. Hence $P(\sim f) = 1$ and by (5) $P(f) = 0$.

Our next result states that equivalent sentences have the same probability:

(7) If $a <=> b$ then $P(a) = P(b)$.

Proof.

First, note that $a \vee \sim b$ is a tautology if $a <=> b$. Assume that $a <=> b$. Then $P(a \vee \sim b) = 1$. Also if $a <=> b$, then $a \vdash \sim\sim b$; so $P(a \vee \sim b) = P(a) + P(\sim b)$. But by (5) $P(\sim b) = 1 - P(b)$, whence $P(a) = P(b)$.

We can now prove the important property of probability functions that they respect the entailment relation; to be precise, the probability of any consequence of a is at least as great as that of a itself:

(8) If $a \vdash b$ then $P(a) \geq P(b)$.

Proof.

If $a \vdash b$ then $[a \vee (b \,\&\, \sim a)] <=> b$. Hence by (7). $P(b) = P(a \vee (b \,\&\, \sim a))$. But $a \vdash \sim(b \,\&\, \sim a)$ and so $P(a \vee (b \,\&\, \sim a)) = P(a) + P(b \,\&\, \sim a)$. Hence $P(b) = P(a) + P(b \,\&\, \sim a)$. But by (1) $P(b \,\&\, \sim a) \geq 0$, and so $P(a) \leq P(b)$.

From (8) it follows that probabilities are numbers between 0 and 1 inclusive:

(9) $0 \leq P(a) \leq 1$, for all a in S.

Proof.

$f \vdash a \vdash t$, where f is any contradiction and t any tautology. Hence by (6), (2), and (8): $0 \leq P(a) \leq 1$.

We shall now demonstrate the general (finite) additivity condition:

(10) Suppose $a_i \vdash \sim a_j$, where $1 \leq i < j \leq n$. Then $P(a_1 \vee \ldots \vee a_n) = P(a_1) + \ldots + P(a_n)$.

Proof.

$P(a_1 \vee \ldots \vee a_n) = P((a_1) \vee \ldots \vee a_{n-1}) \vee a_n)$, assuming that $n > 1$; if not the result is obviously trivial. But since $a_i \vdash \sim a_j$, for all $i \neq j$, it follows that $(a_1 \vee \ldots \vee a_{n-1}) \vdash \sim a_n$, and hence $P(a_1 \vee \ldots \vee a_n) = P(a_1 \vee \ldots \vee a_{n-1}) + P(a_n)$.

Now simply repeat this for the remaining $a_1, \ldots, a_{n-1}$ and we have (10). (This is essentially a proof by mathematical induction.)

Corollary. If $a_1 \vee \ldots \vee a_n$ is a tautology, and $a_i \vdash \sim a_j$ for $i \neq j$, then $1 = P(a_1) + \ldots + P(a_n)$.

Our next result is often called the "theorem of total probability".

(**11**) If $a_1 \vee \ldots \vee a_n$ is a tautology, and $a_i \vdash {\sim}a_j$ for $i \neq j$, then $P(b) = P(b \,\&\, a_1) + \ldots + P(b \,\&\, a_n)$, for any sentence b.
The proof is left to the reader.

A useful consequence of this is the following:

(**12**) If $a_1 \vee \ldots \vee a_n$ is a tautology and $a_i \vdash {\sim}a_j$ for $i \neq j$, and $P(a_i) > 0$, then for any sentence b, $P(b) = P(b \mid a_1)P(a_1) + \ldots + P(b \mid a_n)\,P(a_n)$.

Proof.

A direct application of (4) to (11).

Corollary. $P(b) = P(b \mid c)P(c) + P(b \mid {\sim}c)\,P({\sim}c)$, for any c.

We shall now develop some of the important properties of the function $P(a \mid b)$. Recall that we are assuming in these derivations that the second argument b of $P(a \mid b)$ has positive probability (though this of course is not in practice always going to be the case).

(**13**) Let b be some fixed sentence, and define the function $Q(a)$ of the one variable sentence a to be $P(a \mid b)$. Then $Q(a)$ satisfies axioms 1–3, that is, it is a probability function.
Now define "a is a tautology modulo b" simply to mean "$b \vdash a$" (for then $b \vdash (t \leftrightarrow a)$, where t is a tautology, so that relative to b, a and t are equivalent), and "a and c are exclusive modulo b" to mean "$b \,\&\, a \vdash {\sim}c$"; then

(**14**) $Q(a) = 1$ if a is a tautology modulo b; and the corollary

(**15**) $Q(b) = 1$;

(**16**) $Q(a \vee c) = Q(a) + Q(c)$, if a and c are exclusive modulo b.
The proofs of (13)–(16) are very straightforward and are left for the reader.

We are now in a position to state the results which variously go under the name Bayes's Theorem. This theorem, or rather these theorems, are named after the eighteenth century English clergyman Thomas Bayes. Although Bayes, in a posthumously published and justly celebrated Memoir to the Royal Society of London (1763), derived the first form of the theorem named after him, the second is due to the great French mathematician Laplace.

Bayes's Theorem (first form)

(**17**) $P(a \mid b) = \dfrac{P(b \mid a)\,P(a)}{P(b)}$, where $P(a), P(b) > 0$.

Proof.

$$P(a \mid b) = \frac{P(a \,\&\, b)}{P(b)} = \frac{P(b \mid a)\, P(a)}{P(b)}.$$

This result which, as we have seen, is mathematically trivial, is nonetheless of central importance in the context of so-called Bayesian inference; there *a* is usually the hypothesis to be evaluated relative to empirical data *b*, and this form of Bayes's Theorem thus states that the probability of the hypothesis conditional on the data (or the *posterior probability* of the hypothesis) is equal to the probability of the data conditional on the hypothesis (or the *likelihood* of the hypothesis) times the probability (the so-called *prior probability*) of the hypothesis, all divided by the probability of the data.

Bayes's Theorem (second form)

(18) If $P(b_1 \vee \ldots \vee b_n) = 1$ and $b_i \vdash \sim b_j$ for $i \neq j$, and $P(b_i)$, $P(a) > 0$ then

$$P(b_k \mid a) = \frac{P(a \mid b_k)\, P(b_k)}{\sum_{i=1}^{n} P(a \mid b_i)\, P(b_i)}$$

The proof is straightforward, and is left to the reader.

(19) (Corollary) If $b_1 \vee \ldots \vee b_n$ is a tautology, then if $P(b_i) > 0$ and $b_i \vdash \sim b_j$ and $P(a) > 0$, then

$$P(b_k \mid a) = \frac{P(a \mid b_k)\, P(b_k)}{\sum_{i=1}^{n} P(a \mid b_i)\, P(b_i)}$$

. . .

Probabilistic independence

Two sentences h_1 and h_2 are said to be probabilistically independent (relative to some given probability measure *P*) if and only if $P(h_1 \,\&\, h_2) = P(h_1)P(h_2)$. It follows immediately that, where $P(h_1)$ and $P(h_2)$ are both greater than zero, so that the conditional probabilities are defined, $P(h_1 \mid h_2) = P(h_1)$ and $P(h_2 \mid h_1) = P(h_2)$, just in case h_1 and h_2 are probabilistically independent.

Let us consider a simple example, which is also instructive in that it displays an interesting relationship between probabilistic independence and the so-called Classical Definition of probability. A repeatable experiment is determined by the conditions that a given a coin is to be tossed twice and the resulting uppermost faces are to be noted in the sequence in which they occur. Suppose each of the four possible types of outcome—two heads, two tails, a head at the first throw and a tail at the second, a tail at the first throw and a head at the second—has the same probability, which of course must be one quarter. A convenient way of describing these outcomes is in terms of the values taken by two random variables X_1 and X_2, where X_1 is equal to 1 if the first toss yields a head and 0 if it is a tail, and X_2 is equal to 1 if the second toss yields a head and 0 if a tail.

According to the Classical Definition, or as we shall call it, the Classical Theory of Probability, which we look at in the next chapter (and which should not be confused with the Classical Theory of Statistical Inference, which we shall also discuss), the probability of the sentence "$X_1 = 1$" is equal to the ratio of the number of those possible outcomes of the experiment which satisfy that sentence, divided by the total number, namely four, of possible outcomes. Thus, the probability of the sentence "$X_1 = 1$" is equal to $\frac{1}{2}$, as is also, it is easy to check, the probability of each of the four sentences of the form "$X_i = x_i$", $i = 1$ or 2, $x_i = 0$ or 1. By the same Classical criterion, the probability of each of the four sentences "$X_1 = x_1$ & $X_2 = x_2$" is $\frac{1}{4}$. Hence

$$P(X_1 = x_1 \ \& \ X_2 = x_2) = P(X_1 = x_1)P(X_2 = x_2)$$

and consequently the pairs of sentences "$X_1 = x_1$", "$X_2 = x_2$" are probabilistically independent (we have avoided answering, or trying to answer here, the question of what criteria justify the application of the Classical "definition" . . .).

Notes

1 Pierre Simon de Laplace, *Philosophical Essay on Probabilities* (New York: Dover Publications, 1951), p. 6.

QUESTIONS

1 Show how Bayes' Theorem can be derived from the axioms of probability.

2 Based on the axioms of probability, show that the following equation is true:

P(b) = [P(a) × P(b|a)] + [P(~a) × P(b|~a)].

3 When is *a* "probabilistically independent" of *b*?

David Stove, "Another Attempt to Prove that Induction is Justified: The Law of Large Numbers"

The argument to be advanced here . . . is an attempt to prove the falsity of the *minimal* sceptical thesis about induction. In particular it is an attempt to prove that there is at least one inductive inference, thought by non-sceptics to have *high* probability, which really does so.

The basic idea of this attempted proof is an old one, going back at least to Laplace. In order for the version of it which I give in (iii) below to be properly understood, some account of the history of the argument, and especially of its more recent history, is an essential preliminary.

(i)

Suppose I learn that a certain coin is a fair one: that is, that any time it is tossed the probability of its coming up heads is $\frac{1}{2}$. Then I confidently infer that if it is tossed a large number of times, say 3000 times, it will come up heads about half of those times. I do not infer, with anything like the same degree of confidence, that it will come up heads about half the time if it is tossed a small number of times, say four times.

Everyone else, obviously, makes that same inference, and the same non-inference, as I do. Equally obviously, there is nothing special about the value $\frac{1}{2}$. If we learn that a coin is biased in such a way that at each toss with it the probability of heads is $\frac{1}{3}$, we confidently infer that in a large number of tosses the relative frequency of heads will be about $\frac{1}{3}$, and we do not infer with anything like the same confidence anything about the relative frequency of heads in a small number of tosses. Equally obviously, the kind of inference of which I am speaking is not confined to cases of coins, but is made whenever we learn something of the form "The probability of the event E at each trial is x."

In other words we all believe, or at least we all reason in countless cases as though we believe, "the law of large numbers": that if the probability of the event E at each trial is x, then the probability is extremely high that in a large number of trials E will occur with a relative frequency which is close to x. Nor is this a belief which has become universal only recently, or only as a result of scientific discoveries: the opposite is obviously the case.

David Stove, "Another Attempt to Prove that Induction is Justified: The Law of Large Numbers," *The Rationality of Induction* (Oxford: Clarendon Press, 1986).

Here, then, is a kind of inference—"direct inference," to give it its old name—concerning which everyone believes that the difference between a large and a small number of cases or "trials" makes all the difference to how conclusive the inference is. Everyone believes, for example, that

(64) This coin will come up heads about half the time in 3000 tosses,

is highly probable in relation to

(65) The probability of heads at each toss with this coin is $\frac{1}{2}$;

and everyone believes, on the other hand, that, in relation to (65) it is *not* highly probable that

(66) This coin will come up heads about half the time in four tosses.

It is obvious, moreover, that these beliefs are true.

((65) is, of course, a contingent proposition, and in particular, an assessment of factual probability. But in speaking of the probability of (64) or (66) in relation to (65), we were of course speaking of *logical* probability: the probability of a proposition in relation to another. To make it less likely that the two concepts of probability should be confused with each other in what follows, I will sometimes signal the occurrence of the factual concept of probability in the way that Carnap did, thus: "probability$_2$." But it may be worth while to point out in addition that, although various assessments of factual probability are *mentioned* in this book, none is *asserted*; whereas, of course, many assessments of logical probability are asserted here.)

Human nature is so firmly wedded to belief in the law of large numbers, in fact, that we all have an inveterate tendency to go beyond the law, and to believe that a fair coin, if it is tossed a large number of times, is *certain* to come up heads about half the time. This belief has been reproved as a vulgar error by most of the better sort of writers on probability; and so it is. But the error is by no means confined to the vulgar. It was one of the greatest philosophers of the modern period who wrote that "if you suppose a dye to have any biass, however small, to a particular side, this biass, though, perhaps, it may not appear in a few throws, will certainly prevail in a great number. . . ."[1] Again, what is the frequency interpretation of probability$_2$, but this error, proclaimed as a conceptual truth?

Still, even if this exaggeration of it is false, the law of large numbers itself is true. It is also believed, as I have said, *semper et unique*. Proof of it, however, had to wait until the publication in 1714 of Jacques Bernoulli's *Ars Conjectandi*. That this book does contain such a proof is one of the principal things which entitle the theory of probability, in the period from about 1650 to 1850, to the glorious name of the *classical* theory.

It may well be asked, though, where is the glory? Everyone believes the law of large numbers, everyone always has believed it, and the belief is true. What, then, does a proof of it matter? There is merit in this question, because it is only too easy to misunderstand the nature of Bernoulli's achievement.

What Bernoulli proved for the first time was that direct inference has high probability when the number of trials is large; or, we may say, *a fortiori*, what he did was to prove that, where the number of trials is large, direct inference is justified. Now it is easy to let oneself say, instead of that, that in *Ars Conjectandi* direct inference to large numbers was justified for the first time. To say this makes Bernoulli's achievement much more momentous, of course, but it does so at the price of absurdity, since it implies that before 1714 direct inference to large number was not justified! No, what Bernoulli did was to prove for the first time the proposition—the *truth* of which everyone knew before—*that direct inference to large numbers is justified.*

Now it is true that a proof of a proposition which everyone knew before cannot matter *very* much. It can have a certain importance, however, and Bernoulli's proof does, if only for a reason I will now explain.

Direct inference is not the only kind of inference concerning which everyone thinks that the difference between a small and a larger number of cases makes all the difference to the conclusiveness of the inference. Another kind is what I will call "gamblers' inference."

Every one of us, if he learns that

(67) At all of the 20 tosses with this fair coin it has come up heads,

is disposed to have an increased degree of belief in the proposition

(68) It will not come up heads next time;

whereas we are not so disposed by learning that

(69) At the two tosses with this fair coin it has come up heads.

Yet of course (68) is *not* more probable in relation to (67) than it is in relation to (69). Here, then, is a case of a universal belief, or at least a universal tendency to belief, that the difference between a larger and a small number of trials makes an inference more conclusive, but a case in which we are all *mistaken* in so believing or tending to believe.

Now suppose that some influential philosopher had taken it into his head to maintain that we are all mistaken, in the same way, about *direct* inference too: that the difference which large numbers seem to make to the probability of direct inferences is hallucinatory (as it certainly is in the case of gamblers' inference). This philosopher would have been wrong, of course, and everyone would have known he was wrong. But it could not have been proved, before 1714, that he was wrong, whereas after that date, it could be. Here, then, is a reason why a proof of the law of large numbers has at least a certain conditional importance: it is a disproof of silly philosophical scepticism, should that ever arise, about direct inference.

(Has it ever arisen in fact? In particular, was Hume a sceptic about direct inference, as he was about inductive? He certainly should have been, because of his extreme deductivist bias; but there is more direct evidence as well that he was. Section XI of Book I, Part III of the *Treatise* appears to be a discussion of direct inference, or of something very like it, and a sceptical evaluation of the kind of inference there discussed is certainly implied by the first two sentences of section XIII. It is impossible, however, to be sure of this matter. The main reason is that Hume shows scarcely any interest in the *evaluation* of the inferences he is discussing in XI: his interest is absorbed in their psychodynamics. Anyway, if he was a sceptic about direct inference, no one noticed; whereas everyone, of course, noticed his scepticism about inductive inference.)

As well as direct inference and gamblers' inference, there is a third kind of inference concerning which we all think that the difference between large number of trials or cases and a small number makes all the difference to the probability of the inference. This is what used to be called 'inverse inference', that is, direct inference turned round, or what we call inductive inference. Thus everyone believes that the inference to

(70) The probability$_2$ of heads with this coin is about $\frac{1}{2}$ at each toss

from

(71) This coin came up heads in half of 3000 tosses

is justified, and that the inference to (70) from

(72) This coin came up heads in half of two tosses,

is not. That is, just as everyone thinks and always has thought that direct inference to large numbers is justified, and to small numbers not, so everyone thinks and always has thought that induction *from* large numbers is justified, and from small numbers not. These universal beliefs further resemble the corresponding beliefs about direct inference in being obviously true. And to complete the parallel, there is even an inveterate tendency in the inductive case, as there is in the direct, to go beyond the truth: to believe that, for example, if a coin has come up heads half the time in a large number of tosses, then it is *certain* that the coin is an approximately fair one.

Because of these parallels, and because the theory of probability is, as Laplace said, only 'bon sens reduit au calcul', it was natural to expect, after Bernoulli, that what the theory of probability had done for direct inference to large numbers, it could do for inductive inference from large numbers. There were some people indeed, both before and after Laplace, who thought that the law of large numbers itself proved that induction from large numbers is justified, at the same time as it proved that direct inference to large numbers is justified. That is a natural enough belief, especially if the law of large numbers is formulated as saying, for example, that between the relative frequency of an event in a large number of trials, and the probability of the event at each trial, there is most unlikely to be any wide divergence. Others however, of whom Laplace was one, thought that, as inductive inference is the 'inverse' of direct inference, what was required to prove it justified was a proof of an "inverse," as distinct from the "direct," law of large numbers: the proposition that if the relative frequency of an event E in a large number of trials is x, then the probability is extremely high that the probability of E at each trial is close to x. And Laplace in fact advanced what he claimed was a proof of this proposition.[2]

But whereas Bernoulli's argument for the "direct" law has never been seriously challenged, Laplace's argument for an "inverse" law of large numbers met with a very different reception. At first, indeed, it seemed to carry conviction with most readers, and with some it continued to do so for a long time. (You can find strong traces of it as late as 1892, for example in Karl Pearson's *The Grammar of Science*.) But there was always a critical reaction to it as well, and in the longer run it was this reaction which seemed to prevail entirely. By about the middle of the twentieth century Keynes,[3] Kneale,[4] and other weighty authorities, had pronounced Laplace's argument a tissue of absurdity and confusion.

No one ever doubted the existence of God, it has been said, until the Boyle lecturers tried to prove it; and there is deep truth in this old joke. For it is a fact, although the process is evidently not an entirely rational one, that the failure, or what is believed to be the failure, of an attempt to prove a certain proposition, prompts people to wonder whether the proposition is true at all. Accordingly, Laplace being judged to have failed in his attempt to prove that induction from large numbers is justified, some people began to wonder whether induction, even from large numbers, *is* justified. That large numbers make all the difference to the conclusiveness of *direct* inferences, no one, as I have said, (with the possible exception of Hume), has ever doubted. But now the thought was bound to arise, that perhaps *induction* is different. Perhaps the difference that large numbers seem to make to the conclusiveness of inductive inference is simply a universal hallucination, as it is in the case of gamblers' inference.

The Boyle-lecturers' effect (as we might call it) was assisted in this case by another and much more important historical circumstance: the fact that, between the death of Bernoulli and the birth of Laplace, an influential philosopher *had* taken it into his head to maintain, and with all possible emphasis, what I have just mentioned as a dawning suspicion. To maintain, that is, that in inductive inference the superiority which we all ascribe to a large over a small number of cases is entirely imaginary. This was Hume, of course. "Reason is incapable of any such variation," he wrote, as that by which "we draw, from a thousand instances, an inference which we are not able to draw from one instance . . ."[5]

This cloud, the cloud of scepticism about induction, was scarcely bigger than a man's hand in Laplace's time; and in any case Laplace claimed and was at first widely believed (as I have said) to have dispersed it. But it was not dispersed. On the contrary, by the mid-twentieth century the cloud covered the sky. An influential minority of philosophers (Popper and his followers) actually embraced Hume's inductive scepticism;[6] and even the majority who did not were (as I indicated in Chapter II) "half in love with easeful death" in its sceptical form. The suspicion that the value ascribed to large numbers is illusory in the case of induction, just as it is in the case of gamblers' inference, had penetrated almost every mind. And whether or not anything else could "justify induction," one thing which by 1950 every competent philosopher was supposed to know was that at any rate the theory of probability could not.[7] The Laplacean argument, consequently, seemed to be as dead as a doornail.

It was therefore entirely against the run of play when D.C. Williams published

The Ground of Induction in 1947, a book which in essence resurrected the Laplacean idea, and purported to justify induction by means of a certain version of the law of large numbers. (In fact, since Williams denies the need for any 'inversion' of the law of large numbers, his position is even closer to certain *pre*-Laplacean ideas than it is to Laplace himself.) Williams gives two versions of his central argument. The following is a summary of the second and better version.

Consider a certain class of inferences which are not inductive, but are in fact closely related to direct inferences: a class which Williams calls "proportional syllogisms." These are the instances of the schema

(73) $\frac{m}{n}$ths of the F's are G
x is an F
―――――――――
x is G.

Williams thinks that, while many philosophers are sceptical or uncertain about the probability of inductive inferences, no one is sceptical or uncertain about the probability of proportional syllogisms. If you take any instance of (73), everyone knows that the probability of the conclusion in relation to the premisses is $\frac{m}{n}$ for example, that the probability of the inference

(74) 95% of ravens are black
Abe is a raven
―――――――――
Abe is black

is 0.95. The same holds for inferences which are proportional syllogisms in a slightly widened sense, where the major premiss has an *indefinite* quantifier, such as "The great majority . . ." or "At least $\frac{2}{3}$; . . ." Thus everyone knows, for example, that the inference

(75) At least $\frac{2}{3}$ of ravens are black
Abe is a raven
―――――――――
Abe is black

has high, though indefinite, probability (viz., at least $\frac{2}{3}$).

Now, in view of the existence of this fund of common knowledge, it will be sufficient to justify *inductive* inference, Williams thinks, if it can be shown that there exist inductive inferences which have the same high (even if indefinite) degree of probability as for example (75) has.

This can be proved, Williams thinks, with respect to instances of the schema

(76) $\frac{m}{n}$ths of a large sample S of the F's are G
―――――――――
About $\frac{m}{n}$ths of the population of F's are G.

For there is a purely arithmetical law of large numbers, he says, which states that for any finite population F, any attribute G, and any proportion $\frac{m}{n}$ in which G occurs in F, the vast majority of large samples—samples, say, of 3000 or more—must have approximately the same proportion of G's in them as the population F itself does. (Williams sketches the proof of a micro-instance or two of this law.

Perhaps the best way to approach it first is to try the experiment of imagining the opposite: a population of *F*'s in which most of the large samples are very *unlike* the population in the proportion of *G*'s that they contain.)

Suppose, then, that our experience has been such as to furnish us with a large sample *S* of ravens, of which just 95 per cent are black. By the arithmetical law of large numbers, the vast majority of large samples of ravens must nearly match the raven population with respect to the proportion of black ravens that they contain. Hence any large sample of ravens is almost certain to be one of these near-population-matching, or in other words representative, samples. Hence, by the principle of the proportional syllogism, our large-sample *S* is almost certainly a representative sample. Hence the population of ravens very probably contains about 95 per cent of black ones. "This is the logical justification of induction."[8]

The reception of Williams's book was such as could have been predicted from the state of opinion that I have sketched. It was thought to be an ignorant or a perverse attempt to revive an argument justly discredited long before. After attracting considerable attention, all unfavourable, at the time of its publication, the book was virtually forgotten soon afterwards.

I first read *The Ground of Induction* about 1955, and no other philosophical book has ever influenced me so much. It seemed to me the complete answer, not only to the inductive sceptics, but to the majority of philosophers who nowadays, without being sceptics about induction, are afflicted with "modern nervousness" on that subject. Such people, echoing Hume, ask "Why should I believe that the unobserved resembles the observed? True, I have seen many ravens, and 95 per cent of *them* have been black. But why should I believe that the sample with which nature happens to have furnished me is a *representative* sample of the raven population?" To this question Williams, echoing Laplace, replies: "Because it probably *is* a representative sample. It probably is, because most large samples are representative. And most large samples are, because most large samples arithmetically must be, representative ones." This answer seemed to me, in 1955, to be supremely sane, right, and sufficient. In essence, though not in detail, it seems to me to be so now.

Between then and now, however, I completely lost my initial confidence in Williams's book. This was not owing to any of the published criticisms of it; for these, although numerous, and written in many cases by distinguished philosophers, have all along seemed to me to be entirely worthless. But I slowly became conscious of various distinctions, all of them essential to a defensible version of Williams's argument, which are entirely neglected in his book. (The distinction between logical and factual probability, and the distinction between assessments and principles of probability, are two of them.) These were faults of omission, of course, and therefore not incurable. But finally I did find in the central argument of his book a fault of commission, and one which seemed to me incurable and mortal. As this fault was one which is very far from being peculiar to Williams, I will say what it was.

We often express an assessment of factual probability by saying something of this form: "The probability of an *F* being *G* is such-and-such." Here we use the indefinite article "an" or "a," not as a universal quantifier, nor yet as an existential quantifier, but in a way which is—well, a way peculiar to assessments of factual probability! But often, too, we express an assessment of factual probability by using instead a universal quantifier, and ascribing the probability to each of the individual *F*'s: "Any *F* has a probability such-and-such of being *G*." Thus where we might have said, for example, that the probability of an *F* being *G* is 0.9, or is high, or is close to certainty, we often say instead that:

$$(77)\quad \text{Any } F \left\{ \begin{array}{l} \text{has a probability 0.9 of being} \\ \text{has a high probability of being} \\ \text{is very probably a} \\ \text{is almost certainly} \\ \text{is almost certain to be} \end{array} \right\} G.$$

Analogous schemas exist, of course, whatever may be the value ascribed to the probability: "0.2," "low," or whatever.

It is from instances of schemas like (77), I may observe, that what is called the 'propensity-interpretation' of factual probability draws all its sustenance. And such instances, it must be admitted, abound in science, in everyday life, and in writings about probability, including the preceding pages of this section. They are everywhere, and no statements could appear more innocent. But this appearance, like that of so much else that we say about probability, is deceptive.

One instance of the schema (77) is the generalization, with which biologists have made us all familiar, that

(78) Any mutation is almost certain to be harmful.

This, conjoined with

(79) *M* is a mutation,

entails that

(80) *M* is almost certain to be harmful.

Indeed, how could it not? What is "any" in (78), if it is not a universal quantifier? And what is a universal quantifier, if it does not have syllogistic force? But if "any" in (78) does have syllogistic force, then (78), conjoined, as it consistently can be, with what might perfectly well be true,

(81) *M* is a beneficial mutation,

entails that

(82) *M* is beneficial and almost certain to be harmful.

And (82), unfortunately, either makes no sense at all or is necessarily false.

Now the central argument of Williams's book fairly swarms with instances of the schema (77). (For example: ". . . any sizable sample very probably matches its population in any specifiable respect."[9]) And I thought for some time that such statements are actually indispensable to his argument. I therefore thought that I had detected in that argument a fatal defect: that it could not dispense with statements which, conjoined with truths, can generate necessary falsities or nonsense.

I tried to prove this in a paper which I gave (in a departmental seminar) about five years ago. But in the ensuing discussion Mr R.M. Kuhn (then an undergraduate) convinced me that I was mistaken, not as to the philosophy of the matter, but as to the fact: that Williams's argument *could* be so reconstructed as to be free from any instance of the fatal schema (77).

Soon afterwards Mr Kuhn wrote out at my request his version of Williams's argument. This was the immediate predecessor of my version in (iii) below. Kuhn's version still had, in my opinion, a number of defects. All of these, I think, I have removed. Whether I have not, in this process, introduced new defects of my own into the argument—as I have often done before—remains to be seen.

(ii)

As it is usually formulated, the law of large numbers contains (as we have seen) not just one but two occurrences of the word 'probability' or some synonym of it. But it is possible to formulate the law in a way which does not contain any occurrence of any such word, but is purely mathematical. (Perhaps this is why Keynes said that Bernoulli's law "exhibits algebraical rather than logical insight."[10]) It was just such a purely mathematical law of large numbers, as I have said, that Williams invoked in the second version of his central argument.

What corresponds to Williams's law of large numbers in my version of his argument will likewise be a purely mathematical proposition. But my premiss will be far less general than his was, and the amount of "algebraical insight" required of the reader in order to see that it is true will be much less than that which William's argument demanded. Indeed, the mathematics which my argument requires is, in principle, entirely elementary.

But philosophers are very unused to having any mathematics at all made an essential part of a philosophical argument. There is therefore a serious danger that the mathematical part of my argument, despite its being in principle elementary, will present an obstacle to the philosophical reader. The present section is an attempt to circumvent this danger, by allaying in advance any doubts that a philosopher might have about the one mathematical premiss that I do employ.

Consider, then, a population consisting of just one million ravens, and the large samples of ravens which this population contains.

It is not, of course, meant here, by calling a sample "large," that it is large in relation to the size of the population. "Large" is used here in an absolute, though indefinite, sense. For example, it is a sufficient condition of a sample of our population being a large one, that it contain 3000 ravens.

In this population there must be some particular proportion, either 0 or 1 or something between, of black ravens. On the value of this proportion will depend the value of certain other proportions. One of these is, the proportion of 3000-fold samples which do not differ by more than 3 per cent, in the proportion of black ravens they contain, from the proportion of black ravens in the population itself.

Evidently, this proportion will be a maximum, that is, 1, if the proportion of black ravens in the population is 1; in other words, if all ravens in the population are black. It will be a maximum, similarly, if the proportion of black ravens in the population is 0; that is, if none of them is black. For in either of these cases, no large sample (or any sample) can diverge at all, in its proportion of black ravens, from the proportion of black ravens in the population.

This proportion falls below the maximum, of course, as soon as the proportion of black ravens in the population departs from the extreme cases of 1 and 0. If just 99 per cent of the million ravens are black then 'the chance' (to speak loosely) of a 3000-fold sample diverging by more than 3 per cent in its blackness-frequency from 99 per cent is positive, though small. Similarly if just 1 per cent of the population is black. The proportion (to speak accurately), among the 3000-fold samples, of samples which are thus non-divergent or near-matching, though close to 1, is less than 1 in either of these cases. For in either of these cases the materials from which *not*-near-matching samples can be assembled do exist, though they are not abundant.

This proportion falls still further, obviously, as the blackness-frequency in the population departs still further from the extremes of 1 and 0. The number of 3000-fold samples whose blackness-frequency departs by more than 3 per cent from the blackness-frequency of the population will obviously be far greater, if just 75 per cent of the population is black, for example, than it will be if just 99 per cent of the population is black. For the materials from which such divergent samples can be assembled are far more abundant in the former case than in the latter; while of course the total number of 3000-fold samples included in the population is fixed.

It is clear, therefore, that the 'worst case' for a 3000-fold sample of our population being one which is a near-matcher of the blackness-frequency in the population, is the case in which the latter is just 50 per cent. It is just then that "the chance" (as we say) of such a sample departing by more than 3 per cent from the blackness-frequency in the population is at its maximum. Or, to speak accurately, it is just then that the proportion of near-population-matching 3000-fold samples, to all 3000-fold samples, is at its lowest.

All of this is very obvious. What is not obvious, but in fact surprising, is this: that even this worst case is still a very good one. That is, the proportion, among 3000-fold samples, of those which do not diverge by more than 3 per cent in their blackness-frequency from the blackness-frequency in the population, is still very high even when the population-frequency is 50 per cent.

What *is* that proportion in this case?

The number of 3000-fold samples which a population of a million ravens contains is, of course, simply the number of different combinations, each of 3000 individuals, which can be formed from among a million individuals. The number of different combinations of n individuals which can be formed from m individuals is

$$\frac{m!}{n!\,(m-n)!}$$

("$m!$" is short for "factorial m," which in turn means the product of the numbers

m, $m-1$, $m-2$ . . . , $m-(m-1)$.) So the number of 3000-fold samples in a population of a million is

$$\frac{1{,}000{,}000!}{3000!\ 997{,}000!}.$$

This, then, is the denominator of the fraction we are seeking.

The numerator is, the number of 3000-fold samples in our population which do not diverge in blackness-frequency by more than 3 per cent from 50 per cent.

This number will evidently be the sum of: the number of 3000-fold samples which contains exactly 47 per cent black ones (that is, 1410 black ones); the number which contains exactly 48 per cent black ones (that is, 1440 black ones); and so on, up to the number which contains exactly 53 per cent (that is, 1590) black ones; as well as the number of 3000-fold samples which contain some non-integral percentage of black ravens between these limits of 47 and 53 per cent (such as 1414 black ones).

How is each of these numbers to be arrived at? Well, take for example the number of 3000-fold samples which contain exactly 47 per cent black ones. That number must be the product of: the number of different combinations of 1410 individuals that could be drawn from the 500,000 black ravens; and the number of different combinations of 1590 individuals that could be drawn from the 500,000 non-black ones in the population. That is,

$$\frac{500{,}000!}{1410!\ 498590!} \times \frac{500{,}000!}{1590!\ 498410!}.$$

This, then, is the first of the numbers which are to be summed in the numerator of the fraction we are seeking.

It will be evident to the reader that both the denominator of our fraction, and each of the numbers to be summed in its numerator, is a number so enormous that to calculate its value exactly is in practice out of the question, here or in any other context. But methods of closely approximating such values have been known for a long time.

When these methods of approximation are applied, the denominator of the fraction we seek, that is, the number of 3000-fold samples in a population of a million, turns out to be approximately $10^{8867.9}$. The first of the numbers to be summed in the numerator, that is, the number of 3000-fold samples which contain just 47 per cent black ones, turns out to be approximately $10^{8864.2}$. The sum of all the terms to be summed in the numerator, that is, the number of 3000-fold samples containing between 47 and 53 per cent black ones, turns out to be approximately $10^{8867.9\ -\ 0.00087}$.

That is, in a population of a million ravens just 50 per cent of which are black, the proportion of 3000-fold samples which match within 3 per cent the blackness-frequency in the population is:

$$\frac{10^{8867.9\ -\ 0.00087}}{10^{8867.9}}.$$

But this is very high: in fact more than 99 per cent.

This means that even when the blackness-frequency in the population has that value which makes the proportion of near-matchers among 3000-fold samples the lowest it can be, that proportion is still more than 90 per cent. In other words, *whatever the proportion of black ravens may be in a population of a million, at least nine out of ten 3000-fold samples of that population do not diverge from that proportion by more than 3 per cent in the proportion of black ravens they contain.*

This is, for my purposes, the all-important result. And as the reader has seen, nothing more is *in principle* required to reach it than the elementary theory of combinations. It is true that the mathematics required by the methods of approximation are not elementary; but everything else is.

The result which is italicized above also holds if, with the sample size still fixed at 3000, we consider instead a population of two million, or of three million. In fact it holds independently of any increase in the population-size beyond a million.

The same result will obviously hold *a fortiori* if we consider instead samples which are larger than 3000-fold. (For such samples actually improve the "chance" of a match.) Hence, with a population of a million or more, at least nine out of ten 3000-or-more-fold samples will nearly match the blackness-frequency of the population.

Nor does the above result depend on the population being as *small* as one million. It holds, in fact, however small the population is, as long as it is of such size that it does contain ten 3000-fold samples. Suppose, for example, that the population contains only 3020 ravens. Then it remains true that at least nine out of ten 3000-fold samples are near-matching ones, and true *a fortiori* that at least nine out of ten 3000-or-more-fold samples are near-matchers. For in this case, of course, *all* 3000-or-more-fold samples are near-matching ones.

(iii)

Some abbreviations are needed.

"Pop" will be short for: "the population of ravens, each at least 100 cc in volume and no two overlapping, on earth between 10,000 BC and AD 10,000."

By calling a sample of Pop a "*near*-Pop-matcher with respect to the proportion of black ravens it contains", I mean (as in the preceding section) that the proportion of black ravens in that sample does not differ from the proportion of black ravens in Pop by more than 3 per cent. Similarly for "near" in the proposition E below: "near 95 per cent" means "between 92 and 98 per cent."

Certain propositions are abbreviated by capital letters, as follows:

A: *S* is a 3020-fold sample of Pop.
B: At least $\frac{9}{10}$ths of the 3000-or-more-fold samples in Pop are near-Pop-matchers with respect to the proportion of black ravens that they contain.
C: *S* is a near-Pop-matcher with respect to the proportion of black ravens it contains.
D: Just 95 per cent of the ravens in *S* are black.
E: The proportion of black ravens in Pop is near 95 per cent.

(The propositions A–E are all contingent, since each of them entails that Pop contains at least one raven. None of them, of course, is *asserted* in the argument below. They are simply *mentioned* in certain other propositions, principally assessments of logical probability.)

Hereafter I omit the cumbrous phrase, always intended to be understood after "near-Pop-matcher(s)," 'with respect to the proportion of black ravens that they (it) contain(s)."

The inference from the conjunction of A and D to E is an inductive one. It is also an inference which people who are not sceptics about the induction think has high probability: that is, they think that the conclusion has high probability in relation to the premisses. The following version of William's neo-Laplacean argument is, I think, a proof that the non-sceptics are right in thinking so.

(83) For all x, all $\frac{m}{n}$, all $r > 3000$,
P(x is a near-Pop-matcher$|x$ is an r-fold sample of Pop, and at least $\frac{m}{n}$ths of the 3000-or-more-fold samples in Pop are near-Pop-matchers) $\geq \frac{m}{n}$.

(This premiss is what corresponds in my version to Williams's premiss about the probability of proportional syllogisms: which was that P(x is $G|x$ is F, and $\frac{m}{n}$ths of the F's are G) = $\frac{m}{n}$, for all x, all F, all G, all $\frac{m}{n}$. What (83) says is simply this. Take any inference which is an instance of the schema.

(84) At least $\frac{m}{n}$ths of the 3000-fold samples in Pop are near-Pop-matchers
x is an r-fold sample of Pop
―――――――――――――――――――――――――
x is a near-Pop-matcher;

then, if $r > 3000$, this inference has probability $\geq \frac{m}{n}$.)

It follows from (83) that

(85) P(S is a near-Pop-matcher$|S$ is a 3020-fold sample of Pop, and at least $\frac{9}{10}$ of the 3000-or-more-fold samples in Pop are near-Pop-matchers) $\geq$ 0.9.

That is, in virtue of the above abbreviations,

(86) $P(C|A.B) \geq 0.9$

Now,

(87) Necessarily, if Pop is finite, and large enough to contain ten 3000-or-more-fold samples, then at least $\frac{9}{10}$ of the 3000-or-more-fold samples in Pop are near-Pop-matchers.

(This premiss is what corresponds in my version to Williams's mathematical law of large numbers. Since (87) is entirely lacking in generality, it is, of course, no sort of *law*. But the conditional which it says is necessary is, if what was said in the preceding section is true, an arithematical truth.)

(88) Necessarily, Pop is finite.

(The members of Pop, it will be recalled, are by definition confined to a finite region of space-time, and required to be of a specified minimum size, with no overlaps.)

From (87) and (88) it follows that

(89) Necessarily, if Pop is large enough to contain ten 3000-or-more-fold samples, then at least $\frac{9}{10}$ of the 3000-or-more-fold samples in Pop are near-Pop-matchers.

From the abbreviations above, it is obvious that

(90) Necessarily, if *A* then Pop is large enough to contain ten 3000-or-more-fold samples.

From (90) and (89) it follows that

(91) Necessarily, if *A* then at least $\frac{9}{10}$ of the 3000-or-more-fold samples in Pop are near-Pop-matchers.

That is, in virtue of the abbreviations above,

(92) Necessarily, if *A* then *B*.

It is a principle of logical probability, and in any case obvious, that

(93) If necessarily if p then r, $P(q|p.r) = P(q|p)$.

That is, r is irrelevant to q in relation to p, if it is necessarily true that if p then r.

It follows from (93), (92), and (86) that

(94) $P(C|A) \geq 0.9$.

Now,

(95) $P(C|A.D) \geq P(C|A)$.

That is, "Just 95 per cent of the ravens in *S* are black" is not unfavourably relevant (in Keynes's sense) to "*S* is a near-Pop-matcher," in relation to "*S* is a 3020-fold sample of Pop." This is obvious.

(If we let *D′* be short for "Just 50 per cent of the ravens in *S* are black," then *D′* is unfavourably relevant to *C* in relation to *A*. That is, "*S* is a near-Pop-matcher" is less probable, in relation to "*S* is a 3020-fold sample of Pop and just 50 per cent of the ravens in *S* are black," than it is in relation to the first conjunct of that conjunction. Even this unfavourable relevance is slight in amount: for as we have seen, (94) $P(C|A) \geq 0.9$, and, as the consideration of the "worst case" in the preceding section will have suggested to the reader, $P(C|A.D)$ is *also* ≥ 0.9. But in any case the unfavourable relevance of D' is of course entirely consistent with the not unfavourable relevance of D, which is all that my (95) asserts. To admit it is no more than to acknowledge what is obvious, that where one proposition is not unfavourably relevant, a contrary proposition may be. Indeed, the unfavourable relevance of D' would furnish us with one of the premisses of a *proof* of the not-unfavourable relevance of D, that is, of (95), if it were worth while, as it is not, to prove (95), rather than to take it as a premiss. For it is a principle of logical probability that if r, s, t, etc., are exhaustive and pairwise-exclusive alternatives, then if one of these alternatives is unfavourably relevant to q in relation to p, then at least one other alternative is not so. The possible blackness-frequencies in S are exhaustive and pairwise-exclusive alternatives. Whence if one of them is unfavourably relevant to C in relation to A, at least one other of them is not.)

From (95) and (94) it follows that

(96) $P(C|A.D) \geq 0.9$.

It is a principle of logical probability, and in any case obvious, that

(97) $P(q|p.r) = P(q.r|p.r)$.

That is, a premiss of an inference can always be conjoined with the conclusion *salva probabilitate*.

It follows from (97) that

(98) $P(C|A.D) = P(C.D|A.D)$.

Whence with (96) it follows that

(99) $P(C.D|A.D) \geq 0.9$.

It is obvious, from the abbreviations above, that

(100) Necessarily, if $C.D$ then E.

It is a principle of logical probability, and in any case obvious, that

(101) $P(r|p) \geq P(q|p)$, if necessarily if q then r.

(That is, the probability, in relation to p, of any r such that q necessitates r, cannot be less than the probability of q itself.)

It follows from (101), (100), and (99), that

(102) $P(E|A.D) \geq 0.9$.
(103) The inference from $A.D$ to E is inductive.

So

(104) The inductive inference from $A.D$ to E has high probability.

(iv)

The argument just completed, along with the two arguments of the preceding chapter, forms the core of the rest of this book. Everything that follows is either an extension of one of these three arguments, or a defence of one or more of these arguments or extensions.

While these three arguments are thus all-important for my purposes, they are not as easily surveyable as one would wish. It is not easy for a reader to remember all their premisses. For this reason I here collect, in a form which *is* easily surveyable, all the premisses of each of the three arguments.

To assist the reader further, I have in each case distinguished between those premisses which are principles of logical probability, those which are statements of logical probability, and those which are neither. . . .

The premisses of the argument of Chapter VI:
Principles of logical probability: (93), (97), (101).
Statements of logical probability: (83), (95).
Other premisses: (87), (88), (90), (100), (103).

Notes

1 David Hume, *The Philosophical Works*, ed. Green and Grose (London: Longmans, Green & Co., 1882), vol. 3, p. 175.
2 Cf. I. Todhunter, *A History of the Mathematical Theory of Probability* (Cambridge and London, 1865; reprinted New York: Chelsea Pub. Co., 1965), pp. 554ff.
3 Cf. J.M. Keynes, *A Treatise on Probability* (London: Macmillan, 1921), ch. xxx.
4 Cf. W. Kneale, *Probability and Induction* (Oxford: Clarendon Press, 1949), pp. 201ff.
5 David Hume, *An Enquiry Concerning Human Understanding*, this volume, pp. 307–8.
6 Cf. David Stove, *Popper and After: Four Modern Irrationalists* (Oxford: Pergamon Press, 1982), ch. III.
7 Cf. G.H. von Wright, *The Logical Problem of Induction* (Oxford: Blackwell, 1957), pp. 153, 176.
8 D.C. Williams, *The Ground of Induction* (Cambridge, Mass.: Harvard University Press, 1947), p. 97.
9 *Ibid.*, p. 100.
10 Keynes, *Treatise on Probability*, p. 341.

QUESTIONS

1 What is Stove trying to prove?
2 Give an example of a "direct inference".
3 What does the law of large numbers say?
4 In Stove's example, what is meant by a "near-Pop-matcher"?
5 According to Stove, what proportion of 3000-fold samples taken from a population of a million would be near-Pop-matchers?

DAVID STOVE

FURTHER READING ON INDUCTIVE INFERENCE

Earman, John, *Bayes or Bust?* (Cambridge, Mass.: MIT Press, 1992).

Hempel, Carl, "Inductive Inconsistencies," *Synthese* 12 (1960): 439–69.

Huemer, Michael, "The Problem of Defeasible Justification," *Erkenntnis* 54 (2001): 375–97.

Kornblith, Hilary, *Inductive Inference and its Natural Ground* (Cambridge, Mass.: MIT Press, 1995).

Popper, Karl, *Conjectures and Refutations* (New York: Harper & Row, 1968).

Popper, Karl, *The Logic of Scientific Discovery*, 3rd edn (London: Hutchinson, 1968).

Russell, Bertrand, "On Induction," pp. 60–9 in *The Problems of Philosophy* (Oxford: Oxford University Press, 1959).

Skyrms, Brian, *Choice and Chance: An Introduction to Inductive Logic*, 2nd edn (Belmont, Calif.: Dickenson, 1975).

Stove, David, *Probability and Hume's Inductive Skepticism* (Oxford: Clarendon, 1973).

Stove, David, *Anything Goes: Origins of the Cult of Scientific Irrationalism* (Paddington, Australia: Macleay Press, 1998).

Strawson, P.F., "Hume, Wittgenstein and Induction," in *Skepticism and Naturalism* (New York: Columbia University Press, 1985).

Swinburne, Richard (ed.) *The Justification of Induction* (Oxford: Oxford University Press, 1974).

Williams, D.C., *The Ground of Induction* (Cambridge, Mass.: Harvard University Press, 1947).

7

THE ARCHITECTURE OF KNOWLEDGE

Some beliefs are supported (justified) by other beliefs—I may believe *A* because I believe *B*. These other beliefs may themselves be supported by still further beliefs—perhaps I believe *B* because of *C*—and so on. For a given belief or piece of knowledge, then, we can ask what is the overall structure of the series of reasons for it—the structure of its justification. There are four ultimate possibilities (see Figure 7.1):

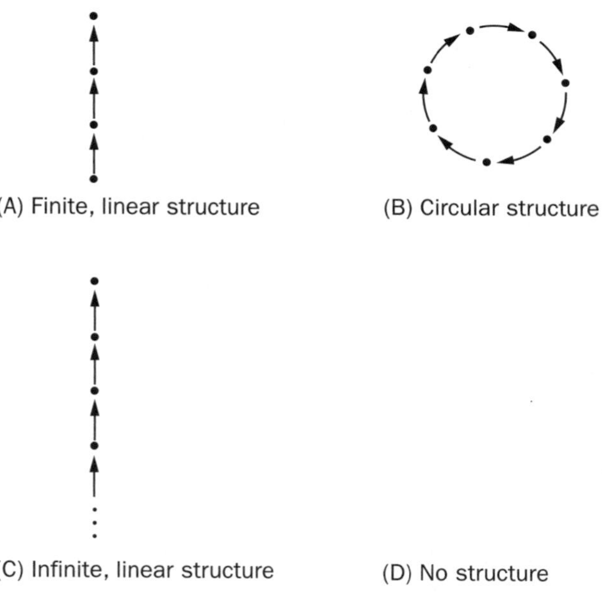

Figure 7.1

(a) There could be a finite series of reasons, none of which repeat. In this case, I come finally to some belief for which I have no further reasons.
(b) There could be a circular series, i.e., one in which, as I state the series of reasons behind A, I would eventually repeat A (or repeat some other proposition that was given as a reason for A).
(c) There could be an infinite regress, i.e., I can go on forever offering new reasons.
(d) There could be no structure (no reasons) at all. This alternative would hold if the belief was simply unjustified.

For each of these possible structures (with the possible exception of (c)), at least one philosopher has held that it is the actual structure of the justification for all of our beliefs. Sextus Empiricus and I.T. Oakley, for instance, have held the *skeptical* position that there is no structure of justification at all—in other words, that all of our beliefs are unjustified, and we have no reasons for believing anything. They arrive at this position by a process of elimination, on the grounds that alternatives (a), (b), and (c) do not seem acceptable. The problem with structure (a) is that it requires an ultimate starting point (this is represented by the dot at the bottom of the diagram for (a)), but, the skeptics think, any such starting point could only be arbitrary, since by definition there is no reason for accepting it. Structure (b) appears to be no better, since it would involve the classic fallacy of circular reasoning. Your beliefs would have structure (b) if, for instance, you believe A on the basis of B, which you accept because of C, which you accept because of A. Nor does structure (c) seem possible, since it would require one to complete an infinite chain of reasoning. Thus, (d) seems the only remaining possibility.

In contrast, Laurence BonJour defends a version of the *coherence theory* of justification (or "coherentism" for short). This theory holds that beliefs are justified by virtue of their coherence with each other (BonJour makes this claim about empirical beliefs, but not about a priori beliefs). To illustrate this, imagine that you are a detective interviewing witnesses to a crime. You interview them separately so they cannot influence each other's answers. Let us say you ask them to report the license plate number of the getaway car that the bank robbers used. If both of them report the same number, then you will conclude that that is the correct number. This would be true even if you initially had no confidence in their veracity (e.g., if you thought they were as likely as not to misreport), since if they were both mistaken or lying, it would be highly unlikely that their answers would cohere; it would be much more likely in that case that they would pick different numbers. Similarly, BonJour thinks, if our perceptual mechanisms were not generally connected to reality, then it would be highly unlikely that our various perceptual beliefs, formed by different senses at different times, would all fit together to give us a coherent picture of the world. The coherence theory is often seen as a sophisticated way of endorsing structure (b) for our justified beliefs: our beliefs are *mutually supporting*, rather than there being one belief or group of beliefs that comes first and confers justification on the others.

Coherentism is usually contrasted with *foundationalism*, which asserts that all beliefs have a justificatory structure of type (a). There are certain starting beliefs, called "foundational beliefs," which do not require any reasons for them, and all the rest of our justified beliefs are based upon them. This view came under attack from various quarters in the twentieth century. In "Has Foundationalism Been Refuted?", William Alston defends foundationalism against some of these attacks, arguing that they depend upon misunderstandings of what foundationalism requires. For instance, it has often been mistakenly assumed that a foundational belief must be immune from later revision, or that a belief with foundational justification can never be false, or that foundational beliefs must be conceived of as "justifying themselves." Critics have then argued that there are no beliefs having these characteristics. Alston responds to the criticisms by showing that one need not make such strong claims in order to be a foundationalist.

Susan Haack has recently proposed a kind of marriage between the traditionally opposed schools of foundationalism and coherentism. Her view, dubbed "foundherentism," holds that some beliefs have some degree of foundational (non-inferential) justification, but that at the same time, these beliefs can also be further justified by their coherence with each other. The analogy is to a crossword puzzle: each entry is supported to some degree by the clue for that entry, *and* entries are also mutually supported by their ability to fit together. She goes on to outline the factors that go into determining the level of justification of a belief. How justified a belief is depends upon how good the subject's evidence is for that belief, which depends, in turn, upon three factors: (a) the degree to which his evidence supports the belief, (b) the degree to which the subject's evidence is itself justified (independently of its support by the belief in question), and (c) the comprehensiveness of the subject's evidence (a belief is better justified by virtue of cohering with a *larger* body of evidence than it is by cohering with a smaller body). For purposes of assessing support relations, Haack proposes to treat a person's evidence as a body of propositions that includes all the propositions the person believes, plus propositions correctly and completely describing the character of the subject's experiences. She believes her theory avoids some of the main problems of both coherentism and foundationalism.

Sextus Empiricus, "The Five Modes"[1]

The later Sceptics, however, teach five modes of suspension. These are the following. The first is based on disagreement. The second is that which produces to infinity. Third, that based on relativity. Fourth, that from assumption. And fifth, the argument in a circle.

That based on disagreement is the one in which we find that in regard to a proposed matter there has arisen in the opinions both of people at large and of the philosophers an unresolved dissension. Because of this dissension we are unable either to choose or to reject anything, and thus we end with suspension of judgement. The mode based on the extension to infinity is the one in which we say that the proof offered for the verification of a proposed matter requires a further verification, and this one another, and so on to infinity, so that since we lack a point of departure for our reasoning, the consequence is suspension of judgement. That based on relativity is that in which, just as we have already said, the object appears thus or thus in relation to the thing judging and the things perceived along with it, while as to its true nature we suspend judgement. The mode from assumption exists when the dogmatists, in their *regressus ad infinitum*, take as their point of departure a proposition which they do not establish by reasoning, but simply and without proof assume as conceded to them. The mode of argument in a circle arises when that which ought itself to be confirmatory of the matter under investigation requires verification from the thing being investigated; at that point, being unable to take either of them to establish the other, we suspend judgement about both.

That it is possible to refer every question to these modes we shall show briefly as follows. The object proposed is either an object of sense or an object of thought; but no matter which it is, it is a disputed point. For some say that the objects of sense alone are true, some say only the objects of thought are true, while others say that some objects of sense and some objects of thought are true. Now, will they assert that the disagreement is resolvable, or irresolvable? If irresolvable, then we have the necessity of suspension granted; for it is not possible to pronounce on things when the dispute about them is irresolvable. But if the dispute is resolvable, then we ask from what quarter the decision is to come. Taking, for example, the object of sense (to fix our argument on this one first), is it to be judged by an object of sense or by an object of thought? If by an object of

Sextus Empiricus, *Scepticism, Man, and God* (Middletown, CT: Wesleyan University Press, 1964).

sense, then, seeing that our inquiry is about objects of sense, that object too will need another as confirmation. And if that other is an object of sense, again it will itself need another to confirm it, and so on to infinity. But if the object of sense will have to be judged by an object of thought, then, since objects of thought also are a matter of dispute, this object, being an object of thought, will require judgment and confirmation. Where, then, is the confirmation to come from? If it is to be confirmed by an object of thought, we shall likewise have an extension *ad infinitum*; but if by an object of sense, the mode of circular reasoning is introduced, because an object of thought was employed for the confirmation of the object of sense and an object of sense for the confirmation of the object of thought.

If, however, our interlocutor should try to escape from these conclusions and claim the right to assume, as a concession without proof, some proposition serving to prove the rest of his argument, then the mode of assumption will be brought in, which leaves him no way out. For if a person is worthy of credence when he makes an assumption, then we shall in each case also be not less worthy of credence if we make the opposite assumption. And if the person making the assumption assumes something which is true, he renders it suspicious by taking it on assumption instead of proving it. But if what he assumes is false, the foundation of what he it trying to prove will be unsound. Moreover, if assumption conduces at all towards proof, let the thing in question itself be assumed and not something else by means of which he will then prove the thing under discussion. But if it is absurd to assume the thing in question, it will also be absurd to assume what transcends it.

But it is evident that all objects of sense are also relative, for they exist as such in relation to those who perceive them. It is clear, then, that whatever sensible object is set before us, it can easily be referred to the five modes. Our reasoning concerning the intelligible object is similar. For if it should be said that it is the subject of an irresolvable disagreement, the necessity of suspending judgement on this matter will be granted us. But in the case of a resolution of the disagreement, if the resolution is reached by means of an object of thought, we shall have recourse to the extension *ad infinitum*; if by means of an object of sense, we shall have recourse to the mode of circular reasoning. For as the sensible again is an object of disagreement, and incapable, because of the extension to infinity, of being decided by means of itself, it will stand in need of the intelligible just as the intelligible also requires the sensible. For these reasons, whoever accepts anything on assumption will again be in an absurd position. But intelligibles are also relative, for they are relative to the intellect in which they appear, whence their name. And if they really were in nature such as they are said to be, there would be no disagreement about them. Thus the intelligible too has been referred to the five modes, so that in any case we must suspend judgment with regard to the object presented.

Such are the five modes taught by the later Sceptics. Their purpose in setting them forth is not to repudiate the ten modes, but to provide for a more diversified exposure of the rashness of the dogmatists by combining these modes with the others.

Note

1 Usually attributed to Agrippa, about whom virtually nothing is known.

QUESTIONS

1 What sort of things does Sextus think we should suspend judgment about?
2 If one of the "dogmatists" claims the right to assume some premise without proof, how would Sextus respond?

I.T. Oakley, "An Argument for Scepticism Concerning Justified Beliefs"

1. Outline of the argument

I shall argue that no beliefs are justified (or reasonable, or rational). I offer no analysis of the term "justified," since this is not required by my argument, and take the notion to be a commonsense one, regularly though unreflectively used by us all. Strictly it is a person at a time who is justified or not in a belief, but for brevity I shall often speak of beliefs being justified. Since a belief may be justified to a greater or lesser extent, I shall stipulate now that when I speak of a belief's being justified, I mean that it is justified to some extent or other, even if only a minimal extent. So in this paper, I shall be arguing that no one is justified in any beliefs even to the most minimal degree.

Consider the claim that person *A* is justified in belief *p*. Now *p*'s being justified (understand throughout: for *A*) either depends on *A*'s being justified in some further belief *q*, or it does not. Let us call beliefs in which *A* is justified and which are such that his being justified in them does not depend on his being justified in any other beliefs, *basic beliefs*. The concept of dependence used here requires, and receives below, further attention. Let us agree for the present merely to so use the term that the relation is transitive. Thus (to adopt a self-explanatory abbreviation), if *Jp* dep *Jq*, and *Jq* dep *Jr*, then *Jp* dep *Jr*.

Someone claiming *A* to be justified in *p* must accept that *p* is either: (1) itself basic, or else dependent on one or more basic beliefs; or (2) a member of a series of an infinite number of different beliefs, justifiedness in each of which is dependent upon justifiedness in its successors, in the series; or (3) *p* is a member of a series of a finite number of different beliefs justifiedness in at least one member of which depends at least partially upon itself. In traditional terms, we must choose between a sort of foundationalism, an infinite regress, or a coherence account of justifiedness. The chain of beliefs upon which *p* depends for its justifiedness either stops, is infinite, or loops back on itself. In what follows, I shall argue against each of the three possibilities, concluding that the chain does not in fact start: *p* is not justified. Before this, however, I turn to the concept of dependence.

I.T. Oakley, "An Argument for Scepticism Concerning Justified Beliefs," *American Philosophical Quarterly* 13 (1976): 221–8.

2. The concept of dependence

I take the concept to be reasonably clear on an intuitive level, though it proves surprisingly difficult to analyse. We will agree, I think, that to say that *p*'s justifiedness depends on *q*'s justifiedness is not the same as saying that *p* was inferred from *q*, or that *q* was the person's reason for *p* (in the context concerned). One may arrive at *p* by inferring it from *q*, but be in the position that one would have been justified in *p* anyway. Further, I shall be presenting examples below of cases where *p*'s justifiedness does depend on *q*'s justifiedness, but where *q* is not what we would normally call a reason or ground for *p*.

The key notion is that if *Jp* dep *Jq*, then *Jq* is necessary for *Jp*. By "necessary" here, we cannot mean logically necessary. The necessity of *Jq* for *Jp* will of course be contingent on there not being to hand, for the person in question, other ways of justifying his belief in *p*, which do not involve being justified in *q*. In such a case, *Jp* might depend on *Jq* or *Jr*.

Regrettably the beliefs justifiedness in which is necessary for *Jp* include some upon which we do not want to say *Jp* depends.[1] Such beliefs are those immediately and obviously entailed by *p*, such as *p* disjoined with any other belief, *q*. Someone not justified in the disjunction would not be justified in *p*, but I take it that we wish to capture a concept of dependence which would not have any *Jp* depending on $J\ (p \vee q)$ where *q* is any belief whatever, but would say that *Jp* dep $J(p \vee q)$ only in such cases as where *J* not-*q* as well. Another obvious point is that justifiedness in *any* belief will clearly be such that justifiedness in some other belief is necessary for it, yet we should not want our account of dependence on its own to rule out the existence of any basic beliefs. (At least I presume we don't. However, should anyone be inclined to accept this quick route to the denial of basic beliefs, I shall be happy enough, and he or she will not have to worry with section 3 below, where I argue that point in detail.)

Ruling out the unwanted cases in which *Jq* is necessary for *Jp* in a non-circular way proves extremely troublesome. However, I take it that we may leave the matter at an intuitive level, and allow that *Jp* dep *Jq* if *Jq* is necessary for *Jp*, provided the necessity does not arise merely in virtue of *p*'s entailing *q* in some very straightforward way.

A final problem about dependence arises from the fact that we would, I think, generally agree that someone may be justified in holding a belief he does not actually hold. The question then arises as to whether *Jp* can ever depend on *Jq* when *q* is not actually held. We need not actually decide this question here, though I shall present examples below some of which seem to me to depend on the justifiedness of unheld beliefs. We need at least to cover this possibility in our arguments, since to show that a belief was basic in the sense of not depending on justifiedness in any other held belief would be fairly uninteresting epistemologically if it were allowed that it might none the less depend on justifiedness in some unheld belief. So in all cases, except where specially indicated, when I speak of *p*'s justifiedness, I shall imply nothing about *p*'s actually being held.

3. Reasons for denying the existence of basic beliefs

My case rests on a consideration of examples, and my contention is that it is impossible to find cases of justified beliefs which do not depend for their justifiedness on the justifiedness of any other beliefs, even when one takes one's examples from the classes of beliefs that seem most promising in this respect: beliefs based on perception of one's immediate physical environment, or beliefs about what are often called our immediate experiences.

For each plausible candidate, *p*, for the status of basicness, I shall seek to show that there is in fact a *q*, such that if *q* were not justified, *p* would not be justified to the least extent. In framing examples to establish this in particular cases, I shall take cases in which: (i) *p* does not entail *q*; (ii) *q* is true, and (iii) where the person, *A*, is not justified in believing *q*, but neither is he justified in believing not-*q*, or, indeed, in any other belief which might imply not-*p*. I shall ask my reader to agree with me that in these cases *A* is not justified in *p*. It will be impossible to put down *A*'s failure to be justified in *p* to *q*'s falsity, or to *A*'s being justified in a further belief such as not-*q* which would constitute a reason for not-*p*. If the agreement I seek as to what we are prepared to say about *p* is in fact forthcoming, I will take the examples to show that *Jp* dep *Jq*. Should the reader reject my examples as failing to provide instances where *q* is true, and where the subject is justified in neither *q* nor not-*q*, I invite him or her to construct examples where this fault is remedied, and to test his or her intuitions on these. Should the reader accept my description of the cases, but fail to agree that in the circumstances *A* would not be justified in *p*, my argument fails.

3.1 Beliefs based on perception

A.J. Ayer states one version of the position I hope to disprove here. He claims that some beliefs are justified

> simply because one is having or has had certain experiences. What, for example, gives me the right to be sure that this is a sheet of paper? Well, partly my seeing what I now do, partly the fact that my past experiences have been such that I can identify pieces of paper when I see them. But it is not necessary that I should believe any propositions about the contents of my visual field . . . or about the character of my past experience. It is enough that I am having the experience that I am and that I have acquired the necessary skill in identifying what I see.[2]

In direct opposition to Ayer's view, I contend that to be justified in a perception-based belief it is not sufficient that someone have the experience that he is having, and have certain discriminatory skills: it is necessary that he be justified in believing, *inter alia*, that he has the relevant skills, and also that there are no special circumstances currently interfering with his exercise of them. Thus his being justified in

p: There is a piece of white paper in front of me

would typically depend on justifiedness in

q: I have the capacity to discriminate pieces of white paper

and

r: *p* was not induced in me by hypnotic suggestion.

Though it would doubtless be rare for someone to be unjustified in *q*, the situation might arise in the case, familiar from other contexts, of the man blind from birth, given his sight by an operation. After limited use of his newly gained faculty, he might indeed possess the discriminatory capacity, but with no feedback on the accuracy of his judgments, be left unjustified in believing either *q* or its negation. In this case, despite *q*'s truth, it seems clear that we should not allow that *Jp*. It is important to note that this is not because he is justified in any belief constituting for him a positive reason for the falsity of *p*. (He has, of course, reason to doubt his justifiedness in *p*, but that is another matter.) Not-*q* would imply not-*Jp*, but he is not justified in the former. Admittedly, the example requires that he be justified in

s: I do not know whether or not I have the capacity to discriminate pieces of white paper,

but *s* does not imply not-*p*, either by itself, or in conjunction with anything else in which we might assume him justified.

Now consider the case where neither *Jr* nor *J* not-*r*, and *r* is in fact true. He is justified in believing

t: Some proportion, between the minutest fraction and the vast majority, of my current beliefs has been induced in me by hypnosis.

This leaves him not justified (even minimally) in *r*, nor in not-*r*, and as a result, I submit, not justified (even minimally) in *p*. His failure to be justified in *p* is traceable only to his failure to be justified in *r*. Even given the belief that beliefs induced by hypnosis are likely to be false, *t* does not imply not-*p*.

At this point, a qualification is called for, since it may reasonably be objected that *Jp* cannot depend on *Jr*, since children who have never heard of hypnosis surely cannot be justified in *r*, yet equally surely are, on occasion, justified in *p*. We might perhaps seek to reply by insisting that one may be justified in a belief one is incapable of formulating. However, I choose the alternative course of shifting ground, and suggesting another belief to replace *r*, upon justifiedness in which *Jp* depends, even for the child. This is

u: There are no factors present of a type which would probably cause me to make mistakes about the presence or absence of white pieces of paper.

Such a belief is regularly justifiedly held not only by children, but by adults who are well aware that there are possible illusion-producing factors of which they know nothing. *Ju* in general derives from beliefs to the effect that such factors would probably manifest themselves in some way (such as the light looking funny, or the appearances of things being contrary to expectation in some way), and to the effect that there are currently no such manifestations. A child who not only knew nothing of hypnosis, but knew nothing at all of factors which induce mistakes in perceptual judgments is not, I suggest, really justified in those judgments. But this case aside, consider someone unjustified in *u*, and also unjustified in not-*u*, in a case where *u* was in fact true. This could arise where someone found himself subject to a number of unexplained sensory illusions in sensory modalities other than sight, and was left in *complete* doubt as to whether or not he might expect illusions of sight as well. Such a situation would not involve his having justified beliefs which implied not-*p*, but he would surely not be justified in *p*.

The examples considered are few, but the way of dealing with them is obviously generalisable without difficulty, not only to perception-based beliefs in general, but also to beliefs based on memory.

3.2 *Beliefs about immediate experiences*

I contend that these beliefs just as much as the perception beliefs just considered, depend for their justifiedness on other beliefs. Let our *p* be *A*'s belief that it *appears* to him too that something is blue, when he has no beliefs about whether there actually exists anything blue, nor about whether it appears to anyone else that anything is blue. Such a belief, I contend, depends for its justification on the justifiedness of

> *q*: There are no factors present of a type which would probably cause error in judgments about immediate experience.

We will of course be justified in *q* if we are justified in believing that beliefs like *p* are incorrigible. But one might believe *p* corrigible, yet be justified in *q*. ("Incorrigible" is used here in the sense in which a belief, if incorrigible, is such that its being believed entails its truth. In fact, if my arguments are correct, the incorrigibility issue is much overrated in epistemology where the important concept is basicness. For that, incorrigibility is neither necessary nor sufficient.)

Suppose that one believed like Reichenbach[3] that statements about one's immediate experiences were corrigible, and that one could fall into error in such beliefs on account of such factors as wishful thinking, and that one's arguments for this position were at least good enough to make us say that one was not justified in believing the contrary. Suppose further that one was not justified in believing that wishful thinking had not led one into error in the case of *p*. Remember that "not justified" here means "not in the least degree justified." This is of course a very unlikely case. In general, even where there is a suspicion that wishful thinking may have entered the picture, one will be justified in thinking that it probably did not. Our hypothetical case is that in which we are not even minimally justified in believing wishful thinking absent. And though very unlikely, the case is possible enough, and could arise, perhaps where one was unhappily aware of a particularly bad record of wishful thinking in similar circumstances. In such a situation then, we are not justified in *q*. *q* might at the same time *be* true: perhaps such statements as *p* are incorrigible, or in any case, our belief that p was indeed uninfluenced by wishful thinking. But despite q's truth, I contend, if we are not justified in q then we must say that we are not justified in p either. For to say that we are not justified in believing p to be in principle free from error, *and* that we are not justified in believing that sources of error have played no part in our believing that p surely makes it quite unjustified to believe p. The principle of this argument is very similar to that of our argument above concerning the perception-based belief that there is a piece of white paper in front of me.

I conclude then, that we have failed to find any basic beliefs in the places where it seemed reasonable to look for them, and that it is therefore appropriate to conclude that there are no such beliefs. (The reader convinced by the above arguments should have no trouble framing for himself arguments of a parallel kind to establish the non-basicness of the truths we label "necessary.")

4. Against a coherence theory of justified beliefs

Such a theory is one which allows that Jp may depend on Jq, and Jq (via, perhaps, a series of other justified beliefs) similarly on Jp. The dependence relation may thus connect a set of beliefs into a circle and thus is not, as might be expected, assymetrical, but is non-symmetrical.

4.1 The viciousness of circularity

Where Jp depends on Jq and vice versa simultaneously, it seems that our immediate intuitive judgment is that neither belief is justified, as this is a case of just what we should call vicious circularity. This point, though an appeal to intuitive judgment, strikes me as having considerable force. Consider the following example, in which, I submit, *A* is unjustified in all the beliefs on the ground that there is circularity of this sort. Suppose *A*'s justifiedness in believing his senses have not been deceiving him for the past week depends on his justifiedness in certain beliefs about the conditions and his perceptual capacities during that week. These in turn depend for justifiedness on certain perception-based beliefs acquired during the past week, which depend for their justifiedness, finally, on the belief with which we started. (I am not here arguing, of course, that we are in fact all in *A*'s position.)

A proponent of the non-symmetry thesis might here defend himself by insisting that there is a crucial difference between fairly small circles, which are relatively accessible to our intuitive judgment, and are clearly to be rejected as vicious, and big circles, embracing very large portions of our corpus of beliefs, about which we do not have any clear intuitions, and which may be accepted as non-vicious. Against this I would argue that, given the transitivity of the dependence relation, big circles can be re-described as little circles merely by leaving out some elements. Thus the distinction does not seem an important one for our purposes. And significantly, it is by no means clear that the circles involved in our actual justifications of our beliefs are going to be especially big, if they exist at all. Have we any reason to expect anything bigger than that described in the example above? It appeared to be a perfectly manageable target for our intuitions. One cannot help feeling that the inaccessibility to our intuitions of the very large circles envisaged is due not to their size but to the fact that they are not articulated.

4.2 *A second argument against the coherence account*

The argument at issue deals mainly with sets of beliefs some of which are unheld. In section 3 above, we argued that experience was never sufficient for justifiedness in a belief *p*, but not that it was never *necessary*. Consider then a set of beliefs containing *p* such that each member of the set depended for justifiedness on nothing more than justifiedness in one or more other members of the set, plus the having by *A* of some experience or experiences from a set of experiences *E*. This is presumably the picture of our justified beliefs that a coherence theorist would wish to present.

The trouble is that for any set of experiences *E*, it will be possible to construct another set of beliefs, not including the belief *p*, and indeed including the belief not-*p*, such that the same dependence relations will obtain. That is, *J* not-*p* will depend, as will all other members of the set, only upon other members of the set, plus parts of *E*. Which is to say that given any set of experiences, plus the coherence theorist's permission to allow circles of justification dependence, we will always be "justified" in both *p* and not-*p*. More strictly, since we shall have equal degrees of "justifiedness" in *p* and not-*p*, we shall be in fact justified in neither. The coherence account thus commits us to the conclusion that no beliefs are justified. I am of course willing to embrace this conclusion, but presume that most would wish to take it as an argument against the account.

A variant of this argument deals with the case where it is not even demanded that experience should enter at some point into our justification of a belief. If we allow this possibility, we allow sets of beliefs where each member depends for justifiedness *only* on justifiedness in other members. Here, a circle of necessity becomes a circle of sufficiency. For any belief *p*, and also for not-*p*, it will be possible to construct sets of beliefs such that *p*, and all other members of the set, depend for justifiedness on no more than justifiedness in other members. In such cases we need not even restrict ourselves to circles with unheld beliefs. Consider *A* who holds

p Each of my houses has been burgled recently
q Each of my houses has been repainted at the same time
r There is a strong correlation between the burglary of my houses and their being re-painted.

Allow that justifiedness in any depends solely upon justifiedness in the other two. On the coherence account, permitting circular dependence, we are immediately committed to saying *A* is justified in all these beliefs, despite the lack of any independent justification for any of them, provided only that he lacks external justification for their negations.

4.3 A third argument against the coherence account

The disastrous surfeit of justified beliefs of the above section could be avoided by someone wishing to restrict our attention to held beliefs, since we relatively seldom actually *hold* more than one set of beliefs to which the same set of experiences would be relevant. I turn then to an argument specifically concerned with sets of held beliefs.

Suppose *A* holds a set, *p*, *q*, *r*, and *s*, such that each member depends only on other members plus some part of a set of experiences, *E*. Now take any further belief held by *A*, *t*, such that (i) *A* is not justified in not-*t*, (ii) justifiedness in *t* would not result in his ceasing to be justified in *p*, *q*, *r*, or *s*, and (iii) *A* does not also hold not-*t*. (If it should be taken as impossible that one should ever hold both a belief and its negation at once, so much the better.)

Now conjoin *t* with each of *p*, *q*, *r* and *s*, to get a new set of conjunctive beliefs, *p* & *t*, *q* & *t*, etc. *A* need not hold this new set in all cases since occasionally one will hold two beliefs and fail to hold the conjunction (again, if this is not accepted, so much the better), but usually he will. Now if he holds the second set and is justified in every member of the first, he will clearly be justified in every member of the second. If *Jp* dep *Jq* and *Jr* and exp e_1, then *Jp* & *t* dep *Jq* & *t* and *Jr* & *t* and exp e_1. And if *Jp* & *t*, then presumably *Jt*.

Thus, acceptance of *A*'s being justified in just one belief by virtue of its membership of a set involving circular dependence relations commits us to calling him justified in any number of further beliefs in which we should never normally call him justified.

I conclude that we have sufficient grounds for rejecting coherence accounts of our justified beliefs.[4]

5. Against infinite regresses

Few seem to have held the view that a belief might be justified in virtue of its membership in an infinite series of beliefs, each depending on its successors (though perhaps the view could gain sympathisers convinced of the inadequacy of coherence accounts and the non-existence of basic beliefs). The reason may be the assumption that a man cannot hold an infinite number of beliefs. However, this is less than clear, and my arguments do not rest on it.

In the first place, acceptance of the infinite series possibility immediately prevents us from drawing a distinction we are very much inclined to draw: that between on the one hand an infinite series of justified beliefs where each depends for its justifiedness on the justifiedness of its successors (*inter alia*, perhaps), and on the other, an infinite series of *un*justified beliefs such that if they *were* justified, each would depend for its justifiedness on the justifiedness of its successors. Furthermore, it becomes a mystery how we can ever know, or be justified in believing, or even simply come to believe, that a particular one of our beliefs is justified or not. In any given case, how do we know that the series of beliefs is infinite as opposed to simply fairly long? We have no direct check, clearly, and it is hard to see what sort of indirect evidence we have to go on, nor on what cues our intuitive judgments might be based.[5]

5.1 *Against infinite series of held beliefs*

Great difficulty is encountered as soon as we start to try to reconstruct even the early stages of a regress. Any attempt to articulate the series seems highly artificial, and, worse still, usually to end up in a circularity at some point or other, or else to involve a series which must come to an end because of the finite age of the believer. I must leave the reader to do most of the thought experiments for himself here, but will mention some of the main possibilities. Beliefs based on perception depend for their justifiedness partly on our justifiedness in other beliefs about our perceptual capacities. These in turn depend for justifiedness on other perception-based beliefs. Now either we already have a circularity here, or else the last mentioned perception-based beliefs are conceived of as different from the initial perception-based belief. And they in turn are conceived of as depending for their justification on justifiedness in beliefs about discriminatory capacities possessed at different times, and these beliefs upon yet other perception-based beliefs. But our temporal finitude does mean we only have a finite number of temporally distinct perceptions, and corresponding perception-based beliefs, and so *that* regress is not infinite.

Some believe that our beliefs about the world can be justified in terms of our beliefs about our own experience, holus bolus, as it were, as a theory is supported by its data. Here, though, we strike a circularity again, as we have already seen that justifiedness in beliefs about our own experiences depends on justifiedness in beliefs about incorrigibility, or about the absence of mistake-inducing factors: i.e., beliefs which are not themselves about immediate experiences.

5.2 *A second argument against infinite series*

The argument now at issue parallels that against coherence in 4.2, and deals in the first instance with series which include unheld beliefs. Assume p to be the head of an infinite series in which each member depends upon its successor and in some cases upon the having of an experience as well. We will always be able to construct a series headed by not-p, and depending upon all the same experiences as were depended upon by the first series.

Thus, let s be a belief somewhere in our series headed by p, and t be the successor of s. Js dep Jt and, say, experience e_1. Thus Jt and e_1 are severally necessary and jointly sufficient for Js. But e_1 and Ju, where u is some other appropriately selected belief, may well be jointly sufficient for J not-s.

To put flesh on the bones, e_1 might be the experience of something white, and we might have

s. There appears something white.
t. *s* is incorrigible.
u. I am currently very liable to mistakes about appearances.

We may conclude that any p and its negation are equally justified, and so we remain justified in no beliefs, held or upheld. As in 4.2, the matter is clearer still if we make no empiricist demand that experience enter into the justification of any belief. For any belief, it will be easy to construct a series extending away from it, each member comprising a conjunction of all the beliefs upon justifiedness in which justifiedness in the member above depends. And if experience need not enter the picture, this means that justifiedness in a member will be sufficient for justifiedness in its predecessor. Thus any belief will be justified by its successor, and, the chain being infinite, there will always be a successor.

Again, as in 4.2, we need not even restrict ourselves at this point to unheld beliefs. Suppose *A* indeed holds the right sort of infinite series, thus:

p: From my front door there extends a long carpet, the first foot-length of which is red.
q: From my front door there extends a long carpet, the first two-foot-length of which is red.
r: From my . . . first three-foot-length of which is red.
Etc., *ad infinitum*.

A does not hold the belief that the carpet is of infinite length. He simply holds an infinite number of beliefs about infinite lengths. Further, let us suppose that *A* is not justified in any belief (about, for instance, the manufacture of carpets, or about the state of affairs in the space extending from his front door) justifiedness in which would be sufficient for his being justified in the negation of any of the beliefs in the above series. Even on this last supposition, we would surely have no inclination at all to say that he was justified in *p*, or any other member of the sequence. Once we permit justification to depend on an infinite series of beliefs, however, we cannot avoid saying that every member of the series is justified.

But the main argument of this section is directed against series with unheld members, and fails against series composed entirely of held beliefs. The subject's simple failure to hold some beliefs will there protect him from the embarrassment of riches otherwise looming. I turn then to an argument directed specifically against series of held beliefs.

5.3 A third argument against infinite series

The argument at issue here parallels the anti-coherence argument of 4.3. Let us suppose *A* justified in *p* in the way envisaged by the regress theorist, that is, as the head of an actually held series each member of which depends for justifiedness on its successors, and perhaps on experiences as well. Conjoin with every member of the series a further belief of *A*'s, *q*, on which we place the same restrictions as those on *t* in 4.3. We get the same result, and for the same reasons. Assuming *A* holds the second series of conjunctive beliefs, and was justified in each member of the first, he will be justified in each member of the second.

Again, then, *A*'s being justified in just one belief by virtue of its membership of the required type of infinite series forces on us an unwanted further set of justified beliefs.

The argument fails, it should be noted, once we allow justifiedness in unheld beliefs. For then we could form a third series by conjoining *not-q* with the members of the first series, arriving thus at justifiedness in both *q* and not *q*. This would leave us unjustified in both, failing independent justification for one or other. This however is just the position we believe ourselves in, and so would be a consequence happily embraced by the proponent of infinite series. This point also underlies the restriction that *A* should not actually believe both *q* and not-*q* (or both *t* and not-*t* in 4.3).

I conclude that we have sufficient reason to reject the infinite regress theorist's account of our justified beliefs.

6. Conclusion: no beliefs are justified

Note that this scepticism does not entail a broader scepticism about knowledge unless one accepts that *Jp* is a necessary condition for knowing *p*. (Some do not.) However, despite this restriction, our scepticism is extremely broad: it embraces beliefs about immediate experiences and it is not merely a claim about the unattainability of certainty, since it maintains we are never justified in a belief to the least degree. I conclude then, with a brief examination of some problems likely to be raised concerning my sceptical position.

First, it might reasonably be insisted here that someone who denies that beliefs are ever justified owes us some account of why we universally think there is a distinction between justified and unjustified, wise and foolish beliefs.

Second, it is said frequently that the sceptic achieves his paradoxical conclusions by means of the verbal trick of defining "knowledge" or "justified" in some non-standard way so that indeed, in this non-standard sense, we have no justified beliefs. This sceptical conclusion then is not paradoxical, since it is *not* the claim that we have no justified beliefs in the sense in which we have always thought we had them.

I will reply to the two points jointly. There is of course an established use of "justified" and "unjustified," but this ordinary use does not establish a different *sense* or *meaning*, separate to that in which we use the term in our conclusion. The difference in fact marked by the justified/unjustified distinction seems to me to be this: a belief is labelled "justified" if it can be supported by beliefs which in the context are currently not in question (by way of similarly unquestioned principles of inference). Questions about justification in general arise only when there is doubt, and we only doubt a little bit of our corpus of beliefs at a time. Until doubt arises, we assume we are justified in believing what we do believe. When doubt does arise, it is settled by reference to that about which doubt has not arisen. This is all very practical and sensible, and in ordinary life we would be foolish to press doubts further than they have to be pressed.

Now if all we mean by "justified belief" is a belief which can be derived from the currently undoubted, then of course there are justified beliefs. But in fact no-one *means* this by "justified belief." Everyone acknowledges that what is currently undoubted *may* not be itself justified (while believing of course that it probably is), and that because of this, what is derived from it *may* not be justified either. The ordinary use of the term is not a use of it in a different *sense* to that in which I have used it. It is convenient—perhaps all we need, as well as all we can, if I am right, hope for—to distinguish that which can be derived from the currently undoubted from that which cannot. But no-one, once the distinction is articulated, would want to say that this is the same as the difference between justified and unjustified.

Lastly, the above discussion provides the basis for a suitable rejoinder to the critic who would turn the conclusion against itself, remarking that if it is true, we cannot be justified in believing it, or indeed the premises from which it is drawn. The convinced sceptic will of course embrace this conclusion, kicking away his ladder along with everything else. But in any case, I will regard my current purpose as fulfilled if my reader accepts that the conclusion is derivable from the currently unquestioned.[6]

Notes

1 This was first pointed out to me by Mr. F.C. Jackson of La Trobe University.

2 A.J. Ayer, "Knowledge, Belief, and Evidence" in A.J. Ayer, *Metaphysics and Common Sense* (London: Macmillan, 1969), p. 121.

3 Hans Reichenbach, "Are Phenomenal Reports Absolutely Certain?", *Philosophical Review* 61 (1952): 147–59.

4 For recent discussions of coherence, see, e.g., Anthony Quinton, *The Nature of Things* (London: Routledge and Kegan Paul, 1973), Ch. 8; Roderick Firth, "Coherence, Certainty and Epistemic Priority," *Journal of Philosophy* 61 (1964): 545–57; Nicholas Rescher, *The Coherence Theory of Truth* (Oxford: Clarendon Press, 1973); and Keith Lehrer, *Knowledge* (Oxford: Clarendon Press, 1974).

5 I owe this point to Mr. Robert Waldie.

6 I have been greatly helped by comments on earlier drafts of this paper made by a large number of people, in particular Dr. R.M. Sainsbury of Oxford University and Mr. F.C. Jackson of La Trobe University. Earlier drafts were read at Dundee, Edinburgh, Aberdeen and Warwick Universities.

QUESTIONS

1 What condition usually thought to be required for knowledge does Oakley say is never satisfied?

2 Suppose I believe there is a white piece of paper in front of me, as a result of seeing it. According to Oakley, what two other propositions does my belief depend on for its justification?

3 Oakley considers a case in which a person has beliefs *p*, *q*, *r*, and *s*, which depend on each other for their justification. He then suggests conjoining each of those beliefs with another, unrelated proposition, *t*. What undesirable consequence does he think results from this, and what theory is this supposed to refute?

Laurence BonJour, *The Structure of Empirical Knowledge*

A basic problem for foundationalism

The fundamental concept of moderate foundationalism, as of empirical foundationalism generally, is the concept of a basic empirical belief. It is by appeal to basic beliefs that the threat of an infinite regress is to be avoided and empirical knowledge given a secure foundation. But a new problem now arises: how can there be any empirical beliefs which are thus basic? For although this has often been overlooked, the very idea of an epistemically basic empirical belief is more than a little paradoxical. On what basis is such a belief supposed to be justified, once any appeal to further empirical premises is ruled out? Chisholm's theological analogy, cited earlier, is most appropriate: a basic empirical belief is in effect an epistemological unmoved (or self-moved) mover. It is able to confer justification on other beliefs, but, in spite of being empirical and thus contingent, apparently has no need to have justification conferred on it. But is such a status any easier to understand in epistemology than it is in theology? How can a contingent, empirical belief impart epistemic "motion" to other empirical beliefs unless it is itself in "motion"? (Or, even more paradoxically, how can such a belief epistemically "move" itself?) Where does the noninferential justification for basic empirical beliefs come from?

This difficulty may be developed a bit by appealing to the account of the general concept of epistemic justification which was presented [earlier]. I argued there that the fundamental role which the requirement of epistemic justification serves in the overall rationale of the concept of knowledge is that of a *means* to truth; and accordingly that a basic constraint on any account of the standards of justification for empirical knowledge is that there be good reasons for thinking that following those standards is at least likely to lead to truth. Thus if basic beliefs are to provide a secure foundation for empirical knowledge, if inference from them is to be the sole basis upon which other empirical beliefs are justified, then that feature, whatever it may be, by virtue of which a particular belief qualifies as basic must also constitute a good reason for thinking that the belief is true. If this were not so, moderate foundationalism would be unacceptable as an account of epistemic justification.

This crucial point may be formulated a bit more precisely, as follows. If we let

Laurence BonJour, *The Structure of Empirical Knowledge* (Cambridge: Harvard University Press, 1985).

ϕ represent the feature or characteristic, whatever it may be, which distinguishes basic empirical beliefs from other empirical beliefs, then in an acceptable foundationalist account a particular empirical belief B could qualify as basic only if the premises of the following justificatory argument were adequately justified:

(1) B has feature ϕ.
(2) Beliefs having feature ϕ are highly likely to be true.
Therefore, B is highly likely to be true.

If B is to actually *be* basic, then presumably premise (1) would have to be true as well, but I am concerned here only with what would have to be so for it to be reasonable to *accept* B as basic and use it to justify other beliefs.

Clearly it is possible that at least one of the two premises of the argument might be justifiable on a purely *a priori* basis, depending on the particular choice of ϕ. It does not seem possible, however, that *both* premises might be thus justifiable. B is after all, *ex hypothesi*, an empirical belief, and it is hard to see how a particular empirical belief could be justified on a purely *a priori* basis. Thus we may conclude, at least provisionally, that for any acceptable moderate foundationalist account, at least one of the two premises of the appropriate justifying argument will itself be empirical.

The other issue to be considered is whether, in order for B to be justified for a particular person A (at a particular time), it is necessary, not merely that a justification along the above lines exist in the abstract, but also that A himself be in cognitive possession of that justification, that is, that he believe the appropriate premises of forms (1) and (2) and that these beliefs be justified *for him*. [Earlier,] I argued tentatively that such cognitive possession by the person in question is indeed necessary, on the grounds that *he* cannot be epistemically responsible in accepting the belief unless *he himself* has access to the justification; for otherwise, *he* has no reason for thinking that the belief is at all likely to be true. No reason for questioning this claim has so far emerged.

But if all this is correct, we get the disturbing result that B is not basic after all, since its justification depends on that of at least one other empirical belief. It would follow that moderate foundationalism is untenable as a solution to the regress problem—and an analogous argument would show weak foundationalism to be similarly untenable.

It will be helpful in the subsequent discussion to have available a slightly more explicit statement of this basic antifoundationalist argument:

(1) Suppose that there are *basic empirical beliefs*, that is, empirical beliefs (a) which are epistemically justified, and (b) whose justification does not depend on that of any further empirical beliefs.
(2) For a belief to be epistemically justified requires that there be a reason why it is likely to be true.
(3) For a belief to be epistemically justified for a particular person requires that this person be himself in cognitive possession of such a reason.
(4) The only way to be in cognitive possession of such a reason is to believe *with justification* the premises from which it follows that the belief is likely to be true.

(5) The premises of such a justifying argument for an empirical belief cannot be entirely *a priori*; at least one such premise must be empirical.

Therefore, the justification of a supposed basic empirical belief must depend on the justification of at least one other empirical belief, contradicting (1); it follows that there can be no basic empirical beliefs. . . .

The elements of coherentism

The very idea of a coherence theory

In light of the failure of foundationalism, it is time to look again at the apparent alternatives with regard to the structure of empirical justification which were distinguished in the discussion of the epistemic regress problem. If the regress of empirical justification does not terminate in basic empirical beliefs, then it must either (1) terminate in unjustified beliefs, (2) go on infinitely (without circularity), or (3) circle back upon itself in some way. As discussed earlier, alternative (1) is clearly a version of skepticism and as such may reasonably be set aside until all other alternatives have been seen to fail. Alternative (2) may also be a version of skepticism, though this is less clear. But the more basic problem with alternative (2) is that no one has ever succeeded in amplifying it into a developed position (indeed, it is not clear that anyone has even attempted to do so); nor do I see any plausible way in which this might be done. Failing any such elaboration which meets the objections tentatively developed earlier, alternative (2) may also reasonably be set aside. This then leaves alternative (3) as apparently the only remaining possibility for a nonskeptical account of empirical knowledge.

We are thus led to a reconsideration of the possibility of a coherence theory of empirical knowledge. If there is no way to justify empirical beliefs apart from an appeal to other justified empirical beliefs, and if an infinite sequence of distinct justified beliefs is ruled out, then the presumably finite system of justified empirical beliefs can only be justified from within, by virtue of the relations of its component beliefs to each other—if, that is, it is justified at all. And the idea of *coherence* should for the moment be taken merely to indicate whatever property (or complex set of properties) is requisite for the justification of such a system of beliefs.

Obviously this rather flimsy argument by elimination carries very little weight by itself. The analogous argument in the case of foundationalism lead to an untenable result; and that failure, when added to the already substantial problems with coherence theories which were briefly noted above, makes the present version even less compelling. At best it may motivate a more open-minded consideration of coherence theories than they have usually been accorded, such theories having usually been treated merely as dialectical bogeymen and only rarely as serious epistemological alternatives.

It will be useful to begin by specifying more precisely just what sort of coherence theory is at issue here. In the first place, our concern is with coherence theories *of empirical justification* and not coherence theories *of truth*; the latter hold that truth is to be simply *identified* with coherence (presumably coherence with some specified sort of system). The classical idealist proponents of coherence theories in fact generally held views of both these sorts and unfortunately failed for the most part to distinguish clearly between them. And this sort of confusion is abetted by views which use the phrase "theory of truth" to mean a theory of the *criteria* of truth, that is, a theory of the standards or rules which should be appealed to in deciding or judging whether or not something is true; if, as is virtually always the case, such a theory is meant to be an account of the criteria which can be used to arrive at a rational or warranted judgment of truth or falsity, then a coherence theory of truth in that sense would seem to be indiscernible from what is here called a coherence theory of justification, and quite distinct from a coherence theory of the very nature or meaning of truth. But if such confusions are avoided, it is clear that coherence theories of empirical justification are both distinct from and initially a good deal more plausible than coherence theories of empirical truth and moreover that there is no manifest absurdity in combining a coherence theory of justification with a *correspondence* theory of truth. Whether such a combination is in the end dialectically defensible is of course a further issue and one to which I will return in the final chapter of this book. . . .

Linear versus nonlinear justification

The initial problem is whether and how a coherence theory constitutes even a *prima facie* solution to the epistemic regress problem. Having rejected both foundationalism and the actual-infinite-regress position, a coherentist must hold, as we have seen, that the regress of empirical justification moves in a circle—or, more plausibly, some more complicated and multidimensional variety of closed curve. But this response to the regress will seem obviously and utterly inadequate to one who approaches the issue with foundationalist preconceptions. Surely, his argument will go, such a resort to circularity fails to solve or even adequately confront the problem. Each step in the regress is a justificatory argument whose premises must be justified *before* they can confer justification on the conclusion. To say that the regress moves in a circle is to say that at some point one (or more) of the beliefs which figured earlier as a conclusion is now appealed to as a justifying premise. And this response, far from solving the problem, seems to yield the patently absurd result that the justification of such a belief depends, indirectly but still quite inescapably, on *its own* logically prior justification: it cannot be justified unless it is already justified. And thus, assuming that it is not justified in some independent way, neither it nor anything which depends upon it can be genuinely justified. Since empirical justification is always ultimately circular in this way according to coherence theories, there can on such a view be in the end no empirical justification and no empirical knowledge.

The crucial, though tacit, assumption which underlies this seemingly devastating line of argument is the idea that inferential justification is essentially *linear* in character, that it involves a one-dimensional sequence of beliefs, ordered by the relation of epistemic priority, along which epistemic justification is passed from the earlier to the later beliefs in the sequence via connections of inference. It is just this linear conception of justification which generates the regress problem in the first place. So long as it remains unchallenged, the idea that justification moves in a circle will seem obviously untenable, and only moderate or strong foundationalism will be left as an alternative: even weak foundationalism cannot accept a purely linear view of justification, since its initially credible beliefs are not sufficiently justified on that basis alone to serve as linear first premises for everything else. Thus the primary coherentist response to the regress problem cannot be merely the idea that justification moves in a circle, for this would be quite futile by itself; rather such a position must repudiate the linear conception of justification in its entirety.

But what is the alternative? What might a nonlinear conception of justification amount to? As suggested briefly [earlier], the main idea is that inferential justification, despite its linear appearance, is essentially systematic or holistic in character: beliefs are justified by being inferentially related to other beliefs in the overall context of a coherent system.

The best way to clarify this view is to distinguish two importantly different levels at which issues of empirical justification can be raised. The epistemic issue on a particular occasion will usually be merely the justification of a single empirical belief, or small set of such beliefs, within the context of a cognitive system whose overall justification is (more or less) taken for granted; we may call this the *local* level of justification. But it is also possible, at least in principle, to raise the issue of the overall justification of the entire system of empirical beliefs; we may call this the *global* level of justification. For the sort of coherence theory which will be developed here—and indeed, I would argue, for any comprehensive, nonskeptical epistemology—it is the issue of justification as it arises at the latter, global, level which is in the final analysis decisive for the determination of empirical justification in general. This tends to be obscured in practice, I suggest, because it is only issues of the former, local, sort which tend to be explicitly raised in actual cases. (Indeed, it may well be that completely global issues are never in fact raised outside the context of explicitly epistemological discussion; but I cannot see that this in any way shows that there is something illegitimate about them.)

It is at the local level of justification that inferential justification *appears* linear. A given justificandum belief is shown to be justified by citing other premise-beliefs from which it correctly follows via some acceptable pattern of inference. Such premise-beliefs may themselves be challenged, of course, with justification being offered for them in the same fashion. But there is no serious danger of an infinite regress at this level, since the justification of the overall system of empirical beliefs, and thus of most of its constituent beliefs, is *ex hypothesi* not at issue. One quickly reaches premise-beliefs which are dialectically acceptable in that particular context and which can thus function there rather like the foundationalist's basic beliefs. (But these *contextually basic beliefs*, as they might be called, are unlikely to be only or even primarily beliefs which would be classified as basic by any plausible version of foundationalism.)

If, on the other hand, no dialectically acceptable stopping point were reached, if the new premise-beliefs offered as justification continued to be challenged in turn, then (according to the sort of coherence theory with which I am concerned) the epistemic dialogue would if ideally continued eventually circle back upon itself, giving the appearance of a linear regress and in effect challenging the entire system of empirical beliefs. At this global level, however, the previously harmless illusion of linearity becomes a serious mistake. According to the envisaged coherence theory, the relation between the various particular beliefs is correctly to be conceived, not as one of linear dependence, but rather as one of mutual or reciprocal support. There is no ultimate relation of epistemic priority among the members of such a system and consequently no basis for a true regress. Rather the component beliefs of such a coherent system will ideally be so related that each can be justified in terms of the others, with the direction of argument on a particular occasion of local justification depending on which belief (or set of beliefs) has actually been challenged in that particular situation. And hence, a coherence theory will claim, the apparent circle of justification is not in fact vicious *because it is not genuinely a circle:* the justification of a particular empirical belief finally depends, not on other particular beliefs as the linear conception of justification would have it, but instead on the overall system and its coherence.

According to this conception, the fully explicit justification of a particular empirical belief would involve four distinct main steps or stages of argument, as follows:

(1) The inferability of that particular belief from other particular beliefs and further relations among particular empirical beliefs.
(2) The coherence of the overall system of empirical beliefs.
(3) The justification of the overall system of empirical beliefs.
(4) The justification of the particular belief in question, by virtue of its membership in the system.

The claim of a coherence theory of empirical justification is that each of these steps depends on the ones which precede it. It is the neglecting of steps (2) and (3), the ones pertaining explicitly to the overall cognitive system, that lends plausibility to the linear conception of justification and thus generates the regress problem. And this is a very seductive mistake: since the very same inferential connections between particular empirical beliefs are involved in both step (1) and step (4), and since the issues involved in the intervening steps are very rarely (if ever) raised in practical contexts, it becomes much too easy to conflate steps (1) and (4), thus leaving out any explicit reference to the cognitive system and its coherence. The picture which results from such an omission is vastly more simple; but the price of this simplicity, according to coherence theories, is a radical distortion of the very concept of epistemic justification—and also, in the end, skepticism or something tantamount to it. . . .

Coherentist observation: an example

Consider then the following example of (putative) observational knowledge: As I sit at my desk (or so I believe), I come to have the belief, among very many others, that there is a red book on the desk. In fact, of course, the content of the belief is a good deal more precise and specific than the formulation just given would suggest: I do not believe simply that there is a red book on the desk, but rather that there is a book of a certain approximate size, of an approximately rectangular shape, which is a certain fairly specific shade of red, and so on. But what matters for the moment is that I do not *infer* that there is a red book on the desk, nor does the belief result from any other sort of deliberative or ratiocinative process, whether explicit or implicit. Rather it simply occurs to me, "strikes me," in a manner which is both involuntary and quite coercive; such a belief is, I will say, *cognitively spontaneous*. It is cognitive spontaneity which marks the belief as putatively observational, as what Sellars calls a "language-entry transition," in a way which can be recognized from within the system of beliefs.

At first glance, such a belief represents as clear a paradigm of an observational belief, indeed of observational knowledge, as one could want. How then is it justified? It is reasonably obvious what the various foundationalist views which were examined earlier and found wanting would say, but what might our envisaged coherentist account of observation offer as an alternative? How might the justification of such a belief, considered as an observation, depend on coherence with or inferability from other beliefs in my overall system of beliefs, on the availability of something like a justificatory argument?

There are several obvious but crucial facts (or at least things which I believe to be facts) concerning the belief and its context which can plausibly serve as the premises of a justificatory argument. Presumably these are things that I know, but what matters for the moment is that I believe them—and that these further beliefs are themselves justified in some manner or other.

First, the belief in question is a cognitively spontaneous belief of a certain, reasonably definite kind K_1, which we may specify, somewhat misleadingly, by saying that it is a visual belief about the color and general classification of a "medium-sized physical object." The reason that this is apt to be misleading is that the term "visual" suggests a classification in terms of causal etiology, whereas what is intended here is a classification concerned only with the intrinsic character and content of the belief, however it may in fact have been caused. Thus hallucinatory or dream beliefs of the right sort could qualify as visual in this sense, despite having been caused in some way having no connection at all with the physiological machinery of vision. We might better describe such beliefs as "putatively visual" or "apparently visual," but I will not bother with this terminological refinement here.

Second, the conditions of observation are of a specifiable sort C_1: the lighting is good, I am reasonably close to the apparent location of the object, my eyes are functioning normally, and so on. It is common to speak of "standard conditions," but these may vary substantially for different sorts of cases; it will thus be less confusing to assume an actual listing of the conditions, though I will not attempt to give a complete one here.

Third, it is a true law of nature concerning me and a large, though indefinite class of relevantly similar observers (where a rough specification of an appropriate sort of observers can be taken to be part of the specified conditions) that our cognitively spontaneous beliefs of that kind in conditions of the sort specified are highly reliable, that is, very likely to be true.

Since I believe all of these things, I am in a position to offer the following justificatory argument for the original belief:

(1) I have a cognitively spontaneous belief of kind K_1 that there is a red book on the desk.

(2) Conditions C_1 obtain.
(3) Cognitively spontaneous visual beliefs of kind K_1 in conditions C_1 are very likely to be true.
Therefore, my belief that there is a red book on the desk is very likely to be true.
Therefore, (probably) there is a red book on the desk.

Obviously this is very far from the end of the matter: if my belief is to be genuinely justified by appeal to this argument, the premises of the argument must themselves be justified; and if the resulting account of observation is to be genuinely coherentist, these further justifications must also make no appeal to basic beliefs. . . . For the moment, the point is that the justification of my original belief is, on this account, not somehow intrinsic or primitive, as would be the case for versions of foundationalism like Quinton's, but is rather dependent on the background and context provided by my other beliefs. This is the basic claim which a coherentist account of observation must make for *all* varieties of observation.

Answers to objections

Answers to standard objections (I) and (II)

The coherentist account of observation and introspection offered in the previous chapter provides the last of the main ingredients needed for the formulation (as opposed to the metajustification) of a coherentist account of empirical justification. In the present chapter I will explore the shape of such a theory in more detail, by considering whether and how it can meet various objections. I begin in this section with a reconsideration of the first two of the standard objections to coherence theories which were formulated [earlier]; this will also yield a significant modification in the theory itself. The second section will then formulate and attempt to answer a number of additional objections which arise in connection with the view in question, following which the final section will summarize the overall position which results and touch briefly on the justification of memory knowledge.

It will prove convenient to consider first objection (II), which alleges that empirical justification, as understood by a coherentist, involves no *input* from the extratheoretic world. In light of the discussion of observation, we are already in a position to see that at least part of this objection is mistaken. It need not be true, as the objection alleges, that coherentist justification is purely a matter of the internal relations within the system of beliefs. For if the system in question contains beliefs to the effect that recognizable kinds of cognitively spontaneous beliefs are likely to be true, and if beliefs of these kinds indeed occur, then such beliefs will be at least provisionally justified in a way which does not depend at all on the relation between their assertive content and the rest of the system. They can thus constitute input in at least the minimal sense of being new elements of the system which are not merely derived inferentially from the earlier elements. And such beliefs need not merely augment the system but may also force the alteration or abandonment of parts of it: either because the (putative) observational belief is directly inconsistent with one or more of the previous beliefs in the system or because such alteration will, in light of the new beliefs, enhance the overall coherence of the system. Of course the observational beliefs could themselves be rejected as a result of such conflict, though if this is done very often, the law which specifies the degree of reliability of that particular sort of observational belief will also have to be revised.

Thus any new observational belief which conflicts with other parts of the system forces a choice between at least two alternative ways of revising the system. The primary basis for making this choice is the relative coherence of the alternatives, though there is another important constraint, of a rather different sort, which will be mentioned momentarily. In this way a coherence theory can allow for a system of beliefs to be tested against the results of (putative) observation and revised accordingly.

There are, however, two important issues with respect to the foregoing suggestion which need to be discussed. First, though such beliefs may constitute input in the minimal sense just specified, is there any reason to think that they genuinely constitute input in the full sense involved in the objection, that is, input from the extratheoretic world? This question can, indeed must, be discussed on two different levels. On an empirical level, operating within the cognitive system, the standard explanation given for the occurrence of such beliefs is that they are *caused* in regular ways by the world; and moreover, it is very hard to think of any alternative explanation which could be offered at this level for the existence of significant numbers of cognitively spontaneous beliefs which are at least largely in agreement with each other. Thus such beliefs will normally be at least *claimed* within the system to constitute extratheoretic input. Of course it can still be asked whether there is any reason to think that such a claim is true; but this is merely a specific case of the general issue of whether coherentist justification is truth-conducive. Thus a complete answer to the input problem will, not surprisingly, depend on the outcome of that later discussion.

The second issue, of more immediate concern, is whether a coherence theory of empirical justification, while perhaps allowing in the way just indicated for the *possibility* of input into the system of beliefs, does not also permit there to be a system of justified empirical beliefs which lacks such input. For suppose that a particular system of beliefs simply fails to attribute a sufficient degree of reliability to enough kinds of cognitively spontaneous beliefs to yield a significant degree of input (or alternatively fails to attribute reliability to those introspective beliefs which are essential for the reliable recognition of other kinds of reliable spontaneous beliefs). One might arbitrarily construct a system of beliefs with this feature; or alternatively, it might be produced gradually (and perhaps unintentionally) if conflicts between putative observations and other beliefs in the system are always settled by rejecting the observations. Such a system would fail to have any effective input from outside the system. But there seems to be no reason why it might not still possess the highest possible degree of coherence and hence be epistemically justified according to the coherentist account offered so far. And this is surely a mistaken, even absurd result.

This point is, I believe, essentially sound. What it shows is that any adequate account of empirical knowledge must *require* putative input into the cognitive system, not merely allow for the possibility of such input. For, as was already argued in the initial statement of objection (II), without input of some sort any agreement which happened to exist between the cognitive system and the world could only be accidental and hence not something which one could have any good reason to expect. Thus, as a straightforward consequence of the idea that epistemic justification must be truth-conducive, a coherence theory of empirical justification must require that in order for the beliefs of a cognitive system to be even candidates for empirical justification, that system must contain laws attributing a high degree of reliability to a reasonable variety of cognitively spontaneous beliefs (including in particular those kinds of introspective beliefs which are required for the recognition of other cognitively spontaneous beliefs).

This requirement, which I will refer to as the *Observation Requirement*, is obviously quite vague, and I can see no way to make it very much more precise without going into vastly more detail than is possible here. The underlying idea is that any claim in the system which is not justified *a priori* should in principle be capable of being observationally checked, either directly or indirectly, and thereby either confirmed or refuted. But whether or not this is so in a given system depends not only on the modes of observation available in that system, but also on the inferential interconnectedness of the system. In a fairly tight-knit system, the Observation Requirement could thus be interpreted less stringently than would be necessary in a looser system.

Notice that the Observation Requirement does *not* stipulate that the cognitively spontaneous beliefs to which reliability is attributed must actually *be* reliable, even as judged from within the system. Nor does it place any restriction on the sort of taxonomy which can be employed in specifying particular classes of such beliefs. Obviously it is part of the background concept of observation that observational beliefs are reliable and also at least implicitly that observational beliefs will fall into something like natural kinds with each kind having a distinctive causal etiology. But these conditions need not be built into the Observation Requirement, since failure to satisfy them will virtually guarantee that the system will not both remain coherent and continue to satisfy the Observation Requirement as stated, at least not in the long run. To attribute reliability to beliefs which are not in fact reliable or to lump together beliefs of very different sorts (which will be affected by different sorts of conditions) is almost certain to lead to eventual incoherence. The Observation Requirement should, however, be understood to include the requirement, common to all adequate theories of knowledge, that a user of the system must make a reasonable effort to seek out relevant, possibly conflicting observations, if his beliefs are to be justified.

Thus understood, the Observation Requirement effectively guarantees that a cognitive system which satisfies it will receive at least apparent input from the world and hence that empirical justification will not depend merely on the internal relations of a static belief system; it thus provides the basic answer to objection (II).

It is important to understand clearly the status of the Observation Requirement within a coherentist position. The need for the requirement is *a priori*: it is, for reasons already indicated in the original discussion of objection (II), an *a priori* truth that empirical knowledge of an independent world is not possible without input from that world; and it also seems to be true *a priori*, in light of my earlier discussion of foundationalism, that such input can only be understood in terms of something very close to Sellars's idea of token credibility which does not derive from type credibility and hence in terms of cognitively spontaneous beliefs which are justified, at least in part, in virtue of that status. Hence, according to a coherence theory, it is an *a priori* truth that a cognitive system must attribute reliability to some members of the general class of cognitively spontaneous beliefs, to the extent indicated, *if* it is to contain empirical knowledge. But for a given system, it is *not* an *a priori* truth that the antecedent of this conditional is satisfied and hence also not an *a priori* truth that its consequent is satisfied—or even that it epistemically ought to be satisfied. Whether any varieties of cognitively spontaneous beliefs are in fact reliable and hence should be recognized as such is an empirical issue to be decided, purely on the basis of coherence, within the cognitive system. It is logically conceivable, relative to a particular system, that no variety of cognitively spontaneous belief is in fact sufficiently reliable and hence that this system will be unable to satisfy the Observation Requirement in the long run while remaining coherent. The Observation Requirement says not that such a situation could occur, but only that if it did occur, there would in consequence be no empirical justification and no empirical knowledge.

Thus the Observation Requirement, as it functions within a coherentist position, might be described, perhaps a bit ponderously, as a regulative metaprinciple, as opposed to a first-level epistemic principle. It does not impinge directly on issues of empirical justification; these are decided entirely be appeal to coherence. Rather the Observation Requirement provides a partial basis for *categorizing* or *classifying* the results yielded by such a system. This is one difference between a coherence theory of the present sort and that version of weak foundationalism which attributes some degree of initial credibility to all cognitively spontaneous beliefs. According to such a foundationalist view, it is true *prior* to any appeal to coherence that cognitively spontaneous beliefs have this minimal degree of credibility—for which no adequate justification is or ever can be offered. Whereas for a coherence theory, *all* epistemic justification of empirical beliefs depends on coherence.

What then would be the status of contingent and superficially empirical beliefs belonging to a coherent system of beliefs which violates the Observation Requirement? I suggest that they be thought of as analogous to beliefs—or at least belief-like states—which are a product of sheer imagination or which are the mental correlate of literary fiction. It is a consequence of the holism which is part and parcel of a coherence theory that the distinction between genuine empirical description and these other categories of thought or discourse is not to be drawn at the level of particular beliefs or statements but only at the level of systems. And the empirical thrust of a cognitive system is precisely the implicit claim that its component beliefs will agree, in general at least, with those classes of cognitively spontaneous beliefs which it holds to be reliable; while one who presents or regards a given body of propositions as purely imaginative or fictional commits himself to no such claim. (Thus the Observation Requirement might be viewed as a kind of rough analogue of the old positivist verifiability criterion of empirical meaningfulness, transmuted so as to apply to systems of beliefs rather than to isolated beliefs or statements.)

We are now also in a position to offer an answer to objection (I), the alternative coherent systems objection. But once it is clear that a coherence theory can allow for, indeed insist upon, the possibility that a cognitive system which is coherent at one time may be rendered incoherent, and thereby in need of revision, by subsequent observational input, this objection needs some major reformulation. If it is to be interesting, the objection cannot be merely that *at a given time* there may be many equally coherent but incompatible systems between which a coherence theory provides no basis for decision. This claim is surely correct but does not constitute an objection to coherence theories, since an analogous claim would also hold for virtually any imaginable theory of knowledge, including all of the standard foundationalist views: on *any* account of the standards of epistemic justification, it is quite possible, even likely, that there will be competing sets of empirical claims which at a particular time are tied for the status of most justified and between which those standards offer *at that time* no basis for decision. This is neither alarming nor particularly surprising. The most that it seems reasonable to expect of an epistemological account is that it make it possible for such ties to be broken *in the long run*.

Thus if it is to constitute a serious objection to a coherence theory of the sort in question here, objection (I) must be interpreted to mean that even in the long run and with the continued impact of (putative) observational beliefs, there will always be multiple, equally coherent empirical systems between which a coherence theory will be unable to decide. But once the possibility of observational input is appreciated, it is no longer clear why this claim should be accepted, or at least why it is thought to be any more plausible in relation to a coherence theory than it is in relation to other theories of knowledge. The basic rationale for the original version of the objection was that alternative coherent systems could, at least in principle, be constructed arbitrarily. But such an arbitrarily constructed system will not in general satisfy the Observation Requirement; and if one should be so constructed as to initially satisfy that requirement, there is no reason to think that it would remain coherent as (putative) observations accumulate, even if it were coherent in the beginning. Thus the possibility of arbitrary invention seems to provide no real support for the envisaged objection.

One useful way to put this point is to say that a coherence theory which incorporates the indicated conception of observation bases justification not on the *static* coherence of a system of beliefs considered in the abstract but rather on the *dynamic* coherence of an ongoing system of beliefs which someone actually accepts. Only such an actually functioning system can contain cognitively spontaneous beliefs and thereby satisfy the Observation Requirement. For this reason, the possibility of arbitrarily constructing a coherent system in the abstract has no bearing on such a theory.

Once the possibility of arbitrary invention is set aside, is there any other reason for thinking that the possibility of alternative coherent systems is a serious problem for this sort of coherence theory? I can think of only one further way of pressing such an objection. According to a coherence theory of the sort in question, the classification of a given sort of cognitively spontaneous belief as reliable and hence as a species of observation is not in any way an *a priori* matter but rather depends entirely on the extent to which such a classification yields a maximally coherent system. But suppose that relative to a given person's cognitive system there are two disjoint classes of cognitively spontaneous beliefs, such that: if the beliefs in one class are classified as observational, one system results and remains coherent in the long run; while if the beliefs in the second class are classified as observational, a different, incompatible system results which is equally coherent and remains equally coherent in the long run; whereas if the beliefs in both classes are classified as observational, a system with a much lower degree of coherence, too low to meet the requirement for justification, results. (There could be more than two such classes, but I will neglect this possibility for the sake of simplicity.) A coherence theory seems to provide no basis for choosing between these two coherent systems. And this might not be so for some versions of foundationalism, depending on just what kinds of cognitively spontaneous beliefs are involved.

Is such a situation a genuine possibility? Could it perhaps be produced by a Cartesian demon, if not in some more ordinary way? The issue is extremely difficult, and I have been unable to devise any really compelling argument in either direction. But there is at least one consideration to be noted. For the situation to work as described, it must be the case that the cognitively spontaneous beliefs in each of the two classes are, when taken separately, strongly in agreement with each other and quite coherent. But then the internal agreement and coherence of these two classes of beliefs are facts which must be explained by *any* total view which such a person might adopt, on pain of serious anomaly and hence greatly reduced coherence. As already briefly suggested, the obvious explanation of the internal agreement and coherence of such a class of beliefs is that it is caused in such a way as to genuinely reflect an objective reality. But if such an explanation is ruled out, as it must be for one of these two classes of beliefs by either of the two cognitive systems in question, then some alternative explanation must be found. And thus for the choice between the two cognitive systems to be genuinely symmetrical in the way supposed by the objection, each would have to have such an alternative, reasonably satisfactory explanation of this sort for the agreement and coherence of the observation beliefs of the other, and the two explanations would have to be equally good (other things being equal). And while such a situation *may* still be a possibility, I can see no reason to think that it is likely enough to constitute a serious objection to our proposed coherence theory.

We have, in any case, obviously come very far from the original version of objection (I). Instead of the claim that there will *always* be indefinitely many equally coherent and incompatible cognitive systems, between which a coherence theory provides no basis for decision, we have now the claim that there *might possibly* be two (or, an even more questionable possibility, more than two) such systems between which a coherence theory could not decide (but for which some foundationalist views *might* provide a basis for decision). This is a very weak objection, if indeed it is still an objection at all.

Thus the first two of the standard and supposedly fatal objections to coherence theories have little real force against a version of coherentism which incorporates the proposed account of observation. This does not mean, of course, that such a position is finally defensible. There remains the third of the standard objections, the problem of truth. But before considering that objection, there are several other serious objections which need to be formulated and assessed.

Some further objections

The first three objections concern the proper classification of the view presented: whether it is genuinely a version of coherentism, and its relation to foundationalism.

Objection 1. The view presented is not genuinely a version of coherentism. Rather it is a version of weak foundationalism in which the foundational beliefs are the person's metabeliefs about the composition of his own system of beliefs, that is, those beliefs specified by the Doxastic Presumption.

Reply. It must be conceded that there is *something* to this objection. Indeed, I have insisted at several points that one's reflective grasp of the composition of one's own system of beliefs provides an essential starting point for this version, or indeed for any plausible version, of coherentism. No nonexternalist appeal to coherence is possible without a grasp of the system of beliefs relative to which coherence is to be judged. This grasp may be, as I have suggested, in part defeasible, but it is not dispensable. And there can be no real objection to characterizing the central role which the metabeliefs that make up this grasp of one's own system of beliefs play for a coherentist position by saying that they constitute the *foundation* of empirical knowledge for such a view, so long as it is clearly understood that "foundation" here does not carry with it the implications which it would possess within a standard foundationalist view. For no claim is being made that these metabeliefs possess any sort of intrinsic or independent justification or warrant of any kind (nor would such a claim be defensible in light of the earlier antifoundationalist arguments). Rather the approximate correctness of these beliefs is an essential presupposition for coherentist justification, and both such justification itself and any resulting claim of likelihood of truth must be understood as relativized to this presupposition. In this respect, then, the present view is fundamentally different from weak foundationalism in a way which makes it only confusing to assimilate the two, in spite of the admitted parallels between them.

Objection 2. The view presented is not genuinely a version of coherentism. It is a version of weak foundationalism in which the initially credible foundational beliefs are just the cognitively spontaneous beliefs. Such beliefs must be regarded as having some small, defeasible degree of justification if coherence with them is to confer justification on anything else; and the effect of the Observation Requirement is to confer on them just such a status.

Reply. Though not entirely without merit, this objection has rather less to be said for it than the preceding one. Obviously the status of cognitively spontaneous beliefs is very special for a view of the sort in question, and obviously that status is conferred at least in part by the Observation Requirement. Moreover, it would be possible to formulate a version of weak foundationalism, or something very close to weak foundationalism, in which cognitively spontaneous beliefs were accorded some degree of initial or independent warrant, and such a view would have fairly close structural similarities to the version of coherentism suggested here.

But in spite of this, the main claims made in the objection are mistaken. First, it is simply not necessary in order for such a view to yield justification to suppose that cognitively spontaneous beliefs have some degree of initial or independent credibility. One way to see this is to consider a parallel example taken, surprisingly enough, from C.I. Lewis. Lewis's account of memory knowledge is a version of weak foundationalism: memory beliefs are claimed to have some antecedent degree of warrant simply by virtue of being memory beliefs, and this is then amplified by appeal to coherence (which Lewis, as we have seen, calls "congruence"). In arguing for his account, Lewis considers the example of "relatively unreliable witnesses who independently tell the same circumstantial story." The point of the example is that: "For any one of these reports, taken singly, the extent to which it confirms what is reported may be slight . . . But congruence of the reports establishes a high probability of what they agree upon, by principles of probability determination which are familiar: on any other hypothesis than that of truthtelling, this agreement is highly unlikely; the story that any one false witness might tell being one out of so very large a number of equally possible choices." And he adds that this result would still follow even if one of the witnesses were to tell a different story. What Lewis does not see, however, is that his own example shows quite convincingly that no antecedent degree of warrant or credibility is required. For as long as we are confident that the reports of the various witnesses are genuinely independent of each other, a high enough degree of coherence among them will eventually dictate the hypothesis of truth telling as the only available explanation of their agreement—even, indeed, if those individual reports initially have a high degree of *negative* credibility, that is, are much more likely to be false than true (for example, in the case where all of the witnesses are known to be habitual liars). And by the same token, so long as apparently cognitively spontaneous beliefs are genuinely independent of each other, their agreement will eventually generate credibility, without the need for any initial degree of warrant.

Secondly, there is no reason why the Observation Requirement should be regarded as in fact conferring such an initial degree of warrant on cognitively spontaneous beliefs. The main point is that it is quite consistent with the Observation Requirement, as explained above, that no cognitively spontaneous belief of any kind might turn out to be warranted: this would be so, for example, if no class of such beliefs turned out to be in internal agreement to any significant degree. But such a result would not seem to be possible for a weak foundationalist view, according to which the largest consistent (or coherent?) class of basic beliefs will seemingly have to be justified to some degree, even if perhaps not enough to satisfy the requirement for knowledge. There is thus a quite fundamental distinction between the two views.

QUESTIONS

1 What is meant by a "basic belief"?
2 According to BonJour, what is required in order for a belief to be "justified"?
3 According to BonJour, what four steps are involved in the justification of an empirical belief?
4 What is a cognitively spontaneous belief?
5 Are cognitively spontaneous beliefs also *basic* beliefs, according to BonJour? (Explain.)

William Alston, "Has Foundationalism Been Refuted?"

The battle over foundationalism in epistemology has recently been escalated with the publication of two works in which that position is subjected to detailed criticism, Frederick L. Will's *Induction and Justification*[1] and Keith Lehrer's *Knowledge*.[2] In both cases, however, the attack is directed to features of the position that are by no means essential to foundationalism and that do not appear in its most defensible form, what I shall call "Minimal Foundationalism". This paper will be devoted to supporting this claim and to suggesting that if one wishes to dispose of foundationalism he must concentrate his fire on its strongest form.

1. Will's criticism

Will formulates foundationalism as follows:

> There is a class of claims, cognitions, that are known in a special direct, certain, incorrigible way; and all epistemic authority resides in these. The philosophical question of the epistemic status of any claim is always a question of the relation of that claim to this class of first cognitions. A claim can be established to be a genuine example of knowledge, or at least a claim worthy of some kind of reasonable adherence, only if it can be disclosed to be, if not a first cognition itself, in some degree authenticated by one or more of such cognitions. It must be possible somehow, beginning with such cognitions, by a finite set of steps in an acceptable procedure to arrive at the claim in question as a conclusion and, by virtue of this, as a justified result. (p. 142)

Elsewhere these "first cognitions" are characterized as "infallible" (p. 203), "indubitable" (p. 172), "self-justifying" (p. 190), and enjoying "logical independence from every other possible cognition" (p. 200). Will's objections to the position are focused on the claims of independence and incorrigibility, the latter understood as the impossibility of justified rejection or revision.

The doctrine advanced concerning these alleged first steps in cognition, like

William Alston, "Has Foundationalism Been Refuted?" *Philosophical Studies* 29 (1976): 287–305.

> that concerning consequent ones, is that . . . in discriminating a quality of one's own visual experience (e.g., the redness of the after-image) one is participating in a practice that extends, and depends for its success upon conditions which extend, far beyond the subject as an individual human being. (p. 197)

And just because of this, one's supposition that one's sensation is of a certain character is liable both to error and to revision.

> If knowing any truth about a sensation, if indeed *having* a sensation of the kind that is specified in that truth, involves the employment and sound working of a vast array of equipment and resource extending far beyond any individual and what can be conceived to be private to him, then the possibility that this equipment and resource is not in place and working soundly cannot be discounted in the philosophical understanding of the knowledge of such truth. If the sound discrimination of the sensation of X, in its character *as* X, can be made only by correctly utilizing something further, say, Y, and if, in a case like this, discrimination of a sensation as X can be made while yet, for some reason, Y is not being used correctly, then a discrimination of X need not be a sound discrimination. (p. 203)

Will's attack on incorrigibility and infallibility embodies a salutary emphasis on the possibility and importance of failings other than error.

> There are a variety of ways in which a discrimination may go wrong without being mistaken, without yielding anything sufficiently close to a good performance to be rightly called an error. And there are also a variety of ways in which a discrimination can exhibit its corrigibility other than by going wrong, by yielding somehow an unsuccessful individual performance. . . . Like every other mode of response, modes of sensory discrimination exhibit their liability to change, improvement, deterioration and obsolescence in the dependence they exhibit at all points upon individual and social needs and the conditions under which these needs are filled. (p. 207)

If I were concerned in this paper with the soundness of Will's criticism, there are a number of matters into which I should have to go. For one thing, there is the question of whether he thinks that the dependence of, for instance, sensory discriminations, on social practices, *itself* contradicts a central tenet of foundationalism, or whether he makes this point only as a basis for showing corrigibility. And this of course depends on how he interprets the *independence* he supposes foundationalism to ascribe to first cognitions. Although he is not as explicit about this as one might wish, there are indications that he supposes foundationalism to be committed to the view that he possibility of first cognitions *in no way* depends on the existence of anything outside one's momentary state of mind (e.g., p. 203); in that case the dependence he (surely correctly) alleges would be itself an argument against the position. Again it is not clear that his vigorous and penetrating attack on incorrigibility really is based on the claim that all cognition depends on social practices. Would not Will's points about the inherent possibility of any procedure's being misused and about the liability of any conceptual scheme to be scrapped for a better one apply even to a disembodied mind that is alone in the universe (assuming, contra Wittgenstein and Will, that one can speak intelligibly of a solipsistic mind as using procedures and conceptual schemes)? But my concern in this paper is limited to showing that even if we freely grant the force of his arguments, a significant brand of foundationalism is left standing.

Let's suppose, then, that Will has shown both that all cognition depends (not just in fact but, as he claims, with a kind of theoretical necessity [pp. 198–99]) on social practices, and that no cognitions are incorrigible. Does that dispose of foundationalism? Hardly. Though foundationalists have often taken their foundations to be incorrigible,[3] they need not have done so in order to be distinctive foundationalists. To flesh out this claim I shall formulate a "Minimal Foundationalism," the weakest, and hence least vulnerable, doctrine that has enough bite (of the right sort) to deserve that title.

It will be useful to build up to the formulation in several stages. In the most unspecific terms a foundationalist is one who supposes that knowledge forms a structure, most components of which are supported by a certain subset of components that are not themselves supported by the former. To make this less metaphorical we have to specify the mode of support involved. Most contemporary formulations (including those of our critics) employ some form of a justified-true-belief conception of knowledge, in that they take something like S's being justified in truly believing that *p* as at least a necessary condition for S's knowing that *p*.[4] In these terms we can specify the relevant mode of support as justification. The rest of knowledge is supported by the foundations and not vice versa, just in that it depends on the foundations for the justification of the beliefs involved, and not vice versa. Two further considerations will enable us to make this formulation more perspicuous.

(1) First a useful bit of terminology. Where what justifies a belief includes[5] the believer's possessing certain other justified beliefs (those that embody his evidence or reasons for the initial belief), we may speak of *mediately (indirectly)* justified belief. And where what justifies a belief does not include any such thing (any other justified belief of that person) we may speak of *immediately (directly)* justified belief. Correspondingly, a case of knowledge in which the justification requirement is satisfied by mediate justification may be called *mediate (indirect) knowledge*; and a case in which the justification requirement is satisfied by immediate justification will be called *immediate (direct)* knowledge.

(2) We should make more explicit just how mediate justification is thought to depend on immediately justified belief. The idea is that although the other beliefs that are involved in the justification of a given belief may themselves be mediately justified, if we continue determining at each stage how the beliefs involved are justified, we will arrive, sooner or later, at a set of beliefs each of which is immediately justified. This will not, in general, be a single line of descent, for typically the mediately justified belief with which we start will rest on several beliefs, each of which in turn will rest on several beliefs. So the general picture is that of multiple branching from the original belief.

Taking account of all this, we may formulate Minimal Foundationalism as follows.

(I) Every mediately justified belief stands at the base of a (more or less) multiply branching tree structure at the tip of each branch of which is an immediately justified belief.

Knowledge seems to have been mislaid in the course of our discussion, but it is easily relocated. Foundationalism is thought of as dealing with knowledge just because one thinks of the justified beliefs in question as satisfying the other requirements for knowledge. One can, if he likes, build into (I) an explicit restriction to cases of knowledge.

(II) In every case of mediate knowledge the mediately justified belief involved stands at the base of a (more or less) multiply branching tree structure at the tip of each branch of which is an immediately justified belief that satisfies the other requirements for knowledge.

The fact remains, however, that the structure definitive of foundationalism comes into the picture via the justification of belief. Hence (I) gives what is essential to the position, and that is what I shall be discussing under the title of "Minimal Foundationalism."

There are certain differences between (I) and Will's formulation that are not directly relevant to our present concerns. For example, Will thinks of foundationalism in terms of how one is to *show* that a nonbasic belief is justified, whereas (I) is in terms of what it is for a nonbasic belief to *be* justified.[6] But of course it follows from (I) that the way to *show* that a nonbasic belief is justified is roughly the way Will specifies. Again, (I) is in terms of "belief," whereas Will uses terms like "claim" and "cognition." It lies outside the purview of this paper to argue that "belief" is the term we need, but I am confident it could be successfully argued.

What *is* directly to the point is that the targets of Will's criticism are not to be found in Minimal Foundationalism. What that position requires of a foundation is only that it be immediately justified, justified by something other than the possession of other justified beliefs. And to say that a certain person is immediately justified in holding a certain belief is to say nothing as to whether it could be shown defective by someone else or at some other time.[7] Still less is it to say that it enjoys the absolute independence opposed by Will. A minimal foundation *is* independent of every other cognition in that it derives its justification from none. But that by no means implies that it is nomologically possible for such a belief to occur without a supporting context of social practices. And it is the latter mode of independence that Will rejects.

Will attempts to show that "absolute" independence and incorrigibility, as well as infallibility, are required if a cognition is to serve as a foundation.

> The crucial aspect of the alleged first cognitions that are taken to be expressed in basic empirical propositions is their logical independence from every other possible cognition. This character of epistemic atoms is essential to them, essential to their role as self-justifying grounds for other claims. If they are not logically independent, other cognitions may serve as grounds for them; and this is incompatible with their role as members of the

> justification sequence with which the sequence of questions must stop, because no more can possibly be asked. From this independence follows their incorrigibility, and given this incorrigibility . . . they will have to be certain in a very strong sense that implies infallibility. (pp. 200–201)

Ten pages earlier there is a similar line of argument, starting from the basic demand for a foundation that it "can be established in utter independence from other claims" (p. 190), which I take to be roughly equivalent to being "members of the justification sequence with which the sequence of questions must stop". Thus we have a chain of alleged implications that runs–*can be established without dependence on other claims→independence from every other cognition→incorrigibility→infallibility*.

As against this I would suggest that neither the starting point nor any of the succeeding links in the chain have been shown to be required by foundationalism.

It may look as if "can be established in utter independence from other claims" is just precisely what we have said Minimal Foundationalism requires of its foundations. However, there is a subtle but highly significant difference between "*is justified* without dependence on other claims" and "can be *established* without dependence on other claims." I might well *be* immediately justified in believing, for example, that I feel depressed, without being able to "establish" this (i.e., *show* that it is true), either with or without dependence on other "claims." In fact it is not at all clear what would count as such a showing; perhaps the strongest candidate would be my showing that I am justified in believing that I feel depressed. But of course to do that requires far more conceptual and dialectical sophistication than would normally be possessed by those who *are* justified in holding such beliefs. In view of that, it is fortunate that Minimal Foundationalism does not require one to be able to *show* that his foundations have the required status, but only that they *do* have them.[8]

In the quotation above "logical independence" is said to be entailed by the capability of being established without reliance on other claims. Perhaps it is, but only in the sense in which a contradiction entails everything. I don't see what sense can be attached to showing or establishing p without adducing some grounds q, not identical with p. If when asked to show that p I simply reiterate my assertion that p, I have clearly not *shown* that p; this follows just from the concept of showing. Even if my belief is self-justifying, so that nothing outside the belief is required to justify me in holding it, what follows from that, if anything follows concerning showing, is that there is no need for me to show that p is true; it certainly does not follow that I *can* show that p just by asserting that p. So the requirement that it be possible to establish that p without dependence on other cognitions is a self-contradictory one. And the more sensible requirement that we have seen to be intrinsic to foundationalism, that the claim *be justified* otherwise than by relation to other cognitions, does *not* entail that the claim is "logically independent of all other possible cognitions." Indeed it is not at all clear what is meant by the latter, but let's take its denial to involve what Will says it involves, viz., that other cognitions may serve as grounds. Does this prevent the putative foundation from being immediately justified? Will thinks so. "Claims are said to be self-justifying ones only when they alone, and no other claims whatever, may be advanced in their support." (p. 201).[9] But I see no merit in this. To say that a belief is immediately justified is just to say that there are conditions *sufficient* for its justification that do not involve any other justified beliefs of that believer. This condition could be satisfied even if the believer has other justified beliefs that could serve as grounds. Overdetermination is an epistemic as well as a causal phenomenon. What fits a belief to serve as a foundation is simply that it doesn't *need* other justified beliefs in order to be justified itself. It can be accepted *whether or not* there are grounds. Clearly the existence of grounds does not prevent its having that status.

As for the next link in the chain, I suppose that if foundations were "logically independent" of other claims in such a way as to render them insusceptible of mediate justification, it would follow by the same token that they could not be shown mistaken on the basis of other claims. But since we have seen no reason to attribute the former to foundations, we are left with no basis for the attribution of incorrigibility. Will elsewhere gives other arguments for incorrigibility, but they also involve features that go beyond Minimal Foundationalism. For example, "incorrigibility derives from the assignment of certain claims to the position of fixed and absolute beginnings in the justification process" (p. 191).[10] And if we require maximal stability for the structure of justification, we shall indeed have to rule out the possibility that any foundation loses its credentials. But all that is required by Minimal Foundationalism is that the mediately justified beliefs a person has at any moment rest (at that moment) on certain immediately justified beliefs. This in no way implies that the set of immediately justified beliefs changes from moment to moment *only* by adding new members. Items can also drop out, whether by refutation or otherwise. That will only mean that mediately justified beliefs that essentially depended on those delinquents will drop out as well.

We may, finally, note that the derivation of infallibility from incorrigibility fares no better.

> Since incorrigibility without truth is a dubious merit for any set of truth claims to have, since incorrigible error is of the worst kind, and since the aspiration to truth of any item in the corpus of human knowledge is taken to depend upon these alleged incorrigible claims, they must, in their splendid isolation, be incorrigibly true. Infallibility as a requirement derives in the theory from incorrigibility. (p. 190)

This may indicate why infallibility is attractive to foundationalists (or any other seeker after truth), but it does nothing to show that a claim *cannot* be incorrigible without being infallible; indeed by acknowledging the conceivability of incorrigible error Will acquiesces in the denial of that.[1] Nor does it do anything to show that only infallible claims can play the foundational role. No doubt, in order to be a foundation a belief must carry a strong presumption of truth; this it enjoys just by virtue of being justified. But that is quite different from *impossibility* of falsity.[12]

II. Lehrer's criticism

Lehrer's formulation of foundationalism runs as follows:

> It is possible to give a more precise characterization of foundation theories by specifying the conditions that must be met for a belief to be basic. The first is that a basic statement must be self-justified and must not be justified by any non-basic belief. Second, a basic belief must either be irrefutable, or, if refutable at all, it must only be refutable by other basic beliefs. Third, beliefs must be such that all other beliefs that are justified or refuted are justified or refuted by basic beliefs. A theory of justification having these features is one in which there are basic beliefs which are self-justified and neither refutable nor justifiable by non-basic beliefs and which justify and refute all non-basic beliefs that are justified or refuted. These basic beliefs constitute the foundation of all justification. (pp. 76–77)

This, like Minimal Foundationalism, is (appears to be) in terms of what it is to *be* justified, rather than what it takes to *show* justification; but, like Will, Lehrer tacks on a requirement of incorrigibility (here interpreted as impossibility of error). As noted in notes 10 and 11, Lehrer claims, like Will, that incorrigibility and infallibility are required for foundations, and devotes a longish chapter (chapter 4) to arguing that there are not nearly enough incorrigible beliefs to serve as foundations for others. In spite of that he goes on in the following chapter to acknowledge the conceivability of a theory built on corrigible foundations. Our task here will be to determine whether his objections against this latter form of the theory tell against Minimal Foundationalism.

Lehrer attacks the theory both on the basic and the nonbasic level. As for the former, he considers whether the beliefs that we need for foundations are "self-justified." After arguing that "independent information" is required for the justification of perceptual beliefs. Lehrer admits that for the justification of some beliefs, for instance, those concerning one's own current states of consciousness, no "information" is required over and above "semantic information" that is needed for understanding the meaning of the statement, and hence that they may be self-justified (p. 111). But *how* is this possible? In particular, "What defence can be given of this epistemological principle telling us that beliefs of this sort are self-justified?" (p. 112). There is a lengthy and, to my mind, persuasive argument against the common position that such principles are true by virtue of the meanings of terms (pp. 112–19). The other alternatives he considers are that "the belief that the principle is true is basic" (p. 121), and that by taking such beliefs to be self-justified we will be able to explain how other beliefs are justified (p. 121). The objection to the first of these alternatives is that: "This manoeuvre, though logically consistent, opens the door to the most rampant forms of speculation. Anyone wishing to argue that he knows anything whatever can then claim that what he knows is a basic belief. When asked to defend this claim, he can again retort that it is a basic belief that this belief is basic, and so on." (p. 152). The second alternative is rejected on the basis of the argument considered below, which seeks to show that foundationalism cannot account for the justification of nonbasic empirical beliefs.

How damaging is this criticism to Minimal Foundationalism? Taking it *à pied de la lettre*, not at all. Minimal Foundationalism does not require that any belief be self-justified, but only that some beliefs be immediately justified; and the former is only one possible form of the latter. A belief is *self*-justified, in a literal sense, if it is justified just by virtue of being held, just by virtue of being the sort of belief it is (e.g., a belief by a person that he is currently thinking so-and-so). But that is by no means the only kind of immediate justification. The following also constitute live possibilities for the justification of, for example, a belief by a person that he currently feels depressed.

(1) Justified by its truth, in other words by the fact that makes it true, the fact that he does now feel depressed.[13]
(2) Justified by the believer's awareness of his feeling depressed, where this is a nonpropositional kind of awareness that does not necessarily involve any belief or judgment, justified or otherwise.[14]
(3) Justified by being formed, or being held, in certain kinds of circumstances, for instance, being wide awake, alert, in full possession of one's faculties.

If what it takes to justify my belief that I am feeling depressed is what is specified by (1), (2), or (3), then more is required than the mere existence of the belief.[15]

But although it is an extremely important point that immediate justification is not confined to self-justification, this is too easy a way with Lehrer's argument. For whatever mode of immediate justification we think attaches to beliefs about one's current states of consciousness, the question can still be raised as to what defense can be given of the epistemological principle that beliefs of this sort are justified under these conditions. This is a profound and difficult problem that must certainly be faced by foundationalism, and I cannot hope to go into it properly here. I shall have to content myself with arguing that Lehrer has not shown this to be a fatal difficulty for Minimal Foundationalism.

First let us note that this is a problem for any epistemology, foundationalist or otherwise, that employs the concept of epistemic justification. It is incumbent on any such epistemology to specify the grounds for principles that lay down conditions for beliefs of a certain sort to count as justified. I believe that a sober assessment of the situation would reveal that no epistemology has been conspicuously successful at this job. Before using this demand as a weapon against foundationalism the critic should show us that the position he favors does a better job.[16]

Rather than spend more time on these legalistic "burden of proof" considerations, I should like to turn to a point that is more directly relevant to my interest in revealing gratuitous accretions to Minimal Foundationalism. My own view as to how foundationalism (or any other epistemology) should test a principle of justification is that it should use empirical evidence to determine whether beliefs approved by the principle are reliable, that is, can be depended on to be (at least usually) correct. I suspect that Lehrer, along with most of my readers, would react to this by saying that whatever the merits of this suggestion for other epistemologies, it is obviously unavailable for foundationalism. Since it is definitive of that position to insist that a foundation does not depend on any other belief for its justification, how can a foundationalist countenance the deployment of empirical evidence to validate the foundations? Well, to see how this is possible we have to uncover a distinction closely analogous to the one mentioned earlier between a basic belief's *being justified* and *being established* (or shown to be justified). The distinction in question is that between (a) knowing (being justified in believing) that I am depressed (when that is a basic belief), and (b) knowing (being justified in believing) that I immediately know (am justified in believing) that I feel depressed. Clearly it is definitive of foundationalism to hold that (a) does not depend on any other beliefs' being justified, but it is in no way essential to foundationalism to deny that (b) is so dependent. Minimal Foundationalism would be committed to the latter denial only if one could not be immediately justified in believing that *p* without also being immediately justified in believing that he is immediately justified in believing that *p*. But why suppose that? Even if justification on the lower level necessarily carries with it justification of the belief that one is so justified, it would not follow that the justification of the higher level belief is *immediate*. It could be, rather, that being justified in believing that *p* automatically puts one in possession of the evidence he needs for being *mediately* justified in believing that he is immediately justified in believing that *p*. And in any event, why suppose that being justified in believing that *p* necessarily carries with it being justified in believing that one is so justified? It would seem that those who have not attained the level of epistemological reflection have no justification for believing anything about their being epistemically justified. And when one does come to be justified in accepting some higher level epistemic belief, is this not typically on the basis of ratiocination? In particular it may be, as Lehrer in effect suggests, that I will have to formulate some general principle of justification and find adequate reasons for accepting it before I can become justified in believing that I am immediately justified in believing that *p*. And in that case perhaps empirical evidence for the reliability of beliefs that satisfy this principle will be the crucial reason in support of the principle.[17]

Let's return to Lehrer's argument that foundationalism can provide no adequate reason for accepting a principle that declares beliefs concerning one's own current conscious states to be immediately justified in some way, for example, to be self-justified. The burden of the last paragraph is that this argument will work only if Lehrer can exclude the possibility of a foundationalist's providing adequate empirical support for such principles. And he can do this only by saddling foundationalism with the gratuitous demand that in addition to basic beliefs' *being* immediately justified, one must be immediately justified in taking them to be immediately justified. Once again the argument tells only against a position that makes claims it need not make in order to be a foundationalism.

On the level of nonbasic beliefs Lehrer's argument proceeds from what he terms "the fundamental doctrine of foundation theories", viz., that "justification, whether it is the self-justification of basic beliefs, or the derivative justification of non-basic beliefs, guarantees truth" (pp. 78–79). When we consider the justification of nonbasic beliefs by evidence, "The consequence which follows is that evidence never *completely* justifies a belief in such a way as to guarantee the truth of the belief unless the probability of the statement on the basis of the evidence is equal to one" (p. 149). Indeed, we can apply the same considerations to basic beliefs. "If we now consider the question of how probable a belief must be in order to be self-justified, an analogous argument shows that the belief must have an initial probability of one" (p. 150). And this implies that practically no contingent beliefs could be justified. "For any strictly coherent probability function, no statement has an initial probability of one unless it is a logical truth and in infinite languages no non-general statement has an initial probability of one unless it is a logical truth. Hence, with the exception of certain general statements in infinite languages, completely justified basic beliefs would have to be restricted to logical truths, and completely justified non-basic beliefs would have to be restricted to logical consequences of completely justified basic beliefs . . . We would be locked out of the realm of the contingent, and skepticism would reign supreme there." (p. 151).

I will not have time to go into the way Lehrer derives these conclusions from the "fundamental doctrine." Again I shall have to restrict myself to considering whether the argument, if valid, is damaging to Minimal Foundationalism. And here that reduces to the question whether Minimal Foundationalism holds that "justification guarantees truth."

Unfortunately it is not at all clear what this is supposed to mean. A natural interpretation would be that justification necessitates truth, that it is impossible for a justified belief to be false. And that seems to be what Lehrer means initially. In the paragraph in which he introduces the "fundamental doctrine," he says, "Basic beliefs are basic because they cannot be false; their truth is guaranteed" (78). But when in the next chapter he comes to recognize the possibility of basic beliefs that are corrigible, he analogizes the epistemic guarantee of truth to a manufacturer's guarantee of soundness, and points out that in neither case is the existence of the guarantee incompatible with the absence of what is guaranteed. (p. 102). But then hasn't the "fundamental doctrine" become vacuous? On *any* (sensible) conception of justification it carries at least a strong presumption of truth. And isn't that as much of a guarantee as a manufacturer's guarantee? It looks at this point as if "guarantee of truth" has become indistinguishable from "justification." But then in chapter 6, where the argument currently under consideration occurs, Lehrer seems to have drifted into a conception midway between "necessitates truth" and "carries a strong presumption of truth," but without telling us just what this is. Indeed the only real clue we have is the claim quoted above, that a belief must have a probability of one if its justification is to guarantee its truth. Perhaps it is something like this: to say that the justification of a belief *guarantees* its truth is to say that it comes as close as possible to necessitating the truth of the belief. But whether or not that is just the way to put it, it is clear that so long as "justification guarantees truth" has the consequence for both basic and nonbasic beliefs alleged by Lehrer in the present argument, that doctrine is no part of Minimal Foundationalism. It is quite possible for some beliefs to be immediately justified and for other beliefs to be mediately justified on the basis of the former, without any of them receiving a probability of one. At least there is nothing in the general notions of immediate and mediate justification to support any such requirement. No doubt, the higher the probability the stronger the justification, but why should a foundationalist have to insist on a maximally strong justification? What is there about *foundationalism*, as contrasted with rival orientations, that necessitates such a demand? The distinctive thing about foundationalism is the *structure* of justification it asserts; and this structure can be imposed on justifications of varying degrees of strength. Once more a band of camp followers has been mistaken for the main garrison.

III. The status of minimal foundationalism

One may grant that Minimal Foundationalism is untouched by the criticisms we have been discussing and yet feel that this is of little import, just because that position is so minimal as to have lost the features that give foundationalism its distinctive contours. My answer to that is simply to point out that when we formulate the main argument for foundationalism, the regress argument, in the only form in which it gives any support to that position, the version that emerges is precisely what I have been calling Minimal Foundationalism. The regress argument may be formulated as follows.

> Suppose we are trying to determine whether S is mediately justified in believing that *p*. To be so justified he has to be justified in believing certain other propositions, *q*, *r*, . . ., that are suitably related to *p* (so as to constitute adequate grounds for *p*). Let's say we have identified a set of such propositions each of which S believes. Then he is justified in believing that *p* only if he is justified in believing each of these propositions. And for each of these propositions, *q*, *r*, . . . that he is not immediately justified in believing, he is justified in believing it only if he is justified in believing some other propositions that are suitably related to it. And for each of these latter propositions. . . .
>
> Thus in attempting to give a definitive answer to the original question we are led to construct a more or less extensive tree structure, in which the original belief and every other putatively mediately justified belief forms a node from which one or more branches issue, in such a way that every branch is a part of some branch that issues from the original belief. Now the question is: what form must be assumed by the structure in order that S be mediately justified in believing that *p*? There are the following conceivable forms for a given branch.
>
> (A) It terminates in an immediately justified belief.
> (B) It terminates in an unjustified belief.
> (C) The belief that *p* occurs at some point (past the origin), so that the branch forms a loop.
> (D) The branch continues infinitely.
>
> Of course some branches might assume one form and others another.
>
> The argument is that the original belief will be mediately justified only if every branch assumes form (A). Positively it is argued that on this condition the necessary conditions for the original belief's being mediately justified are satisfied, and negatively it is argued that if any branch assumes any other form, they are not.
>
> (A) Where every branch has form (A), each branch terminates in an immediately justified belief that is justified without the necessity for further justified beliefs. Hence justification is transferred along each branch right back to the original belief.

(B) For any branch that exhibits form (B), no element, including the origin, is justified, at least by this structure. Since the terminus is not justified, the prior element, which is justified only if the terminus is, is not justified. And since it is not justified, its predecessor, which is justified only if it is, is not justified either. And so on, right back to the origin, which therefore itself fails to be justified.

(C) Where we have a branch that forms a closed loop, again nothing on that branch, including the origin, is justified, so far as its justification depends on this tree structure. For what the branch "says" is that the belief that *p* is justified only if the belief that *r* is justified, and that belief is justified only if . . . , and the belief just before the looping back is justified only if the belief that *p* is justified. So what this chain of necessary conditions tells us is that the belief that *p* is justified only if the belief that *p* is justified. True enough, but that still leaves it open whether the belief that *p is* justified.

(D) If there is a branch with no terminus, that means that no matter how far we extend the branch, the last element is still a belief that is mediately justified if at all. Thus as far as this structure goes, wherever we stop adding elements, we still have not shown that the conditions for the mediate justification of the original belief are satisfied. Thus the structure does not exhibit the original belief as mediately justified.

Hence the original belief is mediately justified only if every branch in the tree structure terminates in an immediately justified belief. Hence every mediately justified belief stands at the base of a (more or less) multiply branching tree structure at the tip of each branch of which is an immediately justified belief.

I do not claim that this argument is conclusive; I believe it to be open to objection in ways I will not be able to go into here. But I do feel that it gives stronger support to foundationalism than any other regress argument. And clearly it yields, at most, Minimal Foundationalism. All that it takes to avoid the three alternatives deemed unacceptable by this argument is a belief at the tip of each branch that is in fact immediately justified. These beliefs do not have to incorrigible, infallible, or indubitable to perform this function. Their justification does not have to "guarantee" their truth in any sense in which that goes beyond just being justified. They do not have to be incapable of mediate justification. They do not even have to be true, though if they were generally false, the structure they support would be of little interest. Their *occurrence* can depend on various external conditions. They do not have to be self-justified, in a strict sense, as contrasted with other modes of direct justification. Nor is it necessary that the believer can show them to be immediately justified; still less is it necessary that he *immediately* know that they are immediately justified. All that is needed to satisfy the demands of the argument is that a belief that *is* immediately justified in some way or other terminate each chain of mediate justification. Since Minimal Foundationalism does guarantee this, it can hardly be maintained that it lacks the distinctive epistemological force characteristic of foundationalism.

Within the confines of this paper I cannot properly support my claim that the above is the only version of the regress argument that supports any form of foundationalism; to do so would involve examining them all. I will, however, say a word about a version that one frequently encounters in both friend and foe, including Will and Lehrer. This is the version that, ignoring the fine print, differs from the above version only in being concerned with *showing justification* rather than with *being justified*.[18] In this second version the argument is that if we start with a mediately justified belief and proceed to show it to be justified by citing its grounds, and then showing them to be justified, and . . . , then again the only alternative to circularity, infinite regress or ending in something not shown to be justified, is to arrive, along each strand of justification, at some belief that can be *shown* to be justified in some way that does not involve adducing other beliefs. This form of the argument does indeed have a conclusion markedly stronger than Minimal Foundationalism, but unfortunately, as pointed out above in another connection, this conclusion is logically incoherent. It is conceptually impossible to *show* that a belief is justified, or show that anything else, without citing propositions we take ourselves to be justified in believing. Hence this form of the argument does not support any form of foundationalism, or any other position.

IV. Conclusion

Will and Lehrer are to be commended for providing, in their different ways, important insights into some possible ways of developing a nonfoundationalist epistemology. Nevertheless if foundationalism is to be successfully disposed of, it must be attacked in its most defensible, not in its most vulnerable, form. Although Will and Lehrer reveal weaknesses in historically important forms of foundationalism, it has been my aim in this paper to show that their arguments leave untouched the more modest and less vulnerable form I have called "Minimal Foundationalism," a form approximated to by the most prominent contemporary versions of the position.[19] It is to be hoped that those who are interested in clearing the decks for an epistemology without foundations will turn their critical weapons against such modest and careful foundationalists as Chisholm, Danto, and Quinton.

Notes

1 Ithaca: Cornell University Press, 1974.

2 Oxford: Clarendon Press, 1974.

3 The case of independence is more complicated. See below for some discussion of this.

4 It often goes unnoticed that the seventeenth-century foundationalists often taken as paradigmatic, Descartes and Locke, were *not* working with any such conception of knowledge, and hence that they did *not* envisage the structure of knowledge as a structure of justification of belief.

5 Only "includes" because other requirements are also commonly imposed in these cases, e.g., that the first belief be "based" on the others, and, sometimes, that the believer realize that these other beliefs do constitute adequate grounds for the first.

6 Talk of a belief "being justified" or the "justification" of a belief is ambiguous. The justification of a belief might be the process of showing it to be justified, or it

might be the status that it is thereby shown to have. Likewise "his belief is justified" might mean that it has been shown to have the status in question, or it might just mean that it does have that status. This ambiguity typically makes it difficult to interpret discussions of epistemic justification. In this paper I shall restrict ". . . is justified" to the latter meaning—*having* the epistemically desirable status. I shall use ". . . is shown to be justified" to express the other concept.

7 Will also argues, in essentially the same way, against the supposition that derived claims can be incorrigible. I take it to be even more obvious that foundationalism need not attribute incorrigibility to nonbasic beliefs, even if it should require basic beliefs to be incorrigible. For the principles of mediate justification might countenance logical connections (e.g., of an inductive sort) that do not transfer incorrigibility.

8 Will's adherence to the stronger requirement is no doubt connected with the fact that he, along with many foundationalists, construes the regress argument in terms of a regress of *showing* justification rather than a regress of *being* justified. See below.

9 Another difficulty with the argument under consideration is the incorrect identification of "immediately justified" (not by relation to other cognitions) and "self-justified." We shall let that pass for now, returning to it in connection with Lehrer where it plays a larger role in the argument.

10 Cf. Lehrer: "If basic beliefs were refutable by non-basic ones, then all that was justified by basic beliefs might be undone if those basic beliefs themselves were refuted. In this case, we would be lacking a foundation for justification" (p. 79). Lehrer cannot be whole-hearted in his advocacy of this argument, for he later acknowledges the possibility of corrigible foundations.

11 Lehrer argues that incorrigibility does entail infallibility; more specifically he argues for the contrapositive: ". . . if the justification of basic beliefs did not guarantee their truth, then such beliefs would be open to refutation on the grounds that, though they are self-justified, they are in fact false" (p. 79). It remains, however, to be shown that the mere possibility of being false necessarily carries with it the possibility that we should be able to show that it is false.

12 Elsewhere Will appeals to Chisholm's notion that what renders a foundation justified is simply the fact that makes is true (p. 201, fn. 5). Where a belief is justified in this way, it cannot be justified without being true. But that is not to say that no such belief can be false. And in any event that is only one possible form of immediate justification. (See below.)

For an illuminating critique of other arguments designed to show that foundations must be incorrigible or infallible; see A.M. Quinton, *The Nature of Things* (London: Routledge & Kegan Paul, 1973), chap. 6.

13 See Sydney Shoemaker, *Self-Knowledge and Self-Identity* (Ithaca: Cornell University Press, 1963), p. 216; and R.M. Chisholm, *Theory of Knowledge* (Englewood Cliffs, N.J.: Prentice-Hall, 1966), pp. 26–27.

14 See B. Russell, *Problems of Philosophy* (London: Oxford University Press, 1912), p. 77; and G.E. Moore, "The Refutation of Idealism," in *Philosophical Studies* (London: Kegan Paul, Trench, Trubner, 1922), pp. 24–25, and "The Nature and Reality of Objects of Perception," in ibid., pp. 70–71.

15 "Self-justified" is often used in an undiscriminating way, to range over more or

less of the terrain of immediate justification. Lehrer himself, just after stressing the requirement that basic beliefs be "self-justified," says that "Empiricists think that experience can guarantee the truth of the basic beliefs" (p. 78). That sounds more like (2).

16 No doubt Lehrer takes himself to have shown this in the exposition of his own position in chap. 8. I cannot discuss that in this paper.

17 In [the previous essay] I explore the differences between Minimal Foundationalism and a kind that requires, for each basic belief, that one also be immediately justified in believing that one is immediately justified in believing it.

It is very common in discussions of foundationalism to state the position so as only to require immediate justification or knowledge at the first level, but then to glide into the stronger requirement. Will's formulation of the position quoted above embodies no requirement that one have immediate knowledge *of* the epistemic status of "first cognitions". But still we find him saying things like "beginning items of knowledge . . . whose philosophical validation as knowledge must be capable of being made out in complete independence of the institution and the instruments of criticism and evaluation that the institution provides" (p. 160) and ". . . a level of foundational items in knowledge, items the status of which as knowledge is in a special way not subject to challenge" (p. 175). In these latter passages he is representing foundationalism as requiring that the *epistemic status* of the foundations be knowable without dependence on other cognitions.

18 Because of the ambiguity pointed out in n. 6, it is often unclear which version is being expounded. But our two authors are unmistakably dealing with the second version. Will indeed, explicitly distinguishes these versions on p. 178, and his criticisms on pp. 183–84 are clearly directed against the second version. For Lehrer's discussion see pp. 15–16 and pp. 155–57.

19 The closest approximation is found in Quinton, *The Nature of Things*. The versions of Chisholm, *Theory of Knowledge*, and Arthur Danto, *Analytical Philosophy of Knowledge* (Cambridge: Cambridge University Press, 1968), are also much closer to Minimal Foundationalism than to the positions attacked by Will and Lehrer.

QUESTIONS

1 What is an "immediately justified belief"?
2 According to Alston, can immediately justified beliefs be supported by other beliefs?
3 Can an immediately justified belief be false?
4 Can an immediately justified belief later be refuted?
5 Must immediately justified beliefs be "self-justified"?
6 According to Alston, has foundationalism been refuted?

Susan Haack, "A Foundherentist Theory of Empirical Justification"[1]

> Let us remember how common the folly is, of going from one faulty extreme into the opposite.[2]

Does the evidence presented establish beyond a reasonable doubt that the defendant did it? Given the evidence recently discovered by space scientists, am I justified in believing there was once bacterial life on Mars? Is scientific evidence especially authoritative, and if so, why? Should we take those advertisements claiming that the Holocaust never happened seriously, and if not, why not? . . . Questions about what makes evidence better or worse, about what makes inquiry better or worse conducted, about disinterestedness and partiality, are of real, daily—and sometimes of life-and-death—consequence.

Of late, however, cynicism about the very legitimacy of such questions has become the familiar philosophical theme of a whole chorus of voices, from enthusiasts of the latest developments in neuroscience, to radical self-styled neo-pragmatists, radical feminists and multiculturalists, and followers of (by now somewhat dated) Paris fashions.

This cynicism is unwarranted; but dealing with it requires something a bit more radical than epistemological business-as-usual. Evidence is often messy, ambiguous, misleading; inquiry is often untidy, inconclusive, biased by the inquirers' interests; but it doesn't follow, as the cynics apparently suppose, that standards of good evidence and well-conducted inquiry are local, conventional, or mythical. And an even half-way adequate understanding of the complexities of real-life evidence and the untidiness of real-life inquiry requires a re-examination of some of those comfortably familiar dichotomies on which recent epistemology has relied—the logical versus the causal, internalism versus externalism, apriorism versus naturalism, foundationalism versus coherentism.

Although the other dichotomies will also come under scrutiny, the main theme here will be that foundationalism and coherentism—the traditionally rival theories of justified belief—do not exhaust the options, and that an intermediate theory is more plausible than either. I call it "foundherentism."

Susan Haack, *The Theory of Knowledge*, 2nd edn, ed. Louis Pojman (Belman, Calif.: Wadsworth, 1998), pp. 283–93.

SUSAN HAACK

The case for foundherentism

Foundationalist theories of empirical justification hold that an empirical belief is justified if and only if it is either a basic belief justified by the subject's experience,[3] or else a derived belief justified, directly or indirectly, by the support of basic beliefs. Coherentist theories of empirical justification hold that a belief is justified if and only if it belongs to a coherent set of beliefs. In short, foundationalism requires a distinction of basic versus derived beliefs and an essentially one-directional notion of evidential support, while coherentism holds that beliefs can be justified only by mutual support among themselves.

The merit of foundationalism is that it acknowledges that a person's experience—what he sees, hears, etc.—is relevant to how justified he is in his beliefs about the world; its drawback is that it requires a privileged class of basic beliefs justified by experience alone but capable of supporting the rest of our justified beliefs, and ignores the pervasive interdependence among a person's beliefs. The merit of coherentism is that it acknowledges that pervasive interdependence, and requires no distinction of basic and derived beliefs; its drawback is that it allows no role for the subject's experience.

Foundationalists, naturally, are keenly aware of the problems with coherentism. How could one possibly be justified in believing that there is a dog in the yard, they ask, if what one sees, hears, smells, etc., plays no role? And isn't the coherentist's talk of mutual support among beliefs just a euphemism for what is really a vicious circle in which what supposedly justifies the belief that *p* is the belief that *q*, and what justifies the belief that *q* the belief that *r*, . . . and what justifies the belief that *z* is the belief that *p*?

Coherentists, naturally, are no less keenly aware of the problems with foundationalism. What sense does it make to suppose that someone could have a justified belief that there is a dog in the yard, they ask, except in the context of the rest of his beliefs about dogs, etc.? Besides, why should we suppose that there *are* any beliefs both justified by experience alone and capable of supporting the rest of our justified beliefs? After all, foundationalists can't even agree among themselves whether the basic beliefs are about observable physical objects, along the lines of "there is a dog," or are about the subject's experience, along the lines of "it now seems to me that I see what looks like a dog" or "I am appeared to brownly." And anyway, only propositions, not events, can stand in logical relations to other propositions; so how *could* a subject's experience justify those supposedly basic beliefs?

As the two styles of theory have evolved, with each party trying to overcome the difficulties the other thinks insuperable, they have come closer together.

Strong foundationalism requires that basic beliefs be fully justified by the subject's experience; pure foundationalism requires that derived beliefs be justified exclusively by the support, direct or indirect, of basic beliefs. But weak foundationalism requires only that basic beliefs be justified to some degree by experience; and impure foundationalism, though requiring all derived beliefs to get some support from basic beliefs, allows mutual support among derived beliefs to raise their degree of justification.

Uncompromisingly egalitarian forms of coherentism hold that only overall coherence matters, so that every belief in a coherent set is equally justified. But moderated, inegalitarian forms of coherentism give a subject's beliefs about his present experience a distinguished initial status, or give a special standing to beliefs that are spontaneous rather than inferential in origin.

In a way, these moderated forms of foundationalism and coherentism lean in the right direction. But the leaning destabilizes them.

Weak foundationalism concedes that basic beliefs need not be fully justified by experience alone; but then what reason remains to deny that they could get more (or less) justified by virtue of their relations to other beliefs? Impure foundationalism concedes that there can be mutual support among derived beliefs; but then what reason remains to insist that more pervasive mutual support is unacceptable? And weak, impure foundationalism allows both that basic beliefs are less than fully justified by experience, and that derived beliefs may be mutually supportive; but now the insistence that derived beliefs can give no support to basic beliefs looks arbitrary, and the distinction of basic and derived beliefs pointless.[4]

Moderated, inegalitarian coherentism concedes that some beliefs are distinguished by their perceptual content or "spontaneous" origin; but isn't this implicitly to concede that justification is not after all a relation exclusively among beliefs, that input from experience is essential?

Not surprisingly, these fancier forms of foundationalism and compromising kinds of coherentism, though more sophisticated than their simpler ancestors, tend to be ambiguous and unstable. On the foundationalist side, for example, under pressure of just the kinds of difficulty my analysis identifies, C.I. Lewis moves from a pure to an impure foundationalism and then, briefly, to a kind of proto-foundherentism.[5] And on the coherentist side, under pressure of just the kind of difficulty my analysis identifies, BonJour tries to guarantee experiential input by adding an "Observation Requirement"—which, however, is ambiguous; on one interpretation it is genuinely coherentist, but doesn't allow the relevance of experience, and on the other it allows the relevance of experience, but isn't genuinely coherentist.[6] (BonJour now acknowledges that, after all, coherentism won't do.)[7]

Neither of the traditionally rival theories can be made satisfactory without sacrificing its distinctive character. The obvious conclusion—although those still wedded to the old dichotomy will doubtless continue to resist it—is that we need a new approach which allows the relevance of experience to empirical justification, but without postulating any privileged class of basic beliefs or requiring that relations of support be essentially one-directional: in other words, a foundherentist theory.

Explication of foundherentism

The details get complicated, but the main ideas are simple.

A foundherentist account will acknowledge (like foundationalism) that how justified a person is in an empirical belief must depend in part on his experience—my version will give a role both to sensory experience, and to introspective awareness of one's own mental states. As coherentists point out, although experience can stand in causal relations to beliefs, it can't stand in logical relations to propositions. But what this shows is not that experience is irrelevant to empirical justification, but that justification is a double-aspect concept, partly causal as well as partly logical in character.

A foundherentist account will acknowledge (like coherentism) that there is pervasive mutual support among a person's justified beliefs. As foundationalists point out, a belief can't be justified by a vicious circle of reasons. But what this shows is not that mutual support is illegitimate, but that we need a better understanding of the difference between legitimate mutual support and vicious circularity—my version will rely on an analogy between the structure of evidence and a crossword puzzle.

Of course, the viability of the foundherentist approach does not depend on my being completely successful in articulating it. No doubt there could be other versions of foundherentism falling within these general contours but differing in their details.

I take as my starting point the following vague, but very plausible, formulation: "A is more/less justified, at *t*, in believing that *p*, depending on how good his evidence is."

By starting from here I take for granted, first, that justification comes in degrees: a person may be more or less justified in believing something. (I also assume that a person may be more justified in believing some things than he is in believing others.)

I also take for granted, second, that the concepts of evidence and justification are internally connected: how justified a person is in believing something depends on the quality of his evidence with respect to that belief.

I assume, third, that justification is personal: one person may be more justified in believing something than another is in believing the same thing—because one person's evidence may be better than another's. (But although justification is personal, it is not subjective. How justified A is in believing that *p* depends on how good his, A's, evidence is. But how justified A is in believing that *p* doesn't depend on how good A *thinks* his evidence is; and anyone who believed the same thing on the same evidence would be justified to the same degree.)

And I assume, fourth, that justification is relative to a time: a person may be more justified in believing something at one time than at another—because his evidence at one time may be better than his evidence at another.

"A is more/less justified, at *t*, in believing that *p*, depending on how good his evidence is." The main tasks, obviously, are to explain "his evidence" and "how good." The double-aspect character of the concept of justification is already in play; for "his," in "his evidence," is a causal notion, while "how good" is logical, or quasi-logical, in character.

The concept of justification is causal as well as logical across the board[8]—its causal aspect is not restricted to experiential evidence alone. Quite generally, how justified someone is in believing something depends not only on *what* he believes, but on *why* he believes it. For example: if two people both believe the accused is innocent, one because he has evidence that she was a hundred miles from the scene of the crime at the relevant time, the other because he thinks she has an honest face, the former is more justified than the latter. In short, degree of justification depends on the quality of the evidence that actually causes the belief in question.

The word "belief" is ambiguous: sometimes it refers to a mental state, someone's believing something [an S-belief];[9] sometimes it refers to the content of what is believed, a proposition [a C-belief]. "A's evidence" needs to be tied somehow to what causes A's S-belief, but must also be capable of standing in logical or quasi-logical relations to the C-belief, the proposition believed.

The idea is to begin by characterizing A's S-evidence with respect to *p*—this will be a set of states of A causally related to his S-belief that *p*; and then to use this as the starting point of a characterization of A's C-evidence with respect to *p*—this will be a set of propositions capable of standing in logical or quasi-logical relations to the C-belief that *p*.

If A initially came to believe that the rock-rabbit is the closest surviving relative of the elephant because a fellow tourist told him he read this somewhere, and later still believes it, but now because he has learned all the relevant biological details, he is more justified at the later time than at the earlier. So, if they are different, "A's S-evidence with respect to *p*" should relate to the causes of A's S-belief that *p* at the time in question rather than to what prompted it in the first place.

What goes on in people's heads is very complicated. There will likely be some factors inclining A towards believing that *p*, and others pulling against it. Perhaps, e.g., A believes that Tom Grabit stole the book because his seeing Grabit leave the library with a shifty expression and a suspicious bulge under his sweater exerts a stronger positive pull than his belief that it is possible that Tom Grabit has a light-fingered identical twin exerts in the opposite direction. Both sustaining and inhibiting factors are relevant to degree of justification, so both will included in A's S-evidence.

In this vector of forces [the causal nexus of A's S-belief that *p*], besides A's present experience and present memory traces of his past experience, and other S-beliefs of his, such factors as his wishes, hopes, and fears will often play a role. But A's desire not to believe ill of his students, say, or his being under the influence of alcohol, although they may affect whether or with what degree of confidence he believes that Grabit stole the book, are not themselves part of his evidence with respect to that proposition.

So "A's S-evidence with respect to *p*" will refer to those experiential and belief-states of A's which belong, at the time in question, to the causal nexus of A's S-belief that *p*. The phrase "with respect to" signals the inclusion of both positive, sustaining, and negative, inhibiting, evidence [respectively, A's S-evidence for *p*, and A's S-evidence against *p*]. A's S-evidence with respect to *p* will include other beliefs of his [A's S-reasons with respect to *p*]; and his perceptions, his introspective awareness of his own mental goings-on, and memory traces of his earlier perceptual and introspective states [A's experiential S-evidence with respect to *p*].

The part about memory needs amplifying. A's experiential S-evidence may include present memory traces of past experience—such as his remembering seeing his car-keys on the dresser. This corresponds to the way we talk of A's remembering seeing, hearing, reading, etc.,. . . . We also talk of A's remembering that *p*, meaning that he earlier came to believe that *p* and has not forgotten it. How justified A is in such persisting beliefs will depend on how good his evidence is—his evidence at the time in question, that is. A person's evidence for persisting beliefs will normally include memory traces of past perceptual experience; my belief that my high-school English teacher's name was "Miss Wright," for instance, is now sustained by my remembering hearing and seeing the name used by myself and others.

Testimonial evidence, in a broad sense—what a person reads, what others tell him—enters the picture by way of his hearing or seeing, or remembering hearing or seeing, what someone else says or writes. Of course, A's hearing B say that *p* will not contribute to his, A's, believing that *p*, unless A understands B's language. But if A believes that *p* in part because B told him that *p*, how justified A is in believing that *p* will depend in part on how justified A is in thinking B honest and reliable. But I anticipate.

A's S-evidence with respect to *p* is a set of states of A causally related to his S-belief that *p*. But in the part of the theory that explains what makes evidence better or worse, "evidence" will have to mean "C-evidence," and refer to a set of propositions. The two aspects interlock: A's C-evidence with respect to *p* will be a set of propositions, and how good it is will depend on those propositions' logical or quasi-logical relations to *p*; but *which* propositions A's C-evidence with respect to *p* consists of, depends on which of A's S-beliefs and perceptual, etc., states belong to the causal nexus of the S-belief in question.

A's C-reasons with respect to *p*, obviously enough, should be the C-beliefs, i.e., the propositions, which are the contents of his S-reasons. For example, if one of A's S-reasons with respect to *p* is his S-belief that female cardinal birds are brown, the corresponding C-reason will be the proposition that female cardinal birds are brown.

But what about A's experiential C-evidence? My proposal is that "A's experiential C-evidence with respect to *p*" refer to propositions to the effect that A is in the perceptual/introspective/memory states that constitute his experiential S-evidence with respect to *p*. Since a perceptual, etc., state can not be part of the causal nexus of A's S-belief that *p* unless A is *in* that state, these propositions are all true. But they need not be propositions that A believes.[10]

So A's experiential C-evidence has a distinctive status. A's C-reasons may be true or may be false, and A may be more or less justified, or not justified at all, in believing them. But A's experiential C-evidence consists of propositions all of which are, *ex hypothesi*, true, and with respect to which the question of justification doesn't arise. (This is the foundherentist way of acknowledging that the ultimate evidence for empirical beliefs is experience—very different from the forced and unnatural way in which foundationalism tries to acknowledge it, by requiring basic *beliefs* justified by experience alone.)

In line with the way we ordinarily talk about the evidence of the senses—"Why do I think there's a cardinal in the oak tree? Well, I can see the thing; that distinctive profile is clear, although the light's not too good, and it's quite far away, so I can't really see the color"—I suggest a characterization of A's experiential C-evidence in terms of propositions to the effect that A is in the sort of perceptual state a normal subject would be in when seeing this or that in these or those circumstances. For example, if A's experiential S-evidence with respect to *p* is his perceptual state, its looking to him as it would to a normal observer seeing a female cardinal bird at a distance of 40 feet in poor light, the corresponding experiential C-evidence will be a proposition to the effect that A is in the kind of perceptual state a normal observer would be in when looking at a female cardinal bird in those circumstances.

Built into my account of experiential evidence is a conception of perception as, in a certain sense, direct. This is not to deny that perception involves complicated neurophysiological goings-on. Nor is it to deny that the judgments causally sustained by the subject's experience are interpretive, that they depend on his background beliefs as well—which, on the contrary, is a key foundherentist thought. It is only to assert that in normal perception we interact with physical things and events around us, which look a certain way to all normal observers under the same circumstances.

You may be wondering why I include the subject's sensory and introspective experience as evidence, but not, say, his extrasensory perceptual experience. Well, the task here is descriptive—to articulate explicitly what is implicit when we say that A has excellent reasons for believing that *p*, that B is guilty of wishful thinking, that C has jumped to an unjustified conclusion, and so on. As those phrases "excellent reasons" and "guilty of wishful thinking," indicate, his other beliefs should be included as part of a subject's evidence, but his wishes should not. Actually, I think it most unlikely there is such a thing as ESP; but it is excluded because—unlike sensory experience, for which we even have the phrase "the evidence of the senses"—it has no role in the implicit conception of evidence I am trying to make explicit.

The concepts of better and worse evidence, of more and less justified belief, are evaluative; so, after the descriptive task of explication, there will be the ratificatory question, whether our standards of better and worse evidence really are, as we hope and believe they are, indicative of truth. But that comes later.

The present task is to explicate "how good" in "how good A's C-evidence is." What factors raise, and what lower, degree of justification?

Foundationalists often think of the structure of evidence on the model of a mathematical proof—a model which, understandably, makes them leery of the idea of mutual support. My approach will be informed by the analogy of a crossword puzzle—where, undeniably, there is pervasive mutual support among entries, but, equally undeniably, no vicious circle. The clues are the analogue of experiential evidence, already completed intersecting entries the analogue of reasons. As how reasonable a crossword entry is depends both on the clues and on other intersecting entries, the idea is, so how justified an empirical belief is depends on experiential evidence and reasons working together.

Perhaps needless to say, an analogy is only an analogy, not an argument. Its role is only to suggest ideas, which then have to stand on their own feet. And there are always disanalogies; there will be nothing in my theory analogous to the solution to today's crossword that appears in tomorrow's newspaper, for instance, nor any analogue of the designer of a crossword.

But the analogy does suggests a very plausible multi-dimensional answer to the question: what makes a belief more or less justified? How reasonable a crossword entry is depends on how well it is supported by the clue and any already completed intersecting entries; how reasonable those other entries are, independent of the entry in question; and how much of the crossword has been completed. How justified A is in believing that *p*, analogously, depends on how well the belief in question is supported by his experiential evidence and reasons [supportiveness]; how justified his reasons are, independent of the belief in question [independent security]; and how much of the relevant evidence his evidence includes [comprehensiveness].

On the first dimension, A's C-evidence may be conclusive for *p*, conclusive against *p*, supportive-but-not-conclusive of *p*, undermining-but-not-conclusive against *p*, or indifferent with respect to *p*/with respect to not-*p*.

Foundationalists often take for granted that evidence is conclusive just in case it deductively implies the proposition in question; but this is not quite right. Inconsistent premisses deductively imply any proposition whatever; but inconsistent evidence is not conclusive evidence for anything—let alone conclusive evidence for everything! Think, for example, of a detective whose evidence is: the murder was committed by a left-handed person; either Smith or Brown did it; Smith is right-handed; Brown is right-handed. Although this deductively implies that Smith did it, it certainly is not conclusive evidence for that belief (let alone conclusive evidence for the belief that Smith did it *and* conclusive evidence for the belief that Brown did it *and* conclusive evidence for the belief that extra-terrestrials did it!).

Deductive implication is necessary but not sufficient for conclusiveness. Evidence E is conclusive for *p* just in case the result of adding *p* to E [the *p*-extrapolation of E] is consistent, and the result of adding not-*p* to E [the not-*p*-extrapolation of E] is inconsistent. E is conclusive against *p* just in case its *p*-extrapolation is inconsistent and its not-*p*-extrapolation consistent. But if E itself is inconsistent, both its *p*-extrapolation and its not-*p*-extrapolation are also inconsistent, so E is indifferent with respect to *p*.

Often, though, evidence is not conclusive either way, nor yet inconsistent and hence indifferent, but supports the belief in question, or its negation, to some degree. Suppose the detective's evidence is: the murder was committed by a left-handed person; either Smith or Brown did it; Smith is left-handed; Brown is left-handed; Smith recently saw the victim, Mrs. Smith, in a romantic restaurant holding hands with Brown. Though not conclusive, this evidence is supportive to some degree of the belief that Smith did it—for, if he did, we have some explanation of why.

The example suggests that supportiveness depends on whether and how much adding *p* to E makes a better explanatory story. But a better explanatory story than what? Conclusiveness is a matter of the superiority of *p* over its negation with respect to consistency. But if *p* is potentially explanatory of E or some component of E, it is not to be expected that not-*p* will be too. So I construe supportiveness as depending on the superiority of *p* over its rivals with respect to explanatory integration; where a rival of *p* is any proposition adding which to E improves its explanatory integration to some degree, and which, given E, is incompatible with *p*.

The word "integration" was chosen to indicate that E may support *p* either because *p* explains E or some component of E, or vice versa—that there is "mutual reinforcement between an explanation and what it explains."[11] (So the concept of explanatory integration is closer kin to the coherentist concept of explanatory coherence than to the foundationalist concept of inference to the best explanation.)

Usually, as conclusiveness of evidence is taken to be the province of deductive logic, supportiveness of evidence is taken to be the province of inductive logic. But at least if "logic" is taken in its now-usual narrow sense, as depending on form alone, this looks to be a mistake. Explanation requires generality, kinds, laws—a motive for the murder, a mechanism whereby smoking causes cancer, and so forth. If so, explanatoriness, and hence supportiveness, requires a vocabulary that classifies things into real kinds; and hence depends on content, not on form alone. (Hempel drew the moral, many years ago now, from the "grue" paradox.)[12] But there is supportive-but-not-conclusive evidence, even if there is no formal inductive logic.

Supportiveness alone does not determine degree of justification, which also depends on independent security and comprehensiveness. Suppose our detective's evidence is: the murder was committed by a left-handed person; either Smith or Brown did it; Smith is right-handed, but Brown left-handed. The detective's evidence is conclusive that Brown did it; nevertheless, he is not well justified in believing this unless, among other things, he is justified in believing that the murder was committed by a left-handed person, that either Smith or Brown did it, etc.

The idea of independent security is easiest to grasp in the context of the crossword analogy. In a crossword, how reasonable an entry is depends in part on its fit with intersecting entries, and hence on how reasonable those entries are, independently of the entry in question. Similarly, how justified a person is in believing something depends in part on how well it is supported by his other beliefs, and hence on how justified he is in believing those reasons, independently of the belief in question.

It is that last phrase—in my theory as with a crossword puzzle—that averts the danger of a vicious circle. The reasonableness of the entry for 3 down may depend in part on the reasonableness of the intersecting entry for 5 across—independent of the support given to the entry for 5 across by the entry for 3 down. Similarly, how justified A is in believing that *p* may depend in part on how justified he is in believing that *q*—independent of the support given his belief that *q* by his belief that *p*.

And, though "justified" appears on the right-hand side of the independent security clause, there is no danger of an infinite regress—any more than with a crossword puzzle. As in the case of a crossword eventually we reach the clues, so with empirical justification eventually we reach experiential evidence. And experiential C-evidence does not consist of other C-beliefs of the subject, but of propositions all of which are, *ex hypothesi*, true, and with respect to which the question of justification does not arise. This is not to deny that, as crossword clues may be cryptic, experiential evidence may be ambiguous or misleading; on the contrary, my account of experiential C-evidence is intended to recognize that it often is. It is only to say that the question of justification arises with respect to a person's beliefs, but not with respect to his experiences.

As how reasonable a crossword entry is depends not only on how well it is supported by the clue and other intersecting entries, and on how reasonable those other entries are, but also on how much of the crossword has been completed, so degree of justification depends not only on supportiveness and independent security, but also on comprehensiveness—on how much of the relevant evidence the subject's evidence includes.

Comprehensiveness promises to be even tougher to spell out than supportiveness and independent security; the crossword analogy isn't much help here, and neither is the nearest analogue in the literature, the total evidence requirement on inductions, which refers, not to the totality of relevant evidence, but to the totality of relevant available evidence—and then there is the further problem that relevance itself comes in degrees.

I am assuming, however, that (degree of) relevance is an objective matter. Naturally, whether I think your handwriting is relevant to your trustworthiness depends on whether I believe in graphology; but whether it *is* relevant depends on whether graphology is *true*.

As this reveals, although relevance, and hence comprehensiveness, is objective, judgments of relevance, and hence judgments of comprehensiveness, are perspectival, i.e., they depend on the background beliefs of the person making them. The same goes for judgments of supportiveness and independent security. How supportive you or I judge E to be with respect to *p*, for example, will depend on what rivals of *p* we happen to be able to think of; but how supportive E *is* of *p* does not. Quality of evidence is objective, but judgments of quality of evidence are perspectival.

Because quality of evidence is multi-dimensional, we should not necessarily expect a linear ordering of degrees of justification; e.g., A's evidence with respect to *p* might be strongly supportive but weak on comprehensiveness, while his evidence with respect to *q* might be strong on comprehensiveness but only weakly supportive. Nor, *a fortiori*, does it look realistic to aspire to anything as ambitious as a numerical scale of degrees of justification. But something can be said about what is required for A to be justified to *any* degree in believing that *p*.

One necessary condition is that there *be* such a thing as A's C-evidence with respect to *p*. If A's S-belief that *p* is caused simply by a blow to the head, or by one of those belief-inducing pills philosophers are fond of imagining, A is not justified to any degree in believing that *p*. Since it is the justification of empirical beliefs that is at issue, another necessary condition is that A's C-evidence should include some experiential C-evidence—present experiential evidence, or memory traces of what he earlier saw, heard, read, etc. This is my analogue of BonJour's Observation Requirement, obviously much more at home in foundherentism than his requirement was in his coherentist theory. (It is not meant to rule out the possibility that some of a person's beliefs may not be sustained directly by experiential evidence, not even by memory traces, but rely on other beliefs and their experiential evidence—as in an unconventional crossword some entries might have no clues of their own but rely on other entries and their clues.)[13] A third necessary condition is that A's C-evidence with respect to *p* should meet minimal conditions of supportiveness, independent security, and comprehensiveness; e.g., it should be better than indifferent in terms of supportiveness. Jointly, these necessary conditions look to be sufficient.

What about the upper end of the scale? Our ordinary use of phrases like "A is completely justified in believing that *p*" is vague and context dependent, depending *inter alia* on whether it is A's particular business to know whether *p*, and how important it is to be right about whether *p*; perhaps it also runs together strictly epistemological with ethical concerns. This vague concept [*complete* justification] is useful for practical purposes—and for the statement of Gettier-type paradoxes. In other philosophical contexts, however, "A is completely justified in believing that *p*" is used in a context-neutralized, optimizing way, requiring conclusiveness, maximal independent security, and full comprehensiveness of evidence [COMPLETE justification].

The account sketched here has been personal, i.e., focused firmly on our friend A. But this is not to deny that in even the most ordinary of our everyday beliefs we rely extensively on testimonial evidence. And where the sciences are concerned, reliance on others' evidence—and hence on the interpretation of others' words and judgments of others' reliability—is absolutely pervasive. (This reveals that not only the social sciences but also the natural sciences presuppose the possibility of interpreting others' utterances: think, e.g., of an astronomer's reliance on others' reports of observations.)

Anyhow, thinking about evidence in the sciences prompts me to ask whether it is possible to extrapolate from my account of "A is more/less justified in believing that *p*" to a concept of justification applicable to groups of people. It might be feasible to do this by starting with the degree of justification of a hypothetical subject whose evidence includes all the evidence of each member of the group, and then discount this by some measure of the degree to which each member of the group is justified in believing that other members are competent and honest.

The ratification of foundherentism

Thus far the task has been to articulate our standards of better and worse evidence, of more and less justified belief. But what do I mean by "our"? And what assurance can I give that a belief's being justified, by those standards, is any indication that it is true?

When I speak of "our" standards of better and worse evidence, I emphatically do not mean to suggest that these standards are local or parochial, accepted in "our," as opposed to "their," community. Rather, I see these standards—essentially, how well a belief is anchored in experience and how tightly it is woven into an explanatory mesh of beliefs—as rooted in human nature, in the cognitive capacities and limitations of all normal human beings.

It is sure to be objected that the evidential standards of different times, cultures, communities, or scientific paradigms differ radically. But I think this supposed variability is at least an exaggeration, and quite possibly altogether an illusion, the result of mistaking the perspectival character of judgments of evidential quality for radical divergence in standards of better and worse evidence.

Because judgments of the quality of evidence are perspectival, people with radically different background beliefs can be expected to differ significantly in their judgments of degree of justification. It doesn't follow that there are no shared standards of evidence. If we think of the constraints of experiential anchoring and explanatory integration rather than of specific judgments of the relevance, supportiveness, etc., of this or that evidence, I believe we will find commonality rather than divergence.

Again, the point is easier to see in the context of the crossword analogy. Suppose you and I are both doing the same crossword puzzle, and have filled in some long central entry differently. You think, given your solution to that long central entry, that the fact that 14 down ends in a "T" is evidence in its favor; I think, given my solution to that long central entry, that the fact that it ends in an "D" is evidence in its favor. Nevertheless, we are both trying to fit the entry to its clue and to other already completed entries. Now suppose you and I are both on an appointments committee. You think the way this candidate writes his "g"s indicates that he is not to be trusted; I think graphology is bunk and scoff at your "evidence." Because of a disagreement in background beliefs, we disagree about what evidence is relevant. Nevertheless, we are both trying to assess the supportiveness, independent security, and comprehensiveness of the evidence with respect to the proposition that the candidate is trustworthy.

But even if I am wrong about this, even if there really are radically divergent standards of evidential quality, it wouldn't follow that there are no objective indications of truth; *variability* of standards does not, in and of itself, imply *relativity* of standards.[14] So those epistemic relativists who have inferred that, since judgments of justification vary from community to community, there can be no objectively correct standards of better and worse evidence, have committed a *non sequitur* as well as relying on a dubious premiss.

As for those who have succumbed to epistemic relativism because they have given up on the concept of truth, I have room here only to say that theirs seems to me an entirely factitious despair.[15] In any case, all that will be required of the concept of truth in what follows is that a proposition or statement is true just in case things are as it says.

Supposing—as I believe, and so do you—that we humans are fallible, limited but inquiring creatures who live in a world which is largely independent of us and what we believe about it, but in which there are kinds, laws, regularities; and supposing—as I believe, and so do you—that our senses are a source, though by no means an infallible source, of information about things and events in the world around us, and introspection a source, though by no means an infallible source, of information about our own mental goings-on; then, if any indication of how things are is possible for us, how well our beliefs are anchored in our experience and knit into an explanatory mesh is such an indication. (And supposing—as I believe, and so, probably, do you—we have no other sources of information about the world and ourselves, no ESP or clairvoyance or etc., then this is the only indication we can have of how things are.)

That last paragraph was nothing like an a priori ratification of foundherentism; for those "supposing" clauses are empirical in character. Assumptions about human cognitive capacities and limitations are *built into* our standards of evidential quality; so the truth-indicativeness of those standards depends on the truth of those empirical assumptions. But neither was that last paragraph much like the appeals to psychology or cognitive science on which some epistemological naturalists of a more extreme stripe than mine propose to rely; for the assumptions referred to in my "supposing" clauses, though empirical, are of such generality as to be rather philosophical than scientific in character.

Those assumptions would surely be presupposed by any conceivable scientific experiment. But they are well integrated with what the sciences of cognition have to tell us about the mechanisms of perception and introspection, and of when and why they are more or less reliable, and with what the theory of evolution suggests about how we came to have the sort of information-detecting apparatus we do. As one would hope, the epistemological part of my crossword—the part where the entries are themselves about crosswords—interlocks snugly with other parts.

But what am I to say to those readers familiar with Descartes' failed attempt to prove "what I clearly and distinctly perceive is true," who are bound to suspect that I must be arguing in a circle? After pointing out that I have not offered a ratificatory argument in which some premiss turns out to be identical with the conclusion, nor an argument relying on a certain mode of inference to arrive at the conclusion that this very mode of inference is a good one—only that, to borrow Peirce's words, by now "the reader will, I trust, be too well-grounded in logic to mistake mutual support for a vicious circle of reasoning."[16]

And what am I to say to readers worried about the Evil Demon, who are bound to object that I have not ruled out the possibility that our senses are not a source of information about the external world at all? After pointing out that since, *ex hypothesi*, his machinations would be absolutely undetectable, if there were an Evil Demon *no* truth-indication would be possible for us—only that my claim is a conditional one: that, if any truth-indication is possible for us, the foundherentist criteria are truth-indicative. (I could discharge the antecedent, and arrive at a categorical conclusion, by adopting a definition of truth along Peircean lines, as the opinion that would survive all possible experiential evidence and the fullest logical scrutiny; but I prefer the more cautious, and more realist, strategy.)

Determined skeptics won't be persuaded; but determined skeptics never are! And the rest of you may notice that foundherentism enables us to sidestep another dichotomy which has—if you'll pardon the pun—bedeviled recent epistemology: *either* a hopeless obsession with hyperbolic skepticism, *or* a hopeless relativism or tribalism preoccupied with "our (local, parochial) epistemic practices." Foundherentism, I believe, provides a more realistic picture of our epistemic condition—a robustly fallibilist picture which, without sacrificing objectivity, acknowledges something of how complex and confusing evidence can be.

Notes

1 This brief statement of foundherentism is based primarily on my *Evidence and Inquiry: Towards Reconstruction in Epistemology* (Oxford: Blackwell, 1993), especially chapters 1, 4, and 10. I have also drawn on material from earlier articles of mine, especially "Theories of Knowledge: An Analytic Framework," *Proceedings of the Aristotelian Society* 83 (1982–3): 143–57 (where foundherentism was first introduced); "C.I. Lewis" in *American Philosophy*, ed. Marcus Singer, Royal Institute of Philosophy Lecture Series, 19 (Cambridge: Cambridge University Press, 1985), pp. 215–39; and "Rebuilding the Ship While Sailing on the Water" in *Perspectives on Quine*, ed. R. Barrett and R. Gibson (Oxford: Blackwell, 1990), pp. 111–27 (where some of the key ideas of foundherentism were developed). I have drawn as well on material from the symposium on *Evidence and Inquiry* published in *Philosophy and Phenomenological Research* 56 (1996): 611–57, and from my "Reply to BonJour," *Synthese* 112 (1997): 25–35.

2 Thomas Reid, *Essays on the Intellectual Powers* (1785) in R.E. Beanblossom and K. Lehrer, eds., *Thomas Reid's Inquiry and Essays* (Indianapolis, Ind.: Hackett, 1983), VI.4.

3 I restrict my attention here to experientialist forms of foundationalism, ignoring, e.g., foundationalist theories of a priori knowledge.

4 My characterization of foundationalism is quite standard; cf. for example, Alston's in E. Sosa and J. Dancy, eds, *Companion to Epistemology* (Oxford:

Blackwell, 1992), p. 144, or Sosa's in "The Raft and the Pyramid," *Midwest Studies in Philosophy* 5 (1980): 23–4. But matters have been confused because, in "Can Empirical Knowledge Have a Foundation?", *American Philosophical Quarterly* 15 (1978): 1–13, and *The Structure of Empirical Knowledge* (Cambridge, Mass.: Harvard University Press, 1986), p. 28, BonJour uses "weak foundationalism" to refer a style of theory that is both weak *and* impure, in my sense, and in addition allows mutual support among basic beliefs and—apparently—allows "basic" beliefs to get support from "derived" beliefs. As my scare quotes indicate, once one-directionality has been so completely abandoned it is unclear that the theory really qualifies as foundationalist at all; certainly the basic/derived distinction has become purely *pro forma*. See also Haack, "Reply to BonJour," *Synthese* 112 (1997): 25–35.

5 See *Evidence and Inquiry*, chapter 2 for details.

6 See *Evidence and Inquiry*, chapter 3 for details.

7 Laurence BonJour, "Haack on Justification and Experience," *Synthese* 112 (1997): 13–15.

8 An idea I first began to work out in "Epistemology *With* a Knowing Subject," *Review of Metaphysics* 33 (1979): 309–36.

9 Expressions introduced in square brackets are my new, technical terms, or special, technical uses of familiar terms.

10 So my theory is not straightforwardly externalist, since A's S-evidence must consist of states of A—states, furthermore, of which A can be aware; but neither is it straightforwardly internalist, since A's experiential C-evidence consists of propositions A need not believe or even conceive.

11 Quine, W.V. and Ullian, J., *The Web of Belief* (New York: Random House, 1970), p. 79.

12 Goodman, N., "The New Riddle of Induction" (1953) in *Fact, Fiction and Forecast*, 2nd edn (Indianapolis, Ind.: Bobbs-Merrill, 1965), pp. 59–83; Hempel, C.G., "Postscript on Confirmation" (1964) in *Aspects of Scientific Explanation* (New York: Free Press, 1965), pp. 47–52.

13 In case a desperate foundationalist is tempted to try seizing on this in hopes of salvaging the derived/basic distinction, let me point out that beliefs without direct experiential evidence could contribute to the support of beliefs with direct experiential evidence; and that this maneuver would identify no plausible *kind* of belief as basic/as derived—think, e.g., of a scientist whose belief that electrons are composed thus and so is sustained by what he sees in the bubble chamber.

14 See also Haack, "Reflections on Relativism: From Momentous Tautology to Seductive Contradiction," *Noûs*, Supplement (1996): 297–315; also in James E. Tomberlin, ed., *Philosophical Perspectives, 10: Metaphysics* (Oxford: Blackwell, 1996), pp. 297–315; reprinted in Haack, *Manifesto of a Passionate Moderate: Unfashionable Essays* (Chicago: University of Chicago Press, 1998), pp. 149–66.

15 I have more to say in "Confessions of an Old-Fashioned Prig" in *Manifesto of a Passionate Moderate*, pp. 7–30.

16 C.S. Peirce, *Collected Papers*, ed. C. Hartshorne, P. Weiss, and A. Burks (Cambridge, Mass.: Harvard University Press, 1931–58), 6.315.

QUESTIONS

1 According to Haack, what do foundationalists believe?
2 What do coherentists believe?
3 What sort of propositions are included in a person's "C-evidence"?
4 What three factors determine how good A's C-evidence for *p* is?

FURTHER READING ON THE ARCHITECTURE OF KNOWLEDGE

Alcoff, Linda, *Real Knowing: New Versions of Coherence Theory* (Ithaca, N.Y.: Cornell University Press, 1996).

Alston, William, *Epistemic Justification* (Ithaca, N.Y.: Cornell University Press, 1989).

Audi, Robert, *The Structure of Justification* (Cambridge: Cambridge University Press, 1993).

BonJour, Laurence, "The Dialectic of Foundationalism and Coherentism," in *The Blackwell Guide to Epistemology*, ed. John Greco and Ernest Sosa (Oxford: Blackwell, 1999), pp. 117–42.

Chisholm, Roderick, *The Foundations of Knowing* (Minneapolis, Minn.: University of Minnesota Press, 1982).

Davidson, Donald, "A Coherence Theory of Truth and Knowledge," in *Reading Rorty*, ed. Alan Malachowski (Cambridge, Mass.: Basil Blackwell, 1990), pp. 120–38.

Descartes, René, *The Philosophical Writings of Descartes*, ed. John Cottingham, Robert Stoothoff, and Dugald Murdoch (Cambridge: Cambridge University Press, 1984).

Fales, Evan, *A Defense of the Given* (Lanham, Md.: Rowman & Littlefield, 1986).

Fumerton, Richard, "Foundationalism, Conceptual Regress, and Reliabilism," *Analysis* 48 (1988): 178–84.

Haack, Susan, *Evidence and Inquiry* (Cambridge, Mass.: Blackwell, 1993).

Howard-Snyder, Daniel, "BonJour's 'Basic Antifoundationalist Argument' and the Doctrine of the Given," *Southern Journal of Philosophy* 36 (1998): 163–77.

Huemer, Michael, "Probability and Coherence Justification," *Southern Journal of Philosophy* 35 (1997): 463–72.

Klein, Peter, "Human Knowledge and the Infinite Regress of Reasons," *Philosophical Perspectives* 13 (1999): 297–325.

Moser, Paul, *Empirical Knowledge*, 2nd edn (Lanham, Md.: Rowman & Littlefield, 1996).

Pollock, John and Joseph Cruz, *Contemporary Theories of Knowledge*, 2nd edn (Lanham, Md.: Rowman & Littlefield, 1999).

Sellars, Wilfred, *Empiricism and the Philosophy of Mind* (Cambridge, Mass.: Harvard University Press, 1997).

Sosa, Ernest, *Knowledge in Perspective* (Cambridge: Cambridge University Press, 1991).

Williams, Michael, *Unnatural Doubts* (Oxford: Blackwell, 1991).

PART III

THE NATURE AND SCOPE OF JUSTIFICATION AND KNOWLEDGE

8

1. THE ANALYSIS OF "KNOWLEDGE"

Analyzing the concept of knowledge has commonly been taken to be one of the central tasks, if not the central task, of epistemology. There are several different uses of "know" (as in "I know John," "I know how to drive," and "I know your phone number"), but the sense that epistemologists have focused on is the sense that refers to *propositional knowledge*, or factual knowledge. This is the sense involved in "I know that 2 + 2 = 4" and "Does John know that the game has been delayed?"

Our question, then, is this: under what conditions does a subject, *S*, know that *p* (where *p* is some proposition)? There is a general agreement among epistemologists on two basic conditions, with disagreements on what further conditions are required. The core of agreement is that in order for a person to count as knowing that *p*, the person must at least believe that *p*, and it must be true that *p*.

But certainly these two conditions are not enough. Take the example of the imprudent gambler, who believes that red is going to come up on the next spin of the roulette wheel, because he just has a hunch. Assume that the gambler does not have ESP and has no reason to believe that he has ESP; however, as chance would have it, the ball does land on red. Did he really *know* that it was going to land on red? No. He believed it, and what he believed was true, but it was just a lucky guess, not knowledge. This sort of case shows the need for at least some third element of knowledge. Traditionally, epistemologists have said that the problem is that the gambler lacks good evidence, or reasons, for believing that the ball will land on red. Thus, the traditional analysis of knowledge, known as the "justified, true belief" theory, is this:

S knows that $p =_{df}$ (i) *S* at least believes that *p*,
(ii) *p* is true, and
(iii) *S* is justified in believing that *p*.

A.J. Ayer is sometimes read (he is so read by Gettier) as defending the justified, true belief theory or something close to it, though in place of (iii) above Ayer would say "*S* has the right to be sure that *p*." In fact, however, Ayer's notion of having the right to be sure differs significantly from the traditional conception of "justification." When Ayer says that S, in order to count as knowing *p*, must have "the right" to be sure that *p*, what Ayer means is that we, the people *attributing* knowledge to S, are thereby expressing a sort of attitude of approval towards *S*'s belief. This fits in with Ayer's emotivist view of the meaning of evaluative terms generally, which we mentioned in Chapter 3. (To see this, review the paragraph in the text that includes the remark,

"The difference is that to say that he knows is to concede to him the right to be sure . . .")

Edmund Gettier famously refuted the justified, true belief theory by means of a type of counter-example now referred to as a "Gettier case." There are two possible kinds of counter-example to a definition. The first kind is one that would show the definition to be too broad; in this case, this would mean an example of something that in fact is not knowledge, but that the definition would count as knowledge. (The above gambler example is a counter-example of this kind to the bare "true belief" analysis.) The other kind is that which would show the definition to be too narrow; in this case, an example of something that in fact is knowledge but that the definition would fail to classify as knowledge. Gettier's counter-examples are of the first kind; in other words, they show that justified, true belief is not *sufficient* for knowledge. Essentially, Gettier uses cases in which a person has a justified, but mistaken, belief that *q* and they validly infer another proposition, *p*, which just happens to be true (even though their reason for believing it was mistaken). In such a case, the person does not really *know p* to be true, even though it is true, they believe it, and they have justification for believing it.

Thus, suppose that Smith is adequately justified in believing that Jones owns a Ford (he has seen Jones driving the Ford, has heard Jones talk about his Ford, has seen the title, etc.). Smith validly infers from this that "Jones owns a Ford, or Brown is in Barcelona." Smith has no idea where Brown actually is—he picked Barcelona at random—but since he believes the first disjunct of that proposition, he thinks the proposition as a whole is true. Now suppose that, improbably enough, Jones actually does not own a Ford (perhaps he just sold it, or it was destroyed, etc.), but, as chance would have it, Brown actually *is* in Barcelona. In this case, intuitively, Smith does *not* know the proposition, "Jones owns a Ford or Brown is in Barcelona," even though he believes it, it is true, and he is justified in believing it.

Gettier's refutation started a cottage industry of knowledge-analyzers. Some epistemologists decided that what was needed was simply a fourth condition to be added onto the justified, true belief theory. Others decided instead to replace the third (justification) condition with something else entirely.

The first new proposal was Michael Clark's proposal to add the condition that *S*'s belief that *p* should be "fully grounded," which means that there are no false beliefs in the chain of reasons *S* has leading to *p*. This effectively eliminates the Gettier cases, that is, it explains why they are not cases of knowledge. Smith's belief that "Jones owns a Ford or Brown is in Barcelona" is not fully grounded, since it is inferred from the false belief that Jones owns a Ford.

Lehrer and Paxson propose a more complicated fourth condition, the condition that there should be no defeaters for *S*'s justification for *p*. A "defeater" for *S*'s justification for believing *p* means, roughly, *a true proposition that, if added to S's evidence, would render S no longer justified in believing p.* Notice how this would account for the Gettier example discussed above: the proposition "Jones does not own a Ford" would be a defeater for Smith's belief "Jones owns a Ford or Brown is in Barcelona," since it is true that Jones does not own a Ford and if Smith added the proposition that Jones does not own a Ford to his beliefs, Smith would no longer be justified in believing "Jones owns a Ford or Brown is in Barcelona." Definitions of knowledge that use a condition generally along these lines are called "defeasibility theories."

The above account of defeaters isn't *quite* right, however; Lehrer and Paxson discuss some hypothetical examples that raise the possibility of what are now called "misleading defeaters." Suppose I see Tom Grabit steal a book from the library. Unbeknownst to me, Tom's mother, Mrs. Grabit, has been going around *saying* that Tom has an identical twin brother who is a kleptomaniac. If there is such a twin, then, intuitively, I do not know (unless I could somehow prove that the person whom I saw was not the twin) that Tom stole the book. But suppose that in fact there is no such twin, and Mrs. Grabit is merely crazy or lying. In this case, intuitively, I *do* have knowledge that Tom stole the book; Mrs. Grabit's false assertions should not defeat this. The proposition "Mrs. Grabit has said that Tom has an identical twin brother who is a kleptomaniac" is a *misleading defeater* (it is a true proposition that, if added to my evidence, makes me no longer justified in believing that Tom stole the book, but, intuitively, it should not count as undermining my knowledge that Tom stole the book). Defeasibility theorists have tried various different ways of defining "misleading defeaters." Lehrer and Paxson's approach is to refine the definition of a defeater as follows:

> If *e* is *S*'s justification for *p*, *d* is a defeater for this justification if and only if (i) *d* is true, (ii) (*e* & *d*) does not justify *p*, (iii) *S* is justified in believing ~*d*, and (iv) if *c* is any logical consequence of *d* such that (*c* and *e*) does not justify *h*, then *S* is justified in believing ~*c*.[1]

Conditions (i) and (ii) are equivalent to the original, rough definition of defeaters given in the preceding paragraph; conditions (iii) and (iv) are technical qualifications needed to meet the counter-examples involving misleading defeaters.

Clark's analysis and the defeasibility analysis are both examples of efforts to fix up the traditional analysis of knowledge by adding a fourth condition. In contrast, authors such as Goldman and Nozick propose to replace the traditional "justification" condition with something else (theories that do this are sometimes called "externalist" theories of knowledge). In Goldman's analysis, the something else is the requirement that there be a "causal connection" between *S*'s belief and the fact that makes the belief true. Goldman's causal theory is most intuitive for the case of perceptual knowledge: I know that there is a table here, because the actual presence of the table *causes* me to have a certain sort of (table-representing) sensory experience, which in turn causes me to believe there is a table here. Thus, my belief is causally connected to the fact that makes it true (namely, the fact that a table is here). Goldman also allows more complicated sorts of "causal connections" (note that being "causally connected" to a belief does not simply mean *causing* the belief). He allows cases in which the fact that makes my belief true causes *evidence* for the belief to be present, and that evidence, in conjunction with background knowledge I already have, causes my belief. He also allows cases in which my belief that *p* and the fact that *p* both have a common cause, as cases of there being an appropriate "causal connection" (this is needed in order to secure knowledge based on induction). One problem for the causal theory, however, is that it is unclear how it can account for a priori knowledge (see Chapter 3); for example, is our knowledge of mathematics explained by our causal relations to mathematical objects?

Robert Nozick's analysis of knowledge starts from the intuitive idea that knowledge "tracks the truth" (as an analogy, imagine a camera that tracks the movement of a ball: as the ball moves to the left, the camera turns to the left; as the ball moves to the right, the camera swings right). His proposal is that *S* knows that *p* when

(i) *S* believes that *p*,
(ii) *p* is true,
(iii) if *p* were false, *S* would not believe that *p*, and
(iv) if *p* were true, *S* would believe that *p*.

This account explains why the Gettier cases are not cases of knowledge: in the "Jones owns a Ford" example, if the proposition "Jones owns a Ford or Brown is in Barcelona" were false, Smith would likely still believe it. Why? Because if the proposition were false, it would be false because of Brown not being in Barcelona. But if Brown were not in Barcelona, Smith would still have believed "Jones owns a Ford or Brown is in Barcelona," since Smith's belief was caused purely by his belief in the first disjunct; Smith did not have any idea where Brown was in the first place, so moving Brown around would not have any effect on Smith's belief. In this case, Smith's belief fails to track the truth; specifically, it fails to satisfy condition (iii) above.

One surprising and much-discussed consequence of Nozick's analysis is the failure of the *closure principle* for knowledge. The closure principle states that if a person knows that *p*, and *p* entails *q*, then he is in a position to know *q* (in technical language, we say that the set of propositions one is in a position to know is "closed under entailment"). Many people consider this principle intuitively obvious, but Nozick rejects it. The key to understanding why is the way he treats condition (iii) above, so it is worth spending a little time to understanding that.

In Nozick's view (and the view of a great many contemporary philosophers), the way one evaluates a statement like "If *A* were the case, *B* would be the case" is something like this: imagine a world pretty much like this one, except that *A* is true in it; then ask whether *B* is also true in such a world. Thus, when asked, "What would happen if I were to drop this pen?", we should imagine a world in which I drop the pen and other things about the world (e.g., the law of gravity, the presence of the Earth, etc.) are pretty much the same. In such a world, the pen falls. We should *not* answer the question by imagining, for example, a world in which I am floating out in space when I drop the pen, in which the law of gravity is absent or is radically different in form, etc. Another way to put the point is this: we look at the "nearby" possible worlds (that is, the scenarios that are otherwise similar to the actual world) in which *A* is true. If *B* is also true in such worlds, then we say that "if *A* were true, *B* would be true."

Thus, consider another example. I now believe that I have two hands. If I did not have two hands, would I still believe that I did? The answer is no. If you imagine a world that is otherwise like the way things are now, except that I lack two hands (perhaps because I had one amputated, or whatever), in such a world I would not now believe I have two hands (because I would just see a stump here, or something like that). Thus, I satisfy condition (iii) for knowing that I have two hands.

Now, consider a science fiction scenario: I am a brain being kept alive in a vat of nutrients, and scientists are stimulating my sensory cortex to produce the illusion of a physical world (something like this happens in the popular movie *The Matrix*, except that there the whole human body is in the vat, rather than just the brain). I now believe that I am not in fact in such a situation; I think I am a normal human being. However, if the brain-in-a-vat scenario obtained, I would still think that it did not (in fact, all of my beliefs would be the same). Therefore, according to Nozick's analysis, I do not *know* that I am not a brain in a vat, because I fail to satisfy condition (iii) with respect to the proposition "I am not a brain in a vat."

This example shows that, if Nozick's theory is correct, the closure principle is false. "I have two hands" entails "I am not a brain in a vat." (A mere brain has no hands.) But while I know I have two hands, I do *not* know, according to Nozick, that I am not a brain in a vat.

All of the above accounts of the meaning of "know" are *invariantist* accounts: they hold that there is a fixed set of conditions that a person must satisfy in order to count as "knowing" something; in other words, that the meaning of "know" is invariant. In contrast, Keith DeRose defends *contextualism*, which holds that the conditions required for someone to count as "knowing" a proposition vary depending on the situation of the person attributing knowledge; in other words, the meaning of the word "know" varies with the context in which it is used. This is similar to the way in which the meaning of an expression such as "this room" varies depending on the speaker's context—it refers to different rooms, depending on where the person using the expression is located at the time. Because of this, it is possible for a person to say, "This room is yellow," and for another person or the same person at another time to say, "This room is grey," without the two statements contradicting each other. If the meaning of "know" is contextual, then it is also possible for one person to say, "*S* knew that *p*" and for another person, or the same person at a different time, to say, "*S* did not know that *p*" (where both are referring to the same person and the same proposition and are speaking of the same time), without genuinely contradicting each other. Both statements could be true, because the context of the second utterance might be different in such a way that the standards for counting as "knowing" are higher in the latter context.

DeRose does not go into detail concerning the contextual factors that affect the standards for knowledge, but he mentions a few factors that contextualists commonly cite. First, it is often thought, among contextualists, that the importance of being right about something can affect the standards for knowledge—if it is very important to be right about whether *p*, then one must have very strong evidence, and must rule out even very improbable alternatives, in order to be truthfully said to "know" *p*. Second, if a certain alternative to *p* has actually been *mentioned* in a conversation, then (many contextualists think) a person must be able to rule out that alternative in order to count as "knowing" *p*. Third, it might be thought (although DeRose is skeptical of this one) that if a particular person is *thinking about* a certain alternative to *p*, then *his* use of "know" will be such that to "know" *p* requires ruling out that alternative.

The contextualist viewpoint has interesting implications for how one should respond to philosophical skepticism (see Chapter 9). Contextualists generally believe that arguments for skepticism depend upon manipulating the conversational context in such a way that the standards for "knowing" are raised to a level much higher than the standards that apply for ordinary, everyday uses of "know."

Note

1 This is my paraphrase of their definition at the end of their section II. I have altered the variables used for the sake of clarity and consistency with this introduction.

A.J. Ayer, "Knowing as Having the Right to be Sure"

The answers which we have found for the questions we have so far been discussing have not yet put us in a position to give a complete account of what it is to know that something is the case. The first requirement is that what is known should be true, but this is not sufficient; not even if we add to it the further condition that one must be completely sure of what one knows. For it is possible to be completely sure of something which is in fact true, but yet not to know it. The circumstances may be such that one is not entitled to be sure. For instance, a superstitious person who had inadvertently walked under a ladder might be convinced as a result that he was about to suffer some misfortune; and he might in fact be right. But it would not be correct to say that he knew that this was going to be so. He arrived at his belief by a process of reasoning which would not be generally reliable; so, although his prediction came true, it was not a case of knowledge. Again, if someone were fully persuaded of a mathematical proposition by a proof which could be shown to be invalid, he would not, without further evidence, be said to know the proposition, even though it was true. But while it is not hard to find examples of true and fully confident beliefs which in some ways fail to meet the standards required for knowledge, it is not at all easy to determine exactly what these standards are.

One way of trying to discover them would be to consider what would count as satisfactory answers to the question How do you know? Thus people may be credited with knowing truths of mathematics or logic if they are able to give a valid proof of them, or even if, without themselves being able to set out such a proof, they have obtained this information from someone who can. Claims to know empirical statements may be upheld by a reference to perception, or to memory, or to testimony, or to historical records, or to scientific laws. But such backing is not always strong enough for knowledge. Whether it is so or not depends upon the circumstances of the particular case. If I were asked how I knew that a physical object of a certain sort was in such and such a place, it would, in general, be a sufficient answer for me to say that I could see it; but if my eyesight were bad and the light were dim, this answer might not be sufficient. Even though I was right, it might still be said that I did not really know that the object was there. If I have a poor memory and the event which I claim to

A.J. Ayer, "Knowing as Having the Right to be Sure," *The Problem of Knowledge* (London: Macmillan, 1956).

remember is remote, my memory of it may still not amount to knowledge, even though in this instance it does not fail me. If a witness is unreliable, his unsupported evidence may not enable us to know that what he says is true, even in a case where we completely trust him and he is not in fact deceiving us. In a given instance it is possible to decide whether the backing is strong enough to justify a claim to knowledge. But to say in general how strong it has to be would require our drawing up a list of the conditions under which perception, or memory, or testimony, or other forms of evidence are reliable. And this would be a very complicated matter, if indeed it could be done at all.

Moreover, we cannot assume that, even in particular instances, an answer to the question How do you know? will always be forthcoming. There may very well be cases in which one knows that something is so without its being possible to say how one knows it. I am not so much thinking now of claims to know facts of immediate experience, statements like "I know that I feel pain," which raise problems of their own. In cases of this sort it may be argued that the question how one knows does not arise. But even when it clearly does arise, it may not find an answer. Suppose that someone were consistently successful in predicting events of a certain kind, events, let us say, which are not ordinarily thought to be predictable, like the results of a lottery. If his run of successes were sufficiently impressive, we might very well come to say that he knew which number would win, even though he did not reach this conclusion by any rational method, or indeed by any method at all. We might say that he knew it by intuition, but this would be to assert no more than that he did know it but that we could not say how. In the same way, if someone were consistently successful in reading the minds of others without having any of the usual sort of evidence, we might say that he knew these things telepathically. But in default of any further explanation this would come down to saying merely that he did know them, but not by any ordinary means. Words like "intuition" and "telepathy" are brought in just to disguise the fact that no explanation has been found.

But if we allow this sort of knowledge to be even theoretically possible, what becomes of the distinction between knowledge and true belief? How does our man who knows what the results of the lottery will be differ from one who only makes a series of lucky guesses? The answer is that, so far as the man himself is concerned, there need not be any difference. His procedure and his state of mind, when he is said to know what will happen, may be exactly the same as when it is said that he is only guessing. The difference is that to say that he knows is to concede to him the right to be sure, while to say that he is only guessing is to withhold it. Whether we make this concession will depend upon the view which we take of his performance. Normally we do not say that people know things unless they have followed one of the accredited routes to knowledge. If someone reaches a true conclusion without appearing to have any adequate basis for it, we are likely to say that he does not really know it. But if he were repeatedly successful in a given domain, we might very well come to say that he knew the facts in question, even though we could not explain how he knew them. We should grant him the right to be sure, simply on the basis of his success. This is, indeed, a point on which people's views might be expected to differ. Not everyone would regard a successful run of predictions, however long sustained, as being by itself a sufficient backing for a claim to knowledge. And here there can be no question of proving that this attitude is mistaken. Where there are recognized criteria for deciding when one has the right to be sure, anyone who insists that their being satisfied is still not enough for knowledge may be accused, for what the charge is worth, of misusing the verb "to know." But it is possible to find, or at any rate to devise, examples which are not covered in this respect by any established rule of usage. Whether they are to count as instances of knowledge is then a question which we are left free to decide.

It does not, however, matter very greatly which decision we take. The main problem is to state and assess the grounds on which these claims to knowledge are made, to settle, as it were, the candidate's marks. It is a relatively unimportant question what titles we then bestow upon them. So long as we agree about the marking, it is of no great consequence where we draw the line between pass and failure, or between the different levels of distinction. If we choose to set a very high standard, we may find ourselves committed to saying that some of what ordinarily passes for knowledge ought rather to be described as probable opinion. And some critics will then take us to task for flouting ordinary usage. But the question is purely one of terminology. It is to be decided, if at all, on grounds of practical convenience.

One must not confuse this case, where the markings are agreed upon, and what is in dispute is only the bestowal of honours, with the case where it is the markings themselves that are put in question. For this second case is philosophically important, in a way in which the other is not. The sceptic who asserts that we do not know all that we think we know, or even perhaps that we do not strictly know anything at all, is not suggesting that we are mistaken when we conclude that the recognized criteria for knowing have been satisfied. Nor is he primarily concerned with getting us to revise our usage of the verb "to know," any more than one who challenges our standards of value is trying to make us revise our usage of the word "good." The disagreement is about the application of the word, rather than its meaning. What the sceptic contends is that our markings are too high; that the grounds on which we are normally ready to concede the right to be sure are worth less than we think; he may even go so far as to say that they are not worth anything at all. The attack is directed, not against the way in which we apply our standards of proof, but against these standards themselves. It has, as we shall see, to be taken seriously because of the arguments by which it is supported.

I conclude then that the necessary and sufficient conditions for knowing that something is the case are first that what one is said to know be true, secondly that one be sure of it, and thirdly that one should have the right to be sure. This right may be earned in various ways; but even if one could give a complete description of them it would be a mistake to try to build it into the definition of knowledge, just as it would be a mistake to try to incorporate our actual standards of goodness into a definition of good. And this being so, it turns out that the questions which philosophers raise about the possibility of knowledge are not all to be settled by discovering what knowledge is. For many of them reappear as questions about the legitimacy of the title to be sure. They need to be severally examined; and this is the main concern of what is called the theory of knowledge.

QUESTIONS

1 According to Ayer, what three conditions are required in order for a person, *S*, to know a proposition, *p*?
2 According to Ayer, what do philosophical skeptics believe? Do they seek to change our use of the word "know"?

Edmund Gettier, "Is Justified True Belief Knowledge?"

Various attempts have been made in recent years to state necessary and sufficient conditions for someone's knowing a given proposition. The attempts have often been such that they can be stated in a form similar to the following.[1]

(a)	S knows that P	*IFF*	(i)	P is true,
			(ii)	S believes that P, and
			(iii)	S is justified in believing that P.

For example, Chisholm has held that the following gives the necessary and sufficient conditions for knowledge:[2]

(b)	S knows that P	*IFF*	(i)	S accepts P,
			(ii)	S has adequate evidence for P, and
			(iii)	P is true.

Ayer has stated the necessary and sufficient conditions for knowledge as follows:[3]

(c)	S knows that P	*IFF*	(i)	P is true,
			(ii)	S is sure that P is true, and
			(iii)	S has the right to be sure that P is true.

I shall argue that (a) is false in that the conditions stated therein do not constitute a *sufficient* condition for the truth of the proposition that S knows that P. The same argument will show that (b) and (c) fail if "has adequate evidence for" or "has the right to be sure that" is substituted for "is justified in believing that" throughout.

I shall begin by noting two points. First, in that sense of "justified" in which S's being justified in believing P is a necessary condition of S's knowing that P, it is possible for a person to be justified in believing a proposition that is in fact false. Secondly, for any proposition P, if S is justified in believing P, and P entails Q, and S deduces Q from P and accepts Q as a result of this deduction, then S is justified in believing Q. Keeping these two points in mind, I shall now present two cases in which the conditions stated in (a) are true for some proposition,

Edmund Gettier, "Is Justified True Belief Knowledge?" *Analysis* 23 (1963): 121–3.

though it is at the same time false that the person in question knows that proposition.

Case I

Suppose that Smith and Jones have applied for a certain job. And suppose that Smith has strong evidence for the following conjunctive proposition:

(d) Jones is the man who will get the job, and Jones has ten coins in his pocket.

Smith's evidence for (d) might be that the president of the company assured him that Jones would in the end be selected, and that he, Smith, had counted the coins in Jones's pocket ten minutes ago. Proposition (d) entails:

(e) The man who will get the job has ten coins in his pocket.

Let us suppose that Smith sees the entailment from (d) to (e), and accepts (e) on the grounds of (d), for which he has strong evidence. In this case, Smith is clearly justified in believing that (e) is true.

But imagine, further, that unknown to Smith, he himself, not Jones, will get the job. And, also, unknown to Smith, he himself has ten coins in his pocket. Proposition (e) is then true, though proposition (d), from which Smith inferred (e), is false. In our example, then, all of the following are true: (*i*) (e) is true, (*ii*) Smith believes that (e) is true, and (*iii*) Smith is justified in believing that (e) is true. But it is equally clear that Smith does not *know* that (e) is true; for (e) is true in virtue of the number of coins in Smith's pocket, while Smith does not know how many coins are in Smith's pocket, and bases his belief in (e) on a count of the coins in Jones's pocket, whom he falsely believes to be the man who will get the job.

Case II

Let us suppose that Smith has strong evidence for the following proposition:

(f) Jones owns a Ford.

Smith's evidence might be that Jones has at all times in the past within Smith's memory owned a car, and always a Ford, and that Jones has just offered Smith a ride while driving a Ford. Let us imagine, now, that Smith has another friend, Brown, of whose whereabouts he is totally ignorant. Smith selects three place-names quite at random, and constructs the following three propositions:

(g) Either Jones owns a Ford, or Brown is in Boston;
(h) Either Jones owns a Ford, or Brown is in Barcelona;
(i) Either Jones owns a Ford, or Brown is in Brest-Litovsk.

Each of these propositions is entailed by (f). Imagine that Smith realizes the entailment of each of these propositions he has constructed by (f), and proceeds to accept (g), (h), and (i) on the basis of (f). Smith has correctly inferred (g), (h), and (i) from a proposition for which he has strong evidence. Smith is therefore completely justified in believing each of these three propositions. Smith, of course, has no idea where Brown is.

But imagine now that two further conditions hold. First, Jones does *not* own a Ford, but is at present driving a rented car. And secondly, by the sheerest coincidence, and entirely unknown to Smith, the place mentioned in proposition (h) happens really to be the place where Brown is. If these two conditions hold then Smith does *not* know that (h) is true, even though (*i*) (h) *is* true, (*ii*) Smith does believe that (h) is true, and (*iii*) Smith is justified in believing that (h) is true.

These two examples show that definition (a) does not state a *sufficient* condition for someone's knowing a given proposition. The same cases, with appropriate changes, will suffice to show that neither definition (b) nor definition (c) do so either.

Notes

1 Plato seems to be considering some such definition at *Theaetetus* 201, and perhaps accepting one at *Meno* 98.

2 Roderick M. Chisholm, *Perceiving: a Philosophical Study* (Ithaca, N.Y.: Cornell University Press, 1957), p. 16.

3 A.J. Ayer, *The Problem of Knowledge* (London: Macmillan, 1956), p. 34.

QUESTIONS

1 According to Gettier, is justified true belief knowledge?
2 What two points about "justification" does Gettier's argument rely on?
3 In Gettier's two examples, what true propositions did Smith not know?

Michael Clark, "Knowledge and Grounds: A Comment on Mr. Gettier's Paper"

In his paper "Is Justified True Belief Knowledge?" (*Analysis* 23.6, June 1963) Mr. Gettier provides two counter-examples which show that it need not be. In each case a proposition which is in fact true is believed on grounds which are in fact false. Since the grounding proposition in each case entails the proposition it justifies (the conclusion), and the grounding proposition, although false, is justifiably believed, the conclusion is also justifiably believed.

Gettier's examples are stronger than they need have been to prove his point. Grounds need not of course entail their conclusions in order to be good grounds. Cases can be devised in which true justified belief fails to be knowledge because a *non-deductive* ground is false. To adapt Gettier's second case, take the proposition

(1) Jones owns a Ford.

Smith believes this because his friend Brown, whom he knows to be reliable and honest, has told him that Jones always has owned one, etc. Now as it happens Brown, despite his general reliability, has made an unusual slip: he has mixed Jones up with someone else. Jones never did have a Ford. However, he just happens to have bought one. So Smith truly believes that he owns one, but he cannot be said to know this since he believes it on false grounds. He is none the less justified both in accepting the grounds and in accepting Jones' past ownership etc. as grounds for the (non-deductive) inference to present ownership.

It is not enough, however, to add the truth of the grounds to a version of the definitions Gettier criticises as a further necessary condition of knowing a proposition. The following definition of knowledge still fails to give conditions which are jointly sufficient:

S knows that p IFF (i) p is true,
(ii) S believes that p,
(iii) S is justified in believing that p, and
(iv) it is on true grounds that S believes that p.

For consider this further adaptation of the example. It is true that Jones always

Michael Clark, "Knowledge and Grounds: A Comment on Mr. Gettier's Paper," *Analysis* 24 (1963): 46–8.

owned a Ford and he still does. Brown, who is known by Smith to be generally reliable and honest, tells Smith that Jones has always owned one. But, in fact, Brown knows nothing about Jones or his Ford; he has just invented what he tells Smith (an act quite out of character), and he happens by chance to be right. Now Smith's belief is not only true and justified, but the grounds on which he holds his belief are true. Yet Brown's wild guess can hardly be regarded as providing Smith with knowledge merely because it happens to be right. In this case, then, the grounds on which Smith believes (1) are true, but the grounds on which he accepts these grounds, *viz.* that Brown knows them, are false; but Brown's general reliability and honesty justify his believing it to be true.

Very often we can go on for quite a long time asking why, asking for the grounds for the grounds, for the grounds for these second-order grounds, and so on, but eventually the question will become logically odd. For example,

(2) "What are your grounds for saying Jones owns a Ford?"
(3) "Brown told me he always has owned one."
(4) "What are your grounds for claiming Brown knows this?"
(5) "He is generally reliable and honest."
(6) "What are your grounds for saying Brown is reliable and honest?"
(7) "I am nearly always with him and I seem to remember no unreliable or dishonest act on his part."

It would clearly be out of order to ask for Smith's grounds for saying he seems to remember. (We might question the reliability of his memory. In this example I assume that we may take his memory to be reliable so that I may avoid having too long a chain of reasons.) If any ground in this chain, that is, either (3) or (5) or (7), is false, we may properly deny that Smith *knows* that Jones owns a Ford. If each ground in this chain is true, then I will say that the belief is "fully grounded". We may now modify the definition under consideration by changing (iv), so that it reads:

(iv)′ S's belief that p is fully grounded,

in which form (i)–(iv)′ jointly will give the necessary and sufficient conditions for knowing that p.

It might be thought that the addition of (iv)′ would enable us to drop (iii). For surely, if p is fully grounded in the sense specified, then S is justified in believing that p. Yet he might believe all the grounds, and they might be good grounds without his seeing that they were *good* grounds; he might be sure of what be believed but not appreciate how the evidence he had for it really justified his belief. (Cf. Cohen, "Claims to Knowledge", *Proc. Arist. Soc., Suppl. Vol.* 1962, p. 35 ff.) In such a case we might want to deny that S was fully justified in his belief, and, if so, we need to retain (iii).

I think that the revised definition illuminates the issue as to whether so-called incorrigible knowledge is to be counted as knowledge at all. If I can't (logically) be wrong, for example, as to whether I am in pain, then, it is claimed, it is not properly a question of knowledge. For knowing entails having found out, and finding out is something which I may fail to do. If I say I am in pain and you ask me how I found out, you have asked an obviously silly question. Now it might be thought that this argument could be met by denying that knowing entails having found out: might I not be born having certain concepts and knowing certain truths? But the need for condition (iv)′ in any definition of knowledge shows that where the question "How did you find out?" is inappropriate the term "know" is also inappropriate. For it is usually just as odd to ask, "On what grounds do you say you are in pain?" Where one knows in virtue of having grounds, it seems plausible to say that it is a case of finding out. To talk of knowledge in the cases in question precludes a unitary definition of knowing, for we should have to say that condition (iv)′ was inapplicable in these cases.

In particular, the question "If I know that p, does it follow that I know that I know that p?" is seen to be odd (unless it is a question about my having the concept of knowing). For, among other things, it asks whether my belief that I know that p is fully grounded. And, among other things, *this* question asks whether the belief's being fully grounded is itself fully grounded, that is, whether the grounds for saying that the complete chain of grounds for p do actually constitute grounds for p, are true. Thus, if p is "He is running away" and my grounds for believing that p are that I am watching him (in this case the chain has only one link), the question is "Why is your watching him a ground for saying what he is doing?" Now this question is very odd; special circumstances might be devised for giving it point, but generally there is no question as to the grounds for this being a good ground which is not silly or of a special, philosophical nature.

QUESTIONS

1 According to Clark, what four conditions are required in order for *S* to know that *p*?
2 Which of those conditions is not satisfied in Gettier's examples?
3 What does it mean for a belief to be "fully grounded"?

justify the grounds, the grounds of the grounds the grounds of the grounds of the grounds etc. no belief ∴ can be fully grounded

Alvin Goldman, "A Causal Theory of Knowing"

Since Edmund L. Gettier reminded us recently of a certain important inadequacy of the traditional analysis of "*S* knows that *p*," several attempts have been made to correct that analysis.[1] In this paper I shall offer still another analysis (or a sketch of an analysis) of "*S* knows that *p*," one which will avert Gettier's problem. My concern will be with knowledge of empirical propositions only, since I think that the traditional analysis is adequate for knowledge of nonempirical truths.

Consider an abbreviated version of Gettier's second counterexample to the traditional analysis. Smith believes

(*q*) Jones owns a Ford

and has very strong evidence for it. Smith's evidence might be that Jones has owned a Ford for many years and that Jones has just offered Smith a ride while driving a Ford. Smith has another friend, Brown, of whose whereabouts he is totally ignorant. Choosing a town quite at random, however, Smith constructs the proposition

(*p*) Either Jones owns a Ford or Brown is in Barcelona.

Seeing that *q* entails *p*, Smith infers that *p* is true. Since he has adequate evidence for *q*, he also has adequate evidence for *p*. But now suppose that Jones does *not* own a Ford (he was driving a rented car when he offered Smith a ride), but, quite by coincidence, Brown happens to be in Barcelona. This means that *p* is true, that Smith believes *p*, and that Smith has adequate evidence for *p*. But Smith does not know *p*.

A variety of hypotheses might be made to account for Smith's not knowing *p*. Michael Clark, for example, points to the fact that *q* is false, and suggests this as the reason why Smith cannot be said to know *p*. Generalizing from this case, Clark argues that, for *S* to know a proposition, each of *S*'s grounds for it must be *true*, as well as his grounds for his grounds, etc.[2] I shall make another hypothesis to account for the fact that Smith cannot be said to know *p*, and I shall generalize this into a new analysis of "*S* knows that *p*."

Alvin Goldman, "A Causal Theory of Knowing," *The Journal of Philosophy* 64, (1967): 357–72.

Notice that what *makes p* true is the fact that Brown is in Barcelona, but that this fact has nothing to do with Smith's believing *p*. That is, there is no *causal* connection between the fact that Brown is in Barcelona and Smith's believing *p*. If Smith had come to believe *p* by reading a letter from Brown postmarked in Barcelona, then we might say that Smith knew *p*. Alternatively, if Jones did own a Ford, and his owning the Ford was manifested by his offer of a ride to Smith, and this in turn resulted in Smith's believing *p*, then we would say that Smith knew *p*. Thus, one thing that seems to be missing in this example is a causal connection between the fact that makes *p* true [or simply: the fact that *p*] and Smith's belief of *p*. The requirement of such a *causal connection* is what I wish to add to the traditional analysis.

To see that this requirement is satisfied in all cases of (empirical) knowledge, we must examine a variety of such causal connections. Clearly, only a sketch of the important kinds of cases is possible here.

Perhaps the simplest case of a causal chain connecting some fact *p* with someone's belief of *p* is that of *perception*. I wish to espouse a version of the causal theory of perception, in essence that defended by H.P. Grice.[3] Suppose that *S* sees that there is a vase in front of him. How is this to be analyzed? I shall not attempt a complete analysis of this, but a necessary condition of *S*'s seeing that there is a vase in front of him is that there be a certain kind of causal connection between the presence of the vase and *S*'s believing that a vase is present. I shall not attempt to describe this causal process in detail. Indeed, to a large extent, a description of this process must be regarded as a problem for the special sciences, not for philosophy. But a certain causal process—viz. that which standardly takes place when we say that so-and-so *sees* such-and-such—must occur. That our ordinary concept of sight (i.e., knowledge acquired by sight) includes a causal requirement is shown by the fact that if the relevant causal process is absent we would withhold the assertion that so-and-so *saw* such-and-such. Suppose that, although a vase is directly in front of *S*, a laser photograph[4] is interposed between it and *S*, thereby blocking it from *S*'s view. The photograph, however, is one of a vase (a different vase), and when it is illuminated by light waves from a laser, it looks to *S* exactly like a real vase. When the photograph is illuminated, *S* forms the belief that there is a vase in front of him. Here we would deny that *S sees* that there is a vase in front of him, for his view of the real vase is completely blocked, so that it has no causal role in the formation of his belief. Of course, *S* might *know* that there was a vase in front of him even if the photograph is blocking his view. Someone else, in a position to see the vase, might tell *S* that there is a vase in front of him. Here the presence of the vase might be a causal ancestor of *S*'s belief, but the causal process would not be a (purely) *perceptual* one. *S* could not be said to *see* that there is a vase in front of him. For this to be true, there must be a causal process, but one of a very special sort, connecting the presence of the vase with *S*'s belief.

I shall here assume that perceptual knowledge of facts is noninferential. This is merely a simplifying procedure, and not essential to my account. Certainly a percipient does not *infer* facts about physical objects from the state of his brain or from the stimulation of his sense organs. He need not know about these goings-on at all. But some epistemologists maintain that we directly perceive only sense data and that we infer physical-object facts from them. This view could be accommodated within my analysis. I could say that physical-object facts cause sense data, that people directly perceive sense data, and that they infer the physical object facts from the sense data. This kind of process would be fully accredited by my analysis, which will allow for knowledge based on inference. But for purposes of exposition it will be convenient to regard perceptual knowledge of external facts as independent of any inference.

Here the question arises about the *scope* of perceptual knowledge. By perception I can know noninferentially that there is a vase in front of me. But can I know noninferentially that the painting I am viewing is a Picasso? It is unnecessary to settle such issues here. Whether the knowledge of such facts is to be classed as inferential or noninferential, my analysis can account for it. So the scope of non-inferential knowledge may be left indeterminate.

I turn next to memory, i.e., knowledge that is based, in part, on memory. Remembering, like perceiving, must be regarded as a causal process. *S* remembers *p* at time *t* only if *S*'s believing *p* at an earlier time is a cause of his believing *p* at *t*. Of course, not every causal connection between an earlier belief and a later one is a case of remembering. As in the case of perception, however, I shall not try to describe this process in detail. This is a job mainly for the scientist. Instead, the kind of causal process in question is to be identified simply by example, by "pointing" to paradigm cases of remembering. Whenever causal processes are of that kind—whatever that kind is, precisely—they are cases of remembering.[5]

A causal connection between earlier belief (or knowledge) of *p* and later belief (knowledge) of *p* is certainly a necessary ingredient in memory.[6] To remember a fact is not simply to believe it at t_0 and also to believe it at t_1. Nor does someone's knowing a fact at t_0 and his knowing it at t_1 entail that he remembers it at t_1. He may have perceived the fact at t_0, forgotten it, and then relearned it at t_1 by someone's telling it to him. Nor does the inclusion of a memory "impression"—a feeling of remembering—ensure that one really remembers. Suppose *S* perceives *p* at t_0, but forgets it at t_1. At t_2 he begins to believe *p* again because someone tells him *p*, but at t_2 he has no memory impression of *p*. At t_3 we artificially stimulate in *S* a memory impression of *p*. It does not follow that *S* remembers *p* at t_3. The description of the case suggests that his believing *p* at t_0 has no causal effect whatever on his believing *p* at t_3, and if we accepted this fact, we would deny that he remembers *p* at t_3.

Knowledge can be acquired by a combination of perception and memory. At t_0, the fact *p* causes *S* to believe *p*, by perception. *S*'s believing *p* at t_0 results, via memory, in *S*'s believing *p* at t_1. Thus, the fact *p* is a cause of *S*'s believing *p* at t_1, and *S* can be said to know *p* at t_1. But not all knowledge results from perception and memory alone. In particular, much knowledge is based on *inference*.

As I shall use the term "inference", to say that *S* knows *p* by "inference" does not entail that *S* went through an explicit, conscious process of reasoning. It is not necessary that he have "talked to himself," saying something like "Since such-and-such is true, *p* must also be true." My belief that there is a fire in the neighborhood is based on, or inferred from, my belief that I hear a fire engine. But I have not gone through a process of explicit reasoning, saying "There's a fire engine; therefore there must be a fire." Perhaps the word "inference" is ordinarily used only where explicit reasoning occurs; if so, my use of the term will be somewhat broader than its ordinary use.

Suppose *S* perceives that there is solidified lava in various parts of the countryside. On the basis of this belief, plus various "background" beliefs about the production of lava, *S* concludes that a nearby mountain erupted many centuries ago. Let us assume that this is a highly warranted inductive inference, one which gives *S* adequate evidence for believing that the mountain did erupt many centuries ago. Assuming this proposition is true, does *S* know it? This depends on the nature of the causal process that induced his belief. If there is a continuous causal chain of the sort he envisages connecting the fact that the mountain erupted with his belief of this fact, then *S* knows it. If there is no such causal chain, however, *S* does not know that proposition.

Suppose that the mountain erupts, leaving lava around the countryside. The lava remains there until *S* perceives it and infers that the mountain erupted. Then *S* does know that the mountain erupted. But now suppose that, after the mountain has erupted, a man somehow removes all the lava. A century later, a different man (not knowing of the real volcano) decides to make it look as if there had been a volcano, and therefore puts lava in appropriate places. Still later, *S* comes across this lava and concludes that the mountain erupted centuries ago. In this case, *S* cannot be said to know the proposition. This is because the fact that the mountain did erupt is not a cause of *S*'s believing that it erupted. A necessary condition of *S*'s knowing *p* is that his believing *p* be connected with *p* by a causal chain.

In the first case, where *S* knows *p*, the causal connection may be diagrammed as in Figure 1. (*p*) is the fact that the mountain erupted at such-and-such a time. (*q*) is the fact that lava is (now) present around the countryside. "B" stands for a belief, the expression in parentheses indicating the proposition believed, and the subscript designating the believer. (*r*) is a "background" proposition, describing the ways in which lava is produced and how it solidifies. Solid arrows in the diagram represent causal connections; dotted arrows represent inferences. Notice that, in Figure 1, there is not only an arrow connecting (*q*) with *S*'s belief of (*q*), but also an arrow connecting (*p*) with (*q*). In the suggested variant of the lava case, the latter arrow would be missing, showing that there is no continuous causal chain connecting (*p*) with *S*'s belief of (*p*). Therefore, in that variant case, *S* could not be said to know (*p*)

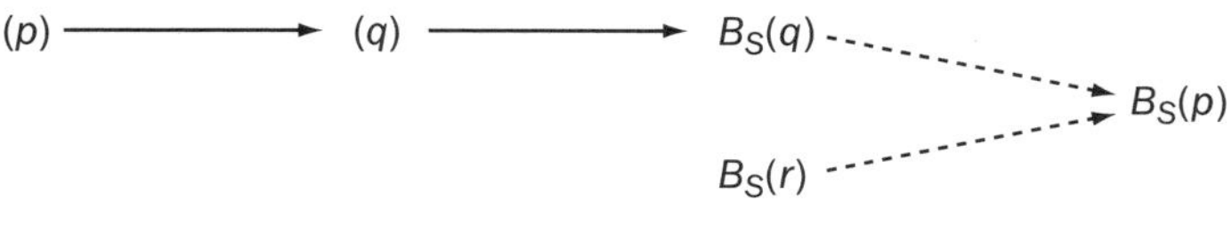

Figure 1

I have said that *p* is causally connected to *S*'s belief of *p*, in the case diagrammed in Figure 1. This raises the question, however, of whether the inferential part of the chain is itself a causal chain. In other words, is *S*'s belief of *q* a cause of his believing *p*? This is a question to which I shall not try to give a definitive answer here. I am inclined to say that inference *is* a causal process, that is, that when someone *bases* his belief of one proposition on his belief of a set of other propositions, then his belief of the latter propositions can be considered a cause of his belief of the former proposition. But I do not wish to rest my thesis on this claim. All I do claim is that, if a chain of inferences is "added" to a causal chain, then the entire chain is causal. In terms of our diagram, a chain consisting of solid arrows plus dotted arrows is to be considered a causal chain, though I shall not take a position on the question of whether the dotted arrows represent causal connections. Thus, in Figure 1, *p* is a cause of *S*'s belief of *p*, whether or not we regard *S*'s belief of *q* a cause of his belief of *p*.[7]

Consider next a case of knowledge based on "testimony." This too can be analyzed causally. *p* causes a person *T* to believe *p*, by perception. *T*'s belief of *p* gives rise to (causes) his asserting *p*. *T*'s asserting *p* causes *S*, by auditory perception, to believe that *T* is asserting *p*. *S* infers that *T* believes *p*, and from this, in turn, he infers that *p* is a fact. There is a continuous causal chain from *p* to *S*'s believing *p*, and thus, assuming that each of *S*'s inferences is warranted, *S* can be said to know *p*.

This causal chain is represented in Figure 2. '*A*' refers to an act of asserting a proposition, the expression in parentheses indicating the proposition asserted and the subscript designating the agent. (*q*), (*r*), (*u*), and (*v*) are background propositions. (*q*) and (*r*), for example, pertain to *T*'s sincerity; they help *S* conclude, from the fact that *T* asserted *p*, that *T* really believes *p*.

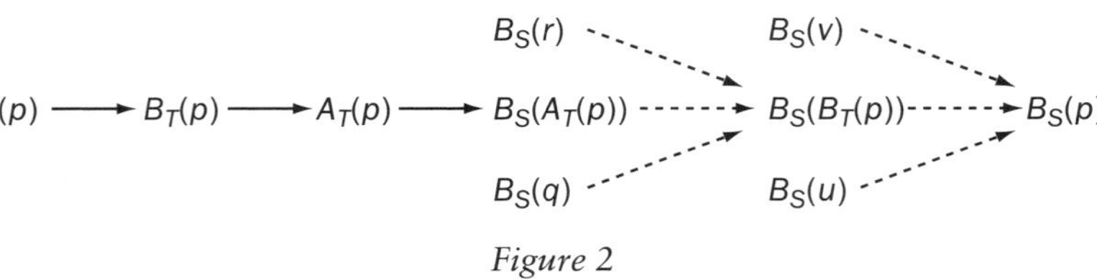

Figure 2

In this case, as in the lava case, *S* knows *p* because he has correctly reconstructed the causal chain leading from *p* to the evidence for *p* that *S* perceives, in this case, *T*'s asserting (*p*). This correct reconstruction is shown in the diagram by *S*'s inference "mirroring" the rest of the causal chain. Such a correct reconstruction is a necessary condition of knowledge based on inference. To see this, consider the following example. A newspaper reporter observes *p* and reports it to his newspaper. When printed, however, the story contains a typographical error so that it asserts not-*p*. When reading the paper, however, *S* fails to see the word "not," and takes the paper to have asserted *p*. Trusting the newspaper, he infers that *p* is true. Here we have a continuous causal chain leading from *p* to *S*'s believing *p*; yet *S* does not know *p*. *S* thinks that *p* resulted in a report to the newspaper about *p* and that this report resulted in its printing the statement *p*. Thus, his reconstruction of the causal chain is mistaken. But, if he is to know *p*, his reconstruction must contain no mistakes. Though he need not reconstruct *every* detail of the causal chain, he must reconstruct all the important links.[8] An additional requirement for knowledge based on inference is that the knower's inferences be warranted. That is, the propositions on which he bases his belief of *p* must genuinely confirm *p* very highly, whether deductively or inductively. Reconstructing a causal chain merely by lucky guesses does not yield knowledge.

With the help of our diagrams, we can contrast the traditional analysis of knowing with Clark's analysis (*op. cit.*) and contrast each of these with my own analysis. The traditional analysis makes reference to just three features of the diagrams. First, it requires that *p* be true; i.e., that (*p*) appear in the diagram. Secondly, it requires that *S* believe *p*; i.e., that *S*'s belief of *p* appear in the diagram. Thirdly, it requires that *S*'s inferences, if any, be warranted; i.e., that the sets of beliefs that are at the tail of a dotted arrow must jointly highly confirm the belief at the head of these arrows. Clark proposes a further requirement for knowledge. He requires that *each* of the beliefs in *S*'s chain of inference be *true*. In other words, whereas the traditional analysis requires a fact to correspond to *S*'s belief of *p*, Clark requires that a fact correspond to *each* of *S*'s beliefs on which he based his belief of *p*. Thus, corresponding to each belief on the right side of the diagram there must be a fact on the left side. (My diagrams omit facts corresponding to the "background" beliefs.)

As Clark's analysis stands, it seems to omit an element of the diagrams that my analysis requires, viz., the arrows indicating causal connections. Now Clark might reformulate his analysis so as to make implicit reference to these causal connections. If he required that the knower's beliefs include *causal beliefs* (of the relevant sort), then his requirement that these beliefs be true would amount to the requirement that there *be* causal chains of the sort I require. This interpretation of Clark's analysis would make it almost equivalent to mine, and would enable him to avoid some objections that have been raised against him. But he has not explicitly formulated his analysis this way, and it therefore remains deficient in this respect.

Before turning to the problems facing Clark's analysis, more must be said about my own analysis. So far, my examples may have suggested that, if *S* knows *p*, the fact that *p* is a cause of his belief of *p*. This would clearly be wrong, however. Let us grant that I can know facts about the future. Then, if we required that the known fact cause the knower's belief, we would have to countenance "backward" causation. My analysis, however, does not face this dilemma. The analysis requires that there be a causal *connection* between *p* and *S*'s belief, not necessarily that *p* be a *cause* of *S*'s belief. *p* and *S*'s belief of *p* can also be causally connected in a way that yields knowledge if both *p* and *S*'s belief of *p* have a *common* cause. This can be illustrated as follows.

T intends to go downtown on Monday. On Sunday, *T* tells *S* of his intention. Hearing *T* say he will go downtown, *S* infers that *T* really does intend to go downtown. And from this *S* concludes that *T will* go downtown on Monday. Now suppose that *T* fulfills his intention by going downtown on Monday. Can *S* be said to know that he would go downtown? If we ever can be said to have knowledge of the future, this is a reasonable candidate for it. So let us say *S* did know that proposition. How can my analysis account for *S*'s knowledge? *T*'s going downtown on Monday clearly cannot be a cause of *S*'s believing, on Sunday, that he would go downtown. But there is a fact that is the *common* cause of *T*'s going downtown and of *S*'s belief that he would go downtown, viz., *T*'s intending (on Sunday) to go downtown. This intention resulted in his going downtown and also resulted in *S*'s believing that he would go downtown. This causal connection between *S*'s belief and the fact believed allows us to say that *S* *knew* that *T* would go downtown.

The example is diagrammed in Figure 3. (*p*) = *T*'s going downtown on Monday. (*q*) = *T*'s intending (on Sunday) to go downtown on Monday. (*r*) = *T*'s telling *S* (on Sunday) that he will go downtown on Monday. (*u*) and (*v*) are relevant background propositions pertaining to *T*'s honesty, resoluteness, etc. The diagram reveals that *q* is a cause both of *p* and of *S*'s belief of *p*. Cases of this kind I shall call *Pattern 2* cases of knowledge. Figures 1 and 2 exemplify *Pattern 1* cases of knowledge.

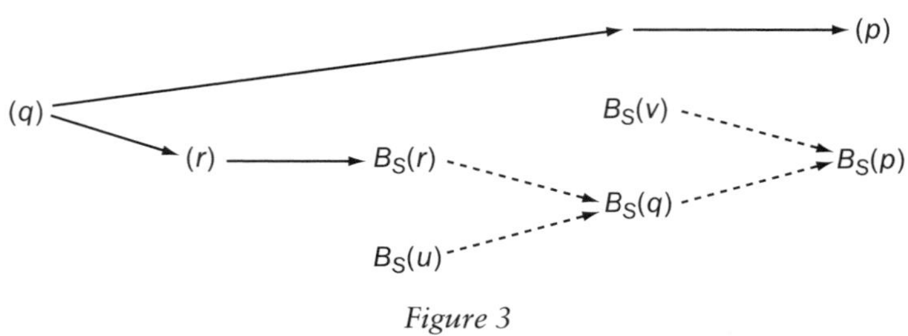

Figure 3

Notice that the causal connection between *q* and *p* is an essential part of *S*'s knowing *p*. Suppose, for example, that *T*'s intending (on Sunday) to go downtown does not result in, or cause, *T*'s going downtown on Monday. Suppose that *T*, after telling *S* that he would go downtown, changes his mind. Nevertheless, on Monday he is kidnapped and forced, at the point of a gun, to go downtown. Here both *q* and *p* actually occur, but they are not causally related. The diagram in Figure 3 would have to be amended by deleting the arrow connecting (*q*) with (*p*). But if the rest of the facts of the original case remain the same, *S* could not be said to know *p*. It would be false to say that *S* knew, on Sunday, that *T* would go downtown on Monday.

Pattern 2 cases of knowledge are not restricted to knowledge of the future. I know that smoke was coming out of my chimney last night. I know this because I remember perceiving a fire in my fireplace last night, and I infer that the fire caused smoke to rise out of the chimney. This case exemplifies Pattern 2. The smoke's rising out of the chimney is not a causal factor of my belief. But the fact that there was a fire in the fireplace was a cause both of my belief that smoke was coming out of the chimney and of the fact that smoke was coming out of the chimney. If we supplement this case slightly, we can make my knowledge exemplify *both* Pattern 1 and Pattern 2. Suppose that a friend tells me today that he perceived smoke coming out of my chimney last night and I base my continued belief of this fact on his testimony. Then the fact was a cause of my current belief of it, as well as an *effect* of another fact that caused my belief. In general, numerous and diverse kinds of causal connections can obtain between a given fact and a given person's belief of that fact.

Let us now examine some objections to Clark's analysis and see how the analysis presented here fares against them. John Turk Saunders and Narayan Champawat have raised the following counterexample to Clark's analysis:[10]

> Suppose that Smith believes
> (p) Jones owns a Ford
> because his friend Brown whom he knows to be generally reliable and honest yesterday told Smith that Jones had always owned a Ford. Brown's information was correct, but today Jones sells his Ford and replaces it with a Volkswagen. An hour later Jones is pleased to find that he is the proud owner of two cars: he has been lucky enough to win a Ford in a raffle. Smith's belief in *p* is not only justified and true, but is fully grounded, e.g., we suppose that each link in the . . . chain of Smith's grounds is true (8).

Clearly Smith does not know *p*; yet he seems to satisfy Clark's analysis of knowing.

Smith's lack of knowledge can be accounted for in terms of my analysis. Smith does not know *p* because his believing *p* is not causally related to *p*, Jones's owning a Ford *now*. This can be seen by examining Figure 4. In the diagram, (*p*) = Jones's owning a Ford now; (*q*) = Jones's having always owned a Ford (until yesterday); (*r*) = Jones's winning a Ford in a raffle today. (*t*), (*u*), and (*v*) are background propositions. (*v*), for example, deals with the likelihood of someone's continuing to own the same car today that he owned yesterday. The subscript "*B*" designates Brown, and the subscript "*S*" designates Smith. Notice the absence of an arrow connecting (*p*) with (*q*). The absence of this arrow represents the absence of a causal relation between (*q*) and (*p*). Jones's owning a Ford in the past (until yesterday) is not a cause of his owning one now. Had he continued owning the same Ford today that he owned yesterday, there would be a causal connection between *q* and *p* and, therefore, a causal connection between *p* and Smith's believing *p*. This causal connection would exemplify Pattern 2. But, as it happened, it is purely a coincidence that Jones owns a Ford today as well as yesterday. Thus, Smith's belief of *p* is not connected with *p* by Pattern 2, nor is there any Pattern 1 connection between them. Hence, Smith does not know *p*.

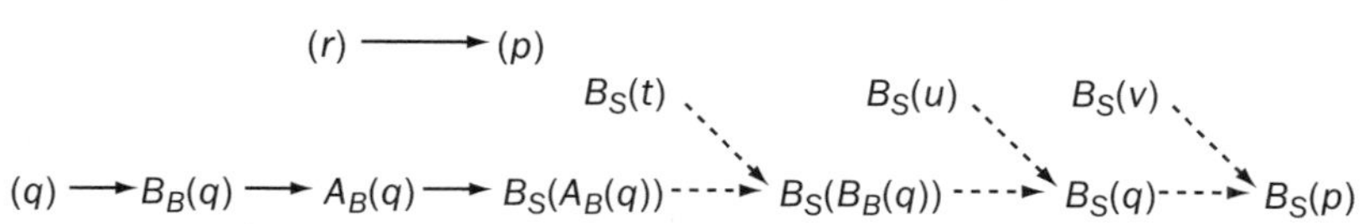

$(r) \longrightarrow (p)$

$B_S(t)$ ⇢ $B_S(B_B(q))$; $B_S(u)$ ⇢ $B_S(q)$; $B_S(v)$ ⇢ $B_S(p)$

$(q) \longrightarrow B_B(q) \longrightarrow A_B(q) \longrightarrow B_S(A_B(q)) \dashrightarrow B_S(B_B(q)) \dashrightarrow B_S(q) \dashrightarrow B_S(p)$

Figure 4

If we supplement Clark's analysis as suggested above, it can be saved from this counterexample. Though Saunders and Champawat fail to mention this explicitly, presumably it is one of Smith's beliefs that Jones's owning a Ford yesterday would *result* in Jones's owning a Ford now. This was undoubtedly one of his grounds for believing that Jones owns a Ford now. (A complete diagram of *S*'s beliefs relevant to *p* would include this belief.) Since this belief is false, however, Clark's analysis would yield the correct consequence that Smith does not know *p*. Unfortunately, Clark himself seems not to have noticed this point, since Saunders and Champawat's putative counterexample has been allowed to stand.

Another sort of counterexample to Clark's analysis has been given by Saunders and Champawat and also by Keith Lehrer. This is a counterexample from which his analysis cannot escape. I shall give Lehrer's example (*op. cit.*) of this sort of difficulty. Suppose Smith bases his belief of

(p) Someone in his office owns a Ford

on his belief of four propositions

(q) Jones owns a Ford
(r) Jones works in his office
(s) Brown owns a Ford
(t) Brown works in his office

In fact, Smith knows q, r, and t, but he does not know s because s is false. Since s is false, not *all* of Smith's grounds for p are true, and, therefore, on Clark's analysis, Smith does not know p. Yet clearly Smith does know p. Thus, Clark's analysis is *too strong*.

Having seen the importance of a causal chain for knowing, it is fairly obvious how to amend Clark's requirements without making them too weak. We need not require, as Clark does, that *all* of S's grounds be true. What is required is that enough of them be true to ensure the existence of at least *one* causal connection between p and S's belief of p. In Lehrer's example, Smith thinks that there are two ways in which he knows p: via his knowledge of the conjunction of q and r, and via his knowledge of the conjunction of s and t. He does not know p via the conjunction of s and t, since s is false. But there is a causal connection, via q and r, between p and Smith's belief of p. And this connection is enough.

Another sort of case in which one of S's grounds for p may be false without preventing him from knowing p is where the false proposition is a dispensable background assumption. Suppose S bases his belief of p on 17 background assumptions, but only 16 of these are true. If these 16 are strong enough to confirm p, then the 17th is dispensable. S can be said to know p though one of his grounds is false.

Our discussion of Lehrer's example calls attention to the necessity of a further clarification of the notion of a "causal chain." I said earlier that causal chains with admixtures of inferences are causal chains. Now I wish to add that causal chains with admixtures of logical connections are causal chains. Unless we allow this interpretation, it is hard to see how facts like "Someone in the office owns a Ford" or "All men are mortal" could be *causally* connected with belief thereof.

The following principle will be useful: *If x is logically related to y and if y is a cause of z, then x is a cause of z*. Thus, suppose that q causes S's belief of q and that r causes S's belief of r. Next suppose that S infers q & r from his belief of q and of r. Then the facts q and r are causes of S's believing q & r. But the fact q & r is logically related to the fact q and to the fact r. Therefore, using the principle enunciated above, the fact q & r is a cause of S's believing q & r.

In Lehrer's case another logical connection is involved: a connection between an existential fact and an instance thereof. Lehrer's case is diagrammed in Figure

5. In addition to the usual conventions, logical relationships are represented by double solid lines. As the diagram shows, the fact *p*—someone in Smith's office owning a Ford—is logically related to the fact *q* & *r*—Jones's owning a Ford and Jones's working in Smith's office. The fact *q* & *r* is, in turn, logically related to the fact *q* and to the fact *r*. *q* causes *S*'s belief of *q* and, by inference, his belief of *q* & *r* and of *p*. Similarly, *r* is a cause of *S*'s belief of *p*. Hence, by the above principle, *p* is a cause of *S*'s belief of *p*. Since Smith's inferences are warranted, even setting aside his belief of *s* & *t*, he knows *p*.

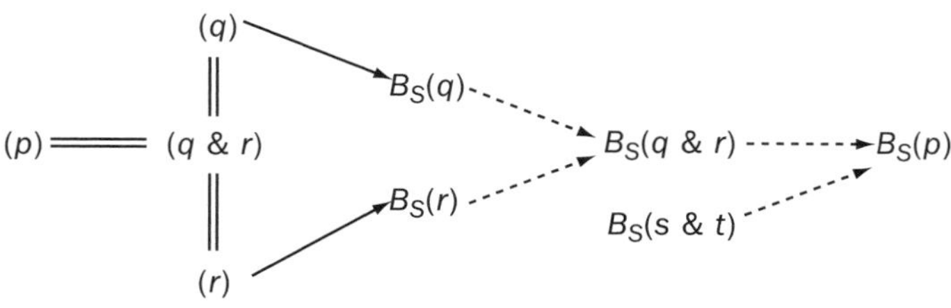

Figure 5

In a similar way, universal facts may be causes of beliefs thereof. The fact that all men are mortal is logically related to its instances: John's being mortal, George's being mortal, Oscar's being mortal, etc. Now suppose that *S* perceives George, John, Oscar, etc. to be mortal (by seeing them die). He infers from these facts that all men are mortal, an inference which, I assume, is warranted. Since each of the facts, John is mortal, George is mortal, Oscar is mortal, etc., is a cause of *S*'s believing that fact, each is also a cause of *S*'s believing that all men are mortal. Moreover, since the universal fact that all men are mortal is logically related to each of these particular facts, this universal fact is a cause of *S*'s belief of it. Hence, *S* can be said to know that all men are mortal. In analogous fashions, *S* can know various other logically compound propositions.

We can now formulate the analysis of knowing as follows:

> *S knows that p* if and only if
> *the fact p is causally connected in an "appropriate" way with S's believing p.*

"Appropriate," knowledge-producing causal processes include the following:

(1) perception
(2) memory
(3) a causal chain, exemplifying either Pattern 1 or 2, which is correctly reconstructed by inferences, each of which is warranted (background propositions help warrant an inference only if they are true)[11]
(4) combinations of (1), (2), and (3)

We have seen that this analysis is *stronger* than the traditional analysis in certain respects: the causal requirement and the correct-reconstruction requirement are absent from the older analysis. These additional requirements enable my analysis to circumvent Gettier's counterexamples to the traditional one. But my analysis is *weaker* than the traditional analysis in another respect. In at least one popular interpretation of the traditional analysis, a knower must be able to justify or give evidence for any proposition he knows. For *S* to know *p* at *t*, *S* must be able, at *t*, to *state* his justification for believing *p*, or his grounds for *p*. My analysis makes no such requirement, and the absence of this requirement enables me to account for cases of knowledge that would wrongly be excluded by the traditional analysis.

I know now, for example, that Abraham Lincoln was born in 1809.[12] I originally came to know this fact, let us suppose, by reading an encyclopedia article. I believed that this encyclopedia was trustworthy and that its saying Lincoln was born in 1809 must have resulted from the fact that Lincoln was indeed born in 1809. Thus, my original knowledge of this fact was founded on a warranted inference. But now I no longer remember this inference. I remember that Lincoln was born in 1809, but not that this is stated in a certain encyclopedia. I no longer have any pertinent beliefs that highly confirm the proposition that Lincoln was born in 1809. Nevertheless, I know this proposition now. My original knowledge of it was preserved until now by the causal process of memory.

Defenders of the traditional analysis would doubtlessly deny that I really do know Lincoln's birth year. This denial, however, stems from a desire to protect their analysis. It seems clear that many things we know were originally learned in a way that we no longer remember. The range of our knowledge would be drastically reduced if these items were denied the status of knowledge.

Other species of knowledge without explicit evidence could also be admitted by my analysis. Notice that I have not closed the list of "appropriate" causal processes. Leaving the list open is desirable, because there may be some presently controversial causal processes that we may later deem "appropriate" and, therefore, knowledge-producing. Many people now doubt the legitimacy of claims to extrasensory perception. But if conclusive evidence were to establish the existence of causal processes connecting physical facts with certain persons' beliefs without the help of standard perceptual processes, we might decide to call such beliefs items of knowledge. This would be another species of knowledge in which the knower might be unable to justify or defend his belief. My analysis allows for the possibility of such knowledge, though it doesn't commit one to it.

Special comments are in order about knowledge of our own mental states. This is a very difficult and controversial topic, so I hesitate to discuss it, but something must be said about it. Probably there are some mental states that are clearly distinct from the subject's belief that he is in such a state. If so, then there is presumably a causal process connecting the existence of such states with the subject's belief thereof. We may add this kind of process to the list of "appropriate" causal processes. The more difficult cases are those in which the state is hardly distinguishable from the subject's believing that he is in that state. My being in pain and my believing that I am in pain are hardly distinct states of affairs. If there is no distinction here between the believing and the believed, how can there be a causal connection between them? For the purposes of the present analysis, we may regard identity as a "limiting" or "degenerate" case of a causal connection, just as zero may be regarded as a "limiting" or "degenerate" case of a number. It is not surprising that knowledge of one's own mental state should turn out to be a limiting or degenerate case of knowledge. Philosophers have long recognized its peculiar status. While some philosophers have regarded it as a paradigm case of knowledge, others have claimed that we have no "knowledge" of our mental states at all. A theory of knowledge that makes knowledge of one's own mental states rather different from garden-variety species of knowledge is, in so far forth, acceptable and even welcome.

In conclusion, let me answer some possible objections to my analysis. It might be doubted whether a causal analysis adequately provides the meaning of the word "knows" or of the sentence (-schema) "*S* knows *p*." But I am not interested in giving the *meaning* of "*S* knows *p*"; only its *truth conditions*. I claim to have given one correct set of truth conditions for "*S* knows *p*." Truth conditions of a sentence do not always provide its meaning. Consider, for example, the following truth-conditions statement: "The sentence 'Team *T* wins the baseball game' is true if and only if team *T* has more runs at the end of the game than the opposing team." This statement fails to provide the meaning of the sentence "Team *T* wins the baseball game", for it fails to indicate an essential part of the meaning of that sentence, viz., that to win a game is to achieve the presumed goal of playing it. Someone might fully understand the truth conditions given above and yet fail to understand the meaning of the sentence because he has no understanding of the notion of "winning" in general.

Truth conditions should not be confused with verification conditions. My analysis of "*S* knows *p*" does not purport to give procedures for *finding out* whether a person (including oneself) knows a given proposition. No doubt, we sometimes do know that people know certain propositions, for we sometimes know that their beliefs are causally connected (in appropriate ways) with the facts believed. On the other hand, it may often be difficult or even impossible to find out whether this condition holds for a given proposition and a given person. For example, it may be difficult for me to find out whether I really do remember a certain fact that I seem to remember. The difficulties that exist for *finding out* whether someone knows a given proposition do not constitute difficulties for my analysis, however.

In the same vein it should be noted that I have made no attempt to answer skeptical problems. My analysis gives no answer to the skeptic who asks that I start from the content of my own experience and then prove that I know there is a material world, a past, etc. I do not take this to be one of the jobs of giving truth conditions for "*S* knows that *p*."

The analysis presented here flies in the face of a well-established tradition in epistemology, the view that epistemological questions are questions of logic or justification, not causal or genetic questions. This traditional view, however, must not go unquestioned. Indeed, I think my analysis shows that the question of whether someone knows a certain proposition is, in part, a causal question, although, of course, the question of what the correct analysis is of "*S* knows that *p*" is not a causal question.

Notes

1 "Is True Justified Belief Knowledge?" *Analysis* (1963): 121–3. I say "reminded" because essentially the same point was made by Russell in 1912. Cf. *The Problems of Philosophy* (Oxford University Press, 1912), ch. XIII, pp. 132 ff. New analyses have been proposed by Michael Clark, "Knowledge and Grounds: A Comment on Mr. Gettier's Paper," *Analysis* 24 (1963): 40–48; Ernest Sosa, "The Analysis of 'Knowledge that *p*'," *ibid.*, 25 (1964): 1–3; and Keith Lehrer, "Knowledge, Truth, and Evidence," *ibid.*, 25 (1965): 168–175.

2 *Op. cit.* Criticisms of Clark's analysis will be discussed below.

3 "The Causal Theory of Perception," *Proceedings of the Aristotelian Society*, supp. vol. 35 (1961).

4 If a laser photograph (hologram) is illuminated by light waves, especially waves from a laser, the effect of the hologram on the viewer is exactly as if the object were being seen. It preserves three-dimensionality completely, and even gives appropriate parallax effects as the viewer moves relative to it. Cf. E.N. Leith and J. Upatnieks, "Photography by Laser," *Scientific American* 212 (June 1965): 24.

5 For further defense of this kind of procedure, with attention to perception, cf. Grice, *op. cit.*

6 Causal connections can hold between states of affairs, such as believings, as well as between events. If a given event or state, in conjunction with other events or states, "leads to" or "results in" another event or state (or the same state obtaining at a later time), it will be called a "cause" of the latter. I shall also speak of "facts" being causes.

7 A fact can be a cause of a belief even if it does not *initiate* the belief. Suppose I believe that there is a lake in a certain locale, this belief having started in a manner quite unconnected with the existence of the lake. Continuing to have the belief, I go to the locale and perceive the lake. At this juncture, the existence of the lake becomes a cause of my believing that there is a lake there. This is analogous to a table top that is supported by four legs. When a fifth leg is inserted flush beneath the table top, it too becomes a cause of the table top's not falling. It has a causal role in the support of the table top even though, before it was inserted, the table top was adequately supported.

8 Clearly we cannot require someone to reconstruct every detail, since this would involve knowledge of minute physical phenomena, for example, of which ordinary people are unaware. On the other hand, it is difficult to give criteria to identify which details, in general, are "important." This will vary substantially from case to case.

10 "Mr. Clark's Definition of 'Knowledge'," *Analysis* 25 (1964): 8–9.

11 Perhaps background propositions that help warrant *S*'s inference must be *known* by *S*, as well as true. This requirement could be added without making our analysis of "*S* knows that *p*" circular. For these propositions would not include *p*. In other words, the analysis of knowledge could be regarded as recursive.

12 This kind of case is drawn from an unpublished manuscript of Gilbert Harman.

"A CAUSAL THEORY OF KNOWING"

QUESTIONS

1. Goldman discusses a case in which *S* believes that a volcano erupted in a certain area, because he sees lava on the ground. In fact, a volcano did erupt there, but the lava was later removed; still later, someone else came and placed new lava on the ground. In this example, does *S* know that a volcano erupted there, according to Goldman? Why or why not?
2. Facts about the future cannot cause our present beliefs. Does this mean that, on Goldman's analysis, we cannot presently *know* any future fact? Why or why not?
3. According to Goldman, if *S* knows that *p*, does it follow that *S* knows that he knows that *p*?

Keith Lehrer and Thomas Paxson, "Knowledge: Undefeated Justified True Belief"

If a man knows that a statement is true even though there is no other statement that justifies his belief, then his knowledge is basic. Basic knowledge is completely justified true belief. On the other hand, if a man knows that a statement is true because there is some other statement that justifies his belief, then his knowledge is nonbasic. Nonbasic knowledge requires something in addition to completely justified true belief; for, though a statement completely justifies a man in his belief, there may be some true statement that *defeats* his justification. So, we must add the condition that his justification is not defeated. Nonbasic knowledge is undefeated justified true belief. These analyses will be elaborated below and subsequently defended against various alternative analyses.[1]

I

We propose the following analysis of basic knowledge: *S* has basic knowledge that *h* if and only if (i) *h* is true, (ii) *S* believes that *h*, (iii) *S* is completely justified in believing that *h*, and (iv) the satisfaction of condition (iii) does not depend on any evidence *p* justifying *S* in believing that *h*. The third condition is used in such a way that it entails neither the second condition nor the first. A person can be completely justified in believing that *h*, even though, irrationally, he does not; and a person can be completely justified in believing that *h*, even though, unfortunately, he is mistaken.[2] Furthermore, the third condition does not entail that there is any statement or belief that justifies *S* in believing that *h*. The analysis, then, is in keeping with the characterization of basic knowledge given above. In basic knowledge, *S* is completely justified in believing that *h* even if it is not the case that there is any statement or belief that justifies his believing that *h*.

There are cases in which a person has some, perhaps mysterious, way of being right about matters of a certain sort with such consistency that philosophers and others have said that the person knows whereof he speaks. Consider, for example, the crystal-ball-gazing gypsy who is almost always right in his predictions of specific events. Peter Unger suggests a special case of this.[3] His gypsy is always right, but has no evidence to this effect and, in fact, believes that he is usually wrong. With respect to each specific prediction, however, the gypsy

Keith Lehrer and Thomas Paxson, "Knowledge: Undefeated Justified True Belief," *The Journal of Philosophy* (1969): 225–37.

impulsively believes it to be true (as indeed it is). Whether or not the predictive beliefs of the ordinary gypsy and Unger's gypsy are cases of knowledge depends, we contend, on whether they are cases of basic knowledge. This in turn depends on whether the gypsies are completely justified in their beliefs. It is plausible to suggest that these are cases of knowledge, but this is only because it is also plausible to think that the gypsies in question have some way of being right that completely justifies their prognostications. We neither affirm nor deny that these are cases of knowledge, but maintain that, if they are cases of knowledge, then they are cases of *basic* knowledge.

It is consistent with our analysis of knowledge to admit that a man knows something even though no statement constitutes evidence that completely justifies his believing it. Philosophers have suggested that certain memory and perceptual beliefs are completely justified in the absence of such evidential statements. We choose to remain agnostic with respect to any claim of this sort, but such proposals are not excluded by our analysis.

II

Not all knowledge that *p* is basic knowledge that *p*, because sometimes justifying evidence is essential. Consider the following analysis of nonbasic knowledge: (i) *h* is true, (ii) *S* believes that *h*, and (iii*) *p* completely justifies *S* in believing that *h*. In this analysis, *p* is that (statement) which makes *S* completely justified in believing that *h*. Note that (iii*), like (iii), does not entail (ii) or (i).

This analysis of nonbasic knowledge is, of course, defective. As Edmund Gettier has shown, there are examples in which some false statement *p* entails and hence completely justifies *S* in believing that *h*, and such that, though *S* correctly believes that *h*, his being correct is mostly a matter of luck.[4] Consequently, *S* lacks knowledge, contrary to the above analysis. Other examples illustrate that the false statement which creates the difficulty need not *entail h*. Consider, for example, the case of the pyromaniac described by Skyrms.[5] The pyromaniac has found that Sure-Fire matches have always ignited when struck. On the basis of this evidence, the pyromaniac is completely justified in believing that the match he now holds will ignite upon his striking it. However, unbeknownst to the pyromaniac, this match happens to contain impurities that raise its combustion temperature above that which can be produced by the friction. Imagine that a burst of Q-radiation ignites the match just as he strikes it. His belief that the match will ignite upon his striking it is true and completely justified by the evidence. But this is not a case of knowledge, because it is not the striking that will cause the match to ignite.

Roderick Chisholm has pointed out that justifications are defeasible.[6] In the examples referred to above, there is some true statement that would defeat any justification of *S* for believing that *h*. In the case of the pyromaniac, his justification is defeated by the true statement that striking the match will not cause it to ignite. This defeats his justification for believing that the match will ignite upon his striking it.

Thus we propose the following analysis of nonbasic knowledge: *S* has nonbasic knowledge that *h* if and only if (i) *h* is true, (ii) *S* believes that *h*, and (iii) there is some statement *p* that completely justifies *S* in believing that *h* and no other statement defeats this justification. The question we must now answer is—what does it mean to say that a statement defeats a justification? Adopting a suggestion of Chisholm's, we might try the following: when *p* completely justifies *S* in believing that *h*, this justification is defeated by *q* if and only if (i) *q* is true, and (ii) the conjunction of *p* and *q* does not completely justify *S* in believing that *h*.[7] This definition is strong enough to rule out the example of the pyromaniac as a case of knowledge. The statement that the striking of a match will *not* cause it to ignite, which is true, is such that when it is conjoined to any statement that completely justifies the pyromaniac in believing that the match will ignite, the resultant conjunction will fail to so justify him in that belief. Given this definition of defeasibility, the analysis of nonbasic knowledge would require that a man who has nonbasic knowledge that *h* must have some justification for his belief that is not defeated by any true statement.

However, this requirement is somewhat unrealistic. To see that the definition of defeasibility under consideration makes the analysis of nonbasic knowledge excessively restrictive, we need only notice that there can be true statements that are misleading. Suppose I see a man walk into the library and remove a book from the library by concealing it beneath his coat. Since I am sure the man is Tom Grabit, whom I have often seen before when he attended my classes, I report that I know that Tom Grabit has removed the book. However, suppose further that Mrs. Grabit, the mother of Tom, has averred that on the day in question Tom was not in the library, indeed, was thousands of miles away, and that Tom's identical twin brother, John Grabit, was in the library. Imagine, moreover, that I am entirely ignorant of the fact that Mrs. Grabit has said these things. The statement that she has said these things would defeat any justification I have for believing that Tom Grabit removed the book, according to our present definition of defeasibility. Thus, I could not be said to have nonbasic knowledge that Tom Grabit removed the book.

The preceding might seem acceptable until we finish the story by adding that Mrs. Grabit is a compulsive and pathological liar, that John Grabit is a fiction of her demented mind, and that Tom Grabit took the book as I believed. Once this is added, it should be apparent that I did know that Tom Grabit removed the book, and, since the knowledge must be nonbasic, I must have nonbasic knowledge of that fact. Consequently, the definition of defeasibility must be amended. The fact that Mrs. Grabit said what she did should not be allowed to defeat any justification I have for believing that Tom Grabit removed the book, because I neither entertained any beliefs concerning Mrs. Grabit nor would I have been justified in doing so. More specifically, my justification does not depend on my being completely justified in believing that Mrs. Grabit did *not* say the things in question.

To understand how the definition of defeasibility must be amended to deal with the preceding example, let us consider an example from the literature in which a justification deserves to be defeated. Suppose that I have excellent evidence that completely justifies my believing that a student in my class, Mr. Nogot, owns a Ford, the evidence consisting in my having seen him driving it, hearing him say he owns it, and so forth. Since Mr. Nogot is a student in my class who owns a Ford, someone in my class owns a Ford, and, consequently, I am completely justified in believing that someone in my class owns a Ford. Imagine that, contrary to the evidence, Mr. Nogot does not own a Ford, that I have been deceived, but that unknown to me Mr. Havit, who is also in my class, does own a Ford. Though I have a completely justified true belief, I do not know that someone in my class owns a Ford. The reason is that my sole justification for believing that someone in my class does own a Ford is and should be defeated by the true statement that Mr. Nogot does not own a Ford.

In the case of Tom Grabit, the true statement that Mrs. Grabit said Tom was not in the library and so forth, should not be allowed to defeat my justification for believing that Tom removed the book, whereas in the case of Mr. Nogot, the true statement that Mr. Nogot does not own a Ford, should defeat my justification for believing that someone in my class owns a Ford. Why should one true statement but not the other be allowed to defeat my justification? The answer is that in one case my justification depends on my being completely justified in believing the true statement to be false while in the other it does not. My justification for believing that Tom removed the book does not depend on my being completely justified in believing it to be false that Mrs. Grabit said Tom was not in the library and so forth. But my justification for believing that someone in my class owns a Ford does depend on my being completely justified in believing it to be false that Mr. Nogot does not own a Ford. Thus, a defeating statement must be one which, though true, is such that the subject is completely justified in believing it to be false.[8]

The following definition of defeasibility incorporates this proposal: when p completely justifies S in believing that h, this justification is defeated by q if and only if (i) q is true, (ii) S is completely justified in believing q to be false, and (iii) the conjunction of p and q does not completely justify S in believing that h.

This definition of defeasibility, though basically correct, requires one last modification to meet a technical problem. Suppose that there is some statement h of which S has nonbasic knowledge. Let us again consider the example in which I know that Tom Grabit removed the book. Now imagine that there is some true statement which is completely irrelevant to this knowledge and which I happen to be completely justified in believing to be false, for example, the statement that I was born in St. Paul. Since I am completely justified in believing it to be false that I was born in St. Paul, I am also completely justified in believing to be false the conjunctive statement that I was born in St. Paul and that q, whatever q is, because I am completely justified in believing any conjunction to be false if I am completely justified in believing a conjunct of it to be false. Therefore, I am completely justified in believing to be false the conjunctive statement that I was born in St. Paul and Mrs. Grabit said that Tom Grabit was not in the library and so forth. Moreover, this conjunctive statement is true, and is such that, when it is conjoined in turn to any evidential statement that justifies me in believing that Tom Grabit removed the book, the resultant extended conjunction will not completely justify me in believing that Tom Grabit removed the book. Hence, any such justification will be defeated.[9] Once again, it turns out that I do not have nonbasic knowledge of the fact that Tom is the culprit.

In a logical nut, the problem is that the current definition of defeasibility reduces to the preceding one. Suppose there is a true statement q such that, for any p that completely justifies S in believing h, the conjunction of p and q does not completely justify me in believing that h. Moreover, suppose that I am not completely justified in believing q to be false, so that, given our current definition of defeasibility, *q* does not count as defeating. Nevertheless, if there is any true statement *r*, irrelevant to both *p* and *q*, which I am completely justified in believing to be false, then we can indirectly use *q* to defeat my justification for believing *h*. For I shall be completely justified in believing the conjunction of *r* and *q* to be false, though in fact it is true, because I am completely justified in believing *r* to be false. If the conjunction of *q* and *p* does not completely justify me in believing that *h*, then, given the irrelevance of *r*, neither would the conjunction of *r*, *q* and *p* justify me in believing that *h*. Hence, my justifications for believing *h* would be defeated by the conjunction *r* and *q* on the current definition of defeasibility as surely as they were by *q* alone on the preceding definition.

The defect is not difficult to repair. Though *S* is completely justified in believing the conjunction of *r* and *q* to be false, one consequence of the conjunction, *q*, undermines my justification but is not something I am completely justified in believing to be false, while another consequence, *r*, is one that I am completely justified in believing to be false but is irrelevant to my justification. To return to our example, I am completely justified in believing to be false the conjunctive statement that I was born in St. Paul and that Mrs. Grabit said that Tom was not in the library and so forth. One consequence of this conjunction, that Mrs. Grabit said that Tom was not in the library and so forth, undermines my justification but is not something I am completely justified in believing to be false, while the other consequence, that I was born in St. Paul, is something I am completely justified in believing to be false but is irrelevant to my justification. The needed restriction is that those consequences of a defeating statement which undermine a justification must themselves be statements that the subject is completely justified in believing to be false.

We propose the following definition of defeasibility: if *p* completely justifies *S* in believing that *h*, then this justification is defeated by *q* if and only if (i) *q* is true, (ii) the conjunction of *p* and *q* does not completely justify *S* in believing that *h*, (iii) *S* is completely justified in believing *q* to be false, and (iv) if *c* is a logical consequence of *q* such that the conjunction of *c* and *p* does not completely justify *S* in believing that *h*, then *S* is completely justified in believing *c* to be false.

With this definition of defeasibility, we complete our analysis of nonbasic knowledge. We have defined nonbasic knowledge as true belief for which some statement provides a complete and undefeated justification. We previously defined basic knowledge as true belief for which there was complete justification that did not depend on any justifying statement. We define as knowledge anything that is either basic or nonbasic knowledge. Thus, *S* knows that *h* if and only if *S* has either basic or nonbasic knowledge that *h*. Having completed our analysis, we shall compare it with other goods in the epistemic marketplace to demonstrate the superiority of our ware.

III

The analysis offered above resembles two recent analyses formulated by Brian Skyrms and R. M. Chisholm. Both philosophers distinguish between basic and nonbasic knowledge, and both analyze knowledge in terms of justification. Moreover, these analyses are sufficiently restrictive so as to avoid yielding the result that a person has nonbasic knowledge when his justification is defeated by some false statement. However, we shall argue that both of these analyses are excessively restrictive and consequently lead to skeptical conclusions that are unwarranted.

Skyrms says that a man has nonbasic knowledge that *p* if and only if he has either derivative or nonderivative knowledge that *p*. He analyzes the latter two kinds of knowledge as follows:

Derivative Knowledge: X has derivative knowledge that *p* if and only if there is a statement "*e*" such that:
(i) *X* knows that *e*
(ii) *X* knows that "*e*" entails "*p*"
(iii) *X* believes that *p* on the basis of the knowledge referred to in (i) and (ii)

Nonderivative Knowledge: X has nonderivative knowledge that *p* if and only if there is a statement "*e*" such that:
(i) *X* knows that *e*
(ii) *X* knows that "*e*" is good evidence for "*p*"
(iii) *X* believes that *p* on the basis of the knowledge referred to in (i) and (ii)
(iv) "*p*" is true
(v) There is no statement "*q*" (other than "*p*") such that:
(a) *X* knows that "*e*" is good evidence of "*q*"
(b) *X* knows that "*q*" entails "*p*"
(c) *X* believes that "*p*" on the basis of the knowledge referred to in (a) and (b) (*op. cit.*, 381)

Later in his paper, Skyrms points out a defect in his analysis of nonderivative knowledge, namely, that the words, "There is a statement '*e*' such that . . ." must be replaced by some such expression as "There is some statement '*e*' consisting of the total evidence of *X* relevant to *p* such that . . ." or else the analysis will lead to trouble (387).

We shall now show why this analysis is unsatisfactory. According to Skyrms, a man who knows that a disjunction is true without knowing any specific disjunct to be true, has nonderivative knowledge of the disjunction (380). Indeed, his analysis of nonderivative knowledge is simply a generalization of his analysis of knowledge with respect to such disjunctions. But his analysis is overrestrictive in the case of our knowledge of disjunctions. Suppose I know that a business acquaintance of mine, Mr. Romeo, arrived in Rochester from Atlanta on either one of two flights, either AA 107 or AA 204. My evidence is that these are the only two flights into Rochester from Atlanta, that Mr. Romeo telephoned earlier from Atlanta to say he would be arriving on one of these two flights, that he is now in Rochester, and that no other flight to Rochester or nearby would enable Mr. Romeo to be in Rochester at the present time. On the basis of this evidence, I may on Skyrms' analysis be said to have nonderivative knowledge that Mr. Romeo arrived on either AA 107 or AA 204. So far so good.

However, suppose that we add to my evidence that, when I meet Mr. Romeo at the airport shortly after the arrival of AA 204 (the later flight), he tells me that he just arrived on AA 204. By Skyrms' analysis I now *lack* nonderivative knowledge that Mr. Romeo arrived on either AA 107 or AA 204. The reason is that condition (v) of his analysis of nonderivative knowledge is no longer satisfied with respect to that disjunction. I now have good evidence that Mr. Romeo arrived on AA 204, and I believe that disjunction on the basis of my knowledge that this evidence is good evidence for the statement "Mr. Romeo arrived on AA 204" and this statement entails "Mr. Romeo arrived on either AA 107 and AA 204." Thus, there is a statement '*q*' that satisfies condition (a), (b), and (c) under (v) where '*p*' is the disjunction.

The consequence that I now lack nonderivative knowledge that Mr. Romeo arrived on either AA 107 or AA 204 would not be fatal if it could be argued that I have derivative knowledge of that disjunction because I know that Mr. Romeo arrived on AA 204. But there is an unmentioned twist of romance in our tale. In fact, Mr. Romeo arrived on the earlier flight, AA 107, and, having entertained his secret love, deceitfully told me he arrived on the later flight. Thus, I do not know that Mr. Romeo arrived on AA 204, because he did not so arrive. By Skyrms' analyses, I have neither derivative nor nonderivative knowledge that Mr. Romeo arrived on either AA 107 or AA 204, and, therefore, I lack nonbasic knowledge of that disjunction. So, as Skyrms would have it, I do not know that Mr. Romeo arrived on either of those flights. However, although there is much of interest that I do not know in this case, I surely do know, on the basis of my original evidence which I may yet brandish with epistemic righteousness, that Mr. Romeo must have arrived on either AA 107 or AA 204. He did so arrive, and my evidence completely justifies me in believing that he did, regardless of the fact that Mr. Romeo spoke with a crooked tongue. Since I do have knowledge of the disjunction, Skyrms' analyses must be rejected.

Chisholm's analysis of knowledge is very similar to ours except for the condition intended to deal with situations in which, though a man has completely justified true belief, his justification is undermined by some false statement. In the sort of cases we have been considering, Chisholm's analysis requires, among other conditions, that if a person knows that *h*, then there is a proposition *p* such that *p* justifies *h* but *p* does not justify any false statement.[10] However, it seems reasonable to suppose that every statement, whatever epistemic virtues it might have, completely justifies at least one false statement. This supposition is supported by the fact that justification in Chisholm's system need not be deductive justification. Any nondeductive justification may fail to be truth-preserving; that is, the conclusion may be false though the premise be true. Thus, though our analysis is in a number of ways indebted to Chisholm's proposals, the foregoing argument is our reason for concluding that Chisholm's analysis would lead to some form of skepticism, that is, to the conclusion that people do not know some things they would generally and reasonably be said to know.

IV

Having indicated our reasons for rejecting those analyses which are most similar to our own, we shall now turn to some analyses that differ from ours in more fundamental ways. Peter Unger has analyzed knowledge as follows: For any sentential value of *p*, (at a time *t*) a man knows that *p* if and only if (at *t*) it is not at all accidental that the man is right about its being the case that *p*.[11] Unger nowhere rules out the possibility that there are some cases in which it is not at all accidental that a man is right simply because he has justification for believing what he does. So it could be that any case that satisfies our conditions for knowledge would satisfy his as well. But there are cases that satisfy his analysis though they fail to satisfy ours.

Let us consider an example. A hologram, or laser photograph, when illuminated by laser light looks three-dimensional even with respect to parallax effects when the viewer shifts his position. Imagine that holography has been so perfected that a laser-illuminated hologram of an object can, under certain observational conditions, be indistinguishable from the real thing.[12] More particularly, suppose that a man, Mr. Promoter, seeking to demonstrate the remarkable properties of laser photography, constructs a boxlike device which contains a vase, a laser photograph of the vase, and a laser source by which the photograph may be illuminated. The device is so constructed that Mr. Promoter by turning a knob may show a viewer the vase or the illuminated laser photograph of the vase, and the visual experience of the viewer when he sees the vase will be indistinguishable from his visual experience when confronted with the photograph. Of course, the very purpose of constructing the device is to arrange things so that people will be completely deceived by the photograph. Now suppose I walk up to the viewer, innocent as the fool who stones the water to destroy his twin, and peer in at the illuminated photograph. Blissfully ignorant of the technical finesse being used to dupe me, I take what I see to be a vase. I believe that the box contains a vase. I am right, there is a vase in the box, and it is not at all accidental that I am right. For Mr. Promoter has constructed the device in such a way that, though I do not see the vase, I will believe quite correctly that there is one there. On Unger's analysis, I know that there is a vase in the box when I see the illuminated laser photograph.

However, it is perfectly apparent that I know nothing of the sort. Any justification I have for believing that there is a vase in the box is defeated by the fact that I do not see a vase in the box but merely a photograph of one. On our analysis it would follow that I do *not* know there is a vase in the box, and that result is the correct one.

Unger might object that it is to some extent accidental that I am right in thinking there is a vase in the box, because I might have had the same visual experiences even if there had been no vase in the box. Hence his analysis yields the same result as ours in this case. But this objection, if taken seriously, would lead us to reject Unger as a skeptic. To see why, imagine that, contrary to the preceding example, Mr. Promoter turns off his device for the day, leaving the knob set so that when I enter the room the vase is before my eyes. I could reach out and touch it if I wished, but good manners restrain me. Nevertheless, there is nothing between me and the vase; I see it and know that it is before my eyes in just the way that I see and know that countless other objects sit untouched before me. However, the statement—I might have had the same visual experience even if there had been no vase in the box—is true in this case as in the former one where I was deceived by the photograph. If this truth shows that my being right in the former case was to some extent accidental, then it would also show that my being right in the present case was to some extent accidental. Therefore, either Unger must agree that the truth of this statement fails to show that my being right in the former case was accidental, in which case his analysis would yield the result that I know when in fact I am ignorant; or he must maintain that its truth shows that my being right in the present case was accidental, in which case his analysis yields the result that I am ignorant when in fact I know. Thus, his analysis is unsatisfactory.

Finally, we wish to consider another kind of theory suggested by Alvin Goldman. His analysis is as follows: *S* knows that *p* if and only if the fact that *p* is causally connected in an "appropriate" way with *S*'s believing that *p* (*op. cit.*, 369). We wish to assert, in opposition to Goldman, that the causal etiology of belief may be utterly irrelevant to the question of what a man knows. Consider yet a third round between Mr. Promoter and me. This time I imagine that I enter as in the first example, where the photograph is illuminated, and become completely and thoroughly convinced that there is a vase in the box. Now imagine that Mr. Promoter, amused with his easy success, tells me that I am quite right in thinking there is a vase in the box, but he then goes on to show me how the device is constructed, removing parts and lecturing about lasers from smirk-twisted lips. With respect to the etiology of my belief that there was a vase in the box, it is possible that my belief was fixed from the time I first looked at the photograph and, moreover, was so firmly and unequivocally fixed that the subsequent revelations neither altered nor reinforced it. This belief is to be *causally explained* by my mistakenly believing that I was seeing a vase when I first entered the room and by the facts about the illuminated laser photograph that caused that erroneous belief. There is no "appropriate" causal connection between the fact that there is a vase in the box and my belief that *p*; so, according to Goldman's analysis, I did not know that there was a vase in the box.

There is something to recommend this result. When I first looked into the device, I did not see the vase, and, consequently, I did not *then* know that there was a vase in the box then. However, after Mr. Promoter's revelations, when I do really see the vase, I do then know that there is a vase in the box. This is not due to any change in the causal etiology of my belief that there is a vase in the box. So, according to Goldman, I still do not know. But Goldman is wrong. I do subsequently know that there is a vase in the box, not because of any change in the causal etiology of the belief, but because I then have some justification for the belief that I formerly lacked. The justification consists of what I learned from Mr. Promoter's demonstration about the box and its contents. In short, there is no reason to suppose that all new evidence that a man could appeal to in order to justify a belief changes the causal etiology of that belief. And such evidence may make the difference between true belief and knowledge.

V

We have contended that our analysis of knowledge in terms of undefeated justified true belief has various advantages over competing analyses. Unlike some of our competitors, we do not presuppose any one theory of justification rather than another. Since current theories of justification are highly controversial, we have employed a notion of justification that is consistent with diverse theories on this subject. By so doing, we hope to have presented a satisfactory analysis of knowledge without waiting for the development of an equally satisfactory theory of justification.

Moreover, the problems that confront a theory of justification can be formulated in terms of the locutions we have introduced in our analysis. For example,

Chisholm has maintained that some statements are self-justifying, and, in our terminology this amounts to answering affirmatively the question whether it is ever the case that some statement *h* completely justifies a person in believing that *h*.[13] Some philosophers have affirmed that all justification must be either inductive or deductive; others have denied this and affirmed that there are other forms of justification as well. In our terminology, this question may be formulated as the question whether, when a statement *p* completely justifies a person in believing *h*, the justified statement must be deduced or induced from the justifying statement or whether there are other alternatives. Finally, philosophers have disagreed about the kind of statement that may justify a man in believing something: whether those statements must be known, or whether they need not be, whether they must include all of a man's evidence, or whether they might exclude some of his evidence, and so forth. We have avoided dogmatically assuming one or the other of these alternatives.

Nevertheless, it may be found that only one theory of justification is suitable to supplement our analysis. Our claim is that, on any satisfactory theory of justification, some knowledge must be undefeated completely justified true belief, and the rest is basic.

Notes

1 This analysis of knowledge is a modification of an earlier analysis proposed by Keith Lehrer, "Knowledge, Truth, and Evidence," *Analysis* 25 (1965): 168–175. It is intended to cope with objections to that article raised by Gilbert H. Harman in "Lehrer on Knowledge," *Journal of Philosophy* 63 (1966): 241–247, and by Alvin Goldman, Brian Skyrms, and others. Criticisms of various alternative analyses of knowledge are given in Lehrer's earlier article, and the reader is referred to that article; such discussion will not be repeated here. The distinction between basic and nonbasic knowledge that is elaborated here was suggested by Arthur Danto in "Freedom and Forebearance," in *Freedom and Determinism* (New York: Random House, 1965), pp. 45–63.

2 Harman's criticism of Lehrer's earlier article rested on his interpreting Lehrer as saying that a person can be completely justified in believing something only if he does believe it. This interpretation leads to problems and is repudiated here.

3 "Experience and Factual Knowledge," *Journal of Philosophy* 64 (1967): 152–173, esp. pp. 165–167; see also his "An Analysis of Factual Knowledge," *Journal of Philosophy* 65 (1968): 157–170, esp. pp. 163–164.

4 "Is Justified True Belief Knowledge?", *Analysis* 33 (1963): 121–123.

5 "The Explication of 'X knows that *p*'," *Journal of Philosophy* 64 (1967): 373–389.

6 *Theory of Knowledge* (Englewood Cliffs, N.J.: Prentice-Hall, 1966), p. 48.

7 Chisholm, "The Ethics of Requirement," *American Philosophical Quarterly* 1 (1964): 147–153. This definition of defeasibility would make our analysis of nonbasic knowledge very similar to one Harman derives from Lehrer's analysis and also one proposed by Marshall Swain in "The Analysis of Non-Basic Knowledge" (unpublished).

8 In Skyrms' example of the pyromaniac cited earlier, the defeating statement is not one which the pyromaniac need believe; Skyrms suggests that the pyromaniac neither believes nor disbelieves that striking the match will cause it to

ignite. Nevertheless, the pyromaniac would be completely justified in believing that striking the Sure-Fire match will cause it to ignite. Hence the statement that striking the match will *not* cause it to light is defeating.

9 A similar objection to Lehrer's earlier analysis is raised by Harman, p. 243.

10 Chisholm; see footnote at end of chap. I, *Theory of Knowledge*, p. 23.

11 "An Analysis of Factual Knowledge," p. 158.

12 Cf. Alvin Goldman, "A Causal Theory of Knowing," *Journal of Philosophy* 64 (1967): 357–372; p. 359.

13 R.M. Chisholm and others, *Philosophy* (Englewood Cliffs, N.J.: Prentice Hall, 1964), pp. 263–277.

QUESTIONS

1 According to Lehrer and Paxson, under what conditions does *S* have basic knowledge that *h*?

2 According to Lehrer and Paxson, under what conditions does *q* defeat *S*'s justification for believing *h*?

3 According to Lehrer and Paxson, under what conditions does *S* have non-basic knowledge that *h*?

Robert Nozick, "Knowledge"

Conditions for knowledge

Our task is to formulate further conditions to go alongside

(1) *p* is true
(2) S believes that *p*.

We would like each condition to be necessary for knowledge, so any case that fails to satisfy it will not be an instance of knowledge. Furthermore, we would like the conditions to be jointly sufficient for knowledge, so any case that satisfies all of them will be an instance of knowledge. We first shall formulate conditions that seem to handle ordinary cases correctly, classifying as knowledge cases which are knowledge, and as nonknowledge cases which are not; then we shall check to see how these conditions handle some difficult cases discussed in the literature.

The causal condition on knowledge, previously mentioned, provides an inhospitable environment for mathematical and ethical knowledge; also there are well-known difficulties in specifying the type of causal connection. If someone floating in a tank oblivious to everything around him is given (by direct electrical and chemical stimulation of the brain) the belief that he is floating in a tank with his brain being stimulated, then even though that fact is part of the cause of his belief, still he does not know that it is true.

Let us consider a different third condition:

(3) If *p* weren't true, S wouldn't believe that *p*.

Throughout this work, let us write the subjunctive "if-then" by an arrow, and the negation of a sentence by prefacing "not-" to it. The above condition thus is rewritten as:

(3) not-$p \rightarrow$ not-(S believes that p).

This subjunctive condition is not unrelated to the causal condition. Often when

Robert Nozick, "Knowledge," *Philosophical Explanations* (Cambridge: Cambridge University Press, 1981).

the fact that p (partially) causes someone to believe that p, the fact also will be causally necessary for his having the belief—without the cause, the effect would not occur. In that case, the subjunctive condition 3 also will be satisfied. Yet this condition is not equivalent to the causal condition. For the causal condition will be satisfied in cases of causal overdetermination, where either two sufficient causes of the effect actually operate, or a back-up cause (of the same effect) would operate if the first one didn't; whereas the subjunctive condition need not hold for these cases. When the two conditions do agree, causality indicates knowledge because it acts in a manner that makes the subjunctive 3 true.

The subjunctive condition 3 serves to exclude cases of the sort first described by Edward Gettier, such as the following. Two other people are in my office and I am justified on the basis of much evidence in believing the first owns a Ford car; though he (now) does not, the second person (a stranger to me) owns one. I believe truly and justifiably that someone (or other) in my office owns a Ford car, but I do not know someone does. Concluded Gettier, knowledge is not simply justified true belief.

The following subjunctive, which specifies condition 3 for this Gettier case, is not satisfied: if no one in my office owned a Ford car, I wouldn't believe that someone did. The situation that would obtain if no one in my office owned a Ford is one where the stranger does not (or where he is not in the office); and in that situation I still would believe, as before, that someone in my office does own a Ford, namely, the first person. So the subjunctive condition 3 excludes this Gettier case as a case of knowledge.

The subjunctive condition is powerful and intuitive, not so easy to satisfy, yet not so powerful as to rule out everything as an instance of knowledge. A subjunctive conditional "if p were true, q would be true", $p \rightarrow q$, does not say that p entails q or that it is logically impossible that p yet not-q. It says that in the situation that would obtain if p were true, q also would be true. This point is brought out especially clearly in recent "possible-worlds" accounts of subjunctives: the subjunctive is true when (roughly) in all those worlds in which p holds true that are closest to the actual world, q also is true. (Examine those worlds in which p holds true closest to the actual world, and see if q holds true in all these.) Whether or not q is true in p worlds that are still farther away from the actual world is irrelevant to the truth of the subjunctive. I do not mean to endorse any particular possible-worlds account of subjunctives, nor am I committed to this type of account. I sometimes shall use it, though, when it illustrates points in an especially clear way.[1]

The subjunctive condition 3 also handles nicely cases that cause difficulties for the view that you know that p when you can rule out the relevant alternatives to p in the context. For, as Gail Stine writes, "what makes an alternative relevant in one context and not another? . . . if on the basis of visual appearances obtained under optimum conditions while driving through the countryside Henry identifies an object as a barn, normally we say that Henry knows that it is a barn. Let us suppose, however, that unknown to Henry, the region is full of expertly made papier-mâché facsimiles of barns. In that case, we would not say that Henry knows that the object is a barn, unless he has evidence against it being a papier-mâché facsimile, which is now a relevant alternative. So much is clear, but what if no such facsimiles exist in Henry's surroundings, although they once did? Are either of these circumstances sufficient to make the hypothesis (that it's a papier-mâché object) relevant? Probably not, but the situation is not so clear." Let *p* be the statement that the object in the field is a (real) barn, and *q* the one that the object in the field is a papier-mâché barn. When papier-mâché barns are scattered through the area, if *p* were false, *q* would be true or might be. Since in this case (we are supposing) the person still would believe *p*, the subjunctive

(3) not-*p* → not-(S believes that *p*)

is not satisfied, and so he doesn't know that *p*. However, when papier-mâché barns are or were scattered around another country, even if *p* were false *q* wouldn't be true, and so (for all we have been told) the person may well know that *p*. A hypothesis *q* contrary to *p* clearly is relevant when if *p* weren't true, *q* would be true; when not-*p* → *q*. It clearly is irrelevant when if *p* weren't true, *q* also would not be true; when not-*p* → not-*q*. The remaining possibility is that neither of these opposed subjunctives holds; *q* might (or might not) be true if *p* weren't true. In this case, *q* also will be relevant, according to an account of knowledge incorporating condition 3 and treating subjunctives along the lines sketched above. Thus, condition 3 handles cases that befuddle the "relevant alternatives" account; though that account can adopt the above subjunctive criterion for when an alternative is relevant, it then becomes merely an alternate and longer way of stating condition 3.

Despite the power and intuitive force of the condition that if *p* weren't true the person would not believe it, this condition does not (in conjunction with the first two conditions) rule out every problem case. There remains, for example, the case of the person in the tank who is brought to believe, by direct electrical and chemical stimulation of his brain, that he is in the tank and is being brought to believe things in this way; he does not know this is true. However, the subjunctive condition is satisfied: if he weren't floating in the tank, he wouldn't believe he was.

The person in the tank does not know he is there, because his belief is not sensitive to the truth. Although it is caused by the fact that is its content, it is not sensitive to that fact. The operators of the tank could have produced any belief, including the false belief that he wasn't in the tank; if they had, he would have believed that. Perfect sensitivity would involve beliefs and facts varying together. We already have one portion of that variation, subjunctively at least: if *p* were false he wouldn't believe it. This sensitivity as specified by a subjunctive does not have the belief vary with the truth or falsity of *p* in all possible situations, merely in the ones that would or might obtain if *p* were false.

The subjunctive condition

(3) not-*p* → not-(S believes that *p*)

tells us only half the story about how his belief is sensitive to the truth-value of *p*. It tells us how his belief state is sensitive to *p*'s falsity, but not how it is sensitive to *p*'s truth; it tells us what his belief state would be if *p* were false, but not what it would be if *p* were true.

To be sure, conditions 1 and 2 tell us that *p* is true and he does believe it, but it does not follow that his believing *p* is sensitive to *p*'s being true. This additional sensitivity is given to us by a further subjunctive: if *p* were true, he would believe it.

(4) $p \rightarrow$ S believes that *p*.

Not only is *p* true and S believes it, but if it were true he would believe it. Compare: not only was the photon emitted and did it go to the left, but (it was then true that): if it were emitted it would go to the left. The truth of antecedent and consequent is not alone sufficient for the truth of a subjunctive; 4 says more than 1 and 2. Thus, we presuppose some (or another) suitable account of subjunctives. According to the suggestion tentatively made above, 4 holds true if not only does he actually truly believe *p*, but in the "close" worlds where *p* is true, he also believes it. He believes that *p* for some distance out in the *p* neighborhood of the actual world; similarly, condition 3 speaks not of the whole not-*p* neighborhood of the actual world, but only of the first portion of it. (If, as is likely, these explanations do not help, please use your own intuitive understanding of the subjunctives 3 and 4.)

The person in the tank does not satisfy the subjunctive condition 4. Imagine as actual a world in which he is in the tank and is stimulated to believe he is, and consider what subjunctives are true in that world. It is not true of him there that if he were in the tank he would believe it; for in the close world (or situation) to his own where he is in the tank but they don't give him the belief that he is (much less instill the belief that he isn't) he doesn't believe he is in the tank. Of the person actually in the tank and believing it, it is not true to make the further statement that if he were in the tank he would believe it—so he does not know he is in the tank.

The subjunctive condition 4 also handles a case presented by Gilbert Harman. The dictator of a country is killed; in their first edition, newspapers print the story, but later all the country's newspapers and other media deny the story, falsely. Everyone who encounters the denial believes it (or does not know what to believe and so suspends judgment). Only one person in the country fails to hear any denial and he continues to believe the truth. He satisfies conditions 1 through 3 (and the causal condition about belief) yet we are reluctant to say he knows the truth. The reason is that if he had heard the denials, he too would have believed them, just like everyone else. His belief is not sensitively tuned to the truth, he doesn't satisfy the condition that if it were true he would believe it. Condition 4 is not satisfied.

There is a pleasing symmetry about how this account of knowledge relates conditions 3 and 4, and connects them to the first two conditions. The account has the following form.

(1)
(2)
(3) not-1 $\rightarrow$ not-2
(4) 1 $\rightarrow$ 2

I am not inclined, however, to make too much of this symmetry, for I found also that with other conditions experimented with as a possible fourth condition there was some way to construe the resulting third and fourth conditions as symmetrical answers to some symmetrical looking questions, so that they appeared to arise in parallel fashion from similar questions about the components of true belief.

Symmetry, it seems, is a feature of a mode of presentation, not of the contents presented. A uniform transformation of symmetrical statements can leave the results nonsymmetrical. But if symmetry attaches to mode of presentation, how can it possibly be a deep feature of, for instance, laws of nature that they exhibit symmetry? (One of my favorite examples of symmetry is due to Groucho Marx. On his radio program he spoofed a commercial, and ended, "And if you are not completely satisfied, return the unused portion of our product and we will return the unused portion of your money.") Still, to present our subject symmetrically makes the connection of knowledge to true belief especially perspicuous. It seems to me that a symmetrical formulation is a sign of our understanding, rather than a mark of truth. If we cannot understand an asymmetry as arising from an underlying symmetry through the operation of a particular factor, we will not understand why that asymmetry exists in that direction. (But do we also need to understand why the underlying asymmetrical factor holds instead of its opposite?)

A person knows that *p* when he not only does truly believe it, but also would truly believe it and wouldn't falsely believe it. He not only actually has a true belief, he subjunctively has one. It is true that *p* and he believes it; if it weren't true he wouldn't believe it, and if it were true he would believe it. To know that *p* is to be someone who would believe it if it were true, and who wouldn't believe it if it were false.

It will be useful to have a term for this situation when a person's belief is thus subjunctively connected to the fact. Let us say of a person who believes that *p*, which is true, that when 3 and 4 hold, his belief *tracks* the truth that *p*. To know is to have a belief that tracks the truth. Knowledge is a particular way of being connected to the world, having a specific real factual connection to the world: tracking it.

One refinement is needed in condition 4. It may be possible for someone to have contradictory beliefs, to believe *p* and also believe not-*p*. We do not mean such a person to easily satisfy 4, and in any case we want his belief-state, sensitive to the truth of *p*, to focus upon *p*. So let us rewrite our fourth condition as:

(4) $p \rightarrow$ S believes that *p* and not-(S believes that not-*p*).

As you might have expected, this account of knowledge as tracking requires some refinements and epicycles. Readers who find themselves (or me) bogged down in these refinements should move on directly to this essay's second part, on skepticism, where the pace picks up. . . .

Skeptical possibilities

The skeptic often refers to possibilities in which a person would believe something even though it was false: really, the person is cleverly deceived by others, perhaps by an evil demon, or the person is dreaming or he is floating in a tank near Alpha Centauri with his brain being stimulated. In each case, the *p* he believes is false, and he believes it even though it is false.

How do these possibilities adduced by the skeptic show that someone does not know that *p*? Suppose that someone is you; how do these possibilities count against your knowing that *p*? One way might be the following. (I shall consider other ways later.) If there is a possible situation where *p* is false yet you believe that *p*, then in that situation you believe that *p* even though it is false. So it appears you do not satisfy condition 3 for knowledge.

(3) If *p* were false, S wouldn't believe that *p*.

For a situation has been described in which you do believe that *p* even though *p* is false. How then can it also be true that if *p* were false, you wouldn't believe it? If the skeptic's possible situation shows that 3 is false, and if 3 is a necessary condition for knowledge, then the skeptic's possible situation shows that there isn't knowledge.

So construed, the skeptic's argument plays on condition 3; it aims to show that condition 3 is not satisfied. The skeptic may seem to be putting forth

R: Even if *p* were false, S still would believe *p*.

This conditional, with the same antecedent as 3 and the contradictory consequent, is incompatible with the truth of 3. If 3 is true, then R is not. However, R is stronger than the skeptic needs in order to show 3 is false. For 3 is false when if *p* were false, S might believe that *p*. This last conditional is weaker than R, and is merely 3's denial:

T: not-[not-*p* → not-(S believes that *p*)].

Whereas R does not simply deny 3, it asserts an opposing subjunctive of its own. Perhaps the possibility the skeptic adduces is not enough to show that R is true, but it appears at least to establish the weaker T; since this T denies 3, the skeptic's possibility appears to show that 3 is false.

However, the truth of 3 is not incompatible with the existence of a possible situation where the person believes *p* though it is false. The subjunctive

(3) not-*p* → not-(S believes *p*)

does not talk of all possible situations in which *p* is false (in which not-*p* is true). It does not say that in all possible situations where not-*p* holds, S doesn't believe *p*. To say there is no possible situation in which not-*p* yet S believes *p*, would be to say that not-*p* entails not-(S believes *p*), or logically implies it. But subjunctive conditionals differ from entailments; the subjunctive 3 is not a statement of entailment. So the existence of a possible situation in which *p* is false yet S believes *p* does not show that 3 is false; 3 can be true even though there is a possible situation where not-*p* and S believes that *p*.

What the subjunctive 3 speaks of is the situation that would hold if *p* were false. Not every possible situation in which *p* is false is the situation that would hold if *p* were false. To fall into possible worlds talk, the subjunctive 3 speaks of the not-*p* world that is closest to the actual world, or of those not-*p* worlds that are closest to the actual world, or more strongly (according to my suggestion) of the not-*p* neighborhood of the actual world. And it is of this or these not-*p* worlds that it says (in them) S does not believe that *p*. What happens in yet other more distant not-*p* worlds is no concern of the subjunctive 3.

The skeptic's possibilities (let us refer to them as SK), of the person's being deceived by a demon or dreaming or floating in a tank, count against the subjunctive

(3) if *p* were false then S wouldn't believe that *p*

only if (one of) these possibilities would or might obtain if *p* were false; only if one of these possibilities is in the not-*p* neighborhood of the actual world. Condition 3 says: if *p* were false, S still would not believe *p*. And this can hold even though there is some situation SK described by the skeptic in which *p* is false and S believes *p*. If *p* were false S still would not believe *p*, even though there is a situation SK in which *p* is false and S does believe *p*, provided that this situation SK wouldn't obtain if *p* were false. If the skeptic describes a situation SK which would not hold even if *p* were false then this situation SK doesn't show that 3 is false and so does not (in this way at least) undercut knowledge. Condition C acts to rule out skeptical hypotheses.

C: not-*p* → SK does not obtain.

Any skeptical situation SK which satisfies condition C is ruled out. For a skeptical situation SK to show that we don't know that *p*, it must fail to satisfy C which excludes it; instead it must be a situation that might obtain if *p* did not, and so satisfy C's denial:

not-(not-*p* → SK doesn't obtain).

Although the skeptic's imagined situations appear to show that 3 is false, they do not; they satisfy condition C and so are excluded.

The skeptic might go on to ask whether we know that his imagined situations SK are excluded by condition C, whether we know that if *p* were false SK would not obtain. However, typically he asks something stronger: do we know that his imagined situation SK does not actually obtain? Do we know that we are not being deceived by a demon, dreaming, or floating in a tank? And if we do not know this, how can we know that *p*? Thus we are led to the second way his imagined situations might show that we do not know that *p*.

Skeptical results

According to our account of knowledge, S knows that the skeptic's situation SK doesn't hold if and only if

(1) SK doesn't hold

(2) S believes that SK doesn't hold
(3) If SK were to hold, S would not believe that SK doesn't hold
(4) If SK were not to hold, S would believe it does not.

Let us focus on the third of these conditions. The skeptic has carefully chosen his situations SK so that if they held we (still) would believe they did not. We would believe we weren't dreaming, weren't being deceived, and so on, even if we were. He has chosen situations SK such that if SK were to hold, S would (still) believe that SK doesn't hold—and this is incompatible with the truth of 3.

Since condition 3 is a necessary condition for knowledge, it follows that we do not know that SK doesn't hold. If it were true that an evil demon was deceiving us, if we were having a particular dream, if we were floating in a tank with our brains stimulated in a specified way, we would still believe we were not. So, we do not know we're not being deceived by an evil demon, we do not know we're not in that tank, and we do not know we're not having that dream. So says the skeptic, and so says our account. And also so we say—don't we? For how could we know we are not being deceived that way, dreaming that dream? If those things *were* happening to us, everything would seem the same to us. There is no way we can know it is not happening for there is no way we could tell if it were happening; and if it were happening we would believe exactly what we do now—in particular, we still would believe that it was not. For this reason, we feel, and correctly, that we don't know—how could we?—that it is not happening to us. It is a virtue of our account that it yields, and explains, this result.

The skeptic asserts we do not know his possibilities don't obtain, and he is right. Attempts to avoid skepticism by claiming we do know these things are bound to fail. The skeptic's possibilities make us uneasy because, as we deeply realize, we do not know they don't obtain; it is not surprising that attempts to show we do know these things leave us suspicious, strike us even as bad faith.[2] Nor has the skeptic merely pointed out something obvious and trivial. It comes as a surprise to realize that we do not know his possibilities don't obtain. It is startling, shocking. For we would have thought, before the skeptic got us to focus on it, that we did know those things, that we did know we were not being deceived by a demon, or dreaming that dream, or stimulated that way in that tank. The skeptic has pointed out that we do not know things we would have confidently said we knew. And if we don't know these things, what can we know? So much for the supposed obviousness of what the skeptic tells us.

Let us say that a situation (or world) is doxically identical for S to the actual situation when if S were in that situation, he would have exactly the beliefs (*doxa*) he actually does have. More generally, two situations are doxically identical for S if and only if he would have exactly the same beliefs in them. It might be merely a curiosity to be told there are nonactual situations doxically identical to the actual one. The skeptic, however, describes worlds doxically identical to the actual world in which almost everything believed is false.[3]

Such worlds are possible because we know mediately, not directly. This leaves room for a divergence between our beliefs and the truth. It is as though we possessed only two-dimensional plane projections of three-dimensional objects. Different three-dimensional objects, oriented appropriately, have the same two-dimensional plane projection. Similarly, different situations or worlds will lead to our having the very same beliefs. What is surprising is how very different the doxically identical world can be—different enough for almost everything believed in it to be false. Whether or not the mere fact that knowledge is mediated always makes room for such a very different doxically identical world, it does so in our case, as the skeptic's possibilities show. To be shown this is nontrivial, especially when we recall that we do not know the skeptic's possibility doesn't obtain: we do not know that we are not living in a doxically identical world wherein almost everything we believe is false.

What more could the skeptic ask for or hope to show? Even readers who sympathized with my desire not to dismiss the skeptic too quickly may feel this has gone too far, that we have not merely acknowledged the force of the skeptic's position but have succumbed to it.

The skeptic maintains that we know almost none of what we think we know. He has shown, much to our initial surprise, that we do not know his (nontrivial) possibility SK doesn't obtain. Thus, he has shown of one thing we thought we knew, that we didn't and don't. To the conclusion that we know almost nothing, it appears but a short step. For if we do not know we are not dreaming or being deceived by a demon or floating in a tank, then how can I know, for example, that I am sitting before a page writing with a pen, and how can you know that you are reading a page of a book?

However, although our account of knowledge agrees with the skeptic in saying that we do not know that not-SK, it places no formidable barriers before my knowing that I am writing on a page with a pen. It is true that I am, I believe I am, if I weren't I wouldn't believe I was, and if I were, I would believe it. (I leave out the reference to method.) Also, it is true that you are reading a page (please, don't stop now!), you believe you are, if you weren't reading a page you wouldn't believe you were, and if you were reading a page you would believe you were. So according to the account, I do know that I am writing on a page with a pen, and you do know that you are reading a page. The account does not lead to any general skepticism.

Yet we must grant that it appears that if the skeptic is right that we don't know we are not dreaming or being deceived or floating in the tank, then it cannot be that I know I am writing with a pen or that you know you are reading a page. So we must scrutinize with special care the skeptic's "short step" to the conclusion that we don't know these things, for either this step cannot be taken or our account of knowledge is incoherent.

Nonclosure

In taking the "short step", the skeptic assumes that if S knows that *p* and he knows that "*p* entails *q*" then he also knows that *q*. In the terminology of the logicians, the skeptic assumes that knowledge is closed under known logical implication; that the operation of moving from something known to something else known to be entailed by it does not take us outside of the (closed) area of knowledge. He intends, of course, to work things backwards, arguing that since the person does not know that *q*, assuming (at least for the purposes of argument) that he does know that *p* entails *q*, it follows that he does not know that *p*. For if he did know that *p*, he would also know that *q*, which he doesn't.

The details of different skeptical arguments vary in their structure, but each one will assume some variant of the principle that knowledge is closed under known logical implication. If we abbreviate "knowledge that *p*" by "Kp" and abbreviate "entails" by the fishhook sign "$\prec$", we can write this principle of closure as the subjunctive principle

P: $K(p \prec q)$ & $Kp \rightarrow Kq$.

If a person were to know that *p* entails *q* and he were to know that *p* then he would know that *q*. The statement that *q* follows by modus ponens from the other two stated as known in the antecedent of the subjunctive principle P; this principle counts on the person to draw the inference to *q*.

You know that your being in a tank on Alpha Centauri entails your not being in place X where you are. (I assume here a limited readership.) And you know also the contrapositive, that your being at place X entails that you are not then in a tank on Alpha Centauri. If you knew you were at X you would know you're not in a tank (of a specified sort) at Alpha Centauri. But you do not know this last fact (the skeptic has argued and we have agreed) and so (he argues) you don't know the first. Another intuitive way of putting the skeptic's argument is as follows. If you know that two statements are incompatible and you know the first is true then you know the denial of the second. You know that your being at X and your being in a tank on Alpha Centauri are incompatible; so if you knew you were at X you would know you were not in the (specified) tank on Alpha Centauri. Since you do not know the second, you don't know the first.

No doubt, it is possible to argue over the details of principle P, to point out it is incorrect as it stands. Perhaps, though Kp, the person does not know that he knows that *p* (that is, not-KKp) and so does not draw the inference to *q*. Or perhaps he doesn't draw the inference because not-$KK(p \prec q)$. Other similar principles face their own difficulties: for example, the principle that $K(p \rightarrow q) \rightarrow (Kp \rightarrow Kq)$ fails if Kp stops $p \rightarrow q$ from being true, that is, if $Kp \rightarrow$ not-$(p \rightarrow q)$; the principle that $K(p \prec q) \rightarrow K(Kp \rightarrow Kq)$ faces difficulties if Kp makes the person forget that $(p \prec q)$ and so he fails to draw the inference to *q*. We seem forced to pile K upon K until we reach something like $KK(p \prec q)$ & $KKp \rightarrow Kq$; this involves strengthening considerably the antecedent of P and so is not useful for the skeptic's argument that *p* is not known. (From a principle altered thus, it would follow at best that it is not known that *p* is known.)

We would be ill-advised, however, to quibble over the details of P. Although these details are difficult to get straight, it will continue to appear that something like P is correct. If S knows that "*p* entails *q*" and he knows that *p* and knows that "(*p* and *p* entails *q*) entails *q*" (shades of the Lewis Carroll puzzle we discuss below!) and he does draw the inference to *q* from all this and believes *q* via the process of drawing this inference, then will he not know that *q*? And what is wrong with simplifying this mass of detail by writing merely principle P, provided we apply it only to cases where the mass of detail holds, as it surely does in the skeptical cases under consideration? For example, I do realize that my being in the Van Leer Foundation Building in Jerusalem entails that I am not in a tank on Alpha Centauri; I am capable of drawing inferences now; I do believe I am not in a tank on Alpha Centauri (though not solely via this inference, surely); and so forth. Won't this satisfy the correctly detailed principle, and shouldn't it follow that I know I am not (in that tank) on Alpha Centauri? The skeptic agrees it should follow; so he concludes from the fact that I don't know I am not floating in the tank on Alpha Centauri that I don't know I am in Jerusalem. Uncovering difficulties in the details of particular formulations of P will not weaken the principle's intuitive appeal; such quibbling will seem at best like a wasp attacking a steamroller, at worst like an effort in bad faith to avoid being pulled along by the skeptic's argument.

Principle P is wrong, however, and not merely in detail. Knowledge is not closed under known logical implication. S knows that *p* when S has a true belief that *p*, and S wouldn't have a false belief that *p* (condition 3) and S would have a true belief that *p* (condition 4). Neither of these latter two conditions is closed under known logical implication.

Let us begin with condition

(3) if *p* were false, S wouldn't believe that *p*.

When S knows that *p*, his belief that *p* is contingent on the truth of *p*, contingent in the way the subjunctive condition 3 describes. Now it might be that *p* entails *q* (and S knows this), that S's belief that *p* is subjunctively contingent on the truth of *p*, that S believes *q*, yet his belief that *q* is not subjunctively dependent on the truth of *q*, in that it (or he) does not satisfy:

(3′) if *q* were false, S wouldn't believe that *q*.

For 3′ talks of what S would believe if *q* were false, and this may be a very different situation than the one that would hold if *p* were false, even though *p* entails *q*. That you were born in a certain city entails that you were born on earth.[4] Yet contemplating what (actually) would be the situation if you were not born in that city is very different from contemplating what situation would hold if you weren't born on earth. Just as those possibilities are very different, so what is believed in them may be very different. When *p* entails *q* (and not the other way around) *p* will be a stronger statement than *q*, and so not-*q* (which is the antecedent of 3′) will be a stronger statement than not-*p* (which is the antecedent of 3). There is no reason to assume you will have the same beliefs in these two cases, under these suppositions of differing strengths.

There is no reason to assume the (closest) not-*p* world and the (closest) not-*q* world are doxically identical for you, and no reason to assume, even though *p* entails *q*, that your beliefs in one of these worlds would be a (proper) subset of your beliefs in the other.

Consider now the two statements:

p = I am awake and sitting on a chair in Jerusalem;
q = I am not floating in a tank on Alpha Centauri being stimulated by electrochemical means to believe that *p*.

The first one entails the second: *p* entails *q*. Also, I know that *p* entails *q*; and I know that *p*. If *p* were false, I would be standing or lying down in the same city, or perhaps sleeping there, or perhaps in a neighboring city or town. If *q* were false, I would be floating in a tank on Alpha Centauri. Clearly these are very different situations, leading to great differences in what I then would believe. If *p* were false, if I weren't awake and sitting on a chair in Jerusalem, I would not believe that *p*. Yet if *q* were false, if I was floating in a tank on Alpha Centauri, I would believe that *q*, that I was not in the tank, and indeed, in that case, I would still believe that *p*. According to our account of knowledge, I know that *p* yet I do not know that *q*, even though (I know) *p* entails *q*.

This failure of knowledge to be closed under known logical implication stems from the fact that condition 3 is not closed under known logical implication; condition 3 can hold of one statement believed while not of another known to be entailed by the first. It is clear that any account that includes as a necessary condition for knowledge the subjunctive condition 3, not-$p \rightarrow$ not-(S believes that p), will have the consequence that knowledge is not closed under known logical implication.

When *p* entails *q* and you believe each of them, if you do not have a false belief that *p* (since *p* is true) then you do not have a false belief that *q*. However, if you are to know something not only don't you have a false belief about it, but also you wouldn't have a false belief about it. Yet, we have seen how it may be that *p* entails *q* and you believe each and you wouldn't have a false belief that *p* yet you might have a false belief that *q* (that is, it is not the case that you wouldn't have one). Knowledge is not closed under the known logical implication because "wouldn't have a false belief that" is not closed under known logical implication.

If knowledge were the same as (simply) true belief then it would be closed under known logical implication (provided the implied statements were believed). Knowledge is not simply true belief, however; additional conditions are needed. These further conditions will make knowledge open under known logical implication, even when the entailed statement is believed, when at least one of the further conditions itself is open. Knowledge stays closed (only) if all of the additional conditions are closed. I lack a general nontrivial characterization of those conditions that are closed under known logical implication; possessing such an illuminating characterization, one might attempt to prove that no additional conditions of that sort could provide an adequate analysis of knowledge.

Still, we can say the following. A belief that *p* is knowledge that *p* only if it somehow varies with the truth of *p*. The causal condition for knowledge specified that the belief was "produced by" the fact, but that condition did not provide the right sort of varying with the fact. The subjunctive conditions 3 and 4 are our attempt to specify that varying. But however an account spells this out, it will hold that whether a belief that *p* is knowledge partly depends on what goes on with the belief in some situations when *p* is false. An account that says nothing about what is believed in any situation when *p* is false cannot give us any mode of varying with the fact.

Because what is preserved under logical implication is truth, any condition that is preserved under known logical implication is most likely to speak only of what happens when *p*, and *q*, are true, without speaking at all of what happens when either one is false. Such a condition is incapable of providing "varies with"; so adding only such conditions to true belief cannot yield an adequate account of knowledge.

A belief's somehow varying with the truth of what is believed is not closed under known logical implication. Since knowledge that *p* involves such variation, knowledge also is not closed under known logical implication. The skeptic cannot easily deny that knowledge involves such variation, for his argument that we don't know that we're not floating in that tank, for example, uses the fact that knowledge does involve variation. ("If you were floating in the tank you would still think you weren't, so you don't know that you're not.") Yet, though one part of his argument uses that fact that knowledge involves such variation, another part of his argument presupposes that knowledge does not involve any such variation. This latter is the part that depends upon knowledge being closed under known logical implication, as when the skeptic argues that since you don't know that not-SK, you don't know you are not floating in the tank, then you also don't know, for example, that you are now reading a book. That closure can hold only if the variation does not. The skeptic cannot be right both times. According to our view he is right when he holds that knowledge involves such variation and so concludes that we don't know, for example, that we are not floating in that tank; but he is wrong when he assumes knowledge is closed under known logical implication and concludes that we know hardly anything.

Knowledge is a real factual relation, subjunctively specifiable, whose structure admits our standing in this relation, tracking, to *p* without standing in it to some *q* which we know *p* to entail. Any relation embodying some variation of belief with the fact, with the truth (value), will exhibit this structural feature. The skeptic is right that we don't track some particular truths—the ones stating that his skeptical possibilities SK don't hold—but wrong that we don't stand in the real knowledge-relation of tracking to many other truths, including ones that entail these first mentioned truths we believe but don't know.

The literature on skepticism contains writers who endorse these skeptical arguments (or similar narrower ones), but confess their inability to maintain their skeptical beliefs at times when they are not focusing explicitly on the reasoning that led them to skeptical conclusions. The most notable example of this is Hume:

> I am ready to reject all belief and reasoning, and can look upon no opinion even as more probable or likely than another . . . Most fortunately it happens that since reason is incapable of dispelling these clouds, nature herself suffices to that purpose, and cures me of this philosophical melancholy and delirium, either by relaxing this bent of mind, or by some avocation, and lively impression of my senses, which obliterate all these chimeras. I dine, I play a game of backgammon, I converse, and am merry with my friends; and when after three or four hours' amusement, I would return to these speculations, they appear so cold, and strained, and ridiculous, that I cannot find in my heart to enter into them any farther. (*A Treatise of Human Nature*, Book I, Part IV, section VII)
>
> The great subverter of Pyrrhonism or the excessive principles of skepticism is action, and employment, and the occupations of common life. These principles may flourish and triumph in the schools; where it is, indeed, difficult, if not impossible, to refute them. But as soon as they leave the

> shade, and by the presence of the real objects, which actuate our passions and sentiments, are put in opposition to the more powerful principles of our nature, they vanish like smoke, and leave the most determined skeptic in the same condition as other mortals . . . And though a Pyrrhonian may throw himself or others into a momentary amazement and confusion by his profound reasonings; the first and most trivial event in life will put to flight all his doubts and scruples, and leave him the same, in every point of action and speculation, with the philosophers of every other sect, or with those who never concerned themselves in any philosophical researches. When he awakes from his dream, he will be the first to join in the laugh against himself, and to confess that all his objections are mere amusement. (*An Enquiry Concerning Human Understanding*, Section XII, Part II)

The theory of knowledge we have presented explains why skeptics of various sorts have had such difficulties in sticking to their far-reaching skeptical conclusions "outside the study," or even inside it when they are not thinking specifically about skeptical arguments and possibilities SK.

The skeptic's arguments do show (but show only) that we don't know the skeptic's possibilities SK do not hold; and he is right that we don't track the fact that SK does not hold. (If it were to hold, we would still think it didn't.) However, the skeptic's arguments don't show we do not know other facts (including facts that entail not-SK) for we do track these other facts (and knowledge is not closed under known logical entailment.) Since we do track these other facts—you, for example, the fact that you are reading a book; I, the fact that I am writing on a page—and the skeptic tracks such facts too, it is not surprising that when he focuses on them, on his relationship to such facts, the skeptic finds it hard to remember or maintain his view that he does not know those facts. Only by shifting his attention back to his relationship to the (different) fact that not-SK, which relationship is not tracking, can he revive his skeptical belief and make it salient. However, this skeptical triumph is evanescent, it vanishes when his attention turns to other facts. Only by fixating on the skeptical possibilities SK can he maintain his skeptical virtue; otherwise, unsurprisingly, he is forced to confess to sins of credulity.

Notes

1 If the possible-worlds formalism is used to represent counterfactuals and subjunctives, the relevant worlds are not those *p* worlds that are closest or most similar to the actual world, unless the measure of closeness or similarity is: what would obtain if *p* were true. Clearly, this cannot be used to explain when subjunctives hold true, but it can be used to represent them. Compare utility theory which represents preferences but does not explain them. Still, it is not a trivial fact that preferences are so structured that they can be represented by a real-valued function, unique up to a positive linear transformation, even though the representation (by itself) does not explain these preferences. Similarly, it would be of interest to know what properties hold of distance metrics which serve to represent subjunctives, and to know how subjunctives must be structured and interrelated so that they can be given a possible worlds representation. (With the same one space serving for all subjunctives?)

One further word on this point. Imagine a library where a cataloguer assigns call numbers based on facts of sort F. Someone, perhaps the cataloguer, then places each book on the shelf by looking at its call number, and inserting it between the two books whose call numbers are most nearly adjacent to its own. The call number is derivative from facts of type F, yet it plays some explanatory role, not merely a representational one. "Why is this book located precisely there? Because of its number." Imagine next another library where the person who places books on the shelves directly considers facts of type F, using them to order the books and to interweave new ones. Someone else might notice that this ordering can be represented by an assignment of numbers, numbers from which other information can be derived as well, for example, the first letter of the last name of the principal author. But such an assigned number is no explanation of why a book in this library is located between two others (or why its author's last name begins with a certain letter). I have assumed that utility numbers stand to preferences, and closeness or similarity measures stand to subjunctives, as the call numbers do to the books, and to the facts of type F they exhibit, in the second library.

2 Descartes presumably would refute the tank hypothesis as he did the demon hypothesis, through a proof of the existence of a good God who would not allow anyone, demon or psychologist, permanently to deceive us. The philosophical literature has concentrated on the question of whether Descartes can prove this (without begging the question against the demon hypothesis). The literature has not discussed whether even a successful proof of the existence of a good God can help Descartes to conclude he is not almost always mistaken. Might not a good God have his own reasons for deceiving us; might he not deceive us temporarily—a period which includes all of our life thus far (but not an afterlife)? To the question of why God did not create us so that we never would make any errors, Descartes answers that the motives of God are inscrutable to us. Do we know that such an inscrutable God could not be motivated to allow another powerful "demon" to deceive and dominate us?

Alternatively, could not such a good God be motivated to deceive itself temporarily, even if not another? (Compare the various Indian doctrines designed to explain our ignorance of our own true nature, that is, Atman–Brahman's or, on another theory, the purusha's nature.) Whether from playfulness or whatever motive, such a good God would temporarily deceive itself, perhaps even into thinking it is a human being living in a material realm. Can we know, via Descartes' argument, that this is not our situation? And so forth.

These possibilities, and others similar, are so obvious that some other explanation, I mean the single-minded desire to refute skepticism, must be given for why they are not noticed and discussed.

Similarly, one could rescrutinize the *cogito* argument. Can "I think" only be produced by something that exists? Suppose Shakespeare had written for Hamlet the line, "I think, therefore I am", or a fiction is written in which a character named Descartes says this, or suppose a character in a dream of mine says this; does it follow that they exist? Can someone use the cogito argument to prove he himself is not a fictional or dream character? Descartes asked how he could know he wasn't dreaming; he also should have asked how he could know he wasn't dreamed. See further my fable "Fiction", *Ploughshares*, Vol. 6, no. 3, Oct. 1980.

3 I say almost everything, because there still could be some true beliefs such as "I exist." More limited skeptical possibilities present worlds doxically identical to the actual world in which almost every belief of a certain sort is false, for example, about the past, or about other people's mental states. See the discussion below in the section on narrower skepticisms.

4 Here again I assume a limited readership, and ignore possibilities such as those described in James Blish, *Cities in Flight*.

QUESTIONS

1 According to Nozick, under what conditions does *S* know that *p*?

2 According to Nozick, do you know that SK is false? Why or why not?

3 What is the closure principle, and does Nozick agree with it?

Keith DeRose, "Contextualism and Knowledge Attributions"

I. Contextualism: initial exposition

Consider the following cases.

> *Bank Case A.* My wife and I are driving home on a Friday afternoon. We plan to stop at the bank on the way home to deposit our paychecks. But as we drive past the bank, we notice that the lines inside are very long, as they often are on Friday afternoons. Although we generally like to deposit our paychecks as soon as possible, it is not especially important in this case that they be deposited right away, so I suggest that we drive straight home and deposit our paychecks on Saturday morning. My wife says, "Maybe the bank won't be open tomorrow. Lots of banks are closed on Saturdays." I reply, "No, I know it'll be open. I was just there two weeks ago on Saturday. It's open until noon."

> *Bank Case B.* My wife and I drive past the bank on a Friday afternoon, as in Case A, and notice the long lines. I again suggest that we deposit our paychecks on Saturday morning, explaining that I was at the bank on Saturday morning only two weeks ago and discovered that it was open until noon. But in this case, we have just written a very large and very important check. If our paychecks are not deposited into our checking account before Monday morning, the important check we wrote will bounce, leaving us in a *very* bad situation. And, of course, the bank is not open on Sunday. My wife reminds me of these facts. She then says, "Banks do change their hours. Do you know the bank will be open tomorrow?" Remaining as confident as I was before that the bank will be open then, still, I reply, "Well, no. I'd better go in and make sure."

Assume that in both cases the bank *will* be open on Saturday and that there is nothing unusual about either case that has not been included in my description of it. It seems to me that (I) when I claim to know that the bank will be open on Saturday in case A, I am saying something true. But it also seems that (2) I am saying something true in Case B when I concede that I *don't* know that the bank

Keith DeRose, "Contextualism and Knowledge Attributions," *Philosophy and Phenomenological Research* 52 (1992): 913–29.

will be open on Saturday. Yet I seem to be in no better position to know in Case A than in Case B. It is quite natural to say that (3) If I know that the bank will be open on Saturday in Case A, then I also know that it will be in Case B.

Is there any conflict here among (1), (2), and (3)? I hope not, because I want to investigate and defend a view according to which all three of them are true. Of course, it would be inconsistent to claim that (1) and (2) are true, and also hold that (4) If what I say in Case A in claiming to know that the bank will be open on Saturday is true, then what I say in Case B in conceding that I don't know that the bank will be open on Saturday is false. But there is a big difference between (3) and (4), and this difference is crucial to the view I want to investigate and defend.

We may, following Peter Unger, call the view I want to investigate a "contextual"[1] theory of knowledge attributions: it is a theory according to which the truth conditions of sentences of the form "S knows that p" or "S does not know that p" vary in certain ways according to the context in which the sentences are uttered.[2] The contextualist can deny (4) even while admitting that I am in no better position to know in Case A than in Case B. The contexts of my utterances in the two cases make it easier for a knowledge attribution to be true in Case A than in Case B.

There are important contextual differences between Case A and Case B which one might think are relevant. First, there is the importance of being right. In Case B, a lot hinges on whether or not the bank will be open on Saturday, while in Case A it is not nearly as important that I be right. One might think that requirements for making a knowledge attribution true go up as the stakes go up.[3]

Second, there is the *mentioning* of a possibility. In Case B my wife raises the possibility that the bank may have changed its hours in the last two weeks. One might think that if this possibility has been mentioned, I cannot truly claim to know that the bank will be open on Saturday on the ground that two weeks ago it was open on Saturday unless I can rule out the possibility that the bank's hours have changed since then. On the other hand, perhaps I don't have to be able to rule out this possibility in order to truly say I know if, as in Case A, no such possibility has not been suggested.[4]

Third, there is the *consideration* of a possibility. Since my wife raised the possibility of the bank changing its hours in Case B, I have that possibility in mind when I utter my sentence. Perhaps, since I am considering this possibility, I must be able to rule it out in order to truthfully claim to know that the bank will be open on Saturday. On the other hand, in Case A I am not considering the possibility, so perhaps I do not have to be able to rule it out in order to truthfully say that I know that the bank will be open on Saturday.[5] (Of course, it must still be *true* that the bank will be open on Saturday in order for me to know that it will be.)

Again following Unger, we may call someone who denies that the types of contextual factors we have just looked at affect the truth conditions of knowledge attributions an "invariantist." According to the invariantist, such features of an utterance of a knowledge attribution do not affect how good an epistemic position the putative knower must be in for the attribution to be true. In considering the Bank Cases, for instance, the invariantist will assert (4), which seems very plausible, and will therefore deny either (1) or (2). Typically, the invariantist will deny (1). In fact, Unger uses the term "invariantism" to denote the position that the standards for true knowledge attributions remain constant *and very high*—as high as they can possibly be. This position I will call "sceptical invariantism," leaving the more general term "invariantism" to denote any position according to which the truth conditions for knowledge attribution do not vary in the way the contextualist claims they do, whether or not the standards are said to be very high. I will then use "non-sceptical invariantism" to refer to a position according to which the standards are held to be constant but relatively low.[6] The *sceptical* invariantist will deny (1). She may admit that I am *warranted in asserting* that I know in Case A or that it is *useful for me to say* that I know, but will insist that what I say in claiming that I know is, strictly speaking, false. On the other hand, similar maneuvers can be used by the *non-sceptical* invariantist to deny (2). A non-sceptical invariantist may admit that I *should not say* that I know in Case B, because my wife mistakenly thinks that I must be able to rule out the possibility that the bank has changed its hours in order to know that the bank will be open on Saturday, and saying that I know will lead her to believe that I can rule out that possibility. Still, my wife *is* mistaken about this requirement, and if I were to say that I knew, I would be saying something that is, though misleading, true. Thus, it is *useful for me to assert* that I *don't* know. But for all its usefulness, my assertion is, strictly speaking, false.

Contextualists, of course, can disagree about what types of features of the context of utterance really do affect the truth conditions of knowledge attributions and to what extent they do so. I will not here enter into this thorny issue, although I have a preference for the more "objective" features—like the importance of being right and what has been said in the conversation—and tend to discount as relevant to truth conditions such "subjective" features as what possibilities the speaker is considering.[7] In this paper I address some *general* issues that confront any contextualist. In Part II, I distinguish between contextualism and a very prominent theory of knowledge which has been called the "relevant alternatives" theory (RA), and in Part III, I respond to an important objection to which *any* form of contextualism seems vulnerable.

By thus isolating and defending contextualism, I will do much to clear the way for contextualist resolutions to sceptical arguments. Contextual theories of knowledge attributions have almost invariably been developed with an eye towards providing some kind of answer to philosophical scepticism. For some sceptical arguments threaten to show, not only that we fail to meet very high requirements for knowledge of interest to philosophers seeking absolute certainty, but also that we don't meet the truth conditions of ordinary, out-on-the-street claims to know. They thus threaten to establish the startling result that we never, or almost never, truly ascribe knowledge to ourselves or to other human beings. According to contextual analysis, when the sceptic presents her arguments, she manipulates various conversational mechanisms that raise the semantic standards for knowledge, and thereby creates a context in which she can truly say that we know nothing or very little. But the fact that the sceptic can thus install very high standards which we don't live up to has no tendency to show that we don't satisfy the more relaxed standards that are in place in ordinary conversations. Thus, it is hoped, our ordinary claims to know will be safeguarded from the apparently powerful attacks of the sceptic, while, at the same time, the persuasiveness of the sceptical arguments is explained.[8]

Many find such contextualist resolutions of sceptical arguments very attractive, especially since their main competition is the sceptical invariantist resolutions according to which the persuasiveness of various sceptical arguments is explained in a way as alarming as it is simple: They seem persuasive because they are indeed sound and successfully establish the startling conclusion that we never or almost never truly ascribe knowledge.[9] But many, while finding the contextualist resolutions a preferable alternative to an unacceptably radical form of scepticism, at the same time feel an initial resistance, closely related to the appeal of (4), to the thought that contextual factors of the types I've mentioned can really affect whether or not a subject knows.[10] While many are willing to accept this thought in order to avoid the sceptical conclusion, there remains a feeling that the contextualist is asking them to swallow pretty hard—although perhaps not quite so hard as the sceptical invariantist would have them swallow. As contextualists have rushed to apply their theories to the problem of scepticism, this initial resistance has not yet been adequately addressed. I will address this resistance, as well as some explicit objections to contextualism that have been raised in the philosophical literature and which are based on the source of this resistance, in Part III below. But first, in Part II, we must carefully distinguish contextualism from RA.

II. Contextualism and 'relevant alternatives"

The most popular form of contextualism, I think it is fair to say, is what has been called the "relevant alternatives" view of knowledge (RA). But we must be careful here. As we shall see, it is a bit tricky to say just in what sense RA is a contextualist view. According to RA, a claim to know that p is made within a certain framework of relevant alternatives which are incompatible with p. To know that p is to be able to distinguish p from these relevant alternatives, to be able to rule out these relevant alternatives to p. But not every contrary of or alternative to p is a *relevant* alternative.[11] In an ordinary case of, say, claiming to know that some animals in a zoo are zebras, to borrow an example introduced by Fred Dretske,[12] the alternative that they are cleverly painted mules is *not* a relevant alternative, and one need not be able to rule it out in order truly to claim to know that the animals are zebras. But in an extraordinary case, that alternative might be relevant. How can it become relevant?

In one of the standard presentations of RA, Alvin Goldman (1976) presents various factors which can affect the range of relevant alternatives. These factors may be divided into two groups. First, there are features of the putative knower's situation; these I will call "subject factors."[13] A subject in an ordinary situation can be truly said to know that what he sees up ahead is a barn even if he cannot rule out the possibility that it is just a barn facade. But, Goldman points out, if there are a lot of such facades in the putative knower's vicinity, then the possibility that what the person is seeing is just a facade *is* a relevant alternative, and the person does not know that he is seeing a barn, even if what he sees happens to be an actual barn (pp. 772–73).

Second, there are features of the speaker's situation, which I will call "attributor factors." Goldman writes, "It is not only the circumstances of the putative knower's situation, however, that influence the choice of alternatives. The speaker's own linguistic and psychological context are also important." Goldman suggests that "if the speaker is in a class where Descartes's evil demon has just been discussed," then certain alternatives may be relevant which ordinarily are not (p. 776).

Insofar as a relevant alternatives theorist allows attributor factors to influence which alternatives are relevant, he is a contextualist. An invariantist can be a relevant alternatives theorist if he allows only subject factors to influence which alternatives are relevant.[14] Consider two situations in which Henry has a good, clear look at what he takes to be—and what, in fact, is—a barn. In Case C there are no barn facades around, but in Case D the area Henry finds himself in is (unbeknownst to him) teeming with barn facades, although Henry is luckily looking at the only actual barn in the area. This does not seem to be a pair of cases in which Henry is in equally good positions to know that what he is seeing is a barn; the conditional, *If Henry knows in Case C, then he knows in Case D* does not seem to be true, so the invariantist can agree that a sentence attributing knowledge to Henry in Case C can be true, while one attributing knowledge to him in Case D is false. And he can use the idea of "relevant alternatives" to explain the difference. Thus, although most versions of RA allow attributor factors to be relevant and are therefore contextualist views, an RA theorist need not be a contextualist.

Of course, in first-person present tense knowledge claims, the attributor of knowledge and the putative subject of knowledge are in the same situation (they are the same person at the same time). If Henry says, "I know that that's a barn," there is no difference between the speaker and the putative knower. In this situation the invariantist RA theorist will allow only factors that attach to Henry qua putative knower (e.g. the presence or lack of facades in his vicinity) to matter in evaluating his claim for truth, while the contextualist will also allow factors that attach to Henry qua attributor of knowledge (such as whether or not the issue of facades has been raised in the conversation) to matter.[15]

Although Goldman draws the distinction between what I am calling subject factors and attributor factors, he does not explain the importance of this distinction. I am stressing it because it is crucial to some of the important claims RA theorists have wanted to make about the *meanings* of knowledge attributions.[16] Gail Stine, for example, writes:

> In Dretske's zoo example, the animal's being a mule painted to look like a zebra is not a relevant alternative. So what one means when one says that John knows the animal is a zebra, is that he knows it is a zebra, as opposed to a gazelle, an antelope, or other animals one would normally expect to find in a zoo. If, however, being a mule painted to look like a zebra became a relevant alternative, then one would literally mean something different in saying that John knows that the animal is a zebra from what one meant originally and that something else may well be false. (Stine (1976), p. 255)

But here we must be very careful. Much depends on *how* the animal's being a painted mule has become a relevant alternative. Suppose that it has become a relevant alternative due to a change in subject factors: There has been a zebra shortage and many zoos (even reputable zoos) *have* been using painted mules in an attempt to fool the zoo-going public. This could come about without the speaker's knowing it. Would one then *mean* something different by saying that John knows that the animal is a zebra? I think not.

The meaning of "meaning," of course, is difficult to get hold of. But there seems to be a fairly straightforward and important sense in which one *does* mean something different if the range of relevant alternatives has been changed by attributor factors but does *not* mean something different if the range of relevant alternatives has been changed only by subject factors. Stewart Cohen, whose version of RA clearly is a contextualist one, writes that he

> construes "knowledge" as an indexical. As such, one speaker may attribute knowledge to a subject while another speaker denies knowledge to that same subject, without contradiction. (Cohen (1988), p. 97)

This lack of contradiction is the key to the sense in which the knowledge attributor and the knowledge denier mean something different by "know." It is similar to the sense in which two people who think they are in the same room but are in fact in different rooms and are talking to each over an intercom mean something different by "this room" when one claims, "Frank is not in this room" and the other insists, "Frank is in this room—I can see him!" There is an important sense in which both do mean the same thing by "this room," in which they are using the phrase in the same sense. But there is also an important sense in which they do not mean the same thing by the phrase; this is the sense by which we can explain the lack of contradiction between what the two people are saying. To use David Kaplan's terminology, the phrase is being used with the same *character*, but with different *content*.[17] Similarly, in Bank Case B from Part I of this paper, when, in the face of my wife's doubt, I admit that I don't know that the bank will be open on Saturday, I don't contradict an earlier claim to know that I might have made before the doubt was raised and before the issue was so important because, in an important sense, I don't mean the same thing by "know" as I meant in the earlier claim: While "know" is being used with the same *character*, it is *not* being used with the same *content*. Or so the contextualist will claim.

But if the range of relevant alternatives is changed by subject factors, the meaning of "know" is not in the same way changed. If very many nearby banks *have* discontinued their Saturday hours in the last two weeks, then it seems that my original claim to know may well have been false, and if I admit that I did not know after this surprising fact about local banks is called to my attention, I will be taking back and contradicting my earlier claim to have known.

Recall the two cases in which Henry has a good, clear look at what he takes to be a barn. (In Case C, there are no barn facades around, but in Case D, the fields are filled with barn facades, but Henry is luckily looking at the only actual barn in the area.) In each case, insert two people in the back seat of the car Henry is driving, and have the first say to the second, "Henry knows that that is a barn." It seems that, in the sense under discussion, what the first person *means* by "knows" in each of the two cases is the same. In Case C what she is saying is true, while in Case D it is false. The presence of the barn facades has changed the *truth value*, but not the *truth conditions* or the meaning (content), of the first person's knowledge attribution.

So attributor factors affect the truth values of knowledge attributions *in a different way* than do subject factors: attributor factors working in such a way that they affect the content of the attribution, but subject factors working in a different way that does not affect its content. These different ways can be explained as follows. Attributor factors set a certain standard the putative subject of knowledge must live up to in order to make the knowledge attribution true: They affect *how good an epistemic position the putative knower must be in to count as knowing*. They thereby affect the truth conditions and the content or meaning of the attribution. Subject factors, on the other hand, determine whether or not the putative subject lives up to the standards that have been set, and thereby can affect the truth value of the attribution *without* affecting its content: They affect *how good an epistemic position the putative knower actually is in.*[18]

To make use of the character/content distinction, the "character" of "S knows that p" is, roughly, that S has a true belief that p and is in a *good enough* epistemic position with respect to p; this remains constant from attribution to attribution. But how good is good enough? This is what varies with context. What the context fixes in determining the "content" of a knowledge attribution is how good an epistemic position S must be in to count as knowing that p. The mentioning of alternatives like painted mules, or barn facades, or changes in banking hours, when there is no special reason for thinking such possibilities likely, can be seen as raising the strength and changing the content of "know" because the ability to rule out such alternatives would only be relevant if one were after a strong form of knowledge (if one were requiring the putative knower to be in a very good position in order to count as knowing).

Subject factors, then, are best construed, not as affecting the truth conditions of knowledge attributions, but rather as affecting whether those truth conditions are satisfied. This fact severely limits RA's prospects for explaining variations in the content of knowledge attributions. RA, for all I've said, may be a helpful tool for determining or explaining why certain attributions of knowledge have the *truth values* they have.[19] Note, however, that for RA to be successful in this capacity, it *must* allow subject factors to affect the range of relevant alternatives, for, as Goldman's barn cases (cases C and D) clearly show and as is evident in any case, subject factors can affect these truth values.

But RA theorists have wanted to make claims about the *meaning* of knowledge attributions[20]. Many of them have thought that the meaning of knowledge attributions changes from case to case depending upon various factors, and they have thought that this change in meaning *amounts to* a change in the range of alternatives that are relevant.[21] But we can now see that the content of a given knowledge attribution cannot be specified by citing what the range of relevant alternatives is, because that range is a function of subject factors (which do not affect the content of the attribution) as well as attributor factors (which do). There can be a drastic change in the range of relevant alternatives from one attribution to another without there being any change in meaning between the two attributions, then, because the change in the range of relevant alternatives can, and often will, be the result of differences in subject factors, which will not have any affect on the meaning of the attribution.[22]

III. The objection to contextualism

Having distinguished contextualism from RA, I will now seek to defend contextualism from a certain type of important objection. The obvious attraction of contextualism, besides (and closely related to) the resolution of sceptical arguments it purportedly provides, is that it seems to have the result that very many of the knowledge attributions and denials uttered by speakers of English are true—more than any form of invariantism can allow for, and certainly more than sceptical invariantism can allow for. Thus, recalling the Bank Cases, contextualism allows us to assert both (1) and (2) and many of us will find both (1) and (2) compelling. Unfortunately, contextualism seems to be vulnerable to a certain type of powerful objection which is closely related to the appeal of (4). Suppose, to recall an example we've already considered, that two people see some zebras in a zoo. Palle Yourgrau constructs the following conversation, and claims that "something is amiss" in it:

A: Is that a zebra?
B: Yes, it is a zebra.
A: But can you rule out its being merely a cleverly painted mule?
B: No, I can't.
A: So, you admit you didn't know it was a zebra?
B: No, I did know then that it was a zebra. But after your question, I no longer know.[23]

This absurd dialogue is aimed at contextualists who think that the mentioning of a possibility incompatible with what one claims to know is enough to require that one rule the possibility out before one can truly claim to know. But this type of attack can work against other contextualists, also. Dialogues much like the above dialogue but with the following last lines seem equally absurd:

B′: No, I did know then that it was a zebra. But now that it has become so important that it be a zebra, I no longer know.
B″: No, I did know then that it was a zebra. But now that the possibility of its being a painted mule has occurred to me, I no longer know.

The general point of the objection is that whether we know something or not cannot depend on, to use Peter Unger's words, "the contextual interests of those happening to use the terms on a particular occasion" (Unger (1984), p. 37).

How shall the contextualist respond? The objection as I have put it forward, though it explains much of the initial resistance many feel toward contextualism, is based on a mistake. The contextualist believes that certain aspects of the context of an attribution or denial of knowledge attribution affect its content. Knowledge claims, then, can be compared to other sentences containing other context-sensitive words, like "here." One hour ago, I was in my office. Suppose I truly said, "I am here." Now I am in the word processing room. How can I truly say where I was an hour ago? I cannot truly say, "I was here," because I wasn't here; I was there. The meaning of "here" is fixed by the relevant contextual factors (in this case, my location) *of the utterance*, not by my location at the time being talked about.

Similarly, the contextualist may admit that the mentioning of the painted mules possibility affects the conditions under which one can truthfully say that one knows an animal to be a zebra: one now must be able to rule out that possibility, perhaps. But the contextualist need not, and should not, countenance the above dialogue. If in the context of the conversation the possibility of painted mules has been mentioned, and *if* the mere mention of this possibility has an effect on the conditions under which someone can be truly said to "know," then any use of "know" (or its past tense) is so affected, even a use in which one describes one's past condition. B cannot truly say, "I did know then that it was a zebra"; that would be like my saying, "I was here." B *can* say, "My previous knowledge claim was true," just as I can say, "My previous location claim was true." Or so I believe. But saying these things would have a point only if one were interested in the truth-value of the earlier claim, rather than in the question of whether in the *present* contextually determined sense one knew and knows, or didn't and doesn't.

Yourgrau writes of the zebra case, "Typically, when someone poses a question regarding whether we really know that P obtains rather than some alternative to P, if we cannot satisfactorily answer the question, we conclude that our earlier claim to know was faulty" (p. 183). But do we? We do not stubbornly repeat ourselves, to be sure: "Still, I know that it is a zebra!" We *might* even say, "I don't know" or "I didn't know." All of this the contextualist can handle. But do we (or should we) admit that our *earlier* claim was *false*? I am on the witness stand being questioned.

Lawyer: Were there any zebras in the zoo on April 23?
Me: Yes.
L: Do you know that?
M: Yes.
L: How do you know?
M: I saw some there.
L: So, you knew that they were zebras?
M: Yes.
L: Could you rule out the possibility that they were only cleverly painted mules?
M: No, I suppose not.
L: So, did you really know that they were zebras?
M: Is there any reason to think that they were painted mules, of all things?
L: Just answer the question!

Well, how should I answer the question? If there is no special reason to think they were painted mules then *I* certainly wouldn't want to admit that I didn't know they were zebras, but maybe I'm just being stubborn. Suppose I do admit it:

M: I guess I didn't *know* that they were zebras.
L: Aha! The witness has contradicted his earlier claim. First he says

> that he knew; now he says he didn't. Now which is it, Mr. DeRose?

Surely something is amiss in *this* dialogue; my lawyer should object. I haven't contradicted my earlier claim, as much as it looks as if I have. It would be as if the following had occurred. While standing in a bright yellow room, I said, "This room is yellow." The lawyer then dragged me by the ear into a room in which all was grey and got me to say, "This room is grey," and now he is jumping all over me: "First he says. 'This room is yellow,' then he says, 'This room is grey.' Which is it?" The contextualist maintains that something very much like this has happened in my original dialogue with the lawyer. Of course, there is room for the invariantist to deny this contextualist claim. But it is *far* from clear that in cases like the one Yourgrau brings to our attention, we should admit that our earlier claim was false or that our later claim contradicts it.

So, the objection that whether we know something or not does not depend on contextual factors of the type we have been considering is based on a mistake. But Unger does not make this mistake when he raises an objection similar to the one we have been considering.[24] He writes of "our belief that the semantics of these expressions ["know" is one of the expressions being considered] is appropriately *independent*, that the conditions do not depend on the contextual interests of these happening to use the terms on a particular occasion" (Unger (1984), p. 37). Insofar as we do have *this* belief, that the conditions *for truly saying* that someone knows do not depend on the sorts of contextual factors we have been discussing, then contextualism goes against at least one of our beliefs. But it seems that much of the appeal of this belief derives from the plausibility of the thesis (with which the contextualist can agree) that whether *we know* something or not does not depend on such factors. The answer to the question, "Does she know?", in whatever context it is asked, including a philosophy paper, is determined by facts independent of contextual factors (or what I have been calling attributor factors). These contextual or attributor factors affect the content of the question, but once the question is asked with a specific content, its answer is determined by subject factors, which are precisely the kinds of factors which *can* very plausibly be thought to affect whether or not the subject knows. Going back to our opening examples, the contextualist can affirm (3) *in any context in which it is uttered:* If I know in Case A, then I know in Case B. Of course, the contextualist must deny (4), and (4) sounds very plausible, but much of the appeal of (4) comes from the plausibility of (3). And since we *must* give up either (1), (2), or (4), those who, like me, find (1) and (2) *very* plausible will be well-motivated to give up (4), especially since (3) can still be affirmed.

In general, then, when it looks as if the contextualist has to say something strongly counter-intuitive, what he must say turns out to be, on the contrary, something fairly theoretical concerning the truth conditions of certain sentences. Do we really have strong intuitions about such things? At any rate, the contextualist can go along with the simple facts that we all recognize: that if I know in Case A, then I know in Case B, and that whether we know something or not does not typically depend on our current interests or on other such contextual factors.[25]

Notes

1 I take the terms "contextualism" and "invariantism" from Unger (1984).

2 The importance of this theory will not be confined to knowledge attributions. For instance, in DeRose (1991) I argue that S's assertion, "It is possible that P," where the embedded P is in the indicative mood, is true if and only if (1) no member of the relevant community *knows* that P is false and (2) there is no relevant way by which members of the relevant community can come to *know* that P is false. As I there argue, there is a great deal of flexibility in the matter of who is and is not to be counted as a member of the relevant community and what is and is not to be counted as a relevant way of coming to know: That these matters are determined by aspects of the contexts in which the statement is made. If, as I am here defending, there is a contextually-determined variation on how good an epistemic position one must be in to count as knowing, then—since epistemic possibilities have entirely to do with what is and is not known and what can and cannot come to be known in certain ways—this variation will affect the content of epistemic modal statements as well: As the standards for knowledge go up, and it becomes harder and harder for a knowledge attribution to be true, it will become easier and easier for an assertion of epistemic possibility to be true.

3 That the importance of being right is an important contextual factor is suggested in Austin (1961), p. 76, fn. 1. Dretske denies the importance of this factor in (1981a), pp. 375–76.

4 David Lewis (1979) stresses this contextual factor, presenting an interesting account of how the mentioning of sceptical possibilities can affect the range of relevant alternatives by means of what he calls a "rule of accommodation." In Chapter 3 (see especially section I) of DeRose (1990). I argue that Lewis's account is not complete, and I locate an independent mechanism of standard changing which, I now believe, is *at least* as important (and probably considerably more important) to the application of contextualism to the problem of scepticism as is the mechanism Lewis has located.

5 Alvin I. Goldman (1976) stresses the importance of what possibilities the speaker is considering.

6 While Unger does not even consider the view that the standards for true knowledge attributions don't change but are held constant at a fairly low level, non-sceptical invariantism is defended (at least conditionally) by Robert Hambourger (1987). Hambourger argues that *if* the standards are constant (Hambourger does not believe that this antecedent is true), then they must be fairly low (pp. 256–57). In the terminology I have introduced, Hambourger is arguing that if some form of invariantism is correct, it must be a form of *non-sceptical* invariantism.

7 My main reason for discounting as relevant to truth conditions the matter of what the speaker is thinking, at least with respect to spoken interactions between people, is that I don't think that one should be able, merely by a private act of one's own thought to drastically "strengthen" the content of "know" in such a way that one can truly say to someone who is quite certain that he is wearing pants, "You don't know you're wearing pants," without there having been anything in the conversation to indicate that the strength of "know" has been raised.

There *might* yet be a fairly tight connection between what raises the truth condition standards and what speakers *tend to* think or perhaps what they *should* think of the standards as being. Perhaps the truth condition standards are what a typical speaker would take them to be or should take them to be, given what has gone on in the conversation. But it seems unfair to one's interlocutor for the truth condition standards of a *public, spoken* knowledge attribution to be changed by an idiosyncratic, private decision. It is far more plausible to suppose that when one is *thinking to one's self* about what is or is not "known," the content of "know" is directly tied to the strength the thinker intends.

8 While, as I've said, contextualist theories (including contextualist versions of RA) are almost invariably developed with an eye towards philosophical scepticism, the most thoroughly worked out contextualist attempts to resolve the problem of scepticism that I am aware of are to be found in Unger (1986), Cohen (1988) (see also Cohen (1987)), and DeRose (1990), especially Chapter 3. Fred Dretske has also applied this type of theory of knowledge to the problem of scepticism in several places. See Dretske (1970), (1971), (1981a), and (1981b).

9 See Unger (1975).

10 A typical objection one meets in presenting contextualism, as I know from personal experience, is: "How can *our* context have anything to do with whether or not *Henry* knows?", where Henry is a character in an example and so is not present in the room.

11 See Goldman (1976), p. 772 Stine (1976), p. 249; and Dretske (1970), p. 1022.

12 See Dretske (1970), pp. 1015–1016.

13 Please note that by "subject factors" I do *not* mean *subjective* (as opposed to objective) factors. I rather mean factors having to do with the putative *subject* of knowledge and her surroundings (as opposed to the attributor of knowledge).

14 Thus, what Goldman calls the "first view" of RA, according to which "a complete specification" of the putative knower's situation determines "a unique set of relevant alternatives" (pp. 775–76), is an invariantist version of RA. Goldman does not endorse this view; he says he is "attracted by the second view" (p. 777), which clearly is a contextualist version of RA.

15 Some factors, I believe, will both affect how good an epistemic position the speaker/putative knower is in *and* (at least according to the contextualist) how good a position he must be in to make his knowledge claims true. Thus, they will be both subject and attributor factors.

16 I further discuss the importance of this distinction between subject factors and attributor factors and the resulting contextualist view according to which content varies in response to attributor factors in Chapter 1 of DeRose (1990). In particular, I there discuss, in addition to the issues treated in the present paper, the advantages such a view according to which content varies over a *range* has over theories like that put forward in Malcolm (1952) according to which there are two distinct senses of "know", a strong sense and a weak one.

17 See Kaplan (1989), esp. pp. 500–507.

18 Unger makes a similar division in (1986), where he distinguishes between the "profile of the context," which corresponds roughly to how good a position the putative knower must be in to count as knowing, and the "profile of the facts,"

which corresponds roughly to how good a position the putative knower actually is in (see esp. pp. 139–40). Unger does not there discuss RA, and so does not use the distinction to distinguish contextualism from RA. He does, however, introduce an important complication which I have ignored in this paper, since it has little effect on the points I'm making here. Unger points out that there are many different aspects of knowledge and that in different contexts, we may have different demands regarding various of these aspects. Thus, for example, in one context, we may demand a very high degree of confidence on the subject's part before we will count him as knowing while demanding *relatively* little in the way of his belief being non-accidentally true. In a different context, on the other hand, we may have very stringent standards for non-accidentality but relatively lax standards for subject confidence. As Unger points out, then, things are not quite as simple as I make them out to be: Our standards are not just a matter of how good an epistemic position the subject must be in, but rather of how good in which respects. Stewart Cohen also suggests a related division, his more closely aligned with the spirit of RA. See note 22 below.

19 Thus what I take to be RA's *basic idea*—that to know that P, one must be able to rule out all of the relevant alternatives to P—may be sound.

20 RA's *basic idea* (see note 19, above) is not about contextual *variations in meanings*. In deed, as I've pointed out, an RA theorist can be an invariantist. It is, then, in going *beyond* this basic idea that RA theorists have, by my lights, gone wrong by tying the meaning of a given attribution too closely to what the range of relevant alternatives is.

21 In addition to the Stine passage we have looked at, see, for example, Goldman (1976), pp. 775–77 (esp. p. 777), where Goldman seems to think that *what proposition is expressed* by a given knowledge attribution is specified by what the range of relevant alternatives is. Something similar seems to be suggested in Lewis (1979), esp. pp. 354–55. Lewis seems to think of the "conversational score" of a given context, with respect to knowledge attributions and epistemic modal statements, to be something that can be specified by giving the range of possibilities that are relevant in that context.

22 A different view which escapes this problem but is still well within the spirit of RA is that the character of "S knows that p" is that S has a true belief that p and can rule out all alternatives to p that are *sufficiently probable*. The context of utterance can then be seen as fixing the content by determining just how probable an alternative must be to count as being sufficiently probable. Something like this alternative view is suggested by Cohen (1988), according to whom context determines "how probable an alternative must be in order to be relevant" (p. 96). (This view is only *suggested* by Cohen because he never says that this probability level for alternative relevance is *all* that context fixes in determining the content of an attribution.) Expanding this idea, we might then take aspects of the putative knower's situation to affect how *probable a given alternative is*. Instead of the meaning being specified by the range of alternatives that are relevant, this view, more plausibly, has it specified by the standards (in terms of probability) alternatives must meet to count as relevant. This still seems more precise than my admittedly vague talk of *how good an epistemic position* one must be in to count as knowing. I fear, however, that this precisification will not work. Among other reasons for doubting that the notion of probability can do all

the work assigned to it here is this: The complication Unger raises about the many different aspects of knowledge (see note 18 above) shows that no single measure like the probability an alternative must have to be relevant can capture all that context does in fixing the content of a knowledge attribution. This probability standard of alternative relevance can be, *at best*, one among several aspects of knowledge the standards for which are fixed by context.

23 Yourgrau (1983), p. 183. The absurdity of such a conversation, along with the worry that it causes problems for theories of knowledge attributions like the one I am investigating, was originally suggested to me by Rogers Albritton, who has been making such suggestions since well before Yourgrau's article came out.

24 Actually, Unger does make this mistake at one point, not about knowledge but about flatness. Throughout his epistemological writings, Unger compares knowledge attributions with claims about the flatness of objects. In (1984). Unger describes an invariantist semantics for "flat" according to which an object must be as flat as possible in order for a sentence like "That is flat" to be true of it, and a contextualist semantics for "flat" according to which how flat something must be in order for a sentence like. "That is flat" to be true of it varies with context, and he claims that there is no determinate fact as to which semantics is correct. In attacking the contextualist semantics for "flat," Unger writes: "How can the matter of whether a given surface is *flat*, in contradistinction to, say, whether it is suitable for our croquet game, depend upon the interests in that surface taken by those who happen to converse about it? This appears to go against our better judgement" ((1984), p. 39). But the contextualist need not and should not claim that "the matter of whether or not a given surface is flat" depends "upon the interests in that surface taken by those who happen to converse about it," although the contextualist *will* say that the truth conditions *for the sentence* "That is flat" do depend upon such contextual interests. I believe that the above passage is just a slip on Unger's part; he is usually more careful in making his attack on contextualism. But it is revealing that Unger makes this slip: It shows how easy it is to confuse the claim (a) that whether or not something is flat or is known does not depend on contextual interests with the claim (b) that the truth conditions for a sentence about flatness or about knowledge do not depend on contextual interests, which does not follow from (a).

25 I am indebted to Robert M. Adams, Rogers Albritton, Peter Unger, and an anonymous referee for *Philosophy and Phenomenological Research* for comments on previous drafts of this paper.

References

Austin, J. L., (1961) "Other Minds," in J. L. Austin, *Philosophical Papers* (Oxford University Press): 44–84.

Cohen, Stewart, (1987) "Knowledge, Context, and Social Standards," *Synthese* 73: 3–26.

——, (1988) "How to be a Fallibilist," *Philosophical Perspectives* 2: 91–123.

DeRose, Keith, (1990) "Knowledge, Epistemic Possibility, and Scepticism," UCLA doctoral dissertation.

——, (1991) "Epistemic Possibilities," *The Philosophical Review* 100: 581–605.

Dretske, Fred, (1970) "Epistemic Operators," *Journal of Philosophy* 67: 1007–1023.

——, (1971) "Conclusive Reasons," *Australasian Journal of Philosophy* 49: 1–22.
——, (1981a) "The Pragmatic Dimension of Knowledge," *Philosophical Studies* 40: 363–78.
——, (1981b) *Knowledge and the Flow of Information* (Cambridge, Massachusetts: MIT Press/Bradford Books).
Goldman, Alvin I., (1976) "Discrimination and Perceptual Knowledgé," *Journal of Philosophy* 73: 771–91.
Hambourger, Robert, (1987) "Justified Assertion and the Relativity of Knowledge," *Philosophical Studies* 51: 241–69.
Kaplan, David, (1989) "Demonstratives," in J. Almog, J. Perry, H. Wettstein, ed., *Themes from Kaplan* (Oxford University Press): 481–563.
Lewis, David, (1979) "Scorekeeping in a Language Game," *Journal of Philosophical Logic* 8: 339–59.
Malcolm, Norman, (1952) "Knowledge and Belief," *Mind* 51: 178–89.
Stine, Gail C., (1976) "Skepticism, Relevant Alternatives, and Deductive Closure," *Philosophical Studies* 29: 249–61.
Unger, Peter, (1975) *Ignorance: A Case for Scepticism* (Oxford University Press).
——, (1984) *Philosophical Relativity* (Minneapolis: University of Minnesota Press).
——, (1986) "The Cone Model of Knowledge," *Philosophical Topics* 14: 125–78.
Yourgrau, Palle, (1983) "Knowledge and Relevant Alternatives," *Synthese* 55: 175–90.

QUESTIONS

1 Of the following statements, which ones does DeRose agree with?

   (1) In Bank Case A, the subject is correct in saying he knows the bank will be open.
   (2) In Bank Case B, the subject is correct in saying he doesn't know the bank will be open.
   (3) If the subject knows the bank will be open in Case A, then he also knows in Case B.
   (4) If what the subject says in Case A is true, then what the subject says in Case B is false.

2 What is the difference between "contextualism" and "invariantism"?
3 What is the difference between "subject factors" and "attributor factors"? Which sort of factor does contextualism say is relevant to the truth of knowledge attributions?

FURTHER READING ON THE ANALYSIS OF "KNOWLEDGE"

Annis, David, "A Contextualist Theory of Epistemic Justification," *American Philosophical Quarterly* 15 (1978): 213–19.
Ayer, A.J., *The Problem of Knowledge* (London: Penguin Books, 1956).

Chisholm, Roderick, *Theory of Knowledge*, 3rd edn (Englewood Cliffs, NJ: Prentice Hall, 1989).

Ginet, Carl, "Contra Reliabilism," *The Monist* 68 (1985): 175–87.

Goldman, Alvin, "What is Justified Belief?" pp. 1–23 in *Justification and Knowledge*, ed. George Pappas (Dordrecht: Reidel, 1979).

Klein, Peter, "A Proposed Definition of Propositional Knowledge," *Journal of Philosophy* 68 (1971): 471–82.

Klein, Peter, "Misleading Evidence and the Restoration of Justification," *Philosophical Studies* 37 (1980): 81–9.

Lehrer, Keith, *Knowledge* (Oxford: Oxford University Press, 1974).

Lewis, David, "Elusive Knowledge," *Australasian Journal of Philosophy* 74 (1996): 549–67.

Lucey, Kenneth (ed.) *On Knowing and the Known* (Amherst, NY: Prometheus, 1996).

Quine, W.V., "Epistemology Naturalized," in *Ontological Relativity and Other Essays* (New York: Columbia University Press, 1969).

Roth, Michael and Leon Galis (eds) *Knowing: Essays on the Analysis of Knowledge* (New York: Random House, 1970).

Russell, Bertrand, "Fact, Belief, Truth, and Knowledge," pp. 142–58 in *Human Knowledge: Its Scope and Limits* (New York: Simon & Schuster, 1948).

Shope, Robert K., *The Analysis of Knowing: A Decade of Research* (Princeton, NJ: Princeton University Press, 1983).

9

SKEPTICISM

Most of the time, epistemologists take it for granted that people have a lot of knowledge about the world around them. I know that the Earth orbits the sun, that Kennedy was assassinated in 1963, that my cat likes milk, and so on. Philosophical skeptics, however, argue that we don't really know many of the things we normally think we know. The most extreme skeptics say that nobody knows anything at all. A slightly less extreme form of skepticism, *external world skepticism*, holds that nobody knows anything about the external world (the world outside of one's own mind). According to this view, then, I don't really know any of the things I just said I did.

Often students fail to see the value in studying skepticism, partly because it seems like such an outlandish and radical thesis. Indeed, very few epistemologists endorse skepticism. Yet the discussion of philosophical skepticism occupies a highly prominent place in the epistemological literature. Why is this? Briefly, the reason is because of the theoretical interest of the arguments for philosophical skepticism. Philosophical skeptics frequently appear able to start from plausible, commonly held assumptions about the nature of knowledge and deduce from these assumptions that we really know little or nothing. Non-skeptical philosophers then face the task of identifying the mistake in these otherwise plausible assumptions.

A case in point is the infamous "brain-in-a-vat" argument. As a bit of background, keep in mind that all of your brain's information about the world comes from electrical impulses that your sense organs and nerves send to the brain. Now, imagine the following scenario. Scientists in a technologically advanced society have figured out how to keep a brain alive, floating in a vat. They have also developed technology for directly stimulating a brain electrically in order to produce a complete set of experiences as of normal life. This technology has been perfected to the point that a person whose brain is so stimulated cannot tell the difference between the artificially induced experiences and the experiences of normal life. All of this is theoretically possible. Which leads us to the question: how do you know that this scenario is not actually true, and that you are not, right now, a brain in a vat?

A strong argument can be made that you *cannot* know this. All of the evidence you have for claims about the external world comes from your sensory experiences. But in the brain-in-a-vat scenario, you would be having the same sort of sensory experiences you are in fact having. Therefore, it seems, your actual sensory experiences are not evidence against the brain-in-a-vat scenario. Therefore, you have no evidence against the brain-in-a-vat scenario. And if you have no evidence against it, it seems to follow that you do not *know* that the brain-in-a-vat scenario does not actually obtain.

Finally, it seems to follow from this that you do not actually know anything about the character of the world around you.

The brain-in-a-vat argument is one instance of a type of skeptical argument sometimes called a "Cartesian skeptical argument" (after Descartes). Other arguments in this family include the dream argument (how do you know you are not having a very realistic and vivid dream right now?) and the deceiving God argument (how do you know that God, or a clever demon, is not deceiving you by planting false sensory images in your mind?). What these arguments have in common is that they each employ a scenario in which most of your beliefs about the external world would be (or might be) false but in which there is an explanation for why everything would *appear* the way it does now.

René Descartes deployed this kind of argument in his first *Meditation*, but note that Descartes is not a philosophical skeptic. Rather, he is using skeptical arguments (which he later tries to refute) in order to establish something about the structure of our knowledge. Descartes thinks that the ultimate foundation of our knowledge should be something that is absolutely indubitable—that is, something we cannot have any grounds for doubting. He uses skeptical arguments to establish that claims about the physical world do not satisfy this condition. Instead, he argues, the foundation of one's knowledge should be propositions about one's own mind—i.e., the propositions "I think," "I exist" (where the "I" refers to my mind), and propositions describing my present conscious mental states. The skeptical scenarios cannot cast doubt on this sort of proposition, for a simple reason: that each of the skeptical scenarios *entails* that I am conscious, that I exist, and that I am having the sort of conscious mental states I am having (recall that a skeptical scenario must explain why things appear to me the way they do). This line of thinking led Descartes to the famous dictum, "I think, therefore I am." Descartes argued that he knows that he exists, despite any skeptical arguments that anyone might bring forward, since he must exist in order to be thinking about the skeptical arguments.

In the later parts of his work, meditations 3–6 (not reprinted here), Descartes tries to establish the existence of the physical world. Essentially, he first tries to prove that God exists, and that God, being perfect, cannot be a deceiver. If God had given me inherently defective cognitive faculties (including the five senses, reason, and intuition), with no way of correcting the error, then God would be a deceiver. It follows that my faculties are not defective in this way, and therefore I can rule out the skeptical scenarios.

Hilary Putnam uses a different strategy to refute the brain in a vat scenario. He argues that the brain-in-a-vat scenario is self-refuting in a sense, because if it were true, it would be impossible for us to entertain it. He arrives at this conclusion through a consideration of the nature of *intentionality*. "Intentionality," in philosophy, is a technical term (note that it is *not* connected to the usual use of the word "intention" in English). Intentionality, in the technical sense, is the property of purportedly being "about" something, or referring to or representing something. For instance, language has intentionality (sentences are about something; words typically refer to something), pictures have intentionality (they depict something), and our thoughts have intentionality (thoughts are about something). Note that each of these things can be intentional even if what they represent does not exist (for instance, a picture of a unicorn has intentionality).

Putnam asks, under what conditions does one thing count as representing something else? Using a series of hypothetical examples, he tries to establish *the causal theory of reference*: this theory holds that a necessary condition for *A* to represent *B* is that *A* should be *causally connected* to *B* in an appropriate way, or at least to things in terms of which *B* could be described. Typically, a person acquires a concept, or learns the use of a word, by directly interacting with examples of the type of thing it refers to (as, for example, when I see a tree). It is also possible to learn a word/idea from other people, but then those other people must have interacted with examples of the type of thing the word refers to. One can also acquire a concept through an explicit definition (e.g., "A unicorn is a horse with a horn on its head"), but then one must first understand the terms in the definition, and ultimately a causal connection to the world must come in at some point (e.g., people have seen horses and horns).

Given the causal theory of reference, we can conclude that if there were a brain in a vat, the brain could not refer to, or think about, brains or vats. The brain might think to itself something like, "I wonder if I am a brain in a vat," but *its* use of "brain" could not possibly refer to brains, since it has never actually seen a brain, nor has it communicated with anyone who has, nor has it perceived anything else in terms of which "brain" might be defined. Similarly, its use of "vat" could not refer to vats. Thus, a brain in a vat cannot entertain the brain-in-a-vat scenario. And therefore, we can conclude that if *we* are now entertaining the brain-in-a-vat scenario, then we are not brains in vats.

Fred Dretske has proposed an answer to the brain-in-a-vat argument that does not require refuting the skeptical scenario. As traditionally understood, the brain-in-a-vat argument goes like this:

1. In general, if I know *p*, and *p* entails *q*, then I can know *q*.
2. I cannot know I am not a brain in a vat.
3. Therefore, I do not know that I have two hands, that I perceive physical objects, etc. (because these claims entail that I am not a brain in a vat).

Dretske argues that it is the *first* premise (known as "the closure principle") that is mistaken. He arrives at this based on his "relevant alternatives" analysis of knowledge, which states that for *S* to know *p* requires that *S* be able to rule out certain kinds of alternatives to *p* (the "relevant alternatives"), but not that *S* be able to rule out all of the *logically possible* alternatives. For instance, in order to know that the bird I am seeing is a Gadwall duck, I must be able to distinguish it from other kinds of bird that actually exist and that could be in this area; but I do not need to be able to distinguish it from some purely hypothetical kind of bird that someone thought up. Notice that any view of this kind, in which the relevant alternatives include less than all of the logically possible alternatives, implies that the closure principle (1) is false.

Peter Klein argues, in contrast, that the brain-in-a-vat skeptic has available a plausible defense of the closure principle, against Dretske's criticism. The main reason why the closure principle seems plausible is that, when I know *p* and *p* entails *q*, then I can simply deduce *q* from *p*, and deducing a conclusion from a known premise seems to be a good way of acquiring knowledge. Note that this means my ability to know *q* would be a consequence, rather than a precondition, of my knowing *p*. However, Klein argues, the skeptic faces a dilemma: if the skeptic defends the closure principle in this way, then he will have no way of defending the *second* premise ("I cannot know I'm not a brain in a vat") without begging the question. In order to justify his second premise, the skeptic would have to rule out every potential way in which I might know (or be justified in believing) that I am not a brain in a vat. According to the defense of the closure principle just suggested, *one* possible way of knowing this would be if I knew I had two hands, and I deduced from this that I am not a brain in a vat. So to show that I do not have *that* way, in particular, of knowing I am not a brain in a vat, it would first have to be established that I cannot know I have two hands. But that is just the conclusion of the argument. So, if the skeptic uses the suggested defense of the closure principle, then his argument will "virtually beg the question"—that is, it will have a premise (2) that cannot be established unless one can first establish the conclusion.

The article by the editor that follows responds to both Klein and Dretske, finding both of their replies to the skeptic implausible when compared with replies that might be made in seemingly analogous cases. It argues that the brain-in-a-vat argument has been mischaracterized and that instead of the closure principle, the skeptic should be taken to be relying on the "preference principle." This is the principle that a person is justified in accepting a hypothesis based on some evidence only if they have grounds for rejecting each incompatible alternative explanation of the evidence. When the skeptic's argument is reformulated using this principle, Dretske's and Klein's responses no longer work. However, a new response to the brain-in-a-vat argument becomes possible. This would be a response based on a direct realist theory of perceptual knowledge. Direct realists believe that we have non-inferentially justified beliefs about the physical world, as a result of perception (see Chapter 1, this volume). A direct realist could accept the preference principle but deny that it had any application to the case of our perceptual beliefs, since these beliefs are not hypotheses inferred from some evidence, but are instead foundational. Although the paper does not establish that direct realism is in fact true, it shows that the skeptic has not refuted the possibility of knowledge of the external world, since the skeptic has not ruled out direct realism; the skeptic has only ruled out an *indirect* realist account of our knowledge of the external world.

Roderick Chisholm discusses a different sort of skeptical argument, the argument based on "the problem of the criterion." This argument in its essence originates with the ancient Greek skeptics, who argued that since our senses sometimes deceive us (as in illusions, hallucinations, mirages), in order for us to really know anything, we must have a general rule, a criterion, for distinguishing the times when our senses are deceiving us from the times when they may be trusted. The skeptics went on to argue that we could not ever know such a criterion to be correct, since we would have to rely on our senses in the course of trying to verify its correctness.

Chisholm's version of the problem is a bit different. Chisholm is concerned with the relationship between our ordinary, common-sense judgments about which particular propositions people know (e.g., I think I know that Kennedy was assassinated in 1963; that my friend knows my phone number, etc.), and our judgments about what, in general, is required in order for someone to know something. He considers three views one might take about this subject:

1. *Methodism:* (Not to be confused with the sect of Christianity of the same name.) This is the view that we should start from judgments about the general require-

ments of knowledge—in other words, from a set of criteria of knowledge—and use those to determine which particular knowledge claims are correct.

2. *Particularism:* This is the view that we should start with our intuitive judgments about which particular propositions particular people know, and use them to construct a theory of the general requirements of knowledge. Such a theory would be justified by its ability to correctly explain why we know the things that we do.
3. *Skepticism:* In the context of Chisholm's article, this is the view that we cannot have justified beliefs *either* about the general criteria of knowledge *or* about which particular propositions we know. This is because we would have to first establish the correct criteria in order to know which particular propositions we know, but we would first have to determine what we know in order to establish the correct criteria of knowledge. We cannot start from either, nor should we engage in circular reasoning, so we must suspend judgment entirely.

Chisholm concedes that none of the above three positions can be established by a non-question-begging argument. Nevertheless, he favors a particularist view, on the grounds that only the particularist is able to recognize all the knowledge that we do in fact have. (Methodists could in theory also do this, but in practice, most methodists have had a very difficult time explaining how we know most of the things we think we know, and have usually been unconvincing when they try.)

We conclude with G.E. Moore's famous defense of common sense against the philosophical skeptics. While other philosophers (particularly indirect realists and methodists) have gone to lengths trying to prove the existence of an external world, Moore says that he can do it quite easily. How? He would hold up his hand and say, while making a certain gesture, "Here is one hand." Then he would hold up his other hand, saying, "And here is another." He would then deduce that there are (at least two) external objects. This, as Moore points out, is analogous to many other proofs that we commonly accept as being perfectly good, rigorous proofs. For instance, suppose someone doubts whether space aliens exist. We might accept photographs of flying saucers, eyewitness reports, and so on as evidence for their existence, though not conclusive evidence. But one thing that would surely count as proof of their existence would be if someone brought us an actual space alien and allowed us to examine him—that, it seems, would be the ideal kind of proof. Similarly, Moore thinks, if someone doubts whether there are external objects, we can prove it to him by simply producing an external object and showing it to him.

Moore's argument would seem appropriate as a response to someone who merely demands, out of the blue, "Prove to me that there are external objects." But it does not seem like much of a response to the specific arguments philosophical skeptics have brought forward to try to show that we do not really know about the external world. The second excerpt from Moore, taken from his article "Hume's Theory Examined," indicates how he would respond to those arguments. Suppose a philosopher gives an argument from two premises, *A* and *B*, to a conclusion *C*. Suppose that the argument is logically valid, so that *if A* and *B* are both true, then *C* must also be true. Moore points out that it would also be valid to argue from *A* and ~*C* (the denial of *C*) to ~*B*, or from *B* and ~*C* to ~*A*. All three of these arguments are valid if and only if *A*, *B*, and ~*C* are jointly incompatible. Which argument is best depends upon which has the more initially plausible premises. If ~*C* is more initially plausible than either *A* or *B*, it would be irrational to accept the first argument; instead, one should accept one of the latter two. Moore thinks that the premises of any skeptical argument are less plausible than the denial of its conclusion. That is, it is more initially plausible that I know, for example, that there is a hand here, than it is that the premises of any given skeptical argument are correct. Therefore, it is rational to reject the premises (that is, to reject their conjunction; this requires only holding that at least one of them is false) of a skeptical argument on the grounds that they lead to the (absurd) conclusion that I don't know there is a hand here. The reader should note the parallel between Moore's position and Chisholm's particularism.

René Descartes, *Meditations on First Philosophy*

Synopsis of the following six Meditations

In the First Meditation reasons are provided which give us possible grounds for doubt about all things, especially material things, so long as we have no foundations for the sciences other than those which we have had up till now. Although the usefulness of such extensive doubt is not apparent at first sight, its greatest benefit lies in freeing us from all our preconceived opinions, and providing the easiest route by which the mind may be led away from the senses. The eventual result of this doubt is to make it impossible for us to have any further doubts about what we subsequently discover to be true.

In the Second Meditation, the mind uses its own freedom and supposes the non-existence of all the things about whose existence it can have even the slightest doubt; and in so doing the mind notices that it is impossible that it should not itself exist during this time. This exercise is also of the greatest benefit, since it enables the mind to distinguish without difficulty what belongs to itself, i.e. to an intellectual nature, from what belongs to the body. But since some people may perhaps expect arguments for the immortality of the soul in this section, I think they should be warned here and now that I have tried not to put down anything which I could not precisely demonstrate. Hence the only order which I could follow was that normally employed by geometers, namely to set out all the premises on which a desired proposition depends, before drawing any conclusions about it. Now the first and most important prerequisite for knowledge of the immortality of the soul is for us to form a concept of the soul which is as clear as possible and is also quite distinct from every concept of body; and that is just what has been done in this section. A further requirement is that we should know that everything that we clearly and distinctly understand is true in a way which corresponds exactly to our understanding of it; but it was not possible to prove this before the Fourth Meditation. In addition we need to have a distinct concept of corporeal nature, and this is developed partly in the Second Meditation itself, and partly in the Fifth and Sixth Meditations. The inference to be drawn from these results is that all the things that we clearly and distinctly conceive of as different substances (as we do in the case of mind and body) are in fact substances which are really distinct one from the other; and this conclusion is drawn in the

René Descartes, *Meditations on First Philosophy*, trans. and ed. John Cottingham (Cambridge: Cambridge University Press, 1996).

Sixth Meditation. This conclusion is confirmed in the same Meditation by the fact that we cannot understand a body except as being divisible, while by contrast we cannot understand a mind except as being indivisible. For we cannot conceive of half of a mind, while we can always conceive of half of a body, however small; and this leads us to recognize that the natures of mind and body are not only different, but in some way opposite. But I have not pursued this topic any further in this book, first because these arguments are enough to show that the decay of the body does not imply the destruction of the mind, and are hence enough to give mortals the hope of an after-life, and secondly because the premises which lead to the conclusion that the soul is immortal depend on an account of the whole of physics. This is required for two reasons. First, we need to know that absolutely all substances, or things which must be created by God in order to exist, are by their nature incorruptible and cannot ever cease to exist unless they are reduced to nothingness by God's denying his concurrence[1] to them. Secondly, we need to recognize that body, taken in the general sense, is a substance, so that it too never perishes. But the human body, in so far as it differs from other bodies, is simply made up of a certain configuration of limbs and other accidents[2] of this sort; whereas the human mind is not made up of any accidents in this way, but is a pure substance. For even if all the accidents of the mind change, so that it has different objects of the understanding and different desires and sensations, it does not on that account become a different mind; whereas a human body loses its identity merely as a result of a change in the shape of some of its parts. And it follows from this that while the body can very easily perish, the mind is immortal by its very nature.

In the Third Meditation I have explained quite fully enough, I think, my principal argument for proving the existence of God. But in order to draw my readers' minds away from the senses as far as possible, I was not willing to use any comparison taken from bodily things. So it may be that many obscurities remain; but I hope they will be completely removed later, in my Replies to the Objections. One such problem, among others, is how the idea of a supremely perfect being, which is in us, possesses so much objective reality that it can come only from a cause which is supremely perfect. In the Replies this is illustrated by the comparison of a very perfect machine, the idea of which is in the mind of some engineer. Just as the objective intricacy belonging to the idea must have some cause, namely the scientific knowledge of the engineer, or of someone else who passed the idea on to him, so the idea of God which is in us must have God himself as its cause.

In the Fourth Meditation it is proved that everything that we clearly and distinctly perceive is true, and I also explain what the nature of falsity consists in. These results need to be known both in order to confirm what has gone before and also to make intelligible what is to come later. (But here it should be noted in passing that I do not deal at all with sin, i.e. the error which is committed in pursuing good and evil, but only with the error that occurs in distinguishing truth from falsehood. And there is no discussion of matters pertaining to faith or the conduct of life, but simply of speculative truths which are known solely by means of the natural light.)[3]

In the Fifth Meditation, besides an account of corporeal nature taken in general, there is a new argument demonstrating the existence of God. Again, several difficulties may arise here, but these are resolved later in the Replies to the Objections. Finally I explain the sense in which it is true that the certainty even of geometrical demonstrations depends on the knowledge of God.

Lastly, in the Sixth Meditation, the intellect is distinguished from the imagination; the criteria for this distinction are explained; the mind is proved to be really distinct from the body, but is shown, notwithstanding, to be so closely joined to it that the mind and the body make up a kind of unit; there is a survey of all the errors which commonly come from the senses, and an explanation of how they may be avoided; and, lastly, there is a presentation of all the arguments which enable the existence of material things to be inferred. The great benefit of these arguments is not, in my view, that they prove what they establish—namely that there really is a world, and that human beings have bodies and so on—since no sane person has ever seriously doubted these things. The point is that in considering these arguments we come to realize that they are not as solid or as transparent as the arguments which lead us to knowledge of our own minds and of God, so that the latter are the most certain and evident of all possible objects of knowledge for the human intellect. Indeed, this is the one thing that I set myself to prove in these Meditations. And for that reason I will not now go over the various other issues in the book which are dealt with as they come up.

First Meditation: *What can be called into doubt*

Some years ago I was struck by the large number of falsehoods that I had accepted as true in my childhood, and by the highly doubtful nature of the whole edifice that I had subsequently based on them. I realized that it was necessary, once in the course of my life, to demolish everything completely and start again right from the foundations if I wanted to establish anything at all in the sciences that was stable and likely to last. But the task looked an enormous one, and I began to wait until I should reach a mature enough age to ensure that no subsequent time of life would be more suitable for tackling such inquiries. This led me to put the project off for so long that I would now be to blame if by pondering over it any further I wasted the time still left for carrying it out. So today I have expressly rid my mind of all worries and arranged for myself a clear stretch of free time. I am here quite alone, and at last I will devote myself sincerely and without reservation to the general demolition of my opinions.

But to accomplish this, it will not be necessary for me to show that all my opinions are false, which is something I could perhaps never manage. Reason now leads me to think that I should hold back my assent from opinions which are not completely certain and indubitable just as carefully as I do from those which are patently false. So, for the purpose of rejecting all my opinions, it will be enough if I find in each of them at least some reason for doubt. And to do this I will not need to run through them all individually, which would be an endless task. Once the foundations of a building are undermined, anything built on them collapses of its own accord; so I will go straight for the basic principles on which all my former beliefs rested.

Whatever I have up till now accepted as most true I have acquired either from the senses or through the senses. But from time to time I have found that the senses deceive, and it is prudent never to trust completely those who have deceived us even once.

Yet although the senses occasionally deceive us with respect to objects which are very small or in the distance, there are many other beliefs about which doubt is quite impossible, even though they are derived from the senses—for example, that I am here, sitting by the fire, wearing a winter dressing-gown, holding this piece of paper in my hands, and so on. Again, how could it be denied that these hands or this whole body are mine? Unless perhaps I were to liken myself to madmen, whose brains are so damaged by the persistent vapours of melancholia that they firmly maintain they are kings when they are paupers, or say they are dressed in purple when they are naked, or that their heads are made of earthenware, or that they are pumpkins, or made of glass. But such people are insane, and I would be thought equally mad if I took anything from them as a model for myself.

A brilliant piece of reasoning! As if I were not a man who sleeps at night, and regularly has all the same experiences while asleep as madmen do when awake—indeed sometimes even more improbable ones. How often, asleep at night, am I convinced of just such familiar events—that I am here in my dressing-gown, sitting by the fire—when in fact I am lying undressed in bed! Yet at the moment my eyes are certainly wide awake when I look at this piece of paper; I shake my head and it is not asleep; as I stretch out and feel my hand I do so deliberately, and I know what I am doing. All this would not happen with such distinctness to someone asleep. Indeed! As if I did not remember other occasions when I have been tricked by exactly similar thoughts while asleep! As I think about this more carefully, I see plainly that there are never any sure signs by means of which being awake can be distinguished from being asleep. The result is that I begin to feel dazed, and this very feeling only reinforces the notion that I may be asleep.

Suppose then that I am dreaming, and that these particulars—that my eyes are open, that I am moving my head and stretching out my hands—are not true. Perhaps, indeed, I do not even have such hands or such a body at all. Nonetheless, it must surely be admitted that the visions which come in sleep are like paintings, which must have been fashioned in the likeness of things that are real, and hence that at least these general kinds of things—eyes, head, hands and the body as a whole—are things which are not imaginary but are real and exist. For even when painters try to create sirens and satyrs with the most extraordinary bodies, they cannot give them natures which are new in all respects; they simply jumble up the limbs of different animals. Or if perhaps they manage to think up something so new that nothing remotely similar has ever been seen before—something which is therefore completely fictitious and unreal—at least the colours used in the composition must be real. By similar reasoning, although these general kinds of things—eyes, head, hands and so on—could be imaginary, it must at least be admitted that certain other even simpler and more universal things are real. These are as it were the real colours from which we form all the images of things, whether true or false, that occur in our thought.

This class appears to include corporeal nature in general, and its extension; the shape of extended things; the quantity, or size and number of these things; the place in which they may exist, the time through which they may endure, and so on.

So a reasonable conclusion from this might be that physics, astronomy, medicine, and all other disciplines which depend on the study of composite things, are doubtful; while arithmetic, geometry and other subjects of this kind, which deal only with the simplest and most general things, regardless of whether they really exist in nature or not, contain something certain and indubitable. For whether I am awake or asleep, two and three added together are five, and a square has no more than four sides. It seems impossible that such transparent truths should incur any suspicion of being false.

And yet firmly rooted in my mind is the long-standing opinion that there is an omnipotent God who made me the kind of creature that I am. How do I know that he has not brought it about that there is no earth, no sky, no extended thing, no shape, no size, no place, while at the same time ensuring that all these things appear to me to exist just as they do now? What is more, just as I consider that others sometimes go astray in cases where they think they have the most perfect knowledge, how do I know that God has not brought it about that I too go wrong every time I add two and three or count the sides of a square, or in some even simpler matter, if that is imaginable? But perhaps God would not have allowed me to be deceived in this way, since he is said to be supremely good. But if it were inconsistent with his goodness to have created me such that I am deceived all the time, it would seem equally foreign to his goodness to allow me to be deceived even occasionally; yet this last assertion cannot be made.

Perhaps there may be some who would prefer to deny the existence of so powerful a God rather than believe that everything else is uncertain. Let us not argue with them, but grant them that everything said about God is a fiction. According to their supposition, then, I have arrived at my present state by fate or chance or a continuous chain of events, or by some other means; yet since deception and error seem to be imperfections, the less powerful they make my original cause, the more likely it is that I am so imperfect as to be deceived all the time. I have no answer to these arguments, but am finally compelled to admit that there is not one of my former beliefs about which a doubt may not properly be raised; and this is not a flippant or ill-considered conclusion, but is based on powerful and well thought-out reasons. So in future I must withhold my assent from these former beliefs just as carefully as I would from obvious falsehoods, if I want to discover any certainty.

But it is not enough merely to have noticed this; I must make an effort to remember it. My habitual opinions keep coming back, and, despite my wishes, they capture my belief, which is as it were bound over to them as a result of long occupation and the law of custom. I shall never get out of the habit of confidently assenting to these opinions, so long as I suppose them to be what in fact they are, namely highly probable opinions—opinions which, despite the fact that they are in a sense doubtful, as has just been shown, it is still much more reasonable to believe than to deny. In view of this, I think it will be a good plan to turn my will in completely the opposite direction and deceive myself, by pretending for a time that these former opinions are utterly false and imaginary. I shall do this until the weight of preconceived opinion is counter-balanced and the distorting influence of habit no longer prevents my judgement from perceiving things correctly. In the meantime, I know that no danger or error will result from my plan, and that I cannot possibly go too far in my distrustful attitude. This is because the task now in hand does not involve action but merely the acquisition of knowledge.

I will suppose therefore that not God, who is supremely good and the source of truth, but rather some malicious demon of the utmost power and cunning has employed all his energies in order to deceive me. I shall think that the sky, the air, the earth, colours, shapes, sounds and all external things are merely the delusions of dreams which he has devised to ensnare my judgement. I shall consider myself as not having hands or eyes, or flesh, or blood or senses, but as falsely believing that I have all these things. I shall stubbornly and firmly persist in this meditation; and, even if it is not in my power to know any truth, I shall at least do what is in my power, that is, resolutely guard against assenting to any falsehoods, so that the deceiver, however powerful and cunning he may be, will be unable to impose on me in the slightest degree. But this is an arduous undertaking, and a kind of laziness brings me back to normal life. I am like a prisoner who is enjoying an imaginary freedom while asleep; as he begins to suspect that he is asleep, he dreads being woken up, and goes along with the pleasant illusion as long as he can. In the same way, I happily slide back into my old opinions and dread being shaken out of them, for fear that my peaceful sleep may be followed by hard labour when I wake, and that I shall have to toil not in the light, but amid the inextricable darkness of the problems I have now raised.

Second Meditation: *The nature of the human mind, and how it is better known than the body*

So serious are the doubts into which I have been thrown as a result of yesterday's meditation that I can neither put them out of my mind nor see any way of resolving them. It feels as if I have fallen unexpectedly into a deep whirlpool which tumbles me around so that I can neither stand on the bottom nor swim up to the top. Nevertheless I will make an effort and once more attempt the same path which I started on yesterday. Anything which admits of the slightest doubt I will set aside just as if I had found it to be wholly false; and I will proceed in this way until I recognize something certain, or, if nothing else, until I at least recognize for certain that there is no certainty. Archimedes used to demand just one firm and immovable point in order to shift the entire earth; so I too can hope for great things if I manage to find just one thing, however slight, that is certain and unshakeable.

I will suppose then, that everything I see is spurious. I will believe that my memory tells me lies, and that none of the things that it reports ever happened. I have no senses. Body, shape, extension, movement and place are chimeras. So what remains true? Perhaps just the one fact that nothing is certain.

Yet apart from everything I have just listed, how do I know that there is not something else which does not allow even the slightest occasion for doubt? Is there not a God, or whatever I may call him, who puts into me the thoughts I am now having? But why do I think this, since I myself may perhaps be the author of these thoughts? In that case am not I, at least, something? But I have just said that I have no senses and no body. This is the sticking point: what follows from this? Am I not so bound up with a body and with senses that I cannot exist without them? But I have convinced myself that there is absolutely nothing in the world, no sky, no earth, no minds, no bodies. Does it now follow that I too do not exist? No: if I convinced myself of something then I certainly existed. But there is a deceiver of supreme power and cunning who is deliberately and constantly deceiving me. In that case I too undoubtedly exist, if he is deceiving me; and let him deceive me as much as he can, he will never bring it about that I am nothing so long as I think that I am something. So after considering everything very thoroughly, I must finally conclude that this proposition, *I am, I exist*, is necessarily true whenever it is put forward by me or conceived in my mind.

But I do not yet have a sufficient understanding of what this "I" is, that now necessarily exists. So I must be on my guard against carelessly taking something else to be this "I", and so making a mistake in the very item of knowledge that I maintain is the most certain and evident of all. I will therefore go back and meditate on what I originally believed myself to be, before I embarked on this present train of thought. I will then subtract anything capable of being weakened, even minimally, by the arguments now introduced, so that what is left at the end may be exactly and only what is certain and unshakeable.

What then did I formerly think I was? A man. But what is a man? Shall I say "a rational animal"? No; for then I should have to inquire what an animal is, what rationality is, and in this way one question would lead me down the slope to other harder ones, and I do not now have the time to waste on subtleties of this kind. Instead I propose to concentrate on what came into my thoughts spontaneously and quite naturally whenever I used to consider what I was. Well, the first thought to come to mind was that I had a face, hands, arms and the whole mechanical structure of limbs which can be seen in a corpse, and which I called the body. The next thought was that I was nourished, that I moved about, and that I engaged in sense-perception and thinking; and these actions I attributed to the soul. But as to the nature of this soul, either I did not think about this or else I imagined it to be something tenuous, like a wind or fire or ether, which permeated my more solid parts. As to the body, however, I had no doubts about it, but thought I knew its nature distinctly. If I had tried to describe the mental conception I had of it, I would have expressed it as follows: by a body I understand whatever has a determinable shape and a definable location and can occupy a space in such a way as to exclude any other body; it can be perceived by touch, sight, hearing, taste or smell, and can be moved in various ways, not by itself but by whatever else comes into contact with it. For, according to my judgement, the power of self-movement, like the power of sensation or of thought, was quite foreign to the nature of a body; indeed, it was a source of wonder to me that certain bodies were found to contain faculties of this kind.

But what shall I now say that I am, when I am supposing that there is some supremely powerful and, if it is permissible to say so, malicious deceiver, who is deliberately trying to trick me in every way he can? Can I now assert that I possess even the most insignificant of all the attributes which I have just said belong to the nature of a body? I scrutinize them, think about them, go over them again, but nothing suggests itself; it is tiresome and pointless to go through the list once more. But what about the attributes I assigned to the soul? Nutrition or movement? Since now I do not have a body, these are mere fabrications. Sense-perception? This surely does not occur without a body, and besides, when asleep I have appeared to perceive through the senses many things which I afterwards realized I did not perceive through the senses at all. Thinking? At last I have discovered it—thought; this alone is inseparable from me. I am, I exist—that is certain. But for how long? For as long as I am thinking. For it could be that were I totally to cease from thinking, I should totally cease to exist. At present I am not admitting anything except what is necessarily true. I am, then, in the strict sense only a thing that thinks; that is, I am a mind, or intelligence, or intellect, or reason – words whose meaning I have been ignorant of until now. But for all that I am a thing which is real and which truly exists. But what kind of a thing? As I have just said—a thinking thing.

What else am I? I will use my imagination. I am not that structure of limbs which is called a human body. I am not even some thin vapour which permeates the limbs—a wind, fire, air, breath, or whatever I depict in my imagination; for these are things which I have supposed to be nothing. Let this supposition stand; for all that I am still something. And yet may it not perhaps be the case that these very things which I am supposing to be nothing, because they are unknown to me, are in reality identical with the "I" of which I am aware? I do not know, and for the moment I shall not argue the point, since I can make judgements only about things which are known to me. I know that I exist; the question is, what is this "I" that I know? If the "I" is understood strictly as we have been taking it, then it is quite certain that knowledge of it does not depend on things of whose existence I am as yet unaware; so it cannot depend on any of the things which I invent in my imagination. And this very word 'invent' shows me my mistake. It would indeed be a case of fictitious invention if I used my imagination to establish that I was something or other; for imagining is simply contemplating the shape or image of a corporeal thing. Yet now I know for certain both that I exist and at the same time that all such images and, in general, everything relating to the nature of body, could be mere dreams [and chimeras]. Once this point has been grasped, to say "I will use my imagination to get to know more distinctly what I am" would seem to be as silly as saying "I am now awake, and see some truth; but since my vision is not yet clear enough, I will deliberately fall asleep so that my dreams may provide a truer and clearer representation." I thus realize that none of the things that the imagination enables me to grasp is at all relevant to this knowledge of myself which I possess, and that the mind must therefore be most carefully diverted from such things if it is to perceive its own nature as distinctly as possible.

But what then am I? A thing that thinks. What is that? A thing that doubts, understands, affirms, denies, is willing, is unwilling, and also imagines and has sensory perceptions.

This is a considerable list, if everything on it belongs to me. But does it? Is it not one and the same "I" who is now doubting almost everything, who nonetheless understands some things, who affirms that this one thing is true, denies everything else, desires to know more, is unwilling to be deceived, imagines many things even involuntarily, and is aware of many things which apparently come from the senses? Are not all these things just as true as the fact that I exist, even if I am asleep all the time, and even if he who created me is doing all he can to deceive me? Which of all these activities is distinct from my thinking? Which of them can be said to be separate from myself? The fact that it is I who am doubting and understanding and willing is so evident that I see no way of making it any clearer. But it is also the case that the "I" who imagines is the same "I." For even if, as I have supposed, none of the objects of imagination are real, the power of imagination is something which really exists and is part of my thinking. Lastly, it is also the same "I" who has sensory perceptions, or is aware of bodily things as it were through the senses. For example, I am now seeing light, hearing a noise, feeling heat. But I am asleep, so all this is false. Yet I certainly *seem* to see, to hear, and to be warmed. This cannot be false; what is called "having a sensory perception" is strictly just this, and in this restricted sense of the term it is simply thinking.

From all this I am beginning to have a rather better understanding of what I am. But it still appears—and I cannot stop thinking this—that the corporeal things of which images are formed in my thought, and which the senses investigate, are known with much more distinctness than this puzzling "I" which cannot be pictured in the imagination. And yet it is surely surprising that I should have a more distinct grasp of things which I realize are doubtful, unknown and foreign to me, than I have of that which is true and known—my own self. But I see what it is: my mind enjoys wandering off and will not yet submit to being restrained within the bounds of truth. Very well then; just this once let us give it a completely free rein, so that after a while, when it is time to tighten the reins, it may more readily submit to being curbed.

Let us consider the things which people commonly think they understand most distinctly of all; that is, the bodies which we touch and see. I do not mean bodies in general—for general perceptions are apt to be somewhat more confused—but one particular body. Let us take, for example, this piece of wax. It has just been taken from the honeycomb; it has not yet quite lost the taste of the honey; it retains some of the scent of the flowers from which it was gathered; its colour, shape and size are plain to see; it is hard, cold and can be handled without difficulty; if you rap it with your knuckle it makes a sound. In short, it has everything which appears necessary to enable a body to be known as distinctly as possible. But even as I speak, I put the wax by the fire, and look: the residual taste is eliminated, the smell goes away, the colour changes, the shape is lost, the size increases; it becomes liquid and hot; you can hardly touch it, and if you strike it, it no longer makes a sound. But does the same wax remain? It must be admitted that it does; no one denies it, no one thinks otherwise. So what was it in the wax that I understood with such distinctness? Evidently none of the features which I arrived at by means of the senses; for whatever came under taste, smell, sight, touch or hearing has now altered—yet the wax remains.

Perhaps the answer lies in the thought which now comes to my mind; namely, the wax was not after all the sweetness of the honey, or the fragrance of the flowers, or the whiteness, or the shape, or the sound, but was rather a body which presented itself to me in these various forms a little while ago, but which now exhibits different ones. But what exactly is it that I am now imagining? Let us concentrate, take away everything which does not belong to the wax, and see what is left: merely something extended, flexible and changeable. But what is meant here by "flexible" and "changeable"? Is it what I picture in my imagination: that this piece of wax is capable of changing from a round shape to a square shape, or from a square shape to a triangular shape? Not at all; for I can grasp that the wax is capable of countless changes of this kind, yet I am unable to run through this immeasurable number of changes in my imagination, from which it follows that it is not the faculty of imagination that gives me my grasp of the wax as flexible and changeable. And what is meant by "extended"? Is the extension of the wax also unknown? For it increases if the wax melts, increases again if it boils, and is greater still if the heat is increased. I would not be making a correct judgement about the nature of wax unless I believed it capable of being extended in many more different ways than I will ever encompass in my imagination. I must therefore admit that the nature of this piece of wax is in no way revealed by my imagination, but is perceived by the mind alone. (I am speaking of this particular piece of wax; the point is even clearer with regard to wax in general.) But what is this wax which is perceived by the mind alone? It is of course the same wax which I see, which I touch, which I picture in my imagination, in short the same wax which I thought it to be from the start. And yet, and here is the point, the perception I have of it is a case not of vision or touch or imagination—nor has it ever been, despite previous appearances—but of purely mental scrutiny; and this can be imperfect and confused, as it was before, or clear and distinct as it is now, depending on how carefully I concentrate on what the wax consists in.

But as I reach this conclusion I am amazed at how [weak and] prone to error my mind is. For although I am thinking about these matters within myself, silently and without speaking, nonetheless the actual words bring me up short, and I am almost tricked by ordinary ways of talking. We say that we see the wax itself, if it is there before us, not that we judge it to be there from its colour or shape; and this might lead me to conclude without more ado that knowledge of the wax comes from what the eye sees, and not from the scrutiny of the mind alone. But then if I look out of the window and see men crossing the square, as I just happen to have done, I normally say that I see the men themselves, just as I say that I see the wax. Yet do I see any more than hats and coats which could conceal automatons? I *judge* that they are men. And so something which I thought I was seeing with my eyes is in fact grasped solely by the faculty of judgement which is in my mind.

However, one who wants to achieve knowledge above the ordinary level should feel ashamed at having taken ordinary ways of talking as a basis for doubt. So let us proceed, and consider on which occasion my perception of the nature of the wax was more perfect and evident. Was it when I first looked at it, and believed I knew it by my external senses, or at least by what they call the "common" sense—that is, the power of imagination? Or is my knowledge more perfect now, after a more careful investigation of the nature of the wax and of the means by which it is known? Any doubt on this issue would clearly be foolish; for what distinctness was there in my earlier perception? Was there anything in it which an animal could not possess? But when I distinguish the wax from its outward forms—take the clothes off, as it were, and consider it naked—then although my judgement may still contain errors, at least my perception now requires a human mind.

But what am I to say about this mind, or about myself? (So far, remember, I am not admitting that there is anything else in me except a mind.) What, I ask, is this "I" which seems to perceive the wax so distinctly? Surely my awareness of my own self is not merely much truer and more certain than my awareness of the wax, but also much more distinct and evident. For if I judge that the wax exists from the fact that I see it, clearly this same fact entails much more evidently that I myself also exist. It is possible that what I see is not really the wax; it is possible that I do not even have eyes with which to see anything. But when I see, or think I see (I am not here distinguishing the two), it is simply not possible that I who am now thinking am not something. By the same token, if I judge that the wax exists from the fact that I touch it, the same result follows, namely that I exist. If I judge that it exists from the fact that I imagine it, or for any other reason, exactly the same thing follows. And the result that I have grasped in the case of the wax may be applied to everything else located outside me. Moreover, if my perception of the wax seemed more distinct after it was established not just by sight or touch but by many other considerations, it must be admitted that I now know myself even more distinctly. This is because every consideration whatsoever which contributes to my perception of the wax, or of any other body, cannot but establish even more effectively the nature of my own mind. But besides this, there is so much else in the mind itself which can serve to make my knowledge of it more distinct, that it scarcely seems worth going through the contributions made by considering bodily things.

I see that without any effort I have now finally got back to where I wanted. I now know that even bodies are not strictly perceived by the senses or the faculty of imagination but by the intellect alone, and that this perception derives not from their being touched or seen but from their being understood; and in view of this I know plainly that I can achieve an easier and more evident perception of my own mind than of anything else. But since the habit of holding on to old opinions cannot be set aside so quickly, I should like to stop here and meditate for some time on this new knowledge I have gained, so as to fix it more deeply in my memory.

Notes

1 The continuous divine action necessary to maintain things in existence.

2 Descartes here uses this scholastic term to refer to those features of a thing which may alter, e.g. the particular size, shape etc. of a body, or the particular thoughts, desires etc. of a mind.

3 Descartes added this passage on the advice of Arnauld (cf. AT vii 215; CSM II 151). He told Mersenne "Put the words between brackets so that it can be seen that they have been added" (letter of 18 March 1641: AT III 335; CSMK 175).

QUESTIONS

1 When Descartes considers the possibility that he might be dreaming, what sort of beliefs does this cast doubt on?

2 What does Descartes think he knows at the end of the Second Meditation?

3 What is the example of the wax supposed to show?

Hilary Putnam, "Brains in a Vat"

An ant is crawling on a patch of sand. As it crawls, it traces a line in the sand. By pure chance the line that it traces curves and recrosses itself in such a way that it ends up looking like a recognizable caricature of Winston Churchill. Has the ant traced a picture of Winston Churchill, a picture that *depicts* Churchill?

Most people would say, on a little reflection, that it has not. The ant, after all, has never seen Churchill, or even a picture of Churchill, and it had no intention of depicting Churchill. It simply traced a line (and even *that* was unintentional), a line that *we* can "see as" a picture of Churchill.

We can express this by saying that the line is not "in itself" a representation[1] of anything rather than anything else. Similarity (of a certain very complicated sort) to the features of Winston Churchill is not sufficient to make something represent or refer to Churchill. Nor is it necessary: in our community the printed shape "Winston Churchill," the spoken words "Winston Churchill," and many other things are used to represent Churchill (though not pictorially), while not having the sort of similarity to Churchill that a picture—even a line drawing—has. If *similarity* is not necessary or sufficient to make something represent something else, how can *anything* be necessary or sufficient for this purpose? How on earth can one thing represent (or "stand for," etc.) a different thing?

The answer may seem easy. Suppose the ant had seen Winston Churchill, and suppose that it had the intelligence and skill to draw a picture of him. Suppose it produced the caricature *intentionally*. Then the line would have represented Churchill.

On the other hand, suppose the line had the shape WINSTON CHURCHILL. And suppose this was just accident (ignoring the improbability involved). Then the "printed shape" WINSTON CHURCHILL would *not* have represented Churchill, although that printed shape does represent Churchill when it occurs in almost any book today.

So it may seem that what is necessary for representation, or what is mainly necessary for representation, is *intention*.

But to have the intention that *anything*, even private language (even the words "Winston Churchill" spoken in my mind and not out loud), should *represent* Churchill, I must have been able to *think about* Churchill in the first place. If lines in the sand, noises, etc., cannot "in themselves" represent anything, then how is it

Hilary Putnam, "Brains in a Vat," *Reason, Truth, and History* (Cambridge: Cambridge University Press, 1981).

that thought forms can "in themselves" represent anything? Or can they? How can thought reach out and "grasp" what is external?

Some philosophers have, in the past, leaped from this sort of consideration to what they take to be a proof that the mind is *essentially non-physical in nature*. The argument is simple; what we said about the ant's curve applies to any physical object. No physical object can, in itself, refer to one thing rather than to another; nevertheless, *thoughts in the mind* obviously do succeed in referring to one thing rather than another. So thoughts (and hence the mind) are of an essentially different nature than physical objects. Thoughts have the characteristic of *intentionality*—they can refer to something else; nothing physical has "intentionality," save as that intentionality is derivative from some employment of that physical thing by a mind. Or so it is claimed. This is too quick; just postulating mysterious powers of mind solves nothing. But the problem is very real. How is intentionality, reference, possible?

Magical theories of reference

We saw that the ant's "picture" has no necessary connection with Winston Churchill. The mere fact that the "picture" bears a "resemblance" to Churchill does not make it into a real picture, nor does it make it a representation of Churchill. Unless the ant is an intelligent ant (which it isn't) and knows about Churchill (which it doesn't), the curve it traced is not a picture or even a representation of anything. Some primitive people believe that some representations (in particular, *names*) have a necessary connection with their bearers; that to know the "true name" of someone or something gives one power over it. This power comes from the *magical connection* between the name and the bearer of the name; once one realizes that a name *only* has a contextual, contingent, conventional connection with its bearer, it is hard to see why knowledge of the name should have any mystical significance.

What is important to realize is that what goes for physical pictures also goes for mental images, and for mental representations in general; mental representations no more have a necessary connection with what they represent than physical representations do. The contrary supposition is a survival of magical thinking.

Perhaps the point is easiest to grasp in the case of mental *images*. (Perhaps the first philosopher to grasp the enormous significance of this point, even if he was not the first to actually make it, was Wittgenstein.) Suppose there is a planet somewhere on which human beings have evolved (or been deposited by alien spacemen, or what have you). Suppose these humans, although otherwise like us, have never seen *trees*. Suppose they have never imagined trees (perhaps vegetable life exists on their planet only in the form of molds). Suppose one day a picture of a tree is accidentally dropped on their planet by a spaceship which passes on without having other contact with them. Imagine them puzzling over the picture. What in the world is this? All sorts of speculations occur to them: a building, a canopy, even an animal of some kind. But suppose they never come close to the truth.

For *us* the picture is a representation of a tree. For these humans the picture only represents a strange object, nature and function unknown. Suppose one of them has a mental image which is exactly like one of my mental images of a tree as a result of having seen the picture. His mental image is not a *representation of a tree*. It is only a representation of the strange object (whatever it is) that the mysterious picture represents.

Still, someone might argue that the mental image is *in fact* a representation of a tree, if only because the picture which caused this mental image was itself a representation of a tree to begin with. There is a causal chain from actual trees to the mental image even if it is a very strange one.

But even this causal chain can be imagined absent. Suppose the "picture of the tree" that the spaceship dropped was not really a picture of a tree, but the accidental result of some spilled paints. Even if it looked exactly like a picture of a tree, it was, in truth, no more a picture of a tree than the ant's "caricature" of Churchill was a picture of Churchill. We can even imagine that the spaceship which dropped the "picture" came from a planet which knew nothing of trees. Then the humans would still have mental images qualitatively identical with my image of a tree, but they would not be images which represented a tree any more than anything else.

The same thing is true of *words*. A discourse on paper might seem to be a perfect description of trees, but if it was produced by monkeys randomly hitting keys on a typewriter for millions of years, then the words do not refer to anything. If there were a person who memorized those words and said them in his mind without understanding them, then they would not refer to anything when thought in the mind, either.

Imagine the person who is saying those words in his mind has been hypnotized. Suppose the words are in Japanese, and the person has been told that he understands Japanese. Suppose that as he thinks those words he has a "feeling of understanding." (Although if someone broke into his train of thought and asked him what the words he was thinking *meant*, he would discover he couldn't say.) Perhaps the illusion would be so perfect that the person could even fool a Japanese telepath! But if he couldn't use the words in the right contexts, answer questions about what he "thought," etc., then he didn't understand them.

By combining these science fiction stories I have been telling, we can contrive a case in which someone thinks words which are in fact a description of trees in some language *and* simultaneously has appropriate mental images, but *neither* understands the words *nor* knows that a tree is. We can even imagine that the mental images were caused by paint-spills (although the person has been hypnotized to think that they are images of something appropriate to his thought—only, if he were asked, he wouldn't be able to say of what). And we can imagine that the language the person is thinking in is one neither the hypnotist nor the person hypnotized has ever heard of—perhaps it is just coincidence that these "nonsense sentences," as the hypnotist supposes them to be, are a description of trees in Japanese. In short, everything passing before the person's mind might be qualitatively identical with what was passing through the mind of a Japanese speaker who was *really* thinking about trees—but none of it would refer to trees.

All of this is really impossible, of course, in the way that it is really impossible that monkeys should by chance type out a copy of *Hamlet*. That is to say that the probabilities against it are so high as to mean it will never really happen (we think). But it is not logically impossible, or even physically impossible. It *could* happen (compatibly with physical law and, perhaps, compatibly with actual conditions in the universe, if there are lots of intelligent beings on other planets). And if it did happen, it would be a striking demonstration of an important conceptual truth; that even a large and complex system of representations, both verbal and visual, still does not have an *intrinsic*, built-in, magical connection with what it represents—a connection independent of how it was caused and what the dispositions of the speaker or thinker are. And this is true whether the system of representations (words and images, in the case of the example) is physically realized—the words are written or spoken, and the pictures are physical pictures—or only realized in the mind. Thought words and mental pictures do not *intrinsically* represent what they are about.

The case of the brains in a vat

Here is a science fiction possibility discussed by philosophers: imagine that a human being (you can imagine this to be yourself) has been subjected to an operation by an evil scientist. The person's brain (your brain) has been removed from the body and placed in a vat of nutrients which keeps the brain alive. The nerve endings have been connected to a super-scientific computer which causes the person whose brain it is to have the illusion that everything is perfectly normal. There seem to be people, objects, the sky, etc; but really all the person (you) is experiencing is the result of electronic impulses travelling from the computer to the nerve endings. The computer is so clever that if the person tries to raise his hand, the feedback from the computer will cause him to "see" and "feel" the hand being raised. Moreover, by varying the program, the evil scientist can cause the victim to "experience" (or hallucinate) any situation or environment the evil scientist wishes. He can also obliterate the memory of the brain operation, so that the victim will seem to himself to have always been in this environment. It can even seem to the victim that he is sitting and reading these very words about the amusing but quite absurd supposition that there is an evil scientists who removes people's brains from their bodies and places them in a vat of nutrients which keep the brain alive. The nerve endings are supposed to be connected to a super-scientific computer which causes the person whose brain it is to have the illusion that . . .

When this sort of possibility is mentioned in a lecture on the Theory of Knowledge, the purpose, of course, is to raise the classical problem of scepticism with respect to the external world in a modern way. (*How do you know you aren't in this predicament?*) But this predicament is also a useful device for raising issues about the mind/world relationship.

Instead of having just one brain in a vat, we could imagine that all human beings (perhaps all sentient beings) are brains in a vat (or nervous systems in a vat in case some beings with just a minimal nervous system already count as "sentient"). Of course, the evil scientist would have to be outside—or would he? Perhaps there is no evil scientist, perhaps (though this is absurd) the universe just happens to consist of automatic machinery tending a vat full of brains and nervous systems.

This time let us suppose that the automatic machinery is programmed to give us all a *collective* hallucination, rather than a number of separate unrelated hallucinations. Thus, when I seem to myself to be talking to you, you seem to yourself to be hearing my words. Of course, it is not the case that my words actually reach your ears—for you don't have (real) ears, nor do I have a real mouth and tongue. Rather, when I produce my words, what happens is that the efferent impulses travel from my brain to the computer, which both causes me to "hear" my own voice uttering those words and "feel" my tongue moving, etc., and causes you to "hear" my words, "see" me speaking, etc. In this case, we are, in a sense, actually in communication. I am not mistaken about your real existence (only about the existence of your body and the "external world", apart from brains). From a certain point of view, it doesn't even matter that "the whole world" is a collective hallucination; for you do, after all, really hear my words when I speak to you, even if the mechanism isn't what we suppose it to be. (Of course, if we were two lovers making love, rather than just two people carrying on a conversation, then the suggestion that it was just two brains in a vat might be disturbing.)

I want now to ask a question which will seem very silly and obvious (at least to some people, including some very sophisticated philosophers), but which will take us to real philosophical depths rather quickly. Suppose this whole story were actually true. Could we, if we were brains in a vat in this way, *say* or *think* that we were?

I am going to argue that the answer is "No, we couldn't." In fact, I am going to argue that the supposition that we are actually brains in a vat, although it violates no physical law, and is perfectly consistent with everything we have experienced, cannot possibly be true. *It cannot possibly be true*, because it is, in a certain way, self-refuting.

The argument I am going to present is an unusual one, and it took me several years to convince myself that it is really right. But it is a correct argument. What makes it seem so strange is that it is connected with some of the very deepest issues in philosophy. (It first occurred to me when I was thinking about a theorem in modern logic, the "Skolem–Löwenheim Theorem", and I suddenly saw a connection between this theorem and some arguments in Wittgenstein's *Philosophical Investigations*.)

A "self-refuting supposition" is one whose truth implies its own falsity. For example, consider the thesis that *all general statements are false*. This is a general statement. So if it is true, then it must be false. Hence, it is false. Sometimes a thesis is called "self-refuting" if it is *the supposition that the thesis is entertained or enunciated* that implies its falsity. For example, "I do not exist" is self-refuting if thought by *me* (for any "*me*"). So one can be certain that one oneself exists, if one thinks about it (as Descartes argued).

What I shall show is that the supposition that we are brains in a vat has just this property. If we can consider whether it is true or false, then it is not true (I shall show). Hence it is not true.

Before I give the argument, let us consider why it seems so strange that such an argument can be given (at least to philosophers who subscribe to a "copy" conception of truth). We conceded that it is compatible with physical law that there should be a world in which all sentient beings are brains in a vat. As philosophers say, there is a "possible world" in which all sentient beings are brains in a vat. (This "possible world" talk makes it sound as if there is a *place* where any absurd supposition is true, which is why it can be very misleading in philosophy.) The humans in that possible world have exactly the same experiences that *we* do. They think the same thoughts we do (at least, the same words, images, thought-forms, etc., go through their minds). Yet, I am claiming that there is an argument we can give that shows we are not brains in a vat. How can there be? And why couldn't the people in the possible world who really *are* brains in a vat give it too?

The answer is going to be (basically) this: although the people in that possible world can think and "say" any words we can think and say, they cannot (I claim) *refer* to what we can refer to. In particular, they cannot think or say that they are brains in a vat (*even by thinking "we are brains in a vat"*).

Turing's test

Suppose someone succeeds in inventing a computer which can actually carry on an intelligent conversation with one (on as many subjects as an intelligent person might). How can one decide if the computer is "conscious"?

The British logician Alan Turing proposed the following test:[2] let someone carry on a conversation with the computer and a conversation with a person whom he does not know. If he cannot tell which is the computer and which is the human being, then (assume the test to be repeated a sufficient number of times with different interlocutors) the computer is conscious. In short, a computing machine is conscious if it can pass the "Turing Test". (The conversations are not to be carried on face to face, of course, since the interlocutor is not to know the visual appearance of either of his two conversational partners. Nor is voice to be used, since the mechanical voice might simply sound different from a human voice. Imagine, rather, that the conversations are all carried on via electric type-writer. The interlocutor types in his statements, questions, etc., and the two partners—the machine and the person—respond via the electric keyboard. Also, the machine may *lie*—asked "Are you a machine", it might reply, "No, I'm an assistant in the lab here.")

The idea that this test is really a definitive test of consciousness has been criticized by a number of authors (who are by no means hostile in principle to the idea that a machine might be conscious). But this is not our topic at this time. I wish to use the general idea of the Turing test, the general idea of a *dialogic test of competence*, for a different purpose, the purpose of exploring the notion of *reference*.

Imagine a situation in which the problem is not to determine if the partner is really a person or a machine, but is rather to determine if the partner uses the words to refer as we do. The obvious test is, again, to carry on a conversation, and, if no problems arise, if the partner "passes" in the sense of being indistinguishable from someone who is certified in advance to be speaking the same language, referring to the usual sorts of objects, etc., to conclude that the partner does refer to objects as we do. When the purpose of the Turing test is as just described, that is, to determine the existence of (shared) reference, I shall refer to the test as the *Turing Test for Reference*. And, just as philosophers have discussed the question whether the original Turing test is a *definitive* test for consciousness, i.e. the question of whether a machine which "passes" the test not just once but regularly is *necessarily* conscious, so, in the same way, I wish to discuss the question of whether the Turing Test for Reference just suggested is a definitive test for shared reference.

The answer will turn out to be "No". The Turing Test for Reference is not definitive. It is certainly an excellent test in practice; but it is not logically impossible (though it is certainly highly improbable) that someone could pass the Turing Test for Reference and not be referring to anything. It follows from this, as we shall see, that we can extend our observation that words (and whole texts and discourses) do not have a necessary connection to their referents. Even if we consider not words by themselves but rules deciding what words may appropriately be produced in certain contexts—even if we consider, in computer jargon, *programs for using words*—unless those programs themselves *refer to something extra-linguistic* there is still no determinate reference that those words possess. This will be a crucial step in the process of reaching the conclusion that the Brain-in-a-Vat Worlders cannot refer to anything external at all (and hence cannot say *that* they are Brain-in-a-Vat Worlders).

Suppose, for example, that I am in the Turing situation (playing the "Imitation Game", in Turing's terminology) and my partner is actually a machine. Suppose this machine is able to win the game ("passes" the test). Imagine the machine to be programmed to produce beautiful responses in English to statements, questions, remarks, etc. in English, but that it has no sense organs (other than the hookup to my electric typewriter), and no motor organs (other than the electric typewriter). (As far as I can make out, Turing does not assume that the possession of either sense organs or motor organs is necessary for consciousness or intelligence.) Assume that not only does the machine lack electronic eyes and ears, etc., but that there are no provisions in the machine's program, the program for playing the Imitation Game, for incorporating inputs from such sense organs, or for controlling a body. What should we say about such a machine?

To me, it seems evident that we cannot and should not attribute reference to such a device. It is true that the machine can discourse beautifully about, say, the scenery in New England. But it could not recognize an apple tree or an apple, a mountain or a cow, a field or a steeple, if it were in front of one.

What we have is a device for producing sentences in response to sentences. But none of these sentences is at all connected to the real world. *If one coupled two of these machines and let them play the Imitation Game with each other, then they would go on "fooling" each other forever, even if the rest of the world disappeared!* There is no more reason to regard the machine's talk of apples as referring to real world apples than there is to regard the ant's "drawing" as referring to Winston Churchill.

What produces the illusion of reference, meaning, intelligence, etc., here is the fact that there is a convention of representation which *we* have under which the machine's discourse refers to apples, steeples, New England, etc. Similarly, there is the *illusion* that the ant has caricatured Churchill, for the same reason. But we are able to perceive, handle, deal with apples and fields. Our talk of apples and fields is intimately connected with our *non-verbal* transactions with apples and fields. There are "language entry rules" which take us from experiences of apples to such utterances as "I see an apple", and "language exit rules" which take us from decisions expressed in linguistic form ("I am going to buy some apples") to actions other than speaking. Lacking either language entry rules or language exit rules, there is no reason to regard the conversation of the machine (or of the two machines, in the case we envisaged of two machines playing the Imitation Game with each other) as more than syntactic play. Syntactic play that *resembles* intelligent discourse, to be sure; but only as (and no more than) the ant's curve resembles a biting caricature.

In the case of the ant, we could have argued that the ant would have drawn the same curve even if Winston Churchill had never existed. In the case of the machine, we cannot quite make the parallel argument; if apples, trees, steeples and fields had not existed, then, presumably, the programmers would not have produced that same program. Although the machine does not *perceive* apples, fields, or steeples, its creator–designers did. There is *some* causal connection between the machine and the real world apples, etc., via the perceptual experience and knowledge of the creator–designers. But such a weak connection can hardly suffice for reference. Not only is it logically possible, though fantastically improbable, that the same machine *could* have existed even if apples, fields, and steeples had not existed; more important, the machine is utterly insensitive to the *continued* existence of apples, fields, steeples, etc. Even if all these things *ceased* to exist, the machine would still discourse just as happily in the same way. That is why the machine cannot be regarded as referring at all.

The point that is relevant for our discussion is that there is nothing in Turing's Test to rule out a machine which is programmed to do nothing *but* play the Imitation Game, and that a machine which can do nothing *but* play the Imitation Game is *clearly* not referring any more than a record player is.

Brains in a vat (again)

Let us compare the hypothetical "brains in a vat" with the machines just described. There are obviously important differences. The brains in a vat do not have sense organs, but they do have *provision* for sense organs; that is, there are afferent nerve endings, there are inputs from these afferent nerve endings, and these inputs figure in the "program" of the brains in the vat just as they do in the program of our brains. The brains in a vat are *brains*; moreover, they are *functioning* brains, and they function by the same rules as brains do in the actual world. For these reasons, it would seem absurd to deny consciousness or intelligence to them. But the fact that they are conscious and intelligent does not mean that their words refer to what our words refer. The question we are interested in is this: do their verbalizations containing, say, the word "tree" actually refer to *trees?* More generally: can they refer to *external* objects at all? (As opposed to, for example, objects in the image produced by the automatic machinery.)

To fix our ideas, let us specify that the automatic machinery is supposed to have come into existence by some kind of cosmic chance or coincidence (or, perhaps, to have always existed). In this hypothetical world, the automatic machinery itself is supposed to have no intelligent creator–designers. In fact, as we said at the beginning of this chapter, we may imagine that all sentient beings (however minimal their sentience) are inside the vat.

This assumption does not help. For there is no connection between the *word* "tree" as used by these brains and actual trees. They would still use the word "tree" just as they do, think just the thoughts they do, have just the images they have, even if there were no actual trees. Their images, words, etc., are qualitatively identical with images, words, etc., which do represent trees in *our* world; but we have already seen (the ant again!) that qualitative similarity to something which represents an object (Winston Churchill or a tree) does not make a thing a representation all by itself. In short, the brains in a vat are not thinking about real trees when they think "there is a tree in front of me" because there is nothing by virtue of which their thought "tree" represents actual trees.

If this seems hasty, reflect on the following: we have seen that the words do not necessarily refer to trees even if they are arranged in a sequence which is identical with a discourse which (were it to occur in one of our minds) would unquestionably *be about trees* in the actual world. Nor does the "program", in the sense of the rules, practices, dispositions of the brains to verbal behavior, necessarily refer to trees or bring about reference to trees through the connections it establishes between words and words, or *linguistic* cues and *linguistic* responses. If these brains think about, refer to, represent trees (real trees, outside the vat), then it must be because of the way the "program" connects the system of language to *non-verbal* input and outputs. There are indeed such non-verbal inputs and outputs in the Brain-in-a-Vat world (those efferent and afferent nerve endings again!), but we also saw that the "sense-data" produced by the automatic machinery do not represent trees (or anything external) even when they resemble our tree-images exactly. Just as a splash of paint might resemble a tree picture without *being* a tree picture, so, we saw, a "sense datum" might be qualitatively identical with an "image of a tree" without being an image of a tree. How can the fact that, in the case of the brains in a vat, the language is connected by the program with sensory inputs which do not intrinsically or extrinsically represent trees (or anything external) possibly bring it about that the whole system of representations, the language-in-use, *does* refer to or represent trees or anything external?

The answer is that it cannot. The whole system of sense-data, motor signals to the efferent endings, and verbally or conceptually mediated thought connected by "language entry rules" to the sense-data (or whatever) as inputs and by "language exit rules" to the motor signals as outputs, has no more connection to *trees* than the ant's curve has to Winston Churchill. Once we see that the *qualitative similarity* (amounting, if you like, to qualitative identity) between the thoughts of the brains in a vat and the thoughts of someone in the actual world by no means implies sameness of reference, it is not hard to see that there is no basis at all for regarding the brain in a vat as referring to external things.

The premisses of the argument

I have now given the argument promised to show that the brains in a vat cannot think or say that they are brains in a vat. It remains only to make it explicit and to examine its structure.

By what was just said, when the brain in a vat (in the world where every sentient being is and always was a brain in a vat) thinks "There is a tree in front of me", his thought does not refer to actual trees. On some theories that we shall discuss it might refer to trees in the image, or to the electronic impulses that cause tree experiences, or to the features of the program that are responsible for those electronic impulses. These theories are not ruled out by what was just said, for there is a close causal connection between the use of the word "tree" in vat-English and the presence of trees in the image, the presence of electronic impulses of a certain kind, and the presence of certain features in the machine's program. On these theories the brain is *right*, not *wrong* in thinking "There is a tree in front of me." Given what "tree" refers to in vat-English and what "in front of" refers to, assuming one of these theories is correct, then the truth-conditions for "There is a tree in front of me" when it occurs in vat-English are simply that a tree in the image be "in front of" the "me" in question—in the image—or, perhaps, that the kind of electronic impulse that normally produces this experience be coming from the automatic machinery, or, perhaps, that the feature of the machinery that is supposed to produce the "tree in front of one" experience be operating. And these truth-conditions are certainly fulfilled.

By the same argument, "vat" refers to vats in the image in vat-English, or something related (electronic impulses or program features), but certainly not to real vats, since the use of "vat" in vat-English has no causal connection to real vats (apart from the connection that the brains in a vat wouldn't be able to use the word "vat", if it were not for the presence of one particular vat—the vat they are in; but this connection obtains between the use of *every* word in vat-English and that one particular vat; it is not a special connection between the use of the *particular* word "vat" and vats). Similarly, "nutrient fluid" refers to a liquid in the image in vat-English, or something related (electronic impulses or program features). It follows that if their "possible world" is really the actual one, and we are really the brains in a vat, then what we now mean by "we are brains in a vat" is that *we are brains in a vat in the image* or something of that kind (if we mean anything at all). But part of the hypothesis that we are brains in a vat is that we aren't brains in a vat in the image (i.e. what we are "hallucinating" isn't that we are brains in a vat). So, if we are brains in a vat, then the sentence "We are brains in a vat" says something false (if it says anything). In short, if we are brains in a vat, then "We are brains in a vat" is false. So it is (necessarily) false.

The supposition that such a possibility makes sense arises from a combination of two errors: (1) taking *physical possibility* too seriously; and (2) unconsciously operating with a magical theory of reference, a theory on which certain mental representations necessarily refer to certain external things and kinds of things.

There is a "physically possible world" in which we are brains in a vat—what does this mean except that there is a *description* of such a state of affairs which is compatible with the laws of physics? Just as there is a tendency in our culture (and has been since the seventeenth century) to take *physics* as our metaphysics, that is, to view the exact sciences as the long-sought description of the "true and ultimate furniture of the universe", so there is, as an immediate consequence, a tendency to take "physical possibility" as the very touchstone of what might really actually be the case. Truth is physical truth; possibility physical possibility; and necessity physical necessity, on such a view. But we have just seen, if only in the case of a very contrived example so far, that this view is wrong. The existence of a "physically possible world" in which we are brains in a vat (and always were and will be) does not mean that we might really, actually, possibly *be* brains in a vat. What rules out this possibility is not physics but *philosophy*.

Some philosophers, eager both to assert and minimize the claims of their profession at the same time (the typical state of mind of Anglo-American philosophy in the twentieth century), would say: "Sure. You have shown that some things that seem to be physical possibilities are really *conceptual* impossibilities. What's so surprising about that?"

Well, to be sure, my argument can be described as a "conceptual" one. But to describe philosophical activity as the search for "conceptual" truths makes it all sound like *inquiry about the meaning of words*. And that is not at all what we have been engaging in.

What we have been doing is considering the *preconditions* for *thinking about, representing, referring to*, etc. We have investigated these preconditions *not* by investigating the meaning of these words and phrases (as a linguist might, for example) but by *reasoning a priori*. Not in the old "absolute" sense (since we don't claim that magical theories of reference are *a priori* wrong), but in the sense of inquiring into what is *reasonably* possible *assuming* certain general premisses, or making certain very broad theoretical assumptions. Such a procedure is neither "empirical" nor quite "a priori", but has elements of both ways of investigating. In spite of the fallibility of my procedure, and its dependence upon assumptions which might be described as "empirical" (e.g. the assumption that the mind has no access to external things or properties apart from that provided by the senses), my procedure has a close relation to what Kant called a "transcendental" investigation; for it is an investigation, I repeat, of the *preconditions* of reference and hence of thought—preconditions built in to the nature of our minds themselves, though not (as Kant hoped) wholly independent of empirical assumptions.

One of the premisses of the argument is obvious: that magical theories of reference are wrong, wrong for mental representations and not only for physical ones. The other premiss is that one cannot refer to certain kinds of things, e.g. *trees*, if one has no causal interaction at all with them,[3] or with things in terms of which they can be described. But why should we accept these premisses? Since these constitute the broad framework within which I am arguing, it is time to examine them more closely.

The reasons for denying necessary connections between representations and their referents

I mentioned earlier that some philosophers (most famously, Brentano) have ascribed to the mind a power, "intentionality", which precisely enables it to *refer*. Evidently, I have rejected this as no solution. But what gives me this right? Have I, perhaps, been too hasty?

These philosophers did not claim that we can think about external things or properties without using representations at all. And the argument I gave above comparing visual sense data to the ant's "picture" (the argument via the science fiction story about the "picture" of a tree that came from a paint-splash and that gave rise to sense data qualitatively similar to our "visual images of trees", but unaccompanied by any *concept* of a tree) would be accepted as showing that *images* do not necessarily refer. If there are mental representations that necessarily refer (to external things) they must be of the nature of *concepts* and not of the nature of images. But what are *concepts*?

When we introspect we do not perceive "concepts" flowing through our minds as such. Stop the stream of thought when or where we will, what we catch are words, images, sensations, feelings. When I speak my thoughts out loud I do not think them twice. I hear my words as you do. To be sure it feels different to me when I utter words that I believe and when I utter words I do not believe (but sometimes, when I am nervous, or in front of a hostile audience, it feels as if I am lying when I know I am telling the truth); and it feels different when I utter words I understand and when I utter words I do not understand. But I can imagine without difficulty someone thinking just these words (in the sense of saying them in his mind) and having just the feeling of understanding, asserting, etc., that I do, and realizing a minute later (or on being awakened by a hypnotist) that he did not understand what had just passed through his mind at all, that he did not even understand the language these words are in. I don't claim that this is very likely; I simply mean that there is nothing at all unimaginable about this. And what this shows is not that concepts *are* words (or images, sensations, etc.), but that to attribute a "concept" or a "thought" to someone is quite different from attributing any mental "presentation", any introspectible entity or event, to him. Concepts are not mental presentations that intrinsically refer to external objects for the very decisive reason that they are not mental presentations at all. Concepts are signs used in a certain way; the signs may be public or private, mental entities or physical entities, but even when the signs are "mental" and "private", the sign itself apart from its use is not the concept. And signs do not themselves intrinsically refer.

We can see this by performing a very simple thought experiment. Suppose you are like me and cannot tell an elm tree from a beech tree. We still say that the reference of "elm" in my speech is the same as the reference of "elm" in anyone else's, viz. elm trees, and that the set of all beech trees is the extension of "beech" (i.e. the set of things the word "beech" is truly predicated of) both in your speech and my speech. Is it really credible that the difference between what "elm" refers to and what "beech" refers to is brought about by a difference in our *concepts*? My concept of an elm tree is exactly the same as my concept of a beech tree (I blush to confess). (This shows that the determination of reference is social and not individual, by the way; you and I both defer to experts who *can* tell elms from beeches.) If someone heroically attempts to maintain that the difference between the reference of "elm" and the reference of "beech" in *my* speech is explained by a difference in my psychological state, then let him imagine a Twin Earth where the words are switched. Twin Earth is very much like Earth; in fact, apart from the fact that "elm" and "beech" are interchanged, the reader can suppose Twin Earth is exactly like Earth. Suppose I have a *Doppelganger* on Twin Earth who is molecule for molecule identical with me (in the sense in which two neckties can be "identical"). If you are a dualist, then suppose my *Doppelganger* thinks the same verbalized thoughts I do, has the same sense data, the same dispositions, etc. It is absurd to think his psychological state is one bit different from mine: yet his word "elm" represents *beeches*, and my word "elm" represents elms. (Similarly, if the "water" on Twin Earth is a different liquid—say, XYZ and not H_2O—then "water" represents a different liquid when used on Twin Earth and when used on Earth, etc.) Contrary to a doctrine that has been with us since the seventeenth century, *meanings just aren't in the head*.

We have seen that possessing a concept is not a matter of possessing images (say, of trees – or even images, "visual" or "acoustic", of sentences, or whole discourses, for that matter) since one could possess any system of images you please and not possess the *ability* to use the sentences in situationally appropriate ways (considering both linguistic factors—what has been said before—and non-linguistic factors as determining "situational appropriateness"). A man may have all the images you please, and still be completely at a loss when one says to him "point to a tree", even if a lot of trees are present. He may even have the image of what he is supposed to do, and still not know what he is supposed to do. For the image, if not accompanied by the ability to act in a certain way, is just a *picture*, and acting in accordance with a picture is itself an ability that one may or may not have. (The man might picture himself pointing to a tree, but just for the sake of contemplating something logically possible; himself pointing to a tree after someone has produced the—to him meaningless—sequence of sounds "please point to a tree".) He would still not know that he was supposed to point to a tree, and he would still not *understand* "point to a tree".

I have considered the ability to use certain sentences to be the criterion for possessing a full-blown concept, but this could easily be liberalized. We could allow symbolism consisting of elements which are not words in a natural language, for example, and we could allow such mental phenomena as images and other types of internal events. What is essential is that these should have the same complexity, ability to be combined with each other, etc., as sentences in a natural language. For, although a particular presentation—say, a blue flash—might serve a particular mathematician as the inner expression of the whole proof of the Prime Number Theorem, still there would be no temptation to say this (and it would be false to say this) if that mathematician could not unpack his "blue flash" into separate steps and logical connections. But, no matter what sort of inner phenomena we allow as possible *expressions* of thought, arguments exactly similar to the foregoing will show that it is not the phenomena themselves that constitute understanding, but rather the ability of the thinker to *employ* these phenomena, to produce the right phenomena in the right circumstances.

The foregoing is a very abbreviated version of Wittgenstein's argument in *Philosophical Investigations*. If it is correct, then the attempt to understand thought by what is called "phenomenological" investigation is fundamentally misguided; for what the phenomenologists fail to see is that what they are describing is the inner *expression* of thought, but that the *understanding* of that expression—one's understanding of one's own thoughts— is not an *occurrence* but an *ability*. Our example of a man pretending to think in Japanese (and deceiving a Japanese telepath) already shows the futility of a phenomenological approach to the problem of *understanding*. For even if there is some introspectible quality which is present when and only when one *really* understands (this seems false on introspection, in fact), still that quality is only *correlated* with understanding, and it is still possible that the man fooling the Japanese telepath have that quality too and *still* not understand a word of Japanese.

On the other hand, consider the perfectly possible man who does not have any "interior monologue" at all. He speaks perfectly good English, and if asked what his opinions are on a given subject, he will give them at length. But he never thinks (in words, images, etc.) when he is not speaking out loud; nor does anything "go through his head", except that (of course) he hears his own voice speaking, and has the usual sense impressions from his surroundings, plus a general "feeling of understanding". (Perhaps he is in the habit of talking to himself.) When he types a letter or goes to the store, etc., he is not having an internal "stream of thought"; but his actions are intelligent and purposeful, and if anyone walks up and asks him "What are you doing?" he will give perfectly coherent replies.

This man seems perfectly imaginable. No one would hesitate to say that he was conscious, disliked rock and roll (if he frequently expressed a strong aversion to rock and roll), etc., just because he did not think conscious thoughts except when speaking out loud.

What follows from all this is that (a) no set of mental events— images or more "abstract" mental happenings and qualities— *constitutes* understanding; and (b) no set of mental events is *necessary* for understanding. In particular, *concepts cannot be identical with mental objects of any kind.* For, assuming that by a mental object we mean something introspectible, we have just seen that whatever it is, it may be absent in a man who does understand the appropriate word (and hence has the full blown concept), and present in a man who does not have the concept at all.

Coming back now to our criticism of magical theories of reference (a topic which also concerned Wittgenstein), we see that, on the one hand, those "mental objects" we *can* introspectively detect—words, images, feelings, etc.—do not intrinsically refer any more than the ant's picture does (and for the same reasons), while the attempts to postulate special mental objects, "concepts", which *do* have a necessary connection with their referents, and which only trained phenomenologists can detect, commit a *logical* blunder; for concepts are (at least in part) *abilities* and not occurrences. The doctrine that there are mental presentations which necessarily refer to external things is not only bad natural science; it is also bad phenomenology and conceptual confusion.

Notes

1 In this book the terms "representation" and "reference" always refer to a relation between a word (or other sort of sign, symbol, or representation) and something that actually exists (i.e. not just an "object of thought"). There is a sense of "refer" in which I can "refer" to what does not exist; this is not the sense in which "refer" is used here. An older word for what I call "representation" or "reference" is *denotation*.

Secondly, I follow the custom of modern logicians and use "exist" to mean "exist in the past, present, or future." Thus Winston Churchill "exists," and we can "refer to" or "represent" Winston Churchill, even though he is no longer alive.

2 A.M. Turing, "Computing Machinery and Intelligence," *Mind* 59 (1950): 433–60, reprinted in A.R. Anderson (ed.), *Minds and Machines* (Englewood Cliffs, N.J.: Prentice Hall, 1964).

3 If the Brains in a Vat will have causal connection with, say, trees *in the future*, then perhaps they can *now* refer to trees by the description "the things I will refer

to as ‘trees’ at such-and-such a future time”. But we are to imagine a case in which the Brains in a Vat *never* get out of the vat, and hence *never* get into causal connection with trees, etc.

QUESTIONS

1 What is “intentionality”?
2 When people on Twin Earth say “water,” what are they referring to, according to Putnam?
3 What conclusion is the Twin Earth example supposed to support?
4 Why, according to Putnam, is the brain in the vat unable to refer to brains or vats?

Fred Dretske, "The Pragmatic Dimension of Knowledge"

Knowing that something is so, unlike being wealthy or reasonable, is not a matter of degree. Two people can both be wealthy, yet one be wealthier than the other; both be reasonable, yet one be more reasonable than the other. When talking about people, places and topics (*things* rather than facts), it makes sense to say that one person knows something *better than* another. He knows the city better than we do, knows more Russian history than any of his colleagues, but doesn't know his wife as well as do his friends. But *factual* knowledge, the knowledge *that* something is so, does not admit of such comparisons.[1] If we both know that today is Friday, it makes no sense to say that you know this better than I. A rich man can become richer by acquiring more money, and a person's belief (that today is Saturday, for example) can be made more reasonable by the accumulation of additional evidence, but if a person already knows that today is Friday, there is nothing he can acquire that will make him know it better. Additional evidence will not promote him to a loftier form of knowledge—though it may make him *more certain* of something he already knew. You can boil water beyond its boiling point (e.g., at 300°F) but you are not, thereby, boiling it better. You are simply boiling it at a higher temperature.

In this respect factual knowledge is *absolute*. It is like being pregnant: an all or nothing affair. One person cannot be *more* pregnant, or pregnant *better than* someone else. Those who view knowledge as a form of justified (true) belief typically acknowledge this fact by speaking, not simply of justification, but of *full*, *complete*, or *adequate* justification. Those qualifications on the sort of justification required to know something constitute an admission that knowledge is, whereas justification is not, an absolute idea. For these qualifiers are meant to reflect the fact that there is a certain threshold of justification that must be equalled or exceeded if knowledge is to be obtained, and *equalling or exceeding this threshold* is, of course, an absolute idea. I can have a better justification than you, but my justification cannot be more adequate (more sufficient, more full) than yours. If my justification is complete in the intended sense, then your justification cannot be more complete.

Philosophers who view knowledge as some form of justified true belief are generally reluctant to talk about this implied threshold of justification. Just how

Fred Dretske, "The Pragmatic Dimension of Knowledge," *Philosophical Studies* 40 (1981): 363–78.

much evidence or justification, one wants to ask, is *enough* to qualify as an adequate, a full, or a complete justification? If the level or degree of justification is represented by real numbers between 0 and 1 (indicating the conditional probability of that for which one has evidence or justification), any threshold less than 1 seems arbitrary. Why, for example, should a justification of 0.95 be good enough to know something when a justification of 0.54 is not adequate? And if one can know *P* because one's justification is 0.95 and know *Q* because one's justification is similarly high, is one excluded from knowing *P and Q* because the justification for their joint occurrence has (in accordance with the multiplicative rule in probability theory) dropped below 0.95?

Aside, though, from its arbitrariness, any threshold of justification less than 1 seems to be *too low*. For examples can easily be given in which such thresholds are exceeded without the justification being *good enough* (by ordinary intuitive standards) for knowledge. For example, if the threshold is set at 0.95, one need only think of a bag with 96 white balls and 4 black balls in it. If someone draws a ball at random from this bag, the justification for believing it to be white exceeds the 0.95 threshold. Yet, it seems clear (to me at least) that such a justification (for believing that a white ball has been drawn) is *not* good enough. Someone who happened to draw a white ball, and believed they drew a white ball on the basis of this justification, would not know that they drew a white ball.

Examples such as this suggest (though they do not, of course, prove) that the absolute, non-comparative, character of knowledge derives from the absoluteness, or conclusiveness, of the justification required to know. If I know that the Russians invaded Afghanistan, you can't know this better than I know it because in order to know it I must already have an optimal, or conclusive justification (a justification at the level of 1), and you can't do better than that. I have explored this possibility in other papers, and I do not intend to pursue it here.[2] What I want to develop in this paper is a different theme, one that (I hope) helps to illuminate our concept of knowledge by showing how this absolute idea can, despite its absoluteness, remain sensitive to the shifting interests, concerns and factors influencing its everyday application. In short, I want to explore the way, and the extent to which, this absolute notion exhibits a degree of contextual relativity in its ordinary use.

To do this it will be useful to briefly recapitulate Peter Unger's discussion of absolute concepts.[3] Although he misinterprets its significance, Unger does, I think, locate the important characteristic of this class of concepts. He illustrates the point with the term *flat*. This, he argues, is an absolute term in the sense that a surface is flat only if it is *not at all bumpy or irregular*. Any bumps or irregularities, however small, and insignificant they may be (from a practical point of view), mean that the surface on which they occur is not really flat. It may be *almost* flat, or *very nearly* flat, but (as both these expressions imply) it is not really flat. We do, it seems, compare surfaces with respect to their degree of flatness (e.g., West Texas is flatter than Wisconsin), but Unger argues that this must be understood as a comparison of the degree to which these surfaces approximate flatness. They cannot both be flat and, yet, one be flatter than the other. Hence, if *A* is flatter than *B*, then *B* (perhaps also *A*) is not really flat. Flatness does not admit of degrees although a surface's nearness to being flat does, and it is this latter magnitude that we are comparing when we speak of one surface being flatter than another.

Unger concludes from this analysis that not many things are really flat. For under powerful enough magnification almost any surface will exhibit *some* irregularities. Hence, contrary to what we commonly say (and, presumably, believe), these surfaces are not really flat. When we describe them as being flat, what we say is literally false. Probably *nothing* is really flat. So be it. This, according to Unger, is the price we pay for having absolute concepts.

If knowledge is absolute in this way, then there should be similar objections to its widespread application to everyday situations. Powerful magnification (i.e., critical inquiry) *should*, and with the help of the skeptic *has*, revealed "bumps" and "irregularities" in our evidential posture with respect to most of the things we say we know. There are always, it seems, possibilities that our evidence is powerless to eliminate, possibilities which, until eliminated, block the road to knowledge. For if knowledge, being an absolute concept, requires the elimination of *all* competing possibilities (possibilities that contrast with what is known), then, clearly we seldom, if ever, satisfy the conditions for applying the concept.

This skeptical conclusion is unpalatable to most philosophers. Unger endorses it. Knowledge, according to him, is an absolute concept that, like flatness, has very little application to our bumpy, irregular world.

I have in one respect already indicated my agreement with Unger. Knowledge *is* an absolute concept (I disagree with him, however, about the source of this absoluteness; Unger finds it in the *certainty* required for knowledge; I find it in the *justification* required for knowledge). Unlike Unger, though, I do not derive skeptical conclusions from this fact. I will happily admit that *flat* is an absolute concept, and absolute in roughly the way Unger says it is, but I do not think this shows that nothing is really flat. For although nothing can be flat if it has *any* bumps and irregularities, what *counts* as a bump or irregularity depends on the type of surface being described. Something is empty (another absolute concept according to Unger) if it has nothing in it, but this does not mean that an abandoned warehouse is not really empty because it has light bulbs or molecules in it. Light bulbs and molecules do not count as *things* when determining the emptiness of warehouse. For purposes of determining the emptiness of a warehouse, molecules (dust, light bulbs, etc.) are irrelevant. This isn't to say that, if we changed the way we used warehouses (e.g., if we started using, or trying to use, warehouses as giant vacuum chambers), they *still* wouldn't count. It is only to say that, given the way they are now used, air molecules (dust particles, etc.) don't count.

Similarly, a road can be perfectly flat even though one can *feel* and *see* irregularities in its surface, irregularities which, were they to be found on the surface of, say, a mirror would mean that the mirror's surface was not really flat. Large mice are not large animals and flat roads are not necessarily flat surfaces. The Flat Earth society is certainly an anachronism, but they are not denying the existence of ant hills and gopher holes.

Absolute concepts depict a situation as being completely devoid of a certain sort of thing: *bumps* in the case of flatness and *objects* in the case of emptiness. The fact that there can be *nothing* of this sort present for the concept to be satisfied is what makes it an absolute concept. It is why if *X* is empty, *Y* cannot be emptier. Nonetheless, when it comes to determining what *counts* as a thing of this sort (a bump or an object), and hence what counts against a correct application of the concept, we find the criteria or standards peculiarly spongy and relative. What counts as a thing for assessing the emptiness of my pocket may not count as a thing for assessing the emptiness of a park, a warehouse, or a football stadium. Such concepts, we might say, are *relationally absolute*; absolute, yes, but only relative to a certain standard. We might put the point this way: to be empty is to be *devoid of all relevant things*, thereby exhibiting, simultaneously, the absolute (in the world "all") and relative (in the word "relevant") character of this concept.

If, as I have suggested, knowledge is an absolute concept, we should expect it to exhibit this kind of *relationally* absolute character. This, indeed, is the possibility I mean to explore in this paper. What I propose to do is to use what I have called relationally absolute concepts as a model for understanding knowledge. In accordance with this approach (and in harmony with an earlier suggestion) I propose to think of knowledge as an evidential state in which *all relevant alternatives* (to what is known) *are eliminated*. This makes knowledge an absolute concept but the restriction to *relevant* alternatives makes it, like *empty* and *flat*, applicable to this epistemically bumpy world we live in.

Why do this? What are the advantages? A partial catalog of benefits follows:

(1) A growing number of philosophers are able to find, or so they claim, a pragmatic, social, or communal dimension to knowledge.[4] A variety of examples indicate, or seem to these philosophers to indicate, that knowledge depends, not *just* on the evidential status of the knower vis-à-vis what is known, but on such factors as the general availability, and proximity, of (misleading) counter-evidence, on the sorts of things that are commonly taken for granted by others in the relevant community, on the interests and purposes of speaker (in claiming to know) and listeners (in being told that someone knows), and the importance or significance of *what* is known or someone's knowing it. I, personally, happen to think that most of these examples show nothing of the kind. These factors affect, not *whether* something is known, but whether it is reasonable to *say* you know or to *think* you know. But, for the moment, I do not want to argue the point. I merely wish to point out that in so far as knowledge *is* a function of such pragmatic, social or communal factors, the present approach to its analysis can absorb this relativity without compromising the absoluteness of knowledge itself. The social or pragmatic dimension to knowledge, if it exists at all, has to do with what *counts* as a relevant alternative, a possibility that must be evidentially excluded, in order to have knowledge. It does not change the fact that to know one must be in a position to exclude *all* such possibilities. It does not alter the fact that one must have, in this sense, an optimal justification—one that eliminates every (relevant) possibility of being mistaken.

(2) Secondly, this approach to the analysis of knowledge helps to avoid the proliferation of *senses* that sometimes threatens to engulf epistemological discussions. We don't have different senses of the verb "to know"—a strong sense here, a weak sense there—but *one* sense with different applications. We don't have two senses of the word "empty"—one for pockets and one for warehouses. We have one sense (or meaning) with a difference in what counts as a thing.

(3) Thirdly, we get a better perspective from which to understand the

persisting and undiminished appeal of skeptical arguments. Most philosophers have experienced the futility of trying to convince a devoted skeptic, or just a newly converted freshman, that we *do* know there are tables and chairs *despite* the possibility of dreams, hallucinations, cunning demons and diabolical scientists who might be toying with our brain on Alpha Centuri (Nozick's example). Somehow, in the end, we seem reduced to shrugging our shoulders and saying that there are certain possibilities that are just too remote to worry about. Our evidence isn't good enough to eliminate these wilder hypotheses because, of course, these wild hypotheses are carefully manufactured so as to *neutralize* our evidence. But dismissing such hypotheses as too remote to worry about, as too fanciful to have any impact on our ordinary use of the verb "to know," is merely another way of saying that for purposes of assessing someone's knowledge that this is a table, certain alternative possibilities are simply not relevant. We are doing the same thing (or so I submit) as one who dismisses chalk dust as irrelevant, or too insignificant, to worry about in describing a classroom as empty. What it is important to realize, especially in arguments with the skeptic, is that the impatient dismissal of his fanciful hypotheses is not (as he will be quick to suggest) a mere *practical* intolerance, and refusal to confront, decisive objections to our ordinary way of talking. It is, rather, a half conscious attempt to exhibit the *relationally* absolute character of our cognitive concepts.

(4) Finally, this approach to the analysis of knowledge gives us the kind of machinery we need to handle the otherwise puzzling examples that are becoming more frequent in the epistemological literature. Consider yet one more example (one *more* because this one, I think, combines elements of several of the more familiar examples). An amateur bird watcher spots a duck on his favorite Wisconsin pond. He quickly notes its familiar silhouette and markings and makes a mental note to tell his friends that he saw a Gadwall, a rather unusual bird in that part of the midwest. Since the Gadwall has a distinctive set of markings (black rump, white patch on the hind edge of the wing, etc.), markings that no other North American duck exhibits, and these markings were all perfectly visible, it seems reasonable enough to say that the bird-watcher *knows* that yonder bird is a Gadwall. He can see that it is.

Nevertheless, a concerned ornithologist is poking around in the vicinity, not far from where our bird-watcher spotted his Gadwall, looking for some trace of Siberian Grebes. Grebes are duck-like water birds, and the Siberian version of this creature is, when it is in the water, very hard to distinguish from a Gadwall duck. Accurate identification requires seeing the birds in flight since the Gadwall has a white belly and the Grebe a red belly—features that are not visible when the birds are in the water. The ornithologist has a hypothesis that some Siberian Grebes have been migrating to the midwest from their home in Siberia, and he and his research assistants are combing the midwest in search of confirmation.

Once we embellish our simple story in this way, intuitions start to diverge on whether our amateur bird-watcher does indeed know that yonder bird is a Gadwall duck (we are assuming, of course, that it *is* a Gadwall). Most people (I assume) would say that he did *not* know the bird to be a Gadwall if there actually were Siberian Grebes in the vicinity. It certainly sounds strange to suppose that he could give assurances to the ornithologist that the bird he saw was *not* a Siberian Grebe (since he knew it to be a Gadwall duck). But what if the ornithologist's suspicions are unfounded. None of the Grebes have migrated. Does the bird-watcher still not know what he takes himself to know. Is, then, the simple presence of an ornithologist, with his false hypothesis, enough to rob the bird-watcher of his knowledge that the bird on the pond is a Gadwall duck? What if we suppose that the Siberian Grebes, because of certain geographical barriers, *cannot* migrate. Or suppose that there really are no Siberian Grebes—the existence of such a bird being a delusion of a crackpot ornithologist. We may even suppose that, in addition to there being no grebes, there is no ornithologist of the sort I described, but that people in the area believe that there is. Or *some* people believe that there is. Or the bird-watcher's *wife* believes that there is and, as a result, expresses skepticism about his claim to know that what he saw was a Gadwall duck. Or, finally, though no one believes any of this, some of the locals are interested in whether or not our birdwatcher *knows* that there are no look-alike migrant grebes in the area.

Somewhere in this progression philosophers, most of them anyway, will dig in their heels and say that the bird-watcher really *does* know that the bird he sees is a Gadwall, and that he knows this despite his inability to justifiably rule out certain alternative possibilities. For example, if there are no look-alike grebes and no ornithologist of the sort I described, but the bird-watcher's wife believes that there are (a rumour she heard from her hairdresser), this does not rob him of his knowledge that the bird he saw as a Gadwall. He needn't be able to rule out the possibility that there are, somewhere in the world, look-alike grebes that have migrated to the midwest in order to know that the bird he saw was a Gadwall duck. These other possibilities are (whether the bird-watcher realizes it or not) simply too remote.

Most philosophers will dig in their heels here because they realize that if they don't, they are on the slippery slope to skepticism with nothing left to hang onto. If false rumours about look-alike grebes and ornithologists can rob an expert bird-watcher of his knowledge that a bird seen in good light, and under ideal conditions, is a Gadwall duck, then similarly false rumours, suspicions or even conjectures about deceptive demons or possible tricks will rob everyone of almost everything they know. One of the ways to prevent this slide into skepticism is to acknowledge that although knowledge requires the evidential elimination of all relevant alternatives (to what is known), there is a shifting, variable set of relevant alternatives. It may be that our bird-watcher does know the bird is a Gadwall under normal conditions (because look-alike grebes are not a relevant alternative), but does not know this if there is a suspicion, however ill-founded it may be, that there exist look-alike grebes within migrating range. This will (or should) be no more unusual than acknowledging the fact that a refrigerator could truly be described as empty to a person looking for something to eat, but *not* truly described as empty to a person looking for spare refrigerator parts. In the first case "empty" implies having no food in it; in the second it implies having no shelves, brackets and hardware in it.

These, then, are some of the advantages to be derived from this approach to the analysis of knowledge. They are, however, advantages that can only be harvested if certain questions can be given reasonable answers: in particular (a) what makes a possibility relevant? (b) If, in order to know, one must rule out all relevant alternatives, how is this "elimination" to be understood? What does it take, evidentially, to "rule out" an alternative? (c) Is it possible, as this type of analysis suggests, for one to know something at one time and, later, not know it (due to the introduction of another relevant alternative) without forgetting it? (c) Can one make it easier to know things by remaining ignorant of what are, for others, relevant possibilities?

These, and many more questions, need answers if this framework for the analysis of knowledge is to be anything more than suggestive. Since I cannot here (or anywhere else, for that matter) provide answers to all these questions, I will try, in the time remaining, to fill in some of the large gaps.

Call the *Contrasting Set* (*CS*) the class of situations that are necessarily eliminated by what is known to be the case. That is, if *S* knows that *P*, then *Q* is in the *CS* (of *P*) if and only if, given *P*, necessarily not-*Q*. In our bird-watcher's example, the bird's being a Siberian Grebe (or any kind of grebe at all) is in the *CS* of our bird-watcher's knowledge, or putative knowledge, that it is a Gadwall duck. So is its being an elephant, a hummingbird, a holographic image, or a figment of his imagination. Furthermore, let us call the set of possible alternatives that a person must be in an evidential position to exclude (when he knows that *P*) the *Relevancy Set* (*RS*). In saying that he must be in a position to exclude these possibilities I mean that his evidence or justification for thinking these alternatives are *not* the case must be good enough to say he *knows* they are not the case. Items in the *CS* that are not in the *RS* I shall call irrelevant alternatives. These are items which, though their existence is incompatible with what is known to be the case, the knower *need not* (though he may) have a justification for thinking do not exist. Under normal conditions (the kind of conditions that I assume prevail in the world today) the possibility of something's being a look-alike grebe, though it is a member of the contrasting set, is not a member of the relevancy set of a bird-watcher's knowledge that what he sees is a Gadwall duck (in the kind of circumstances I described).[5] On the other hand, its being an eagle, a Mallard, or a Loon *are* members of the relevancy set since if the bird watcher could not eliminate these possibilities (sufficient unto knowing that it was not an eagle, a Mallard or a loon) on the basis of the bird's appearance and behavior, then he would not know that it was a Gadwall.

What we are suggesting here is that the *RS* is always a proper subset of the *CS* and, moreover, may not be the same *RS* from situation to situation even though what is known remains the same. The situation can be diagrammed as follows:

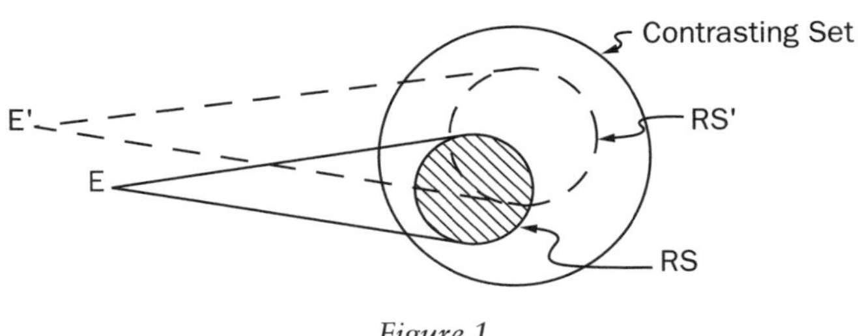

Figure 1

The solid lines indicate a *RS* and the corresponding piece of evidence that would be required to know with this *RS*. With a different *RS* (*RS′*), indicated by dotted lines, different evidence would be required. If Siberian Grebes are in the Relevancy Set, then additional, more elaborate, evidence is required to know that yonder bird is a Gadwall than in the normal situation. Since the bellies are of different color, one might, for example, be able to tell that it was a Gadwall by watching it in flight. The point, however, is that something more would be needed than was available in the original, normal situation.

In terms of this kind of diagram, a skeptic could be represented as one who took *RS* = *CS* in all cases. One's evidence must be comprehensive enough to eliminate all contrasting possibilities—there being no irrelevant alternatives.

Once the mistake is made of identifying *RS* with *CS* the pressure (on non-skeptics) for lowering the standards of justification (requisite for knowing) becomes irresistible. For if in order to know that *P* one must be justified in rejecting *all* members of the *CS* (not just all members of the *RS*), then one can no longer expect very impressive levels of justification for what people know to be the case. If the evidence our bird watcher has for believing the bird to be a Gadwall duck (wing markings, etc.) is also supposed to justify the proposition that it is *not* a look-alike grebe, then, obviously, the justification is nowhere near conclusive. What some philosophers seem inclined to conclude from this is that knowledge does not require conclusive evidence. The reasoning is simple: the bird-watcher knows it is a Gadwall; he doesn't have conclusive reasons (he can't exclude the possibility that it is a look-alike grebe); therefore knowledge does not require conclusive reasons. But this, I submit, is a fallacy, a misunderstanding of what needs to be conclusively excluded in order to know. Such reasoning is analogous to arguing that to be empty an object can have a few hundred things in it, and to conclude this on the basis of the undeniable fact that empty classrooms, warehouses, and buildings generally have at least a hundred things in them.

But what determines the membership of a relevancy set? A relevancy set, you will recall, is a set of situations each member of which contrasts with what is known to be the case, and must be evidentially excluded if one is to know. Are there criteria for membership in this set? I'm now going to stick my neck out by saying what some of the considerations are that determine the membership of these sets. I do not expect much agreement.

(1) The first point has to do with the way we use contrastive focusing to indicate the range of relevant alternatives. I have discussed this phenomenon in another place, so let me give just one example to illustrate the sort of thing I have in mind.[6] Someone claiming to know that Clyde *sold* his typewriter to Alex is not (necessarily) claiming the same thing as one who claims to know that Clyde sold his typewriter *to Alex*. The sentence we use to express what they know is the same, of course, but they reflect, and are designed to reflect, different relevancy sets. A person who knows that Clyde *sold* his typewriter to Alex must be able to rule out the possibility that he *gave* it to him, or that he *loaned* it to him, or (perhaps) that he merely *pretended* to sell it to him. But he needs only a nominal justification, if he needs any justification at all, for thinking it was Alex to whom he sold it. He has to be right about its *being* Alex, of course, but he isn't claiming to have any special justification for thinking it was Alex rather than, say, his twin brother Albert. On the other hand, the person who knows that Clyde sold his typewriter *to Alex* is claiming to know that it wasn't Albert and is, therefore, expected to be in possession of evidence bearing on the identity of the recipient.

But, in this second case, the knower needs only a nominal justification for the belief that Clyde *sold* him the typewriter rather than, say, loaned it to him. He certainly needn't be able to exclude the possibility that the entire transaction was a sham designed to fool the IRS.

(2) A second point, related to the first, is the way the subject term chosen to give verbal expression to what is known often functions to restrict the range of relevant alternatives.[7] Once again, an example will have to suffice. If I say that I could tell that your sister was amused by my funny story, I do not thereby claim to know that she is really your sister, really a human being (rather than a cleverly contrived robot), or really the sort of creature that could experience amusement. These possibilities, though certainly relevant to the truth of what I say in the sense that if they were realized I would not know what I say I know are not possibilities that I need be in an evidential position to exclude to know that your sister was amused by my joke. I was, as it were, *taking it for granted* that she was your sister (hence, a human being, a creature that could experience amusement), and I was claiming to know something about the thing so referred to. On the other hand, if I said that I could tell that the object in the corner (that happened to be your sister) was amused by my funny story, the possibility that it is a robot becomes a relevant alternative, one that I am (by this choice of words) accepting epistemic responsibility for excluding.

(3) Thirdly, in saying that we know we often reveal, either directly or indirectly, *how* we know. I could *see* that the tire was flat, could tell (by the way they *behaved*) that they were in love, *heard* them making plans to go, learned (from the *newspapers*) that the auto workers went out on strike, and used *my pocket calculator* to get the answer. The *way* we come to know, the channel (so to speak) over which we obtain our information, is, I submit, always the locus of irrelevant alternatives. Others can challenge the reliability of this channel (our visual system, our auditory system, the newspapers, the pocket calculator), and if it turns out unreliable in some way they will thereby have discredited our claim to knowledge. But others cannot discredit our claim to knowledge merely by pointing out that the channel over which we received our information *could be* unreliable or that we do not *know* it to be reliable. Possible malfunctions in the channel over which we receive information (combined with a resulting false message) are members of the contrasting set but they are not members of the relevancy set. To say that one can see, by the newspapers, that the auto workers are going on strike is to advance a knowledge claim (that the auto workers are going on strike) on the *assumption* of the newspapers reliability. *If* the newspapers *are* a reliable source of such information, then the claimant does know what he says he knows, and he knows it in the way he says he knows it. One cannot undermine this claim by raising possibilities about deceptive newspaper stories or arguing that the claimant does not know that the newspapers, or this newspaper, is reliable. He never said he did know this. What he did say is that he knew the auto workers were going out on strike while simultaneously disclosing what he was taking for granted which, *if true*, allowed him to know this.

I take the same to be true about our sensory systems when we come to know something by seeing, hearing, tasting and touching. This is the function of our frequent indications (when advancing a knowledge claim) of the manner in which we came to know. We are, by this device, tipping off our listeners, helping them to identify which possibilities are irrelevant to what we are claiming to know.

(4) Fourthly, some people, I am sure, would insist that a pertinent factor influencing the size and membership of the relevancy set is the importance (for speaker and listeners) of what is known or of someone's knowing it. There is a difference between driving by a string of gasoline stations and driving in the middle of the desert. Running out of gas in the first case may be merely an inconvenience; in the latter case it may be a matter of life and death. This makes a difference between knowing (by glancing at your fuel gauge) that you still have some gas in your tank. The implications of being wrong in these two cases are much different—*so* different (some would claim) that additional precautions must be taken (to rule out certain possibilities) in the second case if one is to *know* that one still has some gasoline. And there is even a bigger difference between these cases and knowing that the coolant liquid surrounding the reactor on Three Mile Island is at a safe level by glancing at a similar kind of gauge. The fuel gauge (and associated mechanism) that suffices for knowing that you still have some gasoline (when driving in the city) is just not good enough for knowing that there is sufficient liquid coolant surrounding the reactor. This somewhat paradoxical fact (the fact, namely, that a particular instrument should be good enough to give knowledge in one place, not good enough in another) is to be explained, some would say, by the fact that as the stakes go up, the stakes associated with being right about what one purports to know, so does the size of the relevancy set. There are *more* possibilities that must be eliminated in the nuclear power plant than must be eliminated in the automobile. In particular, a malfunction in the instrument itself must be guarded against in the dangerous situation. If it isn't, one doesn't know.

There is, I admit, some appeal to this point, but I think it mistaken. I see no reason why a standard automobile gauge, transplanted from the automobile to the nuclear power plant, functioning as the *only* indicator of coolant level, should not, assuming it continues to function reliably (as reliably as it did in the automobile), be able to do precisely what the more expensive instruments do—*viz.*, tell the operators that the coolant is at a safe level. I admit that the operators *should not* rely on a single gauge, and certainly not one manufactured under such casual quality control, but if they *do* rely on it, I don't see any basis for denying that they know. They should be nervous, but this nervousness is not to be explained by their failure to know what the coolant level is, but by their uncertainty as to when (due to gauge malfunction) they *stop* knowing it.

(5) Finally, we come to the difficult question, the question of when an alternative (not otherwise excluded as irrelevant by one of the considerations already discussed) is just *too remote* to qualify as relevant. In the case of our bird-watcher, some philosophers, thinking to turn the tables on the skeptic (by drastically diminishing the relevance set), have suggested that an alternative only becomes relevant when there are positive reasons for thinking it is, or may be, realized. Doubt can also be irrational, and if there are no reasons to doubt, mere possibilities are irrelevant to whether what is believed is known.

This, obviously, is an over-reaction. The Wisconsin lakes could be loaded with migrant Siberian Grebes without the bird watcher having any reason to think that such look-alike birds actually existed. His lack of any reason to doubt, his ignorance of the possibility that what he sees is a grebe and not a Gadwall, is irrelevant. The mere possibility is in this case enough to show he doesn't know.

This shows that having a reason (evidence) to think *X* is a genuine possibility is not a necessary condition for *X*'s being a relevant alternative. Perhaps, though, it is sufficient. Perhaps, that is, a reasonable (justified) belief that yonder bird *might* be a look-alike grebe (whether or not this belief is true) is enough to make its being a look-alike grebe a relevant possibility.

But if a person really does believe that the bird could be a grebe, aside from the question of whether or not this belief is reasonable, he surely fails to have the kind of belief requisite to knowing it is a Gadwell. He certainly doesn't think he knows it is a Gadwall. I do not know exactly how to express the belief condition on knowledge, but it seems to me that anyone who believes (reasonably or not) that he *might* be wrong fails to meet it.[8] And so the present suggestion is irrelevant to our problem. It describes conditions in which the subject fails to know but only by robbing him of the belief requisite to knowledge.

It may be thought that the mere presence of evidence that one might be wrong, assuming this evidence does not affect one's willingness to believe, is enough to make the respect in which one (according to this evidence) might be wrong a relevant alternative. This has the unfortunate consequence that one can rob a person, indeed a whole community, of its knowledge by spreading a false rumour. I can, for example, tell the bird-watcher that I just met an ornithologist looking for migrant grebes. Once this message is relayed to the bird watcher, even if he rejects it as a silly fabrication, he no longer knows that the bird he saw was a Gadwall duck. And, as a consequence, the whole community is robbed of its knowledge that their local pond was visited by a rather rare bird (a Gadwall duck). The mere fact that I have given them a reason to think that the bird could be a look-alike grebe,[9] whether or not they accept this as a reason, implies that, lacking evidence that it was not a grebe, they do not know it was a Gadwall.

Without dragging the dialectic out any longer, let me simply say what such considerations suggest to me. They suggest that the difference between a relevant and an irrelevant alternative resides, not in what we happen to *regard* as a real possibility (whether reasonably or not), but in the kind of possibilities that actually exist in the objective situation. Whether or not our bird watcher knows that the bird he sees is a Gadwall depends on whether or not, in some objective sense, it could be a look-alike grebe (or any other similar looking creature). If, as a matter of fact, there are no look-alike grebes, that settles the matter. He knows it is a Gadwall. If there are grebes, but due to certain geographical barriers, they are confined to their Siberian habitat, then, once again, the possibility of the bird's being a grebe, though remaining a logical possibility, is not a relevant possibility. They, the grebes, cannot migrate to the midwest.

If, however, there are grebes, and they can migrate, but just have not done so, the case becomes more ambiguous. I think, however, that we now have a genuine possibility, a relevant alternative. By hypothesis the bird-watcher does not know it is not a migrant grebe, and however improbable this possibility may be, there is nothing the bird watcher has (either in the look of the bird or in general background information) that excludes the possibility that what he is looking at is a migrant grebe. He does not, therefore, know it to be a Gadwall. He will, no doubt, say he knows. And everyone else may agree and, as a result, think *they* know (having been told by someone who knows): But the truth lies elsewhere. It is, I suggest, tantamount to saying that the bottle is empty when there is a drop left. No one is going to quarrel with this description since all the relevant implications (e.g., we can't make another martini) are true. But the claim itself is false.

Notes

1 I know we sometimes say things that suggest a comparison of this sort (e.g., No one knows better than I that there are a lot of mosquitos in the Northwest Territories), but I take such constructions to be describing, not better knowledge, but more direct, more compelling, kinds of evidence.

2 "Conclusive Reasons," *Australasian Journal of Philosophy* 49 (1971): 1–22; and *Seeing and Knowing* (Chicago: University of Chicago Press, 1969).

3 Peter Unger, "A Defense of Skepticism," *Philosophical Review* 80 (1971): 198–219.

4 I have in mind Harman's discussion in *Thought* (Princeton, N.J.: Princeton University Press, 1973) of evidence one does not possess; Goldman's barn example in "Discrimination and Perceptual Knowledge," *Journal of Philosophy* 73 (1976): 771–91; the sorts of examples appearing in various defeasibility analyses of knowledge (see Keith Lehrer and Thomas Paxson, Jr., "Knowledge: Undefeated Justified True Belief," *Journal of Philosophy* 66 (1969): 225–37; and Peter Klein, "A Proposed Definition of Propositional Knowledge," *Journal of Philosophy* 68 (1971): 471–82); Ernest Sosa's recommendation (in "The Concept of Knowledge: How Do You Know?", *American Philosophical Quarterly* 11 (1974): 113–22) that we must depart from the traditional conception of knowledge by putting in relief the relativity of knowledge to an epistemic community (p. 117); and David Annis' "A Contextualist Theory of Epistemic Justification," *American Philosophical Quarterly* 15 (1978): 213–19, in which the basic model of justification (and, presumably, of knowledge) revolves around a person's being able to meet certain objections. The trend here, if this is a trend, seems to be toward the kind of relativity espoused by Thomas Kuhn in his *The Structure of Scientific Revolutions* (Chicago: University of Chicago Press, 1962).

5 Though there are grebes, and some of them look like ducks, there are (to the best of my knowledge) no Siberian Grebes that look like Gadwall ducks. This part of my story was pure invention.

6 In "Contrastive Statements," *Philosophical Review* 81 (1972): 411–37.

7 I tried to describe the way this works with perceptual claims in *Seeing and Knowing*, pp. 93–112.

8 We needn't suppose that for *S* to know that *P*, *S* must believe that he can't be wrong. But it does seem reasonable to insist that if S knows that *P*, he does not believe that he might be wrong. In other words, if the bird-watcher really believes that the bird he sees might be a grebe, then he does not know it is a Gadwall.

9 I assume here that my saying. "There is an ornithologist in the area looking for migrant grebes, a species that looks very much like a Gadwall duck" is *prima facie* evidence that there *is* an ornothologist in the area looking for migrant grebes. If the bird-watcher ignores me (as we are assuming he does), he

nonetheless has been given evidence that the bird he saw might have been a grebe.

QUESTIONS

1 In what way, according to Dretske, is the term "flat" similar to "knows"?
2 According to Dretske, what absolute requirement must one satisfy in order to have knowledge?
3 According to Dretske, why are skeptical hypotheses not "relevant"?

Peter Klein, "Skepticism and Closure: Why the Evil Genius Argument Fails"[1]

Introduction

Skepticism is the view that we lack knowledge in areas commonly thought to be within our ken.[2] One of the most powerful arguments for skepticism employs the Closure Principle and it can be traced at least to Cicero and, later, to Descartes.[3] The purpose of this paper is to show that the Closure Principle cannot be used to motivate skepticism, for *either* the principle is false *or* if the principle is true, the argument for skepticism employing it must, of necessity, beg the question.

Here is a standard argument for skepticism employing the Closure Principle:

1. If a person, *S*, is justified in believing that there is a table before her, then *S* is justified in believing that she is not in one of the skeptical scenarios in which there is no table but it appears just as though there were one.[4]
2. *S* is never justified in believing that she is not in one of the skeptical scenarios in which there is no table but it appears just as though there were one.

Therefore, *S* is never justified in believing that there is a table before her.

This argument for skepticism (from now on called the "main argument") is powerful for at least four reasons: (1) If we are never justified in believing such simple, straightforward, and basic propositions like *there is a table before me*, then hardly any proposition could be justified; and (2) even if (on some accounts) knowledge does not entail justification, it seems almost as disturbing to accede to the conclusion that we are never justified in believing that there is a table before us as it would be to acquiesce to the conclusion that we fail to know such things; and (3) the argument is valid and appears, at least initially, to be sound; and (4) the range of skeptical scenarios can vary from the mundane and local (e.g., normal cases of misperception considered so important by the Pyrrhonians) to the extraordinary and global (e.g., evil demon cases considered so important by the Cartesians).

Peter Klein, "Skepticism and Closure: Why the Evil Genius Argument Fails," *Philosophical Topics* (1995): 213–36.

Nevertheless, I believe that the main argument for skepticism is useless to the skeptic. Many will agree. But they will do so because they think that premise 1 which appeals to an instantiation of the Closure Principle is false; and they have given what seem to be plausible objections to it. I will present an argument for the Closure Principle that avoids those objections and show that *only* an argument of this sort avoids those objections.[5] Nevertheless, the *very reason* why the Closure Principle is true, if indeed it is true, renders the principle useless in motivating skepticism. For in order to vouchsafe the Closure Principle employed in premise 1 in the main argument against various objections, the skeptic must embrace a particular account of internally situated grounds for justified beliefs which is such that there will be no way for the skeptic to argue for premise 2 in the main argument for skepticism without begging the question. In short, the skeptic faces a dilemma: Either the first premise of the main argument cannot be defended or the main argument begs the question.

One cautionary note: My argument does not show that skepticism is incorrect.[6] It merely shows that the family of arguments employing the Closure Principle cannot be used to motivate skepticism. Nevertheless, these arguments constitute a principal weapon, if not *the* principal weapon, in the arsenal developed by the skeptic and, if they can be shown to be worthless, some significant progress will have been made in assessing the power of skepticism.

This paper has three main parts. Part 1 is designed to clarify the Closure Principle and to suggest a possible defense of it based upon internally situated grounds for justified beliefs. In part 2, I argue that *only* a defense of the Closure Principle like the one employed in part 1 can safeguard the Closure Principle against otherwise sound objections. Part 3 is designed to show that, given the requisite type of defense of the Closure Principle, the skeptic is forced to provide an argument for premise 2 of the main argument that is sufficient, by itself, to demonstrate the conclusions of the main argument without employing *either* of the premises of the main argument. In other words, if the Closure Principle is true, the main argument for skepticism begs the question.

Part 1: How might the Closure Principle be defended?

In this part, I want to clarify the Closure Principle and suggest a defense of it. It is *not* crucial for this paper that the proposed defense is adequate or, for that matter, even plausible. What will be crucial to show in part 2 is that without the kind of defense suggested in part 1, the Closure Principle is vulnerable to otherwise sound objections.

Let me begin by noting that premise 1 in the main argument for skepticism does not actually employ a general principle. It simply claims that if *S* is justified in believing a particular proposition (there is a table before her), then *S* is justified in believing another proposition (*S* is not in a skeptical scenario in which there only appears to be a table). But presumably the main argument is only one of many arguments employing an instantiation of a general principle of justification. That is, the main argument is not employed by the skeptic merely to show that we fail to have knowledge about tables! By parity of reasoning, the skeptic also believes that it can be shown that we lack knowledge of trees, our hands, fish, rainbows, etc. In fact, the skeptic takes the first premise to be an instantiation of a general principle roughly like this:

> **(x)(y)[If *S* is justified in believing that x, and x entails y, then *S* is justified in believing that y].**

As stated, the general principle is clearly false. Every necessary truth is entailed by every proposition. But one surely does not want to claim that *S* is justified in believing every necessary truth simply because *S* is justified in believing some randomly chosen proposition. In addition, some entailments might be beyond *S*'s capacity to grasp. Finally, there might even be some contingent propositions that are beyond *S*'s capacity to grasp that are entailed by some propositions that *S* does, indeed, grasp. So, let us simply stipulate that the domain of the propositions in the generalization includes only contingent propositions that are within *S*'s capacity to grasp and that the entailment is "obvious" to *S*. Typically, the skeptical scenarios are posited in such a way as to render it obvious that our ordinary beliefs are false in those scenarios, and it is taken to be a contingent claim that *S* is in the actual circumstances as described in the antecedent and not in the posited skeptical scenario in the consequent. Thus, the stipulated restrictions are in line with the use made of the Closure Principle by the skeptic.

Before suggesting a possible defense of the Closure Principle, one other crucial point must be noted in order to clarify it and its role in the main argument for skepticism. *S*'s being justified in believing a proposition, say p, does *not* entail that *S* actually believes that p. What is meant is that *S has an adequate source of justification for p*. *S* may fail to believe that p because, for example, *S* is epistemically timid or because *S* simply fails to recognize the adequate source of justification. The main argument could have been stated by using "*S* has an adequate source of justification for believing . . ." in place of "*S* is justified in believing . . ." as in the following:

> **(x)(y)[If *S* has an adequate source of justification for believing that x, and x entails y, then *S* has an adequate source of justification for believing that y].**

Although this way of stating the principle would have underscored what I take to be the issue at stake—namely, the adequacy of the sources of justification for beliefs—it is not the standard way of formulating it. I chose the standard way in order to make clear that I intend to be discussing the merits of the principle as it is usually understood.

The crucial point to note is that the main argument for skepticism, if successful, concludes that *S* never has an adequate source of justification for those propositions that we typically think are most evident. Clearly then, in order to assess the validity of the Closure Principle, we must examine the potential sources of justification.

We can conveniently divide the sources of justification into two mutually exclusive and jointly exhaustive types. One source is what I will call "externally situated evidence"—that is, features of the world other than the contents of *S*'s actual beliefs and *S*'s justified beliefs. During a murder investigation, the discovery of fingerprints, eyewitness testimony, letters, and traces of gunpowder may lead a detective to justifiably accuse someone of the crime. These are examples of *externally situated evidence*.

On the other hand, the contents of a person's actual beliefs and justified beliefs can serve as an adequate source of justification for further beliefs. When the detective "puts two and two together" as, for example, when the detective recognizes the consequence of her belief that the murderer's fingerprints match those of a suspect, she may be led to justiably believe the suspect is the murderer. Such potential sources of justification are *internally situated reasons*.[7] Finally, it is possible that a belief could be added, legitimately, to the corpus of justified beliefs on a "mixed" basis, that is based on both sources of justification, i.e., *internally situated reasons* and *externally situated evidence*. For example, by inspecting our current justified beliefs, we could uncover *internally situated reasons* which are such that we justifiably come to believe that only two people remain plausible suspects in the murder case and, then, discover *externally situated evidence* in order justifiably to narrow the list of plausible suspects to only one person. What is provided in answering the question "What justifies *S* in believing that *x*?" determines whether the source is purely external, purely internal, or mixed.

In order to avoid some possible misreadings of my position, it is important to note that as I am using the terms "external" and "internal" (and related terms such as "internalist" and "externalist") they do not refer to general theories of knowledge or justification, namely, what are commonly referred to as "externalism" and "internalism."[8] Rather, as I use these terms, they merely refer to potential *sources* of justification. Some *general* theories of justification (for example, some forms of reliabilism) would hold that a belief is justified just in case it arose in a reliable way; and included among those reliable ways could be various processes of inference, Hence, an adequate *source* of justification endorsed by a *general* externalistic theory of justification would be "internally situated reasons" in my sense.

Now, of course, it is true that some general externalist theories of knowledge eschew the use of "justification" or "justified beliefs" because those terms have such a deontic ring to them.[9] But that causes no real problem here since the entire discussion could be recast using other epistemic terms in place of "justification." For example, the Closure Principle (with the restrictions mentioned above concerning the range of the variables and the obviousness of the entailment) could be recast in many ways, including:

(*x*)(*y*)[If *S* knows that *x*, and *x* entails *y*, then *S* knows that *y*].[10]

Of course, suitable revisions in the main argument for skepticism would have to be made by substituting "knows" (or some linguistic variant) for "is justified in believing." The point I wish to emphasize here is that externalist theories of the *sources* of epistemically acceptable beliefs look to features of the world beyond *S*'s actual beliefs and *S*'s justified beliefs in order to determine whether *S* can expand the corpus of beliefs that are suitable candidates for knowledge.[11] It does not matter whether the term "justification" is employed. What matters is whether it is claimed that the only sources of epistemically acceptable beliefs are external to *S*'s actual beliefs and *S*'s justified beliefs.

Theories about internally situated sources of justified beliefs, on the other hand, focus on the propositions that *S* already believes and those justified for *S* in order to determine whether a new belief can be added to the corpus of beliefs that are suitable candidates for knowledge. A question that typifies such theories is this: In what ways is an epistemic agent justified in expanding her corpus of justified beliefs based on *S*'s actual beliefs and those already justified for *S*?[12]

It is important to note that an internalist with regard to the sources of justification can appeal to *S*'s *justified* beliefs, as well as to *S*'s *actual* beliefs, in order to determine when, if ever, there is an adequate source of justification for a further belief.[13] That the internalist can do so follows from a point mentioned earlier, namely that *S* can be *justified* in believing a proposition without actually believing it. In assessing the Closure Principle, the question *is* whether it is necessary that *S* has an adequate source of justification for a proposition, *q*, whenever *S* has an adequate source of justification for a proposition, *p*, which entails *q*. The question is *not* whether it is necessary that *S* has an adequate source of justification for *q* whenever *S believes* that *p*, and *p* entails *q*. Put another way, the antecedent in the Closure Principle refers to propositions which *S* is justified in believing, not to propositions that *S* believes.

Consider a particular internalist question: If *S* is justified in believing that *p* and *S* is justified in believing that *q*, does *S* (necessarily) have adequate internally situated reasons for being justified in believing that (*p* & *q*)? The answer might seem to be "obviously yes," until it is recognized that, depending upon the probabilities assigned to *p* and to *q* and the method of calculating the probability of a conjunction, the threshold for justification required for each conjunct might be reached without reaching the threshold for the conjunction. (Of course, in some cases, that threshold could be reached and, consequently, the conjunction could be justified.) I might note, in passing, that this fact does not provide *any* evidence against the Closure Principle since that principle concerns the transmission of justification from *one* proposition to another through entailment; it does not concern the transmission of justification from *sets* of justified propositions containing more than one member to another proposition entailed by the set.[14]

This is not the place to discuss the merits of the external, internal, or mixed accounts of the sources of justification. Indeed, they may not be genuine rival theories about the sources of justified beliefs at all. For it seems plausible to suggest that all three types of sources of justification are required in order to have an adequate account of justified beliefs. In addition, for the purposes of this paper it can even be granted that there is no pure form of external source of justification because so-called "background" beliefs are always operative in the justification of beliefs. But that there is a particular type of "pure" internal source of justified beliefs is crucial to any credible defense of the Closure Principle. I hope that will become obvious as the discussion proceeds.

What is important to bear in mind when considering the validity of the Closure Principle is that there are two distinct questions that can be asked:

1. What *externally situated evidence*, if any, provides an adequate source of justification for a belief?
2. What *internally situated reasons*, if any, provide an adequate source of justification for a belief?

At first glance it might seem that developing a comprehensive account of justification and, in particular, providing a full account of the sources of justification would be a prerequisite to answering these two questions as they apply to the Closure Principle. But, luckily, because the Closure Principle assumes in its antecedent that some proposition is already in the corpus of *S*'s justified beliefs, the relevant question is much easier to answer. It is this: Can a new (contingent and graspable) belief be added to the corpus of *S*'s justified beliefs whenever it is obviously entailed by one of the justified (contingent) beliefs already within that corpus?

Putting the question that way suggests a clear, intuitive internalist argument for the Closure Principle: Assume that a belief, *x*, is justified for *S* just in case there is a source of justification (whether an internally situated reason or externally situated evidence or both) in virtue of which *x* is sufficiently likely to be true (from *S*'s point of view).[15] Now, consider a belief, say b_i, such that b_i is justified for *S* and obviously entails another, graspable belief, say b_k. By hypothesis, since *S* is justified in believing that b_i, it is sufficiently likely to be true. Since believing that b_i satisfies that requirement, believing that b_k also satisfies that requirement. For the likelihood of b_k's being true is at least as great as that of b_i's being true. Thus, if believing that b_i is justified for *S*, so is believing that b_k. In short, b_k is justified for *S* because b_i provides an adequate source of justification of b_k for *S*.[16]

This is the argument concerning the internally situated reasons that can provide sources of justified beliefs to which the defender of the Closure Principle can appeal.[17] It strikes me as a plausible argument, but for the purposes of this paper it does not matter whether it is a good argument. The crucial point is that the skeptic has the option of employing such an internalistic defense of the Closure Principle.

Part 2: The defense of the Closure Principle suggested in Part 1 is necessary to save it from the attacks that have been developed against it

When Gettier first introduced the principle that has come to be known as the Closure Principle, it appears that he thought of it as invoking internally situated reasons as adequate sources of justification for expanding the corpus of justified beliefs discussed in part 1. He stated the principle as follows: "For any proposition P, if S is justified in believing P, and P entails Q, *and S deduces Q from P and accepts Q as a result of this deduction*, then S is justified in believing Q."[18] In the language suggested earlier, the principle asserts that whenever *S* has an adequate source of justification for *P*, and *P* entails *Q*, then *S* has an adequate source of justification for *Q* because *P*, itself, is such an adequate source.

Nevertheless, many putative counterexamples have been developed to the Closure Principle, and general theories of knowledge have been proposed in which closure fails. While not denying the validity of the counterexamples or questioning the accounts of knowledge in which closure fails, I do want to show that most of them share a family resemblance, namely, that they ignore the type of defense of the Closure Principle presented in part I that is based upon the adequacy of the internally situated reason that entails an additional proposition for providing a source of justification for expanding the set of justified beliefs to include the entailed proposition. For these objections to the Closure Principle (i.e., the counterexamples and the general theories in which closure fails) rely upon employing an externalist account of the sources of justification and/or knowledge or they fail to note that the internalist can argue that a justified proposition provides an adequate source of justification for any proposition that it obviously entails. More precisely, these objections to the Closure Principle depend upon the fact that *the* externally situated evidence or *the* internally situated reasons that provide an adequate source of justification for a proposition, *p*, do not always provide an adequate source of justification for a proposition, *q*, entailed by *p*. But that fact cannot be used against the Closure Principle if the argument for closure depends upon the claim that in the relevant cases *p*, itself, provides an adequate internally situated reason for expanding the corpus of justified and/or known beliefs to those propositions obviously entailed by *p*.

So, let us turn to the first type of objection—the counterexamples—to the Closure Principle and begin with the one given by Dretske, since it is the most well known and is the prototype of many other purported counterexamples. In the Zebra-in-the-Zoo Case, he points out that there are circumstances in which we are justified in believing that the animal in the zoo is a zebra. The animal is in a pen marked "Zebras" and it looks just like zebras look. He continues as follows:

> Yet something's being a zebra implies that it is not a mule . . . cleverly disguised by the zoo authorities to look like a zebra. Do you know that these animals are not mules cleverly disguised? If you are tempted to say "Yes" to this question, think a moment about what reasons you have, what evidence you can produce in favor of this claim. The evidence you *had* for thinking them zebras has been effectively neutralized, since it does not count toward their *not* being mules cleverly disguised to look like zebras.[19]

Note that the counterexample depends upon the supposed lack of sufficient evidence or reasons for the claim that the animal is not a cleverly disguised mule. In other words, Dretske grants that there is an adequate source of justification for the claim that the animal is a zebra, but he claims that there is no adequate source of justification (available at that moment) for the claim that the animal is not a cleverly disguised mule.

If we restrict the meaning of "evidence" or "reasons" (as used by Dretske) to what I have called *externally situated evidence*, then Dretske is clearly correct. There can be adequate externally situated evidence to justify a proposition, *p*, without there being adequate externally situated evidence to justify a proposition, *q*, entailed by *p*. In addition, the *internally situated reasons* that are adequate for making *p* justified might not be adequate to make *q* justified.[20] For example, the justified belief that *the animals look like zebras and are in a pen marked "Zebras"* cannot be used to justify the claim that the animals are not cleverly disguised mules. But the important point to note is that Dretske has restricted the search for a source of the justification of the entailed proposition in such a way that it precludes finding the entailing proposition—namely, *the animals in the pen are zebras*—as that source.

The Dretske-type purported counterexample aims at a *mistaken target*. It does not aim at the Closure Principle. The Closure Principle does not require that the source of justification for the entailed proposition is anything other than the entailing proposition. Return to Gettier's formulation of the principle: *S* is justified in believing *Q* because *S* deduces it from *P* and accepts *Q* as the result of the deduction. Now, of course, in the statement of the Closure Principle we are using, we have stripped it of the description of the psychological process by which *S* comes to believe the entailed proposition. We did that in order to focus attention on the central question, namely: Does *S* have an adequate source of justification for the entailed proposition? Nevertheless, it is clear from the original formulation of the principle that Gettier thought the entailing proposition provided an adequate source of justification for the entailed one.

Irving Thalberg's formulation of the Closure Principle explicitly attacks what I have called the mistaken target. He says that the principle he is criticizing can be put as follows:

> For any proposition, P, if a person S is justified [by evidence-propositions E_1 . . . E_n which S accepts] in believing P, and P entails Q, and S deduces Q from P and accepts Q as a result of this deduction, then S is justified [by E_1 . . . E_n] in believing Q.[21]

The material in the square brackets is in the original and it illustrates my point convincingly.[22]

The mistaken target is this:

> **(*x*)(*y*)[If *e* is an adequate source of *S*'s justification for *x*, and *x* entails *y*, then *e* is an adequate source of *S*'s justification for *y*].**

The mistaken target is a much stronger principle than the Closure Principle. The mistaken target implies the Closure Principle; but the Closure Principle does not imply the mistaken target. Because the mistaken target is a stronger principle, one might expect that there are counterexamples to it that are not counterexamples to the Closure Principle.

More recently, Robert Audi has given another supposed counterexample to the Closure Principle. I want to quote the argument at some length in order to show that it is yet one more case (albeit in a disguised form) of the way in which the standard objections to the Closure Principle ignore the type of pure internalistic defense available to ground the principle. Here is his argument:

> I add a column of figures, check my results twice, and thereby come to know, and justifiably believe, that the sum is 10,952. As it happens, I sometimes make mistakes, and my wife (whom I justifiably believe to be a better arithmetician) sometimes corrects me. Suppose that, feeling unusually confident, I now infer that if my wife says this is not the sum, she is wrong. But even though I know and justifiably believe that this is the sum, can I on *this basis, automatically* know or justifiably believe the *further* proposition that if she says that it is not the sum, she is wrong? Suppose my checking just twice is enough to give me the *minimum* basis for justified belief and knowledge here. Surely I would then not have sufficient grounds for the further proposition that if she says the answer is wrong, she is wrong.[23]

I emphasized "this basis" in the quotation. The reason for doing so will become apparent shortly.

One might object to Audi's putative counterexample by pointing out, first, that the seemingly entailed proposition is a disguised subjunctive conditional of the form "if my wife were to say that the sum is not 10,952; then she would be wrong." And, second, either the proposition "the sum of the figures in the column is 10,952" is a necessary truth (if the figures are designated rigidly as "the very figures in this very column") or it is a contingent truth (if the figures are designated nonrigidly as "the figures, whatever they are, in the column that I added"). On the one hand, if the proposition is a necessary truth, then this is not an appropriate counterexample to the Closure Principle since that principle concerns only contingent propositions. On the other hand, if the proposition is contingent, then it does not entail the subjunctive claim because in some near possible worlds in which the wife does say that sum is not 10,952, the sum is, indeed, not 10,952 (because the numbers in the column have changed).

Nevertheless, Audi's general point is well taken, namely, there are cases in which there is the minimum amount of *externally situated evidence* available to justify a proposition without there being the minimum amount of such *externally situated evidence* available to justify the entailed proposition. That was the lesson learned from the Zebra-in-the-Zoo Case. One could change Audi's example so as to make the justified proposition clearly a contingent one and the entailed proposition one which asserts that an expert has not truly denied the contingent proposition. For example, the pair of propositions could be: *There will be a snowstorm tomorrow* (based upon reading a local newspaper) and *a meteorologist who said that there will not be a snowstorm is wrong*. In addition, such cases show that if the content of the set of *S*'s relevant justified beliefs is limited to the propositions delineating the externally situated evidence *S* has for a proposition, it is clear that there are cases in which the *internally situated reasons* that justify a proposition, *p*, are not sufficient to justify every proposition entailed by *p*. To generalize, there will be cases in which *the* adequate source of justification for a proposition, *p*, is not *an* adequate source of justification for a proposition, *q*, even when *q* is entailed by *p*. But those cases provide telling evidence against only the *mistaken target* identified earlier; they do not provide evidence against the Closure Principle.

An initially plausible explanation of these cases has been provided by the "relevant-alternatives" account of justification.[24] The suggestion is that *the* source of justification for *p* can be adequate because it makes *p* sufficiently likely relative to *p*'s relevant alternatives without *that source* being adequate to make *q* sufficiently likely relative to *q*'s relevant alternatives, even when *p* entails *q*. In such cases, it is held that the range of relevant alternatives for *q* is larger, or at least different, than the range of relevant alternatives for *p*.

Whether the relevant-alternatives account turns out to be the best explanation of these cases is not important for my purposes. What is crucial to note is that the defenders of the Closure Principle could point out that its validity is not impugned by the existence of such cases or the relevant-alternatives account of them. In order to underscore that point; I emphasized "this basis" in the quotation from Audi. Look back to the quotation and note that the referent of "this" in "this basis" can be either to the *proposition* that the sum is 10,952 or to the *evidence* or *reasons* for the proposition that the sum is 10,952. If it refers to the evidence or reasons, namely, to the fact that one has added the column of figures twice and arrived at the sum 10,952 both times or to the belief that one has done so, then the claim would be that *the* evidence or the *reasons* one has for that proposition are not enough to justify the further claim that the expert is wrong. As I have said, that general point must be granted; but it is not telling against the Closure Principle as it was defended in part 1, for this objection, once again, aims at the mistaken target.

But there is another way of reading Audi's example which does not involve the mistaken target. If "this" in "this basis" refers to the proposition "the sum is 10,952," then the defenders of the Closure Principle should not grant what is being claimed. For it is no longer a question of whether *the* basis for believing that the sum is 10,952 is *an* adequate basis for believing that an expert who disagrees is wrong. Rather, the question is whether the justified proposition "the sum is 10,952" is an adequate basis for justifiably believing that an expert who disagrees is wrong. The defense of the Closure Principle does not require that *the* externally situated evidence and/or *the* internally situated reasons one has for *p* are adequate for *q*, even when *p* entails *q*. It does depend upon the supposed fact that the internally situated reason one has for *q*, namely *p*, is an adequate basis on which to add *q* to the corpus of justified beliefs whenever *p* entails *q*. In terms congenial to the relevant-alternatives account, the defenders of closure could say that it is *p* that is the source of justification for making *q* sufficiently likely relative to *q*'s alternatives, since *p* is incompatible with all of the relevant alternatives to *q*. (All of the alternatives to *q* contain ~*q*.)

What emerges from an examination of the counterexamples examined thus far is that if closure fails, it does so only if there are no pure internalist methods of expanding the set of justified beliefs like the one described in part I.[25] The same conclusion emerges from a brief examination of Robert Nozick's general account of knowledge that is designed to allow for *some* cases in which the corpus of beliefs can be expanded by deduction.[26] It is an example of accounts of knowledge mentioned earlier that eschew "justification" as a necessary condition of knowledge.

A detailed examination of Nozick's account would take us too far afield; however, it is crucial to note the essential role assumed by an externalistic account of the source of justified beliefs.[27] Briefly, Nozick requires that if *S* comes to know *q* via deduction from *p*, then if *q* were false, *S* would not believe *p* (or wouldn't infer *q* from *p*).[28] This condition blocks an unrestricted Closure Principle, even when the method of arriving at a belief is deduction. In Nozick's terminology, *S*'s beliefs may fail to "track" *q* because there will be cases such that if *q* were false, *S* would still believe that *q* (because *S* would still believe that *p* and infer *q* from it). For example, let *p* be "there is a table before *S*" and let *q* be "*S* is not in a skeptical scenario in which there only appears to be a table." The failure of closure occurs on this account of knowledge because *S* can track a proposition, *p*, and although *p* entails *q*, *S* can fail to track *q* because in the near possible worlds for ~*q*, it will still appear that *p*, whereas in the near possible worlds for ~*p*, it will not appear that *p*.

Internalists can (and should) readily grant that tracking does not transmit through deduction; but they can (and should) point out that if *S*'s beliefs track *p*, and p entails q, it is not necessary for S's beliefs to track q in order for S to know q. Put bluntly, the internalist defense of closure is that expanding the corpus of known beliefs to include q by deducing q from a known proposition, p, is permissible on internalist grounds alone. It is not further required that S's beliefs track q.

At this point, I hope it is clear that unless a justified (contingent) proposition can provide an adequate internal basis for every (contingent) proposition that it obviously entails (with the qualifications discussed in note 16), the general Closure Principle fails. However, it is important to recognize that it does not follow immediately from this fact that the skeptic must appeal to this internalistic defense of the *general* principle to vouchsafe the *instantiation* of the general principle in the first premise of the main argument for skepticism. For even if the general principle is susceptible to counterexamples, there might be an *instantiation* of the principle that is not prone to such counterexamples and such that it can be employed by the skeptic. For example, "if S is justified in believing that p, then S is justified in believing p" is an instantiation of the general Closure Principle whose defense does not depend upon the internalistic argument given in part 1. But, of course, that instantiation of the principle will not aid the skeptic's cause. My point is that the mere existence of counterexamples to the *general* principle is not sufficient to show that the skeptic must adopt the suggested internalistic defense of the *instantiated* general principle employed in premise I of the main argument for skepticism.

But a quick look at the skeptic's particular use of the Closure Principle shows that it is tailor-made for the general pattern of the supposed counterexamples. We are not normally required to have evidence against the likelihood of significant, or perhaps even almost universal, deception in order justifiably to add a new belief to the corpus of justified beliefs. In coming to believe that animals in a zoo are what they appear to be, one does not normally have to investigate the possibility that the animals are cleverly disguised to look like something other than what they really are. If something looks like a duck, walks like a duck, and quacks like a duck, then a Dretske-like externalist with regard to the sources of justification will argue that, at least in the usual circumstances, one can justifiably believe that it is a duck. But looking, walking, and quacking like a duck is not an adequate basis on which to justify believing that the duck-like thing isn't a phony duck. A phony duck would look, walk, and quack just like a duck.

To sum up: The recipe for cooking up counterexamples to the general Closure Principle provides an adequate basis for challenging the first premise of the main skeptical argument only if there is no purely internalistic method of expanding the corpus of justified beliefs like that suggested in part I. In addition, Nozick's general account of knowledge blocks closure, at least in those cases in which the skeptic wishes to employ the principle, unless the internalistic method of expanding the corpus of justified beliefs is accepted. Thus, either the skeptic has no adequate defense of the first premise in the main skeptical argument or the skeptic must claim that a justified belief, p, provides an adequate source of justification for anything entailed by p.

Part 3: The main argument for skepticism that depends upon the Closure Principle is useless

So far, I have argued that the instantiation of the Closure Principle employed by the skeptic can be defended only if there is a pure internalist method of expanding the corpus of justified beliefs which is such that whenever a proposition, *p*, is justified for *S*, *p* provides an adequate internally situated reason as a source of justification for every graspable proposition obviously entailed by it. Now, I want to show that if the skeptic embraces this internalistic defense of the Closure Principle, as I have argued she must, the main argument for skepticism is useless because it *must* beg the question.[29] More precisely, my contention is that the main argument *virtually* begs the question—a fallacy virtually equivalent to begging the question and equally as devastating to any argument committing it. Typically it is held that an argument begs the question just in case one of the premises illicitly "contains" the conclusion.[30] Strictly speaking, the skeptic's main argument is not guilty of that fallacy because neither premise 1 nor premise 2 contains the conclusion in the most straightforward way of understanding that term.[31] I define an argument as "virtually begging the question" just in case the conclusion of the argument can be reached by employing only a subargument on behalf of one of the main premises. If the conclusion can be reached, so to speak, before the main argument begins, then the main argument is useless. For the conclusion can be reached without employing any of the main premises. In particular, I think it is clear that the skeptic's subargument for premise 2 of the main argument must be sufficient, by itself, to establish the main conclusion without employing either of the premises of the main argument.

It will be useful to consider an example of an argument that (1) is closely analogous to the main argument for skepticism and (2) clearly commits the informal fallacy of virtually begging the question. Suppose that there are two ways to go by train from New Brunswick, N.J., to Washington, D.C.: (1) You can take the D-train, the "direct train" that stops briefly in Trenton or (2) you can take a train to Trenton, wait there for two hours, and then get a train from Trenton to Washington. Suppose that there are always tickets available from Trenton to Washington and that nothing prevents you from buying such a ticket.

Now, consider this argument:

1*. If a person, *S*, has a way to get to Trenton by train, then *S* has a way to get to Washington by train.
2*. *S* has no way to get to Washington by train.

Therefore, *S* does not have a way to get to Trenton by train.

Since there are two ways to get to Washington, a subargument for premise 2* would be inconclusive if it only demonstrated that *S* did not have a D-train ticket to Washington. For there is an indirect way of getting to Washington, namely, by stopping over in Trenton for two hours. Thus, an argument for 2* must show that *S* does not have any ticket that will get *S* to Trenton by train. But I trust it is clear that although such a subargument for 2* could be sound and valid, it would cause the main argument to virtually beg the question. The main premises (1*, 2*) would become superfluous because the subargument for premise 2* has already shown that *S* does not have a way to get to Trenton by train.

Let us return to the main argument for skepticism and recall premise 2:

2. *S* is never justified in believing that she is not in one of the skeptical scenarios in which there is no table but it appears just as though there were one.

Now, what must the skeptic do in order to demonstrate that premise 2 is true? The typical strategy to support premise 2 looks like this: *S* is not justified in believing that she is not in a skeptical scenario because *S* does not have an adequate source of justification for that belief. After all, so the subargument goes, if she were in a skeptical scenario, it would appear to *S* just like it now does; i.e., that there is a table before her. That is, it is claimed that all of the externally situated evidence and internally situated reasons *S* now has for believing that there is a table before her are not adequate to justify the belief that she is not in a skeptical scenario.

This typical argument for the second premise is reminiscent of the argument *against* the Closure Principle suggested by the Zebra-in-the-Zoo Case and the other counterexamples, and it explicitly employs the reasoning used by Nozick to introduce the tracking condition as a requirement for knowledge. It claims that since the source of justification for *S*'s believing that there is a table before her is not an adequate source of justification for denying that *S* is in a skeptical scenario, *S* is not justified in believing that she is in the skeptical scenario. But, as we have seen, that reasoning conflates the Closure Principle with the *mistaken target*. Further, the skeptic had better be very careful here, for in utilizing the typical subargument for premise 2, the skeptic appears to be appealing to the very intuitions that (mistakenly) provided the basis for rejecting the Closure Principle. Such an argument in support of premise 2 might (mistakenly) be appropriated by the nonskeptic as just one more reason for denying closure.

But more to the point, since the attack on the Closure Principle can be repulsed only by arguing that there is a pure internalistic method of expanding the corpus of justified beliefs like the method described in part 1, the skeptic *cannot* provide a conclusive argument for premise 2 by employing what I called the typical strategy. For even though the reasons or evidence that *S* has for believing that there is a table before her might not provide an adequate source of justification for the denial of the proposition that she is in a skeptical scenario in which it only appears that there is a table, there might be the requisite sort of *internally situated reason* that provides an appropriate source of justification for the denial of the proposition that *S* is in a skeptical scenario—one that is not itself a reason for believing that there is a table before her and, in particular, one that entails the denial of the proposition that *S* is in a skeptical scenario.

It is crucial to recall that in order to defend the Closure Principle, the skeptic *was forced* to include justified propositions among the requisite sort of internally situated reasons that provide an adequate source of justification for further beliefs. The parallel with the Train Tickets Case should be obvious. Just as there are always tickets available from Trenton to Washington, on the internalist grounds we have been considering there are always "inference tickets" available from the claim that there is a table before *S* to the claim that the skeptical scenario does not obtain. Further, just as any subargument sufficient to demonstrate premise 2* (in the Train Tickets Case) must be sufficient to show that *S* does not have a ticket to Trenton, any argument sufficient to demonstrate premise 2 (in the main argument for skepticism) must be sufficient to show that *S* does not have a justified belief which entails that *S* is not in a skeptical scenario.

The moral is this: The defense of the Closure Principle relies upon the claim that there are internalist entailment "inference tickets" available from *S*'s justified beliefs about her surroundings to the denial of the skeptical scenario. Therefore, any subargument for premise 2 sufficient to show that *S* does not have *any* adequate source of justification for the denial of the skeptical scenario must show that *S* does not have a justified belief that entails the denial of the skeptical hypotheses. Of course, such a subargument will be sufficiently strong to establish the main conclusion, namely, that *S* is not justified in believing that there is a table before her. For, ex hypothesi, that proposition entails that *S* is not in a skeptical scenario in which it only appears that there is a table. Thus, premise 1 and premise 2 of the main argument for skepticism are superfluous because the conclusion can be reached simply on the basis of the subargument for premise 2.

Conclusion

The main argument for skepticism fails; and with it many related arguments for skepticism become useless. The specific argument considered in this paper made use of a closure principle employing "justification" as the term of positive epistemic appraisal. Other such terms could be used. Suppose that someone in a Cartesian mood were to claim that knowledge entailed certainty and that since *S* is not *certain* that she is not in one of the skeptical scenarios, she could not be *certain* that there was a table before her.[32] In other words, suppose that the version of a closure principle invoked is: **(*x*)(*y*)[If *S* is certain that *x*, and *x* entails *y*, then *S* is certain that *y*]**. The strategy employed in this paper could be used to show that such an argument would be worthless. For, in order to show that *S* is not certain that she is not in one of the skeptical scenarios, it must be shown that *S* is not certain of any proposition that entails that she is not in such a scenario. If such a subargument could be developed, it would be sufficient to show that she is not certain that there is a table before her. The same outcome applies to arguments employing other terms of positive epistemic appraisal, such as "reasonable," "warranted," "acceptable," "beyond reasonable doubt," "evident," "plausible," and "probable." Thus, the strategy employed in this paper can be generalized to show that the Closure Principle cannot be used to motivate skepticism.

Notes

1 I want to thank David Benfield, Victoria Chapman, Stewart Cohen, Paulo Faria, Richard Foley, Christopher Hill, Brian McLaughlin, Tom Senor, and Jonathan Vogel for their helpful comments on the issues discussed in this paper and/or criticisms of earlier drafts of this paper. I hope I have been able to meet their criticisms; but, no doubt, in some cases they will believe that I have not done so.

2 Actually, there are many forms of skepticism. The form I will be concerned with here is what can be called "Direct Skepticism." It holds that we lack knowledge. Another form, "Iterative Skepticism," holds that we do not know that we know. Finally, a third form can be called "Pyrrhonian Skepticism" since it holds that we have no better reasons for believing any (nonevident) proposition than we do for denying it. Thus, withholding belief appears to be the outcome. I discuss these forms in *Certainty* (Minneapolis: University of Minnesota Press, 1981), esp. pp. 5–11.

3 I think that the best sources of recent discussions about the Closure Principle are *The Possibility of Knowledge*, ed. Steven Luper-Foy (Totowa, N.J.: Rowman and Littlefield, 1987), see esp. the bibliography provided on pp. 324–325; and *Doubting: Contemporary Perspectives on Skepticism*, ed. Michael Roth and Glenn Ross (Dordrecht: Kluwer, 1990).

In the *Academica* (2:26), Cicero points out that some people do have identical twins who cannot be distinguished on the basis of perception alone. In addition, he claims that the "single case of resemblance" will "have made everything doubtful." The point seems to be that if we are justified in believing that we are seeing a chair, for example, we have to be justified in believing that it is not a chair-facsimile. This appears to be a clear use of the Closure Principle.

Although I say the principle can be "traced" to Descartes, I think that the argument for skepticism in the "First Meditation" employs a principle even stronger than the Closure Principle. The argument in the "First Meditation" could be put as follows:

1. If a person, *S*, is justified in believing that there is a table, then *S* is justified in believing the denial of every proposition which makes it somewhat doubtful that there is a table.
2. *S* is not justified in believing the denial of every proposition that makes it somewhat doubtful that there is a table before her. (In particular, at least at the stage of the argument in the "First Meditation," Descartes is not in a position to believe the denial of the proposition that he was created by some thing or some process that lacked the ability to create reliable epistemic equipment, e.g., equipment that delivers the truth when properly used.)

Therefore, *S* is not justified in believing that there is a table.

This employs a stronger principle than the Closure Principle, since Descartes requires that one be justified in denying all grounds for doubting *x* in order to know that *x*. The stronger principle could be put as follows:

Immunity Principle: (*x*)(*y*)[If *S* is justified in believing that *x*, and *y* is the denial of grounds for doubting *x*, then *S* is justified in believing that *y*].

This is stronger because a contrary to *x* would be grounds for doubting *x*, but not all grounds for doubt are contraries. I discuss this principle in "Immune Belief Systems," *Philosophical Topics* 14 (1986): 259–280, and in "Epistemic

Compatibilism and Canonical Beliefs," in *Doubting: Contemporary Perspectives on Skepticism*, pp. 99–120.

4 Ex hypothesi, "there is a table before *S*" entails "*S* is not in one of the skeptical scenarios in which there is no table but it appears just as though there were one."

5 I argued for the principle in *Certainty*, pp. 70–81. But I now think that argument was mistaken. I thought that a defeater of justification for a proposition would defeat every proposition entailing the proposition. But that is false. Consider the following assignments:

e: adequate evidence, ceteris paribus, for believing *p*;
d: an overrider, ceteris paribus, for the justification of *p* by *e*;
r: an overrider, ceteris paribus, of the defeating effect of *d*.
That is, *r*, is a restorer of the justification of *p* by *e*.

I think it is clear that *d* is a defeater of (*e* & *p*), but it is not a defeater of (*e* & *p* & *r*). Thus, the argument in *Certainty* was unsound. One might think that this provides a basis for rejecting Closure on the pure internalist grounds to be discussed later. But it doesn't. One might think that *S* could be justified in believing (*e* & *p* & *r* & *d*) but not justified in believing that (*e* & *p* & *d*) because the former is coherent and the latter is not. It is true that the former is coherent and that the latter is not coherent, but *S* doesn't lose whatever justification she had for *r*, and it remains true, as the pure internalist will claim, that the former provides an adequate source of justification for the latter.

6 In particular, it will not show that an argument for skepticism employing the stronger Immunity Principle (see note 3) faces a similar dilemma.

7 Anthony Brueckner in "Skepticism and Epistemic Closure," *Philosophical Topics* 13 (1985): 89–117, criticized my defense of the Closure Principle in *Certainty*. I had said that justified beliefs can serve as evidence for further beliefs. He correctly pointed out that "evidence" does not typically refer to beliefs. For example, in the Zebra-in-the-Zoo Case (discussed later) the evidence I have is that the animals are in a pen marked "Zebras" and the animals look like zebras. I do not have additional evidence, namely, that the animals are zebras. I think Brueckner may be right about the scope of "evidence" in ordinary discourse. (But see the passage by Dretske quoted later in the main text for some evidence that the use of "evidence" is not so precise.) Thus, in order to avoid that confusion, in this paper I have distinguished between externally situated *evidence* and internally situated *reasons*.

8 I am indebted to Christopher Hill for pointing out the need for this clarification and for some of the terminology employed in describing the two sources of justification.

9 See Alvin Plantinga's discussion of the relationships among internalism, externalism (as those views are typically understood, namely, as referring to general theories of knowledge), and deontology in his book *Warrant: The Current Debate* (Oxford and New York: Oxford University Press, 1993).

10 Other modifications of the principle are required when "knowledge" is substituted for "justification." Since belief does not transmit through entailment, the constraints used by Gettier (discussed later) need to be reintroduced; namely,

that *S* deduces *y* from *x* and accepts *y* as a result of this deduction. Given the interpretation of "*S* is justified in believing *x*" employed throughout this paper, it is not necessary to include these constraints when the consequent does not entail that *S* believes *x*.

11 See, for example, Robert Nozick, *Philosophical Explanations* (Cambridge, Mass.: Harvard University Press, 1981). His account is discussed later.

12 Note that beyond the differences already mentioned in the text concerning my use of "internal" and "external" (namely, that I am using those terms merely to refer to the *sources* of justified beliefs and not to *general* theories of justification), even with regard to the sources of justification, my use of the terms is not quite parallel to the externalist–internalist distinction as normally employed. Typically, "internalism," even with regard to only the sources of justification, refers to a stronger view than the one I am attempting to characterize, because it is usually held that internally situated reasons, if they are to provide a source of justification for *S*, must be "accessible" to *S*. That is, typically it is held that what I am calling "internally situated reasons" are accessible to *S* on the basis of reflection alone. I do not include an accessibility condition in my account of internally situated reasons. But nothing of any significance hangs on employing the weaker notion in this paper. One could add the accessibility condition without affecting the argument. See William Alston, *Epistemic Justification* (Ithaca N.Y.: Cornell University Press, 1989), esp. pp. 185–226, and Alvin Plantinga, op. cit., esp. pp. 3–29, for discussions of the accessibility condition.

13 The justified beliefs can provide a source of further justified beliefs and the actual beliefs can provide overriders. Thus, both play a role in determining whether *S* has an adequate source (i.e., a sufficient source) of justification for further beliefs.

14 In other words, the Closure Principle, alone, does not sanction some of the troublesome inferences in the Lottery Paradox or Preface Paradox.

15 I placed the material in parentheses in order to indicate that the argument for the Closure Principle can be stated in either an objectivist or subjectivist manner. That is, justified beliefs could be those that *are*, indeed, likely to be true given certain procedures for adopting beliefs, or they could be those beliefs that the agent *thinks* are likely to be true given some belief acquisition procedures. I will state the proposed defense of the Closure Principle in the objectivist mode, but it could be transformed into a subjectivist defense of the Closure Principle by adding the parenthetical qualification at the appropriate points.

16 There is an interesting objection to this argument for the Closure Principle that arises from some correspondence with Stewart Cohen (although the correspondence was not about this argument in particular and I am not certain that he would agree with my way of framing the problem): Suppose that *S* comes to believe some proposition, say *p*, on the basis of some source of justification, say a conjunction of *a* and *b*. And suppose further, as is possible, that *p* entails *a*. For example, suppose that *S* comes to justifiably believe *p, that the next card in the deck is the seven of diamonds*, on the basis of *a, that the next card in the deck is a seven*, and *b that the next card is a diamond*. (Let the probabilities of *a* and *b* be sufficiently high so as to permit the conjunction.) Surely, if *S* came to believe that *p*, at least in part, because *S* already justifiably believes that *a*, *S* could not use *p* as an internally situated reason for a source of justification for *a*. For doing so

would be a clear instance of the fallacy of circular reasoning. (The proposition, *a*, is a reason for *p*: so, *p* could not be a reason for *a*.) So, generalizing and returning to the argument for the Closure Principle: b_i cannot always provide an adequate source of justification for b_k even if b_i entails b_k (because b_k might have been one of the internally situated reasons that provided support for b_i).

I have taken the relevant form of the Closure Principle to involve *expanding* S's corpus of justified beliefs. Strictly speaking, the Closure Principle is not restricted to such cases.

There are four responses to this important objection. First, although the Closure Principle is not strictly limited to expanding the corpus of *S*'s justified beliefs, the argument given in the main text for the Closure Principle could be easily modified to account for the case in which the entailed proposition is a source of justification of the entailing proposition. Just rewrite the argument so that the initial conditions are that either b_k (the entailed proposition) is one of the sources of justification for b_i (the entailing proposition) or it isn't. On the one hand, if b_k is among the sources of justification for b_i, then it remains true that if b_i is justified, b_k is justified, because b_k could not be a source of justification (or partial justification) of b_i without b_k, itself, being justified. Otherwise, b_i would be based upon an unjustified source; and reasoning based on arbitrary grounds is as unacceptable as circular reasoning. On the other hand, if b_k is not one of the sources of justification for b_i, then the argument as presented goes through; that is, b_i will provide an adequate, internally situated reason for b_k. I chose not to present the argument in this disjunctive form because it seemed unduly complicated.

Second, and more importantly, if the skeptic were to be appealing to an instantiation of the Closure Principle in this form in the main argument for skepticism (namely, in the form that requires that in order for *S* to be justified in believing that *p*, *S* must *first* be justified in believing all the propositions that *p* entails or, at least, justified in believing the conjunction of the denials of all of the contraries of *p*), it would be susceptible to the Dretske-like counterexamples to be considered later. To jump ahead a bit, Dretske and others have shown that *S* can be justified in believing a proposition, say, *that the animals in the pen are zebras* without *first* being justified in believing *that the animals in the pen are not cleverly disguised mules*. By parity of reasoning and applying this to the main argument for skepticism, I think it is clear that *S* can be justified in believing that there is a table before her without *first* being justified in believing that she is not in one of the skeptical scenarios.

Third, ignoring the Dretske-like counterexamples, suppose the skeptic were, indeed, to be requiring that the sources of justification for a proposition must include all of the propositions that *p* entails (or at least the conjunction of all of the denials of all of the contraries of *p*). That requirement is clearly too strong for the sources of justification for a contingent proposition. For it has the consequence that a source of justification for a contingent proposition is adequate only if it contains a proposition that entails *p*. In order to satisfy that requirement, every proposition that is equivalent to *p* would have to be in the source of justification for *p*. [Or at least $(\sim(\sim p \ \& \ q) \ \& \ \sim(\sim p \ \& \ \sim q))$ would have to be in the source of justification for *p*; for each of the propositions within the inner parentheses is a contrary of *p*, and that conjunction entails *p*.]

Finally, unlike the plausible version of the Closure Principle that we are considering, since this requirement so obviously leads to skepticism, it can be (and should be) rejected by the nonskeptic immediately. For since there are so many, if not infinitely many, contingent propositions (or propositions equivalent to the denials of contraries) that are entailed by any contingent proposition, *p*, the process of coming to be justified in believing a contingent proposition would be so difficult, if not impossible, that the nonskeptic would be entitled to point out that (I) this requirement does not capture our epistemic practices (as the Dretske Zebra-in-the-Zoo Case shows) and (2) if such a principle were recommended as one we *ought* to follow, it would make the acquisition of justified beliefs so difficult, if not impossible, that as a heuristic recommendation for the acquisition of justified beliefs, it would fail on its face.

For a relevant discussion of this issue, see Stewart Cohen's entry "Scepticism," in *Encyclopedia of Philosophy*, ed. Edward Craig (London: Routledge Press, forthcoming). As of the writing of this article, the projected date for the publication of the Routledge encyclopedia is 1997. Also see *Certainty*, esp. pp. 96–104.

17 As I pointed out earlier, I use "internal" and "external" to refer to theories about the *sources* of justified beliefs. By calling this a pure internalistic defense of the Closure Principle. I am calling attention to the fact that the argument depends upon supposing that S's justified beliefs can, in the relevant cases, serve as an adequate source of further justified beliefs. Thus, as mentioned in the main text, under some externalistic general theories of justification this argument for the Closure Principle might be acceptable, if the process of inference is such that it is sufficiently reliable. The argument might be acceptable because some general externalistic theories of knowledge countenance what I am calling internally situated reasons as sources of justification. That they should do so might strike some as odd, but once it is clear that the important distinction I wish to emphasize concerns the *sources* of justified beliefs, that difficulty should disappear.

18 Edmund Gettier, "Is Justified True Belief Knowledge?" *Analysis* 23 (1963): 122; emphasis mine.

19 Fred Dretske, "Epistemic Operators," *Journal of Philosophy* 67 (1970): 1015–1016. Note that Dretske seems to treat "evidence" and "reasons" as synonymous. (See note 7.)

20 It is clear from the Zebra-in-the-Zoo Case that "*x* provides an adequate source of justification for *y*" is not transitive. In that case, one of the propositions (i.e., *the animals in the pen are zebras*) that provides an adequate source of justification for another (i.e., *the animals are not cleverly disguised mules*) does so because it entails it. But the failure of transitivity is more general. Let *c*, *b*, and *o* be chosen as follows:

c: Jones is a clever car thief and stole car *A*;
b: Jones engages in behaviors b_1–b_n.
o: Jones owns car *A*.

Now, if a clever car thief is one who typically engages in behaviors b_1–b_n with regard to cars he or she has stolen and if those behaviors are just those that would lead anyone to justifiably conclude that Jones owns the car (e.g., Jones speaks about buying it, Jones puts it in his or her garage, Jones has a valid looking title), I take it that the following are true:

(1) *c* provides an adequate source of justification for *b*;
(2) *b* provides an adequate source of justification for *o*;
(3) *c* does not provide an adequate source of justification for *o*.

This result obtains if the source of justification in the example is taken to be either an internally situated reason or externally situated evidence and is a direct consequence of justification being defeasible. I discuss this more fully in *Certainty*, esp. pp. 44–70.

21 Irving Thalberg, "Is Justification Transmissible through Deduction?" *Philosophical Studies* 25 (1974): 347–348.

22 Moreover, near the end of the paper, Thalberg suggests that if justification is taken to be "strategic" justification rather than "evidential" justification, then the Closure Principle is valid. Here is what he says:

> The unyielding advocacy of PDJ [his name for the Closure Principle] has persuaded me that a strategical variant of it is acceptable:
> (PDSJ) For any proposition P, if a person S is *evidentially or strategically* justified in believing P, and P entails Q, and S deduces Q from P and accepts Q as a result of this deduction; then S is *strategically* justified in believing Q, *unless Q can be false under more circumstances than P* (ibid., p. 355).

That last qualification in PDSJ is added because Thalberg mistakenly thinks that the Closure Principle would sanction the conjunction of justified beliefs. But as we have already seen, the Closure Principle does not sanction conjunction in general since "P" (in PDSJ) stands for a single proposition, not for a set of propositions containing more than one member. So there is no danger of a conjunction principle arising from the Closure Principle alone. Nevertheless, Thalberg has tacitly granted my point, namely, that the standard objections to the Closure Principle neglect a possible type of internalistic defense of it—what could be called, using his terms, a "strategic" defense of it.

23 Robert Audi, *Belief, Justification, and Knowledge* (Belmont, Calif.: Wadsworth, 1988), p. 77.

24 For accounts of relevant alternatives, see Gail Stine, "Scepticism, Relevant Alternatives, and Deductive Closure," *Philosophical Studies* 29 (1976): 249–261; David Lewis, "Scorekeeping in a Language Game," *Journal of Philosophical Logic* 8 (1979): 339–59 (reprinted in his *Philosophical Papers* [Oxford and New York: Oxford University Press, 1983]); Palle Yourgrau, "Knowledge and Relevant Alternatives," *Synthese* 55 (1983): 55–70: Alvin Goldman, *Epistemology and Cognition* (Cambridge, Mass.: Harvard University Press, 1986); Bredo Johnsen, "Relevant Alternatives and Demon Scepticism," *Journal of Philosophy* 84 (1987): 643–653 (reprinted in *Doubting: Contemporary Perspectives on Skepticism*, pp. 29–37).

25 There are other purported counterexamples to the Closure Principle that have been considered, in part, because they seem to avoid some problems of the

earlier proposals. In "Are There Counterexamples to the Closure Principle?" (in *Doubting: Contemporary Perspectives on Skepticism*, pp. 13–27), Jonathan Vogel examines a case, the Car Theft Case, in which it could be thought that *S* is justified in believing that her car is now parked on Avenue *A* (because she remembers having just parked it there) while not being justified in believing that her car has not been stolen and is no longer on Avenue *A*. He points out that it could be held that in this case, *S* is *not* justified in believing that *her* car was not stolen because she justifiably believes that some cars are stolen and she has *no* evidence that her car is not among those that have been stolen. In contrast, in Dretske's Zebra-in-the-Zoo Case, *S* does not justifiably believe that there have been cases of mules cleverly disguised to look like zebras. Vogel ultimately rejects even the Car Theft Case as a counterexample to the Closure Principle by appealing to "psychological considerations" to explain away the intuitions. According to him, the focus of our attention shifts to new potential defeaters when we consider the proposition that the car has not been stolen. As Vogel says, "the anomalous character of our intuitions about the Car Theft Case may be due to some kind of epistemically important shift rather than to closure failure" (ibid., p. 19). Perhaps psychological shifts can explain away the intuitions in this particular case, although I doubt that those who object to closure will be so sanguine. Nevertheless, unless one supposes that a justified proposition provides an adequate source of justification for all propositions that it obviously entails, there is no way of guaranteeing that all purported counterexamples can be eliminated by appealing to psychological considerations. (I should note that Vogel initially introduces the Car Theft Case as one in which you *know* the antecedent in the entailment but you do not *know* the consequent. But in the article, he does shift to "justification" at some points; for example, see p. 16. For my purposes, the shift is not important, since the cases he considers regarding the possible failure of the Closure Principle depend upon the claim that *S* lacks a justification for the entailed belief and, thus, *S* lacks knowledge.)

26 See Nozick, op. cit.

27 I discuss Nozick's views in "On Behalf of the Skeptic," in *The Possibility of Knowledge*, pp. 267–281. Although I do not discuss the Zebra-in-the-Zoo Case there, I think that this case can be used to show that Nozick's tracking conditions are too strong. On Nozick's view, one of the necessary conditions of *S*'s knowing that *x* is that beliefs about *x* must "track" *x*, and this requires (among other things) that if *x* were false, *S* would not believe that *x* (in near possible worlds). Now, suppose that the zookeeper believes that if she can't at least make it appear that there are zebras in the pen she will lose her job. In other words, the actual world is so constructed that whenever there are no zebras, there will be some things that look like zebras. The zookeeper never has to resort to the ruse, but she would if need be. Hence, in near enough worlds, if the animals in the pen were not zebras, *S* would still believe that they are. But I take it that *S* does know that the animals in the pen are zebras.

28 Nozick, op. cit., p. 231.

29 I want to make clear that I am not arguing, as others have done, that the defender of knowledge can equally well employ the Closure Principle against the skeptic. It has been claimed that just as the skeptic uses the Closure Principle

and modus tollens, the antiskeptic uses the principle and modus ponens. G.E. Moore put it this way:

> I agree with that part of the argument which asserts that if I don't know now that I'm not dreaming, it follows that I don't *know* that I am standing up. . . . But this first part of the argument cuts both ways. For if it is true, it follows that it is also true that if I do *know* that I am standing up, then I do know that I am not dreaming. I can therefore just as well argue: since I do know that I am standing up, it follows that I do know that I am not dreaming. . . . (G. E. Moore, "Certainty," in his *Philosophical Papers* [New York: Collier Books, 1962], p. 242.)

I think it is not absolutely clear from the context that Moore took the proposition "I am dreaming" as shorthand for "I am (in bed) dreaming." If it is not shorthand, this would not be an instantiation of the Closure Principle (since "I am dreaming" does not entail "I am not standing up"); but even if Moore did not take this to be an instance of the Closure Principle but rather took it to be an instance of the Immunity Principle (see note 3), the point I wish to make here is not compromised.

My point, here, is that even though the argument employing the Closure Principle on behalf of the skeptic *must* virtually beg the question and that, therefore, it is useless to the skeptic, it does not follow from this that the principle is useless to the nonskeptic. A full discussion of this point would take us beyond the scope of this paper, but briefly: The type of internalist reasons that make the Closure Principle safe from counterexamples do not force us to grant that an argument which demonstrates conclusively that *S* is justified in believing that there is a table before her would have to show, as part of the defense of one of its premises, that *S* is justified in denying the skeptical hypothesis. For such a denial would not form part of *every* adequate source of justification for the belief in the existence of the table.

30 Note that I say that an argument begs the question if the conclusion is *illicitly* contained in a premise rather than saying that an argument begs the question if the conclusion is contained in a premise. I believe that there are some arguments that do not beg the question but in which the conclusion is "contained" (in a clearly straightforward, intuitive sense) in a premise. Consider this argument:

	Subargument for Premise 1	*Main Argument*
1.1	*S* says "*P* & *Q*."	
1.2	Whatever *S* says is true.	1. *P* & *Q*
		Therefore, *P*.

The main argument given above would be classified as begging the question by most accounts because premise I contains the conclusion. I do not think that it is an instance of begging the question because the argument does not employ the conclusion in an *illicit* manner. It is beyond the scope of this paper to attempt a characterization of what makes the presence of the conclusion in a premise illicit.

31 If the meaning of "contain" were stretched a bit beyond its ordinary sense, then

conclusion could be said to be contained in the subargument. That is, if one ..d suppose that a proposition, *x*, is "contained" within another one, *y*, just in case *x* is strictly implied by *y*, then the distinction between arguments which beg the question and those which *virtually* beg the question would vanish.

32 As I mentioned in note 3, there is a better way to put the Cartesian point.

QUESTIONS

1 What is the closure principle?
2 In the Zebra-in-the-Zoo Case, what is Dretske trying to establish?
3 What is the difference between "externally situated evidence" and "internally situated reasons"?
4 What does it mean for an argument to "virtually beg the question"?

Michael Huemer, "Direct Realism and the Brain-in-a-Vat Argument"

One of the advantages traditionally claimed for direct realist theories of perception over indirect realist theories is that the direct realist is able to avoid skeptical problems to which the indirect realist falls prey.[1] If the only things we are ever directly aware of are the ideas in our own minds, it is asked, then what reason do we have for thinking anything other than ideas exists? How do premises about ideas confirm propositions about physical objects? This is one sort of skeptical worry that the direct realist has an obvious *prima facie* advantage in dealing with.

However, there are other sorts of skeptical problems that direct realism does not seem to particularly help us with, and it is on one of those that I want to focus. Specifically, does the direct realist have an answer to brain-in-a-vat skepticism that is not available to the indirect realist? I claim that the answer is yes.

Before we are in a position to see that, we'll first have to review the brain-in-a-vat argument and explain the distinction between direct and indirect realism. After that, we'll need to look at two contemporary responses to the brain-in-a-vat argument to see why they fail as long as the direct realist account of perception is neglected. Then we'll be able to see how direct realism figures in the refutation of the skeptical argument.

1. Direct and indirect realism

Direct realism is often understood as the view that, in cases of normal perception, we are directly aware of something in the external world. This "something" could include external objects, events, or states of affairs; surfaces of external objects; and/or properties of external objects. Indirect realism is then characterized as the view that, in normal perception, we are only directly aware of internal (mental) phenomena, and we are *indirectly* aware of external phenomena, by means of our awareness of the mental phenomena. These internal, mental phenomena could include mental objects, states, events, and/or properties. So there can be different versions of indirect realism, according to what the theorist says about the nature of the mental phenomena that perception makes us aware of: the indirect realist might hold that what we are directly aware of are sense data, or states

Michael Huemer, "Direct Realism and the Brain-in-a-Vat Argument," *Philosophy and Phenomenological Research* 61 (2000): 397–413.

of "being appeared to" in certain ways, or some other sort of mental phenomena.

That is one traditional way of formulating the issue, but I'm going to use a slightly different formulation here. For our present purposes, what we need is an explicitly epistemological characterization of direct and indirect realism, a characterization in terms of the justification for perceptual beliefs. A person's belief that P is a *perceptual belief* if the (causal) explanation for why he believes that P is that he perceives that P. For instance, the explanation for why I believe that there is a pen here might be that I *see* that there is a pen here, which is a particular way of perceiving that there is a pen here, so I have the *perceptual belief* that there is a pen here. Now we can define indirect realism as the view that, at least in normal cases, perceptual beliefs about the external world are justified, but they depend for their justification on our being aware of certain mental phenomena. So for example, my belief that there is a pen here might depend for its justification on my awareness of a sense datum of a pen, or on my awareness of a state of being appeared to penishly, etc. *Direct realism* is the view that, at least in normal cases, our perceptual beliefs about the external world have justification that does not depend on our being aware of mental phenomena, or anything else that's not in the external world.[2]

2. The brain-in-a-vat argument

The brain-in-a-vat argument goes like this:

(1) If S is justified in believing P and P entails Q, then S is justified in believing Q.[3]
(2) I'm not justified in believing that I'm not a brain in a vat.
(3) That I have a body entails that I'm not a brain in a vat.
(4) Therefore, I'm not justified in believing that I have a body.

It is important to understand that the conclusion of this argument is not merely that I cannot be *absolutely certain* that I have a body. Such a conclusion would be accepted by many philosophers without much excitement. But the argument we're considering is much more interesting. It purports to establish that I don't even have good reason for believing that I have a body. And of course, the assumption is that if you can't justifiably believe that you have a body, then you can't justifiably believe much of anything about the physical world.

A note about the phrase "justified in believing": "S is justified in believing P," as I use the phrase, does not entail that S actually believes P. Rather, it just means that S has available an adequate source of justification for P. S might fail to actually accept some of the propositions that are justified for him, either because S is epistemically timid or because he hasn't noticed the justification he has available. To illustrate the distinction, let's suppose that S knows that P and he also knows that $(P \supset Q)$; however, S has not yet put together these two beliefs and noticed their logical consequence, so S doesn't actually believe that Q. (Presumably, this sort of thing takes place frequently, because we are often aware of certain axioms without being aware of most of the theorems derivable from them.) Nevertheless, S *has available* an adequate justification for Q, insofar as P and $(P \supset Q)$ would provide adequate reason for believing Q, so I would say that S is "justified in believing Q."[4] In general, S is justified in believing P whenever S is in possession of some evidence that, if properly deployed, would lead S to believe P and be justified in doing so.

3. Why direct realism may be irrelevant to the argument

At first glance, it is not obvious how the issue between direct and indirect realism is relevant to this skeptical argument. One could say that, if direct realism is true, it follows that the skeptical argument is unsound, since direct realism as we have defined it involves the claim that we are justified in believing propositions about the external world. But it is equally true that, if *indirect* realism is true, then the skeptical argument is unsound, since indirect realism also involves the claim that we are justified in believing propositions about the external world. So far, no advantage for direct realism is evident. And neither of these observations constitutes a response to the skeptical argument; the skeptic will simply reject both forms of realism as I have formulated them.

One might try arguing that the brain-in-a-vat scenario, as usually described, is impossible, in the sense that the brain in a vat could not really have the same kind of experiences we have. We have experiences of *perceiving* (and hence, being directly acquainted with) external objects. But the brain in the vat doesn't have any *perceptions*. The brain in the vat only has *hallucinations*. According to one faction of direct realists, perceptions and hallucinations do not really share anything in common; they are merely states that *seem* alike to the subject at the time, but this does not show that they actually are intrinsically alike.[5] Thus, John Hyman writes:

> [T]he causal theory is still committed to the Cartesian illusion that "the ordinary notion of perceiving" is a composite notion, which can be divided into its purely mental and its physical components, each of which can exist without the other . . . Against this view I have argued, first, that perceptual experience and illusion are not two species of the same psychological genus and hence the concept of perceiving cannot be dismembered in this way; and second, that there is no epistemological reason for trying to dismember it, since the foundations of empirical knowledge are propositions stating what the speaker perceives.[6]

Supposing that this view is right—namely, that there is no mental state common to both hallucination and veridical perception—does it furnish us with an answer to the brain-in-a-vat argument?

It certainly provides us with a way to object to one way the brain-in-a-vat scenario is commonly described—namely, as a situation in which a being would have the same experiences we presently have, but most of his beliefs about the external world would be false. However, the important question is really whether hallucinations and veridical perceptions can be subjectively indistinguishable (that is, indistinguishable for the subject, at the time). If the direct realist holds that there can not be hallucinations that are subjectively indistinguishable from perceptions, then his theory is just empirically false. We have every scientific reason to believe that if a brain were electrically stimulated in the way described in the brain-in-a-vat scenario, its hallucinations would be subjectively indistinguishable from the perceptions of a normal person. But if the direct realist admits that hallucinations can be subjectively indistinguishable from perceptions, then the skeptic can merely rephrase his challenge: how do we know that what we are actually doing is perceiving things, rather than merely hallucinating? Whether perceptions and hallucinations have a common component isn't what matters; what matters to the skeptic's question is whether we have a way of distinguishing perceptions from hallucinations in our own case. As long as we can't tell the difference, a skeptical worry will remain. All the direct realist has accomplished, so far, is to get the skeptic to reformulate his question.

4. Two contemporary responses

Premise (1) of the skeptical argument is called "the Closure Principle"—the principle that the set of propositions one is justified in believing is closed under entailment. This principle is highly plausible intuitively, but some epistemologists have challenged it.[7] Fred Dretske cites the following case. Imagine you're at the zoo. In a pen clearly marked "zebras," you see some black and white striped equine animals. It seems that you have good reason to believe that those animals are zebras. Surely their zebra-like appearance counts strongly in favor of their being zebras, as does their being in the zebra pen at the zoo. Now, their being *zebras* entails that the animals are not *mules* that have been cleverly disguised by the zoo authorities to look like zebras. Are you justified in believing that the animals are not cleverly disguised mules? Dretske says no:

> If you are tempted to say "Yes" to this question, think a moment about what reasons you have, what evidence you can produce in favor of this claim. The evidence you *had* for thinking them zebras has been effectively neutralized, since it does not count toward their *not* being mules cleverly disguised to look like zebras.[8]

Dretske views this as a counter-example to the Closure Principle: you are justified in believing that the animals are zebras, that they are zebras entails that they are not cleverly disguised mules, but you're not justified in believing that they are not cleverly disguised mules.

What can we say against this? Can we define the intuition behind the Closure Principle? The Closure Principle holds that when S is justified in believing P and P entails Q, S is justified in believing Q. There are at least two reasons why this might be the case. One reason would be that *the very same justification* S has for P also counts as justification for Q—i.e., whatever evidence supports P would also support Q when Q is a logical consequence of P. If that were generally true, then it would follow that the Closure Principle is true. Dretske's example effectively refutes *that* principle. Dretske's example shows that what is evidence for P need not be evidence for every logical consequence of P. The fact that the animals in the pen look like zebras is evidence that they are zebras, but it is not evidence that they aren't mules cleverly disguised to *look like zebras*.

However, another reason for believing the Closure Principle is this: if S is justified in believing P and P entails Q, then *P*, itself, constitutes an adequate reason for believing Q. The idea is simply that deduction is an epistemically permissible way to expand your corpus of beliefs. This idea is probably the real source of the intuition in favor of closure. What Dretske says about his zebra-in-the-zoo case does not address this idea; what he says is only that the evidence you have for thinking the animals are zebras is not evidence against their being cleverly disguised mules. That much seems clear. But Dretske doesn't explain why the fact that *the animals in the pen are zebras* wouldn't be a sufficient reason for thinking that they're not cleverly disguised mules, given that you justifiably believe that the animals are zebras.

Peter Klein has pressed the above point.[9] However, Klein argues that, even though the above reply enables the skeptic to defend premise (1) against Dretske's attack, it nevertheless leaves the skeptic with a problem in defending premise (2). To defend premise (2), what the skeptic has to argue is that I have no available source of justification for the proposition that I'm not a brain in a vat. In defending the Closure Principle, we have just said that when P entails Q and P is justified, P is itself an adequate source of justification for Q—deductive arguments are a source of justification. So the skeptic must argue that, among other things, I don't have *that* kind of justification for believing I'm not a brain in a vat. Since, as premise (3) now assures us, the proposition that I have a body would provide just that sort of adequate justification for thinking I'm not a brain in a vat, the skeptic would have to argue that I don't have that proposition in particular available as a source of justification for thinking I'm not a brain in a vat.

What this means is that, in order to establish premise (2), the skeptic would first have to establish that I'm not justified in believing that I have a body, since that belief, if justified, would be one adequate source of justification for the claim that I'm not a brain in a vat. But that I'm not justified in believing that I have a body is just the conclusion of the argument. So it seems that the skeptical argument begs the question—one of its premises can't be established unless the conclusion is established first.[10]

To put the point another way:[11] suppose I start out thinking that I'm justified in believing I have a body, and the skeptic then proposes to argue me out of this position. He starts by informing me that the Closure Principle is true, because it is epistemically permissible to add to your body of beliefs the deductive consequences of any of your justified beliefs. The skeptic then asserts that I have no available justification for believing I'm not a brain in a vat. I naturally reply, "Yes I do, because I justifiably believe I have a body, which entails that I'm not a brain in a vat, and you just told me that it is epistemically premissible to add to my belief system the deductive consequences of any of my justified beliefs." What will the skeptic say? Why is this not an adequate source of justification for thinking I'm not a brain in a vat? Because I'm *not* justified in thinking I have a body? But that's just the conclusion the skeptic is trying to establish; I'm not going to grant that off hand. So the skeptic needs some other argument for the claim that I'm not justified in thinking I have a body. But if he has such an argument, then he doesn't need to use the brain-in-a-vat argument to begin with, because he would have an independent argument for the same conclusion.

5. What's wrong with these responses?

In short, Dretske's response to the argument is this: Okay, I don't know whether I'm a brain in a vat, but that doesn't matter; I still know that I have a body. And Klein's suggestion is this: Suppose we grant the Closure Principle. Then the skeptic's claim that I'm not justified in believing I'm not a brain in a vat just begs the question.

In spite of what we have said above in the way of philosophical analysis, I think intuition still balks at these responses. It seems as if there must be something wrong with them. It doesn't seem right that I can just admit that I don't know whether I'm a brain in a vat and continue to go on claiming to know all the things I have hitherto thought I knew. But nor does it seem right that the fact that I have two hands could be an adequate proof that I'm not a brain in a vat.

Let's try to articulate why the responses seem wrong. Consider the following two, possibly analogous cases:

> *Case (i) (the courtroom case)*: Imagine that S is on trial for murder. The prosecution offers as evidence the fact that S's blood was found at the scene of the crime along with the victims' blood. The best explanation for this, they say, is that S cut himself while stabbing his victims. The jurors find this argument initially persuasive. However, the defense attorney offers an alternative hypothesis: perhaps S is innocent, and the blood was planted at the crime scene by overzealous police officers seeking to frame S.

We can imagine how jury members might react to the defense hypothesis. Some jurors might feel that, being unable to rule out the alternative hypothesis, they should acquit S. Jurors arguing for a conviction might argue that the defense hypothesis should be rejected because it requires an improbable conspiracy on the part of the police department, because the police had no motive to frame S, and so on. But one thing that a jury member could not be expected to say is the following: "Okay, I agree that we have no reason for rejecting the defense hypothesis. But I still think we should convict S anyway, because we know he did it." Another thing that a juror would probably not come up with is this: "The defense attorney's claim that we can't rule out his hypothesis begs the question, because if we know S is guilty, then we *can* rule out the defense hypothesis."

The first of these unsatisfactory responses parallels Dretske's response to the skeptic. The second parallels Klein's response. If either of these responses were offered, they would probably be met with looks of puzzlement from the other jury members.

> *Case (ii) (the scientific case)*: Two scientists are arguing over the interpretation of quantum mechanics. Physicist A proposes the Copenhagen interpretation, noting that it accounts for a number of weird experimental results. The Copenhagen interpretation is the received view. Physicist B then proposes Bohm's interpretation of quantum mechanics, which is incompatible with the Copenhagen interpretation, noting that Bohm's theory accounts for all of the same experimental results. Now A might be expected to object that Bohm's theory conflicts with relativity, or that it is

> somehow less parsimonious than the Copenhagen interpretation. But one thing A would probably not say is the following: "Okay, I agree that I can't rule out Bohm's theory; for all I know, that may be the right interpretation. But nevertheless, I still know that the Copenhagen interpretation is correct." Nor could we expect A to resort to the following objection: "Your claim that I can't rule out Bohm's theory begs the question, because if I know the Copenhagen interpretation is right, and Bohm's theory conflicts with the Copenhagen interpretation, then I *can* rule out Bohm's theory."

Again, both of these would strike us as illogical replies; yet they are, respectively, analogous to Dretske's and Klein's responses to the brain-in-a-vat argument. If Dretske's or Klein's response to the brain-in-a-vat argument is correct, then one of these absurd replies should be correct in the courtroom case and the scientific case.

Dretske, of course, would challenge the analogy. It is not his view that, in order to know something, one *never* needs to rule out alternative possibilities. Rather, his view is that there are certain kinds of alternatives that one needs to rule out (call them the "relevant alternatives") in order to know something, and there are other kinds of alternatives that one does not need to rule out (the "irrelevant alternatives").[12] Dretske would claim that the brain-in-a-vat hypothesis is an irrelevant alternative, but the defense hypothesis in the courtroom case and Bohm's theory in the scientific case are each *relevant* alternatives. Of course, this claim remains only a promissory note until it is explained what makes an alternative "relevant." According to Dretske, an alternative is relevant only if it is *genuinely possible*, in a certain sense:

> [T]he difference between a relevant and an irrelevant alternative resides, not in what we happen to *regard* as a real possibility (whether reasonably or not), but in the kind of possibilities that actually exist in the objective situation.[13]

Dretske doesn't give a precise analysis of the sense of "possible" he is invoking here, but his discussion makes it clear that it is a sense stronger than logical possibility, stronger than physical possibility, and non-epistemic.[14] Whether something is genuinely possible is supposed to be independent of our beliefs, evidence, and/or knowledge.

Dretske might argue that the brain-in-a-vat hypothesis is an irrelevant alternative, on the grounds that it is not, in his sense, genuinely possible for me to be a brain in a vat (perhaps because no one possesses the technology for keeping a disembodied brain alive, nor for stimulating it in the right ways). As a result, it is not a condition on our knowing about the external world that we rule out the brain-in-a-vat hypothesis. However, Dretske would have difficulty distinguishing this case from the scientific case. In the scientific case, we have two competing physical theories. If one of these theories is true, then the other one is not only false, but physically impossible. If Bohm's theory is true then, for example, it is physically impossible for particles to have indeterminate positions, as required by the Copenhagen theory. This is typical of cases of competing scientific theories. Thus, Dretske's account would imply that the two hypotheses in the scientific case are not both relevant alternatives; whichever theory is false is an irrelevant alternative, because it is not genuinely possible. And therefore, Dretske's theory really would license the conclusion that one could know the Copenhagen interpretation to be true (assuming that it *is* true) even though one has no reason to reject Bohm's interpretation.

6. A reformulation of the skeptic's argument and the direct realist's response

This casts doubt on the validity of Klein's and Dretske's replies. However, all we've done so far is to pump the intuition that there is something wrong with those replies to the skeptic. We haven't actually explained what is wrong with them. Klein's response, at least, seems to work against the skeptical argument as formulated, so we need to reexamine the skeptic's argument.

The problem is that, as we formulated and defended the Closure Principle, your having justification for the claim that you're not a brain in a vat would be a *result* of your having justification for the claim that you have a body. But what the skeptic wants to say is that your having justification for the claim that you're not a brain in a vat is a *precondition* on your having justification for the claim that you have a body—that you need to *first* be in a position to know you're not a brain in a vat *in order* to be justified in believing that you have a body. So the Closure Principle,

(1) If S is justified in believing P and P entails Q, then S is justified in believing Q,

doesn't do justice to the skeptic's motivating idea.

Of course, it would not be acceptable to merely substitute the following, logically stronger principle:

(5) If P entails Q, then a *precondition* on S's being justified in believing P is that S be justified in believing Q.

This principle has no intuitive plausibility. For one thing, it would entail that a precondition on being justified in believing P, for any P, is that one be justified in believing ~~P, and also a precondition on being justified in believing ~~P is that one be justified in believing P; so one could never be justified in believing anything. No, the skeptic needs to say something more specific about the relationship between the brain-in-a-vat hypothesis and the claim that I have a body than that one entails the negation of the other. The skeptic needs to formulate an epistemological principle weaker than the absurd principle (5) above but still entailing that ruling out the brain-in-a-vat hypothesis is a precondition on knowing I have a body. At the same time, we want this epistemological principle, whatever it is, to account for our intuitions about the courtroom case and the scientific case discussed above.

So here's what we're looking for: we want an epistemological principle that, first of all, shows why in the courtroom case, we cannot merely grant that the defense hypothesis of a police conspiracy may be true and still claim to know that S is guilty. It should at the same time explain why, presumably for the same reason, we cannot merely grant that Bohm's interpretation of quantum mechanics may be correct and still claim to know that the Copenhagen interpretation is the right one. The Closure Principle, of course, would satisfy this desideratum. But second, we want the principle to explain why in the courtroom case, the defense attorney's argument does not beg the question, and in the scientific case, the physicist criticizing the Copenhagen interpretation is not begging the question either. This is where the Closure Principle falls short, because it does not tell us why the received view in these cases couldn't count as a source of justification for rejecting the rival hypotheses. Finally, we want our epistemological principle to explain why one *might think* the brain-in-a-vat argument was sound. We don't actually want to make the brain-in-a-vat argument out to *be* sound; in fact, it is a bonus if we can explain why the brain-in-a-vat argument is not sound, even though it might reasonably appear so.

Now consider the following epistemological principle, which I will call the "Preference Principle" (because it concerns the preference of one hypothesis over another):

(6) If E is any evidence and H_1 and H_2 are two incompatible explanations for E, then S is justified in believing H_1 on the basis of E only if S has an independent reason for rejecting H_2.

In this context, an "independent reason" means a reason distinct from H_1 and not justified, directly or indirectly, through H_1. So the idea is that when you're faced with two competing explanations of certain data, you can't accept the one explanation until you have first ruled out the other. One's reasons for rejecting H_2 might include *a priori* reasons, such as that H_2 is significantly less simple than H_1, as well as empirical reasons.

Notice how the Preference Principle is weaker than the principle (5) that we rejected above. (5) would require us to be able to rule out each logical contrary of H_1 (in the sense of having reason to accept its negation), in order to be justified in accepting H_1. Thus, for example, we would have to be able to rule out $(\sim H_1$ & $Q)$, where Q is any arbitrary proposition, as a precondition on being justified in accepting H_1. But the Preference Principle doesn't demand this. It only concerns the alternative *explanations of the data*. If H_1 is an explanation of E, $(\sim H_1$ & $Q)$ will not generally be an explanation of E. For instance, Newton's Theory of Gravity (along with background assumptions) is an explanation for the fact that things fall to the ground when dropped. But the proposition, "Newton's Theory of Gravity is false and my socks are white" is not an explanation for the fact that things fall to the ground when dropped. So in order to accept the Theory of Gravity, we are not required to have an independent reason for rejecting, "the Theory of Gravity is false and my socks are white." This is fortunate, since the only reason I in fact have for rejecting that proposition is the Theory of Gravity.

The Preference Principle seems plausible intuitively, and it satisfies our desiderata. In the courtroom case, the hypothesis that S is guilty and the hypothesis that S was framed by the police are two competing explanations for the fact that S's blood was found at the crime scene, so we cannot accept that S is guilty on the basis of that evidence unless we rule out the other hypothesis.[15] Also, relying on the Preference Principle, the defense attorney is not open to a charge of begging the question. To assert that we have *no reason* for rejecting the defense hypothesis may require begging the question, because in order to establish that we have no such reason, one must first establish that we don't know S is guilty. However, in applying the Preference Principle, the defense attorney only need assert that we have no *independent* reason for rejecting the defense hypothesis, i.e., no reason that is independent of the claim that S is guilty. And to argue that we have no reason *independent of the claim that S is guilty* for rejecting the defense hypothesis clearly does not require one to first establish that we don't know that S is guilty. Similarly, for the scientific case, we have two competing hypotheses, so according to the Preference Principle we must rule out Bohm's theory before we can accept the Copenhagen theory, and we must do so on grounds independent of the Copenhagen theory.

Now when we turn to the brain-in-a-vat argument, we can see why the argument would appear to be sound and non-question-begging—*if* one accepts one of the assumptions of indirect realism. If one accepts that beliefs about the external world are hypotheses for which the evidence is that we have certain sorts of sensory experiences, then the Preference Principle comes into play. Frank Jackson states this view particularly clearly:

> Our beliefs about objects, *all* of them (including the ones about causal links between sense-data and objects), form a theory, "the theory of the external world," which is then justified by its explanatory and predictive power with respect to our sense-data.[16]

Our ordinary, common sense beliefs about the external world, on the one hand, and the brain-in-a-vat hypothesis, on the other hand, are then two competing explanations for the same data. Therefore, just as in the courtroom case and the scientific case, we must rule out the brain-in-a-vat hypothesis in order to be justified in accepting our common sense beliefs about the external world on the basis of that data. So the indirect realist is faced with the responsibility of refuting the brain-in-a-vat hypothesis.

On the other hand, we can also see why we need not accept the brain-in-a-vat argument with its skeptical conclusion—if we adopt a direct realist account of perception. For the direct realist, perceptual beliefs about the external world are foundational; they are not hypotheses posited to explain anything. *Some* beliefs about the external world are hypotheses posited to explain evidence, such as atomic theory or electromagnetic theory; but immediate perceptual beliefs such as "Here is a red, round thing" are not. So the direct realist is in a position to make a principled distinction between, on the one hand, the courtroom case or the scientific case, where alternative hypotheses *do* need to be ruled out; and, on the other hand, the case of our ordinary perceptual beliefs. In the courtroom case and the scientific case, we really do have hypotheses posited to explain certain data, and as a result, the justification of a particular hypothesis depends upon a claim of superiority for that hypothesis over the alternative explanations.

Furthermore, the direct realist is in a position to explain simply how I know I'm not a brain in a vat. When I look at my two hands, for example, I know directly that I have two hands. It follows from this that I am not a brain in a vat. Notice that what is a question-begging argument for the indirect realist is not question-begging for the direct realist. For the indirect realist, the argument just proposed is circular, because I have to start with the mere fact that I have certain sorts of experiences. From there, I don't have any way of getting to the claim that I have two hands except by ruling out the alternative explanations of those experiences. So I can't use the fact that I have two hands to rule out skeptical alternatives. But the argument is *not* circular as proposed by the direct realist, because I'm allowed to *start* from the claim that I have two hands. I'm not required to give an argument for that, so in particular I do not have to give an argument for it that presupposes the conclusion that I'm not a brain in a vat. The conclusion that I'm not a brain in a vat can be justified by a linear argument starting from foundational propositions.

7. Two objections

Objection #1

The direct realist line gets us out of the skeptical problem. But does it perhaps get us too much? There are some circumstances in which we genuinely need to consider alternative "hypotheses" to our perceptual judgements. We do not want our epistemological theory to rule out all such circumstances automatically. We don't want our response to the brain-in-a-vat argument to turn into a recipe for dogmatism with respect to perceptual beliefs.

Here is an example of the sort of circumstance I have in mind. Suppose I am driving late at night. There's a stone wall running along the side of the road. And suppose I seem to see a ghostly white figure at the side of the road walk through the stone wall, at a place where there is no opening. Now I can consider a few different hypotheses. One possibility is that I just saw a ghost walk through a wall. Another possibility is that there was actually an opening in the wall that I somehow did not see, and I saw a person who was walking through it. And a third possibility—the "skeptical" hypothesis if you like—is that there was neither person nor ghost there at all, and I merely hallucinated it. In this circumstance, it seems that I should weight the advantages and disadvantages of the possible explanations for my experience, as the Preference Principle would suggest. In fact the rational conclusion seems to be the "skeptical" one.

But wouldn't my direct realism enable me to resist this, just as it enables me to resist the brain-in-a-vat argument? Suppose I say that I have foundational knowledge that the white figure just walked through the wall, and since this entails that I did not *merely* hallucinate the figure, I can easily rule out that skeptical hypothesis. Isn't this comparable to claiming that since I have foundational knowledge that I have two hands, I can rule out the brain-in-a-vat hypothesis?

The key to unraveling this objection is the notion of *prima facie* justification. The direct realist need not—and should not—hold that perceptual beliefs have a kind of justification that is immune from countervailing considerations. He should hold that the justification attaching to immediate perceptual beliefs is, while foundational, nevertheless defeasible justification. The idea here is similar to the legal concept of presumption: perceptual beliefs may be presumed true unless and until contrary evidence appears. As long as there are no special grounds for doubting a given perceptual belief, it retains its status as justified, but when other, justified or *prima facie* justified beliefs start disconfirming it, the presumption in favor of the perceptual belief can be defeated and the perceptual belief can wind up unjustified.[17]

This is the case in the example just described. I have a certain degree of *prima facie* justification for thinking the ghostly figure just walked through the wall. As I might say, *if I didn't know better*, I would naturally (and reasonably) assume that that is what happened. However, I have a large body of background knowledge, which indicates among other things that people generally can't walk through walls and that ghosts probably don't exist, and this defeats my justification for thinking the figure walked through the wall. It seems clear that this must be the right analysis of the case—as opposed to the view that we always need to rule out the possibility of hallucination before accepting perceptual beliefs—because in cases in which there is no evidence either for or against the hypothesis of hallucination (e.g., if I had merely seen a rabbit sitting by the side of the road), our default assumption is that things are the way they appear.

Now the brain-in-a-vat hypothesis is different. There are no grounds for suspecting that I'm a brain in a vat, in the way that there *are* grounds for suspecting that my seeming ghost sighting is a hallucination. So the presumption in favor of my perceptual belief that I have two hands, for example, remains undefeated, and this belief is therefore available for constructing an argument against the brain-in-a-vat hypothesis.

Objection #2

Does my response to skepticism merely beg the question? The skeptic's position is that we are not justified in believing any contingent propositions about the external world. I have responded to the skeptic by putting forward a direct realist account of perceptual knowledge. In asserting direct realism, I am asserting that we have a certain kind of justification for certain propositions about the external world. So at least part of my direct realist thesis is simply the negation of the skeptical thesis—namely, that we *are* justified in believing some propositions about the external world. Doesn't this mean that my response merely begs the question against skepticism? Obviously, the skeptic will just immediately reject direct realism. How does my asserting direct realism constitute any more of a response to the skeptic's position than just saying, "Skepticism is false"?

In answer to this objection, we need to distinguish two senses in which one might give a "response to the skeptic." One way to respond to the skeptic would be to give a positive argument, addressed to the skeptic, to show that we *do* have knowledge of the external world. This we might term an *aggressive* response to the skeptic. As the above objection shows, I have not given an adequate response of this kind. In fact, I do not believe it is possible to give a non-question-begging, positive argument against skepticism.

However, another sense in which one might be said to respond to the skeptic is this: one might confront an argument produced by the skeptic that tries to show that we *don't* have knowledge of the external world, and show how our common sense beliefs can be defended in the face of that argument. That is, one might demonstrate how the skeptical argument fails to give us a good reason for thinking that we don't know about the external world. We can call this sort of response a *defensive* response to the skeptic.

That is the sort of response I have provided. Given this aim, my asserting direct realism is a legitimate and non-question-begging move. I do not put forward direct realism as a premise from which to prove, positively, that we can know about the external world. That would certainly beg the question. Rather, I argue that the skeptic has only refuted one possible account of our knowledge of the external world, namely, indirect realism. I put forward direct realism by way of showing that there is an alternative account of our knowledge of the external world that is not damaged by the skeptical argument. The point is that if we take the direct realist line, then the skeptic hasn't given us any non-question-begging grounds for changing our position. The skeptic has merely assumed that we will take the indirect realist line.

8. Conclusion

Now let's conclude with a review of what I have and haven't done. I have proposed an epistemological form of direct realism according to which perception gives us a kind of justification for certain beliefs about the external world that is

(a) foundational, in the sense that the perceptual beliefs are not based on any other beliefs, but
(b) defeasible, in the sense that countervailing evidence can rationally require us to revise the perceptual beliefs.

I have not sought to elaborate and argue for this theory in any detail. Rather, I have focused on demonstrating one important advantage that a theory of this kind has over indirect realism, an advantage that has hitherto been overlooked by direct and indirect realists alike. I have shown that, whereas the indirect realist has an obligation of refuting the brain-in-a-vat hypothesis on grounds independent of our common sense beliefs about the external world, the direct realist can easily refute the brain-in-a-vat hypothesis on the basis of his beliefs about the external world. We saw that this does not involve the epistemological direct realist in circular reasoning, since he is able to construct a valid deductive argument starting only from foundational propositions. Finally, we have seen that the direct realist is able to handle the following cases in the intuitively acceptable manner:

(i) The courtroom case, in which we imagine that a jury member arguing for a conviction rejects the defense attorney's alternative explanation of the evidence, on the ground that the defendant is guilty,
(ii) the scientific case, in which a physicist rejects Bohm's interpretation of quantum mechanics on the sole ground that it contradicts the received interpretation, and
(iii) the case of the ghost sighting, where we imagine that I argue that my apparent ghost sighting could not have been a hallucination, since the figure in white really did walk through the wall.

The direct realist can distinguish each of the above examples of bad reasoning from his own reasoning against the skeptic. The first two cases are disanalogous because they both involve hypotheses inferred from evidence, whereas perceptual beliefs are not hypotheses inferred from evidence. The third case is disanalogous because it is a case in which specific reasons for doubting what I appear to have seen have defeated the initial justification for my perceptual belief, but there are no such defeaters for perceptual beliefs *in general*.

Thus, we've revealed a new way in which direct realism comes to our aid in fending off skepticism. I haven't shown that the indirect realist is inevitably committed to skepticism, since the indirect realist might still come up with a way to argue against the brain-in-a-vat hypothesis on *a priori* grounds.[18] The direct realist's advantage is simply that he doesn't need to go down that road—he doesn't have to play the skeptic's game to begin with. Moreover, the direct realist does not make out our knowledge of the external world to be contingent on any abstract, recherché reasoning of which only a small percentage of people in the world are aware. Refuting the brain-in-a-vat hypothesis is not a precondition on having knowledge of the external world, and such knowledge is well within the reach of all normal human beings.[19]

Notes

1 See Thomas Reid, *Inquiry and Essays* (Indianapolis, Ind.: Hackett, 1983), pp. 10–11 and throughout.

2 Compare Richard Fumerton's definition of "epistemological naive realism" in *Metaphysical and Epistemological Problems of Perception* (Lincoln, Nebr.: University of Nebraska Press, 1985), p. 73.

3 This principle will need some qualifications to protect it from easy counterexamples. For instance, if Q is a necessary truth, then P entails Q no matter what Q is, yet it is not apparently the case that, by knowing that the sky is blue, I am justified in believing Gödel's Incompleteness Theorem. We can avoid this problem by restricting the application of the principle to contingent propositions. We can further qualify the principle by restricting it to cases in which S is able to see that P entails Q. (See Peter Klein, "Skepticism, and Closure: Why the Evil Genius Argument Fails," *Philosophical Topics* 23 (1995): 213–36, p. 215.) These qualifications don't affect the skeptical argument or the responses to it discussed below.

4 Compare Peter Klein's remarks, *op. cit.*, p. 216.

5 See, for example, John McDowell, *Mind and World* (Cambridge, Mass.: Harvard University Press, 1996), pp. 111–13; Jonathan Dancy, "Arguments from Illusion," *The Philosophical Quarterly* 45 (1995): 421–38; and John Hyman, "The Causal Theory of Perception," *The Philosophical Quarterly* 42 (1992): 277–96.

6 *Op. cit.*, p. 294.

7 See, e.g., Robert Audi, *Belief, Justification, and Knowledge* (Belmont, Calif.: Wadsworth, 1988), p. 77; and Fred Dretske, "Epistemic Operators," *Journal of Philosophy* 67 (1970): 1007–23. But note that Dretske is discussing the Closure Principle for *knowledge* rather than for *justification*.

8 Dretske, *op. cit.*, p. 1016 (emphasis Dretske's).

9 Klein, *op. cit.*, pp. 218–22.

10 *Ibid.*, pp. 226–28.
11 In conversation, Professor Klein has denied that the argument of this paragraph is equivalent to that of the preceding two, nor to his own argument. I have been unable to understand the significant distinction, but I think the argument of this paragraph is worth considering regardless. If you like, consider it the argument of a hypothetical philosopher, Klein*.
12 See "The Pragmatic Dimension of Knowledge," *Philosophical Studies* 40 (1981): 363–78.
13 *Ibid.*, p. 377 (emphasis Dretske's).
14 Suppose I say, "The roads were covered with snow, so I *couldn't* make it to class." This seems to be the sort of modality Dretske has in mind. Of course, the roads' being snow-covered doesn't make it logically or nomologically impossible for me to come to class. Nor am I making an epistemic claim—I'm not just saying that I know I didn't make it to class. Many uses of modal terms in ordinary language are like this.
15 More precisely, the Preference Principle requires that we *have reason* (that is, have an available justification) for rejecting the alternative hypothesis. It doesn't require that one have actually entertained each alternative hypothesis. It may be true that one must actually entertain and reject each alternative, but that is something the skeptic need not commit to at this point.
16 *Perception: A Representative Theory* (Cambridge: Cambridge University Press, 1977), pp. 143–44.
17 John Pollock also takes this view in his *Contemporary Theories of Knowledge* (Lanham, Md.: Rowman & Littlefield, 1987), pp. 29, 175–79.
18 As Hilary Putnam has done in *Reason, Truth, and History* (Cambridge: Cambridge University Press, 1981), chapter 1.
19 I would like to thank Peter Klein and Brian McLaughlin for their helpful comments on earlier versions of this paper.

QUESTIONS

1 How does Huemer define "direct realism"?
2 What is the "preference principle"?
3 According to Huemer, why does the preference principle *not* apply to the case of the brain-in-a-vat hypothesis and perceptual beliefs?
4 According to Huemer, how does the ghost sighting case differ from ordinary perceptual beliefs?
5 What is meant by a "defensive response" to the skeptic?

Roderick Chisholm, "The Problem of the Criterion"

1

"The problem of the criterion" seems to me to be one of the most important and one of the most difficult of all the problems of philosophy. I am tempted to say that one has not begun to philosophize until one has faced this problem and has recognized how unappealing, in the end, each of the possible solutions is. I have chosen this problem as my topic for the Aquinas Lecture because what first set me to thinking about it (and I remain obsessed by it) were two treatises of twentieth century scholastic philosophy. I refer first to P. Coffey's two-volume work, *Epistemology or the Theory of Knowledge*, published in 1917. This led me in turn to the treatises of Coffey's great teacher, Cardinal D.J. Mercier: *Critériologie générale ou théorie générale de la certitude.*

Mercier and, following him, Coffey set the problem correctly, I think, and have seen what is necessary for its solution. But I shall not discuss their views in detail. I shall formulate the problem; then note what, according to Mercier, is necessary if we are to solve the problem; then sketch my own solution; and, finally, note the limitations of my approach to the problem.

2

What is the problem, then? It is the ancient problem of "the diallelus"—the problem of "the wheel" or "the vicious circle." It was put very neatly by Montaigne in his *Essays*. So let us begin by paraparaphrasing his formulation of the puzzle. To know whether things really are as they seem to be, we must have a *procedure* for distinguishing appearances that are true from appearances that are false. But to know whether our procedure is a good procedure, we have to know whether it really *succeeds* in distinguishing appearances that are true from appearances that are false. And we cannot know whether it does really succeed unless we already know which appearances are *true* and which ones are *false*. And so we are caught in a circle.

Let us try to see how one gets into a situation of this sort.

The puzzles begin to form when you ask yourself, "What can I really know about the world?" We all are acquainted with people who think they know a lot

Roderick Chisholm, "The Problem of the Criterion," *The Foundations of Knowing* (Minneapolis, Minn.: University of Minnesota Press, 1982).

more than in fact they do know. I'm thinking of fanatics, bigots, mystics, various types of dogmatists. And we have all heard of people who claim at least to know a lot less than what in fact they do know. I'm thinking of those people who call themselves "skeptics" and who like to say that people cannot know what the world is really like. People tend to become skeptics, temporarily, after reading books on popular science: the authors tell us we cannot know what things are like really (but they make use of a vast amount of knowledge, or a vast amount of what is claimed to be knowledge, to support this skeptical conclusion). And as we know, people tend to become dogmatists, temporarily, as a result of the effects of alcohol, or drugs, or religious and emotional experiences. Then they claim to have an inside view of the world and they think they have a deep kind of knowledge giving them a key to the entire workings of the universe.

If you have a healthy common sense, you will feel that something is wrong with both of these extremes and that the truth is somewhere in the middle: we can know far more than the skeptic says we can know and far less than the dogmatist or the mystic says that he can know. But how are we to decide these things?

3

How do we decide, in any particular case, whether we have a genuine item of knowledge? Most of us are ready to confess that our beliefs far transcend what we really know. There are things we believe that we don't in fact know. And we can say of many of these things that we know that we don't know them. I believe that Mrs. Jones is honest, say, but I don't know it, and I know that I don't know it. There are other things that we don't know, but they are such that we don't know that we don't know them. Last week, say, I thought I knew that Mr. Smith was honest, but he turned out to be a thief. I didn't know that he was a thief, and, moreover, I didn't know that I didn't know that he was a thief; I thought I knew that he was honest. And so the problem is: How are we to distinguish the real cases of knowledge from what only seem to be cases of knowledge? Or, as I put it before, how are we to decide in any particular case whether we have genuine items of knowledge?

What would be a satisfactory solution to our problem? Let me quote in detail what Cardinal Mercier says:

> If there is any knowledge which bears the mark of truth, if the intellect does have a way of distinguishing the true and the false, in short, *if* there *is* a criterion of truth, then this criterion should satisfy three conditions: it should be *internal, objective*, and *immediate*.
>
> It should be *internal*. No reason or rule of truth that is provided by an *external authority* can serve as an ultimate criterion. For the reflective doubts that are essential to criteriology can and should be applied to this authority itself. The mind cannot attain to certainty until it has found *within itself* a sufficient reason for adhering to the testimony of such an authority.
>
> The criterion should be *objective*. The ultimate reason for believing cannot be a merely *subjective* state of the thinking subject. A man is aware that he can reflect upon his psychological states in order to control them.

Knowing that he has this ability, he does not, so long as he has not made use of it, have the right to be sure. The ultimate ground of certitude cannot consist in a subjective feeling. It can be found only in that which, objectively, produces this feeling and is adequate to reason.

Finally, the criterion must be *immediate*. To be sure, a certain conviction may rest upon many different reasons some of which are subordinate to others. But if we are to avoid an infinite regress, then we must find a ground of assent that presupposes no other. We must find an *immediate* criterion of certitude.

Is there a criterion of truth that satisfies these three conditions? If so, what is it?

4

To see how perplexing our problem is, let us consider a figure that Descartes had suggested and that Coffey takes up in his dealings with the problem of the criterion. Descartes' figure comes to this.

Let us suppose that you have a pile of apples and you want to sort out the good ones from the bad ones. You want to put the good ones in a pile by themselves and throw the bad ones away. This is a useful thing to do, obviously, because the bad apples tend to infect the good ones and then the good ones become bad, too. Descartes thought our beliefs were like this. The bad ones tend to infect the good ones, so we should look them over very carefully, throw out the bad ones if we can, and then—or so Descartes hoped—we would be left with just a stock of good beliefs on which we could rely completely. But how are we to do the sorting? If we are to sort out the good ones from the bad ones, then, of course, we must have a way of recognizing the good ones. Or at least we must have a way of recognizing the bad ones. And—again, of course—you and I do have a way of recognizing good apples and also of recognizing bad ones. The good ones have their own special feel, look, and taste, and so do the bad ones.

But when we turn from apples to beliefs, the matter is quite different. In the case of the apples, we have a method—a criterion—for distinguishing the good ones from the bad ones. But in the case of the beliefs, we do not have a method or a criterion for distinguishing the good ones from the bad ones. Or, at least, we don't have one yet. The question we started with was: How *are* we to tell the good ones from the bad ones? In other words, we were asking: What is the proper method for deciding which are the good beliefs and which are the bad ones—which beliefs are genuine cases of knowledge and which beliefs are not?

And now, you see, we are on the wheel. First, we want to find out which are the good beliefs and which are the bad ones. To find this out we have to have some way—some method—of deciding which are the good ones and which are the bad ones. But there are good and bad methods—good and bad ways—of sorting out the good beliefs from the bad ones. And so we now have a new problem: How are we to decide which are the good methods and which are the bad ones?

If we could fix on a good method for distinguishing between good and bad methods, we might be all set. But this, of course, just moves the problem to a different level. How are we to distinguish between a good method for choosing good methods? If we continue in this way, of course, we are led to an infinite regress and we will never have the answer to our original question.

What do we do in fact? We do know that there are fairly reliable ways of sorting out good beliefs from bad ones. Most people will tell you, for example, that if you follow the procedures of science and common sense—if you tend carefully to your observations and if you make use of the canons of logic, induction, and the theory of probability—you will be following the best possible procedure for making sure that you will have more good beliefs than bad ones. This is doubtless true. But how do we know that it is? How do we know that the procedures of science, reason, and common sense are the best methods that we have?

If we do know this, it is because we know that these procedures work. It is because we know that these procedures do in fact enable us to distinguish the good beliefs from the bad ones. We say: "See—these methods turn out good beliefs." But *how* do we know that they do? It can only be that we already know how to tell the difference between the good beliefs and the bad ones.

And now you can see where the skeptic comes in. He'll say this: "You said you wanted to sort out the good beliefs from the bad ones. Then to do this, you apply the canons of science, common sense, and reason. And now, in answer to the question, 'How do you know that that's the right way to do it?', you say 'Why, I can see that the ones it picks out are the good ones and the ones it leaves behind are the bad ones.' But if you can *see* which ones are the good ones and which ones are the bad ones, why do you think you need a general method for sorting them out?"

5

We can formulate some of the philosophical issues that are involved here by distinguishing two pairs of questions. These are:

A) "*What* do we know? What is the *extent* of our knowledge?"
B) "How are we to decide *whether* we know? What are the *criteria* of knowledge?"

If you happen to know the answers to the first of these pairs of questions, you may have some hope of being able to answer the second. Thus, if you happen to know which are the good apples and which are the bad ones, then maybe you could explain to some other person how he could go about deciding whether or not he has a good apple or a bad one. But if you don't know the answer to the first of these pairs of questions—if you don't know what things you know or how far your knowledge extends—it is difficult to see how you could possibly figure out an answer to the second.

On the other hand, *if*, somehow, you already know the answers to the second of these pairs of questions, then you may have some hope of being able to answer the first. Thus, if you happen to have a good set of directions for telling whether apples are good or bad, then maybe you can go about finding a good one—assuming, of course, that there are some good apples to be found. But if you don't know the answer to the second of these pairs of questions—if you don't know how to go about deciding whether or not you know, if you don't know what the criteria of knowing are—it is difficult to see how you could possibly figure out an answer to the first.

And so we can formulate the position of *the skeptic* on these matters. He will say: "You cannot answer question A until you have answered question B. And you cannot answer question B until you have answered question A. Therefore you cannot answer either question. You cannot know what, if anything, you know, and there is no possible way for you to decide in any particular case." Is there any reply to this?

6

Broadly speaking, there are at least two other possible views. So we may choose among three possibilities.

There are people—philosophers—who think that they do have an answer to B and that, given their answer to B, they can then figure out their answer to A. And there are other people—other philosophers—who have it the other way around: they think that they have an answer to A and that, given their answer to A, they can then figure out the answer to B.

There don't seem to be any generally accepted names for these two different philosophical positions. (Perhaps this is just as well. There are more than enough names, as it is, for possible philosophical views.) I suggest, for the moment, we use the expressions "methodists" and "particularists." By "methodists," I mean, not the followers of John Wesley's version of Christianity, but those who think they have an answer to B, and who then, in terms of it, work out their answer to A. By "particularists" I mean those who have it the other way around.

7

Thus John Locke was a methodist—in our present, rather special sense of the term. He was able to arrive—somehow—at an answer to B. He said, in effect: "The way you decide whether or not a belief is a good belief—that is to say, the way you decide whether a belief is likely to be a genuine case of knowledge—is to see whether it is derived from sense experience, to see, for example, whether it bears certain relations to your sensations." Just what these relations to our sensations might be is a matter we may leave open, for present purposes. The point is: Locke felt that if a belief is to be credible, it must bear certain relations to the believer's sensations—but he never told us *how* he happened to arrive at this conclusion. This, of course, is the view that has come to be known as "empiricism." David Hume followed Locke in this empiricism and said that empiricism gives us an effective criterion for distinguishing the good apples from the bad ones. You can take this criterion to the library, he said. Suppose you find a book in which the author makes assertions that do not conform to the empirical criterion. Hume said: "Commit it to the flames: for it can contain nothing but sophistry and illusion."

8

Empiricism, then, was a form of what I have called "methodism." The empiricist—like other types of methodist—begins with a criterion and then he uses it to throw out the bad apples. There are two objections, I would say, to empiricism. The first—which applies to every form of methodism (in our present sense of the word—is that the criterion is very broad and far-reaching and at the same time completely arbitrary. How can one *begin* with a broad generalization? It seems especially odd that the empiricist—who wants to proceed cautiously, step by step, from experience—begins with such a generalization. He leaves us completely in the dark so far as concerns what *reasons* he may have for adopting this particular criterion rather than some other. The second objection applies to empiricism in particular. When we apply the empirical criterion—at least, as it was developed by Hume, as well as by many of those in the nineteenth and twentieth centuries who have called themselves "empiricists"—we seem to throw out, not only the bad apples but the good ones as well, and we are left, in effect, with just a few parings or skins with no meat behind them. Thus Hume virtually conceded that, if you are going to be empiricist, the only matters of fact that you can really know about pertain to the existence of sensations. "'Tis vain," he said, "To ask whether there be body." He meant you cannot know whether any physical things exist—whether there are trees, or houses, or bodies, much less whether there are atoms or other such microscopic particles. All you can know is that there are and have been certain sensations. You cannot know whether there is any you who experiences those sensations—much less whether any other people exist who experience sensations. And I think, if he had been consistent in his empiricism, he would also have said you cannot really be sure whether there have been any sensations in the past; you can know only that certain sensations exist here and now.

9

The great Scottish philosopher, Thomas Reid, reflected on all this in the eighteenth century. He was serious about philosophy and man's place in the world. He finds Hume saying things implying that we can know only of the existence of certain sensations here and now. One can imagine him saying: "Good Lord! What kind of nonsense is this?" What he did say, among other things, was this: "A traveller of good judgment may mistake his way, and be unawares led into a wrong track; and while the road is fair before him, he may go on without suspicion and be followed by others but, when it ends in a coal pit, it requires no great judgment to know that he hath gone wrong, nor perhaps to find out what misled him."

Thus Reid, as I interpret him, was not an empiricist; nor was he, more generally, what I have called a "methodist." He was a "particularist." That is to say, he thought that he had an answer to question A, and in terms of the answer to question A, he then worked out kind of an answer to question B. An even better example of a "particularist" is the great twentieth century English philosopher, G.E. Moore.

Suppose, for a moment, you were tempted to go along with Hume and say

"The only thing about the world I can really know is that there are now sensations of a certain sort. There's a sensation of a man, there's the sound of a voice, and there's feeling of bewilderment or boredom. But that's all I can really know about." What would Reid say? I can imagine him saying something like this: "Well, you can talk that way if you want to. But you know very well that it isn't true. You know that you are there, that you have a body of such and such a sort and that other people are here, too. And you know about this building and where you were this morning and all kinds of other things as well." G.E. Moore would raise his hand at this point and say: "I know very well this is a hand, and so do you. If you come across some philosophical theory that implies that you and I cannot know that this is a hand, then so much the worse for the theory." I think that Reid and Moore are right, myself, and I'm inclined to think that the "methodists" are wrong.

Going back to our questions A and B, we may summarize the three possible views as follows: there is skepticism (you cannot answer either question without presupposing an answer to the other, and therefore the questions cannot be answered at all); there is "methodism" (you begin with an answer to B); and there is "particularism" (you begin with an answer to A). I suggest that the third possibility is the most reasonable.

10

I would say—and many reputable philosophers would disagree with me—that, to find out whether you know such a thing as that this is a hand, you don't have to apply any test or criterion. Spinoza has it right. "In order to know," he said, "there is no need to know that we know, much less to know that we know that we know."

This is part of the answer, it seems to me, to the puzzle about the diallelus. There are many things that quite obviously, we do know to be true. If I report to you the things I now see and hear and feel—or, if you prefer, the things I now think I see and hear and feel—the chances are that my report will be correct; I will be telling you something I know. And so, too, if you report the things that you think you now see and hear and feel. To be sure, there are hallucinations and illusions. People often think they see or hear or feel things that in fact they do not see or hear or feel. But from this fact—that our senses do sometimes deceive us—it hardly follows that your senses and mine are deceiving you and me right now. One may say similar things about what we remember.

Having these good apples before us, we can look them over and formulate certain criteria of goodness. Consider the senses, for example. One important criterion—one epistemological principle—was formulated by St. Augustine. It is more reasonable, he said, to trust the senses than to distrust them. Even though there have been illusions and hallucinations, the wise thing, when everything seems all right, is to accept the testimony of the senses. I say "when everything seems all right." If on a particular occasion something about *that* particular occasion makes you suspect that particular report of the senses, if, say, you seem to remember having been drugged or hypnotized, or brainwashed, then perhaps you should have some doubts about what you think you see, or hear, or feel, or smell. But if nothing about this particular occasion leads you to suspect what the senses report on this particular occasion, then the wise thing is to take such a report at its face value. In short the senses should be regarded as innocent until there is some positive reason, on some particular occasion, for thinking that they are guilty on that particular occasion.

One might say the same thing of memory. If, on any occasion, you think you remember that such-and-such an event occurred, then the wise thing is to assume that that particular event did occur—unless something special about this particular occasion leads you to suspect your memory.

We have then a kind of answer to the puzzle about the diallelus. We start with particular cases of knowledge and then from those we generalize and formulate criteria of goodness—criteria telling us what it is for a belief to be epistemologically respectable. Let us now try to sketch somewhat more precisely this approach to the problem of the criterion.

11

The theory of evidence, like ethics and the theory of value, presupposes an objective right and wrong. To explicate the requisite senses of "right" and "wrong," we need the concept of *right preference*—or, more exactly, the concept of one state of mind being *preferable*, epistemically, to another. One state of mind may be *better*, epistemically, than another. This concept of epistemic preferability is what Cardinal Mercier called an *objective* concept. It is one thing to say, objectively, that one state of mind is *to be preferred* to another. It is quite another thing to say, subjectively, that one state of mind is in fact preferred to another—that someone or other happens to prefer the one state of mind to the other. If a state of mind A is to be preferred to a state of mind B, if it is, as I would like to say, intrinsically preferable to B, then anyone who prefers B to A is *mistaken* in his preference.

Given this concept of epistemic preferability, we can readily explicate the basic concepts of the theory of evidence. We could say, for for example, that a proposition p is *beyond reasonable doubt t* provided only that believing *p* is then epistemically preferable for S to withholding *p*—where by "withholding *p*" we mean the state of neither accepting *p* nor its negation. It is evident to me, for example, that many people are here. This means it is epistemically preferable for me to believe that many people are here than for me neither to believe nor to disbelieve that many are people here.

A proposition is *evident* for a person if it is beyond reasonable doubt for that person and is such that his including it among the propositions upon which he bases his decisions is preferable to his not so including it. A proposition is *acceptable* if withholding it is *not* preferable to believing it. And a proposition is *unacceptable* if withholding it *is* preferable to believing it.

Again, some propositions are not beyond reasonable doubt but they may be said to have *some presumption in their favor*. I suppose that the proposition that each of us will be alive an hour from now is one that has some presumption in its favor. We could say that a proposition is of this sort provided only that believing the proposition is epistemically preferable to believing its negation.

Moving in the other direction in the epistemic hierarchy, we could say that a proposition is *certain*, absolutely certain, for a given subject at a given time, if that proposition is then evident to that subject and if there is no other proposition that is such that believing that other proposition is then epistemically preferable for him to believing the given proposition. It is certain for me, I would say, that there seem to be many people here and that 7 and 5 are 12. If this is so, then each of the two propositions is evident to me and there are no other propositions that are such that it would be even better, epistemically, if I were to believe those other propositions.

This concept of epistemic preferability can be axiomatized and made the basis of a system of epistemic logic exhibiting the relations among these and other concepts of the theory of evidence. For present purposes, let us simply note how they may be applied in our approach to the problem of the criterion.

12

Let us begin with the most difficult of the concepts to which we have just referred—that of a proposition being *certain* for a man at a given time. Can we formulate *criteria* of such certainty? I think we can.

Leibniz had said that there are two kinds of immediately evident proposition—the "first truths of fact" and the "first truths of reason." Let us consider each of these in turn.

Among the "first truths of fact," for any man at any given time, I would say, are various propositions about his own state of mind at that time—his thinking certain thoughts, his entertaining certain beliefs, his being in a certain sensory or emotional state. These propositions all pertain to certain states of the man that may be said to manifest or present themselves to him at that time. We could use Meinong's term and say that certain states are "self-presenting," where this concept might be marked off in the following way.

A man's being in a certain state is *self-presenting* to him at a given time provided only that (i) he is in that state at that time and (ii) it is necessarily true that if he is in that state at that time then it is evident to him that he is in that state at that time.

The states of mind just referred to are of this character. Wishing, say, that one were on the moon is a state that is such that a man cannot be in that state without it being evident to him that he is in that state. And so, too, for thinking certain thoughts and having certain sensory or emotional experiences. These states present themselves and are, so to speak, marks of their own evidence. They cannot occur unless it is evident that they occur. I think they are properly called the "first truths of fact." Thus St. Thomas could say that "the intellect knows that it possesses the truth by reflecting on itself."

Perceiving external things and remembering are not states that present themselves. But thinking that one perceives (or seeming to perceive) and thinking that one remembers (or seeming to remember) *are* states of mind that present themselves. And in presenting themselves they may, at least under certain favorable conditions, present something else as well.

Coffey quotes Hobbes as saying that "the inn of evidence has no sign-board." I would prefer saying that these self-presenting states are sign-boards—of the inn of indirect evidence. But these sign-boards need no further sign-boards in order to be presented, for they present themselves.

13

What of the first truths of reason? These are the propositions that some philosophers have called "a priori" and that Leibniz, following Locke, referred to as "maxims" or "axioms." These propositions are all necessary and have a further characteristic that Leibniz described in this way: "You will find in a hundred places that the Scholastics have said that these propositions are evident, *ex terminis*, as soon as the terms are understood, so that they were persuaded that the force of conviction was grounded in the nature of the terms, i.e., in the connection of their ideas." Thus St. Thomas referred to propositions that are "manifest through themselves."

An axiom, one might say, is a necessary proposition such that one cannot understand it without thereby knowing that it is true. Since one cannot know a proposition unless it is evident and one believes it, and since one cannot believe a proposition unless one understands it, we might characterize these first truths of reason in the following way:

A proposition is *axiomatic* for a given subject at a given time provided only that (i) the proposition is one that is necessarily true and (ii) it is also necessarily true that if the person then believes that proposition, the proposition is then evident to him.

We might now characterize the *a priori* somewhat more broadly by saying that a proposition is a priori for a given subject at a given time provided that one or the other of these two things is true: either (i) the proposition is one that is axiomatic for that subject at that time, or else (ii) the proposition is one such that it is evident to the man at that time that the proposition is entailed by a set of propositions that are axiomatic for him at that time.

In characterizing the "first truths of fact" and the "first truths of reason," I have used the expression "evident." But I think it is clear that such truths are not only evident but also certain. And they may be said to be *directly*, or *immediately*, evident.

What, then, of the indirectly evident?

14

I have suggested in rather general terms above what we might say about memory and the senses. These ostensible sources of knowledge are to be treated as innocent until there is positive ground for thinking them guilty. I will not attempt to develop a theory of the indirectly evident at this point. But I will note at least the *kind* of principle to which we might appeal in developing such a theory.

We could *begin* by considering the following two principles, M and P; M referring to memory, and P referring to perception or the senses.

M) For any subject S, if it is evident to S that she seems to remember that *a* was F, then it is beyond reasonable doubt for S that *a* was F.

P) For any subject S, if it is evident to S that she thinks she perceives that *a* is F, then it is evident to S that *a* is F.

"She seems to remember" and "she thinks she perceives" here refer to certain self-presenting states that, in the figure I used above, could be said to serve as sign-boards for the inn of indirect evidence.

But principles M and P, as they stand, are much too latitudinarian. We will find that it is necessary to make qualifications and add more and more conditions. Some of these will refer to the subject's sensory state; some will refer to certain of her other beliefs; and some will refer to the relations of confirmation and mutual support. To set them forth in adequate detail would require a complete epistemology.

So far as our problem of the criterion is concerned, the essential thing to note is this. In formulating such principles we will simply proceed as Aristotle did when he formulated his rules for the syllogism. As "particularists" in our approach to the problem of the criterion, we will fit our rules to the cases—to the apples we know to be good and to the apples we know to be bad. Knowing what we do about ourselves and the world, we have at our disposal certain instances that our rules or principles should countenance, and certain other instances that our rules or principles should rule out or forbid. And, as rational beings, we assume that by investigating these instances we can formulate criteria that any instance must satisfy if it is to be countenanced and we can formulate other criteria that any instance must satisfy if it is to be ruled out or forbidden.

If we proceed in this way we will have satisfied Cardinal Mercier's criteria for a theory of evidence or, as he called it, a theory of certitude. He said that any criterion, or any adequate set of criteria, should be internal, objective, and immediate. The type of criteria I have referred to are certainly *internal*, in his sense of the term. We have not appealed to any external authority as constituting the ultimate test of evidence. (Thus we haven't appealed to "science" or to "the scientists of our culture circle" as constituting the touchstone of what we know.) I would say that our criteria are *objective*. We have formulated them in terms of the concept of epistemic preferability—where the location "*p* is epistemically preferable to *q* for S" is taken to refer to an objective relation that obtains independently of the actual preferences of any particular subject. The criteria that we formulate, if they are adequate, will be principles that are necessarily true. And they are also *immediate*. Each of them is such that, if it is applicable at any particular time, then the fact that it is then applicable is capable of being directly evident to that particular subject at that particular time.

15

But in all of this I have presupposed the approach I have called "particularism." The "methodist" and the "skeptic" will tell us that we have started in the wrong place. If now we try to reason with them, then, I am afraid, we will be back on the wheel.

What few philosophers have had the courage to recognize is this: we can deal with the problem only by begging the question. It seems to me that, if we do recognize this fact, as we should, then it is unseemly for us to try to pretend that it isn't so.

One may object: "Doesn't this mean, then, that the skeptic is right after all?" I would answer: "Not at all. His view is only one of the three possibilities and in itself has no more to recommend it than the others do. And in favor of our approach there is the fact that we *do* know many things, after all."

QUESTIONS

1 What is "methodism"?
2 What is "particularism"?
3 What is "skepticism"?
4 Which of these views does Chisholm favor?

G.E. Moore, "Proof of an External World"

In the preface to the second edition of Kant's *Critique of Pure Reason* some words occur, which, in Professor Kemp Smith's translation, are rendered as follows:

> It still remains a scandal to philosophy ... that the existence of things outside of us ... must be accepted merely on *faith*, and that, if anyone thinks good to doubt their existence, we are unable to counter his doubts by any satisfactory proof.

...

It seems to me that, so far from its being true, as Kant declares to be his opinion, that there is only one possible proof of the existence of things outside of us, namely the one which he has given, I can now give a large number of different proofs, each of which is a perfectly rigorous proof; and that at many other times I have been in a position to give many others. I can prove now, for instance, that two human hands exist. How? By holding up my two hands, and saying, as I make a certain gesture with the right hand, "Here is one hand," and adding, as I make a certain gesture with the left, "and here is another." And if, by doing this, I have proved *ipso facto* the existence of external things, you will all see that I can also do it now in numbers of other ways: there is no need to multiply examples.

But did I prove just now that two human hands were then in existence? I do want to insist that I did; that the proof which I gave was a perfectly rigorous one; and that it is perhaps impossible to give a better or more rigorous proof of anything whatever. Of course, it would not have been a proof unless three conditions were satisfied; namely (1) unless the premiss which I adduced as proof of the conclusion was different from the conclusion I adduced it to prove; (2) unless the premiss which I adduced was something which I *knew* to be the case, and not merely something which I believed but which was by no means certain, or something which, though in fact true, I did not know to be so; and (3) unless the conclusion did really follow from the premiss. But all these three conditions were in fact satisfied by my proof. (1) The premiss which I adduced in proof was quite certainly different from the conclusion, for the conclusion was merely "Two human hands exist at this moment"; but the premiss was something far more

G.E. Moore, "Proof of an External World," *Proceedings of the British Academy* 25 (1939).

specific than this—something which I expressed by showing you my hands, making certain gestures, and saying the words "Here is one hand, and here is another." It is quite obvious that the two were different, because it is quite obvious that the conclusion might have been true, even if the premiss had been false. In asserting the premiss I was asserting much more than I was asserting in asserting the conclusion. (2) I certainly did at the moment *know* that which I expressed by the combination of certain gestures with saying the words "There is one hand and here is another." I *knew* that there was one hand in the place indicated by combining a certain gesture with my first utterance of 'here' and that there was another in the different place indicated by combining a certain gesture with my second utterance of "here." How absurd it would be to suggest that I did not know it, but only believed it, and that perhaps it was not the case! You might as well suggest that I do not know that I am now standing up and talking—that perhaps after all I'm not, and that it's not quite certain that I am! And finally (3) it is quite certain that the conclusion did follow from the premiss. This is as certain, as it is that if there is one hand here and another here *now*, then it follows that there are two hands in existence *now*.

My proof, then, of the existence of things outside of us did satisfy three of the conditions necessary for a rigorous proof. Are there any other conditions necessary for a rigorous proof, such that perhaps it did not satisfy one of them? Perhaps there may be; I do not know; but I do want to emphasize that, so far as I can see, we all of us do constantly take proofs of this sort as absolutely conclusive proofs of certain conclusions—as finally settling certain questions, as to which we were previously in doubt. Suppose, for instance, it were a question whether there were as many as three misprints on a certain page in a certain book. A says there are, B is inclined to doubt it. How could A prove that he is right? Surely he *could* prove it by taking the book, turning to the page, and pointing to three separate places on it, saying "There's one misprint here, another here, and another here": surely that is a method by which it *might* be proved! Of course, A would not have proved, by doing this, that there were at least three misprints on the page in question, unless it was certain that there was a misprint in each of the places to which he pointed. But to say that he *might* prove it in this way, is to say that it *might* be certain that there was. And if such a thing as that could ever be certain, then assuredly it was certain just now that there was one hand in one of the two places I indicated and another in the other.

I did, then, just now, give a proof that there were *then* external objects; and obviously, if I did, I could *then* have given many other proofs of the same sort that there were external objects *then*, and could now give many proofs of the same sort that there are external objects *now*.

But, if what I am asked to do is to prove that external objects have existed *in the past*, then I can give many different proofs of this also, but proofs which are in important respects of a different *sort* from those just given. And I want to emphasize that, when Kant says it is a scandal not to be able to give a proof of the existence of external objects, a proof of their existence in the past would certainly *help* to remove the scandal of which he is speaking. He says that, if it occurs to any one to question their existence, we ought to be able to confront him with a satisfactory proof. But by a person who questions their existence, he certainly means not merely a person who questions whether any exist at the moment of speaking, but a person who questions whether any have *ever* existed; and a proof that some have existed in the past would certainly therefore be relevant to *part* of what such a person is questioning. How then can I prove that there have been external objects in the past? Here is one proof. I can say: "I held up two hands above this desk not very long ago; therefore two hands existed not very long ago; therefore at least two external objects have existed at some time in the past, Q.E.D." This is a perfectly good proof, provided I *know* what is asserted in the premiss. But I *do* know that I held up two hands above this desk not very long ago. As a matter of fact, in this case you all know it too. There's no doubt whatever that I did. Therefore I have given a perfectly conclusive proof that external objects have existed in the past; and you will all see at once that, if this is a conclusive proof, I could have given many others of the same sort, and could now give many others. But it is also quite obvious that this sort of proof differs in important respects from the sort of proof I gave just now that there were two hands existing *then*.

I have, then, given two conclusive proofs of the existence of external objects. The first was a proof that two human hands existed at the time when I gave the proof; the second was a proof that two human hands had existed at a time previous to that at which I gave the proof. These proofs were of a different sort in important respects. And I pointed out that I could have given, then, many other conclusive proofs of both sorts. It is also obvious that I could give many others of both sorts now. So that, if these are the sort of proof that is wanted, nothing is easier than to prove the existence of external objects.

But now I am perfectly well aware that, in spite of all that I have said, many philosophers will still feel that I have not given any satisfactory proof of the point in question. And I want briefly, in conclusion, to say something as to why this dissatisfaction with my proofs should be felt.

One reason why, is, I think, this. Some people understand "proof of an external world" as including a proof of things which I haven't attempted to prove and haven't proved. It is not quite easy to say *what* it is that they want proved—*what* it is that is such that unless they got a proof of it, they would not say that they had a proof of the existence of external things; but I can make an approach to explaining what they want by saying that if I had proved the propositions which I used as *premisses* in my two proofs, then they would perhaps admit that I had proved the existence of external things, but, in the absence of such a proof (which, of course, I have neither given, nor attempted to give), they will say that I have not given what they mean by a proof of the existence of external things. In other words they want a proof of what I assert *now* when I hold up my hands and say 'Here's one hand and here's another'; and, in the other case, they want a proof of what I assert *now* when I say 'I did hold up two hands above this desk just now.' Of course, what they really want is not merely a proof of these two propositions, but something like a general statement as to how *any* propositions of this sort may be proved. This, of course, I haven't given; and I do not believe it can be given: if this is what is meant by proof of the existence of external things, I do not believe that any proof of the existence of external things is possible. Of course, in some cases what might be called a proof of propositions which seem like these can be got. If one of you suspected that one of my hands was artificial he might be said to get a proof of my proposition "Here's one hand, and here's another," by coming up and examining the suspected hand close up, perhaps touching and pressing it, and so establishing that it really was a human hand. But I do not believe that any proof is possible in nearly all cases. How am I to prove now that "Here's one hand, and here's another"? I do not believe I can do it. In order to do it, I should need to prove for one thing, as Descartes pointed out, that I am not now dreaming. But how can I prove that I am not? I have, no doubt, conclusive reasons for asserting that I am not now dreaming; I have conclusive evidence that I am awake: but that is a very different thing from being able to prove it. I could not tell you what all my evidence is; and I should require to do this at least, in order to give you a proof.

But another reason, why some people would feel dissatisfied with my proofs is, I think, not merely that they want a proof of something which I haven't proved, but that they think that, if I cannot give such extra proofs, then the proofs that I have given are not conclusive proofs at all. And this, I think, is a definite mistake. They would say: "If you cannot prove your premiss that here is one hand and here is another, then you do not know it. But you yourself have admitted that, if you did not know it, then your proof was not conclusive. Therefore your proof was not, as you say it was, a conclusive proof." This view that, if I cannot prove such things as these, I do not know them, is, I think, the view that Kant was expressing in the sentence which I quoted at the beginning of this lecture, when he implies that so long as we have no proof of the existence of external things, their existence must be accepted merely on *faith*. He means to say, I think, that if I cannot prove that there is a hand here, I must accept it merely as a matter of faith—I cannot know it. Such a view, though it has been very common among philosophers, can, I think, be shown to be wrong—though shown only by the use of premisses which are not known to be true, unless we do know of the existence of external things. I can know things, which I cannot prove; and among things which I certainly did know, even if (as I think) I could not prove them, were the premisses of my two proofs. I should say, therefore, that those, if any, who are dissatisfied with these proofs merely on the ground that I did not know their premisses, have no good reason for their dissatisfaction.

QUESTIONS

1. What are the premises and conclusion in Moore's "proof"?
2. According to Moore, what three conditions must an argument satisfy in order to count as a "proof"?

G.E. Moore, "Hume's Theory Examined"

I think, therefore, those philosophers who argue, on the ground of Hume's principles, that nobody can ever know of the existence of any material object, are right so far as the first step in their argument is concerned. They are right in saying: *If* Hume's principles are true, nobody can ever *know* of the existence of any material object—nobody can ever know that any such object even probably exists: meaning by a material object, an object which has shape and is situated in space; but which *is not* similar, except in these respects, to any of the sense-data which we have ever directly apprehended. But are they also right in the second step of their argument? Are they also right, in concluding: *Since* Hume's principles are true, nobody ever *does* know, even probably, of the existence of any material object? In other words: Are Hume's principles true?

You see, the position we have got to is this. If Hume's principles are true, then, I have admitted, I do *not* know *now* that this pencil—the material object—exists. If, therefore, I am to prove that I *do* know that this pencil exists, I must prove, somehow, that Hume's principles, one or both of them, are *not* true. In what sort of way, by what sort of argument, can I prove this?

It seems to me that, in fact, there really is no stronger and better argument than the following. I *do* know that this pencil exists; but I could not know this, if Hume's principles were true; *therefore*, Hume's principles, one or both of them, are false. I think this argument really is as strong and good a one as any that could be used: and I think it really is conclusive. In other words, I think that the fact that, if Hume's principles were true, I could not know of the existence of this pencil, is a *reductio ad absurdum* of those principles. But, of course, this is an argument which will not seem convincing to those who believe that the principles are true, nor yet to those who believe that I really do not know that this pencil exists. It seems like begging the question. And therefore I will try to shew that it really is a good and conclusive argument.

Let us consider what is necessary in order that an argument may be a good and conclusive one. A really conclusive argument is one which enables us to *know* that its conclusion is true. And one condition, which must be satisfied, if an argument is to enable us to know this, is that the conclusion must really follow from the premisses. Let us see, first, how my argument compares with that of my opponent in this respect.

G.E. Moore, "Hume's Theory Examined," in *Some Main Problems of Philosophy* (New York: Humanities Press, 1953).

My argument is this: I do know that this pencil exists; therefore Hume's principles are false. My opponent's argument on the contrary is: Hume's principles are true; therefore you do not know that this pencil exists. And obviously in respect of the certainty with which the conclusion follows from the premiss, these two arguments are equally good. *If* my opponent's conclusion follows from his premiss, my conclusion must certainly also follow from mine. For my opponent's conclusion does not follow from his premiss, except on one condition, namely, unless the following hypothetical proposition is true: *If* Hume's principles are true, then I do not know that this pencil exists. But if this proposition is true, then *my* conclusion also follows from my premiss. In fact, both arguments depend in this respect on exactly the same hypothetical proposition—the proposition which both I and my opponent have admitted to be true: namely that: If Hume's principles are true, then I do not know that this pencil exists. Neither conclusion follows from its premiss, unless this proposition is true; and each does follow from its premiss, if this proposition is true. And this state of things is an excellent illustration of a principle, which many philosophers are, I think, apt to forget: namely, that the mere fact that one proposition coheres with or follows from another does not by itself give us the slightest presumption in favour of its truth. My conclusion coheres with my premiss, exactly as strongly as my opponent's coheres with *his*. And yet obviously this mere fact does not give the slightest presumption in favour of either.

Both arguments, therefore, equally satisfy the first condition that is necessary to make an argument conclusive. Both equally satisfy the condition that the conclusion must follow from the premiss. What other condition, then, is necessary if an argument is to enable us to *know* that its conclusion is true?

The second condition, that is necessary, is this: Namely that we should *know* the premiss to be true. Obviously, I think, this condition must be satisfied, if the argument is to enable us to *know* that its conclusion is true. It is not sufficient merely that the premiss should *be* true, if we do not *know* that it is so. For suppose that the premiss is true, and the conclusion does follow from it, and *yet* I do not *know* that the premiss is true. How can this state of things possibly enable me to know that the conclusion is true? Obviously so long as this is the whole state of the case, I shall be just as far from *knowing* that the conclusion is true, as if I had never thought of the premiss at all. The argument may be, and is, a good argument in the sense that the conclusion does follow from the premiss, that the premiss is, in fact, true, and that, therefore the conclusion also is in fact true. But it is not a good argument in the sense that it can possibly enable either me or any one else to *know* that the conclusion is true. The mere fact that the premiss *is* true will not, by itself, enable any one whatever to know that the conclusion is so. If anybody whatever is to be enabled by the argument absolutely to *know* the conclusion, that person must himself first absolutely *know* that the premiss is true. And the same holds not only for absolute certainty but also for every degree of probability short of it. If any argument whatever is to enable me to know that its conclusion is in any degree probable, I must first know that its premiss is probable in at least the same degree. In other words, no argument is a good one, even in the sense that it enables us to know its conclusion to have any probability whatever, unless its premiss is at least as certain as its conclusion: meaning by "certain," not merely true or probably true, but *known* to be so.

The only way, then, of deciding between my opponent's argument and mine, as to which is the better, is by deciding which premiss is known to be true. My opponent's premiss is that Hume's principles are true; and unless this premiss not merely *is* true, but is absolutely known to be so, his argument to prove that I do not know of the existence of this pencil cannot be conclusive. Mine is that I do know of the existence of this pencil; unless this premiss not only *is* true, but is absolutely known to be so, my argument to prove that Hume's principles are false cannot be conclusive. And moreover the degree of certainty of the conclusion, in either case, supposing neither is quite certain, will be in proportion to the degree of certainty of the premiss. How is it to be decided which premiss, if either, is known? or which is the more certain?

One condition under which a premiss may be known to be true, is a condition which we have already stated. Namely, any proposition is known to be true, if we have a conclusive argument in its favour; if, that is to say, it does really follow from some premiss or set of premisses already *known* to be true. I say some premiss or *set of premisses*; and this new qualification should be noticed, because it introduces a complication. If any argument from a *single* premiss is to be conclusive, the *single* premiss must, as we have seen, be at least as certain as the conclusion: the conclusion cannot, by the help of any such argument, be known with more certainty than the premiss. But obviously in the case of a set of premisses, the conclusion may be *more* certain than any *single* one of the premisses. Here, too, however, each of the premisses must be known to be at least probable in some degree: no amount of premisses, which were not known to be probable at all, could enable us to know that the conclusion which followed from them all was even in the least degree probable. One way, therefore, in which a proposition can be known to be true, is if it follows from some premiss or set of premisses, each of which is already known to be so with some degree of certainty. And some philosophers seem to have thought that this is the only way in which any proposition can ever be known to be true. They seem to have thought, that is, that no proposition can ever be known to be true, unless it follows from some other proposition or set of propositions already known to be so.

But it is, I think, easy to see that, if this view were true, no man ever has known any proposition whatever to be in the slightest degree probable. For if I cannot know any proposition whatever to be either true or probably true, unless I have first known some other proposition, from which it follows, to be so; then, of course, I cannot have known this other proposition, unless I have first known some third proposition, before *it*; nor this third proposition, unless I have first known a fourth before it; and so on *ad infinitum*. In other words, it would follow that no man has ever known any proposition whatever to be even probably true, unless he has previously known an absolutely infinite series of other propositions. And it is quite certain that no man ever has thus known a really infinite series of propositions. If this view were true, then, neither my argument nor my opponent's argument could possibly be a good argument: neither of them could enable us to know that the conclusion was even in the least degree probable. And the same would be true of every other argument whatsoever. So that if this view—the view that we can never know any proposition whatever, unless we have a good argument for it—were true, then it would follow that we cannot ever know any proposition whatever to be true, since we never can have any good argument for it.

If, therefore, either my argument or my opponent's, or any other argument whatever, is to be a good one, it must be the case that we are capable of knowing at least *one* proposition to be true, *without* knowing any other proposition whatever from which it follows. And I propose to call this way of knowing a proposition to be true, *immediate* knowledge.

. . .

It is certain, then, that if any proposition whatever is ever known by us mediately, or because some other proposition is known from which it follows, some one proposition at least, must also be known by us *immediately*, or *not merely* because some other proposition is known from which it follows. And hence it follows that the conditions necessary to make an argument good and conclusive may just as well be satisfied, when the premiss is only known *immediately*, as when there are other arguments in its favour. It follows, therefore, that my argument: "I know this pencil to exist; therefore Hume's principles are false"; may be just as good an argument as any other, even though its premiss—the premiss that I do know that this pencil exists—is only known immediately.

But is this premiss in fact known by me immediately? I am inclined to think that it is, though this might be disputed, for the following reasons. It must be noticed, that the premiss is: I know that this pencil exists. What, therefore, I am claiming to know immediately is *not*, that this pencil exists, but that I know it to exist. And it may be said: Can I possibly know immediately such a thing as this? Obviously, I cannot know *that* I know that the pencil exists, unless I do know that the pencil exists; and it might, therefore, be thought that the first proposition can only be mediately known—known *merely* because the second is known. But it is, I think, necessary to make a distinction. From the mere fact that I should not know the first, *unless* I knew the second, it does not follow that I know the first *merely* because I know the second. And, in fact, I think I do know *both* of them immediately. This might be disputed in the case of the second also. It might be said: I certainly do not know immediately that the pencil exists; for I should not know it at all, unless I were directly apprehending certain sense-data, and knew that they were signs of its existence. And of course I admit, that I should not know it, unless I were directly apprehending certain sense-data. But this is again a different thing from admitting that I do not know it immediately. For the mere fact that I should not know it, unless certain other things were happening, is quite a different thing from knowing it *only* because I know *some other proposition*. The mere direct apprehension of certain sense-data is quite a different thing from the knowledge of any proposition; and yet I am not sure that it is not by itself quite sufficient to enable me to know that the pencil exists.

But whether the exact proposition which formed my premiss, namely: I do know that this pencil exists; or only the proposition: This pencil exists; or only the proposition: The sense-data which I directly apprehend are a sign that it exists; is known by me immediately, one or other of them, I think, certainly is so. And all three of them are much more certain than any premiss which could be used to prove that they are false; and also much more certain than any other premiss which could be used to prove that they are true. That is why I say that the strongest argument to prove that Hume's principles are false is the argument from a particular case, like this in which we do know of the existence of some material object. And similarly, if the object is to prove *in general* that we do know of the existence of material objects, no argument which is really stronger can, I think, be brought forward to prove this than particular instances in which we do in fact know of the existence of such an object. I admit, however, that other arguments may be more convincing; and perhaps some of you may be able to supply me with one that is. But, however, much more *convincing* it may be, it is, I think, sure to depend upon some premiss which is, in fact, less certain than the premiss that I do know of the existence of this pencil; and so, too, in the case of any arguments which can be brought forward to prove that we do not know of the existence of any material object.

QUESTIONS

1 What is meant by "immediate knowledge"?
2 Why does Moore say that we must have some immediate knowledge?

FURTHER READING ON SKEPTICISM

Audi, Robert, *Belief, Justification, and Knowledge* (Belmont, Calif.: Wadsworth, 1988).

Brueckner, Anthony, "Brains in a Vat," *Journal of Philosophy* 83 (1986): 148–67.

Chisholm, Roderick, *The Foundations of Knowing* (Minneapolis, Minn.: University of Minnesota Press, 1982).

DeRose, Keith, "Solving the Skeptical Problem," *Philosophical Review* 104 (1995): 1–52.

DeRose, Keith and Ted Warfield, *Skepticism: A Contemporary Reader* (New York: Oxford University Press, 1999).

Descartes, René, *The Philosophical Writings of Descartes*, ed. John Cottingham, Robert Stoothoff, and Dugald Murdoch (Cambridge: Cambridge University Press, 1984).

Dretske, Fred, "Epistemic Operators," *Journal of Philosophy* 67 (1970): 1007–23.

Feldman, Fred, "In Defense of Closure," *Philosophical Quarterly* 45 (1995): 487–94.

Foley, Richard, *Working Without a Net* (New York: Oxford University Press, 1993).

Fumerton, Richard, *Metaepistemology and Skepticism* (Lanham, Md.: Rowman & Littlefield, 1995.

Garrett, Brian, "A Sceptical Tension," *Analysis* 59 (1999): 205–6.

Huemer, Michael, *Skepticism and the Veil of Perception* (Lanham, Md.: Rowman & Littlefield, 2001).

Hume, David, *A Treatise of Human Nature* (Buffalo, N.Y.: Prometheus, 1992).

Klein, Peter, *Certainty: A Refutation of Skepticism* (Minneapolis, Minn.: University of Minnesota Press, 1981).

Lehrer, Keith, "Why Not Scepticism?" *Philosophical Forum* 2 (1971): 283–98.

Luper-Foy, Steven (ed.) *The Possibility of Knowledge* (Totowa, N.J.: Rowman & Littlefield, 1987).

Pollock, John and Joseph Cruz, *Contemporary Theories of Knowledge*, 2nd edn (Lanham, Md.: Rowman & Littlefield, 1999).

Stroud, Barry, *The Significance of Philosophical Skepticism* (Oxford: Clarendon, 1984).

Unger, Peter, *Ignorance: A Case for Scepticism* (Oxford: Clarendon, 1975).

Vogel, Jonathan, "Cartesian Skepticism and Inference to the Best Explanation," *Journal of Philosophy* 87 (1990): 658–66.

Williams, Michael, *Groundless Belief*, 2nd edn (Princeton, N.J.: Princeton University Press, 1999).

INDEX

a posteriori knowledge *see* empirical knowledge
a priori knowledge 3, 7–9, 10, 17, 125–30, 142–56, 161–3, 212, 283, 293, 388–9, 534, 599; and causal theory of knowledge 18, 437; and causation 299–301; and induction 212, 263, 311; in mathematics 208–13, 147–51; in science 148–9; *see also* synthetic a priori knowledge
abstract ideas 34, 38, 40, 49, 158
absurdity 70
acquaintance 127, 157, 160–4
acquired perception 61, 234–5
action at a distance 100
additivity principle 345, 348
after-images 77, 81, 403
Alston, William 3, 16–17, 370, 402ff.
analytic propositions *see* analytic–synthetic distinction
analytic–synthetic distinction 7–9, 125–8, 146–9, 152, 176–89, 192
angular size *see* visible magnitude
apparent magnitude *see* visible magnitude
appearances 33, 35, 47, 74, 106, 144, 172, 379, 383, 476, 64–5, 77–8, 150–1, 590–1
argument from illusion *see* illusion
Aristotle 40, 177, 190, 219, 323, 600
artificial language 184–5, 234–5
atheism 44, 46, 49n1, 60, 228
attributor factors 19, 492–7, 500
Austin, J.L. 5, 31, 74ff., 245, 263
Ayer, A.J. 8, 18, 31, 74–83 *passim*, 94, 127, 166ff., 333–4, 377, 435, 440ff., 444
Bacon, Francis 231
basic beliefs 105–6, 375, 391, 401, 417–19, 422; arguments against 377–80, 387–8, 408–11; *see also* foundationalism
Bayes, Thomas: Bayes' Theorem 296, 349–50
Bayesianism 296
behaviorism 89
being 41, 160, 172
belief: dispositional 7, 11–12, 114, 121n15, 253, 264–6; fixation of 276–80; occurrent 104, 253, 264; *see also* thoughts
Berkeley, George 4–5, 8, 28–30, 37ff., 49n1, 54–61 *passim*, 66–8, 158–9
bias 254, 277, 282–7, 306, 417
BonJour, Laurence 8, 9, 15–17, 129–30, 208ff., 370, 387ff., 419, 426, 430n4
brain in a vat 20–2, 438–9, 507–10, 527–34, 575–88

Carnap, Rudolf 8–9, 129, 178–9, 184–5, 187–92, 194ff., 290n14, 353
Carroll, Lewis 11, 253, 256ff., 484
causal theory of knowledge 18, 437, 450ff., 459, 472, 475–6
causal theory of perception 577
causal theory of reference 509, 532–45
causation 30, 48, 154, 341; backward 355; knowledge of 299–301; in memory 97–100
C-belief 420–2, 425
certainty 18, 20, 34, 64, 69, 92, 95
Chisholm, Roderick 22, 23, 283, 387,

414, 444, 465, 466, 468, 470, 473, 510–12, 590ff.
church/barn example (Austin) 78
circular reasoning 16–17, 114, 182, 218, 260, 322, 369–70, 373, 380–3, 389–90, 414, 420, 511, 568–9, 585, 587
Clark, Michael 18, 436–7, 447ff., 450, 455–8
clear and distinct ideas 20, 53
closure principle 21, 23, 438–9, 483–8, 509–10, 552–65, 578–85
Coady, C.A.J. 10, 218, 239ff.
cogito 69, 489n2, 508, 519–20
cognitive meaning *see* verificationism
cognitive synonymy *see* synonymy
cognitively spontaneous beliefs 393–401
coherence theory of justification *see* coherentism
coherentism 15–17, 370–1, 375, 389–401, 417–19, 424, 426; arguments against 380–2; *see also* perception, coherence of
cold, perception of 35, 37–40, 74, 308, 521
color 28, 30, 34, 37–41, 45, 65–6, 69, 71, 74, 144, 151, 154, 302, 304, 422, 516, 521
common sense 5, 22–3, 53, 57–60, 70, 73, 191, 312, 511
concepts 534–7; absolute 540–3; and analyticity 125–6; a priori 144–9; and simplicity 180
confirmation 9, 186–9, 323–31
confirmation theory 323–6; *see also* confirmation
consciousness 529–31; *see also* introspection
contextualism 19, 439, 491–7; objections to 498–500
contradiction 155
contrasting set 545–6
counterfactual analysis of knowledge 19, 437–8, 475–9
courtroom example *see* trial example
criterion of truth *see* problem of the criterion
crossword puzzle example 17, 371, 420–8
Cruz, Joseph 86–7, 104ff.
culpability 115, 118
custom 12, 307–9

deductive inference 12–13, 164, 293–5, 322–4
defeasibility theories 18–19, 436–7, 464–73
defeaters 109, 119–20, 436, 466–8
definitions 9, 179
delusions 71, 75–7
demons *see* evil demon
derivative knowledge 8, 164, 469–70
DeRose, Keith 19, 439, 491ff.
Descartes, René 19–21, 23, 46, 48, 55, 60, 69, 83n8, 414n4, 428, 489n2, 508, 513ff., 528, 552, 592, 605
description, knowledge by 164
direct inference 352–7
direct realism 21–2, 29–31, 260, 510, 575–88; defined 27
dispositional beliefs *see* belief, dispositional
dissolution 20, 295, 321
dreams 22, 69, 71, 77, 80–1, 164, 393, 489n2, 508, 516; memory of 6, 101–2
Dretske, Fred 21, 494, 509–10, 539ff., 558, 562, 578–82
dynamic argument 6, 86, 107–10

Edwards, Paul 13, 294–5, 311ff.
elliptic geometry *see* geometry
emotive meaning 127, 173
empirical knowledge 125–6, 142–3, 395–7; *see also* a priori knowledge
empirical reality 150
empiricism 4, 8, 11, 153, 176ff., 210–12, 253, 594–5; defined 125–6; extreme 127–8; version of foundationalism 260ff; *see also* rationalism
essence 156–7, 177
Euclidean geometry *see* geometry
evil demon 69, 338, 399, 429, 479–83, 489n2, 495, 508, 518, 552
existence 37, 160
explanation *see* inference to the best explanation
explication 179–81
extension (spatial) 38–41, 49, 146, 177, 522; visible vs. tangible 56

extension of a term 177, 535
extensionality 183
external objects 27–8, 33–4, 41–3, 47–9, 55; inconceivability of 29; *see also* matter
externally situated evidence 554–65

faith 231
familiarity 6, 76, 85, 89–90
figure *see* shape
five-minute hypothesis (Russell) 6, 85, 88, 116
flatness 541
forms 125, 156–7
Foster, John 14, 295–6, 333ff.
foundational beliefs 23, 27, 53–4; *see also* foundationalism; intuition; self-evidence
foundationalism 8, 11, 15–17, 260, 370, 375; empiricist version of 259; infinite regress argument for 259–60, 265, 388, 412–14, 608; Lehrer's criticism 408–12; and memory 105; minimal 16, 404–5; moderate 23; weak 16; Will's criticism 402–7
foundherentism 17, 370–1, 419–29
fully grounded beliefs 18, 436, 448–9, 457
Fumerton, Richard 11, 253–4, 259ff.

gambler example 435
gambler's inference 354
Gauss, Carl Friedrich 195–7, 202–3
genetic argument 86, 107–10
genetic defeater 109–12
geometry 9, 126–30, 194–213, 298, 307
Gettier, Edmund 18, 426, 435–6, 444–6, 450, 476, 557; response to 447–9
Gettier examples *see* Gettier, Edmund
ghosts 69, 76, 585–6
God 20, 29, 33, 38, 42, 43, 46, 48, 59–60, 63, 67–8, 116, 144, 171, 231, 508, 514–15, 517–18
Goldman, Alvin 18, 437, 450ff., 472, 494–5, 497
Goodman, Nelson 13–14, 295, 320ff.
grounds for belief 93–5
grue 13–14, 295, 326–9, 425

Haack, Susan 17, 370–1, 417ff.
heat *see* cold
Howson, Colin 14, 296, 344ff.
Huemer, Michael 6–7, 21, 113ff., 575ff.
Hume, David: on abstract ideas 158; on causation 143, 152–3; on empiricism 594–5; on induction 12–13, 293–5, 298ff., 317, 320–1, 330, 354–6; on perception 4, 29–30, 46ff., 60–2, 88; on reasoning 12, 254; on skepticism 487–8, 606–10; on testimony 10, 217–18, 221ff., 239–48, 270ff.
hyperbolic geometry *see* geometry

idealism 27–8, 55, 67, 128, 170–1; defended 37–45
ideas 4, 27–8, 43, 57, 60–3, 67, 160; distinguished from things 45; objects of awareness 32, 37; sources of 32–5, 43
identity, nature of 59
illusion 75–7; argument from 29–31, 48, 60–62, 74–9; stick in water 31, 74, 76–9, 82
images 27, 29, 47–8, 60; in memory 85, 88–9; *see also* ideas; impressions; sense data
immediate knowledge *see* foundational beliefs
impressions 27, 88, 142
indirect realism *see* representationalism
induction 12–14, 143, 153, 217–18, 263, 293ff., 311; defined 293; and total evidence requirement 425–6
inductive/deductive practice 322
inference 11–14, 104–5; and perception 66, 254; rules vs. premises 253; skepticism regarding 254
inference to the best explanation 14, 334–5, 337–42; and beliefs about the external world 27, 31, 42, 71
inferentially justified belief 11–12, 259–68; defined 264–5
infinite regress 16–17, 253, 259, 370, 382–5, 387, 391, 412–14, 425, 592
innate knowledge 7, 125–6, 141
instinctive beliefs 30, 72; and induction 308; and perception 47–9; and testimony 218, 237
intentionality 508, 524–5, 534

internalism 117–18
internally situated reasons 554–65
introspection 5, 7, 10, 24, 28, 51, 408
intuition 7–9, 13, 129–30, 164, 166
invariantist view of knowledge *see* contextualism
"I think, therefore I am" *see cogito*

Johnson, Samuel 29

Kant, Immanuel 7–8; 125–7; on analyticity 176; on existence 172; on knowledge of the external world 602; on synthetic a priori knowledge 126–7, 142ff., 152–6, 208; on transcendent knowledge 167; and transcendental arguments 534
Kekulé von Stradonitz, Friedrich August 126
Klein, Peter 21, 509–10, 552ff., 579–81
knowledge: analysis of 17–19, 92; as justified, true belief 18, 435–6, 494; relevant alternatives theory 21, 294–7, 509, 542–50, 560, 581; structure of 15–17
Kornblith, Hilary 12, 254–5, 275ff.

law of large numbers 296, 352–3, 360
lawlike statements 326–31
laws of nature 44, 59; and induction 14, 296, 334–7; our knowledge of 300; and miracles 217, 223, 229–30, 233n3, 240; *see also* natural necessity
Lehrer, Keith: criticism of Clark 458; on defeasibility theory 18–19, 436–7, 464ff.; on foundationalism 408–12
Leibniz, Gottfried Wilhelm von: monadism 67–8, 158; on truths of reason 176, 598–9; on verificationism 205
linear justification 390–2
Lobachevskian geometry *see* geometry
Locke, John: as methodist 594; on perception 4–5, 28–9, 32ff.; on source of ideas 187; on testimony 10, 217, 219–20
logical positivism 8–9, 127–8, 166–74, 211, 397
lunatics 53

Malcolm, Norman 6, 85–7, 91ff., 502n16
Malebranche, Nicolas de 55
material substance *see* matter
mathematics: axioms of 30, 54; and causal theory of knowledge 437; certainty of 270; demonstrations 35; as empirical 189; knowledge of 440; as synthetic a priori 7–8, 125–7, 143, 145, 147–8, 153; *see also* geometry
matter 58, 60, 66–7; arguments against 39–44, 49; argument for 68–73
matters of fact 176, 294, 298
meaning 9; *see also* synonymy
memory 5–7, 10, 85ff.; and degrees of justification 118–20; definition of 85, 92; dualistic view of 87, 117–18; event vs. factual memory 85; and inference 113–14; involved in reasoning 105–12; and justification 106, 113–20; occurrent 111; pure vs. impure 92; as retention of knowledge 95, 105–6 116–17; seeming memories 106–7; skepticism regarding 97–8, 118; as source of knowledge/justification 96, 106–7, 114–15
mental blackboard 104, 106
metabeliefs 16, 23, 400
metaphysics: problems of 144; skepticism regarding 8, 47, 166–75, 273; as synthetic a priori 127, 149
method of doubt 69, 515–23
methodism 22, 510–11, 594–601
microscopes 52, 65
mind 37, 38–9, 44; *see also* self
mind/body interaction 42, 48
mirages 74–6, 78, 510
mirrors *see* reflections
misleading defeaters 437, 466–7
misreading 77
monads *see* Leibniz, Gottfried Wilhelm von, monadism
monism 158, 170
Moore, G.E. 22–3, 511–12, 573n29, 595–6, 602ff.

naive realism *see* direct realism
nativism 7, 125–6, 141
natural language 234–5, 346

natural necessity 333–5, 533; *see also* laws of nature
necessity 143–4, 533
new riddle of induction 13–14, 295, 326–9
nomological explanatory solution 335; *see also* inference to the best explanation
nondeductive inference 293, 295–6; *see also* induction
non-Euclidean geometry *see* geometry
noninferentially justified belief *see* inferentially justified belief
nonlinear justification *see* linear justification
Nozick, Robert 475ff., 543; on the analysis of knowledge 19, 437–8, 572n27; on the closure principle 21, 438–9, 561–2, 564; on coercive philosophy 290n14
number 40

Oakley, I.T. 15–17, 370, 375ff.
observation requirement 396–8, 400–1, 419, 426
occurrent beliefs *see* belief, occurrent
opinions 219–20
ordinary language philosophy 31
other minds 59–60, 68

pain 34–5, 305; and causal theory of knowledge 460; knowledge of 101, 441, 448–9
paper example (Locke) 35
paradox of the ravens 324–5, 327
particularism 22, 511–12, 594–601
pastness, feeling of 6, 85, 90
Paxson, Thomas 18–19, 436–7, 464ff.
perception 4–5, 10, 23; analysis of 5, 51; and beliefs 4, 15, 51–3; coherence of 35; objects of awareness 27–8; reliability of 47
perceptions 80
perspective 62, 65–6, 70, 74, 76
phenomenalism 4–5; *see also* idealism
philosophers 53, 57–61, 65
philosophy 31, 72–3
physical objects 4, 66; *see also* matter
physician example (Edwards) 313–16
Plato 7, 125, 131ff., 145, 156–7
plausibility judgments 279–81
Poincaré, Jules Henri 202–5, 211
Pollock, John 6, 86–7, 104ff., 120–1
positivism *see* logical positivism
preference principle 510, 583–8
pressure, perception of 66
Price, H.H. 79–82, 248
primary qualities 28–9, 39, 49
primed search 110–12
principle of credulity 10, 218, 237–8, 283
probability 14; axioms 345; conditional 345–6; interpretation of 346; as opposed to knowledge 270–4; probabilistic independence 350–1
problem of projection *see* lawlike statements
problem of the criterion 22, 47, 510–11, 590–601
projectible predicates *see* lawlike statements
proof 16–17, 22, 69, 71, 270–1
proportional syllogism 357, 364
Putnam, Hilary 20, 508–9, 524ff.

qualities 158
Quine, W.V. 8–9, 127–8, 175ff., 263, 290n14, 331n1

rationalism 9, 20, 125–6, 153–4, 159, 317; defended 208–13; moderate 129–30; *see also* a priori knowledge; synthetic a priori knowledge
rationalization 12, 254, 275–87
real magnitude *see* tangible magnitude
real things, idealist account of 43, 59
reason *see* a priori knowledge
reason-giving 275, 279–80
reasoning *see* inference
reductionism 9, 128, 176, 187–9, 240
reflections 74–6, 78, 81
refutation and rebuttal 23
Reid, Thomas 5, 10–11, 30, 51ff. 217–18, 234ff., 283, 595–6
relations 158, 161
relations of ideas 176, 293–4, 298, 303
relevancy set 545–8

relevant alternatives theory *see* knowledge, relevant alternatives theory
representationalism 4–5, 27–8, 30–1, 48, 60–1, 253, 510, 575–6, 584–8
representations 47–8
representative samples 14, 296, 358
resemblance: between ideas and objects 28–9, 39–40, 48; and induction 225, 294–5, 305–6, 312; and intentionality 525, 532; between memories and past states 88; and universals 158, 161
revelation 55, 232
Riemannian geometry *see* geometry
right to be sure 18, 94, 377, 435–6, 441–2, 444, 592
rules of inference *see* inference
Russell, Bertrand: on a priori knowledge 8, 127, 152ff.; on definition 187, 189; on induction 13, 294, 311–18; on memory 6, 85, 88ff., 116; on names 177; on perception 5, 30–1, 64ff.

Saddam example 115, 118
sameness *see* identity
S-belief 420–2
secondary qualities 28–9, 39, 49
second order beliefs *see* metabeliefs
self 69, 154, 522–3; *see also* mind
self-evidence 8, 30, 164; *see also* foundational beliefs; foundationalism; intuition
Senor, Thomas 115, 118
sensation 28, 33–5, 66
sense data 5, 27, 30–1, 66, 74, 79–80, 153, 187–91, 452, 575; causes of 67–8, 70–2; *see also* impressions; images; ideas; representationalism
sensible qualities 32–3, 37–41, 49, 58–9, 161, 164, 302
Sextus Empiricus 15, 370, 372–3
shape 40, 65–6
showing *see* proof
simplicity 71–2, 180, 191–2, 211–13, 301
skepticism 3, 19, 15, 19–24, 28, 46–50, 53, 64, 372–3, 439, 507ff.; about a priori knowledge 211–12; aggressive response to 586; Cartesian 19–20, 23, 46, 399, 508, 516–18, 552, 565–6; and contextualism 493–4; and counterfactual analysis of knowledge 479–83; defensive response to 586–7; external world 507; about memory 97–8, 114; about reasoning 254, 270–87; *see also* induction
Sklar, Lawrence 211–13
soul *see* mind
stick in water example *see* illusion
Stove, David 14, 296–7, 352ff.
subject factors 492–7, 500
subsistence 160
substance 44
substratum 39, 41, 58
synonymy 9, 126, 129, 177–87
synthetic a priori knowledge 7–9, 126–7, 152–3, 210, 262; defended 147–9; rejection of 171; *see also* a priori knowledge; analytic–synthetic distinction
synthetic propositions *see* analytic–synthetic distinction

table example: (Hume) 29–30, 48, 60–2; (Russell) 64–6
tangible magnitude 30, 56, 61–2
taste 40, 82
tautologies *see* analytic–synthetic distinction
testimony 10–11, 52, 70–1, 120, 217ff., 421–2; and causal theory of knowledge 454–6
texture 65
theorem of total probability 349
thoughts: distinguished from beliefs 104; occurrent 104–11
total evidence requirement 425–6
total probability, theorem of 349
tracking condition on knowledge 19, 437–8, 479, 561–2
traditional analysis of knowledge *see* knowledge
transcendental idealism 150–1
trial example: (Reid) 52–3; (Huemer) 580
truth 16, 33
Turing test 529–31
Twin Earth 535

unconditional probability *see* probability
uniformity principle 12–13, 294, 321
unity, concept of 40
universality and a prioricity 143, 154
universals 8, 18, 127, 156–60, 173; knowledge of 160–4
Urbach, Peter 14, 296, 344ff.

verificationism 8–9, 127, 167–8, 212; *see also* logical positivism
virtue 16, 131–5
visible magnitude 30, 56, 61–2

wax example (Descartes) 20, 521–3

zebra example (Dretske) 21, 494–500, 558–60, 578–9